Frameworks for Developing Efficient Information Systems:

Models, Theory, and Practice

John Krogstie
Norwegian University of Science and Technology, Norway

ENGINEERING
SCIENCE REFERENCE

Managing Director:	Lindsay Johnston
Editorial Director:	Joel Gamon
Book Production Manager:	Jennifer Yoder
Publishing Systems Analyst:	Adrienne Freeland
Development Editor:	Joel Gamon
Assistant Acquisitions Editor:	Kayla Wolfe
Typesetter:	Alyson Zerbe
Cover Design:	Jason Mull

Published in the United States of America by
Engineering Science Reference (an imprint of IGI Global)
701 E. Chocolate Avenue
Hershey PA 17033
Tel: 717-533-8845
Fax: 717-533-8661
E-mail: cust@igi-global.com
Web site: http://www.igi-global.com

Library of Congress Cataloging-in-Publication Data

Frameworks for developing efficient information systems : models, theory, and practice / John Krogstie, editor.
     pages cm
 Includes bibliographical references and index.
 Summary: "This book presents research and practices on the advancements in systems analysis and design, offering theoretical frameworks and practical solutions for researchers, practitioners, and academicians to bridge the communication gap between business managers and system designers"--Provided by publisher.
  ISBN 978-1-4666-4161-7 (hardcover) -- ISBN 978-1-4666-4162-4 (ebook) -- ISBN 978-1-4666-4163-1 (print & perpetual access) 1. System design. 2. Information technology. I. Krogstie, John.
  QA76.9.S88F715 2013
  003--dc23
                               2013009179

British Cataloguing in Publication Data
A Cataloguing in Publication record for this book is available from the British Library.

The views expressed in this book are those of the authors, but not necessarily of the publisher.

Table of Contents

Preface xv

Section 1
Process Modeling

Chapter 1
Object-Aware Business Processes: Fundamental Requirements and their Support in Existing
Approaches 1
    Vera Künzle, Ulm University, Germany
    Barbara Weber, University of Innsbruck, Austria
    Manfred Reichert, Ulm University, Germany

Chapter 2
Ontological Description and Similarity-Based Discovery of Business Process Models 30
    Khalid Belhajjame, University of Manchester, UK
    Marco Brambilla, Politecnico di Milano, Italy

Chapter 3
Towards Next Generation Provenance Systems for E-Science 51
    Fakhri Alam Khan, University of Vienna, Austria
    Sardar Hussain, University of Glasgow, UK
    Ivan Janciak, University of Vienna, Austria
    Peter Brezany, University of Vienna, Austria

Section 2
Structural Modeling and Semantics

Chapter 4
Modelling Information Demand in an Enterprise Context: Method, Notation, and
Lessons Learned 77
    Magnus Lundqvist, Jönköping University, Sweden
    Kurt Sandkuhl, University of Rostock, Germany
    Ulf Seigerroth, Jönköping University, Sweden

Chapter 5
Ontology Alignment Quality: A Framework and Tool for Validation.. 99
Jennifer Sampson, Statoil, Bergen, Norway
John Krogstie, Norwegian University of Science and Technology, Norway
Csaba Veres, University of Bergen, Norway

Chapter 6
CbSSDF: A Two-Layer Conceptual Graph Approach to Web Services Description and
Composition – A Scenario-Based Solution Analysis and Comparison with OWL-S........................ 123
Xiaofeng Du, University of Durham, UK
Malcolm Munro, University of Durham, UK
William Song, University of Durham, UK

Chapter 7
Modeling Approach for Integration and Evolution of Information System
Conceptualizations 146
Remigijus Gustas, Karlstad University, Sweden

Section 3
Object-Oriented Modeling

Chapter 8
Ontological Rules for UML-Based Conceptual Modeling: Design Considerations and a Prototype
Implementation 177
Shan Lu, Around America Aviation Group, Canada
Jeffrey Parsons, Memorial University of Newfoundland, Canada

Chapter 9
A Longitudinal Study of Fan-In and Fan-Out Coupling in Open-Source Systems 199
Asma Mubarak, Brunel University, UK
Steve Counsell, Brunel University, UK
Robert M. Hierons, Brunel University, UK

Section 4
Goal and Actor Modeling

Chapter 10
A Method for Eliciting Goals for Business Process Models based on Non-Functional Requirements
Catalogues 226
Evellin Cardoso, Federal University of Espírito Santo, Brazil
João Paulo A. Almeida, Federal University of Espírito Santo, Brazil
Renata S. S. Guizzardi, Federal University of Espírito Santo, Brazil
Giancarlo Guizzardi, Federal University of Espírito Santo, Brazil

Chapter 11
An Approach for E-Service Design Using Enterprise Models 245
Martin Henkel, Stockholm University, Sweden
Paul Johannesson, Stockholm University, Sweden
Erik Perjons, Stockholm University, Sweden

Section 5
Methodology and Tools for Analysis and Design

Chapter 12
What Practitioners Think of Inter-Organizational ERP Requirements Engineering Practices: Focus
Group Results.. 270
Maya Daneva, University of Twente, The Netherlands
Niv Ahituv, Tel-Aviv University, Israel

Chapter 13
The Impact of Regulatory Compliance on Agile Software Processes with a Focus on the FDA
Guidelines for Medical Device Software 298
Hossein Mehrfard, Concordia University, Canada
Abdelwahab Hamou-Lhadj, Concordia University, Canada

Chapter 14
Predicting OSS Development Success: A Data Mining Approach 315
Uzma Raja, University of Alabama, USA
Marietta J. Tretter, Texas A&M University, USA

Chapter 15
Towards Method Component Contextualization 337
Elena Kornyshova, Université Paris I – Panthéon Sorbonne, France
Rébecca Deneckère, Université Paris I – Panthéon Sorbonne, France
Bruno Claudepierre, Université Paris I – Panthéon Sorbonne, France

Compilation of References 369

About the Contributors 398

Index 405

Detailed Table of Contents

Preface xv

Section 1
Process Modeling

Chapter 1

Object-Aware Business Processes: Fundamental Requirements and their Support in Existing
Approaches 1

Vera Künzle, Ulm University, Germany

Barbara Weber, University of Innsbruck, Austria

Manfred Reichert, Ulm University, Germany

Despite the increasing maturity of process management technology not all business processes are adequately supported by it. Support for unstructured and knowledge-intensive processes is missing, especially since they cannot be straight-jacketed into predefined activities. A common characteristic of these processes is the role of business objects and data as drivers for process modeling and enactment. This paper elicits fundamental requirements for effectively supporting such object-aware processes; i.e., their modeling, execution, and monitoring. Imperative, declarative, and data-driven process support approaches are evaluated and how well they support object-aware processes are investigated. A tight integration of process and data as major steps towards further maturation of process management technology is considered.

Chapter 2

Ontological Description and Similarity-Based Discovery of Business Process Models 30

Khalid Belhajjame, University of Manchester, UK

Marco Brambilla, Politecnico di Milano, Italy

Project repositories are a central asset in software development, as they preserve the knowledge gathered in past development activities. Locating relevant information in a vast project repository is problematic, because it requires manually tagging projects with accurate metadata, an activity which is time consuming and prone to errors and omissions. Just like any other artifact or web service, business processes can be stored in repositories to be shared and used by third parties, e.g., as building blocks for constructing new business processes. The success of such a paradigm depends partly on the availability of effective search tools to locate business processes that are relevant to the user purposes. A handful of researchers have investigated the problem of business process discovery using as input syntactical and structural information that describes business processes. This work explores an additional source of information encoded in the form of annotations that semantically describe business processes. Business processes can be semantically described using the so called abstract business processes. These are designated by concepts from an ontology which additionally captures their relationships. This ontology can be built in an automatic fashion from a collection of (concrete) business processes, and this work illustrates how it can be refined by domain experts and used in the discovery of business processes, with the purpose of reuse and increase in design productivity.

Chapter 3

Towards Next Generation Provenance Systems for E-Science 51

Fakhri Alam Khan, University of Vienna, Austria
Sardar Hussain, University of Glasgow, UK
Ivan Janciak, University of Vienna, Austria
Peter Brezany, University of Vienna, Austria

e-Science helps scientists to automate scientific discovery processes and experiments, and promote collaboration across organizational boundaries and disciplines. These experiments involve data discovery, knowledge discovery, integration, linking, and analysis through different software tools and activities. Scientific workflow is one technique through which such activities and processes can be interlinked, automated, and ultimately shared amongst the collaborating scientists. Workflows are realized by the workflow enactment engine, which interprets the process definition and interacts with the workflow participants. Since workflows are typically executed on a shared and distributed infrastructure, the information on the workflow activities, data processed, and results generated (also known as provenance), needs to be recorded in order to be reproduced and reused. A range of solutions and techniques have been suggested for the provenance of data collection and analysis; however, these are predominantly workflow enactment engine and domain dependent. This paper includes taxonomy of existing provenance techniques and a novel solution named VePS (The Vienna e-Science Provenance System) for e-Science provenance collection.

Section 2
Structural Modeling and Semantics

Chapter 4

Modelling Information Demand in an Enterprise Context: Method, Notation, and
Lessons Learned... 77

Magnus Lundqvist, Jönköping University, Sweden
Kurt Sandkuhl, University of Rostock, Germany
Ulf Seigerroth, Jönköping University, Sweden

Information overload is perceived as a common problem in organisations and enterprises, which calls for new organisational and technological approaches for more pertinent and accurate information supply. The paper contributes to addressing this problem by proposing a method for information demand modelling, which contributes to capturing and understanding the information demand of roles in organisations. This method consists to a large extent of an application of enterprise modelling techniques. Illustrated by a case from automotive industries, lessons learned from information demand modelling are presented and discussed. This includes the specific perspective taken in the method for information demand analysis, common challenges experienced in demand modelling, and the validity of recommendations from participative enterprise modelling for information demand modelling. Furthermore, the paper introduces the notation applied for information demand models and discusses refinement process of this notation.

Chapter 5

Ontology Alignment Quality: A Framework and Tool for Validation... 99

Jennifer Sampson, Statoil, Bergen, Norway

John Krogstie, Norwegian University of Science and Technology, Norway

Csaba Veres, University of Bergen, Norway

Recently semantic web technologies, such as ontologies, have been proposed as key enablers for integrating heterogeneous data schemas in business and governmental systems. Algorithms designed to align different but related ontologies have become necessary as differing ontologies proliferate. The process of ontology alignment seeks to find corresponding entities in a second ontology with the same or the closest meaning for each entity in a single ontology. This research is motivated by the need to provide tools and techniques to support the task of validating ontology alignment statements, since it cannot be guaranteed that the results from automated tools are accurate. The authors present a framework for understanding ontology alignment quality and describe how AlViz, a tool for visual ontology alignment, may be used to improve the quality of alignment results. An experiment was undertaken to test the claim that AlViz supports the task of validating ontology alignments. A promising result found that the tool has potential for identifying missing alignments and for rejecting false alignments.

Chapter 6

CbSSDF: A Two-Layer Conceptual Graph Approach to Web Services Description and Composition – A Scenario-Based Solution Analysis and Comparison with OWL-S......................... 123

Xiaofeng Du, University of Durham, UK

Malcolm Munro, University of Durham, UK

William Song, University of Durham, UK

Web services as a new distributed system technology have been widely adopted by industries in the areas, such as enterprise application integration (EAI), business process management (BPM), and virtual organization (VO). However, lack of semantics in the current Web service standards has become a major barrier in service discovery and composition. To tackle the semantic issues of Web services, this paper proposes a comprehensive semantic service description framework – CbSSDF and a two-step service discovery mechanism based on CbSSDF—to help service users to easily locate their required services. The authors give a detailed explanation of CbSSDF, and then evaluate the framework by comparing it with OWL-S to examine how the proposed framework can improve the efficiency and effectiveness of service discovery and composition. The evaluation is carried out by analysing the different proposed solutions based on these two frameworks for achieving a series of tasks in a scenario.

Chapter 7

Modeling Approach for Integration and Evolution of Information System Conceptualizations 146

Remigijus Gustas, Karlstad University, Sweden

Most information systems development methodologies are based on conceptual modeling of static and dynamic views, which are represented by totally different types of diagrams. Understanding of the interplay among interactive, behavioral and structural aspects of specifications is necessary for identification of semantic integrity problems between business process and business data. Typically, semantic inconsistencies and discontinuities between collections of conceptual representations are not easy to detect and to comprehend for information system designers due to static and dynamic aspects of models being visualized in isolation. The goal of this paper is to present a modeling approach for semantic integration and evolution of static and dynamic aspects of conceptual models. Visualization of interplay among structural, interactive and behavioral aspects of computation-neutral representations helps to understand crosscutting concerns and integrity problems of information system conceptualizations. The main advantage of the presented conceptual modeling approach is stability and flexibility of diagrams in dealing with the evolutionary changes of requirements. Therefore, the developed modeling foundation is targeted to both business managers and information system designers for the purpose of computation-neutral integration and evolution of information systems specifications.

Section 3
Object-Oriented Modeling

Chapter 8

Ontological Rules for UML-Based Conceptual Modeling: Design Considerations and a Prototype Implementation 177

Shan Lu, Around America Aviation Group, Canada
Jeffrey Parsons, Memorial University of Newfoundland, Canada

UML is used as a language for object-oriented software design, and as a language for conceptual modeling of applications domains. Given the differences between these purposes, UML's origins in software engineering might limit its appropriateness for conceptual modeling. In this context, Evermann and Wand have proposed a set of well-defined ontological rules to constrain the construction of UML diagrams to reflect underlying ontological assumptions about the real world. The authors extend their work using a design research approach that examines these rules by studying the consequences of integrating them into a UML CASE tool. The paper demonstrates how design insights from incorporating theory-based modeling rules in a software artifact can be used to shed light on the rules themselves. In particular, the authors distinguish four categories of rules for implementation purposes, reflecting the relative importance of different rules and the degree of flexibility available in enforcing them. They propose distinct implementation strategies that correspond to these four rule categories and identify some redundant rules as well as some rules that cannot be implemented without changing the UML specification. The rules are implemented in an open-source UML CASE tool.

Chapter 9

A Longitudinal Study of Fan-In and Fan-Out Coupling in Open-Source Systems 199

Asma Mubarak, Brunel University, UK
Steve Counsell, Brunel University, UK
Robert M. Hierons, Brunel University, UK

Excessive coupling between object-oriented classes is widely acknowledged as a maintenance problem that can result in a higher propensity for faults in systems and a 'stored up' future problem. This paper explores the relationship between 'fan-in' and 'fan-out' coupling metrics over multiple versions of open-source software. More specifically, the relationship between the two metrics is explored to determine patterns of growth in each over the course of time. The JHawk tool was used to extract the two metrics from five open-source systems. Results show a wide range of traits in the classes to explain both high and low levels of fan-in and fan-out. Evidence was also found of certain 'key' classes (with both high fan-in and fan-out) and 'client' and 'server'-type classes with high fan-out and fan-in, respectively. This paper provides an explanation of the composition and existence of such classes as well as for disproportionate increases in each of the two metrics over time. Finally, it was found that high fan-in class values tended to be associated with small classes; classes with high fan-out on the other hand tended to be relatively large classes.

Section 4
Goal and Actor Modeling

Chapter 10

A Method for Eliciting Goals for Business Process Models based on Non-Functional Requirements
Catalogues 226

Evellin Cardoso, Federal University of Espírito Santo, Brazil

João Paulo A. Almeida, Federal University of Espírito Santo, Brazil

Renata S. S. Guizzardi, Federal University of Espírito Santo, Brazil

Giancarlo Guizzardi, Federal University of Espírito Santo, Brazil

While traditional approaches in business process modeling tend to focus on "how" the business processes are performed (adopting a behavioral description in which business processes are described in terms of procedural aspects), in goal-oriented business process modeling, the proposals strive to extend traditional business process methodologies by providing a dimension of intentionality to business processes. One of the key difficulties in enabling one to model goal-oriented processes concerns the identification or elicitation of goals. This paper reports on a case study conducted in a Brazilian hospital, which obtained several goal models represented in i*/Tropos, each of which correspond to a business process also modeled in the scope of the study. NFR catalogues were helpful in goal elicitation, uncovering goals that did not come up during previous interviews prior to these catalogues' use.

Chapter 11

An Approach for E-Service Design Using Enterprise Models 245

Martin Henkel, Stockholm University, Sweden

Paul Johannesson, Stockholm University, Sweden

Erik Perjons, Stockholm University, Sweden

Organisations demand new business models for value creation and innovation that require collaboration with customers and vendors in agile and flexible networks. To realise such networks, organisations are embracing service oriented models and architectures using e-services for business communication. A major issue for a service oriented organisation is to design and offer e-services that are adapted to the needs, wants, and requirements of customers and vendors. This is a challenging task as different customer groups and vendors will have different requirements, which may vary over time, resulting in a large number of e-services. In this paper, the authors suggest enterprise models as being adequate instruments for design and maintenance of e-services. More specifically; an approach for designing e-services based on value and goal models, which will ensure that the constructed e-services will satisfy the needs and wants of customers. A project from the Swedish health care sector is used to demonstrate and evaluate the proposed approach.

Section 5
Methodology and Tools for Analysis and Design

Chapter 12

What Practitioners Think of Inter-Organizational ERP Requirements Engineering Practices: Focus Group Results...270

Maya Daneva, University of Twente, The Netherlands
Niv Ahituv, Tel-Aviv University, Israel

Empirical studies on requirements engineering for inter-organizational enterprise resource planning (ERP) systems have demonstrated that the ERP vendor-provided prescriptive models for ERP roll-outs make tacit assumptions about the ERP adopter's context. This, in turn, leads to the implementation of suboptimal solutions. Specifically, these models assume that ERP implementations happen within a single company, and so they pay only scant attention to the stakeholders' requirements for inter-organizational coordination. Given this backdrop, the first author proposed 13 practices for engineering the ERP co-ordination requirements in previous publications. This paper reports a confirmatory study evaluating those practices. Using an online focus group, the authors collected and analyzed practitioners' feedback and their experiences to understand the extent to which the proposed practices are indeed observable. The study indicated very low variability in practitioners' perceptions regarding 12 of the 13 practices, and considerable variability in their perceptions regarding the role of modeling inter-organizational co-ordination requirements. The contribution of the study is twofold: (1) it adds to the body of knowledge in the sub-area of RE for ERP; and (2) it adds to the practice of using qualitative research methods in empirical RE.

Chapter 13

The Impact of Regulatory Compliance on Agile Software Processes with a Focus on the FDA Guidelines for Medical Device Software 298

Hossein Mehrfard, Concordia University, Canada
Abdelwahab Hamou-Lhadj, Concordia University, Canada

The difficulty of complying with different regulations has become more evident as a large number of regulated businesses are mandated to follow an ever-increasing set of regulations. These regulations often drive significant changes in the way organizations operate to deliver value to their customers. This paper focuses on the impact of the Food and Drug Administration (FDA) regulations on agile software development processes, which in many ways can be considered as just another type of organizational processes. Particular focus is placed on the ability for Extreme Programming (XP) to support FDA requirements. Findings show that XP fails to meet many of the FDA guidelines for medical device software, which increases the risks of non-compliance for organizations that have adopted XP as their main software process. The results of this study can lead the work towards designing an extension to XP for FDA regulations.

Chapter 14

Predicting OSS Development Success: A Data Mining Approach 315

Uzma Raja, University of Alabama, USA

Marietta J. Tretter, Texas A&M University, USA

Open Source Software (OSS) has reached new levels of sophistication and acceptance by users and commercial software vendors. This research creates tests and validates a model for predicting successful development of OSS projects. Widely available archival data was used for OSS projects from Sourceforge.net. The data is analyzed with multiple Data Mining techniques. Initially three competing models are created using Logistic Regression, Decision Trees and Neural Networks. These models are compared for precision and are refined in several phases. Text Mining is used to create new variables that improve the predictive power of the models. The final model is chosen based on best fit to separate training and validation data sets and the ability to explain the relationship among variables. Model robustness is determined by testing it on a new dataset extracted from the SF repository. The results indicate that end-user involvement, project age, functionality, usage, project management techniques, project type and team communication methods have a significant impact on the development of OSS projects.

Chapter 15

Towards Method Component Contextualization 337

Elena Kornyshova, Université Paris I – Panthéon Sorbonne, France

Rébecca Deneckère, Université Paris I – Panthéon Sorbonne, France

Bruno Claudepierre, Université Paris I – Panthéon Sorbonne, France

Method Engineering (ME) is a discipline which aims to bring effective solutions to the construction, improvement and modification of the methods used to develop Information Systems (IS). Situational Method Engineering (SME) promotes the idea of retrieving, adapting and tailoring components, rather than complete methodologies, to the specific context. Existing SME approaches use the notion of context for characterizing situations of IS development projects and for guiding the method components selection from a repository. However, in the reviewed literature, there is no proposed approach to specify the specific context of method components. This paper provides a detailed vision of context and a process for contextualizing methods in the IS domain. This proposal is illustrated with three case studies: scenario conceptualization, project portfolio management, and decision-making.

Compilation of References 369

About the Contributors 398

Index 405

Preface

The area of Information Systems Engineering (ISE) combines organizationally oriented topics often dealt with in Management Information Systems (MIS) with more technical concerns found in Software Engineering (SE). This area bridges different areas of information systems development such as analysis, requirements specification, and design. The *International Journal of Information System Modeling and Design (IJISMD)* publishes original research and practical results on the advances in system analysis and design, and this book is based on the papers published in 2011 in this journal.

The mission of IJISMD is to provide an international forum for modeling experts and design professionals for exchanging innovative ideas. The journal enables presentation of original work on the development of models for blending software and enterprise engineering, managing complexity of design, visualization of integration, and evolution. As we understand, modeling on all levels is an important area. Modeling languages can be divided into classes according to the core phenomena classes (concepts) that are represented and focused on in the language. This has been called the *perspective* of the language (Krogstie 2012), and eight core perspectives have been identified:

1. **Behavioral perspective:** Languages following this perspective go back to the early sixties, with the introduction of Petri-nets. In most languages with a behavioral perspective the main phenomena are "states" and "transitions" between "states." State transitions are triggered by "events".

2. **Functional perspective:** The main phenomena class in the functional perspective is the "transformation." A transformation is defined as an activity, which based on a set of phenomena transforms them to another set of phenomena. This perspective goes back to at least the seventies with DFDs. Modern approaches for process modeling typically combine functional and behavioral modeling.

3. **Structural perspective:** Approaches within the structural perspective concentrate on describing the static structure of a system. The main construct of such languages is the "entity." Data modeling with ER modeling as a standard example can also be traced back to the seventies, but later also other approaches like semantic nets, conceptual graphs, and ontologies can be said to have structural aspects, although ontologies also have powerful means for the representation of rules.

4. **Goal and Rule perspective:** Goal-oriented modeling focuses on "goals" and "rules." A rule is something that influences the actions of a set of actors. In the early nineties, one started to model so-called rule and goal hierarchies, linking rules and goals of different abstraction levels. This is often combined with actor-oriented modeling (see below).

5. **Object-Oriented perspective:** The basic phenomena of object oriented modeling languages are similar to those found in most object oriented programming languages; "Objects" as a specific type of entity with unique id and a local state that can only be manipulated by calling methods of

the object. Objects have a life cycle. The process of the object is the trace of the events during the existence of the object. A set of objects that share the same definitions of attributes and operations compose an object class. Most object-oriented modeling today is done using UML or extensions to UML.

6. **Actor and Role perspective:** The main phenomena of languages within this perspective are "actor" (also termed agent) and "role." The background for modeling in this perspective comes both from organizational science, work on programming languages, and work on intelligent agents in artificial intelligence.

7. **Communication perspective:** The work within this perspective is based on language/action theory from philosophical linguistics. The basic assumption of language/action theory is that persons cooperate within work processes through their conversations and through mutual commitments taken within them. Popular in the nineties in particular, but less work is done within this perspective today.

8. **Topological perspective:** This perspective relates to the topological ordering between the different concepts. The best background for conceptualization of these aspects comes from the cartography and CSCW fields, differentiating between space and place. "Space" describes geometrical arrangements that might structure, constrain, and enable certain forms of movement and interaction; "place" denotes the ways in which settings acquire recognizable and persistent social meaning through interaction.

As we see, there are a number of different approaches to conceptual modeling, each emphasizing different aspects of the perceived reality. Towards the end of the eighties and early nineties, several researchers claimed that one perspective is better, or more natural, than others. Later one has realized that all perspectives might be useful in different settings supporting different goal of modeling. Modeling is usually done in some organizational setting and one can look upon an organization and its information system abstractly to be in a state (the current state, often represented as a descriptive "as-is" model) that are to be evolved to some future wanted state (often represented as a prescriptive "to be" model). Obviously, changes will happen in an organization independent of what is actually planned, thus one might in practice have the use for many different models and scenarios of possible future states, but we simplify the number of possible future states in the discussion below.

The state includes the existing processes, organization and computer systems. These states are often modeled, and the state of the organization is perceived (differently) by different persons through these models. Different usage areas of conceptual models are:

1. **Human sense-making:** The descriptive model of the current state can be useful for people to make sense of and learn about the current perceived situation.

2. **Communication between people in the organization:** Models can have an important role in human communication. Thus, in addition to support the sense-making process for the individual, a model can act as a common framework supporting communication between people both relative to descriptive and prescriptive models.

3. **Computer-assisted analysis:** This is used to gain knowledge about the organization through simulation or deduction, often by comparing a model of the current state and a model of a future, potentially better state.

4. **Quality assurance:** Ensuring that the organization acts according to a certified process developed for instance as part of an ISO-certification process.

5. **Model deployment and activation**: To integrate the model of the future state in an information system directly, making the prescriptive model the descriptive model. Models can be activated in three ways:

   a. Through people, where the system offers no active support.

   b. Automatically, where the system plays an active role, as in most automated workflow systems.

   c. Interactively, where the computer and the users co-operate.

6. To be a prescriptive model to be used in a traditional system development project, without being directly activated.

7. Achieve acceptance of new solutions (either through model deployment or through models being the basis for traditional model deployment) due to the model acting as a common ground.

In the material of the book, we find examples of the six first modeling perspectives, some papers with approaches combining different perspectives, and we have structured this book roughly according to these perspectives, ending with some more general methodologically oriented papers.

PROCESS MODELING

In its modern form, process modeling combines functional and behavioral aspects. Despite the increasing maturity of process management technology, not all business processes are adequately supported by BPM technology and workflow systems. In "Object-Aware Business Processes: Fundamental Requirements and their Support in Existing Approaches," Künzle, Weber, and Reichert investigate support for *unstructured* and *knowledge-intensive* processes. Support for such processes is often missing in traditional approaches and tools, especially since they cannot be *straightjacketed* into predefined activities. A common characteristic of these processes is the role of business objects and data as drivers for process modeling and enactment. This chapter elicits fundamental requirements for effectively supporting such *object-aware processes*, i.e., how to perform their modeling, execution, and monitoring. Imperative, declarative, and data-driven process support approaches are evaluated and how well they support object-aware processes is investigated. A tight integration of process and data as major steps towards further maturation of process management technology is considered.

When process models support a more well-defined process, there is potential for reuse of process knowledge between systems. Belhajjame and Brambilla investigate in the article "Ontological Description and Similarity-Based Discovery of Business Process Models" support for reuse of process models. Just like any other artifact, business process models can be stored in repositories to be shared and used by third parties, e.g., as building blocks for constructing new business processes. The success of such an approach depends partly on the availability of effective search tools to locate business process models that are relevant to the user purposes. A handful of researchers have investigated the problem of business process discovery using as input syntactical and structural information that describes business process models. This work explores an additional source of information encoded in the form of annotations that semantically describe business processes. Business processes can be semantically described using the so called abstract business processes. These are designated by concepts from an ontology which additionally captures the relationships between concepts, and thus also potential relationships between process models.

This ontology can be built in an automatic fashion from a collection of (concrete) business processes, and this work illustrates how it can be refined by domain experts and used in the discovery of business processes, with the purpose of reuse and increase in development productivity.

Process modeling and workflow is utilized in many areas. In "Towards Next Generation Provenance Systems for E-Science," Khan, Hussain, Janciak, and Brezany investigate so called scientific workflow for e-Science. e-Science helps scientists to automate scientific discovery processes and experiments, and promote collaboration across organizational boundaries and disciplines. These experiments involve data discovery, knowledge discovery, integration, linking, and analysis through different software tools and activities. Scientific workflow is one technique through which such activities and processes can be interlinked, automated, repeated, and ultimately shared amongst the collaborating scientists. Workflows are realized by the workflow enactment engine, which interprets the process definition and interacts with the workflow participants. Since workflows are typically executed on a shared and distributed infrastructure, the information on the workflow activities, data processed, and results generated (also known as provenance), needs to be recorded in order to be reproduced and reused. A range of solutions and techniques have been suggested for the provenance of data collection and analysis; however, these are predominantly workflow enactment engine and domain dependent. This chapter includes a taxonomy of existing provenance techniques and a novel solution named VePS (The Vienna e-Science Provenance System) for e-Science provenance collection.

STRUCTURAL MODELING AND SEMANTICS

Structural modeling is often used for representing the data and information in an information system. Information overload is perceived as a common problem in organizations and enterprises, which calls for new organizational and technological approaches for more pertinent and accurate information supply. In "Modeling Information Demand in an Enterprise Context: Method, Notation, and Lessons Learned" by Lundqvist, Sandkuhl, and Seigerroth, the authors address the problem of information overload by proposing a method for information demand modeling, which contributes to capturing and understanding the information demand of roles in organizations. This method consists to a large extent of an application of enterprise modeling techniques. Illustrated by a case from the automotive industry, lessons learned from information demand modeling are presented and discussed. This includes the specific perspective taken in the method for information demand analysis, common challenges experienced in demand modeling, and the validity of recommendations from using participative enterprise modeling for information demand modeling. Furthermore, the paper introduces the notation applied for information demand models and discusses refinement process of this notation.

Recently, Semantic Web technologies, such as ontologies, have been proposed as key enablers for *integrating* heterogeneous data schemas across business and governmental systems. Algorithms designed to align different, but related ontologies have become necessary as differing ontologies proliferate. The paper "Ontology Alignment Quality: A Framework and Tool for Validation" by Sampson, Krogstie, and Veres looks into the need for ontology alignment in this landscape. The process of ontology alignment seeks to find corresponding entities in a second ontology with the same or the closest meaning for each entity in a single ontology. This research is motivated by the need to provide tools and techniques to support the task of validating ontology alignment statements, since it cannot be guaranteed that the results from automated tools are accurate. The authors present a framework for understanding ontology alignment quality and describe how AlViz, a tool for visual ontology alignment, can be used to improve the quality of alignments. An experiment was undertaken to test the claim that AlViz supports the task of validating ontology alignments. A promising result found that the tool has potential for identifying missing alignments and for rejecting false alignments.

Chapter 6

Web services as a new distributed system technology have been widely adopted by different fields in the information systems areas, such as Enterprise Application Integration (EAI), Business Process Management (BPM), and Virtual Organization (VO). However, lack of possibility to represent semantics in the current Web service standards has become a major barrier to provide service discovery and service composition. To tackle the semantic issues of Web services the paper "CbSSDF: A Two-Layer Conceptual Graph Approach to Web Services Description and Composition – A Scenario-Based Solution Analysis and Comparison with OWL-S" by Du, Munro, and Song proposes a comprehensive semantic service description framework—CbSSDF and a two-step service discovery mechanism based on CbSSDF—to help service users to easily locate result when using the approach to retrieve the required services. The authors give a detailed explanation of CbSSDF, and then evaluate the framework by comparing it with OWL-S to examine how the proposed framework can improve the efficiency and effectiveness of service discovery and composition. The evaluation is carried out by analyzing the different proposed solutions based on these two frameworks for achieving a series of tasks following a defined scenario.

Most information systems development methodologies are based on conceptual modeling of static and dynamic views, which are represented by totally different types of diagrams. In "Modeling Approach for Integration and Evolution of Information System Conceptualizations," Gustas points to the need for understanding of the interplay among interactive, behavioral, and structural aspects of specifications to identify semantic integrity problems between business process and business data. Typically, semantic inconsistencies and discontinuities between collections of conceptual representations are not easy to detect and to comprehend for information system designers due to static and dynamic aspects of models being visualized in isolation. The goal of his paper is to present a modeling approach for semantic integration and evolution of static and dynamic aspects of conceptual models. Visualization of interplay among structural, interactive, and behavioral aspects of computation-neutral representations helps to understand crosscutting concerns and integrity problems of information system conceptualizations. The main advantage of the presented conceptual modeling approach is stability and flexibility of diagrams in dealing with the evolutionary changes of requirements. Therefore, the developed modeling foundation is targeted to both business managers and information system designers for the purpose of computation-neutral integration and evolution of information systems specifications.

OBJECT-ORIENTED MODELING

Object-oriented modeling can be said to be another way of combining behavioral, functional, and structural aspects. Although the field of object-oriented modeling has spurred a lot of approaches since it appeared in the late eighties, over the last 10-15 years most work has centered on UML, or extensions to UML. In "Ontological Rules for UML-Based Conceptual Modeling: Design Considerations and a Prototype Implementation" by Lu and Parsons, they look upon how to support different goals of modeling with UML. UML is used both as a language for object-oriented software design, and as a language for conceptual modeling of different applications domains. Given the differences between these goals, UML's origins in software engineering might limit its appropriateness for conceptual modeling. In this context, Evermann and Wand have proposed a set of well-defined ontological rules to constrain the part of the language to be used in construction of UML diagrams to reflect underlying ontological assumptions about the real world. The authors extend their work using a design research approach that examines these rules by studying the consequences of integrating them into a UML CASE tool. The paper demonstrates how design insights from incorporating theory-based modeling rules in a software artifact can be used to shed light on the rules themselves. In particular, the authors distinguish four categories of rules for implementation purposes, reflecting the relative importance of different rules to achieve the underlying goal of the modeling and the degree of flexibility available in enforcing them. They propose distinct implementation strategies that correspond to these four rule categories and identify some redundant rules as well as some rules that cannot be implemented without changing the UML specification. The rules are implemented in an open-source UML CASE tool.

In object-oriented design, excessive coupling between object-oriented classes is widely acknowledged as a maintenance problem that can result in a higher propensity for faults in systems and a 'stored up' future problem. In "A Longitudinal Study of Fan-In and Fan-Out Coupling in Open-Source Systems," Mubarak, Counsell, and Hierons explore the relationship between "fan-in" and "fan-out" coupling metrics over multiple versions of open-source software. More specifically, the relationship between the two metrics is explored to determine patterns of growth in each over the course of time. The JHawk tool was used to extract the two metrics from five open-source systems. Results show a wide range of traits in the classes to explain both high and low levels of fan-in and fan-out. Evidence was also found of certain "key" classes (with both high fan-in and fan-out) and "client" and "server"-type classes with high fan-out and fan-in, respectively. This chapter provides an explanation of the composition and existence of such classes as well as for disproportionate increases in each of the two metrics over time. Finally, it was found that high fan-in class values tended to be associated with small classes; classes with high fan-out on the other hand tended to be relatively large classes.

GOAL AND ACTOR MODELING

While traditional approaches in business process modeling tend to focus on "how" the business processes are performed (adopting a behavioral description in which business processes are described in terms of procedural aspects), in goal-oriented business process modeling, the proposals strive to extend traditional business process methodologies by providing a dimension of intentionality to business processes. One of the key difficulties in enabling one to model goal-oriented processes concerns the identification or elicitation and structuring of the goals themselves. In "A Method for Eliciting Goals for Business Process Models based on Non-Functional Requirements Catalogues," Cardoso, Almeida, Guizzardi, and Guizzardi presents a case study conducted in a Brazilian hospital following such an approach. The case obtained several goal models represented in i*/Tropos, a well-known example of an approach to Goal-Oriented Requirements Engineering (GORE), each of which correspond to a business process also modeled in the scope of the study. Existing catalogues of Non-Functional Requirements (NFR) were helpful in goal elicitation, uncovering goals that did not come up during previous interviews prior to these catalogues' use.

In "An Approach for E-Service Design Using Enterprise Models" by Henkel, Johannesson, and Perjons, the authors look upon value creation and innovation that require collaboration with customers and vendors in agile and flexible networks of *actors*. To realize such networks, organizations are embracing service oriented models and architectures using e-services for business communication. A major issue for a service-oriented organization is to design and offer e-services that are adapted to the needs, wants, and requirements of different actors such as customers and vendors. This is a challenging task as different customer groups and vendors will have different requirements, which may vary over time, resulting in a large number of e-services. In this chapter, the authors suggest using enterprise models as being adequate instruments for design and maintenance of e-services. More specifically, an approach for designing e-services based on *value and goal models,* which will ensure that the constructed e-services will satisfy the needs and wants of customers is presented. A project from the Swedish health care sector is used to demonstrate and evaluate the proposed approach.

METHODOLOGY AND TOOLS FOR ANALYSIS AND DESIGN

Development and evolution of information systems has gone from a focus on structure (e.g. in projects following a waterfall model) and in-house development, to the use of more agile approach utilizing external resources such as packaged and open source systems. One important type of reuse is the use of packaged systems such as ERP-systems. Empirical studies on requirements engineering for inter-organizational Enterprise Resource Planning (ERP) systems have demonstrated that the ERP vendor-provided prescriptive models for ERP roll-outs make tacit assumptions about the ERP adopter's context, e.g. on how they are organized. This, in turn, leads to the implementation of suboptimal solutions when these presumptions do not fit the current organization. Specifically, these models assume that ERP implementations happen within a single company, and so they pay only scant attention to the stakeholders' requirements for inter-organizational coordination. Given this backdrop in the article "What Practitioners Think of Inter-Organizational ERP Requirements Engineering Practices: Focus Group Results" Daneva and Ahituv look in more detail on 13 practices for engineering the ERP coordination requirements proposed by Daneva in previous publications. This chapter reports a confirmatory study evaluating the importance of those practices. Using an online focus group, the authors collected and analyzed practitioners' feedback and their experiences to understand the extent to which the proposed practices are indeed observable. The study indicated very low variability in practitioners' perceptions regarding 12 of the 13 practices, and considerable variability in their perceptions regarding the role of modeling inter-organizational coordination requirements. The contribution of the study is twofold: (1) it adds to the body of knowledge in the sub-area of RE for ERP; and (2) it adds to the practice of using qualitative research methods in empirical RE.

Even if the current approaches to information systems development are more agile, they still have to relate to external legislative and organizational frameworks. In "The Impact of Regulatory Compliance on Agile Software Processes with a Focus on the FDA Guidelines for Medical Device Software" by Mehrfard and Abdelwahab Hamou-Lhadj, the authors address the difficulty of complying with different regulations. This has become more evident as a large number of regulated businesses are mandated to follow an ever-increasing set of standards and regulations. These regulations often drive significant changes in the way organizations operate to deliver value to their customers. This chapter focuses on the impact of the Food and Drug Administration (FDA) regulations on agile software development processes, which in many ways can be considered as just another type of organizational processes. Particular focus is placed on the ability for Extreme Programming (XP) to support FDA requirements. Findings show that XP fails to meet many of the FDA guidelines for medical device software, which increases the risks of non-compliance for organizations that have adopted XP as their main software process. The results of this study can lead the work towards designing an extension to XP for FDA regulation, and might also carry over to support ways of dealing with external regulations in other fields in an agile approach.

One approach for using external resources is the use of Open Source Software (OSS). OSS has reached new levels of sophistication and acceptance by users and commercial software vendors. In "Predicting OSS Development Success: A Data Mining Approach" the authors Raja and Tretter create tests and validate a model for predicting successful development of OSS projects. Widely available archival data was used for OSS projects from Sourceforge.net (SF). The data is analyzed with multiple Data Mining techniques. Initially three competing models are created using Logistic Regression, Decision Trees, and Neural Networks. These models are compared for precision and are refined in several phases. Text Mining is used to create new variables that improve the predictive power of the models. The final model is chosen based on best fit to separate training and validation data sets and the ability to explain the relationship among variables. Model robustness is determined by testing it on a new dataset extracted from the SF repository. The results indicate that end-user involvement, project age, functionality, usage, project management techniques, project type and team communication methods have a significant impact on the development of OSS projects.

Methodologies for information systems development needs to be adaptable. Method Engineering (ME) is a discipline that aims to bring effective solutions to the construction, improvement, and modification of the methods used to develop Information Systems (IS). Situational Method Engineering (SME) promotes the idea of retrieving, adapting, and tailoring methodology components, rather than complete methodologies, to the specific context. Existing SME approaches use the notion of context for characterizing situations of IS development projects and for guiding the method components selection from a repository. However, in the reviewed literature, there is no proposed approach to specify the specific context of method components. In "Towards Method Component Contextualization," Kornyshova, Deneckère, and Claudepierre provide a detailed vision of context and a process for contextualizing methods in the IS domain. This proposal is illustrated with three case studies: scenario conceptualization, project portfolio management, and decision-making.

CONCLUDING REMARKS

One can argue that the main reason why humans have excelled as species is our ability to represent, reuse, and transfer knowledge across time and space. Whereas in most areas of human conduct, one-dimensional natural language is used to express and share knowledge, we see the need for and use of two and many-dimensional representational forms to be on the rise. One such representational form is called *(conceptual) modelling*. A *conceptual model* is traditionally defined as a description of the phenomena in a domain at some level of abstraction, which is expressed in a semi-formal or formal diagrammatical language. Modeling is an important part of both information systems development and evolution, and organizational development in general (e.g. used in enterprise modeling/enterprise architecture). As illustrated in this book, the field of information systems modeling and design includes numerous modeling methods and notations that are typically evolving. Even with some attempts to standardize (e.g. UML for object-oriented software design), new modeling methods are constantly being introduced, many of which differ only marginally from previous approaches. These ongoing changes significantly impact the way information systems, enterprises, and business processes are being analyzed and designed in practice.

Whereas modeling techniques traditionally was used to create intermediate artifacts in systems analysis and design, more and more modeling methodologies take a more active approach to the exploitation of this particular form of knowledge representation. In approaches such as Business Process Management (BPM), Model Driven Architecture (MDA), and Domain Specific Modeling/Domain Specific Modeling Languages (DSM/DSL). Enterprise Architecture (EA), and Active Knowledge Modeling (AKM), the models are used directly to form the information system of the organization. At the same time, similar techniques are used also for sense-making and communication, model simulation, quality assurance and requirements specification in connection to more traditional forms of information systems development as illustrated with the overview of goals of modeling in the introduction.

Given that modeling techniques are used in such a large variety of tasks with very different goals, it is important for appropriate use of the techniques to have a proper overview of different use of modeling, and guidelines for what make a model sufficiently good to achieve the decided goals. An important direction for the field is to extend the work on *quality* of models and modeling languages in this setting, to be able to evaluate and enhance current information modeling methods and methodologies. Evaluation of modeling approaches remains a challenge in the information systems field. Although work has been done in this direction by many researchers over a long period, it is a need to get the results from this research into practical use.

John Krogstie
Norwegian University of Science and Technology, Norway

REFERENCES

Krogstie, J. (2012). *Model-based development and evolution of information systems: A quality approach.* London: Springer. doi:10.1007/978-1-4471-2936-3.

Section 1
Process Modeling

Chapter 1

Object–Aware Business Processes:
Fundamental Requirements and their Support in Existing Approaches

Vera Künzle
Ulm University, Germany

Barbara Weber
University of Innsbruck, Austria

Manfred Reichert
Ulm University, Germany

ABSTRACT

Despite the increasing maturity of process management technology not all business processes are adequately supported by it. Support for unstructured and knowledge-intensive processes is missing, especially since they cannot be straight-jacketed into predefined activities. A common characteristic of these processes is the role of business objects and data as drivers for process modeling and enactment. This paper elicits fundamental requirements for effectively supporting such object-aware processes; i.e., their modeling, execution, and monitoring. Imperative, declarative, and data-driven process support approaches are evaluated and how well they support object-aware processes are investigated. A tight integration of process and data as major steps towards further maturation of process management technology is considered.

DOI: 10.4018/978-1-4666-4161-7.ch001

INTRODUCTION

Business Process Management provides generic methods, concepts and techniques for designing, enacting, monitoring, and diagnosing *business processes* (Van der Aalst, ter Hofstede, & Weske, 2003). When using existing process management systems (PrMS) a business process is typically defined as set of activities representing business functions and having a specific ordering. What is done during activity execution is out of the control of the PrMS. Most PrMS consider activities as black-boxes in which application data is managed by invoked application components (except routing data and process variables). Whether an activity becomes activated during runtime depends on the state of other activities. Generally, a process requires a number of activities to be accomplished in order to terminate successfully. For end-users, PrMS provide process-oriented views (e.g., worklists.)

Existing PrMS have been primarily designed for *highly structured*, *repetitive processes*. By contrast, for *unstructured* and *semi-structured processes* existing PrMS do not provide sufficient support (Silver, 2009). In particular, these processes are driven by user decisions and are *knowledge-intensive*; i.e., they cannot be expressed as a set of activities with specified order and work cannot be *straight-jacketed* into activities (Van der Aalst, Weske, & Grünbauer, 2005). Another limitation of PrMS is their insufficient process coordination support; i.e., process instances cannot be synchronized at a higher-level of abstraction. Consequently, all behavior relevant in a given context must be defined within one process model (Van der Aalst et al., 2000; Müller, Reichert, & Herbst, 2007). This, in turn, leads to a "contradiction between the way processes can be modeled and preferred work practice" (Sadiq et al., 2005). Finally, since application data is managed within black-box activities, integrated access on business processes and data cannot be provided. Due to these limitations many business applications (e.g., ERP systems) do not rely on PrMS, but are hard-coding process logic instead. Resulting applications are both complex to design and costly to maintain, and even simple process changes require costly code adaptations and testing efforts.

To better understand which processes are handled well by existing PrMS and for which support is unsatisfactory, we conducted several case studies. Amongst others we analyzed business applications with hard-coded process logic; e.g., the processes as implemented in the human resource management system *Persis* and the reviewing system *Easychair* (Künzle & Reichert, 2009a, 2009b). Processes similar to the ones we evaluated can be found in many other fields like order handling, healthcare and release management (Müller, Reichert, & Herbst, 2007). A major finding of all case studies was that data objects act as major *driver* for process specification and enactment. Consequently, process support requires *object-awareness*; i.e., business processes and business objects cannot be treated independently from each other. This has implications on the whole process lifecycle since PrMS should consider both object types and their inter-relations. Regarding its execution, on the one hand an *object-aware process* must be closely linked to relevant object instances; i.e., object attributes must process specific values to invoke certain activities or terminate process execution. On the other hand, an object-aware process does not only require certain data for executing a particular activity; i.e., it should be also able to dynamically react on data changes and newly emerging data. Consequently, process progress needs to be aligned with available object instances and their attribute values at runtime.

Regarding end-user functions provided by hard-coded business applications, in addition to a *process-oriented view,* there often exists a *data-oriented view* for managing and accessing data at any point in time. This includes overview tables (e.g., processed object instances) as well as activities that can be optionally executed. The latter are realized based on forms which can be invoked by authorized users to access or change object attributes regardless whether the respective activity is expected to happen during process execution. *Form-based activities* therefore constitute an important part for object management and process execution.

Our overall vision is to enable the modeling, execution and monitoring of object-aware business processes, which provide integrated access to business processes, data and application functions. We aim at the automated and model-driven generation of data-oriented views, process-oriented views and form-based activities at runtime. We also support the integration of arbitrary application components.

Based on the results of our case studies, we have already reported on fundamental challenges (Künzle & Reichert, 2009a, 2009b) and properties of PrMS integrating processes, data and users to provide the needed flexibility. In this paper, we elicit these properties in detail and introduce the requirements for effectively supporting *object-aware processes*. We then evaluate existing process support paradigms along these requirements and discuss which properties are well supported and in which cases additional research is needed to better capture the role of data as driver for process modeling and enactment. Overall, we believe that more profound research on object-aware processes will contribute to overcome some of the fundamental limitations known from existing PrMS.

The remainder of this paper is organized as follows. First, we introduce fundamental properties of object-aware processes and elaborate on the role of data for process enactment in more detail. Following this, we discuss major requirements to support object-aware process management along a realistic example. The main part of the paper discusses the outcomes we obtained when applying imperative, declarative, and current data-driven modeling approaches to tackle the identified requirements. Finally, we close with a summary and outlook.

PROPERTIES OF OBJECT-AWARE BUSINESS PROCESSES

We first describe fundamental properties of object-aware business processes along the main building blocks of existing PrMS (Figure 1). In this context we discuss why objects are the driver for modeling, executing and monitoring these processes.

We first introduce an example of an object-aware process. As illustrated by Figure 2, we use a (simplified) scenario from our case study in the area of human resource management.

Recruitment process: In the context of recruitment applicants may apply for job vacancies via an Internet online form. Before an applicant can send her application to the respective company, specific information (e.g., name, e-mail address, birthday, residence) must be provided. Once the application has been submitted, the responsible personnel officer in the human resource department is notified. The overall process goal is to decide which applicant shall get the job. Since many applicants may apply for a vacancy, usually, different personnel officers handle the applications.

If an application is ineligible, the applicant is immediately rejected. Otherwise, personnel officers may request internal reviews for each applicant. Depending on the concerned functional divisions, the concrete number of reviews may differ from application to application. Corresponding

Figure 1. Building blocks in existing PrMS

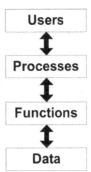

3

Figure 2. Example of a process from the human resource domain

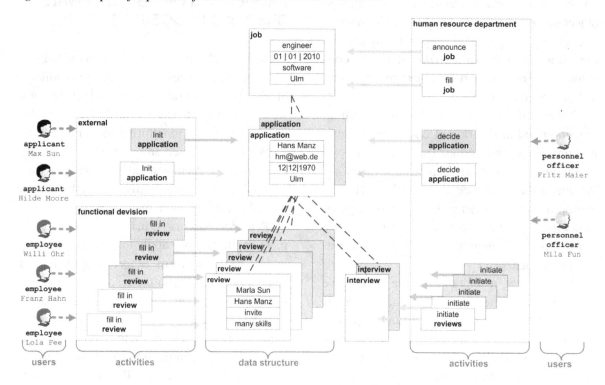

review forms have to be filled by employees from functional divisions until a certain deadline. Employees may either *refuse* or *accept* the requested review. In the former case, they must provide a reason. Otherwise, they make a proposal on how to proceed; i.e., they indicate whether the applicant shall be invited for an interview or be rejected. In the former case an additional appraisal is needed.

After the employee has filled the review form, she submits it to the personnel officer. In the meanwhile, additional applications may have arrived; i.e., different reviews may be requested or submitted at different points in time. In this context, the personnel officer may flag already evaluated reviews. The processing of the application proceeds while corresponding reviews are created; e.g., the personnel officer may check the CV and study the cover letter of the application. Based on the incoming reviews he makes his decision on the application or initiates further steps (e.g., interviews or additional reviews). Further, he does not have to wait for the arrival of all

reviews; e.g., if a particular employee suggests hiring the applicant.

We analyzed additional object-aware processes as implemented in the conference reviewing system *Easychair*. Overall these processes are similar to the recruitment example: scientists may submit papers for a conference and PC chairs request reviews for them. Based on the results of these reviews, some papers are finally accepted, while others are not. In the following we first discuss fundamental properties of object-aware business processes. We illustrate them along our recruitment example. Later on we introduce a second example when discussing characteristic requirements for object-aware processes.

Data

All scenarios we analyzed in our case studies are characterized by a tight integration of process and data: i.e., besides a process-oriented view (e.g., worklists) there exists a data-oriented view that enables end-users to access data at any point in time given the required authorizations. As illustrated in Figure 3a, data is managed based on *object types* which are *related* to each other. Each object type comprises a set of *attributes*. Object types, their attributes, and their inter-relations form a *data structure*.

At runtime the different object types comprise a varying number of inter-related *object instances*, whereby the concrete number can be restricted by lower and upper bounds (i.e., *cardinalities*). Furthermore, object instances of the same object type may differ in both their *attribute values* and *relations* to each other (Figure 3b); e.g., for one application two reviews and for another one three reviews might be requested. We denote an object instance which is directly or transitively referenced by another one as *higher-level* object instance (e.g., an application is a higher-level object instance of a set of reviews). By contrast, an object instance which directly or transitively references another object instance is denoted as *lower-level* object instance (e.g., reviews are lower-level object instances of to an application object).

Activities

Activities can be divided into *form-based* and *black-box* activities. While form-based activities provide *input fields* (e.g., text-fields or check-boxes) for writing and *data fields* for reading selected attribute values of object instances, black-box activities enable complex computations or integration of advanced functionalities (e.g., sending e-mails or invoking web services).

Form-based activities can be further divided into instance-specific activities, batch activities and context-specific activities. *Instance-specific activities* correspond to exactly one object instance (Figure 4, part a). When executing such activity, attributes of that object instance can be read, written or updated using a form (e.g., the form an applicant can use for entering his application data). A *context-sensitive activity* additionally includes fields corresponding to higher-level or lower-level object instances (Figure 4b). When integrating lower-level object instances, usually, a collection of object instances is considered. For example, when an employee fills in a review, additional information about the corresponding application should be provided (i.e., attributes belonging to the application for which the review is requested). Furthermore, employees may change the value for attribute comment of the application object instance. Finally, *batch activities* allow users to change a collection of object instances in one go, i.e., attribute values are assigned to all selected object instances using one form (Figure 4c); e.g., a personnel officer might want to flag a collection of reviews as "evaluated" in one go.

Figure 3. Data structure at build- and runtime

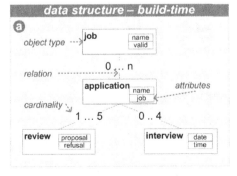
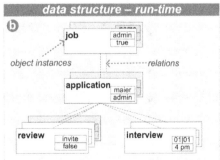

Figure 4. Basic types of form-based activities

Or as soon as an applicant is hired for a job, for all other applications value *reject* should be assignable to attribute decision by filling one form.

Object-aware processes provide a process-oriented view in which *mandatory activities* are assigned to responsible users at the right point in time as well as a data-oriented view in which object instances can be accessed at any point in time using *optional activities*.

Processes

In addition to the *structure* of object types (i.e., their attributes and inter-relations), their *behavior* needs to be considered. Basically, object behavior determines in which order and by whom object attributes have to be (mandatorily) written, and what valid attribute settings are. Thereby, for each object type a set of *states* needs to be defined of which each postulates specific attribute values to be set. More precisely, a state can be expressed in terms of a particular data condition referring to a number of attributes of the respective object type. As example consider object type review and its states as depicted in Figure 5. In state accepted a value for attribute appraisal must be assigned and the value of attribute proposal must either be set to 'reject' or 'invite'. Further, object behavior restricts possible *state* sequences using *transitions*. In particular, for each state possible successor states are defined. Consider the processing of a review in Figure 5c: First, the review must be initiated by a personnel officer. Following this, the employee may either refuse or accept the review.

Figure 5. Object behavior defined based on states and transitions

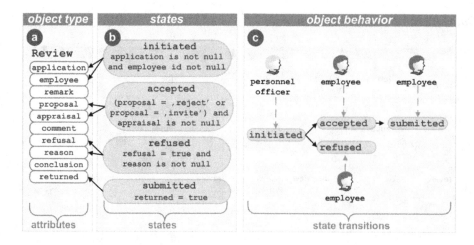

In the latter case, he submits the review back to the personnel officer.

At runtime, for each object type multiple object instances may exist (Figure 6, part a). These object instances may be created or deleted at arbitrary points in time; i.e., the *data structure* dynamically evolves depending on the type and number of created object instances as well as on their relations. Consequently, the individual object instances may be in different states; e.g., several reviews may be requested for a particular applicant. While one of them might be in state initiated, others might have already reached state submitted. Taking the behavior of individual object instances into account, we obtain a complex *process structure* in correspondence to the given data structure (Figure 6b).

Generally, complex processes result from the interactions between instances of different object types:

Object interactions within the recruitment process (Figure 7): A personnel officer announces a job. Following this, applicants may init applications for this job. After submitting an application, the personnel officer requests internal reviews for it. If an employee acting as referee proposes to invite the applicant the personnel officer conducts an interview. Based on the results of reviews and interviews the personnel officer decides in the application. In case of acceptance the applicant is hired.

As can be seen from this scenario, behavior of individual object instances (of same and of different type) needs to be coordinated considering their inter-relations as well as their asynchronous execution. In this context, the dynamic number of object instances must be taken into account (Figure 8); e.g., a personnel officer is not allowed to read the result of a review before the employee has submitted it. Further, the personnel officer may only reject an application immediately if all reviewers propose its rejection.

Activity execution depends on the *behavior* of the processed object instances as well as on their *inter-relations* and thus requires modeling at two abstraction levels.

Figure 6. Data structure and corresponding process structure

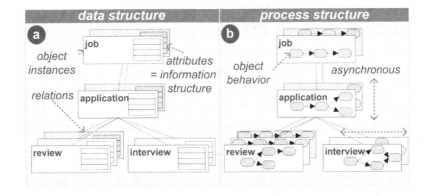

Figure 7. Process definition based on object interactions

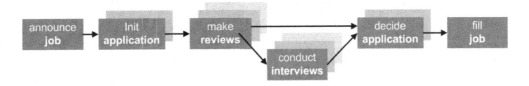

Figure 8. Process structure at build- and runtime

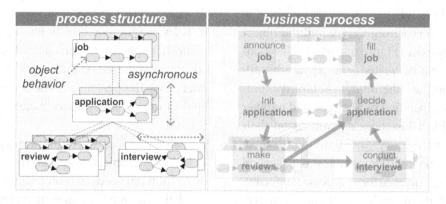

User Integration

Taking the data-oriented view users may optionally access object instances at any point in time and create, read and write them (i.e., executing *optional activities*). The process-oriented view, in turn, provides worklists; i.e., it allows assigning mandatory activities to the right users at the right point in time. If mandatorily required information is missing during process execution, a form-based activity is automatically generated by the system and added to the worklist of the responsible user; e.g., if a review needs to be filled out by an employee a form-based activity with input fields for attributes proposal and appraisal is generated.

Monitoring

The overall state of the process, which is defined in terms of interactions between object instances, should be made transparent. Generally, monitoring the overall process state should provide an aggregated view on the corresponding object instances (Figure 9). Since each object instance may be in a different state, object behavior of each involved object instance needs to be considered in a fine-grained manner.

Figure 9. Aggregated view

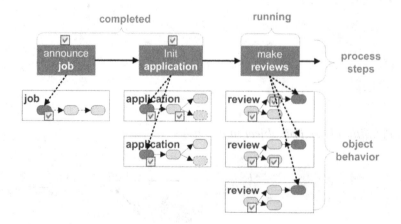

REQUIREMENTS FOR THE IT-SUPPORT OF OBJECT-AWARE PROCESSES

This section elicits fundamental requirements for the support of object-aware processes. We categorize these requirements along the main building blocks of a PrMS (Figure 10). We believe that the poor integration of these building blocks in existing PrMS constitutes a major reason for the insufficient support of object-aware processes and their properties in existing PrMS.

We gathered these requirements in case studies in which we analyzed processes and objects of applications from human resource management, paper reviewing, order handling, and healthcare (Figure 11). Though these requirements are not complete in the sense that they cover all aspects of the object and process lifecycle, their fulfilment is indispensable for enabling the aforementioned properties as well as the automatic generation of runtime components like worklists, overview lists and form-based activities.

Figure 10. Integration of building blocks

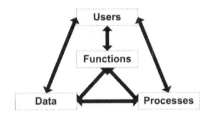

We illustrate the requirements along the introduced recruitment example. We further undergird them using an order handling process in which customers may order different products in an online shop; after such an order is submitted and the resulting bill is paid the seller initiates the shipping of the ordered products. To distinguish between the two scenarios for each requirement we annotate the given examples with 'a' (recruitment process) and 'b' (order handling process) respectively.

Data

R1 (Data integration): Data should be managed in terms of object types comprising object attributes and relations to other object types.
Example 1a: For each job a set of applications may be created. For each application, in turn, several reviews may exist, each having attributes like application, employee, remark, proposal and appraisal.
Example 1b: A shop offers different products. A particular order is always directed to one shop and may comprise several products offered by this shop. Important attributes of a product include its label, price and place of manufacture.

R2 (Access to data): Access to data should be granted at any point given the required authorizations; i.e., not only during the execution of a particular activity.

Figure 11. Fundamental requirements for object-aware processes

	data		activities		processes		user integration
R1	data integration	R5	form-based activities	R10	object behavior	R16	data authorization
R2	access on data	R6	black-box activities	R11	object interactions	R17	process authorization
R3	cardinalities	R7	variable granularity	R12	process-oriented view	R18	differentiation
R4	mandatory information	R8	mandatory and optional activities	R13	flexible process execution	R19	vertical authorization
		R9	control-flow within user forms	R14	re-execution of activities		monitoring
				R15	explicit user decisions	R20	aggregated view

Example 2a: The personnel officer should be allowed to access an application even if no activity is contained in his worklist. Furthermore, if an applicant contacts him to change her address, he should be allowed to update corresponding attributes.

Example 2b: The customer should be allowed to access an order even if no activity is contained in his worklist. For example, he should be allowed to change attribute delivery address even if he has already submitted his order.

R3 (Cardinalities): It should be possible to restrict relations between object instances through *cardinality constraints*.

Example 3a: For each application at least one and at most five reviews may be requested. While for an application two reviews exists, for another one three reviews may be requested.

Example 3b: For each order exactly one payment method must be specified.

R4 (Mandatory information): To reach a particular object instance state from the current one, certain attribute values must be set. For this, a form-based activity with mandatory input fields needs to be assigned to the worklists of authorized users. When executing it, specific input fields referring to mandatorily required attributes have to be filled. Other input fields may be optionally set.

Example 4a: The mandatory form-based activity for requesting a review is accomplished by a personnel officer. When working on this activity, values for object attributes application and employee are mandatory, while other attributes (e.g., remark) are optional.

Example 4b: The mandatory form-based activity for initiating the shipping is accomplished by the seller. When executing this activity, values for object attributes weight and height are mandatory, while other attributes (e.g., express transmission) are optional.

Activities

R5 (Form-based activities): A form-based activity comprises a set of atomic *actions*. Each of them corresponds to either an *input field* for writing or a *data field* for reading the value of an object attribute. Which attributes may be written or read in a particular form-based activity may depend on the user invoking this activity and the state of the object instance. Consequently, a high number of form variants exists. Since it is costly to implement them all, it should be possible to automatically generate form-based activities at runtime.

Example 5a: An employee needs a form-based activity to edit a review; i.e., to assign values to attributes proposal and appraisal. In addition, she can access attributes of the application to which the review refers. As soon as she has submitted her review she may only read attributes proposal and appraisal. If the responsible personnel officer wants to edit the review at the same point in time, he may only write attribute remark.

Example 5b: A customer needs a form-based activity to create an order; e.g., to assign values to attributes shipping address and order date. In addition, the customer may add several products to the order. However, as soon as he has submitted the order he may only change attribute shipping address.

R6 (Black-box activities): To ensure proper execution of black-box activities, we need to be able to define pre-conditions on attribute values of processed object instances. If their input parameters belong to different object instances, their inter-relationships should be controllable. Opposed to form-based activities, which should be automatically generated by the runtime system (R5), for each black-box activity an implementation is required.

Example 6a: Consider a *black-box activity* which compares the skills of an applicant with the requirements of the job. This activity requires input parameters referring to (objects) application, skills, job, and job requirements. It should be ensured that the job is exactly the one for which the applicant applies. Finally, the requirements must comply to the ones of the job and the skills relate to the ones of the applicant.

Example 6b: Consider a *black-box activity* which calculates the total price of an order. This activity requires input parameters referring to the order, products, and shipping method.

R7 (Variable granularity): As discussed, support for instance-specific, context-sensitive, and batch activities is required. Regarding *instance-specific* activities, all actions refer to attributes of one particular object instance, whereas *context-sensitive* activities comprise actions referring to different, but related object instances (of potentially different type). Since *batch activities* involve several object instances of the same type, for them each action corresponds to exactly one attribute. Consequently, the attribute value must be assigned to all referred object instances. Depending on their preference, users should be allowed to freely choose the most suitable activity type for achieving a particular goal. Finally, executing several black-box activities in one go should be supported.

Example 7a: An employee may choose a *context-sensitive activity* to edit a review; i.e., to write attributes proposal and appraisal) and to read attributes of the application. A personnel officer, in turn, may choose a *batch activity* to update several reviews in one go; e.g., to set attribute evaluated for all reviews relating to an application.

Example 7b: A customer may choose a *context-sensitive activity* to edit an order. A seller, in turn, may choose a *batch activity* to initiate the shipping of several products with same weight and height in one go.

R8 (Mandatory and optional activities): Depending on the state of object instances certain activities are mandatory for progressing with the control-flow. At the same time, users should be allowed to optionally execute additional activities (e.g., to write certain attributes even if they are not required at the moment).

Example 8a (Mandatory activity): After a review has been initiated, the assigned employee either must provide or refuse the review; i.e., a form-based activity needs to be mandatorily performed. **(Optional activity)** After a review request has been triggered by the personnel officer (i.e., attributes application and employee are set), he should be further allowed to update object attribute remark. Generally, he may update certain object attributes, while an employee fills in a review.

Example 8b (Mandatory activity): After an order is submitted and the corresponding bill is paid, the seller must initiate the shipping. **(Optional activity)** However, as long as the shipping has not been initiated by the seller, the customer may optionally change the shipping address.

R9 (Control-flow within user forms): Whether certain object attributes are mandatory when processing a particular activity might depend on other object attribute values; i.e., when filling a form certain attributes might become mandatory on-the-fly.

Example 9a: When an employee receives a review request, she either fills the review form as requested by the personnel officer or refuses this task. Consequently, a value needs to be assigned to at least one of the two attributes proposal or refusal. If the employee decides to set attribute proposal, additional object attributes will become mandatory; e.g., if she wants to *invite* the applicant for an interview she has to set attribute appraisal as well. This is not required if she assigns value *reject* to attribute proposal.

Example 9b: If a customer chooses express delivery he must additionally specify a delivery date.

Processes

R10 (Object behavior): It should be possible to determine in which order and by whom object attributes have to be (mandatorily) written, and what valid attribute value settings are. In addition, when executing black-box activities the involved object instances need to be in certain states. Consequently, for each object type its behavior should be definable in terms of states and transitions. In particular, it should be possible to drive process execution based on data and to dynamically react upon attribute value changes. Therefore, it is crucial to map states to attribute values.

Example 10a: An employee may only provide a review for a particular application if the state of the review is initiated. This state is automatically entered as soon as values for attributes employee and application are assigned.

Example 10b: A customer may only order a product if the state of the product is stocked.

R11 (Object interactions): Generally, a process deals with a varying number of object instances of the same and of different object types. In addition, for each processed object instance its behavior must be considered. In this context, it should be possible to process instances in a loosely coupled manner, i.e., *concurrently* to each other and to *synchronize* their execution where needed. More precisely, any process modeling paradigm should allow defining processes with a dynamic number of object instances. First, it should be possible to make the creation of a particular object instance dependent on

the state of the related higher-level object instance (*creation dependency*). Second, during the execution of a higher-level object instance, aggregated information from its lower-level object instances should be accessible; amongst others this requires the aggregation of attribute values from lower-level object instances (*aggregative information*) (Van der Aalst et al., 2000). Third, the executions of different process instances may be mutually dependent (Müller, Reichert, & Herbst, 2007; Van der Aalst et al., 2000); whether an object instance may switch to a certain state depends on the state of another object instance (*execution dependency*). Consequently, processes should be defined in terms of object interactions. Additionally, the integration of black-box activities should possible.

Example 11a: A personnel officer must not initiate any review as long as the corresponding application has not been finally submitted by the applicant (*creation dependency*). Further, individual review process instances are executed concurrently to each other as well as to the application process instances; e.g., the personnel officer may read and change the application while the reviews are processed. Further, reviews belonging to a particular application can be initiated and submitted at different points in time. Besides this, a personnel officer should be able to access information about submitted reviews (*aggregative information*); i.e., if an employee submits her review recommending to invite the applicant for an interview, the personnel officer needs this information immediately. Opposed to this, when proposing rejection of the applicant, the personnel officer should only be informed when other initiated reviews are submitted. Finally, if the personnel officer decides to hire one of the applicants, all others must be rejected (*execution dependency*). In this context, black-box activities become relevant as well (e.g., sending an acknowledgement to an applicant after rejecting his application or comparing the skills of the applicant with the requirements of the job before reviews are initiated.

Example 11b: A seller must not initiate the shipping as long as the corresponding bill has not been paid by the customer (*creation dependency*). A customer should be able to access information about ordered products (*aggregative information*). Finally, if an *ordered* product is not in stock, a reorder by the manufacturer should be initiated (*execution dependency*).

R12 (Process-oriented view): During process execution some activities must be mandatorily executed while others are optional. To ensure that mandatory activities are executed at the right point in time, they must be assigned to the worklists of authorized users.

Example 12a: When a review enters state accepted (i.e., its request was accepted by an employee), a workitem is added to her worklist. When processing it, she has to mandatorily set attributes proposal and appraisal. Furthermore, a personnel officer may optionally change attribute remark of the review.

Example 12b: When an order enters state submitted, a work item is added to the worklist of the customer who has to pay the corresponding bill.

R13 (Flexible process execution): Mandatory activities are obligatory for process execution; i.e., they enforce the setting of object attribute values as required for progressing with the process. In principle, respective attributes can be also set up front by executing optional activities; i.e., before the mandatory activity normally writing this attribute becomes activated. In the latter case, the mandatory activity can be automatically skipped when it is activated.

Example 13a: After the personnel officer has set values for object attributes application and employee, a mandatory activity for filling the review form is assigned to the specified employee. Even if the personnel officer has not completed this review request (i.e., he has specified the respective employee, but not the corresponding application), the selected employee may optionally edit certain attributes of the review. For example, he may refuse the review and set object attribute comment. If the personnel officer has assigned the application, the mandatory activity for providing the review is automatically skipped.

Example 13b: The seller may initiate the shipping before the bill is paid by the customer. If the bill is paid afterwards the mandatory activity for initiating the shipping will be automatically skipped.

R14 (Re-execution of activities): Users should be allowed to re-execute a particular activity (i.e., to update its attributes), even if all mandatory object attributes have been already set.

Example 14a: An employee may change his proposal arbitrarily often until he explicitly agrees to submit the review to the personnel officer.

Example 14b: A customer may change the order arbitrarily often until he explicitly agrees to submit the order to the seller.

R15 (Explicit user decisions): Generally, different ways for reaching a process goal may exist. Usually, the selection between such alternative execution paths is based on history data; i.e., on completed activities and available process-relevant data. In our context, this selection might be also based on explicit user decisions.

Example 15a: A personnel officer may decide whether reviews are requested for a particular application. Only if a review is initiated, a mandatory activity for finalizing the reviews is invoked; i.e., execution of the second activity depends on user a decision.

Example 15b: A customer may decide how many different products he wants to order.

User Integration

R16 (Data authorization): To provide access to data at any point in time, we need to define permissions for creating and deleting object instances as well as for reading/writing their attributes. However, attribute changes contradicting to object behavior should be prevented. For this, the progress of the process has to be taken into account when granting permissions to change objects attributes (Botha, 2002; Wu et al., 2002). Otherwise, if committed attribute values were changed afterwards, object instance state would have to be adjusted to cope with dirty reads. Generally, data permissions should be made dependable on the states as captured by object behavior. This is particularly challenging for context-sensitive and batch activities, since attribute changes have to be valid for all selected instances.

Example 16a: After submitting her review, the employee still may change her comment. However, attribute proposal must not be changed anymore. The personnel officer might have already performed the proposed action. Further, using a batch activity, he may flag several reviews in one go (i.e., assign value *true* to object attribute evaluated). Finally, it must be ensured that the employee can only access reviews she submitted before.

Example 16b: After submitting the order the customer may still change the shipping address. However, since the total price of the order depends on the ordered products, the latter must not be changed anymore.

R17 (Process authorization): For each mandatory activity at least one user or user role should be assigned to it at runtime. Regard-

ing a form-based activity, each user who may execute it must have the permissions for reading/writing corresponding attribute values (Botha, 2002).

Example 17a: An employee who has to fill a review also needs the permissions to set attributes proposal, appraisal, refusal, and appraisal.

Example 17b: A customer who wants to place an order needs the permissions to set corresponding attributes (e.g., shipping address).

R18 (Differentiating authorization and user assignment): When executing mandatory activities particular object attributes have to be set. To determine which user shall execute a pending mandatory activity, her permissions for writing object attributes need to be evaluated. While certain users must execute an activity mandatorily in the context of a particular object instance, others might be authorized to optionally execute this activity; i.e., mandatory and optional permissions should be distinguishable. In particular, a mandatory activity should be only added to the worklists of users having "mandatory permissions". Users with "optional permissions", in turn, may change the corresponding attributes when executing optional activities.

Example 18a: An employee must write attribute proposal if she has accepted the review request. However, her manager may optionally set this attribute as well. The mandatory activity for filling the review form, in turn, should be only assigned to the employee.

Example 18b: The seller must write attribute price before a product can be ordered by a customer. However, the manager of the shop may optionally set this attribute as well. The mandatory activity for filling the product form, in turn, should be only assigned to the seller, but not to the manager.

R19 (Vertical authorization and user assignment): Usually, human activities are associated with actor expressions (e.g., user roles). We denote this as *horizontal authorization.* Users who may work on respective activities are determined at runtime based on these expressions. For object-aware processes, however, the selection of potential actors should not only depend on the activity itself, but also on the object instance processed by it (Rosemann & zur Mühlen, 1997, 2004). We denote this as *vertical authorization.*

Example 19a: A personnel officer may perform activity make decision only for applications for which the name of applicants starts with a letter between 'A' and 'L,' while another officer may perform this activity for applicants whose name starts with a letter between 'M' und 'Z.'

Example 19b: An employee of the seller may initiate the shipping for products having a price lower than 500 euro, while another employee of the seller may perform this activity for products whose price is higher than 500 euro.

Monitoring

R20 (Aggregated view): Process monitoring should provide an aggregated view of all object instances involved in a process as well as their interdependencies.

Example 20a: Consider the decision about a particular application as expressed with attribute decision (based on the results of the reviews). While some reviews might have been already submitted, others might be still processed by an employee. Further, additional reviews might be requested at a later point in time.

Example 20b: Consider different orders referring to the same product. While some orders may have already been completed (i.e., the shipping is completed), others might be still processed. Furthermore, additional orders might be requested at a later point in time.

EVALUATING EXISTING PROCESS SUPPORT PARADIGMS

We evaluate existing approaches along the introduced requirements. We focus on imperative, declarative and data-driven process support paradigms. Other approaches, which are related to our requirements, constitute *extensions* of these paradigms. We base our evaluation on the main characteristics of the approaches. As illustrated in Figure 12, for this purpose we number them consecutively using letters 'A' to 'I'.

As illustrated in Figure 13, only limited support is provided in respect to the support of object-aware processes.

Imperative Approaches

There is a long tradition of modeling business processes in an imperative way. Usually, processes are specified as directed graphs (Weber, Reichert, Rinderle-Ma, 2008). Process steps correspond to different activities which are connected to express precedence relations (Figure 14). For control flow modeling a number of patterns exists, e.g., sequential, alternative and parallel routing, and loop backs (Van der Aalst et al., 2003).

Imperative approaches only provide limited support regarding the requirements raised by object-aware processes. In the following, we discuss the imperative approach along its main characteristics which are numbered using letters 'A' to 'E': hidden information flows (A), flow-based activation of activities (B), actor expressions (C), fixed activity granularity (D), and arbitrary process granularity (E). We evaluate the requirements along these characteristics (Figure 15).

Figure 12. Characteristics of existing approaches

	characteristic	imperative	declarative	data-driven
A	hidden information flows	X	X	
B	flow-based activation	X		
C	actor expressions	X	X	
D	fixed granularity of actvities	X	X	
E	arbitrary granularity of processes	X	X	X
F	constraint-based activation		X	X
G	data integration			X
H	data-driven activation			X
I	advanced role concept			X

Figure 13. Evaluating existing paradigms

+ *supported*
O *partially supported*
- *not supported*

	imperative	declarative	data-driven	
				data
R1	-	-	O	data integration
R2	-	-	O	access to data
R3	O	-	O	cardinalities
R4	-	-	+	mandatory information
				activities
R5	-	-	O	form-based activities
R6	O	O	O	black-box activities
R7	-	-	-	variable granularity
R8	-	+	O	mandatory and optional activities
R9	-	-	-	control-flow within user forms
				processes
R10	O	O	+	object behavior
R11	O	O	O	object interactions
R12	+	+	+	process-oriented view
R13	-	-	+	flexible process execution
R14	-	-	O	re-execution of activities
R15	-	-	+	explicit user decisions
				user integration
R16	-	-	O	data authorization
R17	O	O	+	process authorization
R18	-	-	-	differentiation of authorization and user assignment
R19	-	-	-	vertical authorization
				monitoring
R20	-	-	-	aggregated view

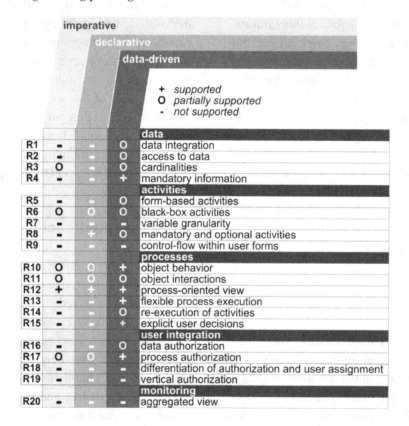

Figure 14. Imperative modeling approach

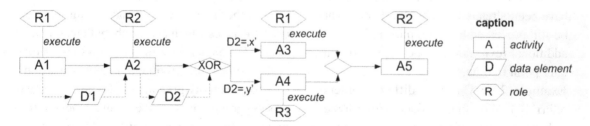

Figure 15. Evaluating the imperative approach

imperative approach

+ supported	**A** hidden information flows
O partially supported	**B** flow-based activation
- not supported	**C** actor expressions
	D fixed granularity of actvities
	E arbitrary granularity of processes

			characteristic
		data	
R1	-	data integration	A
R2	-	access on data	B
R3	O	cardinalities	E
R4	-	mandatory information	A
		activities	
R5	-	form-based activities	A,E
R6	O	black-box activities	A
R7	-	variable granularity	D
R8	-	mandatory and optional activities	B
R9	-	control-flow within user forms	A
		processes	
R10	O	object behavior	E
R11	O	object interactions	E
R12	+	process-oriented view	C
R13	-	flexible process execution	B
R14	-	re-execution of activities	B
R15	-	explicit user decisions	B
		user integration	
R16	-	data authorization	B
R17	O	process authorization	A
R18	-	differentiation of authorization and user assignment	B
R19	-	vertical authorization	A
		monitoring	
R20	-	aggregated view	A

Hidden Information Flows (A)

Usually, imperative approaches enable the explicit definition of data flows between activities based on atomic data elements. The latter are connected with activities (and their parameters) or with routing conditions (Figure 14). Activities themselves are regarded as black-boxes; i.e., application data is usually managed within invoked applications. In particular, there is no explicit link between activities and the object instances they manipulate.

Data. Data integration based on object types, attributes and relations is not supported (i.e., R1 is not met); i.e., the PrMS is unaware of the object instances being accessed during process execution. Further, it cannot control whether required data changes are actually accomplished; i.e., *mandatory information* cannot be realized (i.e., R4 is not met).

Activities. A particular activity usually requires data that has to be provided by preceding activities.

Ideally, this is accomplished according to the modeled data flow. If accessed data elements are not written by previous activities, process execution might be blocked. Opposed to this, if consumed data is not explicitly considered in the modeled data flow, the process instance might proceed though required data is missing. Consequently, it is not possible to automatically invoke a *form-based activity* for requesting missing data from users. Furthermore, the *internal control-flow* of a form-based activity cannot be expressed (i.e., R5 and R9 are not met). Regarding *black-box activities*, in turn, different parameters may belong to attributes of different object instances. However, we cannot control the relations between the object instances to which the parameters of an activity refer (i.e., R6 is not fully supported).

User integration. It cannot be guaranteed that users who own the permission for executing an activity are also authorized to read/write attributes processed by this activity. Thus, *process authorization* is only enabled at activity level (i.e., R17 is not fully met). *Vertical authorization* (i.e., assigning different permissions for the same activity depending on the state of the processed object instance) is not supported (i.e., R19 is not met).

Monitoring. Due to hidden information flows one cannot provide an *aggregated view* on processed object instances (i.e., R20 is not met).

Flow-Based Activation of Activities (B)

Each process step corresponds to one activity being mandatory for process execution (except it is contained in a conditional path). Moreover, activity activation depends on the state of preceding activities, i.e., a particular activity becomes enabled if its preceding activities are completed or cannot be executed anymore (except loop backs).

Data. Data access is only possible when executing activities according to the defined controlflow; i.e., data cannot be accessed independently from process execution (i.e., R2 is not fully met).

Activities. There is no support for *optional activities* enabling data access at any point in time (i.e., R8 is not met).

Processes. Since the activation of an activity solely depends on the completion of other activities, *flexible process execution* (e.g., skipping certain activities if required output data is already available) is not explicitly supported (i.e., R13 is not met).

There is no direct support for *re-executing an activity* as long as the user does not commit its completion (i.e., R14 is not met). Since activity activation only depends on the completion of other activities there is no explicit support for *user decisions* (i.e., R15 is not met).

User integration. Since data can only be accessed when executing mandatory activities, imperative approaches lack sophisticated support

for coordinating processed data and executed processes. Thus, neither proper *data authorization* (i.e., R16 is not met) nor the *distinction between process and data authorization* are considered (i.e., R18 is not met).

Actor Expressions (C)

Human activities are associated with actor expressions (e.g., roles). Based on these expressions activities can be assigned to authorized users at runtime. Further, when a human activity becomes enabled, a corresponding work item is added to worklists of authorized users.

User integration. A *process-oriented view* is provided enabling the execution of activities by the right users at the right point in time (i.e., R12 is met).

Fixed Activity Granularity (D)

Activities are associated with a specific business function implemented at buildtime, thus having a fixed granularity.

Activities. Support of different work practices by enabling instance-specific, context-sensitive and batch activities is not provided; i.e.; a *variable granularity of activities* is not possible (i.e., R7 is not met).

Arbitrary Process Granularity (E)

Imperative approaches do not distinguish between the behavior of individual object instances and the processes coordinating them. Business functions associated with the activities of a process model can be implemented at different levels of granularity. While certain activities are only processing one object instance, others may process several object instances of same/different type. Generally, there exists no elaborated modeling methodology giving advice on the number of object types to be handled within one process definition. Consequently, a process is either defined at a *coarse- or fine-grained level*.

Data. When applying a *coarse-grained process modeling style*, an activity may be linked to several object types. Since object flows are hidden, it is difficult to ensure consistency between process and data modeling. In particular, when modeling a process the creation of object instances cannot be restricted to a varying and dynamic number of object instances based on *cardinalities* (i.e., R3 is not fully met).

Activities. When applying a *fine-grained process modeling style*, activity execution is associated with exactly one process instance. Consequently, only instance-specific activities can be realized, but no context-sensitive or batch activities. Further, it is not possible to automatically generate a *form-based activity* if required data is missing (i.e., R5 is not met).

Processes. When choosing a *fine-grained modeling style* each process definition is aligned with exactly one object type. This way one can ensure that corresponding process instances access one particular object instance of the respective object type at runtime. For this purpose, either one data element for routing the object-ID or several data elements (of which each relates to one attribute) are added to the process model. The activity-centred paradigm of imperative approaches is not appropriate for supporting *object behavior* (i.e., R10 is not fully met). Hidden information flows and the flow-based activation of activities inhibit the dynamic adaptation of the control-flow based on available data. Further, interdependencies between process models cannot be expressed and process instances are executed in isolation to each other. Thus, the definition of *interactions between object instances* is not captured (i.e., R11 is not met). To deal with these requirements the following extensions exist.

Extension 1 (Proclets): Proclets enable process communication and asynchronous process coordination based on message exchanges (Van der Aalst et al., 2000). Using Proclets, however, process coordination cannot be explicitly based on the underlying data structure or on specific data element values. Further, messages can only be exchanged at specific points during process execution (e.g., based on send/receive activities).

Extension 2 (Data-driven process structures): In Corepro, the coordination of processes instances can be based on the relations between involved object instances. Thereby, synchronization constraints are defined based on object states (Müller, Reichert, & Herbst, 2007). However, states are not connected to object attributes. Further, each invoked process is defined imperatively. This leads to the discussed disadvantages like hidden information flows, fixed activity granularity, and arbitrary process granularity.

A *coarse-grained modeling style*, in turn, prohibits *fine-grained control* in respect to *object type behavior* (i.e., R10 is not met). Processes are only defined based on activities and interactions between *object instances* are not considered (i.e., R11 is not met). An interesting extension is object life cycles.

Extension 3 (Object life cycles): To integrate object behavior with processes, an extension of the imperative approach based on object life cycles (OLC) has been proposed (Gerede & Su, 2007; Küster, Ryndina, & Gall, 2007; Redding et al., 2007; Nigam & Caswell, 2003; Liu, Bhattacharya, & Wu, 2007). In particular, the introduction of OLCs target at consistency between process models and process data. For this purpose, an OLC defines the states of an object and the transitions between them in a *separate* *model.* Activities, in turn, are associated with pre-/post-conditions in relation to objects states. However, states are not mapped to attribute values. Consequently, if certain pre-conditions cannot be met during runtime, it is not possible to dynamically react to this. Neither relations between object types nor the varying number of object instances are considered.

Process support involving different object instances can be provided by using sub-processes. Thereby, a sub-process is associated with an activity of the higher-level process instance. However, it is not possible to define relations and synchronization dependencies between different sub-process definitions of the same level. Consequently, processes which are defined based on *object interactions* are not supported (i.e., R11 is not met). This limitation can be addressed by multiple-instantiation patterns (Van der Aalst et al., 2003), which allow specifying the number of instances for a respective activity either at build- or runtime.

Extension 4 (Multiple-instantiation patterns): Regarding multiple-instance activity patterns, new sub-process instances can only be created as long as subsequent activities have not been started; e.g., additional reviews can be instantiated as long as the corresponding application is not further processed. Thus, lower-level process instances

(i.e., sub-process instances) can only be created at a specific point during the execution of the higher-level process instance. Furthermore, except for one variant of the multiple-instantiation pattern, sub-process instances cannot be executed asynchronously to the higher-level process instance. Using multiple-instantiation patterns with synchronization (Figure 16, part a), each sub-process instance must either be completed or skipped before subsequent activities of the higher-level process instance can be triggered. Using multiple-instantiation without synchronization, in turn, the results of these sub-process executions are not relevant for progressing the higher-level process instance (Figure 16b). Finally, interdependencies between sub-processes, which are executed asynchronously to each other (Figure 16c), cannot be taken into account.

Declarative Approaches

Declarative approaches suggest a fundamentally different way of describing business processes (Van der Aalst & Pesic, 2006). While imperative models specify how things have to be done, declarative approaches only focus on the logic that governs the interplay of actions in the process by describing (1) the *activities* that can be performed and (2) the *constraints* prohibiting undesired behavior. In the example from Figure 17, activities

Figure 16. Sub-process execution based on multiple-instantiation

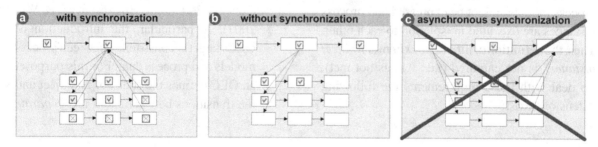

Figure 17. Declarative modeling approach

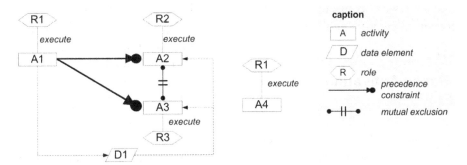

A2 and A3 can only be executed after finishing A1 (Pesic, 2008). Finally, A2 and A3 are mutually exclusive.

Declarative approaches provide limited support for object-aware processes. Many of their characteristics correspond to the ones of imperative approaches: hidden information flows (A), actor expressions (C), fixed activity granularity (D),

and arbitrary process granularity (E). However, they differ in respect to activity activation. While imperative approaches pursue a flow-based activation (B), declarative approaches rely on a constraint-based activation (F) (Figure 18). This leads to better support of optional activities in comparison to imperative approaches. However, the extensions introduced for imperative ap-

Figure 18. Evaluating the declarative approach

declarative approach

+ supported
O partially supported
- not supported

A	hidden information flows
C	actor expressions
D	fixed granularity of actvities
E	arbitrary granularity of processes
F	constraint-based activation

			characteristic
		data	
R1	-	data integration	A
R2	-	access on data	F
R3	-	cardinalities	E
R4	-	mandatory information	A
		activities	
R5	-	form-based activities	A,E
R6	O	black-box activities	A
R7	-	variable granularity	D
R8	+	mandatory and optional activities	F
R9	-	control-flow within user forms	A
		processes	
R10	O	object behavior	E
R11	O	object interactions	E
R12	+	process-oriented view	C
R13	-	flexible process execution	F
R14	-	re-execution of activities	F
R15	-	explicit user decisions	F
		user integration	
R16	-	data authorization	F
R17	O	process authorization	A
R18	-	differentiation of authorization and user assignment	F
R19	-	vertical authorization	A
		monitoring	
R20	-	aggregated view	A

proaches are not applicable to declarative ones. To avoid redundancies, we only discuss the main differences between imperative and declarative approach.

Constraint-Based Activation of Activities (F)

Imperative models take an "inside-out" approach by requiring all execution alternatives to be explicitly specified in the model. Declarative models, in turn, take an "outside-in" approach: constraints implicitly specify execution alternatives as all valid alternatives have to satisfy the constraints (Pesic, 2008). Adding more constraints means discarding some execution alternatives. This results in a coarse up-front specification of a process, which can be refined iteratively during runtime. Typical constraints can be roughly divided into three classes (Sadiq et al., 2005; Van der Aalst & Pesic, 2006): constraints restricting the *selection* of activities (e.g., minimum/maximum occurrence of activities, mutual exclusion), the *ordering* of activities and the use of *resources* (e.g., execution time of activities).

Activities. Adequate support for *optional activities* is provided, i.e., activities can be considered as optional as long as no constraint enforces their execution (i.e., R8 is met).

Arbitrary Process Granularity (E)

Partial support for integrating process instances can be achieved based on sub-processes.

Processes. Since most declarative approaches do not support multiple instantiations, *cardinalities* to higher-level process definitions cannot be expressed (i.e., R3 is not met). It is further not possible to define processes based on *object interactions* (i.e., R11 is not met).

Extension 5 (State-oriented business process modeling): In the state-based extension provided by (Bider, 2002) a state does not necessarily correspond to an object instance. Instead, it rather belongs to a process instance comprising a set of atomic attributes or repeated groups (e.g., lists). States are used to specify the activities which should, can or must be executed; i.e., opposed to declarative modeling, conditions for executing activities are defined based on states rather than on activities. The disadvantages known from declarative approaches still hold: hidden information flows, fixed activity granularity, and arbitrary process granularity. Finally, this approach focuses on modeling functionalities without defining operational semantics; i.e., models cannot be generated.

Data-Driven Approaches

There exist several approaches which support a tighter integration of processes and data (Reijers, Liman, & Van der Aalst, 2003; Vanderfeesten, Reijers, & Van der Aalst, 2008; Müller, Reichert, & Herbst, 2007; Van der Aalst, Weske, & Grünbauer, 2005). Since Case Handling (CH) (Van der Aalst, Weske, & Grünbauer, 2005) satisfies the requirements for object-aware processes best, we focus on CH when evaluating data-driven approaches. Additionally, we refer to the Flower CH tool (Pallas Athena, 2002) in the context of our evaluation. Compared to imperative and declarative approaches the main differences lie in the integration of application data (G), the data-driven execution paradigm (H), and the advanced role concept (I). Like in imperative and declarative approaches, the processes can be defined at arbitrary level of granularity (E). However, the granularity of activities is fixed (D) (Figure 19).

Data Integration (G)

Opposed to activity-centric approaches, CH enables a tighter integration of processes, activities and data (Mutschler, Weber, & Reichert, 2008). As illustrated in Figure 20, CH differentiates between

Figure 19. Evaluating the data-driven approach

		data-driven approach	characteristic
		data	
R1	O	data integration	G
R2	O	access on data	G
R3	O	cardinalities	E
R4	+	mandatory information	G
		activities	
R5	+	form-based activities	G
R6	O	black-box activities	G
R7	-	variable granularity	D
R8	O	mandatory and optional activities	G
R9	-	control-flow within user forms	G
		processes	
R10	+	object behavior	E
R11	O	object interactions	E
R12	+	process-oriented view	I
R13	+	flexible process execution	H
R14	O	re-execution of activities	I
R15	+	explicit user decisions	H
		user integration	
R16	O	data authorization	G
R17	+	process authorization	I
R18	-	differentiation of authorization and user assignment	I
R19	-	vertical authorization	I
		monitoring	
R20	-	aggregated view	G

Legend:
- **+** supported
- **O** partially supported
- **-** not supported
- **D** fixed granularity of actvities
- **E** arbitrary granularity of processes
- **G** data integration
- **H** data-driven activation
- **I** advanced role concept

Figure 20. Case handling

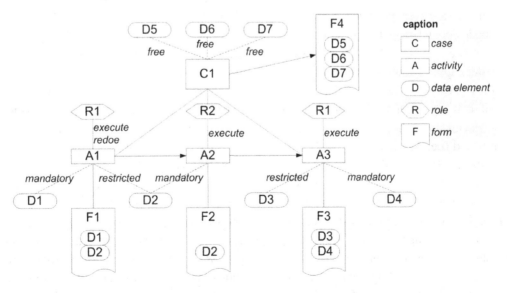

free, restricted and mandatory data elements (Van der Aalst, Weske, & Grünbauer, 2005). Based on *free data elements*, business data not directly relevant for process control or activity inputs can be added to the process model. Free data elements are assigned to the *case description* (i.e., process model) and can be changed at any point in time while modeling the *case* (i.e., the process instance). All other data elements are associated with one or more activities, and are further subdivided into two categories. *Restricted data elements* can only be written in the context of the activities they are assigned to. *Mandatory data elements* require a value to complete the activity to which they belong.

Data. CH only provides atomic data elements; *data integration* in terms of object types and their inter-relations is not considered (i.e., R1 is not fully met). All users involved in a case are allowed to *read* its data elements. Based on a query mechanism, users may access active and completed cases. This enables *access to data* at any point in time. However, the composition of atomic data elements to object types is not considered (i.e., R2 is not fully met). By specifying certain data elements as mandatory, *mandatory information* is supported (i.e., R4 is met).

Activities. Form-based activities can be explicitly defined. However, provided form fields cannot be made dependent on the current process state and user (i.e., R5 is not fully met). Besides this, CH fosters application integration of *black-box activities* (Pesic & Van der Aalst, 2002). However, if activity input parameters refer to different object instances their inter-relations cannot be controlled (i.e., R6 is not fully met). Free data elements enable optional activities, but one cannot define specific *optional activities* for different user roles (i.e., R8 is not fully met). Since dependencies between fields cannot be expressed, no support for controlling the *control-flow within a form* exists (i.e., R9 is not met)

User integration. Regarding *data authorization*, it is not possible to define different access rights for a particular user depending on the progress of the case (i.e., R16 is not met).

Monitoring. Since neither object types/instances nor the relations between them are considered, *aggregated views* cannot be provided (i.e., R20 is not met).

Data-Driven Activation of Activities (H)

Imperative and declarative approaches are both activity-centric. In data-driven approaches (like CH), activities become enabled when data changes. An activity is completed if all mandatory data elements have assigned values.

Processes. Activities can be automatically skipped at runtime if their data elements are provided by other activities; i.e., mandatory data elements are provided by preceding activities. This, in turn, enables *flexible process execution* (i.e., R13 is met). In addition, *user decisions* are supported (Pesic & Van der Aalst, 2002) (i.e., R15 is met).

Advanced Role Concept (I)

CH allows to define who shall work on an activity and who may redo or skip it; for this purpose separate roles exist. Using the redo-role, for example, CH allows actors to execute activities multiple times.

Processes. Based on the execute-role, actors can be assigned to human activities. Further, users may select all cases for which they have to perform an activity. This enables a *process-oriented view* (i.e., R12 is met).

User integration. Since the data elements that are processed during an activity execution are known, fine-grained *process authorization* at the level of single data elements becomes possible (i.e., R17 is met). Despite the introduction of the redo-role, *re-executing* activities arbitrarily often is not possible (i.e., R9 is not fully met).

Example 21 (Re-execution): As illustrated in Figure 21, role R1 may execute or redo activity A1. If all mandatory data elements of a particular activity are available, subsequent activities become enabled immediately. Regarding our example (Figure 21) as long as A2 is not completed (i.e., a value for data element D2 is not set), R1 may redo activity A1. However, after completing subsequent activity A1, redo is only possible if the user is authorized to redo A2 (Figure 21c). Otherwise, A1 cannot be redone any longer.

Regarding mandatory activities, any user owning the *execution-role* for such activity must execute it mandatorily; i.e., no *differentiation between authorization and user assignment* is made (i.e., R18 is not met). Finally, *vertical authorization* based on data element values is not provided (i.e., R19 is not met).

Fixed Activity Granularity (D)

In CH each activity belongs to exactly one process instance, and the granularity of activities is fixed at build-time.

Activities. Users cannot access data element values of other relating cases; i.e., a *variable granularity* of activities to support preferred work practices (e.g., context-sensitive vs. batch activities) is not supported (i.e., R7 is not met).

Arbitrary Process Granularity (E)

CH allows to model processes at arbitrary level of granularity. When described at a *coarse-grained level*, a case definition includes data elements corresponding to different objects. Interdependencies between different cases can be defined based on sub-cases. Further, CH supports multiple-instantiation patterns through dynamic sub-plans (i.e., sub-process instances) (Pesic & Van der Aalst, 2002). This enables instantiation of a dynamically fixed number of sub-process instances. Alternatively, when processes are described at a *fine-grained level*, a "case" can be manually treated in tight accordance with an "object".

Data. Using multiple-instantiation patterns as extension, *cardinalities* between higher-level and lower-level process instances can be taken into account. However, it cannot be ensured that the correct number of sub-processes instances is actually created at runtime (i.e., R3 is not fully met).

Processes. Modeling processes in a *fine-grained manner* means we need to consider each case as object type. This enables support of *object behavior* (i.e., R10 is met). Even if object behavior is not considered in terms of states and transitions, the data-driven execution allows to dynamically react to data changes. As limitation activities always refer to the execution of one particular case. Thus, only instance-specific activities can be realized, but no *varying granularity*; i.e., us-

Figure 21. Re-execution of activities in CH

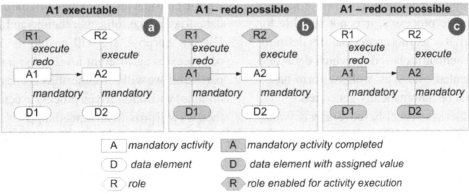

ers cannot choose their preferred work practice (i.e., R7 is not met). Further, we cannot define *interactions between object instances* (i.e., R11 is not met).

When modeling processes at a *coarse-grained level*, similar restrictions for the asynchronous coordination of sub-process instances hold as for imperative approaches. Compared to imperative approaches CH additionally allows users to access data from multiple instances through data containers with a variable number of data elements. Taking literature we cannot conclude that these data enable the data-driven execution of activities that belong to the higher-level process instance; i.e., *interdependencies between asynchronously executed object instances* are not fully supported (i.e., R11 is not fully met).

Further Approaches

The object-process methodology (OPM) (Dori, 2002), considers object types and their interrelations. Furthermore, object behavior can be defined in terms of states and processes enable transitions between them; i.e., states are used as pre-/post-conditions for process execution. However, states are not mapped to individual attribute values what leads to hidden information flows. OPM further allows for different levels of aggregation using zooming functions. There exists no methodology to define the resulting abstraction layers in correspondence to the data structure; i.e., each layer can be defined at an arbitrary level of granularity. In addition, the granularity of activities is fixed. Though OPM considers some properties of object-aware processes, it is not suitable for their support. It is also not appropriate for defining operational semantics based on which data- and process-oriented views as well as form-based activities can be automatically generated.

Finally, there exist goal-based (Soffer & Wand, 2005), decision-oriented, and conversation-oriented process modeling approaches (Nurcan, 2008) which are outside the scope of our evaluation.

Summary and Outlook

We discussed fundamental requirements in respect to the provision of an integrated view on processes and data. Such integration is needed for many applications like *enterprise resource planning* and *customer relationship management*. Further, we showed that the identified requirements go beyond the features of existing modeling approaches. Especially activity-centric approaches show an inherent weakness in respect to object-aware process management. Data-driven approaches, in turn, are more expressive, but have not reached the required maturity level yet. To our knowledge, there exists no approach which provides a well-defined modeling methodology for defining object behavior and interactions. Regarding behavior, object states must be mapped to attribute values and inter-relations must be considered.

To tackle the discussed challenges and requirements, in the *PHILharmonic Flows* project we target at a framework that enables a tight integration of business processes, business data, and users. In our future work we will report on this framework. On the one hand, it retains the well-established principle for separation of concerns; on the other hand, it explicitly considers the relationships between processes, functions, data and users. Furthermore, *PHILharmonicFlows* will address process modeling, execution and monitoring, and will provide generic functions for the model-driven generation of end user components (e.g., form-based activities). Opposed to existing approaches on process and data integration, we want to consider all components of the underlying data structure; i.e., objects, relations and attributes. For this purpose, we will enable the modeling of processes at different levels of granularity. In particular, we will combine object behavior based on states with data-driven process execution. Further, we will provide advanced support for process coordination as well as for the integrated access to business processes, business functions and business data. Our overall vision is to overcome many of the limitations of contemporary PrMS.

REFERENCES

Bider, I. (2002). *State-oriented business process modeling: Principles, theory and practice.* Unpublished doctoral dissertation, Royal Institute of Technology, Stockholm, Sweden.

Botha, R. A. (2002). *CoSAWoE - a model for context-sensitive access control in workflow environments.* Unpublished doctoral dissertation, Rand Afrikaans University, Johannesburg, South Africa.

Dadam, P., & Reichert, M. (2009). The ADEPT project: A Decade of research and development for robust and flexible process support - challenges and achievements. *Computer Science, 23*(2), 81–97.

Dori, D. (2002). *Object-process methodology.* Berlin, Germany: Springer-Verlag.

Gerede, C. E., & Su, J. (2007). Specification and verification of artifact behaviors in business process models. In B. Krämer, K.-J. Lin, & P. Narasimhan (Eds.), *Proceedings of the 5th International Conference on Service-Oriented Computing* (LNCS 4749, pp. 181-192).

Künzle, V., & Reichert, M. (2009a). *Towards object-aware process management systems: Issues, challenges, benefits.* Paper presented at the 10th International Workshop on Business Process Modeling, Development, and Support, Amsterdam, The Netherlands.

Künzle, V., & Reichert, M. (2009b). Integrating users in object-aware process management systems: Issues and challenges. In S. Rinderle-Ma, S. Sadiq, & F. Leymann (Eds.), *Proceedings of the 5th International Workshop on Business Process Design* (LNBIP. 43, pp. 29-41).

Küster, J., Ryndina, K., & Gall, H. (2007). Generation of business process models for object life cycle compliance. In G. Alonso, P. Dadam, & M. Rosemann (Eds.), *Proceedings of the 5th International Conference on Business Process Management* (LNCS 4714, pp. 165 -181).

Liu, R., Bhattacharya, K., & Wu, F. Y. (2007). Modeling business contexture and behavior using business artifacts. In J. Krogstie, A. Opdahl, & G. Sindre (Eds.), *Proceedings of the 19th International Conference on Advanced Information Systems Engineering* (LNCS 4495, pp. 324-339).

Müller, D., Reichert, M., & Herbst, J. (2007). Data-driven modeling and coordination of large process structures. In R. Meersman & Z. Tari (Eds.), *Proceedings of the 15th International Conference on Cooperative Information Systems* (LNCS 4803, pp. 131-149).

Mutschler, B., Weber, B., & Reichert, M. (2008). Workflow management versus case handling: Results from a controlled software experiment. In *Proceedings of the 23rd Annual ACM Symposium on Applied Computing, Special Track on Coordination Models, Languages and Architectures* (pp. 82-89).

Nigam, A., & Caswell, N. S. (2003). Business artifacts - an approach to operational specification. *IBM Systems Journal, 42*(3), 428–445. doi:10.1147/sj.423.0428.

Nurcan, S. (2008). A survey on the flexibility requirements related to business processes and modeling artifacts. In *Proceedings of the 41st Annual Hawaii International Conference on System Science* (p. 378).

Pallas Athena. (2002). The Pallas Athena BV: *Flower user manual.* Apeldoorn, The Netherlands: BuscadorWord. Retrieved from http://word.bienesyautos.com/word-YAWL-Editor-15/2.php

Pesic, M. (2008). *Constraint-based workflow management systems: Shifting control to users.* Unpublished doctoral dissertation, Eindhoven University of Technology, The Netherlands.

Redding, G., Dumas, M., ter Hofstede, A. H. M., & Iordachescu, A. (2008). Transforming object-oriented models to process-oriented models. In A. Ter Hofstede, B. Benatallah, & H.-Y. Paik (Eds.), *Proceedings of the 3rd International Workshop on Business Process Management* (LNCS 4928, pp. 132-143).

Reijers, H. A., Liman, S., & Van der Aalst, W. M. P. (2003). Product-based workflow design. *Management Information Systems*, *20*(1), 229–262.

Rinderle-Ma, S., & Reichert, M. (2007). A formal framework for adaptive access control models. In S. Spaccapietra, P. Atzeni, F. Fages, M.-S. Hacid, M. Kifer, J. Mylopoulos et al. (Eds.), Journal on Data Semantics 9 (LNCS 4601, pp. 82-112).

Rosemann, M., & zur Mühlen, M. (1998). Modellierung der aufbauorganisation in workflow-management-systemen: Kritische bestandsaufnahme und gestaltungsvorschläge. *EMISA-Forum*, *3*(1), 78–86.

Rosemann, M., & zur Mühlen, M. (2004). Organizational management in workflow applications: Issues and perspectives. *Information Technology Management*, *5*(3-4), 271–291.

Sadiq, S., Orlowska, M. E., Sadiq, W., & Schulz, K. (2005). When workflows will not deliver: The case of contradicting work practice. In *Proceedings of the 8th International Conference on Business Information Systems* (pp. 69-84).

Sadiq, S., Sadiq, W., & Orlowska, M. (2005). A framework for constraint specification and validation in flexible workflows. *Information Systems*, *30*(5), 349–378. doi:10.1016/j.is.2004.05.002.

Silver, B. (2009). *Case management: Addressing unique BPM requirements*. Aptos, CA: BPMS Watch. Retrieved from http://www.global360. com/xres/uploads/resource-center-documents/ Case_Management_WP_final.pdf

Soffer, P., & Wand, Y. (2005). On the notion of soft-goals in business process modeling. *Business Process Management Journal*, *11*(6), 663–679. doi:10.1108/14637150510630837.

Van der Aalst, W. M. P., Barthelmess, P., Ellis, C. A., & Wainer, J. (2000). Workflow modeling using proclets. In O. Etzion & P. Scheuermann (Eds.), *Proceedings of the 7th International Conference on Cooperative Information Systems* (LNCS 1901, pp. 198-209).

Van der Aalst, W. M. P., & Pesic, M. (2006). DecSerFlow: Towards a truly declarative service flow language. In F. Leymann et al (Eds.), Dagstuhl Seminar Proceedings: The Role of Business Processes in Service Oriented Architectures (LNCS 4184, pp. 1-23).

Van der Aalst, W. M. P., ter Hofstede, A., Kiepuszewski, B., & Barros, A. (2003). Workflow patterns. *Distributed and Parallel Databases*, *14*(1), 5–51. doi:10.1023/A:1022883727209.

Van der Aalst, W. M. P., ter Hofstede, A., & Weske, M. (2003). Business process management: A survey. In *Proceedings of the 1st International Conference on Business Process Management* (pp. 1-12).

Van der Aalst, W. M. P., Weske, M., & Grünbauer, D. (2005). Case handling: A new paradigm for business process support. *Data & Knowledge Engineering*, *53*(2), 129–162. doi:10.1016/j. datak.2004.07.003.

Vanderfeesten, I., Reijers, H. A., & Van der Aalst, W. M. P. (2008). Product-based workflow support: Dynamic workflow execution. In Z. Bellahsene & M. Leonard (Eds.), *Proceedings of the International Conference on Advanced Information Systems Engineering* (LNCS 5074, pp. 571-574).

Weber, B., Reichert, M., & Rinderle-Ma, S. (2008). Change patterns and change support features - enhancing flexibility in process-aware information systems. *Data & Knowledge Engineering, 66*(3), 438–466. doi:10.1016/j.datak.2008.05.001.

Wu, S., Sheth, A., Miller, J., & Luo, Z. (2002). Authorization and access control of application data in workflow-systems. *Journal of the Association of Intelligent Information Systems, 18*(1), 71–94. doi:10.1023/A:1012972608697.

This work was previously published in the International Journal of Information System Modeling and Design (IJISMD), Volume 2, Issue 2, edited by Remigijus Gustas, pp. 19-46, copyright 2011 by IGI Publishing (an imprint of IGI Global).

Chapter 2
Ontological Description and Similarity–Based Discovery of Business Process Models

Khalid Belhajjame
University of Manchester, UK

Marco Brambilla
Politecnico di Milano, Italy

ABSTRACT

Project repositories are a central asset in software development, as they preserve the knowledge gathered in past development activities. Locating relevant information in a vast project repository is problematic, because it requires manually tagging projects with accurate metadata, an activity which is time consuming and prone to errors and omissions. Just like any other artifact or web service, business processes can be stored in repositories to be shared and used by third parties, e.g., as building blocks for constructing new business processes. The success of such a paradigm depends partly on the availability of effective search tools to locate business processes that are relevant to the user purposes. A handful of researchers have investigated the problem of business process discovery using as input syntactical and structural information that describes business processes. This work explores an additional source of information encoded in the form of annotations that semantically describe business processes. Business processes can be semantically described using the so called abstract business processes. These are designated by concepts from an ontology which additionally captures their relationships. This ontology can be built in an automatic fashion from a collection of (concrete) business processes, and this work illustrates how it can be refined by domain experts and used in the discovery of business processes, with the purpose of reuse and increase in design productivity.

DOI: 10.4018/978-1-4666-4161-7.ch002

INTRODUCTION

The last two decades showed that *business process modeling (BPM)* is the solution of choice of multiple companies and government institutions for describing and enacting their internal and external work procedures. Once modelled, business processes can be made available either publicly or accessible to a specific community to share the know-how between institutions and promote the reuse of existing business processes, e.g., as building blocks for constructing new business processes. The success of such a paradigm depends partly on the availability of a means by which users can locate business processes that are relevant for their purposes.

Another important trend in software development is towards reuse of artifacts and sharing of knowledge. Software models and code repositories play a central role in software development companies, as they accumulate the knowledge and best practices evolved by skilled developers over years. Besides serving the current needs of project development, they have also an archival value that can be of extreme importance in fostering reuse and the sharing of high quality design patterns. In several cases (e.g., the open source community), software project repositories have overcome the boundaries of individual organizations and have assumed a social role in the diffusion of coding and design solutions. State-of-the-practice project repositories mostly support source code or documentation search (Bajracharya, Ossher, & Lopes, 2009; Frakes & Nejmeh, 1987; Holmes & Murphy, 2005). Source code search engines (e.g., Google code, Snipplr, Koders) are helpful if the abstraction level at which development occurs is the implementation code. However, searching project repositories at the source code level clashes with the use of high level models like business process models as the principal artifact to express solutions and design patterns. Therefore, the question arises of what tools to use to leverage the knowledge implicitly stored in repositories

of models, to make them play the same role in disseminating modeling best practices and foster design with reuse.

Approaches to model-driven repository search have been recently explored in the fields UML design (Chen, Madhavan, & Halevy, 2009, Llorens, Fuentes, & Morato, 2004) and business processes. A handful of researchers have investigated the problem of business process reuse based on process similarity and discovery of processes based on search upon repositories. Beeri, Eyal, Kamenkovich, and Milo (2006) proposed a visual query language for discovering business processes modelled using BPEL. Goderis, Li, and Goble (2006) developed a framework for discovering workflows using similarity metrics that consider the activities composing the workflows and their relationships.

The above solutions to business process discovery use as input the workflows that model the business, namely the activities that constitute the business processes and their dependencies in term of control flow. Yet, a workflow is not a complete description of the business processes. In this paper, we argue that a more effective discovery of business processes can be achieved if they are semantically described. Specifically, we show how such information can be encoded within an ontology that can be used for:

- **Abstracting discovery queries:** The user is able to formulate his/her queries in terms of the tasks (semantics) fulfilled by the desired business processes.
- **Exploiting relationships between business processes:** Business processes are inter-dependent. These dependencies can be explicitly described in the ontology in the form of binary relationships (Figure 1) that can be used, amongst other things, for increasing the recall of discovery queries.

Our approach also takes care of automating the classification of business processes within the ontology, in terms of the specification of the processes themselves and of the relations between them. In doing so, our approach prominently considers the topology of the business process and an ontology of activities and decides how to classify BPs based on both aspects. Our approach is neutral with respect to the provenance of the BP models that are analyzed. The analysis can be applied to one process at a time, when it is added to the repository or can be applied to a whole existing repository of processes, not analyzed yet.

The paper is structured as follows. We begin by formally defining business processes. We then introduce the concept of abstract business processes, which can be seen as business processes in which the activities are not associated to processing units responsible for their execution, but are rather described semantically using concepts from an ontology. We present the ontology used for describing business processes, and then show how this ontology can be created and populated in an automatic fashion, starting from a set of concrete business process models. We show how the business process ontology can be used for discovering business processes. We then assess the effectiveness of the solution we propose for describing and querying business process repositories by using workflows from the life science domains. Finally, we compare our solution to existing proposals and close the paper by highlighting our main contributions.

DEFINITION OF BUSINESS PROCESS AND ABSTRACT BUSINESS PROCESS

Business Process

A business process is a collection of interrelated tasks, which aim at solving a particular issue. A business process can be decomposed into several sub-processes, which have their own peculiarities, but also contribute to achieving the goal of the super-process. Execution of tasks is typically constrained by dependency rules among tasks that consist of sequence constraints, branching and merging rules, pre- and post- conditions, event management points, and so on.

A business process can be specified by means of a workflow model, i.e., a visual representation of the correct sequence of tasks that leads to the achievement of the goal. The notations for workflow modelling provide the proper primitives for defining processes, tasks, actors, control flow and data flow between tasks. In our work, we will adopt a particular business process notation, namely BPMN (Object Management Group/ Business Process Management Notation, 2007) for sake of readability and concreteness. However, we propose a general purpose approach, which is valid regardless of the adopted notation. In particular, we based our transformation rules on the concepts and definitions specified by BPDM (Business Process Definition Metamodel) (Object Management Group, 2006), a platform- and notation- independent metamodel for defining business processes.

For specifying processes, we adopt the terminology defined by the Workflow Management Coalition and the Business Process Management Initiative, which provide a workflow model based on the concepts of Process (the description of the supported workflow), Case (a process instance), Activity (the elementary unit of work composing a process), Activity instance (an instantiation of an activity within a case), Actor (a user role intervening in the process), and Constraint (logical precedence among activities and rules enabling activities execution). Processes can be internally structured using a variety of control constructs: sequences of activities, AND-splits (a single thread of control splits into two or more independent threads), AND-joins (blocking convergence point of two or more parallel activities), OR-splits (point in which one among multiple alternative branches is taken), OR-joins (non-blocking convergence point), iterations for repeating the execution of one or more activities, pre- and post-conditions (entry and exit criteria to and from a particular activity). A business process model, according to BPMN, can also include events, that are happenings occurring during the process execution, producing an impact. Events are categorized by type, that includes message, timer, rule, and other events. Gateways are elements that control the flow of the process. They can be used either as decision, splitting, merging, and synchronization points. Various logical behaviours are allowed for the gateways. Activities can express several different behaviours (cycling, compensation, internal sub-process structuring, event catching, and so on). The flow of the process is described by means of arrows that can represent either the control flow, the exchanged messages flow, or the data flow among the tasks. Activities are grouped into pools based on the participant that is in charge of the activity enactment. Typically a participant is identified as an organization that plays some roles. Pool lanes are usually used to distinguish different user types that are involved in the work on behalf of the specific organization.

Figure 1 exemplifies a BPMN workflow diagram specifying the process of online purchase, payment and delivery of goods. The customer can choose the products to purchase, then submits his payment information. At this point, two parallel tasks are executed by the seller employees: the warehouse manager registers the shipping of the order, and a secretary prepares a bill to be sent to the customer.

For the purpose of this paper, we define a business process *bp* by the tuple: <*nameBP, A, CF>*, where:

- *nameBP* is the name identifying the business process.
- *A* is the set of activities composing *bp*. An activity *a* in *A* is defined as <*nameA, roleA>*, where *nameA* is the activity identifier, and roleA is a string determining its role within the business process.
- $CF \subseteq (A \ X \ OP) \ U \ (OP \ X \ A)$ is the controlflow. *OP* is the set of operators used for defining controlflow dependencies between the activities in *A*. Specifically: *OP= {Sequence, AND-split, AND-join, OR-split, OR-join}*.

We say that a business process *bp1* is a *part of* a business process *bp2* if the activities of *bp1* are activities of *bp2*, i.e., $bp1.A \subseteq bp2.A$, the controlflow dependencies of *bp1* are also controlflow dependencies of *bp2*, i.e., $bp1.CF \subseteq bp2.CF$,

Figure 1. Example of business process model expressed in BPMN

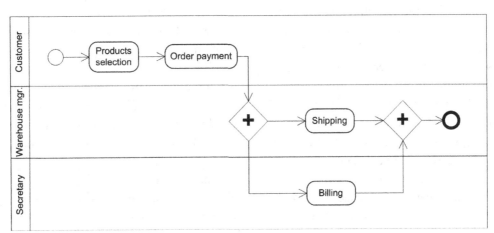

and the controlflow of *bp1* forms a connected directed graph.

Our definition of business process is coherent with WfMC and BPMN, while providing a subset of their full-fledged expressive power. In particular, we consider only the basic aspects of processes, while we omit the others. This is not a major limitation, since the approach can be easily extended to those aspects. Furthermore, empirical studies show that a large part of process specification typically only exploit the basic constructs of the language (Muehlen & Recker, 2008; Recker, 2010). For instance, with respect to the analysis in (Muehlen & Recker, 2008), we cover all the constructs with an occurrence frequency higher than 50%, plus a few more.

ABSTRACT BUSINESS PROCESS

As well as activities and controlflow, the description of a business process can include other aspects like the actors involved, the resources required, etc. However, the purpose of the solution that we report on this article is to facilitate the discovery of business processes using certain aspects (but not all) on the business process, viz. the constituent tasks and their dependencies, and to allow the user to abstract away from the description of other aspects such the actors, roles and resources involved in the business process. To describe the tasks implemented by the activities that compose a business process and their dependencies, we use an abstraction that we termed *abstract business process* as input to the discovery process. Clearly, the solution reported in our work can be extended to support filtering the result of a search using aspects like the actors or resources. For example, we can envisage that once the user obtains a list of business processes that match a given abstract business process, s/he further filters the results using as input parameters like the actors and resources involved in the business processes.

An *abstract business process (ABP)* can be viewed as a representative of a class of *equivalent* business processes. An ABP is instantiated into a concrete business process by specifying the actual resources (e.g., services to be invoked, procedures to be triggered, UIs to be rendered) needed to perform the constituent activities. Business processes are considered equivalent if they share the same set of activities and flow structure. An ABP can be implemented by several concrete business processes, which concretely define the exact behaviour of the tasks and the names of the actors of the process within one (or more) concrete organization(s). Differently from concrete business processes, in which the activities are associated with actors or processing units in charge of their actual execution, in abstract business processes the activities are generic task descriptions, associated with semantic labels that provide information about the capabilities of the processing units able to perform the activities and descriptions of the data to be consumed and produced by the processing units. These descriptions are encoded in the form of annotations that relate the activities of the business process and their inputs/outputs to concepts from ontologies that specify the semantics of these elements in the real world.

An ontology is commonly defined as an explicit specification of a conceptualisation (Gurber, 1993). Formally, an ontology O can be defined as a set of concepts, $O = \{c1,...,cn\}$. The concepts are related to each other using the sub-concept relationship, which links general concepts to more specific ones. For example, *CreditCardPayment* is a sub-concept of *OrderPayment*, for which we write: $CreditCardPayment \leq OrderPayment$. If *CreditCardPayment* is a strict sub-concept of *OrderPayment*, then we write: $CreditCardPayment < OrderPayment$.

The concepts can also be connected by other binary relationships, depending on the specific semantics encoded by the ontology.

To semantically annotate the activities of a business process, we use the task ontology, O_{task}. This ontology captures information about the action carried out by the activities within a domain of interest. In bioinformatics, for instance, an activity can be annotated using a term that describes the *in silico* analysis it performs. Example of bioinformatics analyses include *sequence alignment* and *protein identification*. Another example of a task ontology can be defined in the electronic commerce context. In this case, activities are annotated in terms of business transactions they implement. For instance, business transactions may include *quotation request*, *order confirmation*, and *credit card payment*.

To retrieve the task annotation of service operations we consider the function *task()* defined as follows: *task: ACTIVITY → O_{task}*, where *ACTIVITY* denotes the domain of business process activities. We can now formally define what we intend by an abstract business process.

Abstract business process. An abstract business process *abp* is defined by the pair: <T,CF>, where:

- T is the set of tasks that constitute *abp*: $T \subseteq O_{task}$.
- $CF \subseteq (T \times OP) \cup (OP \times T)$ is the control flow relating the tasks in T.

To map the tasks of two abstract business processes, we consider two classes of functions the domain of which are denoted by *MapEquiv* and *MapSpec*. The functions that belong to *MapEquiv* are used to map same of equivalent tasks (belonging to two ABPs). Let *abp1* and *abp2* be two abstract business processes and let f_{map}: *abp1.T → abp2.T* a function that maps the tasks of *abp1* to those of *abp2*. $f_{map} \in MapEquiv$ iff:

$$\forall t \in abp1.T, task(fmap(t)) \equiv task(t)$$

The functions in *MapSpec* are used to map equivalent or more specific tasks belonging to two ABPs of a given abstract business process to the tasks of another. Let *abp1* and *abp2* be two abstract business processes and let f_{map}: *abp1.T → abp2.T* a function that maps the tasks of *abp1* to those of *abp2*. *fmap* ∈ *MapSpec* iff:

$$\forall t \in abp1.T, task(fmap(t)) \leq task(t)$$

To construct the abstract business process *abp* corresponding to a (concrete) business process *bp*, we use the function *abstractBP()* with the following signature.

abstractBP: BP → ABP

BP denotes the domain of business processes and *ABP* the domain of abstract business processes.

ONTOLOGY FOR DESCRIBING BUSINESS PROCESSES AND THEIR RELATIONSHIPS

To describe business processes, we use an ontology that we call in the rest of this paper the *business process ontology, O_{BP}*. The concepts of this ontology designate abstract business processes. Notice that the purpose of this ontology is quite different with respect to other existing proposals, such as WSMO (http://www.wsmo.org/) or OWL-S (http://www.w3.org/Submission/OWL-S/) (Lara, Roman, Polleres, & Fensel, 2004): while the latter aim at describing processes (or, equivalently, service orchestrations), we focus on defining the relations between the processes. Given a concept c from business process ontology O_{BP}, we use the function *getABP(c)*, the signature of which is illustrated below, to retrieve the abstract business process designated by c.

getABP: O_{BP} → ABP

The concepts in the ontology O_{BP} are related using binary properties that encode relationships between abstract business processes. Specifically, we identify four binary properties to encode process relationships, namely, *equivalence, specialisation, overlap*, and *partOf*.

Process equivalence. Two abstract processes are equivalent iff their respective constituent tasks are equivalent tasks and are connected using the same controlflow. Formally, let *c1* and *c2* be two concepts from the business process ontology O_{BP} that designate the abstract business processes *abp1* and *abp2*, respectively. That is *abp1 = getABP(c1)* and *abp2 = getABP(c2)*. The two concepts *c1* and *c2* are equivalent, for which we write *c1* $\equiv$ *c2*, iff there exists a mapping function f_{equiv}: *abp1.T* $\rightarrow$ *abp2.T* in *MapEquiv* such that:

$$Abp2.CF = \{(f_{equiv}(t), op) \in abp1.CF\} \cup \{(op, f_{equiv}(t)) \in abp1.CF \}$$

As an example, consider two simple abstract processes: *abp1* composed by a sequence of two activities *a1* and *a2; abp2* composed by a sequence of two activities *a3* and *a2*. If *a3* is equivalent to *a1*, we can assert that the two processes are equivalent.

Process specialisation. Let *c1* and *c2* be two concepts from the business process ontology O_{BP} that designate the abstract business processes *abp1* and *abp2*, respectively. *c1* specialises *c2* iff the tasks of *abp1* are equivalent or more specific that the tasks of *abp2*, and that they have the same controlflow. Notice that the concept of "more specific" task applies to the activity ontology and corresponds to the general functional inheritance semantics, that is: the more specific activities in-

herit the properties of the generic ones, but there is no way to enforce that the behviour is actually more specific (this is an undecidable problem in general). Formally, *c1* specialises *c2*, for which we write *c1* < *c2*, iff there exists a mapping function: f_{spec}: *abp1.T* $\rightarrow$ *abp2.T* in *MapSpec* such that:

$$abp2.CF = \{(f_{spec}(t), op), (t, op) \in abp1.CF\} \cup \{(op, f_{spec}(t)), (op, t) \in abp1.CF\}$$

As in the previous example, *abp2* is a specialization of abp1 if *a3* specializes *a1*.

Part-of relationship. Let *c1* and *c2* be two concepts from the business process ontology O_{BP} that designate the abstract business processes *abp1* and *abp2*, respectively. We say that *c1* is *part-of* *c2* iff there exists a concept *c3* that is equivalent to *c1* and that designates abstract business process *abp3 = getABP(c3)* that is *part of abp2*.

As an example, consider two simple abstract processes: *abp1* composed by a sequence of two activities *a1* and *a2;* and *abp2* composed by a sequence of four activities *a4, a1, a2, a3*. We say that *abp1* is part of *abp2* because the latter entirely contains the former.

Process overlap. Two concepts *c1* and *c2* overlaps iff their respective abstract business processes have one or more tasks in common. Let *abp1* and *abp2* the abstract business processes (Figure 2) designated by *c1* and *c2*, respectively. *c1* and *c2* overlap iff:

$$abp1.T \cap abp2.T \neq \varnothing$$

Figure 2. Generation of the business process ontology

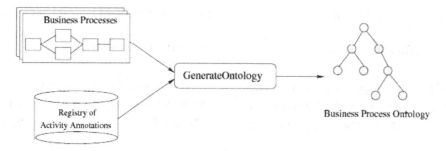

As an example, consider the abstract processes: *abp1* composed by the sequence of activities *a1, a2, a3;* and *abp2* composed by a the sequence *a4, a1, a2, a5*. We say that *abp1* and *abp2* are overlapping because they have some parts in common.

Notice that the *equivalence* property is reflexive, symmetric and transitive, that the *specialisation* and *part-of* properties are both reflexive and transitive, and that the *overlap* property is both reflexive and symmetric.

To manipulate the business process ontology, we assume the existence of the following operations:

- *defineConcept: ABP* → O_{BP}
- *defineProperty: PROPERTYx* O_{BP} *x* O_{BP}→ *Boolean*
- *addInstance: BP x* O_{BP}→ *Boolean*

To define a new concept *c* that represents an abstract business process *abp* in the business process ontology, we use the operation *defineConcept(abp)*. The operation returns the concept defined. The operation *defineProperty(p,c1,c2)* defines a property *p in Property* between the concepts *c1* and *c2*. *Property* denotes the domain of binary properties in the business process ontology:

Property = {equivalence, specialisation, part-of, overlap}.

Business processes are defined as instances of the concepts in the business process ontology. Specifically, a business processes *bp* can be defined as an instance of a concept *c* iff *c* designate the abstract business process *abp* corresponding to *bp*: i.e., *abp = abstractBP(bp)*. To define *bp* as an instance of the concept *c*, we use the operation *addInstance(bp,c)*. The operation returns true if it is executed successfully and false, otherwise.

CREATING AND POPULATING THE ONTOLOGY

The business process ontology is created and populated in an automatic fashion, starting from a set of annotated business processes. Figure 2 illustrates the generation process: given a set of business processes together with semantic annotations describing the tasks of their constituent activities, the concepts of the business process ontology are defined and the binary properties that relate the concepts in the business process ontology are automatically inferred. Furthermore, (concrete) business processes are defined as instances of the ontology concepts, thereby allowing the business process ontology to be used for business process discovery later on. Table 1 presents the algorithm whereby the business process is created.

Notice that the automated part of our approach stands in the correct classification of business processes, in terms of the specification of the processes within the BPO ontology and the generation of the relations between the processes. In doing so, our approach prominently considers the topology of the business process and the activity ontology and decides how to classify BPs based on both aspects. Notice also that further concrete descriptions of activities could be exploited (e.g., pre- and post- conditions, user roles, parameters

Table 1. Algorithm for building and populating the business process ontology

```
Algorithm GenerateOntology
input BP
output O_BP
begin
1 for each bp ∈ BP do
2 abp = abstractBP(bp)
3 if (there is c in O_BP, abp = getABP(c))
4 then
5 addInstance(bp,c)
6 else
7 c:= defineConcept(abp)
8 addInstance(bp,c)
9 deriveAndAssertProperties(c)
end
```

and so on). In this phase we decided to keep the process definition simple, but extensions can be applied at will.

For each business process *bp*, the corresponding abstract process *abp* is built *(line 2)*. If the business process ontology contains a concept *c* that designates the abstract business process *abp*, *(line 3)*, then *bp* is defined as an instance of *(line 5)*. If not, then a new concept is defined within the business process ontology to represent the abstract business process *abp*, *(line 7)*, and *bp* is defined as an instance of the concept defined, *(line 8)*. Furthermore, the binary properties that relate the newly defined concept *c* to other concepts in the business process ontology are derived and asserted using the *deriveAndAssertProperties(c)* subroutine, *(line 9)*. This subroutine operates as follows. The abstract process designated by the concept *c* is compared to the abstract business processes designated by other concepts in the business process ontology. If the two abstract processes are found to be equivalent (see section 3) then an *equivalence* property is defined by the respective concepts in the business process ontology. The *specialisation*, *part-of* and *overlap* are defined in a similar fashion.

DISCOVERYING BUSINESS PROCESSES

Most of existing proposals to business process discovery adopts the following paradigm. The user first formulates a query specifying the business process of interests by describing the activities that compose the business processes (e.g., specifying the processing units in charge of the activities execution) and the controlflow that connects them. A matching operation is then performed in order to choose from the repository of available business processes, business processes that match the user query. Our approach to business process discovery is illustrated in Figure 3.

We adopt a different approach that exploits information about business processes and their relationship encoded within the business process ontology. It consists of the following three steps.

1. **Query specification:** The objective of this step is to design an abstract business process. To do so, the user makes use of the task ontology, the concepts of which are used to annotate business process activities. Specifically, the user chooses tasks of relevance from this ontology. S/he then specifies the way they are to be coordinated using controlflow operators. Users can also

Figure 3. Process of business process discovery

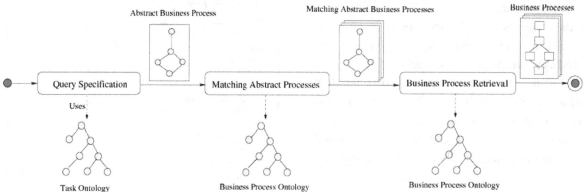

reuse an existing business process that they specified previously as a starting point, and then add/remove tasks and modify the controlfow according to their needs.

2. **Matching business processes:** This step is performed automatically, and consist in matching the abstract business process specified by the user against the business process ontology. This step will be presented in detail later in this section. The output of this step is one or multiple abstract business processes.

3. **Business process retrieval:** Given the abstract business processes output by the previous step, their business processes instances are retrieved from the repository of business process specifications. It is worth mentioning that the relationships between abstract business processes and their respective business process instances are stored within the business process ontology.

We will now focus on business process matching. Given *abp*, an abstract business process representing the user query, *What are the abstract business processes that match abp?*

We identify two classes of matching between abstract business processes that we derive from the binary properties relating the concepts of the business process ontology. Consider that *c* is the concept in the business process ontology designating the abstract business process *abp* representing the user query.

- **Strong matching:** The abstract business processes that match *abp* are those designated by the concepts equivalent or more specific than *c*. This is the strongest degree of matching. The business process obtained as a result of the query have the same controlflow as the abstract business process specified by the user, and their ac-

tivities perform tasks that are equivalent or more specific than those specified by the user.

- **Loose matching:** Users may not get a business process they are looking for by using *strong* matching, and, therefore, may wish to relax their queries. In this case, the following loose form of matching can be used. The abstract business processes that match *abp* are those designated by concepts that are *part-of c*, concepts that *c* is *part-of*, and concepts that *overlaps* with. Using this form of matching, the user may get business processes that contain the target business process as a part of the retrieved process, for example.

If needed, additional classes of matching can be defined, by specifying customized matching rules, specified as queries on the ontology and on the bp structures. Obviously, the result of the matching is heavily influenced by the matching logic, therefore the designer must be careful in defining new matchings. Indeed, newly introduced partial matchings can lead to extraction of processes that are dramatically different from the ones the user is looking for.

As well as describing business processes, the business process ontology can be used for ranking the business processes returned as a result to user's query. Specifically, we use the ontology to derive a partial order between business processes. To illustrate this, consider two business processes *bp1* and *bp2*. Using our approach *bp1* is ranked before *bp2* if the abstract business process of *bp2* is a subclass of the abstract business process of *bp1*. That is abstractBP($bp2$) < abstractBP($bp1$). The rationale behind this is the fact that the overall task that can be carried out by business processes instances of *bp2* may be much more specific than what the user was asking for. Using the above approach, we derive a partial ranking between business processes. Indeed, two business process may be ranked equally. This is specifically the case when:

(abstractBP(bp1) ≡ abstractBP(bp2)) or
not ((abstractBP(bp1) < abstractBP(bp2))
or (abstractBP(bp2) < abstractBP(bp1)))

In addition to the criterion discussed above, we can use an additional source for ranking, in particular when business processes are retrieved using loose matching. To illustrate this, consider that the user specified an abstract business process *abp1*, and that a set of business process *BPR* were retrieved using the loose matching strategy. The business processes in *BPR* that are instances of *abp1* or one of its sub-concepts will be ranked higher than those that are instances of abstract business processes that linked to *abp1* using either the overlap or part-of relationship.

IMPLEMENTATION EXPERIENCE AND VALIDATION OF THE APPROACH

The solution reported in this paper raises the following questions:

- Can we automatically create an ontology that describes existing business processes and the relationships between them using the algorithm presented?
- Does the business process ontology created provide useful information? In other words, does it help end users in identifying the business processes that meet their requirements?

Typically, if the ontology created is composed of concepts that are independent from each other, by which we mean that they are not related using the properties we advocated in this paper, then this implies that the approach we describe is not applicable in practice. On the other hand, if the concepts in the ontology created are related by dependencies, then this mean that the ontology created can be beneficial for end users when exploring and querying business processes.

To answer the above questions, we built a prototypical implementation of our approach and we conducted an experiment in which we used business processes from the domain of bioinformatics. The next subsections summarize our work and the outcomes of our evaluation.

IMPLEMENTATION OF THE APPROACH

Our implementation experience consists of the development of a prototype application that manages ABP repositories and automatically generates process properties according to the approach described in Section 4.

To perform a first evaluation, we defined a set of RDF concepts for describing the business processes, the contained tasks and the control flow that connects them. The implementation relies on Sesame (http://www.openrdf.org) as a repository technology for RDF and on SPARQL as a query language. The repository stores the description of tasks (and their equivalence/specialization relationships with other tasks), the description of business processes (in terms of control flows that include the task list and the precedence constraints), and the (equivalence, overlap, partof, and specialization) relationships between processes. Besides the main APIs for querying the repository and for storing new concepts, a business process comparison method has been implemented at the purpose of generating automatically the relationships between business processes, according to the following scenario: when a new business process needs to be stored in the repository, we assume that its task list and control flow is fully specified in RDF. For each task, the list of equivalent and specializing tasks must be provided too. For instance, the following example shows the definition of task *T4* as equivalent to *T3* and specialization of *T2*.

```
<rdf:Description rdf:about= "http://
www.polimi.it/BPdisc/rdf/T4">
<activity:id> T4
</activity:id>
<activity:equivalent> T3
</activity:equivalent>
<activity:specializes> T2
</activity:specializes>
</rdf:Description>
```

Given these inputs about a business process, the comparison procedure, implementing the algorithm described in Figure 2, automatically generates the properties of the process, in terms of relationships to the other processes already stored in the repository. The outcome of the algorithm is a piece of RDF structured as shown in the following example. In the example, *BP6* is defined as implemented by the Control Flow *CF3*, equivalent to *BP5* and part of *BP9*.

```
<rdf:Description rdf:about= "http://
www.polimi.it/BPdisc/rdf/BP6">
<process:id> BP6
</process:id>
<process:control-flow> CF3
</process:control-flow>
<process:equivalence> BP5
</process:equivalence>
<process:part-of> BP9
</process:part-of>
</rdf:Description>
```

The complexity of the generation algorithm is linear with the number of business processes already stored in the system and quadratic in the number of activities and control flows for each business process (this is due to the fact that containment must be checked taking any activity as a starting point).

The prototype and some sample RDF documents are available online at: http://dbgroup.como. polimi.it/brambilla/bpmrdf.

A second implementation using OWL ontologies and repositories is ongoing too. In that case, the Protégé repository and API is used. A simplified OWL ontology can be found online at this url: http://dbgroup.como.polimi.it/brambilla/bpmowl.

VALIDATION: APPLICATION TO BIOINFORMATICS BUSINESS PROCESSES

Workflows are currently widely used in the bioinformatics field as a means for specifying and enacting *in silico* experiments. As a result, a wide range of popular scientific workflow workbenches have been developed and are now used by the life science community. For the purposes of our experiment, we used 23 workflows that were created in the context of eScience projects, namely, ISPIDER (http://www.ispider.manchester.ac.uk), myGrid (http://www.mygrid.org.uk) and DDBJ (http://www.ddbj.mig.ac.jp).

Some of the web services that embody the activities that constitute those workflows were annotated using the myGrid task ontology. Figure 4 illustrates a fragment of this ontology. For the purposes of our experiment, we annotated the activities associated with non annotated web services. Using the algorithm presented in section 4, we then automatically generated the business process ontology illustrated in Figure 5. Notice that the number of concepts in this ontology is 11 instead of 23, which is the number of business processes used as input for the ontology creation. This is because some of the concepts, i.e., abstract business processes, in the businesses ontology created are associated with multiple workflows.

Notice also that the concepts in the created business process ontology are linked to each other using the specialisation, part-of and overlap relationships. This is a positive result, since it

Figure 4. A fragment of the task ontology as displayed using Protégé

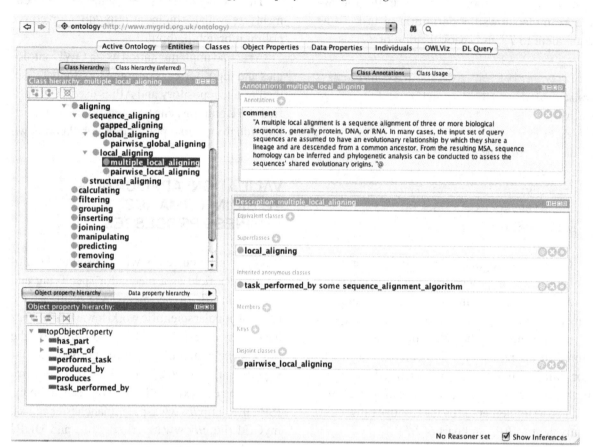

Figure 5. Business process ontology, which was automatically built given a collection of workflow definitions

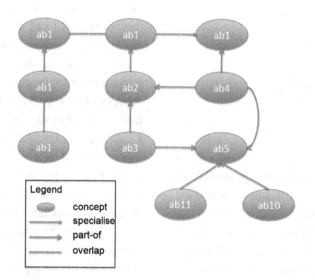

shows that business processes are in practice dependent, and that the ontology automatically created captures (at least some of) these dependencies.

To further assess the effectiveness of our solution, we used the business process ontology (Figure 4) created for evaluating the following queries:

Q1: Returns the business processes instances of the concept *ab1*.

Q2: Returns the business processes instances of *ab1* and its subconcepts.

Q3: Returns the business processes instances of the concept *ab1*, its subconcepts, and the concepts *abp1* is part-of.

Q4: Returns the business processes instances of the concept *ab1*, its subconcepts, and the concepts that are part-of *abp1*.

Q5: Returns the business processes instances of the concept *ab1*, its sub-concepts, and the concepts that overlap with *abp1*.

The objectives intended by evaluating the above queries is two-fold. Firstly, to see whether the use of the business process ontology for guiding the query process allows increasing the recall of the results by using the notion of abstract business process and the specialisation property. This feature is examined by the queries Q1 and Q2. Secondly, to see whether the ontology can be used for exploring the dependencies between business processes by using the part-of and overlap relationships. This feature is examined using the queries Q3, Q4 and Q5.

Figures 5 and 6 illustrate the number of business processes returned for each of the above queries. It shows an increase in recall compared to the case where the queries are evaluated relying only on structural information of business processes. For example, it shows that the number of business processes that are equivalent to or specialises the abstract business process abp_1 is 6. Also, the ontology can be used for exploring the dependencies between business processes thanks to the specialisation, part-of and overlap properties.

For instance, by considering the abstract business processes of which ab_1 is part-of, the number of business processes returned increases from 6 to 8.

Figure 6. Chart showing the number of business processes returned when evaluating the queries

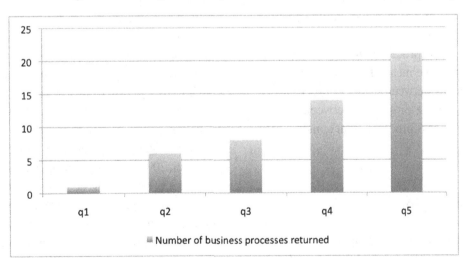

To summarise, the validation we conducted using business processes from the life sciences domain shows the effectiveness of the solution we propose for describing and discovering business processes. Specifically, the validation shows that:

- The ontology used for capturing semantic information about business processes and their relationships can be created in an automatic fashion.
- The concepts in the business process ontology created are highly dependent in the sense that they are related using the specialisation, overlap and part-of properties advocated in this paper.
- The use of the ontology for evaluating business process discovery queries significantly increases the recall of queries. This can be explained by the fact the business processes we used as input to the experiment do not overlap in terms of activities. In other words, the web services implementing the activities are different. Therefore, a search that uses as input a (concrete) business process will return at most one business process, whereas a search that uses an abstract business process has the potential of returning more than one results since different web services can implements the same tasks.
- The business process ontology can be used as an effective means for exploring the dependencies between business processes by relying on the properties between the abstract business processes that constitute the ontology.

RELATED WORK

Recently, many proposals have attempted to facilitate the discovery of business processes, and more in general of software models and artifacts. This section analyses and compares these proposals to ours, by considering the different categories of contributions.

BPM Formalization and Ontologies

Business process formalization has been widely studied. Various proposals map business process languages like BPMN to Petri-Nets (Dijkman, Dumas, & Ouyang, 2008), Linear-time Temporal Logic (Brambilla, Deutsch, Sui, & Vianu, 2005), or executable orchestration languages like BPEL (Ouyang, Dumas, Aalst, Hofstede, & Mendling, 2009). Our definitions are perfectly aligned with these studies, however, we are not interested in execution semantics. The work (Honda, Yoshida, & Carbone, 2008) builds on the concept of type abstraction based on a global view for defining generic processes, abstracting the details of the implementation of tasks. We apply a similar approach by adopting the activity ontology and allowing abstract business processes to include abstract tasks that could be specialized and then implemented in different ways.

In the *definition of process ontologies*, researchers recognize the deficiencies of ontological definition of business process modeling languages (Recker, 2010). Some ontology proposals already exist: the Business Process Modelling Ontology (BPMO) defines the link between processes and organisations. BPMO is the superset of the EPC and BPMN ontologies, by defining the common concepts of the two ontologies. A binding of BPMO has been developed for within the WSMX framework (Dimitrov, Simov, Stein, & Konstantinov, 2007; Hepp, Leymann, Domingue, Wahler, & Fensel, 2005). However, proposals like WSMO or OWL-S () cover the description of processes (or, equivalently, service orchestrations), whilst our approach focuses on defining the relations between the processes (and possibl can be applied to those descriptions). Other works adopt an ontology-based approach to modelling language comparison (Recker, Rosemann, Indulska & Green, 2009), for pattern analysis (Soffer, Wand & Kaner, 2007), and so on.

BPM Discovery

Workflow similarity is an enabling issue for content-based business process discovery. Aalst and Basten (2002) posed the basis of the concepts of inheritance between business processes, that we exploit in the relationships described in our ontology (in the BPO thanks to the *extends* relation) and between activities (in the activity ontology). Other works, like (Van Glabbeek, 2001), defined the formal foundations and the semantics of business processes and similarities, on which we base our definitions. Wombacher and Rozie (2006) and Hidders, Dumas, Aalst, Hofstede, and Verelst (2005) investigated graph similarity metrics for equivalence and ranking for workflow discovery. The work presented in (Ehrig, Koschmider, & Oberweis, 2007) defines similarity based on synoms and homonyms in process elements. In our work, besides workflow structure, we also use semantic information that describe the activities.

Most of the approaches to *BPM discovery* only apply graph-based comparison or XML-based querying on the business process specifications, disregarding ontology-based similarity discovery. Beeri, Eyal, Kamenkovich, and Milo (2006) proposed BP-QL, a visual query language for querying and discovering business processes modelled using BPEL. However, the work allows querying only the process structures through queries on XML. Lu and Safiq (2006) proposes a way for comparing and retrieving business process variants based on the differences in the model topology between the variants.

Goderis, Li, and Goble (2006) developed a framework for discovering workflows using similarity metrics and ranking that consider the activities composing the workflows and their

relationships. In their approach, they reduce the problem to a graph matching problem, thus adapting existing algorithms for this purpose. Their approach receives as input two BPEL models and evaluates the distance between them.

The work of Zhuge (2002) is instead closer to our approach: it presents an inexact matching approach based on SQL-like queries on ontology repositories. The focus is on flexible workflow process reuse, based on a multi-valued process specialization relationship. The matching degree between two workflow processes is determined by the matching degrees of their corresponding sub-processes or activities, and the matching degree between two activities is determined by the activity-distance between them in the activity-ontology repository. Differently from us, the ontology cannot be automatically built from the workflow models and does not include explicit relationships between business processes.

Kiefer, Bernstein, Lee, Klein, and Stocker (2007) propose the use of semantic business processes to enable the integration and interoperability of business processes across organizational boundaries. They offer an imprecise query engine based on iSPARQL to perform the process retrieval task. Beco, Cantalupo, Giammarino, Matskanis, and Surridge (2005) specified the language OWL-WS (OWL for workflow and services) for describing ontologies of workflows and services, but the language was mainly used for specifying adaptive business processes. Markovic, Pereira, and Stojanovic (2008) proposed a framework for flexible queries on BP models, for providing better results when too few processes are extracted. Awad, Polyvyanyy, and Weske (2008) proposes the BPMN-Q query language for visual semantic queries over BPMN models.

Dumas, Garcia-Bañuelos, and Dijkman (2009) offer a good overview of recent works on similarity based search of business processes. The discussed works have a very similar focus to ours, although different techniques are applied. Most of them can be assimilated to schema matching approaches. In some sense, our work falls in this class too: indeed, we try to match activities and flows of two different models.

Our approach is complementary to the proposal by Ma, Wetzstein, Anicic, Heymans, and Leymann (2007). Indeed, our approach allows to automatically generate the business prrocess ontology that describes and classifies business processes. This ontology can be used as input by the repository developed by Ma, Wetzstein, Anicic, Heymans, and Leymann (2007) to provide users with a means for searching for business processes.

SOFTWARE COMPONENT DISCOVERY

Retrieval of software components, intended as mere code artifacts or as described pieces of software, is a broader and well established discipline. Back to the '90s, Agora (Seacord, Hissam, & Wallnau, 1998) was a search engine based on JavaBeans and CORBA technologies that automatically generates and indexes a worldwide database of software artifacts. Platzer and Dustdar (2005) propose a method for discovery and analysis of Web services based on a Vector Space Search Engine. The work described in (Inoue, Yokomori, Yamamoto, Matsushita, & Kusumoto, 2005) proposes a graph-representation model of a software component library, based on analyzing actual usage relations of the components. The approach described in (Khalifa, Khayati, & Ghezala, 2008) combines formal and semi-formal specification to describe behaviour and structure of components.

Software Model Discovery

Some approaches exist that address the problem of model search for UML projects. Some early works based on XML documents for indexing (Gibb, McCartan, O'Donnell, & Sweeney, 2000).

The work described in Gomes, Pereira, Seco, Carreiro, & Bento1 (2004) offers model retrieval facilities of artifacts stored in a central knowledge base and classified with WordNet terms. The paper (Llorens, Fuentes, & Morato, 2004) proposes a retrieval framework allowing designers to retrieve information on UML models based on XML representation. Schemr (Chen, Madhavan, & Halevy, 2009) implements a novel search algorithm, based on a combination of text search and schema matching techniques for retrieving database conceptual models.

Another branch of research applies information retrieval (IR) techniques to models and code together, to trace the association between artifacts (Settimi, Cleland-Huang, Ben Khadra, Mody, Lukasik, & DePalma, 2004; Antoniol, Canfora, Lucia, & Casazza, 2000).

Source Code Search

Several communities and on-line tools exist for sharing and retrieving code, such as *Google code*, *Codase* (http://www.codase.com), *Snipplr* (http://snipplr.com), *Koders* (http://www.koders.com) and others, where projects are stored together with their associated documentation, used for answering keyword searches. Keyword queries are directly matched to the code or the metadata, with support of regular expressions, wildcards, concept restriction, and metadata search.

Research works widely applied IR techniques (Frakes & Nejmeh, 1987) and structural context techniques (Holmes & Murphy, 2005) for improving productivity and reuse of software, but also for quickly identifying code bugs (Williams & Hollingsworth, 2005). The Sourcerer Project (Bajracharya, Ossher, & Lopes, 2009) provides an infrastructure for large-scale indexing and analysis of open source code.

CONCLUSION

In this paper we presented an approach for describing, storing, and discovering Business Processes. Building on existing formal definitions, we extended the concept of similarity between process models by exploiting ontology definitions and the concept of abstract business process. To validate our approach we implemented a prototype system and we evaluated it on a scenario in the bioinformatics field.

An abstract business process can be seen as a representative of a class of concrete business processes, having the same structure although defined in different contexts or organizations. Queries based on ABPs allow reuse and matching of business process models, thus saving time and reducing cost of implementation of enterprise workflows.

Thanks to ontology-based comparison, we can evaluate the similarity between processes in a more flexible way with respect to traditional approaches, and therefore identify more potential similarities, for instance based on activity descriptions that are semantically close.

Ongoing and future works include: the investigation of query specification, the integration of our discovery approach with a BP modeling environment such as WebRatio BPM (http://www.webratio.com) (Brambilla, Butti, & Fraternali, 2010; Brambilla, Dosmi, & Fraternali, 2009); another validation based on a testbed in the banking field, where some real applications are being developed for an application for managing leasing requests for major European bank; and the extension of the approach to further similarity relationships between processes and tasks. We also intend to compare our method to existing proposals for business process discovery.

REFERENCES

Acerbis, R., Bongio, A., Brambilla, M., & Butti, S. (2007). Web ratio 5: An eclipse-based case tool for engineering web applications. In L. Baresi, P. Fraternali, & G.-J. Houben (Eds.), *Proceedings of the 7th International Conference on Web Engineering* (LNCS 4607, pp. 501-505).

Antoniol, G., Canfora, G., de Lucia, A., & Casazza, G. (2000). Information retrieval models for recovering traceability links between code and documentation. In *Proceedings of the International Conference on Software Maintenance* (p. 40). Washington, DC: IEEE Computer Society.

Awad, A., Polyvyanyy, A., & Weske, M. (2008). Semantic querying of business process models. In *Proceedings of the Conference on Enterprise Distributed Object Computing* (pp. 85-94). Washington, DC: IEEE Computer Society.

Bajracharya, S., Ossher, J., & Lopes, C. (2009, May). Sourcerer: An internet- scale software repository. *In Proceedings of the ICSE Workshop on Search-Driven Development-Users, Infrastructure, Tools and Evaluation* (pp. 1-4). Washington, DC: IEEE Computer Society.

Beco, S., Cantalupo, B., Giammarino, L., Matskanis, N., & Surridge, M. (2005). OWL-WS: A workflow ontology for dynamic grid service composition. In *Proceedings of the First International Conference on e-Science and Grid Computing* (pp. 148-155). Washington, DC: IEEE Computer Society.

Beeri, C., Eyal, A., Kamenkovich, S., & Milo, T. (2006). Querying business processes. In *Proceedings of the 32nd International Conference on Very Large Data Bases* (p. 343-354).

Belhajjame, K., & Brambilla, M. (2009). Ontology-based description and discovery of business processes. In *Proceedings of the 10th Workshop on Business Process Modeling, Development, and Support* (LNBIP 29, pp. 85-98).

Ben Khalifa, H., Khayati, O., & Ghezala, H. (2008, December 15). A behavioral and structural components retrieval technique for software reuse. In Proceedings of Advanced Software Engineering and its Applications (pp. 134–137). Washington, DC: IEEE Computer Society. doi:doi:10.1109/ASEA.2008.45 doi:10.1109/ASEA.2008.45.

Brambilla, M., Butti, S., & Fraternali, P. (2010). Web ratio BPM: A tool for designing and deploying business processes on the web. In B. Benatallah, F. Casati, G. Kappel, & G. Rossi (Eds.), *Proceedings of the 10th International Conference on Web Engineering,* (LNCS 6189, pp. 415-429).

Brambilla, M., Deutsch, A., Sui, L., & Vianu, V. (2005). The role of visual tools in a web application design and verification framework: A visual notation for LTL formulae. In D. Lowe & M. Gadedke (Eds.), *Proceedings of the 5th International Conference on Web Engineering* (LNCS 3579, pp. 557-568).

Brambilla, M., Dosmi, M., & Fraternali, P. (2009). Model-driven engineering of service orchestrations. *In Proceedings of the IEEE World Conference on Services-I* (pp. 562-569). Washington, DC: IEEE Computer Society.

Ceri, S., Fraternali, P., Bongio, A., Brambilla, M., Comai, S., & Matera, M. (2002). *Designing data-intensive web applications*. San Francisco, CA: Morgan Kaufmann.

Chen, K., Madhavan, J., & Halevy, A. (2009). Exploring schema repositories with schemr. In *Proceedings of the 35th SIGMOD International Conference on Management of Data* (pp. 1095-1098).

Dayal, U., Whang, K.-Y., Lomet, D., Alonso, G., Lohman, G., Kersten, M., et al. (Eds.). (2006, September 12-15). In *Proceedings of the 32nd International Conference on Very Large Data Bases,* Seoul, Korea. New York, NY: ACM Press.

Dijkman, R., Dumas, M., & Ouyang, C. (2008). Semantics and analysis of business process models. *Information and Software Technology, 50*(12), 1281–1294. doi:10.1016/j.infsof.2008.02.006.

Dimitrov, M., Simov, A., Stein, S., & Konstantinov, M. (2007). A BPMO based semantic business process modelling environment. In *Proceedings of the Workshop on Semantic Business Process and Product Lifecycle Management* (Vol. 251).

Dumas, M., Garcia-Banuelos, L., & Dijkman, R. M. (2009). Similarity search of business process models. *A Quarterly Bulletin of the Computer Society of the IEEE Technical Committee on Data Engineering, 32*(3), 23–28.

Ehrig, M., Koschmider, A., & Oberweis, A. (2007). Measuring similarity between semantic business process models. In *Proceedings of the Fourth Asia-Pacific Conference on Conceptual Modelling,* Darlinghurst, Australia (pp. 71-80).

Frakes, W. B., & Nejmeh, B. A. (1987). Software reuse through information retrieval. *SIGIR Forum, 21*(1-2), 30–36. doi:10.1145/24634.24636.

Gibb, F., McCartan, C., O'Donnell, R., Sweeney, N., & Leon, R. (2000). The integration of information retrieval techniques within a soft- ware reuse environment. *Journal of Information Science, 26*(4), 211–226. doi:10.1177/016555150002600402.

Goderis, A., Li, P., & Goble, C. A. (2006). Workflow discovery: The problem, a case study from e-science and a graph-based solution. In *Proceedings of the International Conference on Web Services* (pp. 312-319). Washington, DC: IEEE Computer Society.

Gomes, P., Pereira, F. C., Paiva, P., Seco, N., Carreiro, P., & Ferreira, J. L. et al. (2004). Using wordnet for case-based retrieval of uml models. *AI Communications, 17*(1), 13–23.

Gruber, T. (1993). A translation approach to portable ontology specifications. *Knowledge Acquisition, 5*(2). doi:10.1006/knac.1993.1008.

Hepp, M., Leymann, F., Domingue, J., Wahler, A., & Fensel, D. (2005). Semantic business process management: A vision towards using semantic web services for business process management. *In Proceedings of the IEEE International Conference on e-Business Engineering* (pp. 535-540). Washington, DC: IEEE Computer Society.

Hidders, J., Dumas, M., Van der Aalst, W. M. P., ter Hofstede, A. H. M., & Verelst, J. (2005). When are two workflows the same? In *Proceedings of the Australasian Symposium on Theory of Computing* (pp. 3-11).

Holmes, R., & Murphy, G. C. (2005). Using structural context to recommend source code examples. In *Proceedings of the 27th International Conference on Software Engineering* (pp. 117-125). New York, NY: ACM Press.

Honda, K., Yoshida, N., & Carbone, M. (2008). Multiparty asynchronous session types. In *Proceedings of the 35th Annual ACM SIGPLAN-SIGACT Symposium on Principles of Programming Languages* (p. 273-284). New York, NY: ACM Press.

Inoue, K., Yokomori, R., Yamamoto, T., Matsushita, M., & Kusumoto, S. (2005). Ranking significance of software components based on use relations. *IEEE Transactions on Software Engineering, 31*(3), 213–225. doi:10.1109/TSE.2005.38.

Kiefer, C., Bernstein, A., Lee, H. J., Klein, M., & Stocker, M. (2007). Semantic process retrieval with iSPARQL. In *Proceedings of the 4th European Conference on the Semantic Web: Research and Applications* (pp. 609-623).

Lara, R., Roman, D., Polleres, A., & Fensel, D. (2004). A conceptual comparison of WSMO and OWL-S. In L.-J. Zhang & M. Jeckle (Eds.), *Proceedings of the European Conference on Web Services* (LNCS 3250, pp. 254-269).

Llorens, J., Fuentes, J., & Morato, J. (2004). UML retrieval and reuse using XMI. In *Proceedings of the IASTED International Conference on Software Engineering* (pp. 740-746).

Lu, R., & Sadiq, S. (2006). Managing process variants as an information resource. In *Proceedings of the 4th International Conference on Business Process Management* (pp. 426-431). Washington, DC: IEEE Computer Society.

Markovic, I., Pereira, A. C., & Stojanovic, N. (2008, February). *A framework for querying in business process modelling*. Paper presented at the Multikonferenz wirtschaftsin- formatik.

Muehlen, M., & Recker, J. (2008). How much language is enough? Theoretical and practical use of the business process modeling notation. In Z. Bellahsène & M. L´eonard (Eds.), Advanced Information Systems Engineering (LNCS 5074, pp. 465-479).

Object Management Group. (2006). *Business process definition metamodel*. Retrieved from http://www.omg.org/technology/documents/br_pm_spec_catalog.htm#BPDM

Object Management Group (OMG)/Business Process Management Initiative. (BPMI) (2007). *Business process management notation (BPMN) 2.0*. Retrieved from http://www.bpmn.org

Ouyang, C., Dumas, M., Van Der Aalst, W. M. P., ter Hofstede, A. H. M., & Mendling, J. (2009). From business process models to process-oriented software systems. *ACM Transactions on Software Engineering and Methodology, 19*(1), 1–37. doi:10.1145/1555392.1555395.

Platzer, C., & Dustdar, S. (2005). A vector space search engine for web services. In *Proceedings of the Third European Conference on Web Services* (p. 62). Washington, DC: IEEE Computer Society.

Recker, J. (2010). Opportunities and constraints: The current struggle with BPMN. *Business Process Management Journal*, 181–201. doi:10.1108/14637151011018001.

Recker, J., Indulska, M., Rosemann, M., & Green, P. (2010). The ontological deficiencies of process modeling in practice. *European Journal of Information Systems*, *19*(5), 501–525. doi:10.1057/ejis.2010.38.

Recker, J., Rosemann, M., Indulska, M., & Green, P. (2009). Business process modeling: A comparative analysis. *Journal of the Association for Information Systems*, *10*(4), 333–363.

Seacord, R. C., Hissam, S. A., & Wallnau, K. C. (1998). Agora: A search engine for software components. *IEEE Internet Computing*, *2*(6), 62–70. doi:10.1109/4236.735988.

Settimi, R., Cleland-Huang, J., Ben Khadra, O., Mody, J., Lukasik, W., & De- Palma, C. (2004). Supporting software evolution through dynamically retrieving traces to UML artifacts. In *Proceedings of the 7th International Workshop on Principles of Software Evolution* (pp. 49-54). Washington, DC: IEEE Computer Society.

Soffer, P., Wand, Y., & Kaner, M. (2007). Semantic analysis of flow patterns in business process modeling. In G. Alonso, P. Dadam, & M. Rosemann (Eds.), *Proceedings of the 5th International Conference on Business Process Management* (LNCS 4714, pp. 400-407).

Van der Aalst, W. M. P. (2003). Inheritance of business processes: A journey visiting four notorious problems. In H. Ehrig, W. Reisig, G. Rozenberg, & H. Weber (Eds.), Advances in Petri net Technology for Communication-Based Systems (LNCS 2472, pp. 383-408).

Van der Aalst, W. M. P., & Basten, T. (2002). Inheritance of workflows: An approach to tackling problems related to change. *Theoretical Computer Science*, *270*(1-2), 125–203. doi:10.1016/S0304-3975(00)00321-2.

Van Glabbeek, R. (2001). The linear time - branching time spectrum I: The semantics of concrete, sequential processes. In Berstra, J. A., Ponse, A., & Smolka, S. A. (Eds.), *Handbook of Process Algebra* (pp. 3–99). Amsterdam, The Netherlands: Elsevier. doi:10.1016/B978-044482830-9/50019-9.

Williams, C. C., & Hollingsworth, J. K. (2005). Automatic mining of source code repositories to improve bug finding techniques. *IEEE Transactions on Software Engineering*, *31*(6), 466–480. doi:10.1109/TSE.2005.63.

Wombacher, A., & Rozie, M. (2006). Evaluation of workflow similarity measures in service discovery. In Service Oriented Electronic Commerce (LNCS 4275, pp. 51-71).

Zhuge, H. (2002). A process matching approach for flexible workflow process reuse. *Information and Software Technology*, *44*(8), 445–450. doi:10.1016/S0950-5849(02)00022-8.

This work was previously published in the International Journal of Information System Modeling and Design (IJISMD), Volume 2, Issue 2, edited by Remigijus Gustas, pp. 47-66, copyright 2011 by IGI Publishing (an imprint of IGI Global).

Chapter 3
Towards Next Generation Provenance Systems for E-Science

Fakhri Alam Khan
University of Vienna, Austria

Sardar Hussain
University of Glasgow, UK

Ivan Janciak
University of Vienna, Austria

Peter Brezany
University of Vienna, Austria

ABSTRACT

e-Science helps scientists to automate scientific discovery processes and experiments, and promote collaboration across organizational boundaries and disciplines. These experiments involve data discovery, knowledge discovery, integration, linking, and analysis through different software tools and activities. Scientific workflow is one technique through which such activities and processes can be interlinked, automated, and ultimately shared amongst the collaborating scientists. Workflows are realized by the workflow enactment engine, which interprets the process definition and interacts with the workflow participants. Since workflows are typically executed on a shared and distributed infrastructure, the information on the workflow activities, data processed, and results generated (also known as provenance), needs to be recorded in order to be reproduced and reused. A range of solutions and techniques have been suggested for the provenance of data collection and analysis; however, these are predominantly workflow enactment engine and domain dependent. This paper includes taxonomy of existing provenance techniques and a novel solution named VePS (The Vienna e-Science Provenance System) for e-Science provenance collection.

DOI: 10.4018/978-1-4666-4161-7.ch003

INTRODUCTION

The main theme of e-Science (Schroeder, 2008) is to promote collaboration amongst researchers across their organizational boundaries and disciplines - to reduce coupleness and dependencies and encourage modular, distributed, and independent systems. This has resulted in dry-lab experiments also known as in-silico experiments (Cavalcanti et al., 2005). Unlike wet-lab experiments, the dry-lab experiments enable a researcher to plan an experiment, locate suitable activities via resource directories, combine them into a workflow, and execute it. e-Science workflows (Taylor et al., 2006) are used to specify the execution order of tasks (i.e. activities). A task may take data input, process it, and produce data output. Real world workflows are complex in nature and may contain several hundreds of activities. Scientists need their experimental activities to be recorded in order to be re-usable and re-producible, similar to the used annotation and book logging in wet-lab experiments. Workflow provenance (Khan et al., 2008) describes the workflow service invocations during its execution, information about services, input data, and data produced to help keeping track of workflow activities (Simmhan et al., 2005). It gives not only insight into the workflows, but enables re-execution of workflows as well. Provenance of workflows includes information about the underlying infrastructure, input and output of workflow activities, their transformations, and context used. e-Science workflows are typically executed on a distributed and dynamic infrastructure provided by different institutions - i.e. resources may join and leave continuously. Therefore, provenance, metadata, and annotations of workflows are of paramount importance for reliable and trustworthy e-Science workflows. There is a strong need to propose and build a provenance system that is in-line with the e-Science core theme of modularity and de-coupleness, which ultimately means domain and application independent provenance system. Key requirements for e-Science

provenance systems are interoperability, domain independence, lightweight, visualization, and report generation. Interoperability means that an e-Science provenance system should readily work across different domains, applications, and workflow enactment engines.

However, the existing research and development work is mainly focused on provenance collection tightly coupled with the workflow enactment engines, often specific to their projects. With the growing e-Science infrastructures there is a strong need for a provenance system that works across multiple domains and enactment engines. We call such a system loosely coupled provenance system. Not only portability is an important issue to address, but also the performance impact of the provenance collection process on the overall infrastructure as well, as provenance collection is an additional task to the core computational processing in e-Science workflows so that it should be lightweight.

The major contribution of this paper is twofold. First, various possible ways and scenarios through which provenance can be collected are discussed. Taxonomy of existing work according to those scenarios is elaborated based on the coupling of the provenance system to a concrete workflow enactment engine. Secondly, the Vienna e-Science Provenance System (VePS) focusing on workflow enactment engine independence, domain independence, portability, and less performance overhead is introduced together with its design, architecture, and the performance evaluation of our prototype implementation.

The rest of the paper is organized as follows. First, the concepts and terminologies used in our approach are introduced, and then the taxonomy of existing solutions for a provenance system is discussed. Introduction to the VePS architecture, design, and implementation is provided. Next we detail and share performance evaluation, experiences, and observed issues. Finally, we conclude our work and outline future development directions.

CONCEPTS AND TERMINOLOGY

e-Science is a science or research theme that exploits Grid- or Cloud-based solutions more often called e-Infrastructure. The term e-Infrastructure is used for the technology that supports research undertaken comprising of distributed and on-demand computing software. e-Science provides researchers with shared access to large data collections, advanced ICT tools for data analysis, large scale computing resources, and high performance visualization, among other examples. According to Greenwood et al. (2003):

e-Science is the use of electronic resource instruments, sensors, databases, computational methods, and computers by scientists working collaboratively in large distributed project teams in order to solve scientific problems.

The term workflow originated from the business community, where it was used as an administrative concept for managing operations often referred to as a business process, delivering services from one participant agent to another (van der Aalst et al., 2003). e-Science in particular has taken advantage of workflows based on distributed and Grid technology (Taylor et al., 2006). Workflows typically order the tasks associated with e-Science, e.g. which services will be executed and how they will be coupled together to meet the requirements of the end user. The workflow tasks are described by a document called *workflow document* that specifies the sequence of tasks (activities), control structure, and data being used. Fox defines a workflow as: "The automation of the processes, which involves the orchestration of a set of Grid services, agents, and actors that must be combined together to solve a problem or to define a new service" (Fox & Gannon, 2006). A Scientific Workflow Management System (SWfMS) enables scientists to design and execute their workflows. A scientist's experiment is realized via invoking the tasks specified in the workflow document with the specified data by the SWfMS component known as workflow enactment engine, thus enabling the generation of results.

Scientists performing experiments in wet-labs often record their experiment procedures in notebooks in order to make them verifiable and reproducible for other scientists. These notes include specifying (who): the person performed the experiment, (what and how): materials and techniques used in the experiment, (why): the purpose of the experiment, and (what): the results produced (Zhao et al., 2003). Scientists are not only interested in the results of experiments but also to know "how to" perform these experiments themselves. Similarly many experiments performed through *in silico* workflows involve hundreds or thousands of steps getting inputs and producing outputs. The outputs are not likely to be interesting, trustable, and useful for scientists if they cannot themselves verify, validate, share, and reuse these experiments. Furthermore, workflows involving a large number of steps executing across multiple, distributed resources may have a large number of parameter settings making them infeasible and/or difficult for users to define. To address this, provenance needs to be captured. Provenance (also referred to as lineage and pedigree) has been defined by computer scientists in different ways depending upon the domain in which it is applied (Braun et al., 2008). Greenwood et al. (2003) defines provenance in the context of scientific workflows as "metadata recording the process of experiment workflows, annotations, and notes about the experiments." Provenance allows to keep a record of the workflow activities invoked, the services and databases used, their version and parameter settings, the datasets used and generated, etc. In the context of workflows, provenance can be described as the documentation of workflows that led to a particular result. They can then be used to answer questions like who (person), how (procedure), what, and which resources were used in the workflow (Rajbhandari et al., 2006).

The On-Line Monitoring tools (Schroeder, 1995) are systems with the goal to validate the execution conditions and execution events in order to make systems fault tolerant. If some execution condition is violated, the On-Line Monitoring tool issues a notification to the system. On-Line Monitoring tools tend to be integral part of the underlying system or tools that are executed. Provenance systems can be classified as a special class of On-Line Monitors with the functionality to collect data on activities executed, data processed, and results produced. Unlike On-Line Monitoring tools, for provenance systems, it is not necessary to be integral part of the underlying infrastructure. Moreover, provenance systems will not issue a notification to the system if a workflow or some activity fails. It will record the failure event in the provenance database for the future use to trace what went wrong during the experiment.

PROVENANCE SCENARIOS AND TAXONOMY

The major aim of this detailed taxonomy is to identify the strengths and weaknesses of the state of the art e-Science provenance systems. Our observations, systemic analysis, and scenarios done during the development of this taxonomy will help to identify the issues required to address in order to propose optimal e-Science provenance systems. We systematically create scenarios and evaluate a set of state of the art e-Science provenance systems: (1) Taverna provenance framework, (2) WEEP Engine provenance framework, (3) Kepler provenance framework, (4) Kickstart provenance system of the Virtual Data System (VDS), and (5) Karma provenance framework. For the purpose of systematic evaluation of provenance systems, we have developed the following list of characteristics (properties):

(p1) Domain independence (interoperability): Indicates the ability of a provenance system to collect provenance information across different scientific workflow management systems.

(p2) Flexibility (user control): Indicates the ability of the user or scientist to activate or deactivate provenance data collection.

(p3) Usability: Indicates the ease of integration of a provenance system into workflow enactment engine or SWfMS. The usability of a provenance system increases with its ability to collect provenance data without requiring major modifications.

(p4) Workflow enactment engine overhead: Indicates the additional workload on the SWfMS as result of activating provenance collection.

(p5) Workflow document overhead: Indicates the additional workload on the workflow document designer as result of activating provenance collection.

We propose a scoring system to quantify our opinion and associate grades to properties. The following grades are used in our scoring system for quantifying how well a provenance system supports a property:

0 (Worst): For properties $p1$, $p2$, and $p3$ it indicates that a property is not supported, whereas for properties $p4$ and $p5$ it introduces the worst possible overhead.

1 (Poor): Indicates that there is a little support for a property.

2 (Sufficient): Indicates that a property is sufficiently supported but with a possibility to improve it considerably.

3 (Good): Indicates that there is a good support for a property with some improvements needed.

4 (Very good): Indicates that there is a very good support for a property but some minor improvements are needed.

5 (Excellent): Indicates the perfect grading.

There are numerous existing techniques and surveys (Simmhan et al., 2005; Bose & Frew, 2005; Freire et al., 2008; Tan, 2004) conducted on the provenance collection and some are coming up with promising results. But all of them describe the provenance and provenance collection from a different perspective. We propose a taxonomy of existing provenance techniques based on two main categories - *Listener mode provenance scenarios* and *Monitoring mode provenance scenarios*. In listener mode provenance scenarios, the provenance module is fully dependent on a workflow enactment engine and is somehow controlled by the workflow enactment engine itself, whereas in the monitoring mode provenance scenarios, the provenance system acts autonomously and independently of the workflow enactment engine, client(s), and activities.

Listener Mode Provenance Scenarios

Much of the state of the art on e-Science provenance falls into this scenario. *Listener mode provenance* means that such a provenance system relies on notifications and information that the workflow enactment engine passes onto it, that is it depends on the workflow enactment engine in one way or the other. Main functionalities of such a provenance system include passively listening to workflow enactment engine notifications, parsing data from notifications, storing the provenance data, and visualization of provenance data. However, the main disadvantage of these systems is that they become highly domain and scenario specific and are hard to apply to other workflow enactment engines except for which they are designed. In the following subsections,

we describe possible listener mode provenance scenarios and correspondingly categorize the state of the art provenance systems.

Embedded Provenance System Scenario

In such a scenario the provenance module forms an integral part of the hosting workflow enactment engine. In other words, the workflow enactment engine itself internally keeps logs of all workflow activities. An advantage of having such a provenance system is that the user or researcher is freed from the plugging-in of the provenance service or system and does not have to care about the provenance recording. On the other hand, it is the workflow enactment engine designer and developer who suffer from extra burden. Moreover, such a system does not fit into e-Science as it is tightly coupled to workflow enactment engines, resulting in less portability and flexibility. Portability in the sense that such a provenance system cannot exist except the workflow enactment engine for which it is designed. Flexibility is lost because the users have no control on provenance activation and/or deactivation. The interaction procedure of this scenario is as follows:

1.   The user or client searches a service directory (e.g. UDDI) for desired services and composes a workflow in a specified language. The most commonly used workflow composition language is Business Process Execution Language (BPEL) (OASIS, 2007).

2.   The client submits the composed workflow (workflow document) to the workflow execution engine for execution (enactment). Upon reception of the workflow document by the workflow enactment engine, the engine parses the workflow document and starts invoking the Web services in the order as specified by the workflow document.

3. Whenever the workflow execution engine takes some action (e.g. invokes a Web service, receives a response from an invoked Web service etc.), it passes the provenance related information to the provenance component and the provenance component transforms it into a specific format and stores it in a database.

4. The client can view, query, and visualize the workflow provenance information.

The Taverna Freefluo (Greenwood et al., 2004) workflow enactment engine uses the SCUFL language (Simple Conceptual Unified Flow Language) for enacting different types of services in a workflow such as WSDL services, SOAPLab services (Senger et al., 2003), Talisman Services (Oinn, 2003), and local applications. For provenance collection within the Taverna workbench, there is an event listener embedded in the workflow enactor (i.e. Freefluo) that receives provenance information such as service names, URIs, parameters, input and output data, as well as user annotations (Zhao et al., 2008). The WEEP Engine (Janciak et al., 2008) also supports embedded provenance collection. It maintains a simple database in which it stores the activities names, time, and type. As depicted in Figure 1, alongside other workflow enactment engine components (EE-Components), the workflow

enactment engine has the provenance component and a database for storing provenance data as well. A summary of evaluation of properties for the Taverna provenance framework and the WEEP Engine provenance framework is shown in Table 1.

Provenance Service Specified in Workflow Document

In this section we consider the scenario where the provenance system is designed as a Web service, which carries out its listening activities outside the workflow enactment engine. To invoke this provenance service and to enable the workflow enactment engine to start communicating with this service, it is included as an activity in the workflow specification document itself. Upon submission of the workflow document to the workflow enactment engine, the engine first invokes the provenance service and then passes that activity information as input to the service. The provenance service

Table 1. Summary of evaluation properties for WEEP Engine and Taverna provenance frameworks

	p1	p2	p3	p4	p5
Taverna provenance framework	1	0	4	1	3
WEEP Engine provenance framework	1	0	4	0	4

Figure 1. Provenance as an integral part of workflow enactment engine

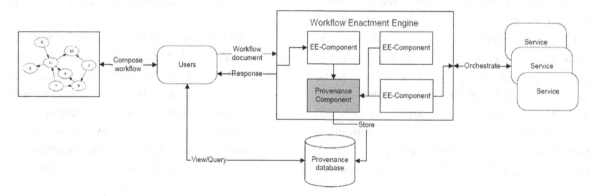

upon receiving this information transforms it into a specific format and stores it in provenance store. The interaction procedure of this scenario is as follows:

1. The client or user selects a suitable provenance service from available provenance services through the Web services directory. The selected provenance service is put into the workflow document as first service, as it is necessary to activate provenance service before any workflow activity is performed.
2. The client or user selects the services which perform the computational processing user needs and composes a workflow of the provenance service and other desired Web services.
3. The client submits the workflow document to the workflow enactment engine for workflow enactment. The engine parses the document and invokes the provenance service. The invocation of this service creates a communication link between the service and engine.

The engine uses this communication link to share any activity and/or data information with the service.

4. The workflow enactment engine invokes other services as described by the workflow document. During these invoke and response events the engine shares provenance information with the provenance service.
5. Upon reception of provenance information, the provenance service transforms it into a suitable format and stores it.

Details of this scenario are explained in Figure 2. Advantage of including the provenance service as part of the workflow document is the ease of integration and more user control over provenance collection. Thereby, if the user does not want the provenance system to be active, she/he can easily remove it from the workflow document.

This scenario has two flavors: (a) Provenance service is included in the workflow document as an indispensable activity; and (b) Provenance service is included in the workflow document but

Figure 2. Provenance service specified in workflow document

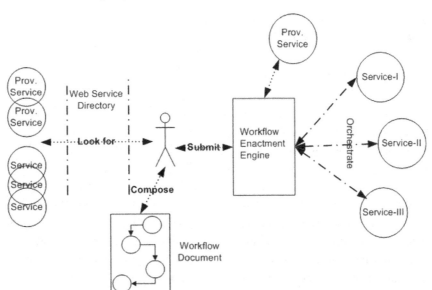

is parameterized; that is included into the workflow document, but on choice. Some of the disadvantages of having such a provenance system are:

- It is difficult to trace the sources of errors because the failure of the workflow causes the provenance system to fail as well.
- It introduces extra load on workflow and workflow designer because the workflow designer has to include the provenance service alongside experimental services as well.
- It introduces extra burden on workflow enactment engine because the engine has to invoke one extra service, resulting in higher response time.

The Kepler provenance framework (Altintas et al., 2006) provides a provenance recorder as a component which can be configured with the workflow in the Kepler system. However, it is provided as a plug-in and when it is used it becomes part of workflow definition. The grades scored by Kepler provenance framework against evaluating properties are shown in Table 2.

Provenance Service Invoked by the Workflow Enactment Engine Itself

In this scenario the provenance service (provenance module) is not introduced as an activity in the workflow specification document but the workflow enactment engine itself is aware of *when* and *how* to invoke it. The interaction steps for this scenario are:

1. The client composes a workflow document in a specified workflow language consisting of Web services which confirm to client needs. It is important that the client does not need to include provenance service in the workflow document. The client is only concerned about the services that he needs

Table 2. Summary of evaluation properties of Kepler provenance framework

	p1	p2	p3	p4	p5
Kepler provenance framework	2	3	2	1	2

for the experiment and the workflow enactment engine will take care of provenance.

2. The client submits the workflow document to the workflow enactment engine. Upon reception of the document, the engine automatically invokes the provenance service and subscribes itself.

3. The workflow enactment engine now parses the workflow document and enacts the workflow as per workflow document. The engine shares the provenance information with the provenance service whenever there is an invoke or a response activity.

4. The provenance service collects the received provenance information in a specific format and stores it in the provenance database.

The advantage of such a provenance system is that the workflows as well as the workflow designer are freed from burden of provenance service inclusion in the workflow document. Moreover, in this scenario it is possible to trace out the problem if a workflow fails. Disadvantage of such a system is introduction of extra load on the workflow enactment engine when comparing to the scenario *provenance service specified in workflow document*. The workflow enactment engine always has to be aware of the provenance system. Furthermore, such a provenance system offers less user control. Whenever new workflow is submitted to the workflow enactment engine, the engine automatically enacts the provenance service, leaving the user with fewer options.

Kickstart (Vockler et al., 2006) is an example of such a provenance system. It is distributed as part of the Virtual Data System (VDS) (Clifford et al., 2008). Kickstart lies between the scheduler and applications and communicates with the provenance system to transfer the information with a functionality of provenance tracking. The summary of Kickstart scoring points is shown in Table 3.

EPR of the Enactment Engine is Supplied by Either the User or the Engine Itself

One possible scenario can be that provenance is collected by a third service (module, activity) which is independent of the workflow enactment engine but, to communicate with enactment engine the provenance service needs EPR (End Point Reference) of the enactment engine, which may be supplied by the workflow enactment engine itself or by the user as shown in Figure 3. Interaction procedure is as follows:

Table 3. Summary of evaluation properties of Kickstart provenance system

	p1	p2	p3	p4	p5
Kickstart provenance system of VDS	1	1	3	1	3

1. The client or user submits a workflow document to the workflow enactment engine. The engine parses the workflow document, assigns a unique EPR to the workflow, and creates an instance of it.

2. The user/engine retrieves the workflow EPR and provides it to the provenance service.

3. When the provenance service receives the workflow EPR, it subscribes itself to the activities and notifications of the workflow enactment engine.

4. The workflow enactment engine enacts (executes) the workflow and provides notifications on the workflow activities to the provenance service.

5. The provenance service on receiving these notifications parses provenance information from these notifications and stores it.

In cases where the EPR is provided by the workflow enactment engine, the provenance system becomes dependent on the engine. The workflow enactment engine needs to be aware of the provenance service as well. In the scenario where the EPR is passed to the provenance system by the user or researcher, it is highly error prone. Moreover, it exerts extra burden on the user to keep track of the enactment engine EPR.

Figure 3. Enactment engine EPR is provided by the user or the enactment engine

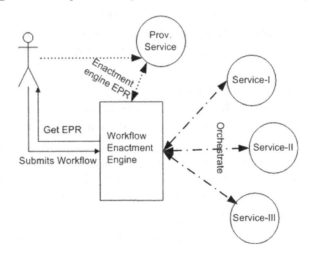

Karma (Simmhan et al., 2008) is one example that relies on a notification broker, also called notification bus. The enactment engine as well as all the services, activities, and clients need to publish notifications to the broker. These notifications are collected by the Karma provenance collection system from the broker. To enable Karma provenance framework to issue notifications, it needs modifications on the server side. Evaluation points of the Karma provenance framework are shown in Table 4.

MONITORING MODE PROVENANCE SCENARIOS

In contrast to the passive *listener mode* provenance systems the *monitoring mode* provenance systems are more active. These systems work like an agent to monitor the workflow enactment engine and the underlying architecture, rather than to depend heavily on workflow enactment engines. Apart from having a workflow enactment engine independent provenance system which can work across multiple domains, other benefits are:

- **Simplicity:** The provenance system does not require any modifications on the workflow enactment engine side. Therefore, it is easier and simpler to enable/disable the monitoring mode provenance system.
- **Efficiency:** The provenance system runs independent of the workflow enactment engine and therefore, the engine performs efficiently.
- **Tracing Errors:** If the enactment engine starts malfunctioning or fails, the prov-

Table 4. Summary of evaluation properties of Karma provenance framework

	p1	p2	p3	p4	p5
Karma provenance framework	3	3	1	2	1

enance system can track and log the enactment engine activities. This will help in determining what actually went wrong.

- **Portability:** Since provenance system is independent of workflow enactment engine, it can work across multiple engines and become highly portable.
- **Tracing Malicious Activities:** If there is some malicious or controversial activity performed by either workflow or the enactment engine, it can be tracked by the provenance system.

Besides these advantages, the issues in realizing such a provenance system are that their implementation is not so much straight forward. The workflow enactment engine can execute many workflows in parallel (many instances of the same workflow) and hence it is very difficult for an independent provenance system to know which activity belongs to which workflow (or instance), which makes it even harder to trace and distinguish them. One possible solution might be to get provenance collected irrespective of workflow. That is all engine activities are logged in a specific format and then this log is mined/semantically analyzed to group activities of the same workflows together. In the following sub-sections we develop possible scenarios of workflow enactment engine independent provenance systems.

Provenance Service Local to the Enactment Engine and is Used by a Single User

In this scenario the provenance collection service and the workflow enactment engine will be running on the same server with the same middleware and on a local desktop system. The benefits of having the workflow enactment engine and provenance module/service local to the user are: (a) Easy to differentiate between different users workflows as only one user a time execute workflows; (b) Such a system has less complexity in terms of having multiple instances or different threads for different workflows; and (c) More user control as the user can enable or disable provenance for a certain workflow.

Workflow Enactment Engine is Shared by Multiple Users

In this scenario the engine runs on some portal, and the provenance service is deployed on the same middleware and multiple users submit their workflows simultaneously to the engine. Figure 4 visualizes this scenario. In this figure it is shown that although the provenance service is local to the workflow enactment engine, it is fully independent of the engine and acts as an intelligent agent to collect provenance. Some open issues with this provenance system are:

- If the workflow enactment engine is designed such that it creates a separate thread for different workflows then how do we differentiate the provenance information that emanates from the same engine?
- If different instances of the workflow enactment engine along with workflow are cre-

ated, then how will the provenance service behave? Should it create different threads or instances to process different workflows activities? In other words should it create a provenance service instance for every workflow or a single provenance service instance should handle provenance for all workflows on a shared infrastructure?

- Where to store the provenance information? If the provenance data is stored on a portal from where the workflow is submitted to the engine then it seems comparatively easy but more security threats are there because of being shared by multiple users.
- It is quite difficult and challenging to differentiate between different workflow activities i.e. which activity belongs to which workflow?

Evaluation Summary

Figure 5 describes our taxonomy and the systems that fall into these scenarios and their coupleness to workflow enactment engine. From Figure 5 it is evident that Taverna and the WEEP Engine are

Figure 4. Enactment engine independent provenance: multiple users

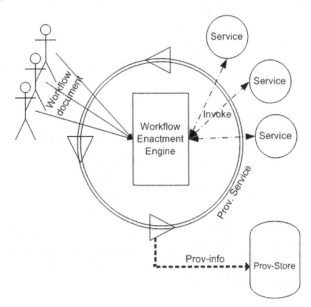

Figure 5. Provenance taxonomy and scenarios

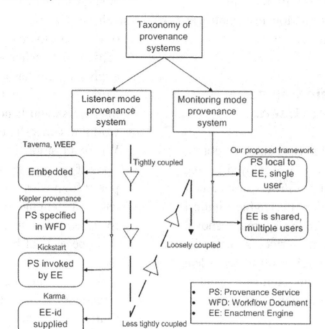

the most tightly coupled provenance systems. The tight coupleness of provenance systems decreases in Kepler, Kickstart, and Karma respectively. Currently, in existing e-Science systems the Karma has the least tightly coupled provenance system. It is also essential to understand that the future lies in a fully independent e-Science provenance system and is one area which needs to be addressed.

The dark areas in Table 5 represent lack of proper support by the provenance systems against the evaluating properties, whereas the brighter areas represent better or excellent support of properties.

The three properties (domain independence, flexibility, and workflow enactment engine overhead) have average score less than 2 (i.e. less than sufficient). This indicates that most state of the art e-Science provenance systems have not addressed these properties.

VePS: ARCHITECTURE, DESIGN, AND IMPLEMENTATION

The Open Provenance Model (OPM) (Moreau et al., 2010) has tried to standardize the provenance collection, but despite their efforts, most provenance systems for e-Science revolve around workflow enactment engine. The fundamental design of e-Science provenance system needs to be changed. It has to come out of the passive mode (passively listening to scientific workflow management system notifications) and has to adapt a more active and intelligent mode. Keep-

Table 5. Evaluation summary

	p1	p2	p3	p4	p5
Taverna provenance framework	1	0	4	1	3
WEEP Engine provenance framework	1	0	4	0	4
Kepler provenance framework	2	3	2	1	2
Kickstart provenance system of VDS	1	1	3	1	3
Karma provenance framework	3	3	1	2	1
Average property score	1.6	1.4	2.8	1.0	2.6

ing in mind these characteristics, we propose and design a workflow enactment engine independent provenance system named Vienna e-Science Provenance System (VePS). Apart from the workflow enactment engine independent provenance collection, the VePS provenance framework is capable of workflow visualization as well.

The VePS shares the middleware i.e., Apache Axis2 (Jayasinghe, 2008) with the engine (i.e. both the VePS and engine are deployed onto the same middleware). The VePS records the workflow activities, whereas multiple users and clients can submit and execute their workflows. We have chosen Apache Axis2 as the middleware because of its stability, popularity, maturity, healthy user community, and its ability to keep evolving to cater changes in the technology and user requirements (Azeez, 2008). Provenance information such as service name(s), method(s) invoked, input data name(s), input data type, input data value, output data names, and values are collected by the VePS provenance framework.

The VePS provenance framework consists of four components, namely *Provenance Interceptor*, *Provenance Parser*, *Provenance Transformer*, and *Visualizer* as shown in Figure 6. Apart from the *Provenance Interceptor*, the remaining components work outside of the underlying infrastructure and hence put less performance burden on workflow execution. The *Provenance Interceptor* component's role is to catch messages passing through the middleware and asynchronously pass these intercepted messages to the *Provenance Parser*. This component extracts and collects the provenance information from the received messages. The collected provenance information is passed to the *Provenance Transformer* component, which transforms it into a well defined XML structure and stores it. The *Visualizer* component is used to visualize the provenance information and produce a provenance information report.

From the sequence diagram shown in Figure 7, it can be seen that on submission of a workflow document to the workflow enactment engine, it

Figure 6. VePS architecture: showing the four main components namely- Provenance Interceptor, Provenance Parser, Provenance Transformer, and Visualizer

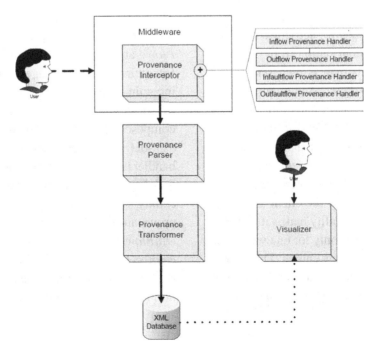

Figure 7. Sequence diagram showing the calls for submission of workflow document to the workflow enactment engine, the enactment engines' invoke and response messages to the Web services through Axis2, provenance handlers interception of SOAP messages, parsing of provenance information, and transforming the provenance information into a well structured XML document

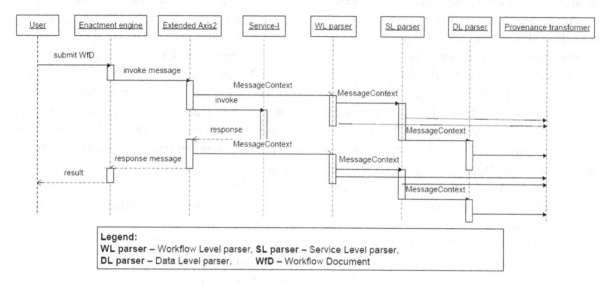

parses the document and generates an invoke message. Upon reception of a message by Axis2, it transforms it into a SOAP message and sends an invoke request to the desired service. Before the delivery of the invoke message, provenance handlers intercept this message and asynchronously deliver it to the *Provenance Parser*. This component parses workflow, activities, and data relevant provenance information from the intercepted messages. This data is then sent to the *Provenance Transformer* component, which properly structures the data and stores it in an XML document. From the VePS framework (as shown in Figure 6), it is clear that it no longer depends on the workflow enactment engine, as it lies at the middleware level to intercept communication messages between the client and components (services). This ability makes it possible to collect provenance not only for one workflow enactment engine but for any engine. This makes VePS portable and domain independent. More fine-grained details of the *Provenance Interceptor*,

Provenance Parser, Provenance Transformer, and *Visualizer* components are discussed in the following sub-sections.

Provenance Interceptor

The Apache's Axis2 architecture has defined four flows, namely *InFlow, OutFlow, InFaultFlow*, and *OutFaultFlow*. All communication (incoming SOAP messages, outgoing messages, incoming faulty messages, and outgoing faulty SOAP messages) pass through them. Each flow is composed of two types of phases, pre-defined and user-defined, which in turn consist of handlers. A handler is the smallest component in the Axis2 and is defined as the message interceptor. The *Provenance Interceptor* component consists of four provenance handlers *InFlowProvenanceHandler, OutFlowProvenanceHandler, InFaultFlowProvenance-Handler*, and *OutFaultFlowProvenance-Handler*. The provenance handlers are integrated into Axis2 with the functionality to intercept the underlying communication between the workflow enactment engine and services passing through Axis2 as shown in Figure 8.

The handlers work like 'T' pipes. They catch the underlying SOAP communication messages and forward them to the *Provenance Parser*. The VePS provenance framework continuously monitors the engine as well as the workflow status through the middleware. The ability of the *Provenance Interceptor* to function independently of the workflow execution engine, clients, and activities makes it domain and application independent. It also means that the VePS is no longer coupled tightly to workflow enactment engine and hence can work across multiple engines. A brief introduction to the provenance handlers is given below.

InFlowProvenanceHandler: It is specifically designed for the *InFlow* of Apache's Axis2 and is added into *InFlowProvenancePhase*, which is then added into the user defined section as shown in Figure 8(a). The core functionalities of *InFlowProvenanceHandler* are: (i) collection of the request SOAP messages passing through the system (middleware) and (ii) extraction of the target service URI. Upon collection of SOAP

messages and WSDL URIs', they are passed onto the *Provenance Parser* component for off line processing and extraction of provenance information asynchronously. The *InFlowProvenanceHandler* and the rest of provenance handlers resemble 'T' pipes in their functionality that is all the SOAP messages pass through them and they intercept these SOAP messages and pass them to the other components of the provenance system for off line processing without any delay. *InFlowProvenanceHandler* collects provenance information such as activity name(s), invocation time, operation invoked, input(s), etc. The code in Listing 1 shows part of axis2.XML, where the *InflowProvenancePhase* is attached after the system predefined phases, whereas the *OutflowProvenancePhase* is attached before the system predefined phases.

OutFlowProvenanceHandler: The outflow of Apache's Axis2 is designed to facilitate the response messages, which means that response SOAP messages always pass through Axis2 outflow (except for the faulty response messages). To enable the interception of response messages and collect provenance information about time consumed by activities and data used, we developed *OutFlowProvenanceHandler*. In functional-

Figure 8. Extended Axis2 with four provenance handlers for inflow, outflow, infaultflow, and outfaultflow

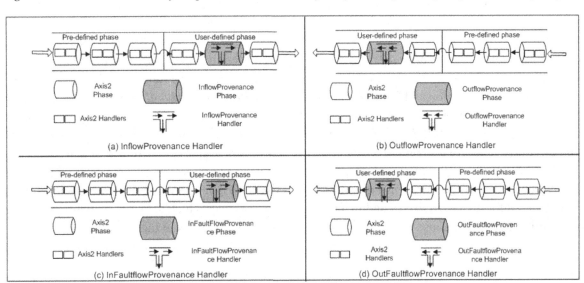

Listing 1. Part of Axis2.XML with provenance handlers

```
<phaseOrder type="InFlow">
        <!--System predefined phases-->
        <phase name="Transport"/>
        <phase name="Addressing">
        <phase name="Security"/>
        <phase name="PreDispatch"/>
        <phase name="Dispatch"
class="org.apache.axis2.engine.DispatchPhase"/>
        <phase name="RMPhase"/>
        <!--System predefined phases-->
        <phase name="OperationInPhase"/>
        <phase name="soapmonitorPhase"/>
        <phase name="InflowProvenancePhase"/>
</phaseOrder>
<phaseOrder type="OutFlow">
        <!--user can add his own phases to this area-->
        <phase name="soapmonitorPhase"/>
        <phase name="OperationOutPhase"/>
        <phase name="OutflowProvenancePhase"/>
        <!--system predefined phase-->
        <!--these phase will run irrespective of the service-->
        <phase name="RMPhase"/>
        <phase name="PolicyDetermination"/>
        <phase name="MessageOut"/>
        <phase name="Security"/>
</phaseOrder>
```

ity, this handler resembles to the *InFlowProvenanceHandler* except the fact that it is integrated into the *OutFlow* of Apache's Axis2 as shown in Figure 8(b). The *OutFlowProvenanceHandler* intercepts all the response SOAP messages going through *OutFlow*, and passes them along with WSDL URIs to the *Provenance Parser*. This handler is part of the *OutFlowProvenancePhase*, which is then plugged into the Axis2 *OutFlow* operation phase section.

OutFaultFlowProvenanceHandler: In cases where there occur some errors, these error messages go through *InFaultflow* and *OutFaultflow* of Apache's Axis2. To enable us to catch these error messages, two handlers (*OutFaultFlowProvendanceHandler* and *InFaultFlow-Provenance-Handler*) are proposed, designed, and integrated into Axis2 fault flows as shown in Figure 8(d). Provenance information on errors and/or faults is helpful in tracing the cause of errors (if there

are any) and to know what actually went wrong. The *OutFaultFlow-ProvenanceHandler* collects outgoing faulty responses and forwards them to the *Provenance Parser* component. It is added to the *OutFaultFlowProvenancePhase*, which is itself added to the Axis2 *OutFaultFlow*.

InFaultFlowProvenanceHandler: Like *OutFaultFlowProvenanceHandler*, this handler does the same processing but for the faulty requests, and is ordered into *InFaultFlow-ProvenancePhase*, which then becomes part of *InFaultFlow* as shown in Figure 8(c). Core functionalities of the *InFaultFlowProvenanceHandler* are: (i) interception of faulty requests, (ii) forwarding faulty request to the *Provenance Parser* component for extraction of provenance information from these faulty requests. Provenance information about faulty requests is useful in determining if there were any requests for resources which were not available or if there were faulty URI's in the workflow document.

Provenance Parser

The *Provenance Parser* is the second core component of the VePS and resides outside of the Axis2 middleware core. The provenance data parsing is performed off-line to the middleware system. This keeps the overhead to minimum and enables the VePS to exert less computational burden on the workflow enactment engine, middleware, and services. The *Provenance Parser* is the `go to' component for a provenance handler. The intercepted requests, responses, or faulty messages are forwarded to the provenance parsers by provenance handlers. After receiving these SOAP message objects and WSDL documents, they are parsed. The relevant provenance information such as sender, receiver, time, operation name, input, and output data type are collected. This filtered provenance data is sent to the *Provenance Transformer* component. The *Provenance Parser* component has three sub-parsers: *Workflow Level Parser*, *Service Level Parser*, and *Data Level Parser*. These three sub-parsers collect information about workflow, services, and data exchanged respectively:

- **Workflow Level Parser:** It collects workflow level provenance information such as workflow input(s), output(s), activities names, start time, and termination time of the workflow. This provenance information is useful in determining the invocation sequence of workflow services (activities).
- **Service Level Parser:** It gathers information about individual activities. Provenance information such as description of service parameters, input(s)/output(s) data to the activity, and invocation interface are included.
- **Data Level Parser:** For every workflow, multiple *Data Level Parsers* are designed. Each single data file used by a service is associated with one of them. It collects detailed provenance information on data used, such as number of rows, mean, variance, unit, size, etc.

Provenance Transformer

Data without proper structure and storage is useless. For this reason, the *Provenance Transformer* component has been developed. XML is chosen to store and share provenance information because of its portability, platform independence, vendor independence, and system independence (Bray et al., 2004). The main role of the *Provenance Transformer* is to identify the provenance category, transform the data into a well designed XML format, and write it into its exact hierarchy. The component also lies outside the Axis2 architecture and performs all of its computation off-line to the underlying infrastructure. The provenance XML document generated is shown in Listing 2.

The root element '*Provenance*' has an attribute '*numberOfFields*,' which contains information about the total number of services executed by a workflow. Every activity (a service call) specified in a workflow document is represented by an element named '*Service*' in the provenance XML document. Data about service name, execution (successful/failed) are stored as attributes '*name*' and '*success*' of the *Service* element. The Service element has two child elements: '*invocation*' and '*response*'. The invocation element contains provenance data about service execution. The time of service invocation and the name of the method invoked are represented by attributes `*method-Name*' and '*time*' respectively. Every invocation element has child element(s) named '*InputData*.' The number of *InputData* elements depends on the number of parameters passed to the service. For every corresponding parameter an '*InputData*' element is created. It contains information on parameter name, type, and value, whereas the response element contains data about activities results and responses. Every response element has '*OutputData*' child element. The '*OutputData*' element represents result data type and value. For details of the provenance XML refer to Listing 2.

Listing 2. XML document generated by the VePS

```xml
<?xml version="1.0" encoding="UTF-8"?>
<Provenance numberOfFields="5">
    <!--Provenance XML document-->
    <Service name="SIServiceNew" parallel="false" parallelTo="none" success="true">
        <invocation methodName="executeSI" source="127.0.0.1" target="http://localhost:8080/axis2/services/SIServiceNew" time="1277392647250">
            <InputData name="Input_Output" type="string" value="http://www.par.univie.ac.at/~khan/test-data/si/si-data_original.xml"/>
            <InputData name="StandardInput" type="string" value="http://www.par.univie.ac.at/~khan/test-data/si/si-standard_input.xml"/>
        </invocation>
        <response methodName="executeSI" time="1277392649484">
            <OutputData name="return" type="string" value="Z:/public_html/test-data/si-generated/StandardOutput1.xml"/>
        </response>
    </Service>
    <Service name="KFServiceNew" parallel="false" parallelTo="none" success="true">
        <invocation methodName="executeKF" source="127.0.0.1" target="http://localhost:8080/axis2/services/KFServiceNew" time="1277392649781">
            <InputData name="StandardOutput" type="string" value="http://www.par.univie.ac.at/~khan/test-data/kf/StandardOutput1.xml"/>
        </invocation>
        <response methodName="executeKF" time="1277392650437">
            <OutputData name="return" type="string" value="file://Z:/public_html/test-data/kf-generated/StandardOutput_AfterKF.xml"/>
        </response>
    </Service>
    <Service name="FFTServiceNew" parallel="false" parallelTo="none" success="true">
        <invocation methodName="executeFFT" source="127.0.0.1" target="http://localhost:8080/axis2/services/FFTServiceNew" time="1277392650562">
            <InputData name="Input" type="string" value="http://www.par.univie.ac.at/~khan/test-data/fft/StandardOutput_AfterKF.xml"/>
        </invocation>
        <response methodName="executeFFT" time="1277392650765">
            <OutputData name="return" type="string" value="file://Z:/public_html/test-data/fft-generated/fft1.xml"/>
        </response>
    </Service>
    <Service>
    <Service>
</Provenance>
```

Visualizer

A provenance system is incomplete and ineffective without proper visualization and presentation. We have not addressed querying capabilities as main focus was on collection of provenance information independent of workflow enactment engine. However, we developed a simple validation application for presenting collected provenance data. The *Visualizer* is the fourth and the last core component of the VePS. It takes as input the provenance *XML* document, parses it, and produces a provenance information report on workflow. The report contains information such as total number of services in the workflow, successfully invoked services, unsuccessful services, name of the service with maximum processing time, name of the service with minimum processing time, and names of the services having maximum and minimum number of parameters.

Apart from provenance report generation, there is a visualization component as well, which visualizes the workflow with help of boxes and lines. The start and end of the experiment is indicated by small circles labeled as *Process Start* and *Process End* respectively. The small rectangular boxes represent services within the workflow and the directed lines show their sequence of execution. The interface (method name) and *partnerLink* of the services is represented with the help of large boxes as shown in Figure 9, which gives a snapshot of the sequential NIGM workflow being visualized. Benefit of such visualization includes; quick understanding of the experiment. This means that just by looking at the visualized workflow the scientist gets idea about the activities, their sequence, and interfaces without going into their programming and XML details.

EVALUATION, EXPERIENCES, AND ISSUES

The performance overhead is an important indicator of a system's scalability and acceptability. Greater the performance overhead of a system the less scalable a system is, and less scalability means less suitability for e-Science infrastructure

Figure 9. Visualized workflow via VePS

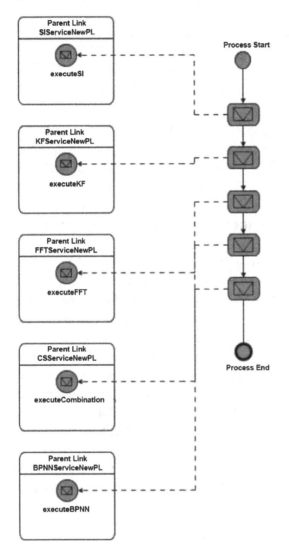

and vice versa. For these reasons, we evaluated the VePS for performance overhead (internal as well as external overhead) on a real world NIGM workflow (Non-Invasive Glucose Measurement Workflow) (Elsayed et al., 2008), and share the results. The impact of high volumes of input data on the VePS performance is examined and the domain independence is validated against the Taverna (Greenwood et al., 2004) and Kepler (Ludäscher et al., 2006) workflow management systems. Furthermore, we also detail the experience gained through testing and discuss the issues that were encountered.

VePS Performance Evaluation

The NIGM workflow consists of five Axis2 Web services. NIGM first preprocess, clean, and transform the input data through System Identification (SI) (Ljung, 1999), Kalman Filtering (KF) (R. E. Kalman, 1960), and Fast Fourier Transformation (FFT) (Bochner & Chandrasekharan, 2001). The transformed data is merged through Combination Service (CS) and finally the Back Propagation Neural Network model (BPNN) is applied to predict the glucose value in human blood. To execute experiments, we used Apache Tomcat version 6.0.18 and deployed Apache Axis2 version 1.3 into Tomcat with the WEEP Engine (version 1.2.1) deployed as a service. A WS-BPEL workflow document which contained the sequential invocation of SI, KF, FFT, CS, and BPNN Services respectively was submitted to the WEEP Engine which orchestrated the workflow.

For performance overhead measurement, the workflow was executed hundred times with the provenance system and without it. A comparison of the result of workflows orchestrated *with provenance* and *without provenance* was performed. The results of performance overhead are shown in Table 6, which reflects that the VePS has on average 4.35% performance overhead with a standard deviation of 18.52. In the worst case a performance overhead of 121ms was recorded, whereas in the best case the overhead was 40ms. Furthermore, it is significant to know the overhead caused by the *provenance handlers* as well as by the *parsers*. The overhead generated by the *provenance handlers* will influence the workflow execution time and is of principal importance for the developers of e-Science applications. Greater the Axis2 overhead, greater are possibilities that developers will be reluctant to embrace such a provenance system into their applications. Whereas, less Axis2 overhead will signify that more and more developers will be attracted (that is because such a system will not hugely affect response time) to include such provenance system into their applications across different domains.

Table 6. Provenance system performance overhead

Description	Best Time (ms)	Worst Time (ms)	Mean Time (ms)	Avg. Overhead (time)	Percent Overhead	Standard Deviation
With Provenance	1805	2035	1920	80	4.35%	18.52
Without Provenance	1765	1914	1840			

On the other hand, the *parsers* (provenance system internal) overhead will affect the scalability of the provenance system. The results of this comparison are shown in Figure 10. It is essential to understand that out of the total overhead only 10.6% is caused by *provenance handlers*. This reflects that the VePS will not have major performance overhead on workflow execution and is encouraging to be integrated across different e-Science applications. On the other hand *parsers* overhead is somewhat high and will have negative consequences on scalability. The reason for such a low Axis2 overhead is that the parsing is performed off line and only SOAP message interception is done in-line to the underlying e-Science infrastructure. We further compared the performance of provenance parsers for *invoke* and *response* calls, and found out that provenance collection for *invoke* caused more overhead than that of *response* as shown in Figure 11. Experimental results of the VePS are promising as it has less overhead on middleware and hence on the workflow execution, which makes it attractive for integration into different domains and workflows.

Impact of Large Volumes of Data

The scientific workflows are usually data intensive and involve complex computations over large volumes of data. It is important for any provenance system to perform well in such scenarios. For this reason we measure the impact of large volumes of data on the VePS. For the NIGM workflow which takes paired values of measurements, ten groups of input data starting from the 10K (Ten thousand paired values) up to 100K were prepared. The time consumed by the VePS to collect provenance for the data of different volume is shown in Figure 11. It can be seen from the Figure 11 that the volume of data being processed has no

Figure 10. Provenance system overhead (internal overhead) vs. Axis2 overhead

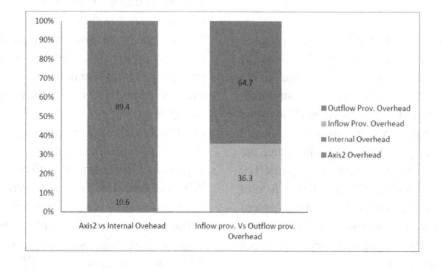

Figure 11. Impact of input data volume on the VePS provenance framework

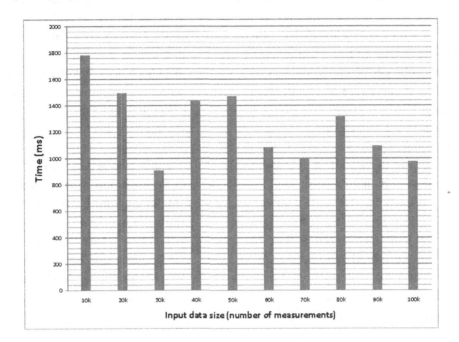

relation or impact on the VePS performance. The impact of input data chart shown in Figure 11 can be divided into two groups. First the 30K, 60K, 70K, 90K, and 100K group which consumes almost 1000ms time, whereas the rest of input data measurements form the second group which takes on the average 1400ms. The reason for this no impact is that the VePS stores a reference to the data resource being used and does not copy or replicate the input data into provenance information. This makes the VePS ideal for scientific workflows consuming large volumes of data but on the other hand if the original data resource is modified or removed then the VePS would not be able to reproduce the same workflow.

Interoperability and Domain Independence Evaluation

The Taverna and Kepler workflow management systems were used to check the interoperability and domain independence of the VePS provenance system. Both are well described and matured scientific workflow management systems and are capable of enacting Web services based workflows. The Taverna is mainly used in bio-informatics whereas the Kepler is broadly used in astronomy. The NIGM workflow was composed in the visual designers provided by these systems and the workflow was executed. The VePS captured the provenance of the workflow executed by these workflow management systems without making any modifications to the Taverna or Kepler engines. This proves that the VePS is capable of collecting provenance information from any Web service based workflow management system and is domain independent. The only disadvantage of the VePS provenance framework is that it is dependent on the Apache Axis2 middleware system and it will not capture provenance for non Web service based scientific workflow management systems.

Experiences

A brief discussion on the experiences that were learned from the development and performance evaluation of the VePS provenance framework is provided as follows:

- This technique is fairly lightweight in the sense that it only catches the *MessageContext* object in-line and all other processing is done off line. Furthermore, it promises to be performance efficient as it lies on the middlleware and apart from intercepting SOAP messages everything is done off-line to the middleware.

- Since recording of provenance information is independent of the workflow enactment engine, it can work for different engines and across different application domains.

- The VePS collects provenance information on errors and faults, which can be used to trace sources of errors, if there occurs any.

- Since the provenance information is captured at the Axis2 layer, which leaves the workflow enactment engine and the server from extra processing of sending and saving provenance information, it is quite advantageous in scenarios where the engine runs on some remote server and portal is used to submit the workflows.

- The VePS exerts less burden on clients, workflow designers, and workflow enactment engine developers as it frees them from caring (integrating, activating) provenance system into their experiments (workflows, applications).

Issues

Through experiments a number of issues were encountered in realizing a provenance system that complies with the real essence of e-Science. Below a brief description of these issues is listed, which if addressed will result in e-Science provenance system that fully satisfies the e-Science requirements.

- **Differentiation of workflow activities in single workflow execution engine and one workflow at a time:** This is the most basic scenario. In this scenario a workflow execution engine is deployed onto server with ability to execute one workflow at time. We currently address this scenario and collect provenance information about workflow activities names, time, input(s), output(s), parameters names, etc. After collecting provenance information at the middleware level it is transformed into the XML and then workflow report along with visualization is generated.

- **Differentiation of workflow activities in single workflow execution engine and multiple workflows scenario:** The biggest issue we have explored is to differentiate between different workflow activities. When multiple workflows are executed in parallel the VePS fails to distinguish between them. This results the issue, How to differentiate activity *a* of workflow *A* from activity *b* of workflow *B*?

- **Differentiation of workflow activities in multiple workflow execution engines and multiple workflows scenario:** Consider the scenario that workflow execution engine is running on a remote server and accessed through a portal and hence shared by many users. How to design a provenance collection module so that every individual's workflow activities are efficiently collected. The VePS currently is based on working directly on the application server and it cannot differentiate multiple workflows running on a server at the same time or having multiple execution engines enacting workflows.

- **Security issues:** The workflows enacting services having strong security requirements like encryption and decryption will require to manipulate data at the application level and hence at the middleware level we will not be able to intercept and see what data is sent and received.

- **De-coupleness from middleware:** The VePS is independent of workflow execution engine but it still depends on the middleware (which is in our case Apache's Axis2). How to make a provenance system fully independent? This is a future research direction on provenance for e-Science and is our ultimate goal. One possible solution is to make provenance as some intelligent plug-in, which can easily be integrated into any application server on the fly.

CONCLUSION AND DISCUSSION

In this paper, a thorough study of state-of-the-art e-Science provenance systems was conducted. Possible scenarios of provenance collection were presented and a unique taxonomy of state of the art provenance systems on basis of their dependence on workflow management systems was created. A systematic evaluation criterion was created based on properties such as domain independence, flexibility, usability, workflow enactment engine overhead, and workflow document overhead. From the taxonomy and evaluation we arrived at the conclusion that existing provenance systems are more domain, application, and workflow management systems dependent and hence are less portable. From the taxonomy it was also concluded that for provenance systems to be in line with the e-Science core theme of interoperability, it needs to be workflow enactment engine and application independent.

Keeping in mind the characteristics of domain and application independence we proposed a solution namely – VePS (The Vienna e-Science Provenance System), for collecting provenance information for e-Science applications based on Web services. The VePS records the workflow provenance in a well designed XML structure and is dependent on the Apache Axis2 middleware system. The VePS provenance system has the advantage to be workflow enactment engine independent, lightweight, and can be applied to various application domains.

The overhead of the VePS was measured and it resulted in a minute value (i.e. < 5%). Less performance overhead makes the VePS suitable for e-Science research as less overhead makes it suitable for integration into difference applications. Large volumes of input data have little or no impact on the VePS, as it only collects references to the data resources. Furthermore, VePS successfully collected provenance information from the Taverna and Kepler scientific workflow management systems and hence proved to be domain and workflow engine independent.

In the future, this approach will be extended to generate a BPEL workflow document from the provenance information which will help make the e-Science experiments fully reproducible. It will also be interesting to extend this work and try to propose and implement a provenance system that is not only loosely coupled to the workflow enactment engine but to the underlying middleware systems as well.

REFERENCES

Altintas, I., Barney, O., & Jaeger-Frank, E. (2006). Provenance collection support in the kepler scientific workflow system. In *Proceedings of the IPAW Conference* (pp. 118-132).

Azeez, A. (2008). *Axis2 popularity exponentially increasing*. Retrieved from http://afkham.org/2008/

Ballinger, K., Ehnebuske, D., Ferris, C., Gudgin, M., Liu, C. K., Nottingham, M., et al. (2006). *WS-I basic profile version 1.1*. Retrieved from http://www.ws-i.org/Profiles/BasicProfile-1.1.html

Bochner, S., & Chandrasekharan, K. (2001). *Fourier transforms*. Princeton, NJ: Princeton Book Company.

Bose, R., & Frew, J. (2005). Lineage retrieval for scientific data processing: A survey. *ACM Computing Surveys*, *37*(1), 1–28. doi:10.1145/1057977.1057978.

Braun, U., Shinnar, A., & Seltzer, M. (2008). Securing provenance. In *Proceedings of the 3rd Conference on Hot Topics in Security*, Berkeley, CA (pp. 1-5).

Bray, T., Paoli, J., Sperberg-McQueen, C. M., Maler, E., Yergeau, F., & Cowan, J. (2004). *Extensible markup language (XML) 1.1*. Retrieved from http://www.w3.org/TR/2004/REC-xml11-20040204/

Cavalcanti, M. C., Targino, R., Baião, F., Rossle, S., Bisch, P. M., & Pires, P. F. et al. (2005). Managing structural genomic workflows using Web services. *Data & Knowledge Engineering*, *53*, 45–74. doi:10.1016/S0169-023X(04)00112-0.

Chopra, V., Li, S., & Genender, J. (2007). *Professional apache tomcat 6*. New Delhi, India: Wiley.

Clifford, B., Foster, I., Voeckler, J.-S., Wilde, M., & Zhao, Y. (2008). Tracking provenance in a virtual data grid. *Concurrency and Computation*, *20*(5), 565–575. doi:10.1002/cpe.1256.

David, P., & Spence, M. (2007). *Designing institutional infrastructure for e-science*. Retrieved from http://www.stanford.edu/group/siepr/cgi-bin/siepr/?q=system/files/shared/pubs/papers/pdf/07-23.pdf

Elsayed, I., Han, J., Liu, T., Woehrer, A., Khan, F. A., & Brezany, P. (2008). Grid-enabled non-invasive blood glucose measurement. In M. Bubak, G. Dick van Albada, J. Dongarra & P. M.A. Sloot (Eds.), *Proceedings of the 8th International Conference on Computational Science, Part I* (LNCS 5101, pp. 76-85).

Fox, G., & Gannon, D. (2006). Workflow in grid systems. *Concurrency and Computation*, 1009–1019. doi:10.1002/cpe.1019.

Freire, J., Koop, D., Santos, E., & Silva, C. T. (2008). Provenance for computational tasks: A survey. *Computing in Science & Engineering*, *10*(3), 11–21. doi:10.1109/MCSE.2008.79.

Greenwood, M., Glover, K., Pocock, M. R., Wipat, A., & Li, P. (2004). Taverna: A tool for the composition and enactment of bioinformatics workflows. *Bioinformatics (Oxford, England)*, *20*(17), 3045–3054. doi:10.1093/bioinformatics/bth361.

Greenwood, M., Goble, C., Stevens, R., Zhao, J., Addis, M., Marvin, D., et al. (2003). Provenance of e-science experiments – experience from bioinformatics. In *Proceedings of the UK e-Science All Hands Meeting* (pp. 223-226).

Janciak, I., Kloner, C., & Brezany, P. (2008, September 29-October 1). Workflow enactment engine for WSRF-compliant services orchestration. In *Proceedings of the 9th IEEE/ACM International Conference on Grid Computing* (pp. 1-8).

Jayasinghe, D. (2008). *Quickstart apache axis2*. Birmingham, UK: Packt Publishing.

Kalman, R. E. (1960). A new approach to linear filtering and prediction problems. *ASME - Journal of Basic Engineering*.

Khan, F. A., Han, Y., Pllana, S., & Brezany, P. (2008). Provenance support for grid-enabled scientific workflows. In *Proceedings of the International Conference on Semantics, Knowledge and Grid* (pp. 173-180).

Ljung, L. (1999). *System identification - theory for the use*. Upper Saddle River, NJ: Prentice Hall.

Ludäscher, B., Altintas, I., Berkley, C., Higgins, D., Jaeger, E., & Jones, M. et al. (2006). Scientific workflow management and the Kepler system: Research articles. *Concurrency and Computation*, *18*, 1039–1065. doi:10.1002/cpe.994.

Moreau, L., Clifford, B., Freire, J., Futrelle, J., Gil, Y., & Groth, P. et al. (2010). The open provenance model core specification (V1.1). *Future Generation Computer Systems, 27*(6), 743–756. doi:10.1016/j.future.2010.07.005.

OASIS. (2007). *The WS-BPEL 2.0 specification*. Retrieved from http://www.oasis-open.org/committees/download.php/10347/wsbpel-specification-draft-120204.htm

Oinn, T. M. (2003). Talisman - rapid application development for the grid. *Bioinformatics (Oxford, England), 19*(1), 212–214. doi:10.1093/bioinformatics/btg1028.

Rajbhandari, S., Wootten, I., Ali, A. S., & Rana, O. F. (2006). Evaluating provenance based trust for scientific workflows. In *Proceedings of the Sixth IEEE International Symposium on Cluster Computing and the Grid* (pp. 365-372).

Schroeder, B. A. (1995). On-line monitoring: A tutorial. *Computer, 28*(6), 72–78. doi:10.1109/2.386988.

Schroeder, R. (2008). e-Science as research technologies: Reconfiguring disciplines, globalizing knowledge. *Social Sciences Information. Information Sur les Sciences Sociales, 47*(2), 131–157. doi:10.1177/0539018408089075.

Senger, M., Rice, P., & Oinn, T. (2003). Soaplab - a unified Sesame door to analysis tools. In *Proceedings of the UK e-Science All Hands Meeting* (pp. 509-513).

Simmhan, Y. L., Plale, B., & Gannon, D. (2005). A survey of data provenance in e-science. *SIGMOD Record, 34*, 31–36. doi:10.1145/1084805.1084812.

Simmhan, Y. L., Plale, B., & Gannon, D. (2008). Karma2: Provenance management for data-driven workflows. *International Journal of Web Services Research, 5*(2), 1–22. doi:10.4018/jwsr.2008040101.

Tan, W.-C. (2004). Research problems in data provenance. *A Quarterly Bulletin of the Computer Society of the IEEE Technical Committee on Data Engineering, 27*(4), 45–52.

Taylor, I. J., Deelman, E., Gannon, D. B., & Shields, M. (Eds.). (2006). *Workflows for e-science: Scientific workflows for grid*. New York, NY: Springer.

van der Aalst, W. M. P., ter Hofstede, A. H. M., & Weske, M. (2003). Business process management: A survey. In M. Weske (Ed.), *Proceedings of the International Conference on Business Process Management* (LNCS 2678, p. 1019).

Vockler, J. S., Mehta, G., Zhao, Y., Deelman, E., & Wilde, M. (2006). Kickstarting remote applications. In *Proceedings of the 2nd International Workshop on Grid Computing Environments in conjunction with Super-Computing* (pp. 76-85).

Zhao, J., Goble, C., Greenwood, M., Wroe, C., & Stevens, R. (2003). Annotating, linking and browsing provenance logs for e-science. In *Proceedings of the Workshop on Semantic Web Technologies for Searching and Retrieving Scientific Data* (pp. 158-176).

Zhao, J., Goble, C., Stevens, R., & Turi, D. (2008). Mining Taverna's semantic web of provenance. *Concurrency and Computation, 20*(5), 463–472. doi:10.1002/cpe.1231.

This work was previously published in the International Journal of Information System Modeling and Design (IJISMD), Volume 2, Issue 3, edited by Remigijus Gustas, pp. 24-48, copyright 2011 by IGI Publishing (an imprint of IGI Global).

Section 2
Structural Modeling and Semantics

Chapter 4
Modelling Information Demand in an Enterprise Context:
Method, Notation, and Lessons Learned

Magnus Lundqvist
Jönköping University, Sweden

Kurt Sandkuhl
University of Rostock, Germany

Ulf Seigerroth
Jönköping University, Sweden

ABSTRACT

Information overload is perceived as a common problem in organisations and enterprises, which calls for new organisational and technological approaches for more pertinent and accurate information supply. The paper contributes to addressing this problem by proposing a method for information demand modelling, which contributes to capturing and understanding the information demand of roles in organisations. This method consists to a large extent of an application of enterprise modelling techniques. Illustrated by a case from automotive industries, lessons learned from information demand modelling are presented and discussed. This includes the specific perspective taken in the method for information demand analysis, common challenges experienced in demand modelling, and the validity of recommendations from participative enterprise modelling for information demand modelling. Furthermore, the paper introduces the notation applied for information demand models and discusses refinement process of this notation.

DOI: 10.4018/978-1-4666-4161-7.ch004

1. INTRODUCTION

Accurate, pertinent and readily available information is essential to problem solving situations, decision-making and knowledge-intensive work. A prerequisite for providing relevant information in a timely manner is the understanding of the information demand; different actors in enterprises have as well as the information flow aiming at meeting this information demand. The intention of this paper is to contribute to understanding information flow problems in enterprises by proposing a method for information demand analysis and by discussing experiences of using this method in an industrial context. For this purpose, the paper integrates, the conceptual development of a method, lessons learned and approaches from two different research directions: *enterprise modelling* (EM) and information logistics.

Since development of the early approaches and methods, one of the traditional application purposes of *enterprise modelling* has been to understand the current situation in an enterprise or organisation under consideration, in order to find problem areas and to propose improvements (Harmon, 2009). A multitude of methods, approaches, tools and work practices aiming at this purpose were developed in areas such as business process reengineering (Davenport, 1993), process improvement (Humphrey, 2007), enterprise knowledge modelling (Lillehagen & Krogstie, 2008), or organisational renewal (Burke, 1994). This large body of knowledge is one basis for the work presented in this paper.

The second field laying the foundations for our work is the area of *information logistics* (Deiters, Löffeler, & Pfenningschmidt, 2003). Information logistics addresses the challenge of improving information flow in enterprises and organisations. Routine activities and well-defined workflows are supported by sophisticated solutions, like enterprise information systems or production planning systems. But for deviations from daily routine, ad-hoc processes, work in distributed, structur-

ally changing teams or seemingly unstructured innovation activities, quickly finding the right information for a given purpose often is a challenge. The analysis of information demand and the development of context models – to be more precise information demand context models – have been found a useful contribution when addressing this problem.

The focus of the paper is on lessons learned from applying the proposed information demand modelling method in industrial cases. The remainder of this paper is structured as follows: The next section (Section 2) elaborates on the background and previous research results forming the starting point for our work. This includes the objectives of information logistics and a conceptualisation of the term information demand. Section 3 discusses the used conceptualisation of methods and introduces a method for information demand modelling, which also is based on the conceptualisation of information demand presented in Section 2.2. Section 4 illustrates the use of the information demand modelling method in an industrial case and discusses information flow problems detected. Section 5 discusses and reflects on selected experiences from the industrial case. We have put focus on the evolution of different parts of the method according to the notion of method in Section 3 and in this paper we direct special attention to the notation used for capturing the information demand. Furthermore, the validity of enterprise modelling practices for information demand context modelling is investigated. Section 6 summarises the work and gives an outlook on future activities.

2. BACKGROUND AND PREVIOUS RESULTS

The work presented in this paper continues research in information logistics, in particular information demand modelling. This section briefly summarises this research, which includes a short introduction to the field of information logistics and related work in information demand modelling (Section 2.1), and the conceptualisation of information demand used in this paper with its origin (Section 2.2).

2.1. Information Logistics

Accurate and readily available information is essential in decision-making situations, problem solving and knowledge-intensive work. Recent studies show that information overload is perceived as a problem in industrial enterprises (Öhgren & Sandkuhl, 2008). An example of a problem in relation to information overload is, in relation to different roles, to find the right information needed for a work task (Öhgren & Sandkuhl, 2008). It is expected that an improved information supply would contribute significantly to saving time and most likely to improving productivity.

The research field information logistics addresses the above mentioned challenge in information supply by using principles from material logistics, like just-in-time delivery, in the area of information supply. The main objective of information logistics is improved information provision and information flow. This is based on demands with respect to the content, the time of delivery, the location, the presentation and the quality of information. The scope can be a single person, a target group, a machine/facility or any kind of networked organisation. The research field information logistics explores, develops, and implements concepts, methods, technologies, and solutions for the above mentioned purpose.

A core subject of demand oriented information supply is how to capture the needs and preferences of a user in order to get a fairly complete picture of the demand in question. In addition to the context-based approach presented in Section 2.2, user profiles and situation-based demand models have been found useful for this purpose.

User profiles have been subject to research in information systems and computer science since more than 25 years. User profiles are usually created for functionality provided by a specific application. They are based on a predefined structured set of personalisation attributes and assigned default values at creation time. Adaptation of such profiles requires either an explicit adjustment of the preference values by the user (Kotinurmi, 2001), or involves deducing attribute values through logging and interpreting of user actions (Setten, Veenstra, & Nijholt, 2002). Some approaches aim at a generalisation of user profiles for a whole application domain. The objective is to enable different services to use the same profile for adapting appearance or behaviour. A frequently discussed approach is the W3Cs standardisation activity for Composite Capabilities and Preference Profiles and Device Independence (Klyne et al., 2004). Instead of a fixed set of attributes, this approach aims at extensible structures for profiles based on a common predefined vocabulary and a set of rules.

A *situation-based* approach was proposed for implementing demand-oriented message supply (Meissen, Pfennigschmidt, Voisard, & Wahnfried, 2004). The basic idea is to divide the daily schedule of a person into situations and to determine the optimal situation for transferring a specific message based on the information value. This approach defines a situation as an activity in a specific time interval including topics and location relevant for the activity. Information value is a relation between a message and a situation, which is based on relevance of the topics of a message for the situation, utility of the message in specific situations and acceptance by the user. Situation-based description of information demand allows for a more sophisticated capturing of user demands as compared to user profiles. The situation captures aspects of individual information demand like time, location and content. The information value relation adds further dimensions like acceptance and offers a way of deciding on when to supply information. However, this approach is subject to the same criticisms as user profiles: the task of defining situations and topics is requiring considerable efforts and has the danger of getting inaccurate over time.

2.2. Information Demand

The understanding and definition of the term information demand used in this paper is based on work performed during 2005-2007, which also contributed to a deeper understanding of how information is used with regards to work-related tasks. During March – June 2005, an empirical investigation was carried out in Sweden aimed at studying how information is used in Swedish authorities and small- and medium sized enterprises. The main objective of this investigation was to identify the connection between information use and different work related aspects, such as work processes, resources, and organisational structures. The purpose behind doing so was to achieve better understanding of the information demands that motivate demand-driven information supply.

The investigation, which comprised 27 interviews with individuals from three different organisations, The Swedish Board of Agriculture, Kongsberg Automotive, and Proton Engineering, the latter two suppliers within the automotive industry, was performed as a series of semi-structured interviews. For purposes relevant to the intended use of the results in other research projects, these 27 individuals were chosen in such a way that they constituted a sample of all levels of the investigated organisations, i.e. from top-level management via middle management down to production- and administrative personnel. Among the results of the investigation were a definition of information demand and a conceptualisation of this term.

Information demand will be used throughout this paper with the following meaning:

Information demand is the constantly changing need for relevant, current, accurate, reliable,

and integrated information to support (business) activities, when ever and where ever it is needed (p. 59).

Information demand has a strong relation to the context in which such a demand exists. The organisational role having the demand and for what task the information is demanded as well as the setting in which such tasks are performed are important aspects for understanding information demand. Thus, the concept of information demand context has been defined both conceptually and as the core of the method with respect to modelling, evaluating and analysing of information demand. We will use the following definition in this paper:

An Information Demand Context is the formalised representation of information about the setting in which information demands exist and comprises the organisational role of the party having the demand, work tasks related, and any resources and informal information exchange channels available, to that role.

Figure 1 illustrates the core concepts defining an information demand context and their relations. An information demand context includes role and responsibilities, tasks, resources and in particular information as core concepts. The above conceptualisation of information demand will be used when introducing the method for information demand analysis in Section 3.

Related work on information demand analysis primarily can be found in the areas of information retrieval and information systems development. In information retrieval, information demand is closely related to information need, which Saracevic (1975) defines as "a psychological state associated with uncertainty, and with the desire to know the unknown." In order to more operationalize this term for use in design and evaluation of information systems, the notion of relevance was introduced. Ingwersen (1992) and Saracevic (1996) consider several types of relevance, e.g.

Figure 1. Context-related concepts with respect to information demand

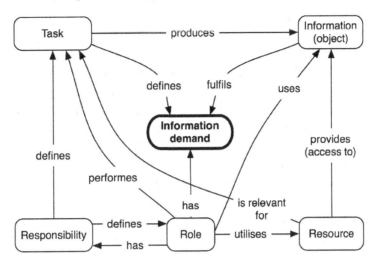

algorithmic, topical, and cognitive relevance, but rather focus on evaluating these relevance types than modelling the user's demand.

In information systems development a lot of work has been done in analysing information requirements as part of requirements elicitation. Early work in the area from Davis (1982) proposes different strategies for information requirement determination. Flynn and Jazi (1994) presented an approach for organizational requirements engineering linking together organizational and information systems modelling in order to identify information requirements for different task characteristics and managerial structures. Many contemporary methods for enterprise modelling acknowledge the importance of making relationships and dependencies between organization structure, tasks and information requirements explicit. Examples for such methods are EKD (Bubenko, Jr., Brash, & Stirna, 1998) and IRTV (Lillehagen & Krogstie, 2009). However, these approaches do not consider all aspects of an information demand context and do not provide modelling or analysis procedures for this purpose.

Furthermore, the use of context information is discussed in various areas of computer science and information systems development. Examples are the use of context representations in informa-

tion logistics (Haselhoff, 2001), decision support systems (Smirnov, Pashkin, Chilov, & Levashova, 2005), and in ubiquitous computing (Dey, 2000). Experiences from these areas show the need for of considering the lifecycle of contexts. Haselhoff (2001) for example uses abstract contexts and operational contexts to distinguish between modelling context information at design time and configuring context information for operational use. Such lifecycle considerations will also be necessary for information demand contexts, but are outside the scope of this paper.

3. METHOD SUPPORTED INFORMATION DEMAND ANALYSIS

Understanding and conceptualising information demand is an important contribution to improved information flow, but far from sufficient. Next necessary steps to take are to define how to capture information demand in a real-world case and how to develop information logistics solutions for such a case. This section introduces the main constituents of a proposed method for information demand analysis (Section 3.2). But in order to do so it is also important to understand and conceptualise methods as a support for action on a general level, in this case the notion of methods that have been used during generation and validation of the proposed method (Section 3.1).

3.1. Methods as Support for Action

All actions are performed based on some motive and rational. There can be several things influencing, guiding and inspiring us, when we perform actions. The sources of guidance and influence can be more or less explicit. The support can be of a tacit nature in terms of different experiences that we have and that we are recalling in the actual work situation, in this paper information demand analysis. The support can also be explicitly formulated as different method descriptions that we follow. In this paper we focus on the method support for performing information demand analysis and in order to conceptualise this we present our view on the concept of "notion of methods."

In our view methods are supposed to give us explicitly formulated guidance for cause of actions in terms of different method descriptions that we follow to achieve certain results. Somewhere between experiences and methods we recognise theories that can inform our actions without giving such explicit prescriptive directives as methods. Theories can help us to direct attention towards certain concepts and structure of concepts (focal areas). In this case the conceptualisation of information demand is built into the method for information demand analysis as a focal area. In addition to this we can also use computerised tools as guidance for actions since methods in many cases is implemented in different tools. The use of methods, theories and tools can therefore be regarded as action knowledge that we can agree with and seek support from during information demand analysis. During modelling there is usually a need to document different aspects and many methods therefore include rules for representation, which often is called modelling techniques or notations, which has a central part in this paper. Methods also provide procedural guidelines, which

many times are tightly coupled to notation. The procedure involves some meta-concepts as process, activity, information, and object, which are parts of the prescribed work procedure. They are also parts of the semantics of the notation. The concepts are the glue and the overlapping parts between work procedure and notation. Methods can thus be crystallised into: *Perform action A, in order to reach goal G.*

It has now been stated that procedure, notation and concepts are the constituents of methods. When there is a close link between procedure, notation, and concepts, it is referred to as method component (Röstlinger & Goldkuhl, 1994). The concept of method component is similar to the concept Method Chunk (Ralyté, Backlund, Kühn, & Jeusfeld, 2006) and (Mirbel & Ralyté, 2006) and the notion of method fragment (Brinkkemper, 1995). Methods are often a compound of several method components (focal areas), which could be referred to as methodology (Avison & Fitzgerald, 1995), These different method components together form a structure called a framework, which gives the phase structure of a method, which for this case can be seen in Figure 2.

All methods build on some implicit (tacit) or explicit perspective. A perspective includes values, principles and categories (with definitions), which are expressed in the method and its method components. The perspective is the conceptual- and value basis of the method and its rationality. The earlier presented conceptualisation of context-related concepts with respect to information demand in Figure 1 are typical aspects that appear on the perspective level but which will have impact on both the framework and the method components.

An additional aspect of methods is labelled co-operation principles; i.e. how different persons (roles) interact and co-operate when performing method-supported actions. Co-operation principles have to do with roles and division of work in the process. This aspect is labelled collection principles and it is conceptually important to

Figure 2. The notion of methods used during method development (Goldkuhl, Lind, & Seigerroth, 1998)

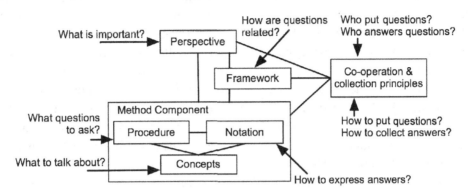

distinguish between a procedure ("what question to ask"), a co-operation principle ("who is asking the question") and a collection principle ("how is the answer collected"). A method component (with procedures) can be used together with different co-operation and collection principles, as e.g. seminars, brainstorm sessions, interviews and questionnaires. In this case the participative dimension will be important in the proposed method. The central parts of the presented notion of methods are illustrated in Figure 2 (Goldkuhl & Cronholm, 1993; Goldkuhl, Lind, & Seigerroth, 1998; Röstlinger & Goldkuhl, 1994). This notion of methods is the conceptual base that we have used for structuring the proposed method for information demand analysis during development and application.

A framework gives methods the overall structure divided into phases with main results that tells us what to do and in what order. The framework is governed by the perspective which depicts epistemological, ontological, theoretical and practical standpoints for the method, e.g. socio-technical view, component based, process orientation, participation. Method components will in contrast to framework also give instruction about how to perform a certain work step in terms of a method component, e.g. the method component process analysis is executed through the procedure instructions – notation rules – and

the focused concepts. If we for example in the perspective have depicted that the method is process oriented then this need to be secured on the method component level through that we have a method component that address concepts that are included in the process theory which is expressed in the perspective. The cooperation and collection principles will, based on the perspective, and how different parts are related in the framework, give instructions about how to capture knowledge about a specific focal area, e.g. information demand, process, problem, goals, etc.

3.2. A Method for Information Demand Analysis

The proposed method for information demand analysis, which is presented in this section, was developed from 2006-2008 in the R&D project InfoFlow that included 7 industrial and academic partners. The basis for the method development is the understanding of the term information demand (Section 2.2), three industrial cases from the InfoFlow project (Lundqvist, 2008; Lundqvist & Seigerroth, 2008; Lundqvist, Seigerroth, & Stirna, 2008), and requirements derived from these cases (Lundqvist, Sandkuhl, Seigerroth, & Stirna, 2008). This section is dedicated to the main features of the proposed method following the notion of methods presented in Section 3.1.

From cooperation point-of-view, analysing information demand relies on a co-design perspective as collaborative modelling with stakeholder participation during the information demand modelling sessions. Since information demand has a close relation to roles (as actor) in a practice we need to ensure that the designated roles also are represented during the information demand modelling sessions (cooperation principles according to the notion of method). Therefore it is considered as important that the modelling is performed in cooperation with the actual individuals having the roles that are to be modelled. A traditional way to address information demand modelling is to do this through process modelling but since the stance for our approach is role-based we argue that a process oriented approach would have the risk to move the focus away from many of the relevant aspects of information demand. This is an important part in the perspective of the proposed method.

As described earlier in Section 2, understanding information demand requires understanding of information demand contexts in terms of a number of dimensions. In Figure 3, an overview

of a framework for achieving such understanding is presented. Since context is considered central to information demand analysis, method support for modelling such contexts is at the core of the framework. However, in order to be able to perform any meaningful context modelling a clear scope is needed. Consequently, the information demand analysis starts with scoping activities. Also, depending on the requirements and needs relevant for the specific case additional aspects of information demand might be analysed and modelled. The focus in this article is however on the information demand context modelling as highlighted in the framework below.

Scoping as a prerequisite for information demand context modelling is the process of defining the area of analysis and is done with the purpose of selecting parts of an organisation to be subjected to analysis. This phase also include the identification of the roles (individuals) relevant for the continued information demand analysis. Scoping should also set the scene for identification and understanding of the organisations problems, goals, intentions, and expectations to motivate

Figure 3. An overview of the process of analysing information demand

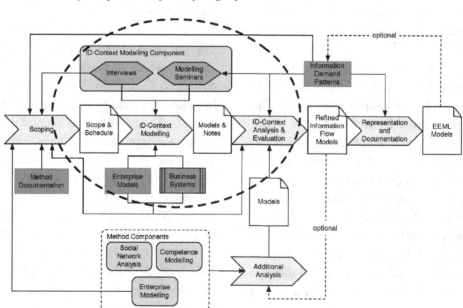

them to engage in the information demand analysis.

Information Demand Context Modelling

Information demand context modelling is mainly performed through participative activities such as joint modelling seminars where the participants themselves are involved in the actual manufacturing of different models. This process is usually supported and facilitated by a method expert who could be an internal or external person. As illustrated in Figure 3, the conceptual focus is in this phase on information demand within a defined scope. The key to context modelling is to identify the interrelationship between roles, tasks, resources and information. No regards are given to the sequence of activities and resource availability, etc. The evolvement of the notation for information demand context modelling as a part of this method component will be presented in Section 5.1.

Information Demand Context Analysis and Evaluation

Once the necessary knowledge about the information demand contexts is obtained it can be used for a number of different purposes. One purpose is evaluation, where different aspects of information demand can be evaluated in relation to roles, tasks, resources and information. It is also suitable to address the results from the modelling session with respect to motivation and purposes expressed during the scoping activities. Focusing on information demand contexts only provide an initial view of information demand without any consideration given to such aspects as individual competence, organisational expectations and requirements in terms of goals, processes etc. Depending on the intentions behind the analysis further activities might be required. The method provides a number of method components supporting such activities. Since the main focus of the method presented here is on information demand it utilises existing procedures and notations for such additional aspects rather than defining new ones. Consequently, if the method user wishes to investigate such additional aspects of information demand, he or she can do this by using subsets of the other methods, notations and languages. Examples of such methods are presented below.

- **Enterprise Knowledge Development (EKD):** A method for generating knowledge about organisational functioning and reasons for change by analysing traditional enterprise aspects in a participative manner with support of a number of description techniques and guidelines.
- **I-star (i*):** A method that can be used for modelling social networks in terms of the concepts typically found within the area of enterprise modelling.
- **Unified Enterprise Competence Modelling Language (UECML):** An extension to the Unified Enterprise Modelling Language focusing on modelling competence with respect to mainly roles and activities.

Whilst no further details on utilising these methods, notations and languages are given in this paper but the results from doing so always have to be evaluated with respect to the contexts identified during the previous phase. The reasoning behind this is simply that the proposed method is not a method for analysing traditional enterprise aspects. Its only goal is to identify and understand the information demand within an organisation. Everything that is done, as part of the analysis efforts, should therefore also be focused on the role-based nature of information demand. Doing so requires one to relate any knowledge gained to the information demand contexts. That is to say, such additional aspects are only relevant in the sense that they influence the initial view on information demand generated by the context modelling and analysis. Examples of this might be individual competence that differentiates between the information needed by two separate individuals having the same role and performing the same tasks within an organisation. Consequently, this phase of the process has to be iterated for every additional analysis activity that is performed to ensure that the strong relation to the contexts is maintained.

4. CASE STUDY IN INFORMATION DEMAND ANALYSIS

4.1 Industrial Application Case

Within InfoFlow, modelling of information demand context was performed in a number of industrial cases in order to collect experiences from various situations and domains and to iteratively develop and improve the method. This section will briefly discuss one of these cases in order to expose typical modelling purposes, the process of modelling, the organisational setting, and results. The industrial case selected is taken from manufacturing industries and focuses on engineering change management within one of the industrial partners of the InfoFlow project. Proton Finishing (henceforth Proton) is a sub-supplier to different first-tier suppliers in automotive and telecommunication industries and performs various surface treatment services of metal components. Surface treatment in this context includes different technical or decorative coatings to achieve certain functionality or appearance.

In the Proton case four major activities were conducted in accordance with the list below. These activities had the focus of engineering change management in the finishing production process where Proton is a subcontractor to many different OEMs in the automotive industry. The challenge for Proton is to handle the continuously incoming changed specifications for the products that they are producing for the OEM. Not implementing the

changes in time would lead to products with wrong characteristics and economic consequences. The major activities in this case were:

1. General modelling of how Proton was handling change management in the production processes. The major results from this activity were descriptions of Proton's processes and a number of described change areas.
2. Validation of process descriptions, prioritisation of change areas, and planning of how to proceed.
3. Detailed process modelling and refinement of improvement areas at Proton.
4. Information demand analysis of a specific part of Proton's sales process (from quotation to production planning).

In this paper, focus is the fourth activity in the list above since it has served as the major basis for development of a method component for information demand context modelling. Usually a number of scoping activities precede the context modelling, but this was not needed here since the scope already was defined in activity 1, 2, and 3. The fourth activity, the actual modelling, was divided into two main activities, (1) interviews, and (2) an information demand modelling seminar. During these two activities the following persons were involved, two researchers from Jönköping University, one consultant from SYSteam Management and four persons from Proton (head of quality, sales representative, technical support/ technical in-house sales, and production planner).

The interviews were performed in a semi-structured manner during two hours where one researcher was guiding the interview and the other researcher together with the consultant took notes. The interviews were also recorded as basis for later analysis and further development of the information demand analysis method. The main purpose with the interviews was to set the stage and decide the focus for the next activity; a seminar during which an initial version of the method (a method hypothesis) for information demand analysis, was tested.

During this modelling seminar one researcher acted as modelling facilitator to move the modelling activities forward. The major purpose of the modelling seminar was to describe the information demand for different roles based on their assignments in the sales process. The modelling seminar was performed in a participative way where the representatives from Proton were actively involved in the modelling. The modelling was performed on plastic sheets with sticky notes and whiteboard markers. The other researcher and the consultant participated during the modelling seminar by observing, documenting and asking questions regarding clarification of aspects of the domain that was in focus. The result from the modelling seminar was the empirical foundation to a method component for information demand context modelling, specifying a number of procedures, a notation and a number of concepts on which to focus. The result from the seminar has also been used by the head of quality at Proton to elucidate and share knowledge amongst the employees about certain dimensions in the change management process. The models have served as an instrument to develop shared knowledge amongst roles at Proton about different aspects of the practice in terms of information demand and information flow.

Figure 4 is part of an information demand model developed in the Proton case focusing on the sales process (from quotation to production planning). This information demand model was

Figure 4. Excerpt of an information demand model from the Proton case

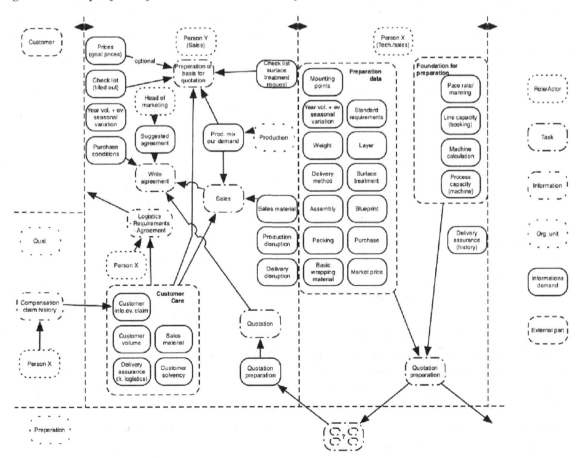

developed by applying a method hypothesis where the initial constructs (Section 2.2) for information demand analysis were tested. The method hypothesis was at this state constituted by initial notation rules that captured the constructs of information demand that has been described earlier. Together with this we also had the initial instructions for work procedures and cooperation principles formulated. Both the initial notation and instructions were largely based on general ideas and approaches from various enterprise modelling methods put in relation to the understanding gained throughout the preceding empirical investigation.

4.2. Common Problems Related to Information Demand

Most organisations have problems related to information demand in some way or another and quite a few of these problems also seem to be independent of organisation or domain. When analysing information flow problems observed in the different industrial cases of the InfoFlow project, such as the case briefly presented in Section 4.1, we have observed different kinds of problems, which shall be summarised in this section. In the following, we will use the term "actor" for a person involved in information-intensive work in an organisation.

One problem category observed is superfluous or irrelevant information, i.e., information is provided to an actor who does not need this information or the information is created without meeting any demand. The reason for this often is that the actor once needed the information, but the information demand changed over time. The effect is unnecessary efforts spent on gathering and providing the information. Furthermore, the receiving actor will have to spend time on sorting out the information and this might contribute to growing perception of information overload One example for this from the first industrial case is the administrator who every month spends a couple of days computing statistics for the sales department. These statistics were used to plan the

sales department work for the next month, but nowadays reports from an ERP-system are used instead. The administrator is however not aware that the information is no longer needed. Another example is the construction department, which produces a lot of drawings and specifications to be used by the production department. They are not certain that all these documents are needed anymore, but they do not dare stop producing them if someone actually does need them.

Another common problem observed is a *gap in the information flow*. The information is supplied, but the roles needing the information are not receiving it or are not aware that they need the information. One reason can be that the actors supplying the information are not aware of all roles that need the produced information and therefore do not distribute it accordingly. Another reason can be that the roles in demand of the information do not know where the information is available or how it is distributed. A third reason is that the information is supplied through a gateway role, i.e., the only purpose for this role to get the information is to supply it to any role needing it. A final reason might be lack in technical support; information is simply not stored in a way that supports the proper distribution of it. An example for this is customer relationship related information. The production department has all information regarding any problems the customers have had with the delivery of their products, but this information does not reach the sales department sometimes resulting in awkward situations with customers and possible loss of sales as a consequence. Another example is the specification of the raw material in an ERP-system needed by the purchase department and the production planners. The relevant information is gathered by the warehouse personnel upon arrival and then handed to the machine operators to input it into the ERP-system. As the operators have no need for this information on their own, this task is always down prioritised and consequently raw material is always specified too late.

It is also very common that information is gathered and provided at the wrong time (*wrong timing*). The reason for this often is that roles, which easily can gather information at the correct time, are not aware that they should. The receiving roles are forced to store the information for later use. At the point in time when they would need the information, they don't find it any more, forgot that they received it or assume that the received information meanwhile is outdated. An example for this is customer invoice information. It is practical to, when the sale is made, gather the information about where to send the invoice. Most sales department however, does not do this because they are not thinking about invoicing as one of their activities and are therefore not aware of what information is needed. This results in the roles performing the invoicing trying to find this information when the invoice should be sent. At that time it is much harder to get the information.

Another common problem is the use of *outdated and/or incorrect information*. This is often due to that individuals do not use the correct source of information. They can be asking another person who they think has the most recent information or information stored elsewhere. One very common example of this is the use of outdated contract templates. The correct templates are often stored on the intranet but people tend to use the latest contract they wrote as a template resulting in faulty contracts.

5. REFLECTIONS AND DISCUSSION

5.1. Initial and Enhanced Notation for Information Demand Models

In enterprise modelling and information demand analysis the models as such (models as artefacts) will have a central place. One important constituent of a model is the notation, i.e., what symbols (visualisations) are used to represent different concepts. In this section we will present how the notation for information demand context modelling has evolved based on application in case studies.

Figure 4 in Section 4.1 is part of an information demand model developed in the Proton case and focusing on the sales process (from quotation to production planning) (see Section 2.1 for description of the Proton case). The evaluation of this application of the method prototype generated a number of issues to be taken into account for further development of the method, see bullets below. The identified deficiencies in the method were:

- The produced models were a result from a process informed modelling approach with a conspicuous sequential division of the domain, i.e. the transformation of input into output and the process sequence is dominant in the model.
- The produced models showed a functional decomposition in the division of the modelled domain, i.e. the division in the figure is closely related to the organisations functional structure.
- The models were manifested by a dualistic description of role relationships in relation to information demand, i.e., the focus is mainly on two immediate roles in relation to specific transitions in the process, see first bullet above.
- The models had an unclear description of interaction between different roles, i.e., the relation between coordination and transformation is unclear.
- The models had a fragmented structure of action objects (information need) lacking somewhat in context, i.e., some individual action objects are without relations to roles or actions and some action objects are grouped into categories without specified relations to roles or actions.

- The models included a variety of relations where the differences between these relations were unclear, i.e., different types of relations are expressed in the same way.
- The models lacked some temporal dimension that needed to be expressed explicitly in a certain situations.

Based on the application of the method prototype in the Proton case the method and the notation were refined in order to deal with the deficiencies identified. Beside the deficiencies presented above, the analysis also pointed out the need for refinement of the conceptual model for information demand, which has been presented earlier in Figure 1. The refinements of the notation are a result of addressing the deficiencies identified through the Proton case. The refinements of the notation have been manifested through the usage of another case from an academic setting; planning and giving an academic course (Figure 5 and Figure 6). The refinements of the method and the notation were tested in a new case since we did not have access to Proton at the time. Figure 5 details the various notational parts while Figure 6 provides an overview of a model to illustrate the general layout and structure.

The method and the notation were developed in the following dimensions.

- Elicitation of role and task as central unit of analysis to address information demand.
- A pluralistic description of role relationships in terms of information demand.
- Enhancement of and a clear division between three dimensions in the models; (1) Operations, (2) Coordination and Management, and (3) Administration and Support.
- A coherent structure of action objects (information need) based on the role relationships.
- Typification of different role relationships.
- The temporal dimension can be expressed through notes connected to activities or action objects.

Elicitation of role and task has helped us to move away from a process oriented analysis and/or functional decomposition which can restrain the focus information demand. This has also helped to utilise the expression for a more pluralistic description of the relations (interaction) between different roles when performing different tasks, in this example to give a course. In order to create a more understandable structure in the information demand model we have also made a division between three dimensions; (1) Operations, (2) Coordination and Management, and (3)

Figure 5. Developed notation for ID-context modelling

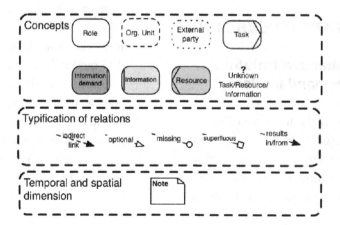

Figure 6. An example of the refined notation for modelling information demand contexts

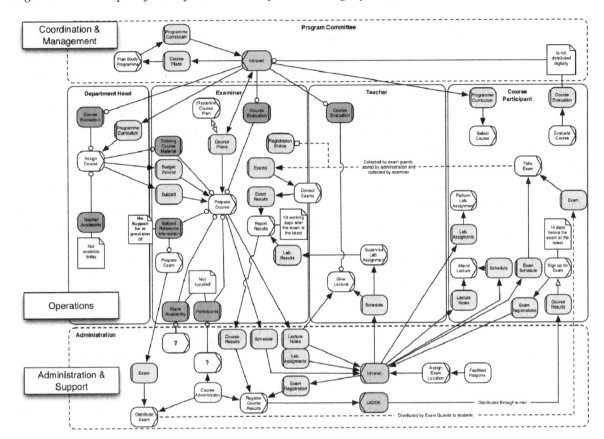

Administration and Support. Operations are manly focusing on the core practice and the assignment, for example to give a course or as in the Proton case, from quotation to production planning. Coordination and management constitute the coordination structure, which will govern the practice and information demand explicit, in this case for giving a course. Administration and support have helped us to elicit different types of support that is needed in order to fulfill the information demand in this specific situation. The typification of the role relations has given the possibility to express a richer picture in the model, which in turn has increased the understanding of the information demand. In addition to this there has also been a general development of the notation in terms of distinguishing different dimensions of information demand, see Figure 6.

Visualising information demand and flow in this manner has helped reducing the effects of deficiencies related to information gathered at the wrong time as the visualisation in itself facilitates the understanding of the information demand in a wider organisational perspective. According to the representatives from Proton taking part in the modelling process there is also an inherent value in grouping information by role independently of processes as this gives an overview of each roles general situation with respect to information flow.

In relation to the earlier presented common problems related to information demand (Section 4.2) we argue that these problems can be elucidated and somewhat handled through these refinements of the method. Superfluous or irrelevant information can for instance be shown through the elicitation of role and task since the needed information (action object) will be specified in direct relation to a role's mission to perform a specific task. This is further supported by the introduction of the relationship *superfluous* that allows for unneeded or unwanted information objects, in relation to work tasks, to be singled out and identified in the model. Gaps in information flow can also be identified in this way and through that the pluralistic relationships between roles are made explicit. In the pluralistic relationships we can address the interaction logic between rules in the value chain, which will shed light upon gaps in the information flow. In cases such as this as well as for when needed information is not part of a value chain, and therefore not easily identified, the new relationship *missing* allows for such information objects to be incorporated into the model. The timing problem can be addressed through the temporal dimension in the notation (notes connected to activities or action objects). The outdated and/or incorrect information can partly be elucidated through the division between; (1) Operations, (2) Coordination and Management, and (3) Administration and Support. This division will show whether the right information will be provided through operative interaction or if it is to be found in the governing structures (Coordination and Management) or, as pointed out in the example of common problems, if the information can/should be retrieved from infrastructural support, like information systems.

5.2. Method Evaluation

To ensure that the developed method is useful and applicable from an industrial point-of-view some thought has to go into both its design and its actual use. This suitability assessment with respect to intended use may be done continuously throughout the development process in an iterative manner or it may be done after development of its various parts in an incremental manner. Partly due to the notion of method used as the foundation for development but also due to the empirical nature of the research project, it is the authors' view that an iterative development-evaluation-development approach it better suited, mainly as this allows continuous switching between generation and validation under the influence of both theoretical and empirical input and feedback.

Goldkuhl (1999) propose three different views on grounding of method generation and validation, *internally, theoretically,* and *empirically*. Actual evaluation of the method and its part accordingly to this idea can of course be done in and from several different ways and perspectives. Siau and Rossi (2008) argues for mainly two classes of techniques for doing so, *empirical* and *theoretical*. During method development, techniques and approaches from both classes have been used as illustrated in Table 1.

5.3. Validity of Practices from Enterprise Modelling Perspective

Information demand analysis in the industrial case presented in Section 4.1 (with focus on context modelling) was conducted in a participative manner since it was considered as best practice for the problem at hand and it created a shared understanding of the current situation (Lind & Seigerroth, 2003). The researchers involved were also experienced in this way of working. Information demand context modelling is similar to enterprise modelling, but still a different approach due to the different perspective taken. Thus, it should be examined whether proven experiences and recommendations for participative modelling can be transferred to context modelling. This section will present the lessons learned in this area by discussing how and to what extent the recommendations for participative modelling proposed by Stirna et al. (2007) were used in the context modelling cases.

Table 2 shows the recommendations published in Stirna et al. (2007) and compares them to the experiences from the four context modelling cases performed in the InfoFlow project (Section 3.2).

Table 1. Generation and validation of IDA

	Generation	Validation
Internally	Reflective discussions where the emerging internal structure and content of IDA was questioned and developed.	Evaluation of method consistency in terms of interrelationships of its various parts.
Theoretically	Use of a theoretically sound and valid method notion to provide a conceptual structure for IDA. Relating concept definitions to existing methods and established knowledge.	Comparison of developed method against existing method notions and method theory. Analysis of validity in comparison to existing methods practices (Section 5.3).
Empirically	Interview-based investigation for deriving method focus, conceptual foundation, and requirements. Practical application of the evolving method together with industrial partners. Development of support documentation (method handbook) together with industrial partners.	Several test cases for evaluating the usefulness of the method in industrial cases (Section 4). Industrial method use and evaluation by external parties by means of a method evaluation framework, NIMSAD. Industrial use and evaluation of method handbook.

The recommendations were divided into five groups, which are reflected in the table. When describing the experiences, we have used

- "Confirmed" if the recommendation was applied in the cases and usefulness for information demand analysis was confirmed,
- "Not applied" if the recommendation was not applied, i.e. no statement can be made regarding validity for context modelling
- "Insufficient data" if the number of cases was too small in order to confirm the validity. However, this does not necessarily mean that the recommendation is not valid.
- "Modified" if the recommendation was enhanced or changed.
- "Not confirmed" if the recommendation was found to be not valid for information demand analysis.

The overall impression is – not surprisingly – that an overwhelming part of the recommendations for participative modelling were found useful and accurate for context modelling. However, the number of cases this result is based on was rather few. Furthermore, there is the danger of a certain bias regarding utility of the original recommendations, since the authors of this paper and the authors of the recommendations (Stirna, Persson, & Sandkuhl, 2007) have a close working relationship.

6. SUMMARY AND FUTURE WORK

The paper presented lessons learned and practices from information demand modelling based on several industrial cases. The modelling approach used is a newly developed method for this purpose, which takes a role-centric view and focuses on capturing the role's tasks and responsibilities and the information required for these tasks and responsibilities. The method consists of several method components, which to a large part are grounded in enterprise modelling traditions.

The paper puts a specific focus on the development of the notation used for capturing information demand context. Evolution of the notation was an integrated part of the method development processes and included consolidation of the essential modelling primitives and their interrelationships. Furthermore, lessons learned and practices of information demand modelling are presented and discussed. This includes the specific perspective taken in the method for information demand analysis, common challenges experienced in demand modelling, and the validity of recommendations from participative enterprise modelling for context modelling and practices of context modelling.

Table 2. Comparison of recommendations and experiences

Recommendation from Stirna, Persson, and Sandkuhl (2007)	Experiences from Information Demand Analysis and Context Modelling	Comments and Explanations
1. Assess the organisational context.		
Try to understand the organisation's *power and decision-making structure* before starting participative modelling sessions	Confirmed, but only in one of the cases	3 out of the 4 cases were part of the InfoFlow project and the project partners' organisation structures were well known. Only in the 4th case, this recommendation was applied at an organisation not familiar to the researchers involved. For this organisation, we followed the recommendation by scheduling additional discussions with different members of the management.
Organisational culture has significant impact on the results and effects of enterprise modelling. To understand the culture is important.	Insufficient data.	The culture in the 4 cases perceived to be quite similar. All 4 organisations seem to have a well-established interaction and knowledge sharing culture. Thus, there is an insufficient basis to confirm or reject the recommendation.
Schedule interviews with stakeholders before starting the project: This may reveal hidden agendas.	Confirmed.	Not all participants were interviewed before the modelling sessions, but most of them, which proved to be a good preparation for the modelling sessions. The interviews revealed different objectives of the participants with respect to the project and helped to establish a positive attitude towards the modelling session.
2. Assess the problem at hand.		
The problem statement provided by an organisation may not be the actual problem. Interview key decision makers or conduct participative enterprise modelling (EM) sessions for understanding the actual problem.	Confirmed.	Both ways were used, i.e. interviews with decision makers in some cases and EM sessions in other cases. EM sessions were used when the problems in daily work were obvious, but the causes of these problems were unclear.
Understand the complexity of the project (fairly simple, complex or wicked)	Insufficient data.	Too few cases were considered. One case can be classified as fairly simple, the other 3 cases as complex, but none of them can be categorised as wicked problem.
3. Assign roles in the modelling process.		
Modelling facilitator	Confirmed.	Modelling facilitator was used in all cases. This role is considered as very important. The modelling facilitator also participated in the stakeholder interviews before the modelling sessions.
Tool operator	Modified: the computerised enterprise modelling tool was used after the session.	The role of tool operator was assigned and the tool operator participated in the sessions. During the sessions, plastics and post-its were used instead of a computerised tool, in order to jointly develop the enterprise model. The tool operator acted rather as documenting assistant and as assisting facilitator. The actual use of the enterprise modelling tool was performed after the session.
Modelling participant/domain expert	Confirmed.	The cases confirmed the essential importance of participants with domain knowledge in the modelling sessions.
4. Acquire resources for the project in general and for preparation efforts in particular.	Confirmed, but only in one of the cases.	In 3 out of 4 cases, the resources were already assigned, since they were part of the resources of the InfoFlow project. In one case, the resources for preparation efforts were also taken from InfoFlow, but for the enterprise modelling sessions and their preparation had to be agreed on with the organisation under consideration.

continued on following page

Table 2. Continued

Recommendation from Stirna, Persson, and Sandkuhl (2007)	Experiences from Information Demand Analysis and Context Modelling	Comments and Explanations
5. Conduct modelling sessions.		
Define clear objectives of practical value	Confirmed.	The objectives of the modelling were always related to case situated information demand and information flow issues. The objectives were discussed during the preparation with the stakeholders and when starting the modelling sessions.
Use a modelling notation that everyone understands	Confirmed.	The notation was introduced very thoroughly by a walk-through of the modelling results. The participants were encouraged to ask questions and contribute to explaining the models.
Do not "train" the modelling participants in method knowledge	Confirmed.	No training was performed or offered, since this would not contribute to information demand modelling.
Keep everyone involved and focused	Confirmed.	This was perceived as essential for success of the sessions. Moderation techniques encouraging involvement of all participants were applied.
Do not accept unknown participants	Not applied.	There were no unknown participants (which are called "intruders" in the original recommendation) to be taken care of.
Problem owner should not dominate the seminar	Not confirmed.	In all modelling seminars, there were several problem owners, i.e. dominance of only a few participants was not an issue.
Establish a common vocabulary	Confirmed.	The participants in the cases to a large extent already had a joint vocabulary. However, clarifications of terms sometimes were necessary.
Develop models in parallel	Not applied.	The computerised models were developed after the sessions. However, the "plastic and post-it" versions were developed in parallel.
Make concrete decisions in the session	Confirmed.	The decisions made primarily concerned changes in information flow and also included the next steps to take
Model should deliver a solution	Not applied.	The enterprise models developed aimed in all cases at creating a joint understanding. Solution development was outside the scope of the cases.
Make sure that everyone knows what will happen after the seminar	Confirmed.	All sessions concluded with preparation of an action list regarding the following activities.

Future work in the area will primarily target the further validation and refinement of the method for information demand analysis. Furthermore, the various notations used in the method need to be additionally evaluated to ensure efficacy, communicability, and correctness. While some effort already has been put into this, such work has to be better integrated with existing ideas and theories (Moody, 2009). Important input is expected from consultants applying the method in daily practice.

The method is documented in a Swedish and an English handbook, which supports dissemination on national and international level. In order to collect the consultants' experiences, a prolongation of the InfoFlow project was established in April 2010 involving 6 industrial and academic partners from Sweden and Germany.

Furthermore, the lifecycle of context information demand will be investigated, which has to include various perspectives. Context models will have to be adapted to organisational changes regarding task and responsibilities for the roles under consideration. Such changes might be initiated as a result of information demand modelling and analysis or by an alignment of organisational structures and processes to new business objectives. Another lifecycle perspective has to address changes in the actual demand of specific individuals. This aspect partly is already addressed in information demand patterns for recurring contexts and information supply patterns for implementing organisational and technical changes for specific patterns.

ACKNOWLEDGMENT

Some parts of the research presented were financed by the Swedish Knowledge Foundation (KK-Stiftelsen) through grant 2005/0252, project "Information Logistics for SME (InfoFlow)."

REFERENCES

Avison, D. E., & Fitzgerald, G. (1995). *Information systems development: Methodologies, techniques and tools*. New York, NY: McGraw Hill.

Brinkkemper, S. (1995). Method engineering: Engineering of information systems development methods and tools. *Information and Software Technology, 37*.

Bubenko, J. A. Jr, Brash, D., & Stirna, J. (1998). *EKD user guide*. Stockholm, Sweden: Stockholm University.

Burke, W. W. (1994). *Organisational development - a process of learning and changing*. Reading, MA: Addison-Wesley.

Davenport, T. H. (1993). *Process innovation: Reengineering work through information technology*. Boston, MA: Harvard Business School Press.

Davis, G. B. (1982). Strategies for information requirements determination. *IBM Systems Journal, 21*(1), 1982. doi:10.1147/sj.211.0004.

Deiters, W., Löffeler, T., & Pfenningschmidt, S. (2003). The information logistical approach toward a user demand-driven information supply. In Spinellis, D. (Ed.), *Cross-media service delivery* (pp. 37–48). Boston, MA: Kluwer Academic.

Dey, A. K. (2000). *Providing architectural support for building context-aware applications*. Unpublished doctoral dissertation, Georgia Institute of Technology, Atlanta, GA.

Flynn, D., & Jazi, M. D. (1994). Organisational and information systems modeling for information systems requirements determination. In P. Loucopoulos (Ed.), *Proceedings of the 13th International Conference on Entity-Relationship Approach* (LNCS 881, pp. 79-93).

Goldkuhl, G. (1999). *The grounding of usable knowledge: An inquiry in the epistemology of action knowledge*. Linköping, Sweden: Linköping University.

Goldkuhl, G., & Cronholm, S. (1993, June 14-16). *Customizable CASE environments: A framework for design and evaluation*. Paper presented at the COPE IT/NordDATA Workshop, Copenhagen, Denmark.

Goldkuhl, G., Lind, M., & Seigerroth, U. (1998). Method integration: The need for a learning perspective. *IEEE Software, 145*(4).

Harmon, P. (2009). The scope and evolution of business process management. In vom Brocke, J., & Rosemann, M. (Eds.), *Handbook on business process management*. New York, NY: Springer.

Haselhoff, S. (2001). Optimising information flow by means of context: Models and architecture. In *Proceeding of the Informatik Conference* [Wirtschaft und Wissenschaft in der Network Economy].

Humphrey, W. S. (2007). Software process the improvement – a personal view: How it started and where it is going. *Software Process Improvement and Practice, 12*, 223–227. doi:10.1002/spip.324.

Ingwersen, P. (1992). *Information retrieval interaction*. London, UK: Taylor Graham.

Klyne, G., Reynolds, F., Woodrow, C., Ohto, H., Hjelm, J., Butler, M. H., et al. (2004). *Composite capability/preference profiles (CC/PP): Structure and vocabularies 1.0*. Retrieved from http://www.w3.org/TR/2004/REC-CCPP-struct-vocab-20040115/

Kotinurmi, P. (2001). *User profiles and their management*. Retrieved from http://www.tml.tkk.fi/Studies/Tik-111.590/2001s/papers/paavo_kotinurmi.pdf

Lillehagen, F., & Krogstie, J. (2008). *Active knowledge modeling of enterprises*. New York, NY: Springer. doi:10.1007/978-3-540-79416-5.

Lillehagen, F., & Krogstie, J. (2009). *Active knowledge modeling of enterprises*. New York, NY: Springer.

Lind, M., & Seigerroth, U. (2003). Team-based reconstruction for expanding organisational ability. *Journal of the Operational Society, 54*, 119–129. doi:10.1057/palgrave.jors.2601474.

Lundqvist, M. (2008). *InfoFlow application case: Experiences from modelling activities at Kongsberg automotive*. Jönköping, Sweden: Jönköping University.

Lundqvist, M., Sandkuhl, K., Seigerroth, U., & Stirna, J. (2008). Method requirements for information demand analysis. In *Proceedings of the 2nd International Conference on Adaptive Business Systems*.

Lundqvist, M., & Seigerroth, U. (2008). *InfoFlow application case: Experiences from modelling activities at proton finishing*. Jönköping, Sweden: Jönköping University.

Lundqvist, M., Seigerroth, U., & Stirna, J. (2008). *InfoFlow application case: Experiences from modelling activities at SYSteam management*. Jönköping, Sweden: Jönköping University.

Meissen, U., Pfennigschmidt, S., Voisard, A., & Wahnfried, T. (2004). Context- and situation-awareness in information logistics. In W. Lindner, M. Mesiti, C. Turker, Y. Tzitzikas, & A. I. Vakali (Eds.), *Proceedings of the Workshops on Current Trends in Database Technology* (LNCS 3268, pp. 448-451).

Mirbel, I., & Ralyté, J. (2006). Situational method engineering: Combining assembly-based and roadmap-driven approaches. *Requirements Engineering, 11*, 58–78. doi:10.1007/s00766-005-0019-0.

Moody, L. D. (2009). The "physics" of notation: Towards a scientific basis for constructing visual notations in software engineering. *IEEE Transactions on Software Engineering, 35*(6), 756–779. doi:10.1109/TSE.2009.67.

Öhgren, A., & Sandkuhl, K. (2008). Information overload in industrial enterprises - results of an empirical investigation. In *Proceedings of the ECIME Conference*, London, UK.

Ralyté, J., Backlund, P., Kühn, H., & Jeusfeld, M. A. (2006). Method chunks for interoperability. In D. W. Embley, A. Olivé, & S. Ram (Eds.), *Proceedings of the 25th International Conference on Conceptual Modeling* (LNCS 4215, pp. 339-353).

Röstlinger, A., & Goldkuhl, G. (1994). *På väg mot en komponentbaserad metodsyn*. Paper presented at the VITS Höstseminarium, Linköping, Sweden.

Saracevic, T. (1975). Relevance: A review of and a framework for the thinking on the notion in information science. *Journal of the American Society for Information Science and Technology, 26*(6).

Saracevic, T. (1996). Relevance reconsidered. In Ingwersen, P., & Pors, N. O. (Eds.), *Information science: Integration in perspective* (pp. 201–218). Copenhagen, Denmark: Royal School of Library and Information Science.

Setten, M., Veenstra, M., & Nijholt, A. (2002). Prediction strategies: Combining prediction techniques to optimize personalization. In *Proceedings of the Conference on Adaptive Hypermedia - Personalization in Future TV*, Malaga, Spain.

Siau, K., & Rossi, M. (2008). Evaluating techniques for system analysis and design modelling methods – a review and comparative analysis. *Information Systems Journal, 21*(3), 249–268. doi:10.1111/j.1365-2575.2007.00255.x.

Smirnov, A., Pashkin, M., Chilov, N., & Levashova, T. (2005). Ontology–based knowledge repository support for healthgrids. In *Proceedings of Healthgrid* (pp. 47–56). From Grid to Healthgrid.

Stirna, J., Persson, A., & Sandkuhl, K. (2007). Participative enterprise modelling: Experiences and recommendations. In J. Stirna, A. Persson, & K. Sandkuhl (Eds.), *Proceedings of the 19th International Conference on Advanced Information Systems Engineering* (LNCS 4495, pp. 546-560).

This work was previously published in the International Journal of Information System Modeling and Design (IJISMD), Volume 2, Issue 3, edited by Remigijus Gustas, pp. 75-95, copyright 2011 by IGI Publishing (an imprint of IGI Global).

Chapter 5
Ontology Alignment Quality:
A Framework and Tool for Validation

Jennifer Sampson
Statoil, Bergen, Norway

John Krogstie
Norwegian University of Science and Technology, Norway

Csaba Veres
University of Bergen, Norway

ABSTRACT

Recently semantic web technologies, such as ontologies, have been proposed as key enablers for integrating heterogeneous data schemas in business and governmental systems. Algorithms designed to align different but related ontologies have become necessary as differing ontologies proliferate. The process of ontology alignment seeks to find corresponding entities in a second ontology with the same or the closest meaning for each entity in a single ontology. This research is motivated by the need to provide tools and techniques to support the task of validating ontology alignment statements, since it cannot be guaranteed that the results from automated tools are accurate. The authors present a framework for understanding ontology alignment quality and describe how AlViz, a tool for visual ontology alignment, may be used to improve the quality of alignment results. An experiment was undertaken to test the claim that AlViz supports the task of validating ontology alignments. A promising result found that the tool has potential for identifying missing alignments and for rejecting false alignments.

INTRODUCTION

Ontologies are a promising technology for supporting data interoperability by providing a basis for integrating separate domains through the identification of logical connections or constraints between data schemas. Furthermore, ontologies are well suited for defining shared conceptualizations in order to support the interoperability of heterogeneous and inter-organizational sources of information. Through automated reasoning ontologies provide the flexibility required for

DOI: 10.4018/978-1-4666-4161-7.ch005

navigating through different levels of abstraction and querying the overall body of knowledge about business processes. Interoperability problems arise from the fact that developers of information systems use different vocabularies to express the information contained in the systems even when describing the same domain. In many cases, applications require information from multiple information sources. However, an application can only use information from two software systems completely and accurately, if precise semantic correspondences among the data from the two systems can be made. Ontology alignment tools such as Chimæra (McGuinness, 2000), FOAM (Ehrig, 2005), OMEN (Mitra et al., 2005) and Prompt (Noy & Musen, 2003) help establish semantic correspondences between data entities contained in different software systems.

The overall research process that was followed is shown in Figure 1. The research questions we address in this paper are as follows.

1. How can we define ontology alignment quality?
2. Does visualization improve ontology alignment quality and how?

To maintain quality throughout the research we applied the design-science research guidelines developed by Hevner et al. (2004). Design-science research requires the use of rigorous methods in both the development and evaluation of the designed artifact. Since artifact quality depends on the selection of appropriate techniques to develop or construct a theory, we based our framework for ontology alignment quality on a well established quality framework (Krogstie et al., 1995; Lillehagen & Krogstie, 2008).

The core subject of the paper is ontology alignment, whereby we develop two design science artifacts, a framework and a visualization tool. We define ontology alignment quality as a framework comprising: semantic, syntactic,

Figure 1. The research process

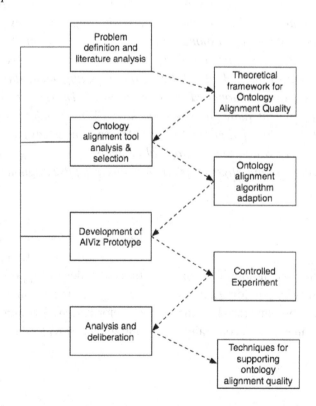

pragmatic and social quality dimensions. According to Denning (1997) and Tsichritzis (1998) artifacts built in design science research are rarely full-grown information systems that are used in practice. Instead, artifacts are innovations that define the ideas, practices, technical capabilities, and products through which the analysis, design, implementation, and use of information systems can be effectively achieved.

It is well known that evaluation is an important component of the research process. Evaluation of a design artifact requires the definition of appropriate metrics and the gathering and analysis of appropriate data. We designed and undertook a controlled experiment to perform the evaluation of the visual ontology alignment tool. Hevner et al. (2004) claim that a controlled experiment is a relevant evaluation method for designed artifacts. We found that the evaluation phase provided essential feedback to what Hevner et al. (2004) refers to as the 'construction' phase. Accordingly a design artifact is complete and effective when it satisfies the requirements and constraints of the problem it was meant to solve. The evaluation of the prototype tool resulted in promising results for supporting ontology alignment tasks such as: checking candidate alignments and locating missing alignments.

We briefly mention related work in the next section, from this study we found that only a few tools offer visualization facilities for ontology alignment. In response to research question 1, we define quality in ontology alignment using the linguistic concepts of syntax, semantics and pragmatics. Using these concepts a theoretical framework for ontology alignment quality is then presented. Following terminology definition, we briefly describe the functionality provided by the tool. Moreover, we describe how we improve the presentation and quality of ontology alignment results for the FOAM algorithm through the use of information visualization techniques. We undertook an experimental evaluation of the prototype tool, to determine whether visualization helps

improve ontology alignment quality. Results of the experiment are presented. Finally, in the last Section, we summarize our work, present our conclusions and discuss future work.

Before we describe the framework and tool, we will briefly discuss an alignment example, together with challenges a user may face when evaluating ontology entity pairs.

Ontology Alignment Example and Challenges

In Figure 2 we show a simple example of possible alignments between entities in two ontologies. Candidate alignment pairs are shown as dotted lines between the concepts. Question marks are placed over pairs which may or may not be similar.

A user interacting with an ontology alignment tool such as Prompt or FOAM, must analyze candidate alignments such as 'cat' and 'feline' and determine whether to accept or reject them, as well as create additional alignments that the tool may have missed. Potential entity pairs might have many of the same properties, yet for some reason humans are able to judge that the properties are misleading in doing a comparison. For example, in an animal transport company example both 'owner' and 'pet' might have similar properties such as 'name' and 'address', but they are certainly not similar concepts! Similarly the 'exporter' and the 'owner' may have the same properties, but are also not necessarily good candidates for alignment.

A number of ontology management algorithms, Momis (Beneventano et al., 2001), Glue (Doan et al., 2004), Chimæra (McGuinness, 2000), FOAM (Ehrig, 2005), IFMap (Kalfoglou & Schorlemmer, 2002), OLA (Euzénat, 2004), Onion (Mitra, 2000) Prompt (Noy & Musen 2003), SAMBO (Lambrix & Tan, 2006) S-Match (Giunchigli et al., 2004), all establish similarity between entities through a comparison of features. By features we mean all object and datatype properties, such as having a name, address, and so on. But it can also be

Figure 2. A highly schematic example

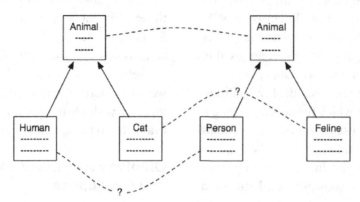

additional properties like for example instances belonging to a class. Even when performing a structural comparison, these algorithms use the features of the parents, children and sibling entities to establish similarity. However, a number of cognitive scientists (Davenport & Keane, 1999; Goldstone & Son, 2005; Larkey & Markman, 2005) have argued that feature based models of similarity cannot adequately explain similarity judgments, yet every technique for computing similarities in ontology alignment relies on such models. We therefore expect these techniques to fail in the same ways that models of feature based human similarity judgment fail. First, we expect that featural overlap will sometimes lead to the wrong conclusion (e.g. 'owner' and 'pet'. Both might have a name and address, for example). Second, we expect that some cases of similarity will be missed.

For the same reasons cognitive scientists found feature based models of similarity to be problematic, automated ontology alignment algorithms, based on feature comparison, can also incorrectly match entities. Therefore, user interaction is necessary to help accept, reject and correct candidate alignments and to find missing pairs. But user validation of ontology alignment entity pairs is difficult given how the results are presented in existing tools. With this motivation, we designed a visual tool to help support such alignment tasks. The tool AlViz (described in

Section 4) presents alignment results visually, and introduces relevant information in the form of various contextual cues.

By showing the relevant alignment status of entire neighborhoods we allow similarities and contrasts in groups of entities to be illuminated. Furthermore, we claim that by providing information about what kind-of-thing an entity is, based on the neighborhoods it occupies, the tool, adds extra features thereby supporting the pluralistic process of similarity judgment. In a first pilot evaluation of our tool we found visualization to help identify missing pairs and to help find more suitable matches.

There are a number of application areas in business and government that already benefit from semantic technologies for facilitating organizational data interoperability. Semantic Web technologies have been put in place to integrate data and services between government agencies and to provide services to citizens. Database administrators find ontologies useful because they form a basis for integrating separate databases through identification of logical connections or constraints between schemas. An important step in data integration is the identification of related entities between different ontologies. Using ontology alignment tools a data administrator can identify entities that are related between ontologies that describe the data in local databases to a global ontology that describes the domain. When an alignment is established between global and local ontologies, end users can link to the source databases through a query that shields the user from the heterogeneity between the underlying databases.

Ontologies have been used for database cleaning, semantic database integration, consistency and data mining (Miller & Xu, 2001). In the medical domain research has been undertaken towards the definition and standardization of terminologies. The complexity of the terminologies used in medicine and the strong need for quality control has also led to the development of ontologies that feature complex concept definition. Some of these ontologies are available in OWL (e.g. FMA, http://sig.biostr.washington.edu/projects/fm/) and can be seen as one of the first OWL applications that have been used in real life applications. It is well recognized that a single universal terminology for the medical domain is neither possible nor beneficial, because different tasks and viewpoints require different, often incompatible conceptual choices. Because different communities make use of different proposed standards, the need for ontology alignment is important for enabling the exchange of information between these different communities.

While the content of the Web is designed for humans to read, the Semantic Web is striving towards making the content also available for machines to interpret and manipulate. The main idea of the Semantic Web is to enrich the current contents of Web pages with descriptions, which can be parsed by computer programs for automated reasoning. The enrichment is achieved by annotating Web contents with ontologies. To do this, data on the Web is "tagged" with entities of an ontology to help clarify the meaning and to establish relationships to other data. However, different websites are unlikely to be annotated using the same ontology. Hence, querying and integrating data from multiple sources on the Semantic Web requires establishing semantic correspondences between entities of their ontologies,

so that the data can be unified and consistently integrated. Pastor et al. (2004) remark web applications require precise semantics and a number of technologies and languages have been proposed to achieve such a goal. In addition they describe how most of the web applications running on the web have a "mostly unknown semantic structure, and all independent of each other" (Pastor et al., 2004). Given the decentralized nature of the Semantic Web, there are an increasing number of independently developed ontologies, making the task of manually identifying and encoding such correspondences in mediators or agents unfeasible. Hence, semi-automatic support in ontology alignment is vital to the success of the Semantic Web (Do, 2006).

RELATED WORK

Ontology Alignment

To enable integration of heterogeneous data schemas a number of ontology management tools have been proposed, e.g. Momis (Beneventano et al., 2001), Glue (Doan et al., 2004), Chimæra (McGuinness, 2000), FOAM (Ehrig, 2005), IF-Map (Kalfoglou & Schorlemmer, 2002), OLA (Euzénat et al., 2004), OMEN (Mitra et al., 2005), Onion (Mitra et al., 2000) Prompt (Noy & Musen 2003), SAMBO (Lambrix & Tan, 2006), and S-Match (Giunchigli et al., 2004). Unfortunately the different tool makers do not use consistent terminology, referring to the process variously as: ontology matching, ontology mapping, ontology alignment, ontology integration and ontology merging (Euzénat & Shvaiko, 2007). Ontology merging is where two different ontologies within the same domain are merged into a single unifying ontology. For example, PROMPT (Noy & Musen, 2003) was originally developed as an ontology merging tool. PROMPT is an interactive tool which allows the user to give some information about relatedness of concepts and uses this information to determine the next operation and to identify potential conflicts. The tool relies on a linguistic matcher to give initial suggestions of potential mappings which are then refined and updated in later stages. PROMPT leaves the user in control of making the decisions, it makes suggestions that a user can choose to follow or not. AnchorPROMPT (Noy & Musen, 2001) considers similarity between class hierarchies, and the use of similarity scores in determining the potential match between classes.

FOAM (Ehrig, 2005) is an ontology mapping algorithm that combines different similarity measures to find one-to-one mapping candidates between two or more ontologies. FOAM is based on heuristics (similarity) of the individual entities (concepts, relations, and instances). The results are presented as pairs of aligned entities. Ehrig et al. (2005) describe how a range of similarity measures are used in FOAM for finding alignments between entities ranging in increasing semantic complexity such as: entities, semantic nets, description logics, restrictions and rules. The similarity computation of FOAM is achieved by using a wide range of similarity functions. Once the individual measures are calculated for each entity description (e.g. URI, RDF/S primitives or domain specific features) they are input to the similarity aggregation using a sigmoid function. FOAM produces as output a set of actual mappings and a set of questionable mappings that require user verification.

Recently FOAM has been integrated into the Protégé ontology management framework as a tab-widget. The FOAM tab implements a Protégé interface for the FOAM algorithm developed by Ehrig (2005). Recently work has progressed towards extending the plugin framework for PROMPT (Falconer et al., 2006). Indeed, the author's extensions to the PROMPT framework are beneficial to our research because they also implement and use the mapping tool FOAM as a plugin. According to (Falconer et al., 2006) the new PROMPT framework is to help address two

fundamental issues. First how can we satisfy the cognitive support requirements in one environment? Second, how can we close the gap between mapping algorithm research and mapping users? The authors claim that by

supporting user interface extension points in PROMPT, experts and developers in Human Computer Interaction can incorporate their ideas and tools to help decrease the cognitive load on end users of mapping tools.

Their timely research also aims to help the algorithm researcher. They continue,

By using these extensions, researchers (or software developers) can easily incorporate their algorithms into PROMPT, allowing the research to be available under one consistent user interface (Falconer et al., 2006).

Chimæra (McGuinness, 2000) is another interactive ontology merging tool, similar to PROMPT, however, since it uses only a class hierarchy in its analysis it does not locate all the mappings that PROMPT establishes. When using Chimæra a user can bring together ontologies developed in different formalisms, during which s/he can request an analysis or guidance from the tool. Chimæra can, for example, point out to the user a class in the merged ontology that has two slots obtained from the different source ontologies or has two subclasses that came from the different ontologies.

GLUE (Doan et al., 2004) is a system that uses machine-learning techniques to semi-automatically find mappings between heterogeneous ontologies. The multiple learners within the GLUE system use concept instances and the taxonomic structure of ontologies. GLUE uses a probabilistic model to combine the results from the different learners. The result of the matching is a set of similarity measures, specifying whether concepts in one ontology O1 are similar to concepts in the other ontology O2. Onion (ONtology compositION) (Mitra et al., 2000) is another architecture which supports a scalable framework for ontology integration. The main innovation in ONION is that it uses articulations of ontologies to interoperate among ontologies. An articulation generation function in ONION is a matching or alignment algorithm between ontologies.

Ontology Management and Visualization

Several ontology management tools incorporate visualization techniques e.g. OLA (Euzénat et al., 2004), Jambalaya (Storey et al., 2001), and PromptViz. These tools mainly use simple types of visualizations such as two-dimensional trees or graphs. Most often the nodes stand for concepts and the edges represent relationships between concepts. Ontology visualization is a promising approach as long as we are able to provide additional benefit to the ontology engineer. One of the key uses of visualization in knowledge engineering tools is to help users navigate ontologies. Such visualization tools aim to help users comprehend and navigate large information spaces. To achieve this, different types of graph layouts are often used in order to display the ontology from different perspectives e.g. Jambalaya (Storey et al., 2001). Ontology navigation is also important for ontology alignment, as users need to understand the structural context related to the candidate alignments they must validate. However, in ontology alignment the focal point of the navigation is the entities involved in the alignments, and not always the entire information space (Falconer et al., 2006). Therefore, we need to provide a way to highlight entities involved in an alignment, as well as those entities in the 'neighborhood.'

A number of graph-based visualization plug-ins exist for Protégé (Grosso et al., 1999), for example OntoViz (Sintek, 2007) was one of the earlier tools developed for visualizing frame based ontologies. OntoViz is Protégé plug-in that visualizes ontologies with the use of the graph visualiza-tion software called Graphviz. Graphviz (Gansner & North, 2000), is a generic graph visualization toolkit that has also been used for tools such as IsaViz and RDFViz. While OntoViz may be useful for graphically representing small ontologies or ontology fragments, the graphs become jumbled when the complexity of the ontology increases. Fluit et al. (2004) also found that the "scalability of the visualization is quite poor" and "it is hard to understand the visualization as soon as more relations are added". Relevant parts of an ontology can be selected using check boxes. The linking of the two views is very useful and helps with navigation, however the tool does not provide any zooming functionality, hence it is difficult to get an overview of the overall structure of the entire ontology.

RDF Gravity (Goyal & Westenthaler) is an RDF Graph Visualization Tool developed by the Knowledge Information Systems group at the Salzburg Research organization. Four main features of this tool are: graph visualization (renderers, zoom and selection), filters to enable specific views of a graph, full text search and query support, visualizing multiple RDF files. An interesting aspect of this tool is that it allows a user to include multiple files and then query or visualize the RDF triples from multiple files within the same graph. A powerful feature of the tool is the ability to filter out and visualize specific parts of RDF graphs. Graphs generated using this tool becomes rather cluttered with a large number of nodes are visible, this is partly due to the display of node names.

OntoSphere3D is another Protégé plug-in for ontologies navigation and inspection using a 3-dimensional hyper-space where information is presented on a 3D view-port enriched by several visual cues. The authors use an interesting 3D approach to tackle space allocation problems for visual ontology models. This is a promising visualization technique providing information at the global and detail level of single ontology.

Recently (Gilson et al., 2008) proposed a novel approach for automatic generation of visualizations from domain-specific data available on the web. They combine a probabilistic ontology mapping technique based on OMEN (Ontology Mapping Enhancer) (Mitra et al., 2005). The authors have since developed SemViz which is a tool that generates appropriate visualizations automatically from a large collection of popular web pages for music charts without prior knowledge of these web pages (Gilson et al., 2008).

From an analysis of the state of the art we have found there are a number of ontology tools applying visualization techniques, however these techniques are not primarily for supporting the alignment of ontologies. In this area, most tool support is textual in nature. Thus the AlViz-tool that we present here is one of the first to our knowledge to support visual ontology alignment. On the other hand it builds upon existing alignment algorithms. To judge the potential improvement of such an approach compared to the textual approaches, we need to have a clear understanding on ontology alignment quality.

UNDERSTANDING ONTOLOGY ALIGNMENT QUALITY

In 1994, Lindland et al. devised a first version of a framework for understanding conceptual model quality. They observed that previous lists of desirable properties for conceptual models did not provide a "systematic structure for evaluating them." Consequently they proposed a framework that not only identified major quality goals, but gave the means for achieving them. The framework is based on the semiotic concepts of syntax, semantics and pragmatics, in recognition that modeling is essentially making statements in some (semi) formal languages. Later Krogstie et al. (1995) extended the framework (called SEQUAL) and since then it has been useful in a wider context for understanding quality in areas such as enterprise modeling (Krogstie & Arnesen, 2004), interactive

modeling (Krogstie & Jørgensen, 2002), requirements engineering (Krogstie, 1999) and evaluating modeling languages such as UML (Krogstie, 2001) and BPMN (Nysetvold & Krogstie, 2006). It has also been used for the evaluation of ontologies (Lin et al., 2004; Hella & Krogstie, 2010). Here we apply the framework to ontology alignment to formally define ontology alignment quality with the goal of determining how, and with what tools, we can improve the quality of a set of ontology alignments. One of the techniques we suggest for improving the quality of ontology alignment, which we will describe in the next Section, is information visualization.

The framework is depicted in Figure 3. On the left hand side of Figure 3 we represent the different quality dimensions relating to ontology 1 (O_1), and on the right hand side we represent quality dimensions relating to ontology 2 (O_2). We represent the ontology alignment statements for convenience as O_A, while recognizing that O_A is not an ontology, but a set of statements relating ontology 1 (O_1) to ontology 2 (O_2). In our research we specifically focus on the quality of the ontology alignments, represented in the lower half of Figure 3.

Here we describe the important components of the framework for ontology alignment quality. Like Krogstie et al. (1995) we take a set-theoretic approach to the different quality aspects. Throughout the framework we represent both the human and technical participants (e.g. data integration agents) in the alignment process, we do not show these participants as direct components of Figure 3; instead we focus on the participant's knowledge K_A (T_A for technical participants) of the alignment.

To make the discussion more concrete, we will use examples of ontology alignment statements from Table 1, which includes some of the candidate alignments from two ontologies used in the evaluation. These ontologies will be described in more detail in the evaluation section, so for now

Figure 3. Theoretical framework for ontology alignment quality

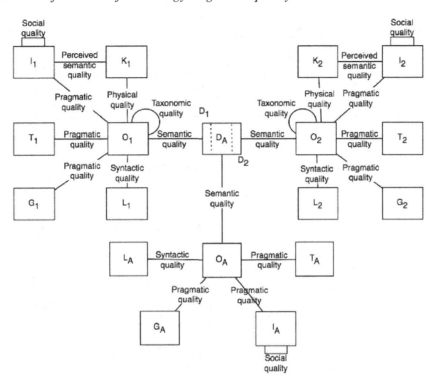

Legend

O_1 and O_2 - ontology 1, ontology 2.

I_1 and I_2 - set of all statements the social actors perceive ontology 1 and ontology 2 consist of.

K_1 and K_2 - set of all relevant, explicit knowledge statements of the participants involved in the ontology development.

T_1 and T_2 - set of ontology statements interpreted by each technical actor.

G_1 and G_2 - set of goals for which ontology 1 and ontology 2 were created.

L_1 and L_2 - language extension - set of possible statements according to the ontology language.

D_1 and D_2 - set of statements about domain 1 and domain 2.

O_A - set of all alignment statements between O_1 and O_2.

I_A - set of all statements the social actors perceive the ontology alignments consist of.

T_A - set of all alignment statements interpreted by each technical actor.

G_A - set of goals for which ontology 1 and ontology 2 were aligned.

L_A - set of possible statements according to the ontology alignment language.

D_A - set of statements about the two overlapping domains 1 and 2.

it is sufficient to note that the first is a pair of ontologies is in the domain of census demographic data, and the second is from tourism.

In the next subsections we describe important aspects of the framework. We focus on pragmatic and semantic quality and how we improve ontology alignment quality from a pragmatic and semantic perspective in this paper. Brief discussion of physical and syntactic quality can be found

in (Sampson, 2007). However, we argue that addressing physical and syntactic quality is relatively trivial compared to improving pragmatic and semantic quality. Moreover, taxonomic and social quality are outside the scope and topics for future work, first because taxonomic quality is related to the quality of the individual ontologies and second because social quality is facilitated through collaborative tools.

Table 1. Suggested alignments for population and tourism ontologies

Population1	Population2	Travel1	Travel2
University_Qualification	Tertiary_Qualification	Activity	Activity
Samoyed	Samoyed	Frequent_Flyer_Scheme	Milage_Scheme
Programming	Java_Programming	Urban_Area	Urban
Qualification	Qualification	Campground	Camping
Indian	Indian	Guest	Guest
Leadership	Leader	Art_Gallery	Art_Gallery
Chocolate	Chocolate	LodgingRating	Rating
German	Norway	Singapore	Singapore
Construction	Non_fiction	Rock_Climbing	Climbing
State_School	State	BudgetAccommodation	Accommodation
European	European	Organization	Location
Domestic_Cat	Cat	Airline	Airline_Company
House	House	National_Park	Landmark
Commercial_Property	Commercial_Property	Winery	Winery
Animal	Animal	Theme_Park	Theme_Park
Fishing	Fishing	BudgetHotel	Budget
Ancestry	Geneology	Boat	Cruiseboat
North_American	North_America	Capital	Capital_City
Human	Person	Ballooning	Hot_Air_Balloon
Skill	Skill	RuralArea	Rural
African	African	Farmland	Farm_Country
Property	Private_Dwelling	Car	Automobile
Country	Country	Mountain	Mountain

Pragmatic Quality

Pragmatic quality is the correspondence between the ontology alignment statements and the audience interpretation (the degree to which the alignment pairs have been understood). For example, in Table 1 a set of candidate alignment pairs are shown which would typically require interpretation if they are to be validated. How can we improve the understandability of such a set of alignments? First of all we can make the type of relation that holds between the pairs explicit (e.g. similar domain and range over relations, equal super classes, syntactically equal labels etc). In this way we provide the "audience" with justification of why

the alignment pair exists. For example 'Singapore' and 'Singapore' have syntactically identical labels, but in these ontologies it so happens that one represents the airline, while the other, the country. It would clearly be of benefit to explicitly state that the alignment is purely syntactic; otherwise unwarranted assumptions could be made about their semantic similarity.

While complete comprehension is an ideal goal, it is unrealistic to assume that each audience member will understand all alignment pairs. Therefore, it is necessary to introduce the notion of feasibility. Feasible comprehension refers to the notion that not all alignment pairs may have been correctly understood by all audience members, i.e.

$$(\exists \; l) \; (I_{Al} \setminus O^{l}_{A}) U \; (O^{l}_{A} \setminus I_{Al}) = S_{Al} \neq \emptyset$$

where there is no statement $s \; E \; S_{Al}$ such that the benefit of determining the misunderstanding corresponding to s exceeds the drawback of determining where the misunderstanding occurs. Pragmatic quality can be measured through the subjective measure of pragmatic correctness, that is: the two ontologies and the relations between them are a) understandable and b) understood. We argue that a graphical representation of ontology alignment data may be an important means to improve pragmatic quality of the set of alignments.

Semantic Quality

Semantic quality concerns the validity and completeness of the ontology alignment. The semantic quality of the set of alignments is the correspondence between O_A and the alignment domains D_A. Validity means that the set of alignment statements are regarded as correct and relevant for the two overlapping domains. Whereas completeness requires that the set of alignments statements contains all the necessary statements about the two overlapping domains. A definition for the validity of the ontology alignment as

$$\text{validity}_{\text{align}} = 1 - (\#(O_A \setminus D_A)) / \#O_A$$

where given a perfect mapping the value returned would be 1, indicating that all statements are valid.

We define completeness of the ontology alignment as:

$$\text{completeness}_{\text{align}} = 1 - (\#(D_A \setminus O_A)) / \#D_A$$

Similarly, given a perfect mapping the value returned would be 1, indicating that the set of alignment statements is complete.

Krogstie et al. (1995) comment that "total validity and completeness cannot be achieved for anything but extremely simple and highly intersubjectively agreed domains", so like Krogstie et al. (1995) we introduce the notion of feasibility. In doing so we determine the time to terminate an alignment process is not when the alignment is 'perfect', but when it has reached a state where further aligning will be less beneficial than applying the alignments currently suggested. Accordingly, a relaxed validity and completeness is defined:

- **Feasible validity:** $O_A \setminus D_A = R \neq \emptyset$, where there is no statement $r \; E \; R$ such that the benefit of performing a delete of r from O_A exceeds the drawback of eliminating the invalidity of r.

Furthermore, a definition for feasible completeness for ontology alignment is as follows:

- **Feasible completeness:** $D_A \setminus O_A = S \neq \emptyset$, where there is no statement $s \; E \; S$ such that the benefit of inserting s in O_A in a syntactically complete way exceeds the drawback of adding the statement s.

The goal is therefore to help improve the semantic quality of a set of ontology alignment pairs by reducing the effort involved in adjusting the statements in the automatic alignment. We go some way to achieving this goal through the development of a visual tool for helping human experts 'judge' the completeness and validity of the ontology alignment pairs. In the next section we briefly describe the tool for improving the quality of a set of ontology alignment pairs like those shown in Table 1). Currently, we focus on how we can improve semantic quality using visualization.

The framework is to formally define what we mean by ontology alignment quality. It should be emphasized that we don't generally assign numbers to these metrics, however we can develop tools to help minimize or maximize the different metrics. In the next section we will describe one such tool, designed specifically for improving completeness and validity of alignment pairs.

A Note about Perceived Quality

The model in Figure 3 includes the notion of perceived quality, for the ontologies themselves. This is an important notion when applied to modeling in general (Krogstie et al., 1995). In modeling, semantic quality is usually checked through human perception (i.e. the person validating the model) making judging questions like, "is there something wrong in this model?" (perceived validity) or "is there something missing?" (perceived completeness). This is based on the judge's own knowledge of the domain. On the other hand in the context of ontology alignment, there is no such preconceived knowledge. What is being judged is the sensibility of the alignment itself as generated by the alignment algorithm, while the validity and completeness of the underlying ontologies are assumed. We therefore address the semantic quality of the alignment rather than the perceived semantic quality.

IMPROVING ONTOLOGY ALIGNMENT QUALITY USING VISUALIZATION

As described above information visualization techniques have been recommended as one possible means for addressing some of the problems related to validating ontology alignment results. We recommend information visualization techniques for improving the quality of a set of ontology alignment statements, because visualization helps by shifting some parts of the cognitive work load to perception abilities (Lanzenberger & Sampson, 2006). By using visual metaphors, visualization aids the interpretation and understanding of complex data in order to provide the user with relevant information, such as how entities in two ontologies are related.

With the quality framework as a foundation we designed and implemented a prototype tool, AlViz, which extends current approaches to ontology alignment. The purpose was not to propose another algorithm for alignment, but rather to provide ontology engineers with a visual representation of alignment results to enable understanding, agreement and validation of the results.

AlViz is a multiple-view visual ontology alignment tool that uses J-trees and small world graphs. The purpose of the tool is to assist a user (ontology engineer or domain expert) in the process of validating complex alignment decisions and determining whether to accept or reject candidate alignment pairs. We also aim to help users find missing alignments (or correct invalid, proposed alignments). Missing alignments may be between concepts that have not already been associated to another concept or corrections to the suggested alignments based on responses from the validation check. To accomplish these tasks the user does not necessarily need to understand the complex semantics of ontologies, s/he does not need to be an ontology engineer, but has to understand the meaning of the aligned entities. We believe that these tasks are necessary for improving the semantic quality of an ontology alignment.

The development of AlViz is incremental, and as such the first version of the tool was primarily focused on testing the hypothesis that visualization is useful for validating ontology alignments, finding missing alignments and for improving the quality of the results. Due to the complexity of the task at hand and the number of features necessary, we prioritized the tool functionality so as to achieve a testable first version (i.e., a proof of concept). These functionality details have been described in (Lanzenberger & Sampson, 2006; Sampson & Lanzenberger, 2006). A number of extensions to the tool would be necessary to fully integrate it with Protégé (Grosso, 1999) and to complete additional requirements.

A screenshot of AlViz is shown in Figure 4. Two types of views are important for visual ontology alignment namely, J-Trees (shown on the left hand side and commonly known as class browsers in Protégé) and small world graphs (shown on the right hand side). While J-Trees are very useful, they become cluttered and do not provide adequate overview functionality when dealing with large or complex ontologies. Because of these problems with J-Trees we also use small world graphs (van Ham & van Wijk, 2004) as a second visualization type. Ingram's (Ingram, 2005) small world graph implementation is applied as a new technique for visualizing ontologies in AlViz.

In the screen shot, nodes represent concepts (classes) and the edges represent is-a relations. However, the final implementation will allow for different relationships to be selected by the user (e.g. part-of). Colors are used to represent the following relations between pairs of classes in an ontology. Unfortunately the colors cannot be reproduced in the journal article, but readers should instead note that the shades of grey in the figures were actually distinct colors in the actual display.

1. **Equal labels only (Yellow):** This is where concept names are the same or similar, according to a well defined edit distance metric. Edit distance is used for comparing concept labels by calculating the number of changes needed to transform one string into another one. This means that labels can either be exactly the same or they can be only slightly similar requiring a number of changes to make them equivalent. Some concept labels are more similar than others (shorter edit distance).

2. **Labels are similar and some shared properties (Pink):** The class names are similar

Figure 4. AlViz Screenshot: In this view the spheres represent classes and are differentiated according to the similarity type. The slider to the right adjusts the level of detail. In this screen shot we show the lowest level of detail.

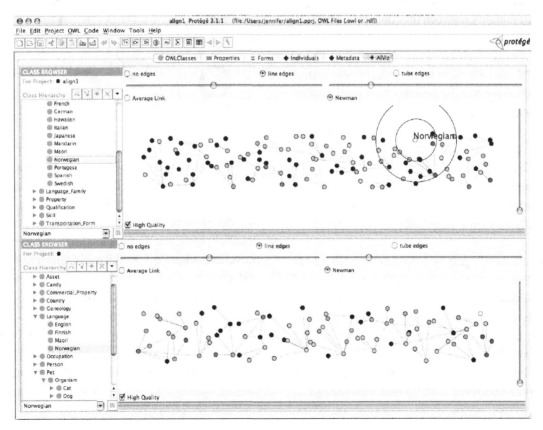

and the concepts have similar data or object properties. Object properties represent relations between concepts such that they are used to link individuals to individuals (e.g. has_itinerary) whereas data properties link individuals to data values (e.g. customer name).

3. **Labels similar and some shared properties plus they may have other similar features (e.g. superclasses, subclasses or instances) (Green):** Concepts can obviously be related in more than one way e.g. through having similar super classes and / or similar sub classes, having the same instances and also having similar data and object properties.

4. **Equal concepts, the labels are the same and most of the properties are the same or very similar (Red):** Concepts are most likely to be equal when the class names are the same and the data and object properties are the same or very similar. (Obviously if they are also similar in other ways this strengthens the equality between the concepts). The next relation is a special case similarity:

5. **Broader-than and Narrower-than (Magenta):** Broader-than: a concept in one ontology may be broader than a concept in another ontology. That is, concept x of ontology 1 is broader than concept y of ontology 2 if the sub class of concept x is equal to (the superclass) of concept y. Narrower-than means: if the superclass of concept x is equal to (the subclass) of concept y then concept x is narrower than concept y.

Small world graphs help a user to examine the structure of the ontology more intuitively. This method uses clusters to group the nodes of a graph showing a specific level of detail, shown in Figures 5 and 6 using Ingram's (Ingram, 2005) small world graphs.

Changing the level of detail (the size of the clusters) is achieved using a slider on the right-

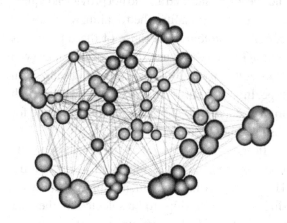

Figure 5. Small world graph for a tourism ontology (Sampson & Lanzenberger, 2006)

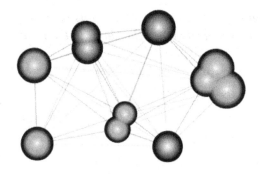

Figure 6. Highly clustered small world graph of the same tourism ontology (Sampson & Lanzenberger, 2006)

hand side of the small world graph. In the tool, ontology classes are represented in the graphs as spheres of different colors. Colors represent different types of similarity between nodes in the two different ontologies, and when the level of detail changes, the dominant color represents the prevailing kinds of similarity in that cluster of nodes.

Visualizing ontology alignment data presents a number of distinct challenges compared to ontology visualization. First, we are dealing with the visualization of two ontologies, therefore problems with displaying and understanding large ontologies are exacerbated. To alleviate this problem we provide two techniques for visualizing the same data (J-trees and small world graphs) and we use clustering (applying the slider on the right hand side to change the number of nodes displayed). Second, we found that it is important to make explicit the way in which entities between the ontologies are related. To achieve this we use color, also we use clustering to show the structure of the graph.

A third requirement is to provide ontology engineers with standard information visualization techniques such as zooming, detail and overview. In our implementation the clustering mechanism of the small world graphs is a useful technique for zooming, together with the fish-eye lens (shown in Figure 4 highlighting the node 'Norwegian'). AlViz supports 'linking and brushing', this means that when a node is selected in one view it is also highlighted in all other views, this feature maintains context between the related ontologies. The fourth requirement was to support the task of validating ontology alignments through the use of information visualization techniques.

We found that the tool helps with rejecting inappropriate alignments such as 'Ballooning' which is a subclass of 'Activity' in Travel1, versus 'Hot Air Balloon' which is a subclass of 'Transport' in Travel2.

In addition the tool helps draw attention to black nodes occurring within a cluster of colored nodes, thereby helping an ontology engineer discover missing alignments. In this way ontology engineers can make careful decisions when using the tool. The fifth requirement was to use information visualization techniques to support the task of identifying missing alignment pairs.

In the next section we describe the experiment where we found that the tool has potential for improving the completeness and validity of a set of ontology alignments.

EVALUATION: CONTROLLED EXPERIMENT

An experiment was designed to establish whether participants using AlViz are able to identify more missing alignments and eliminate 'false' alignments, compared to those without AlViz. This led us to the following hypotheses:

H1: AlViz users perform better at the task of finding alignments missed by the automated tool, compared to those users without AlViz.
H2: AlViz users perform better at the task of accepting or rejecting questionable alignments, compared to those users without AlViz.

A controlled experiment with the purpose of determining whether AlViz helps facilitate semantic quality was undertaken. We used two sets of ontologies, the first set of ontologies Population1 and Population2 were created based on a census data model and the second set of ontologies Travel1 and Travel2, are based on a travel ontology from the Protégé OWL ontologies library (http://protege.cim3.net/file/pub/ontologies/travel/travel.owl) and an e-tourism (http://e-tourism.deri.at/ont/e-tourism.owl) ontology. Participants were asked to check a list of candidate alignments and to decide whether to accept or reject the proposed match. A subset of the proposed alignments for both sets of ontologies is shown in Table 1.

We measured the benefit of AlViz by comparing the results obtained after using AlViz, as compared to the alternative method of verifying alignments using textual displays and class browsers available in the ontology management tool Protégé and the plug-in OntoViz (Sintek, 2007). The independent variable is the tool used for evaluating the validity and completeness of the alignments, and the dependent variables are the number of missing alignments found and the number of agreements between subjects on alignment decisions. We were aware that individual users may respond with different interpretations of the same information visualization. However, we were particularly interested in how the visualized ontologies help with identifying missing alignments and checking proposed alignments.

We ran a within-subjects experiment and counter-balanced each condition, to ensure that our results were not biased due to task order and differences in the ontologies, several conditions were controlled. Namely, we had to ensure that order of the task was rotated along with the ontologies. This resulted in a number of experimental conditions:

1. AlViz first using Tourism ontologies and Protégé second using Population ontologies.
2. Protégé first using Tourism ontologies and AlViz second using Population ontologies.
3. AlViz first using Population ontologies and Protégé second using Tourism ontologies.
4. Protégé first using Population ontologies and AlViz second using Tourism ontologies.

Dependent variables were measured through the participants recording their decisions for each question, by observation and through subject result analysis. We also collected demographic data about the participants through an experiment questionnaire. There were 8 subjects in the main experiment and two subjects in the pilot experiment. All participants were employees at the Norwegian University of Science and Technology from the following working groups: information systems, knowledge based systems, database systems and software engineering. The participants had a range of different experiences in ontologies and conceptual modeling, and four participants had prior IT industry experience.

In both cases, alignments suggested by an automatic tool were given to the participants as a list of paired concepts. The participants were asked to check each pair of concepts for validity. By validity we mean that: all the ontology align-

ment statements (the paired concepts and their relations) are correct and relevant for the domain as interpreted by the participants. The participants would either accept or reject the decision to align the pairs if they believed the alignment was valid. Where appropriate the participants were asked to justify their answer. In addition the participants were asked to suggest new alignments which the tool may have missed. Missing alignments may be between concepts that have not already been associated to another concept or corrections to the suggested alignments based on the participant's responses from the validation check. When using AlViz to do this task the participants could check the nodes that are black, this means there is no relation (or related concept) according to the automated tool.

Documentation and brief training was given to each participant to describe the features of AlViz and the Protégé plug-in OntoViz (Sintek, 2007). When the participants used Protégé's OntoViz they were able to execute two versions of Protégé so both ontologies could be viewed at the same time. It was also important to describe the different alignment relations between concepts used in our tool AlViz.

Pilot Experiment

Before commencing with the main experiment a pilot experiment was undertaken with two participants. The goal of the pilot experiment was to obtain first feedback on the usefulness of visualization for validating candidate ontology pairs and to, most importantly, evaluate the experiment design. The pilot experiment was invaluable as it resulted in a number of changes to the experiment design. In particular, the pilot study showed that the task of validating the alignments was too long therefore the list of concepts to be checked was shortened. The pilot was also useful in helping identify a small number of software bugs.

Quantitative Analysis

We used the statistics program 'R' (http://www.rproject.org/index.html) to complete t-tests and an ANOVA. The most promising result we achieved was a marked improvement in discovering missing alignments (concept pairs not discovered by the automated tool). A number of the participants noticed that it was significantly easier to discover new alignments when using AlViz. For example, the concepts Accommodation and Budget Accommodation were matched as candidate alignment pairs by the FOAM algorithm, because both their labels are similar and they have similar properties. However, a better match would be between the concepts Accommodation and Lodging, for the following reason. Budget Accommodation is, intuitively, likely to be a specialization of the concept Accommodation in the matching ontology. Then, since Budget Accommodation is a subclass of Lodging in its own ontology, it seems like Lodging and Accommodation are the best alignments. The automated algorithm missed this simply because of the orthographic differences. These are the types of alignments we hope AlViz will help discover.

First we calculated the mean and standard deviation for all missing alignments identified by the participants using AlViz and Protégé. The results were as follows: AlViz mean(SD): 4.625(1.598) and Protégé mean(SD): 0.875(0.835), notably lower than that of AlViz. The number of new alignments, determined by the participants and collapsed over ontologies is shown in Table 2.

Next we undertook a Welch Two Sample t-test giving the probability that the difference between the two means is caused by chance. We were seeking to test the hypothesis that we expect participants to find more missing alignments using AlViz than without. Our hypothesis are: H0= performance will be equal between participants using AlViz and participants using Protégé, when performing the task of identifying missing alignments. H1 = participants using Alviz will perform better than participants using Protégé, when performing the task of identifying missing alignments.

The two sample t-test results were as follows: $t(10) = 5.88$, $p < 0.05$. Since p is less than 0.05 we can reject the null hypothesis, H0, which means that the difference between the means is not caused by chance. That is, the experimental manipulation had a significant effect such that subjects who used AlViz performed better at identifying missing alignments than subjects who used Protégé on its own.

We found that AlViz supports the task of identifying missing alignments in a number of ways, for example, nodes that are black have no relation according to the automated tool. Participants were then able to check black nodes (with colored neighbor nodes) to see if there were any related nodes in the other ontology. Furthermore, having identified concepts with only similar labels that are clearly different the participants were often able to find better matches using AlViz. Whereas using just Protégé graphs the task was significantly harder as there are no visual clues to help the user with the task. While AlViz is a prototype tool, the result we achieved is important. Most state of the art automated tools for ontology alignment are not able to pick up all matches between entities in ontologies, however, by using AlViz we can support the alignment task by making it easier to find missing matches between concepts.

Determining whether AlViz helps participants accept or reject questionable alignments was also interesting. We know that the set of questionable alignments generated by FOAM must contain some candidate alignments that should be rejected. We aim to see if our tool helps with this task. In

Table 2. Total number of new alignments for all participants

	Tourism	Population
AlViz	19	18
Protégé	3	4

Table 3 we show the number of questionable alignments accepted by participants (i.e. agree to align).

Through an ANOVA (analysis of variance) on this data it is possible to determine whether the means among the two groups are equal. The ANOVA results show there was a significant interaction $p < 0.05$ between ontologies and visualization for questionable alignments. By analyzing questionable alignments we find that in the Tourism domain (where we aligned a Travel.owl ontology with an e-tourism.owl ontology), we would have expected the participants to *reject* 4 out of the 5 questionable alignments (i.e. alignments that where actually questionable according to the Foam algorithm, i.e. not relating to Table 3). Whereas in the Population domain, (where we aligned two ontologies relating to people and animals i.e. Population1 and Population2) we would have expected the participants to have *accepted* 4 out of the 5 questionable alignments. The total counts for questionable alignments accepted by subjects for each ontology, are shown in Table 3. We can see from these results, that when using AlViz, participants checking the Tourism alignments, decided to reject the alignments more. In our opinion this is an appropriate response. To explain this reasoning we will briefly discuss each questionable alignment.

First we start with the tourism ontologies. The concept pairs (Singapore, Singapore) are 'questionable' because, while sharing the same name they are different concepts - in this pair of ontologies one refers to the country and the other the airline. Similarly the pairs (Theme Park, Theme Park) and (Winery, Winery) share the same names and some related properties, however in the first

Ontology (Travel.owl), 'Theme Park' and 'Winery' are subclasses of the concept 'Company', whereas in the second ontology (e-Tourism.owl) 'Theme Park' and 'Winery' are subclasses of the concept 'Tourist Attraction'. Interestingly more participants argued that they should not be aligned when using AlViz (but they noted that there is a relationship between them). The concept pairs 'Rock Climbing' and 'Climbing' also have similar labels and some similar properties however, their hierarchies are different, that is the subclass/superclass structure is different.

The concept pairs 'Capital' and 'Capital City' have similar labels and similar superclasses, however the properties are not the same. All participants agreed that the concepts should be aligned. As mentioned previously, comparing Align1.owl and Align2.owl (population ontologies) we would have expected the participants to have accepted 4 out of the 5 questionable alignments. For example, the concepts 'University Qualification' and 'Tertiary Qualification' both have similar labels and some similar properties. In this case we would agree with the majority of participants that the concepts should be aligned. Using AlViz they all agree to align 'University Qualification' and 'Tertiary Qualification', when using just Protégé one participant disagreed.

Three out of four participants agreed that the concepts 'Animal' and 'Organism' should be aligned when using AlViz and Protégé. We also agree with this decision because in these ontologies the concepts have highly similar properties. Also from the context of the ontologies we can see that the concepts are related, because the subclasses and siblings are related. Figure 4 shows how the concepts share similar properties (subclasses inherit parent properties - not shown explicitly in the figures).

Similarly with 'Ancestry' and 'Geneology', while we recognize that the concept names have different meanings -in the context of these particular ontologies they are quite similar as the properties and the subclasses are highly similar.

Table 3. Number of questionable alignments accepted by subjects

	Tourism	Population
Visualization (AlViz)	6	16
No Visualization (Protégé)	14	13

All participants using AlViz agreed they should be aligned, whereas only one participant agreed when using Protégé. Moreover, the concept pairs 'North American' and 'North America' also have the same properties and are subclasses of 'Ancestry' and 'Geneology'. Participants using AlViz, following the same reasoning as their previous decision, agreed with the decision to align. However two of the participants using Protégé did not agree to align the concepts. The questionable match between concepts 'Human' and 'Person' is also interesting. All participants using Protégé agreed that the concepts should be aligned, however only one participant agreed using AlViz. We argue that in this case you would not align 'Human' with 'Person' because they have some different properties and their subclasses are quite different. Overall we found that AlViz helps a user reject a candidate alignment when the super-classes of the entities involved are different.

Regarding our research hypothesis, we accept H1 - that AlViz users perform better at the task of finding alignments missed by the automated tool, compared to those users without AlViz. This was supported through our quantitative analysis and through informal discussions with the participants. However, further studies would be necessary to conclusively argue in support of H2, that - AlViz users perform better at the task of accepting or rejecting questionable alignments. However when using AlViz the participants who checked the Tourism alignment set, decided to reject questionable alignments more. In our opinion this was an appropriate response. A conclusion from our experiment results was that our tool helps support a user deciding to reject 'false' candidate alignments, when the super-classes of the entities involved are different.

In terms of improving completeness we obviously make it easier to find missing alignments. As mentioned previously we don't generally assign numbers to validity and completeness, but we do have a sense of the measure from our experiment. For example, before using AlViz, there might

have been 5 missing alignments. How do we know this? Clearly because the participants were able to locate them by using AlViz. This means that "completeness" was lower before because there were 5 missing alignments and now, there are none. Well, we don't really know that there are none, but at least we know there are 5 less! So completeness increased, which was the aim.

Qualitative Analysis

The participants were asked to provide comments regarding their overall satisfaction of using AlViz when compared to using the Protégé plug-in OntoViz (Sintek, 2007) for validating the set of candidate alignments. Some participants commented that they were able to complete the alignment validation tasks faster when using AlViz. For example some participants expressed that the node color coding helped with alignment decision making as it provided immediate information as to whether it was necessary to check the concept data and object properties or not. It was also clear from a qualitative perspective that the participants were able to use the visualization to help check the alignment pairs. One participant commented that it was quite obvious that without AlViz it was difficult to find missing pairs; another remarked that the experiment tasks were easier to complete using AlViz than without. When using the visual tool the participants were able to apply and learn strategies for checking alignments so the task actually became easier.

Threats to Validity

In assessing how generalizable these results are, it is necessary to consider the various kinds of validity and how they relate to our experiment. The threat to internal validity is minimized by random selection of subjects, counter balancing of experimental stimuli, and by specifying the research question in a somewhat general way. That is, in this initial study we were interested in whether or not AlViz improves alignment quality. We were not interested in more detailed questions about, for example, which aspect of the visualization is most useful. It would be more difficult to establish specific causal relationships between such detailed aspects of a visualization and alignment decisions. The external validity is also protected to the extent that we only claim that AlViz will help people in their deliberations when they evaluate ontology alignments. The anecdotal evidence from our randomly selected subjects shows that this was indeed the case. In addition, even though the pattern of results was qualitatively different in the two ontologies, the deliberation process which results in the acceptance or rejection of suggested alignments was similarly enhanced in both cases.

One potential problem is the size of the ontologies. In a real world setting with much larger ontologies there might be differences in how the tool is used. Yet our claim is that the zooming functionality will allow people to isolate fragments of large ontologies to deal with them in more manageable chunks whose size is not dissimilar to our test ontologies.

Finally the construct validity is provided by the theoretical framework, where we argue that one way to increase the quality of the alignment is to decrease the difficulty of evaluating the alignment statements. This is precisely what the results show.

CONCLUSION

Understanding how we can improve ontology alignment quality is important because ontologies and their alignments are the building blocks for data interoperability. Along with a framework for ontology alignment quality we have identified a number of important aspects for checking and improving alignment results. Our work is based on quality types originally described in Lindland et al. (1994) and Krogstie et al. (1995). Definitions for aspects in the quality framework are presented,

but in general we don't assign absolute numbers to the metrics, instead we describe ways in which they can be improved. While the framework encompasses a number of quality dimensions, we focused our research on semantic quality and the notions of completeness and validity.

We have developed a tool AlViz, to help improve the quality of a set of ontology alignments. The tool uses two visualization techniques: J-Trees and small world graphs to help make relations between two ontologies explicit. Through a simple, controlled experiment we showed that the tool helps with completeness and validity. The experiment indicates that AlViz provides novel, new information to help human judges decide if a pair of concepts should be aligned. Since the similarity between related nodes is made explicit using the linking and brushing technique, AlViz provides immediate visual cues for users assessing whether two nodes should indeed be aligned. We found that participants were able to find missing alignments more easily than those using the fully developed Protégé plug-in OntoViz (Sintek, 2007). In terms of validity we were able to show that our tool helps a user reject a candidate alignment, when the superclasses of the entities involved are different.

Despite the prototype nature of the tool, and the number of participants in the experiment, it was clear that the tool helped participants validate the set of alignments. We claim this is important, as so far our attempt is one of the first to help humans solve complex alignment decisions, that is, those that an algorithm either misses completely or defines as 'questionable'. While we recognize the limitations with our work, we believe that the results provide initial evidence that the concept of using information visualization for presenting alignment results is not only novel but also beneficial. Implementation of AlViz is ongoing, our goal is to produce a comprehensive and practical tool for visualizing complex ontology alignment data. We plan to undertake more experiments to evaluate our research, and most importantly to use the tool to assist with business and government interoperability. Since the development of the research prototype and conduct of the experiments described in this paper, further development (http://sourceforge.net/projects/alviz/) work has been completed at the Institute of Software and Technology and Interactive Systems at the Vienna University of Technology.

ACKNOWLEDGMENT

The authors would like to thank Professor Arne Sølvberg for his invaluable contributions to this research. We would also like to acknowledge Monika Lanzenberger from the Vienna University of Technology, and Slaven Banovic for their work with AlViz. Thanks also to Marc Ehrig for making the Foam ontology alignment algorithm open source and available for use, and to Stephan Ingram from the University of British Columbia for making the small world graph algorithm available. This work was conducted using the Protégé resource, which is supported by grant LM007885 from the United States National Library of Medicine.

REFERENCES

Beneventano, D., Bergamaschi, S., Guerra, F., & Vincini, M. (2001). The MOMIS approach to information integration. In *Proceedings of the International Conference on Enterprise Information Systems* (pp. 194-198).

Davenport, J., & Keane, M. T. (1999). Similarity and structural alignment: You can have one without the other. In *Proceedings of the Twenty First Annual Conference of the Cognitive Science Society* (pp. 132-137).

Do, H. H. (2006). *Schema matching and mapping-based data integration*. Unpublished doctoral dissertation, Universität Leipzig, Leipzig, Germany.

Doan, A., Madhaven, J., Domingos, P., & Halevy, A. (2004). Ontology matching: A machine learning approach. In Staab, S., & Studer, R. (Eds.), *Handbook on ontologies* (pp. 397–416). New York, NY: Springer.

Ehrig, M. (2005). *Foam - framework for ontology alignment and mapping*. Retrieved from http://www.aifb.uni-karlsruhe.de

Ehrig, M., Haase, P., Stojanovic, N., & Hefke, M. (2005) Similarity for ontologies - a comprehensive framework. In *Proceedings of the 13th European Conference on Information Systems*.

Euzénat, J., Loup, D., Touzani, M., & Valtchev, P. (2004).Ontology alignment with OLA. In *Proceedings of the 3rd EON Workshop at the 3rd International Semantic Web Conference*.

Euzénat, J., & Shvaiko, P. (2007). *Ontology matching*. Berlin, Germany: Springer-Verlg.

Falconer, S., Noy, N., & Storey, M. A. (2006). Towards understanding the needs of cognitive support for ontology mapping. In *Proceedings of the Workshop on Ontology Matching at the International Semantic Web Conference*.

Fluit, C., Sabou, M., & van Harmelen, F. (2004). Supporting user tasks through visualization of light-weight ontologies. In Staab, S., & Studer, R. (Eds.), *Handbook on ontologies* (pp. 415–434). New York, NY: Springer.

Gansner, E. R., & North, S. C. (2000). An open graph visualization system and its applications to software engineering. *Software, Practice & Experience, 30*(11), 1203–1233. doi:10.1002/1097-024X(200009)30:11<1203::AID-SPE338>3.0.CO;2-N.

Gilson, O., Silva, N., Grant, P. W., & Chen, M. (2008). From web data to visualization via ontology mapping. *Computer Graphics Forum, 27*(3). doi:10.1111/j.1467-8659.2008.01230.x.

Giunchigli, F. Shvaiko, P., & Yatskevich, M. (2004). S-match: An algorithm and an implementation of semantic matching. In C. J. Bussler, J. Davies, D. Fensel, & R. Studer (Eds.), *Proceedings of the First European Semantic Web Symposium on the Semantic Web: Research and Applications* (LNCS 3053, pp. 61-75).

Goldstone, R. L., & Son, J. (2005). Similarity. In Holyoak, K., & Morrison, R. (Eds.), *Cambridge handbook of thinking and reasoning* (pp. 13–36). Cambridge, UK: Cambridge University Press.

Goyal, S., & Westenthaler, R. (2003). *RDF gravity (RDF graph visualization tool)*. Retrieved from http://semweb.salzburgresearch.at/apps/rdf-gravity/index.html

Grosso, E., Eriksson, H., Fergerson, R., Tu, S., & Musen, M. (1999). Knowledge-modeling at the millenium the design and evolution of Protégé-2000. In *Proceedings of the 12th International Workshop on Knowledge Acquisition, Modeling and Management*.

Hella, L., & Krogstie, J. (2010). A structured evaluation to assess the reusability of models of user profiles. In *Proceedings of the Conference on Exploring Modeling Methods in Systems Analysis and Design*.

Hevner, A. R., March, S. T., Park, J., & Ram, S. (2004). Design science in information systems research. *Management Information Systems Quarterly, 28*(1), 75–105.

Ingram, S. F. (2005). *An interactive small world graph visualization*. Retrieved from http://www.cs.ubc.ca/~sfingram/cs533C/small_world.pdf

Kalfoglou, Y., & Schorlemmer, M. (2002). Information flow based ontology mappings. In *Proceedings of the 1st International Conference on Ontologies, Databases and Application of Semantics*.

Kotis, K., & Lanzenberger, M. (2008). Ontology matching: Current status, dilemmas and future challenges. In *Proceedings of the International Conference on Complex, Intelligent and Software Intensive Systems* (pp. 924-927).

Krogstie, J. (1999). Using quality function deployment in software requirements specification. In *Proceedings of the Fifth International Workshop on Requirements Engineering: Foundations for Software Quality*.

Krogstie, J. (2001). Using a semiotic framework to evaluate UML for the development of models of high quality. In Krogstie, J. (Ed.), *Unified modeling language: Systems analysis, design and development issues* (pp. 89–106). Hershey, PA: IGI Global. doi:10.4018/9781930708051.ch006.

Krogstie, J., & Arnesen, S. (2004). Assessing enterprise modeling languages using a generic quality framework. In Krogstie, J., Siau, K., & Halpin, T. (Eds.), *Information modeling methods and methodologies*. Hershey, PA: IGI Global. doi:10.4018/978-1-59140-375-3.ch004.

Krogstie, J., & Jørgensen, H. D. (2002). Quality of interactive models. In A. Olive, M. Yoshikawa, & E. S. K. Yu (Eds.), *Proceedings of the First International Workshop on Advanced Conceptual Modeling Techniques* (LNCS 2784, pp. 351-363).

Krogstie, J., Lindland, O., & Sindre, G. (1995). Towards a deeper understanding of quality in requirements engineering. In J. Iivari, K. Lyytinen, & M. Rossi (Eds.), *Proceedings of the 7th International Conference on Advanced Information Systems Engineering* (LNCS 932, pp. 82-95).

Lambrix, P., & Tan, H. (2006). Sambo - a system for aligning and merging biomedical ontologies. *Journal of Web Semantics, 4*(3), 196–206. doi:10.1016/j.websem.2006.05.003.

Lanzenberger, M., & Sampson, J. (2006) Alviz - a tool for visual ontology alignment. In *Proceedings of the 10th International Conference on Information Visualization* (pp. 430-440).

Larkey, L. B., & Markman, A. B. (2005). Processes of similarity judgment. *Cognitive Science, 29*(6), 1061–1076. doi:10.1207/s15516709cog0000_30.

Lillehagen, F., & Krogstie, J. (2008). *Active knowledge modeling of enterprises*. New York, NY: Springer. doi:10.1007/978-3-540-79416-5.

Lin, Y., Sampson, J., & Hakkarainen, S. (2004). An evaluation of UML and OWL using a semiotic quality framework. In Siau, K. (Ed.), *Advanced topics in database research* (*Vol. 4*, pp. 178–200). Hershey, PA: IGI Global.

Lindland, O. I., Sindre, G., & Sølvberg, A. (1994). Understanding quality in conceptual modelling. *IEEE Software, 11*(2), 42–49. doi:10.1109/52.268955.

McGuinness, D., Fikes, R., & Wilder, S. (2000). An environment for merging and testing large ontologies. In *Proceedings of the 7th International Conference on Principles of Knowledge Representation and Reasoning* (pp. 483-493).

Miller, S., & Xu, H. (2001) Integrating a heterogenous distributed data environment with a database specific ontology. In *Proceedings of the International Conference on Parallel and Distributed Computing Systems.*

Mitra, P., Kersten, M., & Wiederhold, G. (2000). Graph oriented model for articulation of ontology independencies. In *Proceedings of the 7th International Conference on Extending Databases Technology.*

Mitra, P., Noy, N., & Jaiswal, A. (2005). Ontology mapping discovery with uncertainty. In Y. Gil, E. Motta, R. Benjamins, & M. A. Musen (Eds.), *Proceedings of the 4th International Semantic Web Conference* (LNCS 3729, pp. 537-547).

Noy, N., & Musen, M. (2001). Anchor-prompt: Using non local context for semantic matching. In *Proceedings of the Workshop on Ontologies and Information Sharing at IJCAI.*

Noy, N., & Musen, M. (2003). The prompt suite: Interactive tools for ontology merging and mapping. *International Journal of Human-Computer Studies, 59*(6), 983–1024. doi:10.1016/j.ijhcs.2003.08.002.

Nysetvold, A. G., & Krogstie, J. (2006). Assessing business process modeling languages using a generic quality framework. In Siau, K. (Ed.), *Advanced topics in database research series* (*Vol. 5*, pp. 79–93). Hershey, PA: IGI Global. doi:10.4018/978-1-59140-935-9.ch005.

Pastor, O., Fons, J., Torres, V., & Pelechano, V. (2004). Conceptual modelling versus semantic web: the two sides of the same coin? In *Proceedings of the Workshop on Application Design, Development and Implementation Issues in the Semantic Web.*

Sampson, J. A. (2007). *Comprehensive framework for ontology alignment quality*. Unpublished doctoral dissertation, Norwegian University of Science and Technology, Trondheim, Norway.

Sampson, J. A., & Lanzenberger, M. (2006). Visual ontology alignment for semantic web applications. In J. F. Roddick, V. R. Benjamins, S. Si-said Cherfi, R. Chiang, C. Claramunt, R. A. Elmasri et al. (Eds.), *Proceedings of the 1st International Workshop on Advances in Conceptual Modeling: Theory and Practice* (LNCS 4231, pp. 405-414).

Sintek, M. (2007). *Ontoviz tab: Visualizing protégé ontologies*. Retrieved from http://protegewiki.stanford.edu/index.php/OntoViz

Storey, M., Musen, M., Silva, J., Best, C., Ernst, N., Fergerson, R., et al. (2001). Jambalaya: Interactive visualization to enhance ontology authoring and knowledge acquisition in Protégé. In *Proceedings of the International Workshop on Interactive Tools for Knowledge Capture.*

van Ham, F., & van Wijk, J. J. (2004). Interactive visualization of small world graphs. In *Proceedings of the IEEE Symposium on Information Visualization* (pp 199-206).

Vitvar, T., Kerrigan, M., van Overeem, A., Peristeras, V., & Tarabanis, K. (2006). Infrastructure for the semantic pan-european e-government services. In *Proceedings of the AAAI Spring Symposium on the Semantic Web meets eGovernment.*

This work was previously published in the International Journal of Information System Modeling and Design (IJISMD), Volume 2, Issue 3, edited by Remigijus Gustas, pp. 1-23, copyright 2011 by IGI Publishing (an imprint of IGI Global).

Chapter 6
CbSSDF:
A Two–Layer Conceptual Graph Approach to Web Services Description and Composition – A Scenario–Based Solution Analysis and Comparison with OWL–S

Xiaofeng Du
University of Durham, UK

Malcolm Munro
University of Durham, UK

William Song
University of Durham, UK

ABSTRACT

Web services as a new distributed system technology have been widely adopted by industries in the areas, such as enterprise application integration (EAI), business process management (BPM), and virtual organization (VO). However, lack of semantics in the current Web service standards has become a major barrier in service discovery and composition. To tackle the semantic issues of Web services, this paper proposes a comprehensive semantic service description framework – CbSSDF and a two-step service discovery mechanism based on CbSSDF—to help service users to easily locate their required services. The authors give a detailed explanation of CbSSDF, and then evaluate the framework by comparing it with OWL-S to examine how the proposed framework can improve the efficiency and effectiveness of service discovery and composition. The evaluation is carried out by analysing the different proposed solutions based on these two frameworks for achieving a series of tasks in a scenario.

DOI: 10.4018/978-1-4666-4161-7.ch006

1. INTRODUCTION

Service description, discovery and composition are three major research topics in the research fields of Web Services and Service Science. In the past decade, enormous research effort in Web services has been spent on service description (Paolucci et al., 2003: Du et al., 2007), discovery (Ludwig & Reyhani, 2005; Paolucci et al., 2003; Song & Li, 2005; Song et al., 2009), and composition (Agarwal et al., 2005; Du et al., 2006). In order to effectively and efficiently perform Web service discovery and composition, a comprehensive service description framework is essential. There are several semantic service description frameworks proposed to provide semantic rich service descriptions, such as OWL-S (Martin et al., 2004), WSDL-S (Akkiraju et al., 2005), and WSMF (Fensel & Bussler, 2002). The main idea of these works is to build a semantic layer either on the top of or to be integrated into the WSDL documents to semantically describe the capabilities of Web services so that a software agent or other services can reason about the service's capabilities and knows how to interact with it.

However, the problems still exist in the current study of semantic service description and discovery:

- **Insufficient usage context information:** Usage context information of a service represents an informative surrounding in which the service is invoked or applied. Current semantic Web service description frameworks are mostly focusing on the ontology based data and capability semantics of Web services. They do not sufficiently address the usage context information of a service. Although there is some research work (Maamar et al., 2005, 2007; Medjahed et al., 2007) addressing Web services context, they mainly study the runtime environmental context, and hence help very little in allocation of the required

services at the stage of service discovery. The usage context of a service includes the information about how a service is used and its relationships with other services. This kind of context information can be helpful for service users to locate their required services.

- **Precise service specifications:** In order to locate a required service, the current service discovery requires precisely defined technical specifications for the required service, such as service input and output data types and service capabilities in WSDL and OWL-S. This kind of information is difficult for a service user to provide at the preliminary stage of service discovery, especially when the service user is not a domain expert in the required service area.

- **Insufficient information about inter-relationships among services:** The current work inadequately addresses the inter-service relationships. A Web service needs to interact with other Web services to achieve its capabilities. If we consider each service as an isolated individual and ignore its relationships with other Web services, the efficiency of service discovery and composition for this service will decrease.

- **Lack of incomplete information handling:** Although some of the existing work support rules in service description and composition (Martin et al., 2004; Orriens et al., 2003; Charfi & Mezini, 2004), these rules are based on monotonic logic and reasoning which are not suitable for handling incomplete information.

To address the above problems, we introduce a new concept, termed as Service Usage Context (SUC), to describe a service's usages at both the conceptual level and instance levels (to be discussed in Section 2), and based on SUC, a new, comprehensive description framework, called

Context-based Semantic Service Description Framework (CbSSDF). CbSSDF aims to improve the semantic capability of service discovery and simplify the service composition process. It contains these main components: a set of Service Conceptual Graphs (S-CGs) and a Semantic Service Description Model (SSDM). The set of S-CGs gives an abstract description of the relationships between services and concepts. S-CG is the implementation of the conceptual level SUC. The formalism behind S-CG is conceptual graphs (Sowa, 1984). SSDM gives a comprehensive semantic description of a service through different semantic aspects. It also addresses the instance level SUC of services.

1.1. Service Usage Context

The term "context" is frequently referred to in the computer science literature, whose meaning is mainly based on each individual researcher's understanding (and its usage is implicit). There are a lot of researches focusing on the term "context" or "contextual situation" and providing various definitions, which we discuss as follows:

Dey and Abowd (2000) define context as "any information that can be used to characterize the situation of an entity. An entity is a person, place, or object that is considered relevant to the interaction between a user and an application, including the user and applications themselves"; Brown et al. (1997) define context from the user's perspective as users' location, who the users are with, what the time of day is, etc.; Ryan et al. (1997) consider the information about the computers environment as context, such as location, time, temperature, or user identity etc.

These definitions demonstrate that the "context" is a very complex term and is interpreted from many different perspectives. However, in our work, context does not focus on the physical environment as most of the researchers do. The context taken into account here is the usage context of Web services, called the Service Usage Context

(SUC), the information that can help service users to understand and use Web services.

The SUC is proposed in the belief that the identification of meaning of a concept mainly stems from its contexts, i.e. its relationships to other concepts (Guha et al., 2004). In some cases, it is difficult to learn the genus of a concept and it is even more difficult to find properties to differentiate this concept from the other concepts in the same genus. In this situation, we need to describe how the concept can be applied in instance usage scenarios, i.e. the schemata, in order to make its type definition understandable. We take the definition of a "hammer" for an example. If a person is told that "a hammer is a type of tool with heavy rigid head and a handle", he may or may not be able to infer what the tool is for. However, if we say "a hammer can strike nails into wood", at least he is proposed one way to use a hammer despite not knowing clearly and exactly what a hammer is. Sometimes the type definition of a concept is not important when only the concept's functionalities are of interest. For a hammer's user, as long as the hammer can achieve the user's requirements, e.g. knocking nails into wood, it is the right thing for the user.

Web services encapsulate discrete functionalities of each service to achieve certain desired goals. To fully describe Web services, only using type definition, such as in ontology, is insufficient. The descriptions need to comprise type definitions (i.e. ontology) of services and schemata (i.e. the SUC). In our approach, we consider not only the type definition of a service, but also how the service is used in various usage contexts. The SUC can help service users to better understand services and better match services with their requirements. The SUC emphasises that parts can only make sense for a whole (Fensel et al., 2007). Two levels of the SUC are presented in our work. We define the conceptual level SUC (T-*Context*) to represent the usage context of a service and the conceptual relationships between the service and other services and entities. To define the instance level service interactions, we use the instance level service usage context (A-*Context*).

The key issue to be addressed in this paper is how to semantically define the service usage contexts so that the discovery and composition of services become more efficient and easier for the end users of the services.

1.2. Organisation of the Paper

The rest of the paper is organised as follows. First we introduce a semantic description framework for web services which focuses on services and their context in Section 2. The framework consists of two main levels of semantic description: a concept graph for services which is based on Sowa's concept graph, discussed in Section 2.1 and a semantic description model which supports a refined service search, discussed in Section 2.2. Section 3 focuses on the implementation concerns of the service discovery and composition. We first discuss how an S-CG is used to represent the services and queries conceptually, where the graph matching method is analysed in Section 3.1. Then we discuss the second step of the service comparison and retrieval with the refined semantic description model in Section 3.2. As OWL-S is widely accepted as the major ontology language for describing web services, it is of course the first choice to compare the proposed context semantic service description framework with OWL-S. In Section 4 we compare the two methods in three different aspects, i.e. locating an atomic service, locating a composite service, and constructing a composed service. It is obvious, in comparison with OWL-S, that the proposed approach is better when a large amount of services are available for matchmaking and selection since the two step filtering mechanism can greatly eliminate the irrelevant and less related services and when a dynamic service composition is required for constructing a composite service because our method provides not only ontological reasoning as does by OWL-S but also the semantic inter-

service relationships. We conclude the paper in Section 5 by summarising the research work and main contributions and point out the research directions for the future. With the number of web services increasing at an exponential rate, an efficient and effective way of discovery and composition of services become more and more crucial to successful use of the services over the web, enriching service description with profound semantic is indispensable.

2. CONTEXT BASED SEMANTIC SERVICE DESCRIPTION FRAMEWORK

Context-based Semantic Service Description Framework (CbSSDF) is a comprehensive framework for Web services by describing service capabilities and service usage contexts (SUC). The framework aims to improve the semantic capability of service discovery and automate the service composition process. It contains three main components: a set of Service Conceptual Graphs (S-CGs), a Semantic Service Description Model (SSDM), and a set of non-monotonic rules represented in Defeasible Logic (Nute, 1994). The set of S-CGs gives an abstract description of the relationships between the instance services (called A-*Context*) and concept services (called T-*Context*). The formalism for S-CGs is based on conceptual graphs (Sowa, 1984). The SSDM attempts to describe a service through different semantic aspects, including the A-*Context* of services. The Defeasible Logic aims at addressing the issue of incompleteness of knowledge acquired for describing services.

2.1. Service Conceptual Graphs

Only using the technical description such as in WSDL or OWL-S is not sufficient comprehensively describe a service, as discussed previously. Two services that are technically compatible do not necessarily mean that they can work together – their combination may be logically incorrect. The SUC information, especially for the T-*Context*, of a service tells how the service is conceptually or logically related to other services and entities in a business domain and under what context the service should be used. In CbSSDF, the T-*Context* is implemented using the Service Conceptual Graphs (S-CG). Each S-CG can be considered as a conceptual usage scenario. It describes a way in which the service can be used.

The key point of having S-CGs in the service description is to bridge the gap between the technical detail of a service and the conceptual understanding of the user's needs for the service. By having S-CGs, when a service user searches for a service, he or she can first express their demands in a conceptual way, e.g. in a natural language query, without worrying about any technical details. These requirements will be converted into conceptual graphs which are further matched with the S-CGs in the service repository to find out which services are the most relevant. Then, based on the found conceptual services, service users will provide technical specifications, if they can, to refine the result. We call this a two-step service discovery, which will be discussed in Section 4.

The S-CG representation is based on the conceptual graph (CG) formalism and it is an implementation of the T-*Context*. As discussed in Sowa (1984), the perception process in a person's mind is the process of associating percepts with concepts and assembling concepts with conceptual relations. The result of the perception process is a map or graph of concepts linked by conceptual relations that can be formally represented in the CGs. In other words, the CGs can closely represent people's mind and perceptions. This is the main reason why we choose the CG based formalism to represent the T-*Context*. Further reasons that we choose CG as the representation formalism include: a) the CG makes a clear separation between ontological knowledge (the type definition) and factual, contextual knowledge (the schemata) (Mugnier, 2000); b) the CG is logically equivalent to the first order logic (FOL), which means that it has the full expressiveness of FOL (Kerdiles & Salvat, 1997); c) the CG supports direct mappings from and to natural language with a direct translation between natural language and symbolic logic (Sowa, 1984), which is useful when dealing with natural language based service queries; and d) the graph based modelling is easy to be understood by both end users and reasoning systems, and from the computational viewpoint, a graph homomorphism problem has less complexity than logic deduction (Mugnier, 2000). For the details of the CG formalism, readers refer to Sowa (1984).

In the following, we give the definition of S-CG and its basic properties, which are based on the CG formalism. An S-CG is a simple CG, which means that it does not contain co-reference links and nested context (Sowa, 1984). Similar to a CG, an S-CG is defined over a *support* $\mathcal{G} = (T_C, T_R, \phi, t)$, where, T_C and T_R are two partially ordered finite sets, respectively of concept types and relation types; ϕ is a set of individual markers and T_C, T_R, and ϕ are pairwisely disjoint; t is a mapping from ϕ to T_C. For the detailed definition of $\mathcal{G}$, readers can refer to Chein and Mugnier (1992). In the S-CG case, T_C includes domain concepts and service concepts; ϕ includes the individuals of domain concepts and the instance services of service concepts. Formally, an S-CG is defined.

Definition 3.1: An S-CG g_s, defined over a support $\mathcal{G}$, is a binary $((C_{gs} \cup R_{gs}, E_{gs}), l_{gs})$, where:
- $(C_{gs} \cup R_{gs}, E_{gs})$ is a bipartite graph, where C_{gs} and R_{gs} are node sets, respectively of concept nodes and of relation nodes, and E_{gs} is a set of edges.
- l_{gs} is a labelling function of nodes and edges. A concept node $c_{gs} \in C_{gs}$ is labelled by an ordered pair $(type(c_{gs}), marker(c_{gs}))$, where $type(c_{gs}) \in T_c$, $marker(c_{gs}) \in \phi \cup \{*\}$. A relation

node $r_{gs} \in R_{gs}$ is labelled by $type(r_{gs})$, where $type(r_{gs}) \in T_R$. The edge labelling is omitted in the S-CG.

The example in Figure 1 illustrates a simple usage scenario for a money transfer service. This S-CG involves two service concepts, the Money_Transfer service and the Currency_Conversion service. Related to the two service concepts are some more concepts, for example "Currency", "Bank", and "Country". The relation nodes, such as "AGNT", "REQ", "GEN", and "LOC", describe relationships between these concepts. A larger S-CG that describes a complicated scenario can be created for a complex business service through joining together simple S-CGs.

For each T-*Context* we define an owner service concept associating with the T-*Context* and the owner service concept's corresponding instance services are owner services. However, in its actual implementation, i.e. S-CGs, all the service concepts addressed in an S-CG are the owner of the S-CG depending on which instance service the S-CG has been assigned to. This is to avoid the situation where duplicate S-CGs are created for each service and to reduce the redundancy and complexity of the T-*Context* implementation.

As S-CG is based on the CG formalism, all the properties, rules, and operations that are applicable to the CGs are also applicable to S-CGs. In the following, we will summarize some of the important operations on CGs and basic properties of S-CGs.

Specialization and *generalization* are two important CG operations that are essential to the CG matching and reasoning (Mugnier, 2000), see Sowa, (1984) for related definitions.

As S-CGs are used to match with CGs generated from a service user's query to locate relevant services, we now make a brief analysis of the relationship between an S-CG and a CG generated from a query through the following theorems and definitions.

Theorem 2.1: Let u be an S-CG, v a generated CG from a service query, and ϕ an operator that can convert a CG into its equivalent logic formulas. If $u \leq v$, then $\phi u \Rightarrow \phi v$.

Proof. As S-CGs are simple CGs, the proof proposed by Sowa (1984) is applicable here.

Definition 2.2: Let u be an S-CG and v a generated CG from a service query. If $u \leq v$ or $\phi u \Rightarrow \phi v$, then the service query is called *conceptually satisfiable* by the S-CG u.

Theorem 2.2: For any two CGs u and v, where $u \leq v$, there must exist a mapping $\pi: v \rightarrow u$, where $\pi_u v$ is a sub-graph of u called a projection of v on u. The projection operator π has the following properties:

- For each concept c in v, $\pi_u c$ is a concept in $\pi_u v$ such that $type(\pi_u c) \leq type(c)$, "$\leq$" here represents the subtype relationship between concepts. If c is an individual concept, then $referent(\pi_u c) = referent(c)$.

Figure 1. An example of an S-CG

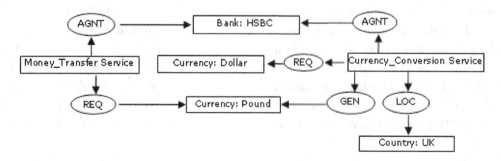

○ For each relation r in v, $\pi_u r$ is a conceptual relation in $\pi_u v$ such that $type(\pi_u r) = type(r)$. If the i-th arc of r is linked to a concept c in v then the i-th arc of $\pi_u r$ must be linked to $\pi_u c$ in $\pi_u v$.

Proof. See Sowa (1984) for detail.

Theorem 2.3: Let u be an S-CG and v a generated CG from a service query. If v has a projection on u, i.e. $\pi: v \rightarrow u$, then the service query must be *conceptually satisfiable* by u.

Proof. According to Theorem 2.2, if $\pi: v \rightarrow u$, u must be identical to or a specialisation of v, i.e. $u \leq v$. By Definition 2.2, if $u \leq v$, the service query is *conceptually satisfiable* by u.

Theorems 2.1 and 2.3, and Definition 2.2 together describe how to verify whether a service query is conceptually satisfiable by an S-CG. Conceptual satisfiability is an important concept. It supports to identify whether a service request from the end users is within or beyond a service provider's business domain. If a service request is not conceptually satisfiable by an S-CG, there is no need to search for the instance services that associate with the S-CG. The S-CG u in the above theorems and definitions does not necessarily exist in a service repository. It can be dynamically generated by joining existing S-CGs. If a service request is conceptually satisfiable this does not necessarily mean that the instance services associated with the S-CG can actually achieve the service request. It only suggests that these instance services are relevant to the request and may possibly propose a full or partial solution. In other words, conceptual satisfiability is an important evidence for judging whether an instance service is relevant to a service query/requirement.

2.2. Semantic Service Description Model

More often than not, a service query cannot be satisfied by a single service, instead through a composition of several services. How to correctly and efficiently construct a composite service to meet the user's need that cannot be met by a single service is the major task in service discovery and composition. Service discovery and composition techniques based on current semantic service description frameworks (Paolucci et al., 2002; Wu et al., 2003) search for and compose services in an isolated manner, that is, the current techniques locate services individually, without considering the inter-service relationships, thus for each participating service in a composite service, the same searching and planning procedure has to be carried out repetitively. In order to improve the efficiency of service composition with more accurate results, we propose a semantic service description model (SSDM) as a component of the CbSSDF. SSDM addresses four types of semantics (Cardoso & Sheth, 2006) associated with a service, i.e. the data semantics, the functional semantics, the non-functional semantics, and the execution semantics. In SSDM, the data semantics deal with semantically annotated inputs and outputs of a service. The functional semantics are captured by a service ontology and pre-conditions and effects. The non-functional semantics are represented through the service metadata. The execution semantics are addressed through the internal structure of a service. SSDM can also implement the A-*Context* to improve the efficiency of service composition.

In the SSDM, the A-*Context* of a service is implemented through a set of Common Usage Patterns (CUPs). A CUP describes how an instance service (the owner service of an A-*Context*) can be composed with other instance services in a scenario or a part of a scenario. It complies with the owner service's T-*Context*, which means that for the owner service and the other services in a CUP, their service concepts must appear together in at least one of the owner service's S-CGs. The whole collection of CUPs of a service collectively represents how this service can interact/be composed with other services at the instance level. A CUP is formally defined as below:

Definition 2.3: Given a service s_k, a CUP of s_k (the owner service of the CUP) is defined as a binary $p=(S, \mathcal{L})$, where:

- $S=\{s_1, s_2, \ldots, s_n\}$: A set of services that directly interact with s_k. Let x be the number of inputs of s_k and y be the number of outputs of s_k, we have $n \leq (x + y)$. If $s_k \in S$, it means that s_k can be composed with its duplicated copy or it is in a loop control structure.

- $\mathcal{L}$: A set of service links that link the services in S with s_k.

- Let G_{sk} be the set of S-CGs of s_k, then $\exists g_{sk} \in G_{sk} \mid p \text{ a } g_{sk}$.

The expression "p a g_{sk}" is read as "p complies with g_{sk}", which means that for all the instance services in p, their service concepts or service concepts' super concepts must appear in g_{sk}.

According to the definition, a CUP describes only the relationships between the owner service and services that directly interact with the owner service. The indirect relationships are not described in a CUP because they can be inferred from the other service's CUPs.

A CUP can be considered as a segment of a workflow. Service composition is about constructing suitable workflows and therefore we can say that CUPs can make the service composition process more efficient. The reason is that assembling segments of workflows in the service composition process is quicker than assembling individual services. In the following we use an example to illustrate how a CUP is generated.

First we consider a few of example services shown in Table 1.

From the above diagram, we can obtain the CUPs of each service through their service links. For example, s4's CUPs are ({s2}, { l (s4, s2) | s4.out1 << s2.in1 }) and ({s3}, {1(s4, s3) | s4.out1 << s3.in1 }).

SSDM is proposed based on definitions of atomic service and composite service and the definition of CUP. In SSDM, we assume that all the services are composite services and an atomic service is a special case of the composite service. Formally, the SSDM is defined as follows:

Definition 2.4: Given a service s_k, its SSDM is a 7-tuple (*IO*, *PE*, *M*, O, *Str*, *C*, *B*), where,

- *IO*: Inputs and outputs of s_k, including their data types and semantics.

- *PE*: A set of rules that describe preconditions and effects of s_k.

- *M*: A set of metadata that describe non-functional attributes of s_k, such as the quality of service (QoS), the service provider information, and the natural language based service description, etc.

- O: A service ontology that defines the service concept of s_k.

- *Str:* The internal structure of s_k, which contains a set of services, control structures, and the data flow. An empty internal structure means that s_k is an atomic service.

- *C*: A set of CUPs associated with s_k.

- *B*: The service grounding information of s_k.

A graphical illustration of the SSDM is shown in Figure 2 and the notations used in Figure 3 are listed:

1. Service$_k$ is the described service.
2. Concept$_s$ can be either the direct or ancestor service concept of Service$_k$ in a service ontology.
3. S_i-S_{i+1}...-S_n are the sub-services of Service$_k$.

Table 1. An example of services expressed in common usage patterns (CUPs)

Web Services	Service Concept	Inputs	Outputs
Money_Transfer (s_1)	Banking_Service	*Input$_1$:* Data Type: *Double* Concept: *Currency: Pound* *Input$_2$:* Data Type: *Account* Concept: *Bank_Account* *Input$_3$:* Data Type: *Account* Concept: *Bank_Account*	*Output$_1$:* Data Type: *Boolean* Concept: *Transfer_Status*
Money_Transfer (s_2)	Banking_Service	*Input1:* Data Type: Double Concept: *Currency: Dollar* *Input$_2$:* Data Type: *Account* Concept: *Bank_Account* *Input$_3$:* Data Type: *Account* Concept: *Bank_Account*	*Output$_1$:* Data Type: *Boolean* Concept: *Transfer_Status*
Currency_Conversion (s_3)	Financial_Tool	*Input$_1$:* Data Type: Double Concept: *Currency: Dollar*	*Output$_1$:* Data Type: *Double* Concept: *Currency: Pound*
Currency_Conversion (s_4)	Financial_Tool	*Input$_1$:* Data Type: Double Concept: *Currency: Euro*	*Output$_1$:* Data Type: Double Concept: *Currency: Dollar*

Based on their input and output data types, the services can be connected as shown in Figure 2.

Figure 2. An example of CUPs

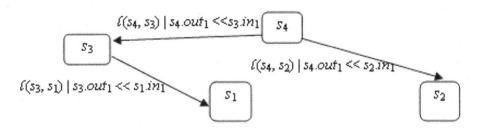

Figure 3. A graphical illustration of SSDM

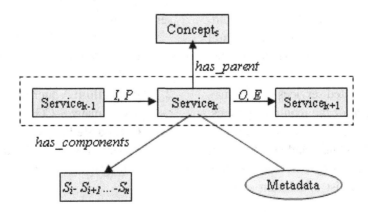

4. Service$_{k-1}$ and Service$_{k+1}$ represent the services that are linked to Service$_k$ through service links in a CUP.

5. *I* and *P* are the inputs and pre-conditions, and *O* and *E* are the outputs and effects.

6. Services within the dashed border rectangle represent a CUP of Service$_k$.

3. S-CG BASED SERVICE DISCOVERY

Currently, semantic service search engines and the ordinary UDDI service search engine all require technical details of the required services. To use these service search engines, service users need sufficient domain knowledge about the request services in order to provide technical specifications. However, more often than not, service users are not domain experts in the required service's area and therefore, it is very hard for them to provide the technical specifications at the very beginning of the service discovery process. Consequently, these service search engines have to carry out searching with inadequate requirement information and therefore return inaccurate results.

To solve this problem, we propose an enhanced (two-step) service discovery mechanism based on the CbSSDF based service description. S-CGs in the CbSSDF, i.e. the T-*Context*, help the service search engine to locate services by using their concepts and conceptual relations, so in the first step a service user only needs to describe their requirements or scenarios in natural language without worrying about any technical detail. The search engine will then convert the natural language query into a CG and match with the S-CGs in the service repository to locate the relevant services. The located services may or may not be an exact match for the required services. However, the match suggests that these services are relevant to the user's query and therefore may provide a solution to the query. After the first step, the service user gets a list of relevant services

with their technical descriptions attached. These service descriptions can act as hints to assist the user in providing detailed technical specifications according to their own situation. The second step is to refine the result from the first step using the provided technical specification, generate composite services, and rank the results according to their degree of similarity to the specification.

3.1. S-CG Based Service Retrieval

In this step, the aim of the service search engine is to find the relevant services from the service repository. This can be achieved by using the CG matching mechanism (Montes-y-Gómez et al., 2001). A service query is first converted into a CG and then matched with the S-CGs in the service repository. As discussed previously in Section 2.2, if a service query is conceptually satisfiable, its CG must have a projection (Sowa, 1984) on at least one S-CG. Therefore, in this step, we aim to finding an S-CG that contains the projection of the query CG. This S-CG can be either an existing S-CG in the service repository or a join of existing S-CGs. There are many well developed algorithms (Croitoru & Compatangelo, 2006; Chein & Mugnier, 1992) that can be used to check for CG projections. In the first step we look for relevance rather than exactitude, this means that our CG matching method can be much more flexible than the formal CG projection checking methods proposed in the literature. There are six situations in which an S-CG's corresponding services can be considered as relevant to a service query:

1. **Exact Match:** A query CG is exactly matched with one or more S-CGs.
2. **Projection:** A query CG has a projection in one or many S-CGs.
3. **Composite Projection:** A query CG has a projection in an S-CG that is generated by joining existing S-CGs.

4. **Overlap:** A query CG has overlap concepts or relations with one or many S-CGs.

5. **Concept Match:** A query CG has only concept nodes matched with one or more S-CGs' concept nodes.

6. **Relation Match:** A query CG has only relation nodes matched with one or more S-CGs' relation nodes.

In the six situations, the relevance level of services is gradually decreases from "Exact match" to "Relation match." We use an algorithm to categorise services in the repository into the different relevance situations and then we perform the CG similarity calculation to calculate the actual relevance degree of the services in each situation. The algorithm is shown in Listing 1. The relevance levels are from 1 to 6, 1 represents "Exact match" and 6 represents "Relation match." In order to improve performance, "Composite projection" is checked last and only on the services that are confirmed as relevant this is because if a set of S-CGs have no common concepts with a query CG, the derived graphs from them will not contain a projection of the query CG.

After the relevance level categorisation process is completed, the actual relevance/similarity degree to the service query of each relevant service under each relevance level needs to be computed, except services with relevance level "1". The relevance/similarity degree is calculated using the CG similarity measurement method.

The method we use to compute the CG similarity is proposed by Montes et al. (Montes-y-Gómez et al., 2001). According to Montes et al., the similarity between two CGs, u and v, consists of a concept similarity S_c and a relation similarity S_r. The concept similarity S_c is calculated using the Dice coefficient (Frakes & Baeza-Yates, 1992) expression:

$$S_c = 2 \times \frac{\sum\limits_{c \in \cup o}(weight(c) \times \beta(\pi_u c, \pi_v c))}{\sum\limits_{c \in u}(weight(c) + \sum\limits_{c \in v} weight(c)}$$

where O is a set of common overlap graphs of u and v; $\cup O$ is the union of all of the common overlap graphs of u and v; $\pi_u c$ and $\pi_v c$ represent the concepts coming from graphs u and v; $weight(c)$ is the importance factor of the concept type c. Its value can be various in different applications. Currently, we distinguish two types of concepts, i.e. a domain concept and a service concept. See Listing 1.

The set of common overlaps O represents all common elements between u and v. The overlaps include not only the direct overlaps of the two graphs, but also the common generalisation of the two graphs.

The $\beta(\pi_u c, \pi_v c)$ function in the above expression computes the semantic similarity between the two concepts $\pi_u c$ and $\pi_v c$, defined as in Box 1.

The first condition indicates that the two concepts are exactly the same. The second condition indicates that the two concepts have the same type but refer to different instances, where the term *depth* represents the number of levels in the ontology tree that contain both concepts. The third condition indicates that the two concepts have different types, where, d_c represents the distance from the least common super-type of $\pi_u c$ and $\pi_v c$ to the root of the ontology; $d_{\pi uc}$ and $d_{\pi vc}$ represent the distances from $\pi_u c$ and $\pi_v c$ to the root of the ontology.

The relation similarity S_r is calculated using the following expression:

$$S_\gamma = \frac{2m(o)}{m_c(u) + m_c(v)}$$

where, $m(o)$ is the number of the relation nodes in the common overlap graphs of u and v; $m_c(u)$ and $m_c(v)$ are the numbers of the relation nodes of the common overlap graphs of u and v and the overlap graphs' adjacent relation nodes. To examine the similarity between two relations, we need to compare not only the two relations themselves, but also the neighbour relations that linked to these two relations.

Listing 1. CG similarity based service relevance classification algorithm

```
List relevantServices = null;
CG q = query.CG;
S = {s_1, s_2, ..., s_n}; //the service repository
for each s∈S do
{       if projectionCheck(q, s.S-CG) = = true then
        {       if exactMatch(q, s.S-CG) = = true then
                {       s.setRelevanceLevel(1);
                        relevantService.add(s);
                        continue;
                }
                else
                {       s.setRelevanceLevel(2);
                        relevantService.add(s);
                        continue;
                }
        }
        if overlapCheck(q, s.S-CG) = = true then
        {       s.setRelevanceLevel(4);
                relevantService.add(s);
                continue;
        }
        if commonConceptCheck(q, s.S-CG) = = true then
        {       s.setRelevanceLevel(5);
                relevantService.add(s);
                continue;
        }
        if commonRelationCheck(q, s.S-CG) = = true then
        {       s.setRelevanceLevel(6);
                relevantService.add(s);
                continue;
        }
}
if compositeProjectionCheck(q, relevantServices.S-CGList) = = true then
{       List participatedSerivces = compositeProject.getServices()
        for each s∈participatedSerivces do
        {       if s.getRelevanceLevel() != 1 or s.getRelevanceLevel() != 2 then
                        s.updateRelevanceLevel(3);
        }
}
```

Box 1.

$$\beta(\pi_u c, \pi_v c) = \begin{cases} 1 & \text{if type}(\pi_u c) = type(\pi_v c) \text{ and referent } (\pi_u c) = referent(\pi_v c) \\ depth / (depth + 1) & \text{if type } (\pi_u c) = type(\pi_v c) \text{ and referent } (\pi_u c) \neq referent(\pi_v c) \\ 2d_c / d_{\pi_o c} + d_{\pi_v c}) & \text{if type } (\pi_o c) \neq type(\pi_v c) \end{cases}$$

The actual relevance/similarity degree expressions under different situation are shown in Box 2.

The first condition applies when two CGs only have common concept nodes, i.e. the "Concept match" situation. The second condition applies when two CGs only have common relation nodes, i.e. the "Relation match" situation. The last condition applies when two CGs have overlap, i.e.

Box 2.

$$Sim = \begin{cases} S_c = 2\left(\sum_{c \in \bigcup O}(weight(c) \times \beta(\pi_u c, \pi_v c))\right) \Big/ \left(\sum_{c \in u} weight(c) + \sum_{c \in v} weight(c)\right) & if\ S_r = 0\ and\ S_c \neq 0 \\ S_r = \dfrac{2m(o)}{m_c(u) + m_c(v)} & if\ S_c = 0\ and\ S_r \neq 0 \\ \\ S_c \cdot S_r & if\ S_c \neq 0\ and\ S_r \neq 0 \end{cases}$$

the "Overlap" situation. However, the "Projection", and the "Composite Projection" situations are special cases of overlap, thus the last condition is also applicable on these situations.

After this step, the services in the service repository have been categorised as either relevant services or irrelevant services. The relevant services will be passed to the second step of the two-step service discovery mechanism for further refinement. These services have the potential to satisfy the service requirements. However, the irrelevant services will also be considered during the service composition process when relevant services cannot fully fulfill service requirements.

3.2. SSDM Based Service Composition

The second step aims to refine the result from the first step. The refinement is based on semantic distance and technical detail matching between a user's specification and service attributes in each service's SSDM description. The major difference between the two-step service discovery method and the traditional service discovery methods is that by having the result from the first step, service users are edified and therefore able to provide further technical detail to describe their particular needs. Even if the service users still cannot provide the full technical specification, partial detail is acceptable and the step two can be repeated until an appropriate result is found.

As discussed previously in Section 3.3, the attributes provided in SSDM for service description are inputs, outputs, pre-conditions, effects, the service internal structure, CUPs, and the service metadata. If we use a vector v to represent the attributes of a service, then we can build up a $t \times m$ vector space V, where t is the number of terms in v and m is the number of services in a service repository (or the candidate services from step one). The vector space V is represented: in Box 3.

Here, the columns of V are service attribute vectors, the rows of V are term vectors, a_{ij} is the i-th attribute term of service j, and t represents the number of service attributes addressed in SSDM. A user requirement can also be represented as a vector $r = (q_1, q_2, ..., q_t)$. Then, we apply the cosine similarity method to measure the distance between the service user's specification and the service attributes in SSDM. The cosine similarity method (Berry et al., 1999) uses the cosine value of the angle between two vectors to

Box 3.

$$V = \begin{pmatrix} a_{11} & a_{12} & . & . & a_{1m} \\ a_{21} & a_{22} & . & . & a_{2m} \\ . & . & . & . & . \\ . & . & . & . & . \\ a_{t1} & a_{t2} & . & . & a_{tm} \end{pmatrix}$$

measure the similarity between these two vectors. The cosine value of the angle is computed using the formula in Box 4.

Here, m is the number of services in the service repository (or the candidate services from step one), t is the number of attributes addressed in SSDM, a_{ij} is the i-th attribute term of service j, and q_i is the ith term addressed in a query. A smaller angle represents a higher similarity between two vectors.

However, many attributes addressed in SSDM contain sub-attributes, such as inputs, outputs, the service internal structure, CUPs, and the service metadata. For example the service metadata attribute has many sub-attributes, such as the service provider's information, the service subject area, the region of the service, and versioning information. These sub-attributes themselves can also be considered as vector spaces. Therefore, V is actually a vector space with sub-spaces. A vector v_j in V is graphically illustrated in Figure 4.

Each line or arrow in Figure 4 represents an attribute or a sub-attribute of a service. In reality, there should be many service vectors like v_j in the cube, i.e. V. We treat V and its sub-spaces as a tree structure and use a recursive algorithm to compute the cosine similarity between a service specification and each service attribute vector and its sub-vectors. Finally, an overall similarity degree for each service is calculated and the result services are ranked according to the similarity degree.

The cosine similarity calculation and the vector space model try to find the most suitable services for a service requirement. However, there are many cases where a service requirement cannot be satisfied by a single service, i.e. the required service does not exist in the service repository. In these cases, we need to employ the service composition approach (Dustdar & Schreiner, 2005) to dynamically construct composite services to fulfill the service requirement. In the following, we discuss how CbSSDF can facilitate the service composition process and improve its efficiency.

One of the most common approaches for service composition is to use AI planning techniques (Sirin et al., 2004; Zhang et al., 2004). Planning is about producing state changes through actions in order to achieve a desired goal (Yang, 1997). A planning problem can be defined.

Figure 4. A graphical representation of part of the vector space V

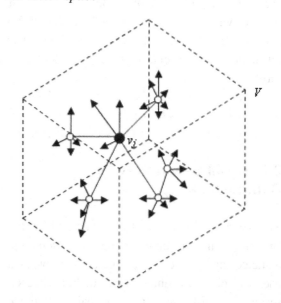

Box 4.

$$\cos\theta_{vr} = \left(\frac{v_j \bullet r}{\left\| v_j \right\|_2 * \left\| r \right\|_2} \right)^m_{j-1} = \left(\frac{\sum_{i-1}^{t} a_{ij} q_i}{\sqrt{\sum_{i-1}^{t} a_{ij}^2} * \sqrt{\sum_{i-1}^{t} q_i^2}} \right)^m_{j-1}$$

Definition 3.1: A planning problem is a 5-tuple (X, U, f, x_I, X_G), where:

- X: is a set of states that represents all the distinct situations in a planning domain. X is finite or countably infinite and $X \neq \varnothing$
- U: is a set of actions. Each action $u_i \in U$ produces a new state x' after applied on the current state x, $x, x' \in X$.
- f: is a state transition function. $x' = f(x, u)$
- x_I: is an initial state, $x_I \in X$.
- X_G: is a set of goal states, $X_G \subset X$.

A planning algorithm's task is to find a sequence of actions in U that can transform an initial state x_I to a desired goal state x_g, $x_g \subset X_G$, which is formally represented as:

$$f(f(f(...f(x_I, u_I)...), u_{n-1}), u_n) \subseteq X_G,$$
$$u_i \in U, 1 \leq i \leq n$$

From the expression we can see that the time complexity of a planning algorithm is dependent on the number of steps required to achieve the goal and the number of candidate actions for each step. Using the Forward-Chaining Total-Order (FCTO) planning algorithm as an example, the worst case time complexity of FCTO (Yang, 1997) is:

$$T(FCTO) = O(B^N {}_* t)$$

where B is the number of candidate actions for each step, N is the number of steps in a plan for achieving the goal, and t is the average time spent by a planner on each step. However, irrespective of which planning algorithm is used, the time complexity is always related to N and B. If either of these two numbers can be decreased, especially N, the time complexity of the planning algorithm would be decreased.

In the Web service composition situation, a candidate service can be considered as an action, its pre-conditions are the states before its execu-

tion and effects are the states after its execution. A composite service can be considered as a plan to achieve a goal. The complexity of the service composition process can be higher than that of a normal planning task because in the existing service description frameworks, a composite service planner cannot determine which services are the potential candidates for the next step, therefore it has to check the whole service repository for each step it makes towards the composite service. This situation is improved using CbSSDF. The service composition process can become much more efficient by using the information provided in each service's SSDM. The key component for facilitating service composition is the CUP. Each service has a set of CUPs associated with it. These CUPs improve service composition efficiency by reducing the number of potential candidate services to be considered for each step in a composite service and most importantly reducing the number of steps that the composite service planner takes to achieve the goal, see the analysis:

- **Reducing the number of potential candidates:** In the set of CUPs for a service, all services that can potentially interact with the service based on the input, output data type compatibility and the pre-condition and effect constraint, have been listed. Let N be the number of services in a service repository S, S_c a set of services in the set of CUPs of a service s, and $N_C = |S_c|$, we always have $N_C \leq N$, if $s \in S$ and $S_c \subseteq S$. It is very unlikely that $N_C = N$, unless a service can interact with all other services in a service repository. Therefore, in most cases, $N_C < N$.

- **Reducing the number of steps:** Under the existing service description frameworks, when a composite service planner constructs a plan to achieve a goal, it takes more steps to reach the goal as the existing service descriptions do not provide the information about inter-relationships between services. However, under CbSSDF, a composite service planner can construct a plan much faster than before because of the additional information provided in the CUPs. Each CUP can be considered as a fragment of a plan (or a workflow). When a service is located, its CUPs can tell the service planner what the possible services are for the next step. Therefore, the number of steps to reach a goal can be cut in half compared with the planning process under the existing service descriptions. Let B_C be the number of steps that a planner need to go through to construct a composite service under CbSSDF, and B the number of steps under the existing service descriptions, we have $B_C = B/2$, if $B \geq 2$.

According to the above analysis, the time complexity expression for the FCTO algorithm under CbSSDF, can be rewritten as below:

$$T(FCTO) = O((B/2)^N_C *t)$$

4. SCENARIO BASED COMPARISON WITH OWL-S

To evaluate our framework, we make a scenario based comparison and analysis on how the CbSSDF based solution tackles problems, such as query interpretation, service discovery, and service planning and composition. We also consider whether the situation has been improved and by how much in comparison with existing service description frameworks. We set up the scenario with three tasks for the comparison and analysis to be based on. The three tasks include atomic service discovery, composite service discovery, and dynamic composite service generation. We choose OWL-S as representative of the existing semantic Web service description frameworks for comparison purposes. The reasons for choosing OWL-S are: (1) it is comparable to CbSSDF; (2)

it is a relatively mature research work in semantic Web service area; (3) it is an extension to OWL and therefore, the features provided by OWL are directly inherited by OWL-S for describing the semantics of services.

Suppose we have a student who wants to find a Web service to calculate the volume of a cone. He knows how this can be done, but he wants a Web service do it for him. He proposes a query as follows:

Cone volume calculation service: multiply a cone's base circle area by its height and divide by 3

This query states which kind of service he is looking for and how the service should work. Now let us analyse what the possible situations of the returned results are:

- One or many existing atomic services from the service repository are located for the requirement.
- One or many existing composite services from the service repository are located for the requirement.
- There are no existing services that can satisfy the requirements, but a composite service is constructed dynamically for the requirement.
- No (satisfiable) result returned, i.e. neither existing services nor dynamically constructed composite services can fully satisfy the requirement.

4.1. Locating an Existing Atomic Service

In the first task, we assume that there is at least one atomic service in the service repository that can satisfy the requirements, i.e. performs the calculation of the volume of a cone. This task requires a service description framework has the capability to support query interpretation and specification matchmaking.

The comparison result for these two different solutions for solving task 1 is listed in Table 2.

From the comparison result shown in Table 2, we can see that for locating a single atomic service, there is no significant difference between these two solutions. They both require the service user to propose a query followed by a detailed technical specification of the required service. However, In the CbSSDF based solution, the matchmaking can be performed based on imprecise information, such as the natural language query. The service user can provide technical specification later based on the interim results. The OWL-S based solution requires the service user to give technical specification of required services at the very beginning of the search. It could be a difficult task for the service user to give detailed technical specification of a required service, especially when the service user is not a domain expert in the required service area.

4.2. Locating an Existing Composite Service

In the second task, we assume that in the service repository there is at least one composite service that can perform the calculation of the volume of a cone. This task requires a service description framework has the capabilities to support query interpretation, specification matchmaking, and internal structure and sub-services matching with composite services if it is applicable.

The comparison result for these two different solutions for solving task 2 is listed in Table 3.

The comparison result in Table 3 shows the difference between these two solutions in dealing with composite service discovery. In the CbSSDF based solution, the rich service description enables service users to be able to use extra information, such as the internal structure composite services, to more precisely locate required services. In reality, it is not necessary for a user to know whether the required service is an atomic service or a composite service. However, if the user does know, the extra information can be used to obtain better search result. In the OWL-S based solution, composite service and atomic service are not distinguished from the service user's perspective. The advantage of this is that it can make the service discovery and service description simpler. From the CbSSDF point of view, it tries to use all the available information to assist service discovery. The disadvantage of this is that it increases the complexity of service description and discovery.

Table 2. The comparison of CbSSDF and OWL-S based solutions for task 1

CbSSDF Based Solution	OWL-S Based Solution
1. Query Interpretation	
A given query Q is converted into a CG: $Q \grave{E} CG$ (Image file: image_in_table 2.TIF)	A given query Q is converted into a set of concepts: $Q \grave{E} C=\{c_1, c_2, ..., c_n\}$
2. Match Making	
Step one: From CG matching a set of relevant services $S_r=\{s_1, s_2, ..., s_n\}$ can be obtained. Then the services in S_r are ranked according to their S-CGs' similarity to the query CG.	Not Applicable.
Step two: Based on the further technical specification provided by service users, S_r is refined, ranked according to similarity, and returned to the service user. The specification matching is performed based on the attributes addressed in SSDM, such as IOPE, service concept, metadata, internal structure, and CUPs.	Matchmaking cannot be performed based on natural language query. Therefore, the technical specification is required at the same time when the query is proposed. The matchmaking is performed based IOPE and metadata. A set of result service is returned to the service user and they are ranked according to the similarity to the specification.

Table 3. The comparison of CbSSDF and OWL-S based solutions for task 2

CbSSDF Based Solution	OWL-S Based Solution
1. Query Interpretation	
A given query Q is converted into a CG: $Q \models CG$ The same graph as in Table 2	A given query Q is converted into a set of concepts: $Q \models C=\{c_1, c_2, ..., c_n\}$
2. Matchmaking	
Step one – CG Matching: From CG matching a set of relevant services $S_r=\{s_1, s_2, ..., s_n\}$ can be obtained. Then the services in S_r are ranked according to their S-CGs' similarity to the query CG.	Not Applicable.
Step two – Specification Matching: Based on the further technical specification provided by service users, S_r is refined, ranked, and returned to the service user. However, in this step, if the service user is familiar with the required services and able to provide the internal sub-services' detail, the result can be more accurate. For example, if service s is a composite service and consists of s_i and s_j, then s_i and s_j's details can also be used to locate s.	The internal details of services are hidden from service users in OWL-S based solution, thus for a service user, the atomic service and the composite service are not distinguished. For this reason, the matchmaking process in this task is exactly the same as the one described in task 1.

However, the complex service description can be compensated by more accurate service discovery result.

4.3. Dynamically Constructing Composite Service

In the third task, we assume that there is no existing service that can perform the calculation of the volume of a cone. Therefore, a composite service needs to be dynamically constructed by using the existing services in the service repository.

This task requires a service description framework has the capabilities to support not only query interpretation, specification matchmaking, but also service planning during the service composition process.

The comparison result for these two different solutions for solving task 3 is listed in Table 4.

In the situation of dynamic composite service construction, the CbSSDF based solution can fully reveal its advantages. Comparing to OWL-S based solution, the information provided by CbSSDF can much improve the performance of service composition and the accuracy of the result. The inter-relationship between services addressed in CUPs can narrow down the number of candidate

services in each step of planning. As each CUP can be considered as a segment of a plan, the actual steps of a plan to reach the desired goal is also reduced. The general rules and domain specific rules can be used to not only describe the pre-conditions and effects of services, but also inspect the correctness of generated composite services.

In OWL-S based solution, each service has been treated completely individually. The potential inter-relationship between services in the real world has been ignored. One of the consequences of this is slow performance because during the planning phase, each task's possible candidate services are the entire collection of services in the service repository rather than the services that are relevant and compatible to the service in the previous task.

4.4. Discussion of Scenario Based Comparison

By analysing the two different approaches through the three tasks, we have found the pros and cons of these two solutions, summarised as following:

- In dealing with atomic service discovery, these two solutions have no considerable

Table 4. The comparison of CbSSDF and OWL-S based solutions for task 3

CbSSDF Based Solution	OWL-S Based Solution
1. Query Interpretation	
A given query Q is converted into a CG: $$Q \grave{E} CG$$ The same graph as in Table 2	A given query Q is converted into a set of concepts: $$Q \grave{E} C=\{c_1, c_2, ..., c_n\}$$
2. Matchmaking	
Step one – CG Matching: From CG matching a set of relevant services $S_r=\{s_1, s_2, ..., s_n\}$ can be obtained. The set of services are ranked according to their S-CGs' similarity to the query CG. The CG matcher will also join single S-CGs together into larger S-CGs in order to achieve maximum match.	Not Applicable.
Step two – Specification Matching: Based on the further technical specification provided by service users, S_r is refined and ranked. If there is no matched service or matched with very low similarity rate, the system will start service planning to generate composite services.	Based on the further technical specification provided by service users, the OWL-S based solution will try to find a set of best matched services. If there is no matched service or matched with very low similarity rate, service composition will be attempted.
3. Planning and Composition	
The planning is based on reduced service range S_r, i.e. the relevant services are considered first in the planning. When a service is located, its CUPs can tell the planner where to go next. Only the services in its CUPs are compatible, therefore, there is no need to go through all the services in the repository.	The planning is based on assuming all the services in the whole service repository are candidate services. The planner in OWL-S based solution need to go through the whole service repository every time when locating a service for a task.
4. Rule Evaluation	
The pre-conditions and effects of each service are evaluated during service planning process. The general rules and domain specific rules are evaluated to filter out invalid composite services.	The pre-conditions and effects of each service are evaluated during service planning process.

difference. However, in the CbSSDF solution, the two-step service discovery mechanism gives service users the flexibility to search services by imprecise information first, such as natural language, and then give the precisely specified technical information later to refine the result if they can. In the OWL-S solution, the service users have to provide precisely specified technical information at the very beginning of each search, which may be hard for the users who are not familiar with the technical details of the required services.

- In the OWL-S solution, the composite service and the atomic service are not distinguished in service user's perspective. Therefore, for a service user, there is no

difference in the way he searches for an atomic service or a composite service. The advantage of this is that it makes the searching process simpler and the user does not need to be aware of the difference between composite service and atomic service.

- One of the principles of CbSSDF is to use all the possible information to assist service discovery. Therefore, if the service users know the internal detail of composite services they are looking for, they can provide relevant information, which can make the discovery result more accurate. However, the disadvantage of this is that it increases the complexity of service description.
- When dynamically composite services construction is required, the advantages of

CbSSDF based solution emerge. First of all, the two-step service discovery mechanism can filter out irrelevant services by CG matching so that the candidate services for service composition are reduced. Secondly, CUPs can further reduce the number of candidate services in each step of service planning. They can also reduce the number of steps that a planner needs to reach the goal state.

- A significant defect of the OWL-S solution is that it does not consider the inter-relationship of services. The consequence of it is that no matter in which stage of a planning process, the planner has to search through the whole service repository for candidate services.

5. CONCLUSION

The goal of this paper is to present a comprehensive semantic Web service description framework and compare it with the existing Web service description framework (OWL-S) to examine how it increase the efficiency and effectiveness of the Web service discovery and composition.. However, some issues still exist, such as insufficient context information, precise requirements required to locate services, insufficient information about inter-relationships among services, and insufficient incomplete information handling

To address the above issues, we proposed a Context based Semantic Service Description Framework (CbSSDF) that provides service usage context (SUC) information about services, adequate semantics of services, and a non-monotonic rule system for handling incomplete information. We also proposed a two-step service discovery mechanism based on CbSSDF to demonstrate how the proposed framework can improve service discovery and composition. The main contributions of the paper are summarised as follows:

1. A new concept of service context, i.e. the Service Usage Context (SUC), is proposed.
2. A Context based Semantic Service Description Framework (CbSSDF) is proposed to address not only the semantics of Web services, but also the SUC.
3. A two-step service discovery mechanism is proposed to give service users much more flexibility to search for their required services.

The result of the scenario based comparison between CbSSDF and OWL-S shows that the CbSSDF based solution can improve the users' service searching experience by the two-step service discovery mechanism and increase the efficiency and effectiveness of service discovery and composition by embedding SUC and the richer semantics in SSDM. The major defect of CbSSDF is the complexity because it addresses richer semantics and the SUC information. However, the more accurate service discovery results compensate the complexity defect. The performance evaluation has not been addressed in this paper. However, in our previous work (Du et al., 2008) we have proposed some of the evaluation results on service discovery result accuracy, system performance, and system scalability.

However, there are still more improvement work can be done to enhance CbSSDF. The followings are a list of work that can improve the applicability and performance of the framework and will be addressed in the future.

- A descriptive language needs to be created to represent the CbSSDF. At the moment, the CbSSDF descriptions in the prototype are stored in a database for demonstration purposes only.
- Quality of Service (QoS) needs to be considered in the service description. QoS is a very important criterion in the service selection process. A service matched with

a user's requirement does not necessarily mean that the service is the right service for the user. It is a right service only if it provides the user with the desired QoS in terms such as the cost, performance, and stability.

REFERENCES

Agarwal, S., Handschuh, S., & Staab, S. (2005). Annotation, composition and invocation of semantic web services. *Journal of Web Semantics*, *2*(1).

Akkiraju, R., Farrell, J., Miller, J., Nagarajan, M., Schmidt, M., Sheth, A., & Verma, K. (2005). *Web service semantics – WSDL-S*. Retrieved from http://lsdis.cs.uga.edu/projects/METEOR-S/WSDL-S

Baader, F., Horrocks, I., & Sattler, U. (2002). Description logics for the semantic web. *Künstliche Intelligenz*, *16*(4), 57–59.

Brewka, G. (2001). On the relationship between defeasible logic and well-founded semantics. In T. Eiter, W. Faber, & M. Truszcynski (Eds.), *Proceedings of the 6th International Conference on Logic Programming and Nonmonotonic Reasoning*, Vienna, Austria (LNCS 2173, pp. 121-132).

Brown, P. J., Bovey, J. D., & Chen, X. (1997). Context-aware applications: From the laboratory to the marketplace. *IEEE Personal Communications*, *4*(5), 58–64. doi:10.1109/98.626984.

Cardoso, J., & Sheth, A. (Eds.). (2006). *Semantic web services, processes and applications (Semantic web and beyond: Computing for human experience)* (*Vol. 3*). New York, NY: Springer. doi:10.1007/978-0-387-34685-4.

CGXML. (2008). *Framework for conceptual knowledge processing*. Retrieved from http://tockit.sourceforge.net/cgxml/index.html

Charfi, A., & Mezini, M. (2004). Hybrid web service composition business process meet business rules. In *Proceedings of the 2nd International Conference on Service-Oriented Computing*.

Chein, M., & Mugnier, M. L. (1992). Conceptual graphs: Fundamental notions. *Revue d'Intelligence Artificielle*, *6*(4), 365–406.

Dey, A., & Abowd, G. (2000, April). Towards a better understanding of context and context-awareness. In *Proceedings of the Workshop on the What, Who, Where, When and How of Context-Awareness*, Hague, The Netherlands.

Du, X., Song, W., & Munro, M. (2006, August 31-Spetember 2). Using common process patterns for semantic web services composition. In *Proceedings of the 15th International Conference on Information System Development* Budapest, Hungary.

Du, X., Song, W., & Munro, M. (2007, August 29-31). Semantic service description framework for addressing imprecise service requirements. In *Proceedings of the 16th International Conference on Information System Development*, Galway, Ireland.

Du, X., Song, W., & Munro, M. (2008, August 25-27). A method for transforming existing web service descriptions into an enhanced semantic web service framework. In *Proceedings of the 17th International Conference on Information System Development*, Paphos, Cyprus.

Dustdar, S., & Schreiner, W. (2005). A survey on web services composition. *International Journal of Web and Grid Services*, *1*(1), 1–30. doi:10.1504/IJWGS.2005.007545.

Editor, O. W. L.-S. (2008). *Related projects*. Retrieved from http://owlseditor.semwebcentral.org/related.shtml

Fensel, D., & Bussler, C. (2002). The web service modeling framework WSMF. *Electronic Commerce Research and Applications, 1*(2), 113–137. doi:10.1016/S1567-4223(02)00015-7.

Fensel, D., Lausen, H., Polleres, A., Bruijn, J., & Stollberg, M. Roman, D., & Domingue, J. (2007). Enabling semantic web services: The web service modeling ontology. New York, NY: Springer.

Guha, R., McCool, R., & Fikes, R. (2004, November). Contexts for the semantic web. In S. A. McIlraith, D. Plexousakis, & F. van Harmelen (Eds.), *Proceedings of the Third International Semantic Web Conference*, Hiroshima, Japan (LNCS 3298, pp. 32-46).

Kerdiles, G., & Salvat, E. (1997). A sound and complete proof procedure based on tableaux and projection. In D. Lukose, H. Delugach, M. Keeler, L. Searle, & J. Sowa (Eds.), *Proceedings of the Fifth International Conference on Conceptual Structures: Fulfilling Peirce's Dream* (LNCS 1257, pp. 371-385).

Ludwig, S., & Reyhani, S. (2005). Semantic approach to service discovery in a grid environment. *Journal of Web Semantics, 3*(4).

Maamar, Z., Benslimane, D., Thiran, P., Ghedira, C., Dustdar, S., & Sattanathan, S. (2007). Towards a context-based multi-type policy approach for web services composition. *Data & Knowledge Engineering, 62*(2), 327–351. doi:10.1016/j.datak.2006.08.007.

Maamar, Z., Mostefaoui, S. K., & Yahyaoui, H. (2005). Toward an agent-based and context-oriented approach for web services composition. *IEEE Transactions on Knowledge and Data Engineering, 17*(5), 686–697. doi:10.1109/TKDE.2005.82.

Martin, D., Burstein, M., Hobbs, J., Lassila, O., McDermott, D., McIlraith, S., et al. (2004). *OWL-S: Semantic mark-up for web services.* Retrieved from http://www.daml.org/services/owl-s/1.0/owl-s.html

Medjahed, B., & Atif, Y. (2007). Context-based matching for web service composition. *Distributed and Parallel Databases, 21*(1), 5–37. doi:10.1007/s10619-006-7003-7.

Mindswap. (2008). *OWL-S API.* Retrieved from http://www.mindswap.org/2004/owl-s/api/

Montes-y-Gómez, M., Gelbukh, A., López-López, A., & Baeza-Yates, R. (2001). Flexible comparison of conceptual graphs. In H. C. Mayr, J. Lazansky, G. Quirchmayr, & P. Vogel (Eds.), *Proceeding of the 12th International Conference and Workshop on Database and Expert Systems Applications* (LNCS 2113, pp. 102-111).

Mugnier, M. (2000). Knowledge representation and reasonings based on graph homomorphisms. In G. Mineau & B. Ganter (Eds.), *Proceedings of the 8th International Conference on Conceptual Structures* (LNAI 1867, pp. 172-192).

Orriens, B., Yang, J., & Papazoglou, M. P. (2003). A framework for business rule driven web service composition. In *Proceedings of the 4th International Workshop on Conceptual Modeling Approaches for e-Business Dealing with Business Volatility.*

Paolucci, M., Kawamura, T., Payne, T., & Sycara, K. (2002). Semantic matching of web services capabilities. In I. Horrocks & J. Hendler (Eds.), *Proceedings of the 1st International Semantic Web Conference* (LNCS 2342, pp. 333-347).

Paolucci, M., Sycara, K., & Kawamuwa, T. (2003, May 20-24). Delivering semantic web services. In *Proceedings of the Conference on World Wide Web*, Budapest, Hungary (pp. 829-836).

Rock, A. (2000). *Deimos: Query answering defeasible logic system.* Retrieved from http://www.cit.gu.edu.au/~arock/defeasible/Defeasible.cgi

Rule, M. L. (2008). *The rule markup initiative.* Retrieved from http://www.ruleml.org/

Ryan, N., Pascoe, J., & Morse, D. (1997). Enhanced reality fieldwork: The context-aware archaeological assistant. In Gaffney, V., van Leusen, M., & Exxon, S. (Eds.), *Computer applications in archaeology*. Oxford, UK: British Archeological Reports.

Song, W., Du, X., & Munro, M. (2009). A concept graph approach to semantic similarity computation method for e-service discovery. *International Journal of Knowledge Engineering and Data Mining*, *1*(1).

Song, W., & Li, X. (2005). A conceptual modeling approach to virtual organizations in the grid. In H. Zhuge & G. C. Fox (Eds.), *Proceedings of the Fourth International Conference on Grid and Cooperative Computing* (LNCS 3795, pp. 382-393).

Sowa, J. F. (1984). *Conceptual structures: Information processing in mind and machine*. Reading, MA: Addison-Wesley.

SRML. (2001). *Simple rule markup language*. Retrieved from http://xml.coverpages.org/srml.html

Strang, C. J. (2005). Next generation systems architecture — The matrix. *BT Technology Journal*, *23*(1). doi:10.1007/s10550-005-0107-1.

Wu, D., Parsia, B., Sirin, E., Hendler, J., & Nau, D. (2003). Automating daml-s web services composition using shop2. In *Proceedings of the 2nd International Semantic Web Conference* (pp. 195-210).

Yang, Q. (1997). *Intelligent planning: A decomposition and abstraction based approach*. Berlin, Germany: Springer Verlag.

Zhang, J., Zhang, S., Cao, J., & Mou, Y. (2004, September 15-18). Improved HTN planning approach for service composition. In *Proceedings of the IEEE International Conference on Services Computing* (pp. 609-612).

This work was previously published in the International Journal of Information System Modeling and Design (IJISMD), Volume 2, Issue 4, edited by Remigijus Gustas, pp. 82-103, copyright 2011 by IGI Publishing (an imprint of IGI Global).

Chapter 7
Modeling Approach for Integration and Evolution of Information System Conceptualizations

Remigijus Gustas
Karlstad University, Sweden

ABSTRACT

Most information systems development methodologies are based on conceptual modeling of static and dynamic views, which are represented by totally different types of diagrams. Understanding of the interplay among interactive, behavioral and structural aspects of specifications is necessary for identification of semantic integrity problems between business process and business data. Typically, semantic inconsistencies and discontinuities between collections of conceptual representations are not easy to detect and to comprehend for information system designers due to static and dynamic aspects of models being visualized in isolation. The goal of this paper is to present a modeling approach for semantic integration and evolution of static and dynamic aspects of conceptual models. Visualization of interplay among structural, interactive and behavioral aspects of computation-neutral representations helps to understand crosscutting concerns and integrity problems of information system conceptualizations. The main advantage of the presented conceptual modeling approach is stability and flexibility of diagrams in dealing with the evolutionary changes of requirements. Therefore, the developed modeling foundation is targeted to both business managers and information system designers for the purpose of computation-neutral integration and evolution of information systems specifications.

DOI: 10.4018/978-1-4666-4161-7.ch007

INTRODUCTION

Information system architectures can be defined on various granularity levels and expressed by modeling views, which are normally represented by using different types of diagrams. It is common to the industrial versions of system analysis and design methods to distinguish disparate views and dimensions of enterprise architecture (Zachman, 1987). The Zachman framework can be viewed as taxonomy for understanding of different types of diagrams. It defines various dimensions of business application and data architectures such as What, How, Who, Where, When and Why. Integrity of different architecture views and dimensions is a fundamental problem in most Information System (IS) methodologies. Semiformal IS modeling methods such as structured analysis and design (Gane & Sarson, 1979; DeMarco, 1979; Yourdon & Constantine, 1979) are plagued by the paradigm mismatch between static and dynamic types of diagrams, which represent business processes and business data in isolation.

Object-oriented design (Booch et al., 1999) languages were introduced to overcome the integrity problems of static and dynamic aspects. Unified Modeling Language (UML) (OMG, 2010) provides various types of diagrams, which are applied for representation of interactive, behavioral and structural aspects of information system specifications. Every modeling approach, which covers a collection of different diagrams, must contain a systematic method for detection of inter-model inconsistency and incompleteness. The static and dynamic aspects of IS specifications are complimentary and they cannot be analyzed in isolation. The structural aspects describe characteristics of objects, which are invariant in time. The interactive and behavioral aspects describe dynamic characteristics of objects over time. All object-oriented design languages are based on collections of meta-models (Glinz, 2000). There is often semantic discontinuity and overlapping in IS specifications, because static and dynamic

constructs of meta-models and notations do not fit perfectly. Semantic integrity of diagrams is difficult to achieve in this situation. This problem was addressed in the development of the Archi-Mate language, which can be used for bridging from business to Information Technology (IT) layers of enterprise system architecture (Jonkers et al., 2004). A number of ontologically grounded modeling rules proposed by Evermann and Wand (2009) are necessary to achieve integrity among UML diagrams. However, enforcing these rules using such de facto standard as UML is still quite problematic. Principles of interplay among UML constructs, which define semantics of business processes and business data, are not completely clear.

Working with the collections of meta-models is more cumbersome for the achievement of semantic modeling quality (Lindland et al., 1994). Semantic integrity problems can be measured in terms of semantic inconsistency and incompleteness between specifications on various levels of abstraction. Inter-model consistency is hard to achieve for non-integrated model collections. Modeling techniques that are realized as collection of models are more difficult to comprehend for system analysis experts who are responsible for business alignment with implementation-oriented architectural descriptions of enterprise systems. UML was developed with the ultimate goal of unifying the best features of the graphical modeling languages and creating a de facto industry standard for object-oriented software design. Recently, UML started to evolve into a language for business and enterprise modeling. However, the decomposition principles and principles of separation of crosscutting concerns (Jacobson & Ng, 2005) are ambiguous in UML. This situation contributes to a more complicated process for introducing and managing evolutionary changes of information system conceptualizations. Semantic integration principles of interactive, structural and behavioral aspects of IS specifications are not completely clear in UML. The treatment of these deficiencies would require modification of the UML foundation. Introducing fundamental changes in UML, with the purpose of integration of collection of models, is a complex research activity. However, such attempts would allow using UML as a computation-neural conceptual modeling language. It is necessary for understanding and reasoning about enterprise system architectures (Finkelstein, 2004) across organizational and IT system boundaries. It is recognized that UML support for such task is vague, because semantic integration principles of different diagram types are lacking (Harel & Rumpe, 2004).

Understanding the needs of an enterprise organizational system in the early analysis stages of a system development projects requires knowledge about stakeholders, their goals, interactions, and alternative actions (Horkoff & Yu, 2010). i* models are intended to facilitate analysis of the system domain with an emphasis on social aspects by providing a graphical description of actor intentions and actor dependencies in terms of tasks or resource exchange (Yu, 1997). Such models offer a way to systematically capture essential information about business processes in a graphical form, which constantly evolves through continued elicitation. Gordijn et al. (2006) uses comparisons of i*-like models to e3 value models for requirements analysis of enterprise models and networks. Value models capture the essential characteristics of business models that can be represented as compositions of organizational components and value exchange activities. The explicit modeling of interactions and value flows is crucial in system development. Interactions, which are represented by data, decision or material flows, are very useful for information system architects to comprehend the details of crosscutting concerns and to provide smooth transition from system analysis to system design.

Most conceptual modeling methods that are intended for business process modeling do not use explicitly the concept of value flow. Value models, which include resource exchange activities among actors, can be viewed as fundamental design guidance for the alignment of organizational processes with the supporting IT operations. The declarative nature of value flows is very useful from a system analysis point of view for the simple reason that they have very little to do with the dependencies between business activities (Johannesson et al., 2010). In other words, the particular strength of value flows is their usefulness for separation of crosscutting concerns among organizational and technical subsystems. Each value flow between a service requester and a service provider can be further analyzed in terms of internal behavioral and structural changes of objects. Flow modeling constructs are quite comprehensible for business experts and thus they are suitable for discussing new configurations of business processes with enterprise architects, IS designers and even system users. Typically, stakeholders distinguish among the past, current and future conceptualizations of processes that can be expressed on different levels of abstraction. Nevertheless, most business process modeling methods do not deal with the notion of value flow, which demonstrates value exchange among actors involved in business processes (Gordijn et al., 2000).

Data flow modeling in terms of Data Flow Diagrams (DFD) was the strength of structured analysis and design methods (Gane & Sarson, 1979; Yourdon & Constantine, 1979). UML also supports various types of associations between classes, actors and use cases, or between objects such as software or hardware components. However, UML and DFD are not suitable for modeling direct associations between actors, which can be captured by value models. Modeling value and data flows between organizational enterprise subsystems is awkward in UML. It is not completely clear how coordinating service interactions, which are necessary for the initiation of value flows, can be explicitly defined by the conventional IS analysis and design methods. The DEMO method provides a strong foundation for interaction based thinking (Dietz, 2006). However, the DEMO modeling foundations are currently not rooted in the traditional IS modeling techniques. It would be quite beneficial to explicitly capture coordinating interaction, data or value flow dependencies in interplay with the conventional conceptual modeling constructs. Interaction dependencies (Gustas, 2010) are very useful for the development of an integrated graphical representation of business process and business data. Service interaction flows are also important for the identification of essential crosscutting concerns in business processes, which span across organizational and technical system boundaries.

Clear decomposition principles allow designers to construct systems that have a comprehensible structure. The separation of crosscutting concerns contributes to more flexible ways for introducing evolutionary extensions to meet evolving needs of stakeholders. In the software engineering community, many scholars believe in use-case-driven approach (Jacobson & Ng, 2005). They recommend use cases as a technique for the separation of crosscutting concerns, since the realization of use cases touches several classes. Information system designers often focus on business use case modeling. A business use case is described in computation-free terminology, which characterizes the business process that is used by actors to achieve their goals (e.g., paper review process management, payment processing). In more general terms, use case is a unit of functionality that a system can provide for organizational or technical actors. It can be specified by conceptualizing interactions, activities, and state changes in various classes of objects. A coherent use case represents information system functionality that typically helps to achieve one goal. Many business activities are complex processes, which can be defined by communication actions between actors involved. Every actor may play two roles: either agent or recipient. A use case is the specification of a set of actions performed by a system, which yields an observable result for one or more actors (OMG, 2010). Such actors are both requesters and consumers of results. Use cases are performed by a system and they are suitable to represent functionality of computerized system. Such requirement typically enforces early implementation-related modeling decisions. This is one of the reasons why computation neutral alignment of business processes with use cases is difficult to achieve or to comprehend for business modelers who are not thinking in use-case-oriented terms. Quite often business activities do not match well with the implementation-oriented functionality of use cases. It is difficult to separate crosscutting concerns of business activities between organizational actors and to link them to the conventional diagram types, which express related behavioral effects of IT operations.

An enterprise system is a composition of organizational and technical (software and hardware) subsystems. Every subsystem partitions an enterprise system into parts, which can be loosely coupled with other subsystems without detailed knowledge of their internal structure. In UML, a subsystem, as a behavioral unit, may also be interpreted by designers as a container. Containers of model elements are components, packages and subsystems. Subsystems sometimes can be interpreted as classes, which are composed of more specific classes and characterized by a set of their own associations, operations and attributes. The system decomposition must be strictly partitioned. Designers should not be allowed to allocate model elements in two different places. Furthermore, UML does not provide clear superimposition principles of active (subsystems, actors, components) and passive elements (meta-classes, classes, objects). There is very little research done on how the structural aspects and state dependent behavior of objects and components should be combined together. The lack of the semantic integrity among different types of diagrams creates difficulties in detection of discontinuities and breakdowns in business processes, because the knowledge on orchestration or choreography of business interactions is missing.

The isolation of IS architecture views and dimensions creates difficulties in detecting inconsistencies among requirements by business experts, who determine the organizational strategies. Consequently, the traditional information system methodologies are not able to bridge a communication gap among business experts and IT-system designers. A semantically integrated model provides several advantages. The integrity control rules can be introduced directly into the model. Particular views and specific types of diagrams, which define the structural, behavioral or interactive aspects, can be generated by producing projections of an integrated model. The ArchiMate standard (Lankhorst et al., 2010) of The Open Group can be considered as a strong candidate for the interaction based reasoning. The purpose of the ArchiMate language was improved alignment of business models with the application specific design. Despite of this fact, the lack of conceptual modeling approach, which can be used for detection of semantic integrity problems among various types of specifications, is the cornerstone of frustration for information system architects.

This paper demonstrates how interaction dependencies among organizational components can be integrated with the behavioral and structural aspects of IS conceptual representations. Conceptual models that put into a foreground service interactions should make sense not just for IS designers in implementation-oriented domains, but also for business modeling experts, which are focused on the computation-neutral analysis of organizations. The presented modeling approach shares many similarities with the ontological foundation of service process (Ferrario & Guarino, 2008) as well as similarities with the basic principles of an ontological framework developed by Bunge (Bunge, 1979). In this paper, we present a modeling approach for semantic integration and evolution of interactive, structural and behavioral aspects of conceptual models. The traditional IS methodologies are quite weak in integrating interaction dependencies with the related behavioral effects and representing consequences if commitments in delivering value flows are broken. Early graphical representations of IS conceptualizations can be defined in terms of interaction flows (Gustas & Gustiene, 2009) among enterprise components that keep system viable. Modeling of service interactions is crucial from system analysis and design point of view for several reasons. Explicit interaction modeling helps to develop integrated graphical representation of business process and business data, which is very relevant for reasoning about the interplay of behavioral and structural aspects of information system specifications. Identification of interaction dependencies between actors is important for motivating object transition events and effects. Interaction models also provide enterprise architects with a clear understanding of crosscutting concerns and help them to move smoothly from IS analysis to design, without requirement to represent a complete solution.

MODELING OF INTERACTIVE AND BEHAVIORAL ASPECTS

Many textbooks in the area of systems analysis and design recommend concentrating first on the structural aspects of domain modeling that are based on specification of classes, attributes and associations. The second step is typically the analysis of behavioral aspects of the domain that are expressed in terms of events, state transitions and their related effects. Finally, it is recommended to start modeling interactive aspects. Interactions are often considered as the third leg of the modeling tripod (Blaha & Rumbaugh, 2005). State modeling can be viewed as reductionist projection of behavior, because both states and interactions are necessary to describe behavior fully. Separation of modeling views creates difficulties in detecting semantic integrity problems in various collections of diagrams, because the dependencies between interaction events and effects of structural changes are missing.

Many designers consider drawing use case diagrams as an excellent starting point of system analysis. However, use case diagrams are typically not augmented with a specification of business events, which advance business process states and help stakeholders to understand related behavioral effects. Therefore, many world-class modelers downplay use case diagrams in the early requirement engineering phases. Instead they focus on writing scenarios (Larman, 2009). Another problem is that a use case diagram enforces early implementation related decisions about a technical system boundary and its environment, which is defined in terms of organizational and technical actors. Any conceptual representation should follow the basic conceptualization principle (Griethuisen, 1982) in representing only computation-neutral aspects that are not influenced by possible implementation solutions. Violation of this principle results in a higher complexity and a reduced flexibility of diagrams. In other words, the comprehensibility of domain is compromised for technical reasons. We believe that analyzing interplay of the interactive, behavioral and structural aspects of IS specifications helps to introduce a new approach to conceptual modeling. One of the goals of this paper is to question the conventional way of system analysis and design. We will demonstrate a different way of reasoning in modeling interplay of static and dynamic relations among concepts. A small case study on a conference review management system will be used as a running example to illustrate modeling constructs and their expressive power. The initial graphical description of a conference review management system components and their interactions are defined by the sequence diagram, which is presented in Figure 1.

This diagram matches our initial description of a conference management system. It is as follows: One of the authors plays the role of *contact person* who *submits* a paper to a conference. The responsibility of a conference program committee (*PC*) *chair* is to *appoint reviewers* for every submission. The *reviewer* is obliged to *return review* of the paper to the *PC chair* on time. Depending on the reviewing outcome, the *PC Chair* is authorized to *accept* or *reject* a submitted paper. If the paper is accepted, then revision instructions are sent to the corresponding *contact person*. Otherwise, reviewer comments are included in the rejection letter. It is important to note that this brief natural language specification explains the organizational process and data resources in interplay with each other. However, the modeling techniques of most conventional approaches project the static and dynamic aspects of IS specifications into different types of diagrams.

There are a few unconventional features related to the diagram, which is presented in Figure 1. The boxes such as: Contact_Person: PC_Chair and: Reviewer are roles, not objects in the traditional understanding of object-oriented design. Contact Person, PC Chair and Reviewer are organizational

Figure 1. Main interactions of a conference review management system

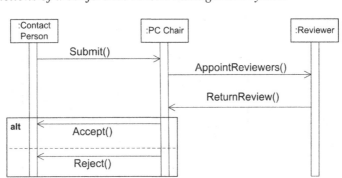

components, which are called actors in UML. Actors are typically placed outside the technical system boundary in a use case diagram. The second violation of common rules is that the presented actions Submit, AppointReviewers, ReturnReview, Accept and Reject are not use cases in the traditional understanding. A use case typically represents functionality, which is performed by the system, to yield an observable result to one particular actor (Jacobson & Ng, 2005). Note that every interaction presented in the sequence diagram is related to two actors: agent and recipient. Thus, the corresponding communication action spans few swimlanes of activity diagram.

Use case, sequence or activity diagrams with swimlanes can be used to represent the dynamic aspects of processes. Business modeling experts typically split higher level business related actions either into more detailed activities or use cases, which fit one of the UML diagram types. System designers express business related activities in terms of the bottom level operations, which manipulate only one type of object. All business activities, which are presented in the previous diagram, are communication actions, which cannot be placed precisely on a single swimlane of activity diagram, because a communication action binds two actors. For instance, the meaning of

requirement 'The *reviewer* is obliged to *return review* of the paper to the *PC chair* on time' can be explained as follows:

- Reviewer is an agent, who is responsible for triggering the *Return Review* action,
- PC Chair is a recipient of *Review* flow, which is delivered by using this action.

An example of a corresponding lower granularity activity diagram with swimlanes is represented in Figure 2.

As it is illustrated in the presented activity diagram, one business interaction between two organizational actors is broken down into sub-activities, which span across two swimlanes. The presented higher granularity business process states such as *Submit*, *Appoint Reviewers*, *Return Review*, *Accept* and *Reject* do not fit the syntactic constructs of the language. Another distinctive feature of the return review action is that it should be triggered concurrently by one or more reviewers, which were appointed by the PC Chair for a specific paper. In other words, this action is multiple. Multiplicity of processes is difficult to express in conventional modeling approaches. Multiple and iterative invocation are two different things.

Figure 2. Lower granularity activities in a conference review management system

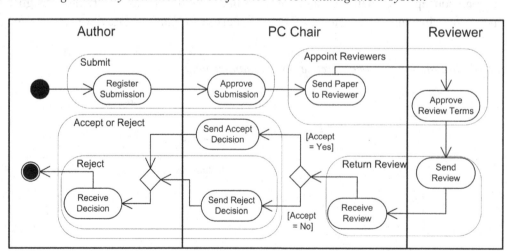

Communication actions are represented by super activities, which should be excluded from the presented activity diagram. The finer granularity activities such as *Register Submission, Approve Submission*, etc., can be included without any problems into activity diagram. In summary, the higher granularity process states must be excluded from UML diagrams for two major reasons:

1. All these activities do not fit well the use case definition (OMG, 2010), because they are communication actions between two actors. Designers normally place focus on a use case functionality, which is performed by the system.
2. Designers are interested in the bottom level operations, which are invoked on one type of object. The identification of object-oriented operations is crucial in designing class, state and sequence diagrams. The presented com-

munication actions can be decomposed into several operations, which are able to change structural properties of different objects.

Although the described higher granularity business process states do not fit well the constructs of a use case diagram, they represent the communication actions, which are crucial for understanding the crosscutting concerns of an enterprise system. Interaction flows between actors cannot be explicitly captured by a use case diagram. An example of the convoluted design, which is built by using lower granularity activities, is presented in Figure 3.

Many designers consider a use case diagram as an excellent picture of the system context. The problem is that the presented diagram cannot explicitly capture the semantic details of the interaction links that are denoted by complementary dash arrows in two opposite directions. The

Figure 3. Use case diagram, which is composed of the lower granularity activities

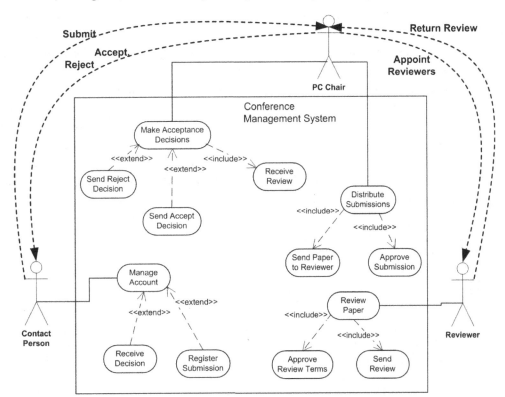

presented interaction dependencies cannot be expressed by the use case diagram, which represents a boundary between the technical system and its environment. The environment is defined in terms of organizational and technical actors, which are placed outside a boundary. For example, Contact Person, PC Chair and Reviewer represent the organizational actors of the conference management system. Such use case representation is more implementation-oriented as compared with the diagram presented in Figure 1. The use case diagram represent functionality (see *Distribute Submissions*, *Review Paper*, *Manage Account* and *Make Acceptance Decisions*), which is not explicitly linked with the initially introduced communication actions: *Submit*, *Appoint_Reviewers*, *Return_Review*, *Accept* and *Reject*. Therefore, such use case centered thinking would create difficulties in detecting dependencies among business activities. It is not clear how the presented use cases can be aligned with the interaction flows, which are illustrated in Figure 1.

Parallel, sequential, exclusive or iterative use case execution can be specified by using activity diagrams. Normally, this type of specification is not associated with use case diagrams. There are two important reasons for staying away from use case diagrams in the initial phase of conceptual modeling. They are as follows:

1. Use case diagrams cannot explicitly capture interaction flows between actors. In the presented example (see Figure 3), use cases require distinguishing between sub-processes, which are relevant for each individual actor. If the presented core communication actions cannot be captured by use case diagrams, then the continuity of service interactions is not easy to comprehend and to trace by using other the types object-oriented diagrams.

2. It is not completely clear how to integrate interactive, structural and behavioral aspects together with use cases in a single view.

Business activities typically involve communication actions between agents and recipients. Communication actions can be defined by interaction flows, which are crucial for understanding the crosscutting concerns between various organizational or technical system components. Interactive aspects must be explicitly captured by information systems specifications, because they provide a natural way of decomposition into business process states. Interaction flows are important for motivating state transition events and effects. The presented five interactions (see Figure 1) can be viewed as triggering events in various state transition diagrams. State diagrams define behavior of various classes of objects. Behavioral aspects can be represented as series of events, which may occur in one or more possible states. State transitions are triggered by events, which specify the permissible ways for changes to occur. Graphical example of the corresponding state transition diagram is presented in Figure 4.

This diagram represents states and state transitions of a *Paper* class object. State transitions are associated with events, which originate from

Figure 4. Events and transitions of a paper object

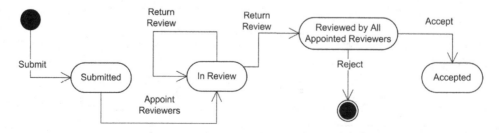

five interactions in a conference management system. Communication actions in this diagram are interpreted as triggering events: *Submit, AppointReviewers, ReturnReview, Accept* and *Reject*. The main problem with this diagram is that it does not represent how state transitions are related to service commitments between actors (Chopra et al., 2010). Interactions and states are necessary to describe behavior fully. However, use case diagrams just partially visualize interactive side of business processes, which are not augmented with specification of state related behavior. Some more details can be described by using activity, state and class diagrams. The main goal of the next three sections is to demonstrate dependencies between interaction flows and related structural changes of objects. These dependencies will serve as a basis for the integration of different types of diagrams.

DEPENDENCIES BETWEEN ACTORS

The ontological principles developed by Bunge (1979) are fundamental for the motivation of various conceptual modeling constructs of our integrated modeling approach. Bunge suggests viewing a system as composition of subsystems, which are understood as interacting components. Every subsystem can be loosely coupled by interactions to other subsystems. When subsystems interact, they cause certain things to change. Changes can be manifested via properties. Any subsystem can be viewed as an object, but not every object is a subsystem. According to Bunge, just interacting things (which cause objects to change) can be viewed as subsystems. It is quite beneficial to analyze interactions between subsystems for keeping track of crosscutting concerns and for justification of subsystems. It should be noted that the basic underlying principle in UML is to provide separate projections, which are represented by the interactive, behavioral and structural views of models.

Enterprise systems can be analyzed as compositions of technical and organizational components, which can be represented by various types of actors. Organizational components are interacting subsystems such as individuals, organizations and their divisions or roles, which denote groups of people. Technical components are represented by enterprise subsystems such as machines, software and hardware. An instance of an actor is an autonomous subsystem. Its existence can only be justified by a set of interaction dependencies with the other subsystems that keep the enterprise system viable. Only actors are able to initiate communication actions, which manipulate objects. This view is a bit different from Bunge's work, but it is fundamental in modeling of organizations (Dietz, 2006). Passive concepts in our approach are denoted by classes of objects, which represent data at rest. All passive concepts are characterized by mandatory attributes. Objects of passive concepts can be affected by interacting subsystems, which are able to perform specific services on request.

The ontological foundation of our modeling approach is based on the set of semantic dependencies between active concepts, which are viewed as enterprise actors. Actors are represented by subsystems that are non-overlapping in functionality. Active concepts can be related by the static dependencies such as inheritance, composition and classification (Gustas, 2010; Gustas & Gustiene, 2009; Gustas & Gustiene, 2008). The graphical notation of semantic dependencies is presented in Figure 5.

Figure 5. Notation of semantic dependencies between actors

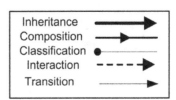

Conceptual models, which include material, information or decision flows, are not difficult to understand for business professionals and for information system designers. Interaction dependencies are helpful for clarifying why actors are willing to exchange value flows with each other. The majority of conceptual modeling methods are not able to capture explicitly interaction flows between actors. Actions and flows can be viewed as fundamental elements for defining business scenarios. A scenario is an excellent means for describing the order of interactions. Each interaction dependency between actors can be analyzed separately as is required by the principle of separation of crosscutting concerns. In such a way, service interactions provide a natural way of process decomposition. Interaction dependency between two actors B and C, which is represented by R (B → C), indicates that the subsystem denoted by B is able to perform action R on one or more subsystems of C. For example, the PC Chair is entitled to Appoint Reviewers. This de-

pendency can be represented as follows: AppointReviewers (PC chair → Reviewer). It does not mean that a reviewer must always accept to review every paper, which is appointed by the PC chair. But if the reviewer accepts the *Appoint Reviewers* action, then he enters into a commitment (Chopra et al., 2010) to *Return Review* into the opposite direction (see Figure 6). Sending of the review flow (see Figure 7) by Reviewer to PC chair can be triggered by Return Review communication action, which is represented by the following interaction dependency: ReturnReview (Reviewer → PC chair). If so, then the Reviewer, which is viewed as an organizational subsystem, is using the Return Review action for satisfying social commitment for PC chair. The Return Review action can be implemented in various ways. For instance, the review can be sent using a post office or an e-mail service. In our case, a conference management system is used for this purpose.

Figure 6. Dependencies among actors in a conference management system

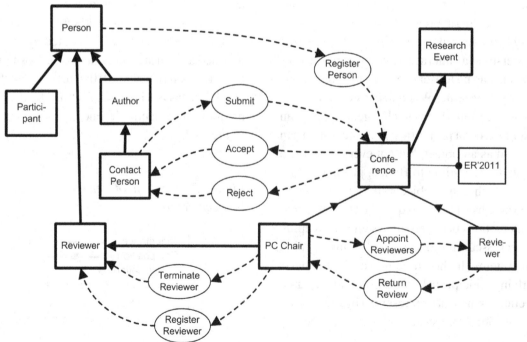

Figure 7. Main actors and interactions in a conference management system

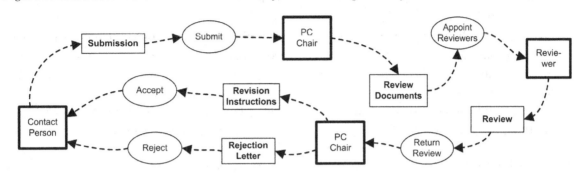

Actors are specialized or decomposed by using inheritance, classification and composition dependencies. Inheritance dependency ($\Rightarrow$) and composition dependencies (—>—) can be used for reasoning about sharing the static and dynamic dependencies between active and passive concepts. Square rectangles will be used for the representation of active concepts. Active concepts are actors, which are connected by the interaction dependencies. For example, interaction dependencies are inherited or propagated by the following semantic links:

Contact Person $\Rightarrow$ Author, Reviewer $\Rightarrow$ Person, PC chair $\Rightarrow$ Reviewer,

PC chair —>— Conference, Reviewer —>— Conference.

Interaction, composition, classification and inheritance dependencies of a conference management system are represented in Figure 6.

The classification dependency ($\bullet$—) specifies objects or subsystems as instances of concepts. Classification is often referred to as instantiation, which is the reverse of a classification. It should be noted that in the object-oriented approaches, classification is a more restricted relation. It can only be defined between an object and a class. A class cannot play the role of an object. Instances of concepts propagate to the more generic concepts in the inheritance hierarchy. This feature is defined by the following rule:

If A $\bullet$— B and B $\Rightarrow$ C then A $\bullet$— C.

Here: $\Rightarrow$ is inheritance dependency and $\bullet$— is classification dependency.

Actors have their own instances, which play the role of subsystems. For example, ER'2011 is an instance of the *Conference* concept. Instances can be basic or derived. If (ER'2011$\bullet$— Conference) and (Conference $\Rightarrow$ Research Event) then (ER'2011$\bullet$— Research Event).

Every instance of an actor is a subsystem, which is characterized by the set of possibilities and obligations that are defined for this actor. Conceptual models of service interactions can be used to analyze actor possibilities and obligations, which are represented by the interaction dependencies. For instance, the Submit action can be viewed as a possibility for sending a submission to ER'2011 by a Contact Person. Submission approval is typically delegated to the PC chair. If the submission is approved, then the PC chair is obliged to Appoint Reviewers.

Composition dependency (—>—) as presented in this paper, differs significantly from the object-oriented composition. It is a much stricter form of aggregation, which allows just either 1 or 1..* multiplicities between parts of the same whole. Other cases of conventional composition are not legal. It means that parts and wholes cannot be optional. The most important distinctive features of the presented composition dependency, which differentiates it from the other type's whole-part dependencies, are as follows:

1. A part is existence dependent on a whole,
2. If a whole has a single part, then this part has an identical lifetime with the whole,
3. If a whole has more than one part, then the creation of the first part is coincident with the creation of the whole, the creation and removal of additional parts can take place any time, but the removal of the last part is coincident with removal of the whole (Guizzardi 2007),
4. Coincident creation and removal of a whole together with all parts is a special case of composition,
5. A part can belong to only one whole of the same type. It should be noted that the optional cases of aggregation and composition can always be transformed into this stricter type of composition with the help of special modeling techniques (Gustas, 2010).

Composition hierarchies can be used for the detection of inconsistent interaction dependencies between actors. Interaction links between loosely coupled actors on the lower level of decomposition are propagated to the compositional wholes. Loosely coupled actors do not belong to the same decomposition hierarchy and they are linked exclusively by the interaction dependency. The composition links can be used for reasoning about derived interaction dependencies between actors on the higher granularity levels of specification. The interaction dependencies between actors, which are placed in two different composition hierarchies, are characterized by the following inference rules:

1. If A —>— B and R(A → C) then R(B → C),
2. If A —>— B and R(C → A) then R(C → B).

For example, if Contact Person submits a paper to PC chair, then it is submitted to a conference as well. This fact can be derived by the following rule: If (PC chair —>— Conference) and Submit(Contact Person → PC Chair) then Submit(Contact Person → Conference). The concept of Conference is decomposed into such organizational components as PC Chair and Reviewer. Initiation of the Accept or Reject action is delegated to PC Chair. Note that service interactions, which are specified on different granularity levels, must be consistent. Actors, actions and flows of consistent service interactions cannot be contradictory. For instance, service interaction flows, which are represented in Figure 7, are consistent with the dependencies of the previous conceptualization. The interaction dependencies in Figure 6 are incomplete, because they are not representing types of information flows that are exchanged between actors.

The inheritance dependency between two actors indicates that they share the static and dynamic similarities. The more specific actors always inherit composition and interaction dependencies from the more generic actors. In the object-oriented approaches, the inheritance applies just for attributes, relationships, constraints and operations. In our modeling approach, inheritance dependency can be used for sharing service interactions of more general actors. Inheritance can also be used for sharing the mandatory attributes of passive classes of objects. Interaction dependencies are inherited according to the following inference rules:

1. If A ⇒ B and R(B → C) then R(A → C),
2. If A ⇒ B and R(C → B) then R(C → A).

If an Author is a Person, then Author inherits all service interaction links, which are specified for the Person concept (see the diagram in Figure 6). For example, if (Author ⇒ Person) and Register Person(Person → Conference) then Register Person(Author → Conference). It means that not only a person has possibility to register to a conference. An author can register to a conference as well.

The composition and inheritance dependencies can be used for the detection of inconsistent interaction dependencies on various levels of abstraction (Gustas, 2010). Adding more specific actors must always be justified by the new possibilities or obligations, which can be specified in terms of complementary interaction links. It must be noted that the presented inference rules are useful, but not sufficient for reasoning about inconsistency of service interactions. To understand the deep semantics of service interactions, the behavioral effects and related structural changes of objects should be analyzed together. How to express interplay between business interactions and structural changes in various classes of objects is discussed in the next section.

INTERACTION FLOWS AND STRUCTURAL CHANGES OF OBJECTS

Interaction flows are the special types of passive concepts that represent moving things between actors. Actors may represent organizational and technical components, which are denoted by square rectangles. Actions are represented by ellipses. In our modeling approach, the solid rectangles are used for the denotation of material flows and light boxes will indicate information flows. A hard copy of conference proceedings can be viewed as a material flow that can be delivered to a contact person by a publisher. There are no material flows in the presented graphical description of a conference management system. Only five types of information flows were identified. Actions can be performed by actors. They are necessary for transferring flows between subsystems. In general, an action with a missing information or material flow is understood as a decision or control flow. Various information flows among actors of a conference management system are illustrated in Figure 7.

A contact person has possibility to deliver a submission to PC chair. If the submission is accepted, the responsibility of a conference PC chair is to trigger the *Appoint Reviewers* action, which is used to send the review documents to reviewers. The reviewer is obliged to deliver review to PC chair by triggering the *Return Review* action. The PC Chair is authorized to either *Accept* or *Reject* a submitted paper by informing a contact person with a special letter. The main difference of this diagram in comparison with the previously presented sequence diagram (see Figure 1) is that it additionally shows information flows between various actors. Note that the information flow structure can be also represented by event parameters attached to messages in a sequence diagram. Nevertheless, there are many other fundamental differences between these two types of diagrams, which will be introduced below.

Two kinds of interactions between actors can be distinguished. Interaction flows can be transferred by production and coordination actions (Dietz, 2006). Service requests can be viewed as coordination actions, which are initiated by service requesters. Coordination actions are necessary to make a commitment regarding the corresponding production action. Production actions are normally performed by service providers. The production actions are capable of bringing value to service requester. For example, the *appoint reviewers* action can be viewed as coordination act, which corresponds to service request. The *return review* action can be considered as a production act, because the *review* flow brings value to PC chair. Both service requesters and service providers are viewed as actors, which represent subjects characterized by different goals. Actors are active concepts, which together with interaction flows can be used for understanding the essential organization of an enterprise system. Active and passive entities are considered as disjoint ontological categories, but they represent two different sides of a concept (Gustas, 2010).

Classes, associations and attributes are the most fundamental object-oriented constructs used in UML class diagrams. They are stemming from the conventional conceptual modeling approaches, which were developed to capture how various entities or data types are linked with each other in a conceptual schema. Classes can be understood as a passive side of concept that represents data at rest. Relationships between passive concepts are represented by associations. In the presented example, various classes of objects can be identified according to the initial description of a conference management system. They are as follows: Contact_Person, Submitted_Paper, Reviewing, Reviewer, Review, Accepted_Paper. Structural properties of objects in UML can be defined by attributes, associations, inheritance, aggregation and composition relations between classes, which represent passive concepts. Associations are characterized by association ends and multiplicities (see class diagram in Figure 8).

Domain states can be defined as a collection of attribute values and links an object has with other types of objects. The presented five communication actions (*Submit*, *Appoint Reviewers*, *Return Review*, *Accept* and *Reject*) can be viewed

as triggering events, which can be explicitly linked with various state transition effects. In UML, state transition diagrams define the behavior of objects. State transitions are triggered by events, which specify the permissible ways for various structural changes of objects to occur. The following types of effects can be distinguished in the object-oriented design (Martin & Odell, 1998):

1. Creation or termination of an object,
2. Classification or declassification of an object,
3. Connection or disconnection of a link between two objects.

Effects can be represented by various UML diagrams in a variety of ways. For instance, creation and termination of objects can be represented by transitions from an initial state and to a final state. Connection and disconnection events can be specified by using sequence diagrams. Object interaction sequences are defined in terms of operations. Classification and declassification effects can be implemented by using sequences of object creation, connection, disconnection and termination operations. Classes, associations

Figure 8. Main classes and associations in a conference review management system

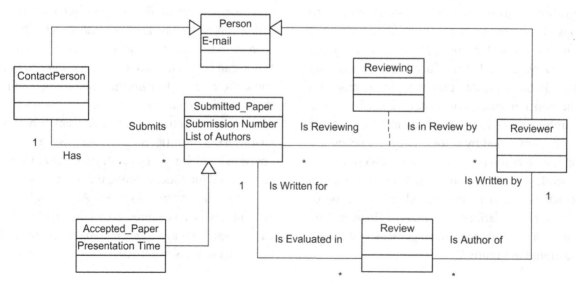

and attributes are necessary for specification the resulting structural changes of objects.

In this section, we will use a natural language text for the specification of all necessary structural changes, which can be viewed as triggering effects of a conference management system. Five sets of behavioral effects, which are resulting from the presented communication actions (see Figure 7), will be further integrated with the structural changes of objects. These structural changes can be explained by the class diagram, which express the static aspects a conference review management system. Structural changes of objects will be explained on the basis of the associations, classes and their attributes, which are represented in Figure 8.

The first event (1) is *Submit* (see Figure 7). It creates the following effects:

1.1. Creation of a submitted paper object, which is characterized by a Submission Number and List of Authors. We assume that an object in the ContactPerson class is already created by the *Register Person* action. The focus of this section is exclusively on effects of communication actions, which are represented in Figure 7. We also assume that designers are interested just in one property of a contact person object. It is represented by the E-mail attribute.

1.2. Creation of a connection link between ContactPerson and Submitted_Paper objects with references in two opposite directions.

The association end names are used for representation of links between two classes of objects. We assume that *Submit* event triggers creation of *Submits* and *Has* references into two opposite directions.

Appoint Reviewers is the second event (2), which triggers creation of object links in the Reviewing association class. Object links are represented by two association ends: *Is Reviewing* and *Is in Review by*. This action is necessary for linking every submitted paper with three or more appointed reviewers. We assume that objects of the *Reviewer* class are created by other communication actions, which are not included into our initial description (for instance, the twelfth figure represents possibility for PC Chair to register a new reviewer).

The related effects of *Return Review* event (3) include creation and termination of objects that can be described as follows:

3.1. Creation of an object in the Review class.

3.2. Creation of references between Submitted_Paper and Review objects in two opposite directions, which are represented by the association end names: *Is Written for* and *Is Evaluated in*,

3.3. Creation of references between Reviewer and Review objects, which are represented by the association end names: *Is Author of* and *Is Written by*,

3.4. Termination of the corresponding object link in the Reviewing association class, which is represented by the association end names: *Is in Review by* and *Is Reviewing*.

The related triggering effects of *Accept* event (4) are as follows:

4.1. Creation of an object in the Accepted Paper class with an additional property of *Presentation Time* (note that the properties *Submission Number* and *List of Authors* are copied from the Submitted Paper object),

4.2. Creation of references between Accepted_Paper and Review objects, which are represented by the association end names: *Is Written for* and *Is Evaluated in*,

4.3. Creation of references between Contact Person and Accepted Paper objects, which are represented by the association end names: *Has* and *Submits*.

4.4. Removal of *Is Written for* reference from a Review to Submitted_Paper object,

4.5. Removal of *Submits* reference from a Contact Person and Submitted Paper object,

4.6. Termination of a redundant object from the Submitted_Paper class.

The triggering effects of the *Reject* event (5) are as follows (this action may differ significantly depending on design decisions). We assume that (in case of rejection) all related information of submitted paper object must be removed:

5.1. Removal of a corresponding reference *Submits* from the Contact Person to Submitted Paper object,

5.2. Removal of corresponding references *Is Author of* from Reviewer to the corresponding Review objects of submitted paper,

5.3. Termination of the Submitted Paper object,

5.4. Termination of all Review objects, which are linked with the corresponding Submitted Paper object.

Each set of the described effects must be synchronized. Otherwise, a situation of data inconsistency may arise. A number of activity or sequence diagrams can be developed for representation of semantic details of the behavioral effects in terms of object-oriented operations. Such diagrams would look very complex and clumsy. However, the semantics of all structural changes can be integrated and visualized in a concise way. We will present these described effects in a single

diagram in interplay with the interaction flows, which are represented in Figure 7.

Behavioral and structural aspects of interactions can be analyzed in terms of reclassification, creation or termination effects. When two subsystems interact one may affect the state of each other (Evermann & Wand, 2009). Structural changes of objects can be defined in terms of object properties. Interaction dependency R(A → B) between two active concepts A and B indicates that A subsystem can perform action R on one or more B subsystems. An action between actors typically manipulates properties of some objects (Gustas & Gustiene, 2009). Otherwise, this action is not useful. Property changes may trigger objects' transitions from one class to another. The internal changes of objects can be expressed by using transition links (—>) between two classes, which represent passive concepts. The graphical notation of the reclassification construct is represented in Figure 9.

Two kinds of fundamental changes occur in a reclassification action: the removal of an object from a pre-condition class and creation of an object in a post-condition class. A reclassification construct with a missing post-condition class is used for representation of termination of object in a pre-condition class. A construct without a precondition class represents object creation in a post-condition class. For example, the *Submit* action can be defined as a creation event and the *Reject* action can be viewed as a termination event.

Figure 9. Construct for representation of reclassification event

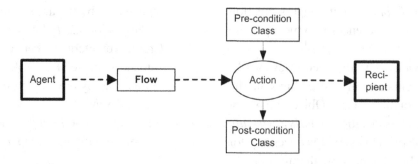

Appoint Reviewers, *Return Review* and *Accept* are reclassification events. Object creation or reclassification without any properties does not make any sense. So, various types of static and dynamic dependencies between classes are used to define mandatory properties of objects. The lack of a noteworthy difference between a pre-condition and post-condition class indicates that the specification of a communication action is either incomplete or a communication action is not purposeful. The pre-condition and post-condition classes are typically characterized by two different sets of mandatory attributes, which are sufficient for representing the permissible ways in which changes may occur. The static dependencies such as inheritance, composition, single-valued and multi-valued mandatory attributes are sufficient to visually recognize and comprehend the details of various interaction effects. The graphical notation of concept dependencies is presented in Figure 10.

One significant difference of the presented modeling approach in comparison with the traditional methods is that all dependencies are nameless. Objects are defined exclusively in terms of their properties. The association end names are eliminated in our modeling approach. The main reason for introducing nameless attribute dependencies is improving stability of conceptualizations. If concepts are used to model an association end, then the resulting diagrams may be unstable. From the evolutionary perspective, any concept may be interpreted as an attribute, association end or a class. In the presented modeling approach, the interpretation of a concept as a class, attribute or association is flexible. The interpretation depends on the collection of dependencies, which are specified at the specific moment of time. Additionally, any concept can be specialized by using special conditions or states. Class can also be viewed as an exclusive complete generalization of other concepts.

The presented set of semantic dependencies is sufficient for the unambiguous specification of creation, reclassification or termination effects. These effects are fundamental for the integration of behavioral and structural aspects of interactions into a single conceptual representation. Rules for analysis of creation, termination and reclassification effects are presented in the next section. One of the challenges of this paper is to demonstrate how to integrate the semantics of all five types of events and five set of related structural changes of objects into a single conceptual representation of reasonable size. The remaining part of this paper presents the modeling approach, which combines interactive, behavioral and related structural object changes into one type of computation-neutral diagram. The outcome of an integration process may result in a huge diagram. It can be divided in smaller diagrams according to the principles of decomposition and principles of separation of crosscutting constraints. Any integrated diagram can be also projected into the isolated subsets of structural, behavioral or interactive viewpoints.

Figure 10. Graphical notation of dependencies between concepts

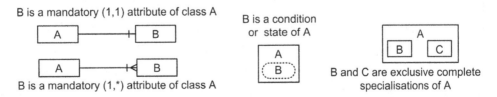

INTEGRATION OF OBJECT BEHAVIOR AND STRUCTURAL ASPECTS OF INTERACTION EFFECTS

One of the most general ontological definitions of a system is provided by Bunge (1979). It served as a theoretical basis for understanding the notions of organization and enterprise ontology (Dietz, 2006). Bunge's ontological foundation is important for the motivation of semantic integration and decomposition principles of our conceptual modeling method. They are as follows:

- An enterprise system is a composition of subsystems, which are represented by various actors.
- Every actor can be loosely coupled by interaction dependencies to other actors.

- When subsystems interact, they cause certain things to change. Changes are manifested via properties.

The behavioral, interactive and structural dependencies of the previously analyzed diagrams can be merged into a single conceptual representation, which is presented in Figure 11. This conceptualization integrates the semantic details of sequence, state transition, class diagrams (see Figures 1, 2, 4, and 8) and includes all interaction flows (see Figure 7) with related five sets (1, 2, 3, 4, 5) of object creation/termination effects, which are listed in the previous section.

Only computation-neutral details of the use case (see the diagram in Figure 3) specification are included in this representation. A transition arrow from or to an action represents a control flow, which defines termination and/or creation

Figure 11. Interactive, behavioral and structural aspects of a conference management system

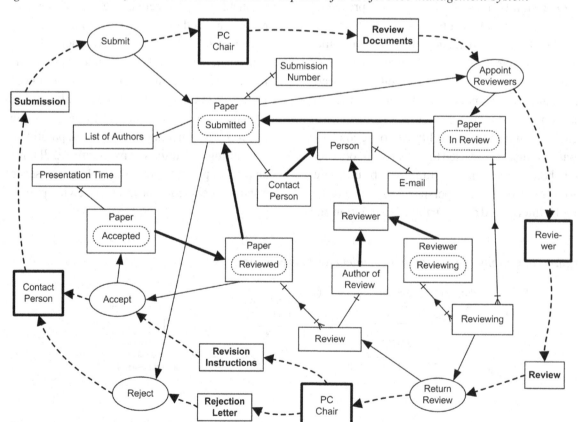

of various types of objects. A diagram showing object transitions and flows with states has most of the advantages of activity, state, sequence and class diagrams without most of their disadvantages when analyzed in isolation. Each action is used to superimpose interaction and object transition effects in a single diagram. Various combinations of the presented dependencies are fundamental for understanding sequences, alternatives, synchronizations or iterations of object creation, reclassification and termination effects. Semantics of interaction effects cannot be analyzed separately from the static aspects of the presented conceptualization.

Composition, inheritance and mandatory attribute dependencies are used for the understanding of creation and termination effects. We will present three types of rules for reasoning about structural changes of objects in relation to the presented set of semantic dependencies between concepts. These rules are divided into three different groups, which can be associated to:

1. Objects and their properties,
2. Composites and their parts and
3. Generalization hierarchies of objects.

Inheritance dependencies (⇒) are useful for reasoning about alternatives of communication action effects. The first group of rules can be used for understanding of the creation and termination effects of objects, which are propagated in the specific generalization hierarchy. Object creation and termination rules (Rule 1.1 and Rule 1.2) can be explained as follows:

Rule 1.1: Objects of more specific classes cannot be created prior creation to more generic objects of classes, which are dependent on other creation actions. For example, a Paper[Accepted] object cannot be created by *Accept* action prior to Paper[Reviewed] object is created by the *Return Review* action. Paper[Reviewed] object cannot be created

prior to a Paper[Submitted] by the *Submit* action. A Paper[in Review] class cannot be created by the *Appoint Reviewers* action prior it is created in the more generic class Paper[Submitted] by the *Submit* action. Corollary: objects, which are instances of more general classes represented as complete generalizations, must be created in one of the more specific non-overlapping classes.

Rule 1.2: Termination of an object in an inheritance hierarchy requires termination of all its specializations. For instance, the termination of a Person object would cause termination of Reviewer, Author of Review and/or termination of a Contact Person (see diagram in Figure 11).

Composition dependencies (—>—) are useful for reasoning about synchronization and iteration of object creation, reclassification and termination effects. Four rules (2.1, 2.2, 2.3, 2.4) can be used for understanding the creation/termination effects of composites and parts. These rules are as follows:

Rule 2.1: Creation of an object requires creation of all its compositional parts. For instance, the *Appoint Reviewers* action requires synchronous creation of Paper[In Review] together with at least one associated object of Reviewing. Note that reviewing object represents reified review process, which links one Paper object and one Reviewer object in the state of Reviewing.

Rule 2.2: Termination of an object requires termination of all its compositional parts. For example, the *Reject* action requires termination of Paper[Submitted] as well as Paper[Reviewed] together with all Review objects as compositional parts.

Rule 2.3: Creation of the first part requires creation of a compositional whole. For example, if the *Return Review* action creates the first Review of a Paper object, it is necessary to synchronously create a Paper[Reviewed] object.

Rule 2.4: Termination of the last part requires termination of a compositional whole. For instance, if the *Return Review* action terminates the last Reviewing object, it is necessary to terminate a compositional whole of a Paper object in Review state (Paper[in Review]). Composition dependency is a strict form of aggregation, which allows just either 1 or 1..* multiplicities between parts and wholes. Other cases of conventional composition are not legal. It means that parts and wholes cannot be optional, a part is always existent dependent on a whole, creation of the first part is coincident with the creation of the whole, and removal of the last part is coincident with the removal of the whole.

The attribute dependencies are useful for reasoning about the sequences of object creation, reclassification and termination effects. So, the third group of rules (3.1 and 3.2) is important for understanding sequences of manipulation effects with objects and their properties. These rules are as follows:

Rule 3.1: A property, which is viewed as an object on its own cannot be created prior to the creation of the object itself. Such objects are represented by the concepts, which are viewed as classes and at the same time as mandatory attributes of other classes.

Rule 3.2: Removal of a mandatory object property causes termination of the object. Corollary: termination of an object, which is viewed as a property of another object, is causing the termination of that object.

Any interaction link can be used for instantiation or removal of objects together with their properties. Some properties are interpreted as objects on their own. Property can play a role of an object, if it is characterized by its own properties. Such objects must be created, prior to be linked as properties of other objects. For example, a Contact Person is a property of Paper [Submitted]. It is also an object, because any Contact Person object is characterized by E-mail, which is inherited from a Person. The instantiation of a Submitted Paper attribute such as Contact Person cannot be accomplished prior to creation of a Contact Person object. The conceptualization, which is presented in Figure 12, can be considered as a consistent extension of the previous diagram. It represents possible ways of creation and termination of various kinds of *Person* objects in a conference review management system.

Note that if the interaction dependencies in Figure 11 are taken into account, then the Submit

Figure 12. Complementary interactions in a conference management system

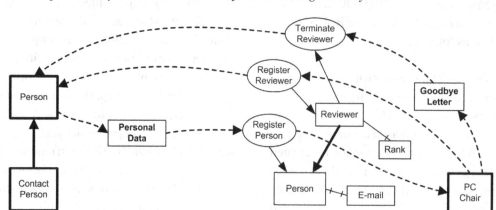

communication action requires, in the first step, creation of a Person object by using the *Register Person* action. Thus, this action can be viewed as the decomposition (like a use case inclusion) of the *Submit* action. If the *Register Person* action is missing, then the effects of *Submit* action can be described as follows:

1. Create a Person with E-mail property,
2. Create Paper [Submitted] with such properties as Submission Number, List of Authors and Contact Person, which is reclassified by using exactly one object of Person (see Figure 11). The *Register Reviewer* action can be also viewed as an optional extension of the *Register Person* action.

Termination of an object requires removal of object properties that are defined by the mandatory attributes of a precondition class. For example, the *Terminate Reviewer* action will cause the removal of Rank, but it is not supposed to remove the E-mail property, because an object of Person is not terminated. Sometimes, termination of object may cause removal of it as a property of another object. The removal of one essential property of an object may be sufficient for violation of some mandatory dependency links, which would cause its termination. Note that termination of an object (it causes removal all its properties) does not mean termination of dependent objects. For example, Contact Person is a property of Paper[Submitted]. Termination of Paper[Submitted] with its contact person property does not mean termination of a Contact Person object, which is characterized by the E-mail property. Nevertheless, the removal of a Person or a Contact Person object would cause termination of the associated Paper[Submitted] objects. In some cases, post-condition class constraints may override termination of a precondition class object. One such a case is the reclassification action with a post-condition class, which is either specialization of the precondition class or the precondition class is viewed as a mandatory

attribute of the postcondition class. In such a case, the inheritance or attribute dependency requires preservation of a precondition class object. For example, the action *Appoint Reviewers* requires the preservation of Paper[Submitted] object. Paper[Submitted] object in this case plays the role of a precondition in the *Appoint Reviewers* action. Yet another example of preservation is the Paper[Reviewed] class in the *Accept* action. Quite often objects are not preserved (see Reviewing class in Figure 11). They may pass several classes and then are terminated.

EVOLUTION OF DIAGRAMS

Conceptual modeling of service interactions is useful for keeping the track of crosscutting concerns among organizational and technical components. We have demonstrated the integrated modeling approach on a small scale example, which represents conceptualization of two service interaction loops in a conference review management system. The first service interaction loop can be specified as follows:

if Submit(Contact Person → PC Chair)
then Accept(PC Chair → Contact Person),
otherwise Reject(PC Chair → Contact Person).

The second service interaction loop is:

if Appoint Reviewers(PC Chair → Reviewer)
then Return Review(Reviewer → Contact Person).

Let us extend the initial description of a conference management system by introducing the following requirement: *a contact person should have a possibility to withdraw a submitted paper at any time*. The *Withdraw* communication action can be viewed as an alternative behavior of a Contact Person. Withdrawal basically means cancellation of a Submit action. It can be expressed by the following interaction dependency:

Withdraw(Contact Person → PC Chair).

Taking into account such new requirement would cause a very simple extension of the integrated diagram, which is represented in Figure 11. The extended diagram contains a new withdraw action between Contact Person and PC chair. It is presented in Figure 13.

The withdraw action is necessary for the termination of Paper[Submitted]. All triggering effects of withdraw action can be visually recognized by using the presented three groups of rules, which are presented in the previous section. The introduced extension looks trivial, because the static dependencies are not affected by introducing this additional requirement. Nevertheless, equivalent changes required to the UML diagrams, which are affected by introducing this new require-

ment, are quite substantial. There are four sets of effects, which can be visually recognized by analyzing the states of a Paper object (see diagram in Figure 13) such as Submitted, In Review, Reviewed and Accepted. Changes that are required to be introduced into activity diagram are presented in Figure 15. It is obvious that the previous state transition diagram (see diagram in Figure 4) needs to be extended with four different Withdraw events, which are marked by numbers 1, 2, 3, 4 in Figure 14.

There are four sets of termination effects, which are not reflected in this diagram. They can be visually recognized by analyzing four states of a paper concept in Figure 13. Four new sequence diagrams have to be introduced for the representation of the semantic details of these effects. Before we go into the further details of object

Figure 13. Four cases of withdrawal in a conference management system

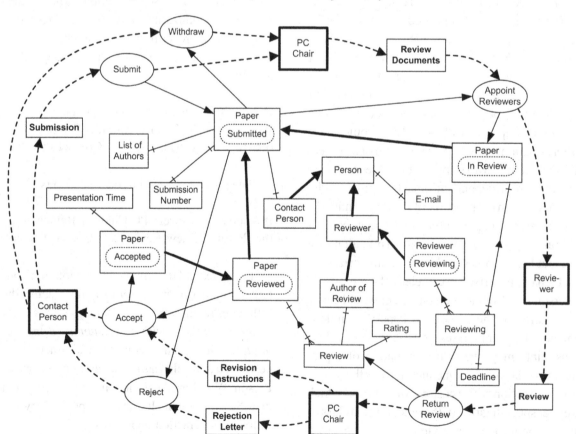

Figure 14. Four cases of withdrawal in a conference management system

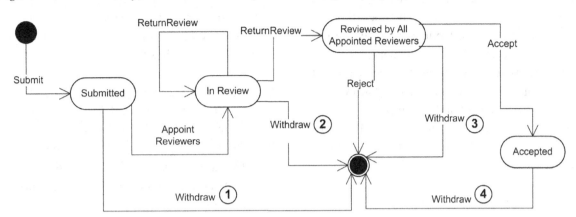

Figure 15. Activity diagram with four different withdraw actions

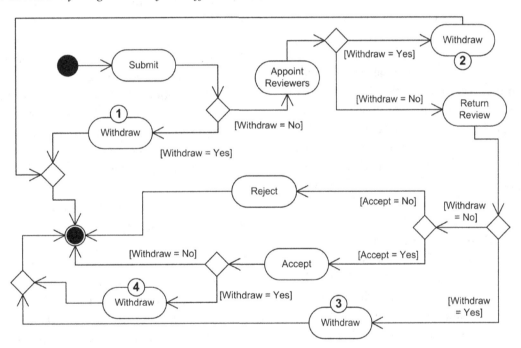

creation/termination effects, some important discrepancies between states, which are presented in the diagrams, should be explained. All states of the state transition diagram are exclusive as it is required by a state chart of this type (Harel, 1987). In object-oriented approaches, objects can be exclusively in one state at a time, unless more complex nested or composite states (Blaha & Rumbaugh, 2005) are introduced. It is not difficult to see that the domain states of the integrated diagram such as *In Review* and *Reviewed* are overlapping (see Figure 13). That is why we have introduced the state '*Reviewed by All Appointed Reviewers*', which is exclusive to the other states in the state transition diagram (see Figure 14 and Figure 4). Note that all states such as Submitted, In Review, Reviewed and Accepted of the integrated diagram (Figure 13) are overlapping. For example, a paper can be *in Review, Reviewed* and *Submitted* at the same time. Sometimes, it is difficult to avoid the overlapping states. In our example, the overlapping naturally depends on the order of initiated interactions between actors. It means that various combinations of states will be caused by the created and terminated objects in the related generalization hierarchies. These hierarchies are defined by the inheritance dependencies such as:

Paper[In Review] ⇒ Paper[Submitted]),

Paper[Reviewed] ⇒ Paper[Submitted]),

Paper[Accepted] ⇒ Paper[Reviewed]).

For instance, the *Return Review* action is multiple. Several reviews can be created for each paper in any order. Nevertheless, the *Return Review* is designed to create one Review object at a time by the assigned Reviewer. This action can only be triggered for each *Paper* object, which appears *In Review* state. Note that the Paper[In Review] concept is linked by the composition dependency with several reified processes of *Reviewing*. Reviewing is also a pre-condition class, which tells us that the *Return Review* action can be repeated (1:M times) for each Paper in Review state (see composition link). In order to represent these semantic details in a state transition diagram, it is necessary to introduce a super state Submitted and to show somehow that a Paper object additionally can be in two states (In Review and Reviewed) at the same time. The overlapping states of the integrated diagram are intrinsic to a conference review management domain, because the appointed reviewers in reality would never return their reviews at the same moment of time. In contrary, all states in Figure 14 are exclusive. So, a *Submitted* Paper cannot be accepted and reviewed at the same time. We will explain the related termination effects of the withdraw action by using associations, classes and their attributes,

which are presented by the class diagram in Figure 8. The triggering effects, which are represented by Withdraw #1 transition (see Figure 14), can be described as follows:

1.1. Termination of the *Submitted Paper* object, which is characterized by a Submission Number and List of Authors,
1.2. Removal of the connection reference from *Contact Person* to *Submitted Paper* object, which is represented by the association end *Submits*.

The triggering effects, which are represented by Withdraw #2 transition (see Figure 14), are as follows:

2.1. The same effects as described in step 1.1,
2.2. The same effects as described in step 1.2,
2.3. Termination of all object links in the *Reviewing* association class must be performed with corresponding *Submitted Paper* object, which includes removal of *Is Reviewing* reference from *Reviewer*.

The following effects are relevant for the Withdraw #3 transition:

3.1. Removal of a reference *Is Author of* from *Reviewer* to *Review* object and termination of a corresponding objects in *Review* class,
3.2. Termination of all object links in the *Reviewing* association class must be performed with a corresponding *Submitted Paper* object, which includes removal of *Is Reviewing* reference from *Reviewer* object,
3.3. The same effects as described in step 1.1,
3.4. The same effects as described in step 1.2.

The triggering effects of step 3.1 and 3.2 can be exclusive, or both steps can be performed with all *Reviewing* and *Review* objects, which are linked with a corresponding *Submitted Paper* object. The removal of properties depends on whether the paper is not reviewed by any reviewer, reviewed by all reviewers or it is still in review by some, but not all reviewers.

Triggering effects, which are represented by Withdraw #4 transition, can be described as follows:

4.1. Removal of a reference *Is Author of* from *Reviewer* to *Review* object,
4.2. Termination of the corresponding *Review* objects,
4.3. Removal of the reference *Submits* from *Contact Person* to *Accepted Paper* object,
4.4. Termination of an *Accepted_Paper* object.

The first version of the activity diagram (see Figure 2) must be substantially extended for the reason of the additional withdrawal requirement. The presented four variations of withdraw actions must be added together with corresponding decision symbols for evaluation of withdrawal conditions after execution of *Submit*, *Appoint Reviewers*, *Return Review* and *Accept* actions. The problem is that the *Withdraw* action cannot be located in one place of the activity diagram, because of the variations in triggered effects. One could argue that such the UML activity diagram extensions, as an interruptible activity region, might be used to represent the Withdraw action. Nevertheless, this construct would totally fail in representing the semantics of four sets of previously listed effects, which are all captured by the integrated diagram in Figure 13. The extended activity diagram together with the corresponding four withdrawal activities and withdrawal conditions is represented in Figure 15.

The presented example demonstrates that even simple evolutionary changes may require significant re-design of object-oriented diagrams. Semantic integration of interactive, behavioral and structural aspects of objects in a single diagram is the advantage of the presented modeling approach. The extensions of a single integrated conceptualization with one alternative action were quite

insignificant. The most important feature of the presented modeling approach is the stability and flexibility of diagrams in dealing with evolutionary changes in the process of system analysis and design. Separating and merging various dimensions of crosscutting concerns is more comprehensive and more effective in the integrated diagrams in comparison with the conventional object-oriented modeling techniques.

CONCLUSION

The conventional information systems analysis and design methods project the structural, interactive and behavioral dimensions of IS specifications into totally different types of diagrams. Most information system design methodologies fail to link interactions with motivating triggering effects, because of separation of static and dynamic aspects of conceptual models. Such separation creates difficulties in the detection of semantic inconsistency and incompleteness of conceptual representations. UML individual diagram types are clear enough, but the semantic integration principles are quite vague. Therefore, the object-oriented diagrams are difficult to apply for business logics alignment with computation-specific design for making both organizational and technical system parts more effective. The presented modeling approach introduces a single type of diagram. It is capable to capture, in concise form, the semantics of the behavioral effects and structural changes, which are justified by the interaction flows across organizational and technical system boundaries. The similarity of conceptual models before and after adding complimentary requirements, demonstrates the stability of the proposed modeling approach when compared with the UML models.

The basic underlying principle in UML is to provide separate models for different modeling dimensions. It is not so easy to superimpose the interactive, structural and behavioral aspects of IS specifications, which are represented using a number of incompatible diagrams. There is a lack of research on how the structural aspects and state dependent behavior of objects should be combined with the use case models. Classes and their associated state machines are regarded as realization of use cases. The possibility to conceptualize interactions, behavior and effects of structural changes in a single type of diagram is not the only benefit of the presented modeling approach. If diagrams are used to communicate unambiguously semantic details of a conceptualized system, then optional properties should be proscribed (Gemino, 1998). The decline in cognitive processing performance, that occurs when optional attributes and relationships are used, appears to be substantial (Bodart et al., 2001). Properties in our modeling approach are expressed as mandatory attribute values. So, the integrated diagrams are able to unambiguously communicate structural changes in various classes of objects.

The presented modeling method puts in the foreground the interaction dependencies between actors. Interaction flows help IS designers to separate the crosscutting concerns of enterprise system components and to semantically integrate the static and dynamic aspects of conceptualizations into a holistic representation. Such integrated modeling approach follows the basic conceptualization principle in representing only computational-neutral aspects, which are not influenced by any implementation related details. Conceptual models, which are centered on material, information and decision flows, are not difficult to understand for business professionals as well as information system designers. Service interactions are helpful for clarifying why actors are willing to exchange business objects with each other. The majority of conventional methods, including object-oriented approaches, are not able to capture explicitly the interaction flows between actors. Actions and flows in the proposed modeling method are viewed as the fundamental elements for defining business scenarios. Each interaction dependency can be analyzed separately as it is required by

the principle of separation of concerns. In such a way, interaction flows provide the natural way of decomposition into business process states. Such computation-neutral representations are easier to comprehend for business experts without a technical background. So, they are more suitable for bridging the communication gap among IS designers and business process integrators.

One of the most important advantages of the presented conceptual modeling approach is stability and flexibility of diagrams in dealing with evolutionary changes of requirements. Our studies demonstrate that separation and merging of crosscutting concerns in the integrated diagrams is more efficient in comparison with the conventional modeling techniques. This was demonstrated on one simple example of a conference review management system. The semantically equivalent changes required for representing one alternative communication action by the traditional activity, state transition and sequence diagrams were quite substantial. It should be noted that there are a number of other modeling approaches, which focus on analyzing interactivity. A starting point of the enterprise modeling language ArchiMate (Lankhorst et al., 2010) as well as the DEMO approach (Dietz, 2006) is stemming from this modeling tradition. Nevertheless, just few emerging approaches are making attempts to express the deep semantics of interplay (Dori, 2002) between dynamic and static aspects of IS conceptualizations.

Analyzing various diagrams in isolation creates difficulties in detecting requirement conflicts by business experts, who determine the organizational strategies. Consequently, information system methodologies are not able to bridge a communication gap among business experts and IT-system designers. The presented modeling approach for semantic integration of static and dynamic aspects provides several advantages. It is based on a single diagram type and therefore the semantic integrity rules are embedded directly into the modeling foundation. The particular views, which define structural, behavioral or interactive aspects, can be generated by producing the desired projections of an integrated model. Currently, the lack of conceptual modeling approach, which can be used in information system development industry for the detection of semantic integrity problems among various types of diagrams, is the cornerstone of frustration for enterprise system integrators and IS architects. Our initial studies demonstrate that a single semantically integrated model suits better for detection of discontinuity, inconsistency and incompleteness of IS specifications. The proposed modeling principles can be used to significantly reduce enterprise system architecture evolution complexity.

ACKNOWLEDGMENT

The author is grateful to Dr. Giancarlo Guizzardi for his accurate, fundamental and extensive comments on the initial version of this paper.

REFERENCES

Blaha, M., & Rumbaugh, J. (2005). *Object-Oriented Modeling and Design with UML*. London: Pearson.

Bodart, F., Patel, A., Sim, M., & Weber, R. (2001). Should Optional Properties be used in Conceptual Modeling? A Theory and three Empirical Tests. *Information Systems Research*, *12*(4), 384–405. doi:10.1287/isre.12.4.384.9702.

Booch, G., Rumbaugh, J., & Jacobson, I. (1999). *The Unified Modeling Language User Guide*. Reading, MA: Addison Wesley Longman, Inc..

Bunge, M. A. (1979). Treatise on Basic Philosophy: *Vol. 4. Ontology II: A World of Systems*. Dordrecht, The Netherlands: Reidel Publishing Company.

Chopra, A. K., Mylopoulos, J., Dalpiaz, F., Giorgini, P., & Singh, M. P. (2010). Requirements as Goals and Commitments Too. In *Intentional Perspectives on Information System Engineering* (pp. 137–153). Berlin: Springer. doi:10.1007/978-3-642-12544-7_8.

De Marco, T. (1979). *Structured Analysis and System Specification*. Upper Saddle River, NJ: Prentice Hall.

Dietz, J. L. G. (2006). *Enterprise Ontology: Theory and Methodology*. Berlin: Springer. doi:10.1007/3-540-33149-2.

Dori, D. (2002). *Object-Process Methodology: A Holistic System Paradigm*. Berlin: Springer.

Evermann, J., & Wand, Y. (2009). Ontology Based Object-Oriented Domain Modeling: Representing Behavior. *Journal of Database Management*, *20*(1), 48–77.

Ferrario, R., & Guarino, N. (2008). Towards an Ontological Foundation for service Science. In *Proceedings of the First Future Internet Symposium (FIS 2008)*, Vienna, Austria (pp. 152-169). Berlin: Springer.

Finkelstein, C. (2004). Enterprise Integration Using Enterprise Architecture. In Linger, H., (Eds.), *Constructing the Infrastructure for the Knowledge Economy* (pp. 43–82). New York: Kluwer Academic/Plenum Publishers.

Gane, C., & Sarson, T. (1979). *Structured System Analysis*. Upper Saddle River, NJ: Prentice Hall.

Gemino, A. (1998). To be or maybe to be: An empirical comparison of mandatory and optional properties in conceptual modeling. In *Proceedings of the Ann. Conf. Admin. Sci. Assoc. of Canada* (pp. 33-44). Saskatoon, Canada: Information Systems Division.

Glinz, M. (2000). Problems and Deficiencies of UML as a Requirements Specification Language. In *Proceedings of the 10-th International Workshop on Software Specification and Design,* San Diego (pp. 11-22).

Gordijn, J., Akkermans, H., & van Vliet, H. (2000). Business Process Modeling is not Process Modeling. In Conceptual Modeling for E-Business and the Web (LNCS 1921, pp. 40-51). New York: Springer.

Gordijn, J., Petit, M., & Wieringa, R. (2006). Understanding Business Strategies of Networked Value Constellations Using Goal- and Value Modeling. In *Proceedings of the 14ᵗʰ IEEE International Conference on Requirements Engineering* (pp. 129-138). Washington, DC: IEEE Press.

Guizzardi, G. (2007). Modal Aspects of Object Types and Part-Whole Relations and the de re/de dicto distinction. In *Proceedings of the 19ᵗʰ International Conference on Advanced Information Systems Engineering,* Trondheim, Norway (LNCS 4495). Berlin: Springer Verlag.

Gustas, R. (2010). A Look behind Conceptual Modeling Constructs in Information System Analysis and Design. *International Journal of Information System Modeling and Design, 1*(1), 79–108.

Gustas, R., & Gustiene, P. (2008). Pragmatic – Driven Approach for Service-Oriented Analysis and Design. In *Information Systems Engineering: From Data Analysis to Process Networks* (pp. 97–128). Hershey, PA: IGI Global.

Gustas, R., & Gustiene, P. (2009). *Service-Oriented Foundation and Analysis Patterns for Conceptual Modeling of Information Systems. Information System Development: Challenges in Practice, Theory and Education (Vol. 1).* New York: Springer.

Harel, D. (1987). Statecharts: A Visual Formalism for Complex Systems. *Science of Computer Programming, 8,* 231–274. doi:10.1016/0167-6423(87)90035-9.

Harel, D., & Rumpe, B. (2004). Meaningful Modeling: What's the Semantics of 'Semantics'? *IEEE Computer,* 64-72.

Horkoff, J., & Yu, E. (2010). Interactive Analysis of Agent-Goal Models in Enterprise Modeling. *International Journal of Information System Modeling and Design, 1*(4).

Jacobson, I., & NG, P.-W. (2005). *Aspect-Oriented Software Development with Use Cases.* Upper Saddle River, NJ: Pearson Education.

Johannesson, P., Andersson, B., & Weigand, H. (2010). Resource Analysis and Classification for Purpose Driven Value Model Design. *International Journal of Information System Modeling and Design, 1*(1), 56–78.

Jonkers, H., Lankhorst, M., van Buuren, R., Bonsangue, M., & van der Torre, L. (2004). Concepts for Modeling Enterprise Architectures. *International Journal of Cooperative Information Systems, 13*(3), 257–287. doi:10.1142/S0218843004000985.

Lankhorst, M. M., Proper, H. A., & Jonkers, H. (2010). The Anatomy of the Archimate Language. *International Journal of Information System Modeling and Design, 1*(1), 1–32.

Larman, C. (2009). *Applying UML and Patterns: An Introduction to Object-Oriented Analysis and Design and Iterative Development* (3rd ed.). Upper Saddle River, NJ: Pearson Education.

Lindland, O. I., Sindre, G., & Solvberg, A. (1994). Understanding Quality in Conceptual Modeling. *IEEE Software, 11*(2). doi:10.1109/52.268955.

Martin, J., & Odell, J. J. (1998). Object-Oriented Methods: A Foundation (UML ed.). Upper Saddle River, NJ: Prentice-Hall.

OMG. (2010). *Unified Modeling Language Superstructure, version 2.2.* Retrieved January 19, 2010, from www.omg.org/spec/UML/2.2/

van Griethuisen, J. J. (1982). *Concepts and Terminology for the Conceptual Schema and Information Base (Rep. No. ISO TC97/SC5/WG5, No 695).* ISO.

Yourdon, E., & Constantine, L. L. (1979). *Structured Design.* Upper Saddle River, NJ: Prentice Hall.

Yu, E. (1997). Towards Modeling and Reasoning Support for Early-Phase Requirements Engineering. In *Proceedings of the 3rd IEEE International Symposium on Requirements Engineering* (pp. 226-235). Washington, DC: IEEE Press.

Zachman, J. A. (1996). *Enterprise Architecture: The Issue of the Century.* Database Programming and Design Magazine.

This work was previously published in the International Journal of Information System Modeling and Design (IJISMD), Volume 2, Issue 1, edited by Remigijus Gustas, pp. 45-73, copyright 2011 by IGI Publishing (an imprint of IGI Global).

Section 3
Object–Oriented Modeling

Chapter 8

Ontological Rules for UML-Based Conceptual Modeling:
Design Considerations and a Prototype Implementation

Shan Lu
Around America Aviation Group, Canada

Jeffrey Parsons
Memorial University of Newfoundland, Canada

ABSTRACT

UML is used as a language for object-oriented software design, and as a language for conceptual modeling of applications domains. Given the differences between these purposes, UML's origins in software engineering might limit its appropriateness for conceptual modeling. In this context, Evermann and Wand have proposed a set of well-defined ontological rules to constrain the construction of UML diagrams to reflect underlying ontological assumptions about the real world. The authors extend their work using a design research approach that examines these rules by studying the consequences of integrating them into a UML CASE tool. The paper demonstrates how design insights from incorporating theory-based modeling rules in a software artifact can be used to shed light on the rules themselves. In particular, the authors distinguish four categories of rules for implementation purposes, reflecting the relative importance of different rules and the degree of flexibility available in enforcing them. They propose distinct implementation strategies that correspond to these four rule categories and identify some redundant rules as well as some rules that cannot be implemented without changing the UML specification. The rules are implemented in an open-source UML CASE tool.

DOI: 10.4018/978-1-4666-4161-7.ch008

INTRODUCTION

Recently, a significant stream of information systems research has focused on developing and evaluating guidelines for conceptual modeling in information systems development. Much of that work has focused on justifying and evaluating prescriptions derived from ontology (e.g., Burton-Jones & Meso, 2006; Burton-Jones & Weber, 1999; Evermann & Wand, 2006; Gemino & Wand, 2005; Parsons & Wand, 2008). The primary research methodology used to evaluate ontologically derived modeling guidelines has been laboratory experimentation. Most prior work has evaluated the *usefulness* of modeling rules or guidelines by comparing the differences between following versus not following the rules, on measures of recall, comprehension, and problem-solving among readers of diagrams (Gemino & Wand, 2004). In this paper, we propose a complementary approach for assessing modeling rules. Specifically, we propose to examine the *feasibility* of automating the enforcement of modeling rules in software and to highlight design decisions that need to be made in the course of incorporating rules into a modeling tool. This kind of evaluation can also provide insights on the consistency and potential usefulness of such rules.

We evaluate a set of ontologically grounded modeling rules proposed by Evermann and Wand (2001a, 2001b) and Evermann (2003) to constrain the use of the Unified Modeling Language (UML) for conceptual modeling. Although the origins and initial focus of the UML lie in the area of object-oriented software design, it has evolved into a language for *conceptual modeling* – representing aspects of a real-world domain for which a system is required (Evermann, 2003; Burton-Jones & Meso, 2006). In this context, the UML is used as a language for communicating between clients and developers in understanding and eliciting requirements, and also for documenting the outcome of analysis (Dobing & Parsons, 2006, 2008).

UML was developed as a language for software design (Booch et al., 2005). As a result, extending UML for use in conceptual modeling has raised questions about its appropriateness for that purpose. More generally, the applicability of object-oriented modeling in the early development phases is controversial (Kobryn, 2002). In addition, the UML in its entirety is very complex (Siau & Cao, 2001). In speaking of earlier versions of UML, Kobryn noted that "although UML 1.x has enjoyed widespread acceptance, its shortcomings include: excessive size and gratuitous complexity" (Kobryn, 2002). UML 2.0 and later versions have increased this level of complexity.

Against this backdrop, several researchers have proposed approaches to constraining the use of UML to conform to certain underlying principles. Such work is grounded in the view that, since conceptual modeling involves representing aspects of the real world, *ontology*, the branch of philosophy dealing with the nature and structure of the real world, is an appropriate foundation to guide UML-based conceptual modeling. Accordingly, researchers have proposed ontological rules that would constrain the construction of UML diagrams to ensure they properly reflect underlying ontological assumptions. If followed, these constraints effectively impose a method for using the UML for conceptual modeling that reduces the degree of freedom available to an analyst in creating a model. The outcome of following this method should be a model that is sound with respect to the ontological foundation on which the rules are based.

Two such approaches, based on alternative ontological foundations, are noteworthy. First, the OntoUML language (Guizzardi, 2005) proposes an approach to improving ontological fidelity. OntoUML is based on foundational ontological concepts based on an ontological theory originating in the General Formalized Ontology (GFO) that underlies the General Ontological Language (Degen et al., 2001), and which integrates what later became known as the Unified Foundational Ontology (UFO) (Guizzardi & Wagner, 2010). A complementary tool has been developed to supporting the underlying ontological foundation (Benevides & Guizzardi, 2009). Second, using a foundational ontology based on Bunge (1977, 1979), Evermann and Wand (2001a, 2001b) and Evermann (2003) provide ontology-based guidance for using the UML in conceptual modeling, manifested as a set of rules and corollaries. However, they do not provide a tool to enforce these rules in constructing models.

In this paper, we focus on the approach proposed by Evermann and Wand. We believe that manually enforcing the set of complex rules they propose is impractical. Simply remembering and applying the rules would be a challenge in a real systems development project. Moreover, Evermann and Wand do not analyze their rules in the following senses: (1) How can the rules be implemented in a UML tool to support conceptual modeling? (2) Are there redundancies in the rules? (3) Are any of the rules already implied by the UML specification? (4) Are there any internal inconsistencies or contradictions among the rules?

To illustrate how ontological rules for using UML in conceptual modeling can be enforced effectively, this paper examines the extent to which, and in what manner, Evermann and Wand's rules might be implemented in a UML CASE tool. In addition, we hope to gain insights about the collection of rules by considering how they might

be implemented. We explore methods to check UML diagrams as they are being constructed, detect when violations of one or more rules occur, and take appropriate action depending on the violation. We do so by developing a method to implement the rules. The remainder of this paper is structured as follows. First, we briefly summarize the parts of the UML relevant to conceptual modeling and introduce Evermann and Wand's ontological rules. Next, we explain the approach taken in analyzing and implementing the ontological rules, followed by a conclusion and possible areas of future research.

ONTOLOGICAL RULES FOR CONCEPTUAL MODELING WITH UML

Elements of UML Relevant to Conceptual Modeling

We assume that readers have basic knowledge of the UML and therefore do not explain UML concepts here. Since our research is based on Evermann and Wand's ontological rules, we (and they) focus on diagrams related to those rules for conceptual modeling purposes, rather than consider all diagrams in the language. Our research covers the three types of UML diagrams indicated in Table 1.

Table 1. UML diagrams and components covered in this research

Diagrams	Describe	Diagrams	Components Included
Static structure	Static structure of things	Class diagram	Class, Attribute, Operation, Association, Binary association, Association class, N-ary association, Composition, Link, Generalization.
Change	Change within things	Statechart diagram, Activity diagram	State, Composite states, Events, Simple transitions, Transitions to and from Concurrent states, Transitions to and from Composite states, Submachine states, Synch states, Action state, Subactivity state, Call states, Swimlanes.
Interaction	Interaction between things	Sequence diagram, Collaboration diagram	Interactions, Messages, Stimulus

Ontological Foundations

In addition to analyzing and examining the suitability of UML for conceptual modeling, Evermann and Wand have proposed constraints (rules) to make UML better suited for that purpose (Evermann & Wand, 2001a, 2001b; Evermann, 2003). They point out that conceptual modeling involves representing aspects of the real world domain of interest. When people use UML for conceptual modeling, the goal is to describe and help people to understand the real world. Therefore, we need a theory to describe the real world, against which to map UML constructs. Ontology is the branch of philosophy dealing with the nature and structure of the real world. Ontology defines constructs that describe what the world consists of and how the world works.

There are several possible ontologies that can be used as a foundation for conceptual modeling. Evermann and Wand's research uses Mario Bunge's ontology (Bunge, 1977, 1979) as adapted by Wand and Weber (1990, 1993). There has been some debate about the appropriateness of using Bunge's ontology and its adaptation by Wand and Weber for conceptual modeling (see: *Scandinavian Journal of Information Systems*, 18(1) http://iris. cs.aau.dk/index.php/volume-18-40200641-no-1. html). Nevertheless, many researchers have continued to find this approach valuable since (Evermann & Wand, 2001, p. 3):

- It is well formalized;
- It has been successfully adapted to diverse topics in information systems modeling and shown to provide a good benchmark for the evaluation of modeling languages and methods (e.g., Green & Rosemann, 2000; Irwin & Turk, 2005; Opdahl & Henderson-Sellers, 2002);
- It has been used to suggest an ontological meaning to object concepts (Wand, 1989; Parsons & Wand, 1997); and

- It has been empirically shown to lead to useful outcomes (Burton-Jones & Meso, 2006; Gemino & Wand, 2005).

Bunge's ontology introduces basic concepts to describe the world, including: Thing, Property, State, Change, Law, and Interaction. The world consists of things that possess properties. Properties are either intrinsic to one thing or mutual to several things. Everything has states defined by the specific values of its properties. States change as the property values change. All these changes follow rules, which are called transition laws. Everything can change. Change is either qualitative, in which a thing acquires or loses properties, or quantitative, in which property values of a thing changes. Two things are said to interact when they act on each other.

Evermann and Wand's Ontological Rules

Following Bunge's ontology, Evermann and Wand propose three groups of ontological rules – static rules, change rules, and interaction rules – based on an ontological commitment in which "our world consists of a static structure of things with their properties, changes in things and interactions of things" (Evermann, 2003, p. 37). In this section, we present an example of each kind of rule. The complete list of rules and corollaries is provided in Appendix 1. We use the original numbering scheme from Evermann (2003) below for ease of cross-referencing. Details of the derivation of the rules and corollaries are available in Evermann (2003).

Static Rules

Rule 1: Only substantial entities in the world are modeled as objects.

In Bunge's ontology, "thing" is the basic element in the world and it refers to "substantial entity" (Bunge, 1977, p. 110). Substantial entities are material things that physically exist in the world. They can be seen, heard, or felt by humans. For example, a 'book' is a material thing, whereas a 'job' and an 'order' are not. Instead, ontologically such concepts can be modeled in terms of mutual properties of several things (e.g., a 'job' is a mutual property of an employee and an employer), and are dealt with in Rule 2 and Corollary 3 (see Appendix 1). Moreover, Bunge's concept of *property precedence* (possessing a specific property implies possessing a more general one) can be used to understand the connection between general mutual properties (such as 'job' or 'employment') and specific manifestations of these mutual properties such as 'Salary' (Parsons & Cole, 2004).

Change Rules

Rule 21: A UML-state represents a specific assignment of values to the attributes and attributes of association classes of the objects for which the state is defined.

According to ontology, a thing can be represented by state functions, whose values are determined by properties of the thing (Bunge, 1977, p. 126). That is, states of things associate with properties of things. The different property value sets correspond to different states. In Evermann and Wand's research, UML-states and UML-state transitions are mapped with ontology's states and ontology's state transitions, respectively. Also, "there exist no states which are independent of attributes because properties express all the characteristics of a thing" (Evermann, 2003, p. 71). Thus, states cannot be described independent of properties of things. For example, a 'Person' object has an attribute of 'location.' Different values of 'location' specify different states of the 'Person.'1 A value of 'office' implies state of 'work'; a value of 'bus' implies state of 'travel; and a value of 'home'

implies state of 'rest.' (Note that 'work,' 'travel,' and 'home' are high-level composite states that can be decomposed into sub-states.)

In addition, properties consist of intrinsic properties and mutual properties, which are represented by attributes of ordinary and association classes respectively. Since mutual properties are properties of all of the "participating" objects, a state can (and usually does) represent a set of values that are partially in an object class (intrinsic properties) and partially in an association class (mutual properties).

Interaction Rules

Rule 33: For every class of objects between which message-passing is declared, there exists an association class.

Interactions are expressed by message-passing, where a "message defines a particular communication between instances that is specified in an interaction" (OMG, 2003, p. 2-119). That is, when message-passing exists, there is an interaction. According to Bunge (1977, p. 259), "two different things X and Y interact iff each acts upon the other." That means both objects participating an interaction undergo changes. Since "change may be quantitative, in which case the values of one or more properties is changed" (Evermann, 2003, p. 33), property values of both objects should change. Also because every property must lawfully relate to other properties (Bunge, 1977, p. 77), the changes of both objects must obey laws. That is, an interaction must lawfully change properties of both participating objects. However, a law is any restriction on the possible values of properties of a thing (Bunge, 1977, p. 129). A law only constrains property values of a single object (Evermann, 2003, p. 32). Therefore, in order for an interaction to change property values while satisfying laws in both objects, it must change the mutual properties of participating objects. Mutual properties can be mapped to association classes (Rule 3). Thus, for every class of objects between which message-passing is declared, there exists an association class. For example, a 'Company' interacts with an 'Employee' by promotion. This promotion interaction changes the value of mutual property 'salary' of both 'Company' and 'Employee.'

The above examples illustrate the three kinds of rules proposed by Evermann and Wand. There are in total 36 rules and 39 corollaries (see Appendix 1 for a complete list and Evermann (2003) for derivation of rules).

ANALYZING AND IMPLEMENTING ONTOLOGICAL RULES

To implement the ontological rules, we chose ArgoUML (CollabNet, Inc., 2003) from among several existing UML CASE tools available and supporting UML 1.5 when the project began. Our choice was motivated by several factors. First, ArgoUML supports the function of critiquing designs. Critiques are activated when the program launches. When users draw UML diagrams, the system can detect mistakes and advise users. ArgoUML's native critiquing is based on UML syntax. Our research extends the critiquing function to apply Evermann and Wand's ontological rules during diagram construction. Second, ArgoUML is open source software. Thus, unlike a proprietary product, it is relatively easy to add our desired functionality to the tool. A disadvantage of using ArgoUML in this project has been the fact that, as an ongoing project, it did not fully realize the UML specification. As a result, the implementation of some rules had to be adapted to account for this. In future work, this could be overcome by providing an implementation based on the UML 2.0 metamodel implemented using the EMOF framework (e.g., Benevides & Guizzardi, 2009), thereby providing tool independence and an approach that is usable by any tools that

support the UML metamodel. Such an approach has the advantage that the rules can be expressed declaratively using OCL.[2]

Categorizing Rules by Priority

Examination of the rules and corollaries shows clearly that there are important differences in how they can be implemented practically within a UML CASE tool. For example, some rules are critical in the sense that failing to detect and correct violations *as they occur* during the construction of a diagram can lead to problems that are difficult or impossible to rectify later. In other cases, rule violations cannot reasonably be detected without human guidance and interpretation, and implementation support is primarily a matter of flagging possible violations. After analyzing all rules and corollaries, we identified four implementation approaches and categorize each rule and corollary under one of them.

The first category (CRITICAL) is for rules that specify that something must be or must not be modeled in a particular way (e.g., Rule 1). For rules of this type, the violation warning must be shown immediately to prevent further problems, and the cause of the violation must be resolved before proceeding. Otherwise, problems resulting from the violation could compound in the development of the model, and require a series of additions to the model to be "undone" to resolve the violation. Thus, as soon as the rule is violated, the system should alert the user. In the CRITICAL approach, the implementation displays a dialogue informing users of the violation and resets the related model element so that the user can reenter correct information. For example, in Rule 1, when a non-substantial noun is detected (by a method such as the one described later), the system will display a violation warning as well as clear the string of the non-substantial noun in the diagram and wait for the new input string. Thus, the user cannot continue until he/she supplies a substantial noun as a class name. Figure 1 shows the response to violation of a CRITICAL rule in the current implementation. As can be seen, failure to detect and correct a situation as it occurs could lead to a model that violates fundamental ontological considerations (as reflected in Evermann and Wand's rules) and cannot easily be corrected without reconstructing a diagram from scratch.

Not all violations are easy to detect or correct. In some cases, it is not reasonable to delete the violating diagram element as in the CRITICAL approach. For example, "Sets of mutual properties must be represented as attributes of association classes" (Rule 3). If the system requires that the current violation be corrected before new model elements can be added, a problem arises. For example, if mutual properties are mistakenly defined for object classes, deleting them does not resolve the violation as a new association class needs to be defined and the mutual attributes added to this class. If the system prevents the

addition of an association class until the violation is corrected, the result is a form of deadlock.

In such cases, even though the rules indicate conditions that must be true in an ontologically sound representation, a CRITICAL implementation approach will result in a system that inhibits the modeler from working effectively on developing a diagram. To prevent this, we adopt what we call a high priority approach (HIGH): that is, once a rule violation occurs, the system displays a dialogue to warn the user. However, it does not clear anything in diagrams. Instead, it keeps the violating input and gives the user the option to correct it later (or even not to change it at all). To prevent the user from forgetting about the violation and to avoid continually displaying dialogues indicating the same violation, this violation is put into a HIGH priority reminder list. That means the popup dialogue will be shown only once for each violation instance of a rule. The system continues examining the diagram in real time in

Figure 1. CRITICAL rule violation warning

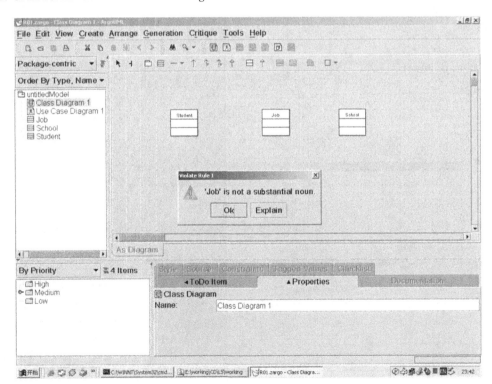

a background process. If the user does not change the input, the violation message will remain in the reminder list, but the violation will not interfere with the task of diagram construction. If the issue is resolved as the diagram is constructed, the violation is deleted from the reminder list. The user can check the list at any time to view all outstanding HIGH violations.

To illustrate, Rule 3 discussed above is designated HIGH priority. The system should inform users as soon as the violation appears. Thus, we design this feature to display a dialogue when it finds the same attribute in two associated classes, indicating the possibility that mutual properties might be modeled improperly (see Figure 2). However, this violation cannot be corrected immediately. The user needs to create an association and put this attribute in that association class (and, since this can be complex, might wish to defer the task). During that period, the system should

not trigger further warnings of this violation. To accommodate this, the rule is stored in a high priority reminder list (see Figure 3).

The approach in this rule (as well as in some others) is imperfect. It can indicate a violation when in fact there is none. Consider the example "customer buys book from bookstore." Both customer and bookstore may have the intrinsic attribute "name," which are homonyms that refer to the different properties customer name and bookstore name. However, this situation still appears to violate rule 3 in our approach. To accommodate situations such as this, our approach also allows for human control over the process: designers can dismiss reminders of violations that are erroneously detected (see Figure 4). Even so, we maintain that providing alerts to potential violations is useful, as it allows designers to create the necessary association class and add the "offending" attributes to it. Otherwise, the designer might

Figure 2. HIGH priority rule violation warning

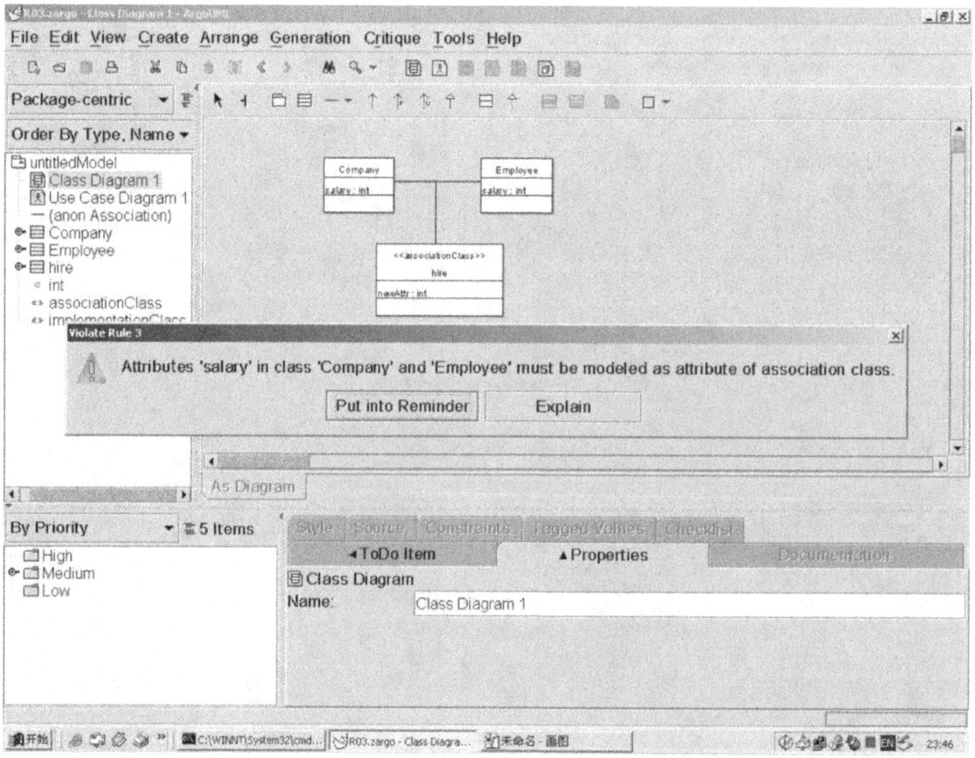

Figure 3. HIGH priority reminder item

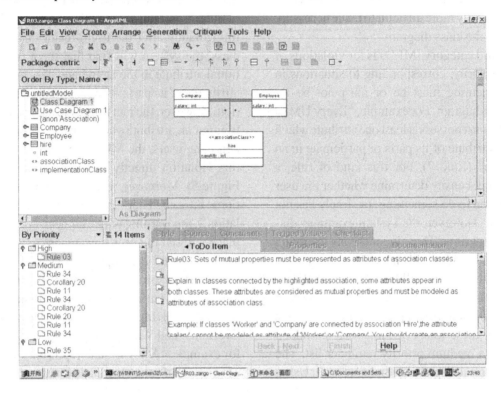

Figure 4. Resolution of HIGH priority violation by dismissal

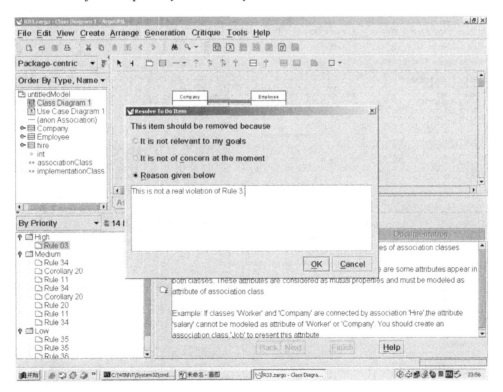

only become aware of violations much later, making it potentially more difficult to make necessary changes to the class diagram.

The third category (MED) is for violations of medium priority, corresponding to situations in which something must be or must not be included in a diagram. For example, "Every UML-aggregate must possess at least one attribute which is not an attribute of its parts or participate in an association" (Rule 7). For this kind of rule, a system cannot easily determine whether the user has forgotten to do something, or simply has not done it yet. However, the system examines diagrams in real time. Thus, in situations involving rules of the kind "A must have B", as soon as A is created, the system will find there is no B in A before a user can input B. In this case, the system should not display a dialogue saying, A must have B. Instead, these kinds of violations are added directly to a medium priority reminder list. The system does not display any dialogue at all. Using

this MED approach, we can keep track of the violation without interrupting users. In Rule 7, immediately after the user creates an aggregate class, the system will find that there is no additional attribute in the aggregate class beyond the attributes of its parts. The system detects a violation. However, the fact is that the user has no time to input an attribute yet. To avoid confusing and annoying users, the MED approach simply adds this violation directly to the reminder list (see Figure 5). Moreover, if the user models an additional attribute later (thereby correcting the 'violation'), the warning will disappear. All this takes place without the user's awareness.

We call the fourth approach low priority (LOW) reminders. These do not entail violation warnings, but consist of reminders. Such situations are based on rules involving newly proposed structures (by Evermann and Wand) that do not exist in UML[3]; for example, "A UML-state represents a specific assignment of values to the attributes and attributes

Figure 5. MED priority reminder item

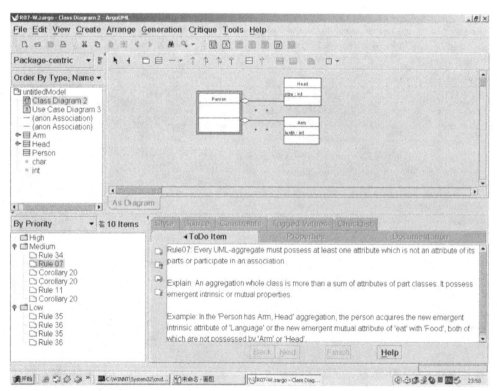

of association classes of the objects for which the state is defined" (Rule 21). There is no way for a program to detect violations of this kind of rule. In this case, the program will display reminders to users and ask users whether they want to keep this reminder. If the user indicates, the system will put the reminder into the LOW reminder list (see Figure 6). In Rule 21, because there is no mechanism connecting states and attribute values in UML, we use the LOW approach. The program gets all states and state machines to which they belong. Then it gets the model element owning the state machine and reminds users to follow this rule.

Although we have implemented these categories of rules to provide warnings or messages to modelers in most cases when violations are detected, we recognize that in an alternate implementation violations (other than CRITICAL) could simply be recorded for review by the modeler at a later time. Indeed, it would be useful in future research to examine empirically the effects of immediate notification (versus review after a

model is created) on both the quality of the models and modeler satisfaction with the modeling tool.

Selective Rule Implementation

We did not implement all rules and corollaries proposed by Evermann and Wand. Specifically, our analysis of how certain rules might be implemented identified four general cases in which rules or corollaries did not need to be implemented: (1) those *invariably enforced* when others are followed; (2) those that provide a *solution* to violations of others; (3) those that are *inconsistent* with the UML specification; and (4) those that are impossible to violate and thus are *redundant*. One of the contributions of this research is to analyze the rules and corollaries for the purpose of design and implementation, and to evaluate the coverage and consistency of the rules on that basis. Thus, the implementation of artefacts to support the rules provides a way of assessing the rules. We explain each case with examples.

Figure 6. LOW priority reminder item

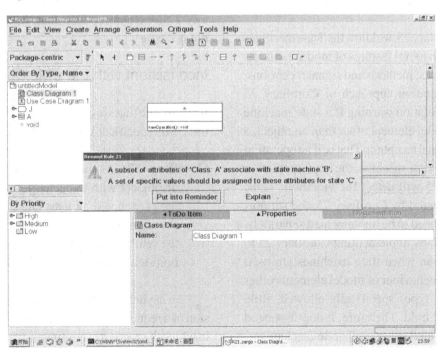

Enforced by Following Another Rule

Evermann and Wand's rules are derived by interpreting how UML can be used to support conceptual modeling based on ontological concepts. With a large set of rules and corollaries, it is possible that some cannot be violated if others are followed. This can be analyzed by examining each rule or corollary in terms of the requirements to implement a mechanism to enforce it in relation to other rules. Here we consider an example that shows the approach used to identify cases where one rule is enforced by following another. Consider:

Rule 29: An operation is not directly specified by state machines. Instead, the methods that implement an operation are specified by state machines.

vs.

Corollary 25: A state chart either expresses the external behavior of an object (SC0), a method, a signal reception or is a composite state contained in another state machine.

From Corollary 25, we know that state machines represent behavioural features of model elements including objects, methods and signal receptions. The implementation approach of Corollary 25 will show a violation warning if a state machine specifies a model element other than an object, a method or a signal reception. That is, if an operation is specified by state machine, the implementation of Corollary 25 will detect the violation. Thus, Rule 29 is covered by Corollary 25 and support for it does not need to be implemented separately. In other words, by implementing Corollary 25 to show a violation when state machines are used to express the behaviour of model elements other than the three types specifically allowed, Rule 29 will always hold. Therefore, it does not need to be implemented using a separate mechanism.

Solution to Violation of Another Rule

Our analysis of Evermann and Wand's rules shows that some rules actually propose mechanisms to redress violations of other rules. Thus, if a mechanism is implemented to detect or prevent a violation of a rule of the former type, a violation of a rule of the latter type will not occur (indeed, the solution offered by the latter rule might be suggested as a way of resolving a detected violation). Consider:

Corollary 3: If an association class of an n-ary association is intended to represent substantial things, the association should instead be modeled as one with arity (n+1).

vs.

Corollary 2: An association class cannot represent substantial entities or composites of substantial entities.

Corollary 2 specifies that an association class cannot represent substantial things. Corollary 3 actually offers a solution to a violation of Corollary 2. If we enforce Corollary 2, Corollary 3 is not necessary.

Inconsistent with the UML Specification

It is possible that some rules are inconsistent with the UML specification. Consider:

Corollary 37: Asynchronous communication of objects with expected response implies the existence of at least one state transition caused by the object acted upon, signifying the return interaction after the state transition signifying the original communication.

"An asynchronous invocation is the transmission of a request from a requestor to a target object in which the requestor continues execution immediately, without waiting for a reply" (OMG, 2003, pp. 2-312). The motivation of this corollary is that even though the acting object does not wait for a reply, the acted object may still return a reply, which is considered the "expected response" (Evermann, 2003, p. 127). However, UML specifies that "it is permissible to asynchronously invoke a request to a procedure that eventually issues a reply; the reply message is simply discarded" (OMG, 2003, pp. 2-312). One may argue that if the reply message actually sends some useful information, it should not just be discarded. However, "if the invocation is repliable, a subsequent reply by the invoked execution is transmitted to the requesting object as an asynchronous request" (OMG, 2003, pp. 2-322). That is, the response actually invokes another new communication. This is because "the target object might later communicate to the requestor, but any such communication must be explicitly programmed and it is not part of the asynchronous invocation action itself" (OMG, 2003, pp. 2-312). As we can see, there is no "expected response" for asynchronous communication. The motivation of this corollary is unnecessary in view of the UML specification. Thus, there is no need to implement support for it in our modeling tool.

Note also that within the UML specification, issues of synchronous and asynchronous communication can be considered a response to message-passing as a mechanism for object interaction in object-oriented programming languages. In that context, such considerations need not even be included in discussions of using UML for conceptual (real world) modeling. Nevertheless, we have discussed it here as it arises in Evermann and Wand's analysis and we have considered whether and how their rules can be implemented in a UML modeling tool.

Redundant

It might not be possible to violate some rules if the UML specification is followed. Consider:

Corollary 18: All states in an activity diagram must be states of the same object.

In UML, "an activity graph is a special case of a state machine" (OMG, 2003, pp. 2-172). In addition, UML specifies that a state machine is a behavior that specifies the sequence of states of an object. That is, an activity diagram only represents one object. Consequently, all states in an activity diagram must be states of the same object. Thus, it is impossible to violate this corollary; it is redundant.

Supporting Features of the Implementation

To support the analysis and implementation of the ontological rules, we have also used several other approaches: query for required information; use of a dictionary; and alternatives to proposed changes of UML. The following examples illustrate these approaches. These approaches are not theoretically-driven, but reflect compromises that are embedded in design decisions when attempting to enforce a set of abstract rules in the context of a design task involving humans and information technology.

Query for Required Information

Our implementation uses the approach of querying users for required information. When our program needs more information to determine whether a rule has been followed or violated, it asks users. Consider Rule 5. It is difficult to find a way for a program to tell whether attributes in an association class come from the same interaction. Once the program finds an association class, it gets all attributes from that association class and asks users whether these attributes are from one interaction (and provides an example to illustrate the concept). If the user indicates that they are not from the same interaction, the program issues a violation warning.

Use of a Dictionary or Domain Vocabulary

Consider again Rule 1. We can map "substantial entity" into human language, or into a domain vocabulary of terms. "Entities" can be mapped to nouns. In practice, such a repository is likely to be domain specific and would need to be developed as a collaborative effort among members of a community concerned with that domain. In the absence of a generally-agreed repository of substantial nouns for a domain, we used a naïve approach to enable our implementation to determine whether a noun is substantial or not. First, classify all nouns in a dictionary into two groups: Substantial and Non-substantial. Then, create a file to store those nouns. When checking UML diagrams, the program gets the "object" and searches for a match in the file. If an object is "Non-substantial", the program shows the violation. If an object cannot be found in our database, the program asks the user whether that object is substantial or not (with an explanation). The program will add the new substantial or non-substantial noun to its database. Note that using this general approach, we can substitute arbitrary lists of nouns with a more sophisticated ontology developed by a community of practitioners for a specific domain.

This approach clearly has limitations. If the user uses an abbreviation for an object name or a class name, the system cannot find it in the database. However, we propose an approach to mitigate this problem. A word stemming algorithm can be adopted. If the user's input is similar to a word in our database, the system can ask the user whether the input is the same as the database's word. Other problems with this approach include multiple word senses. Therefore, we propose that alternative approaches can be used, such as WordNet (http://wordnet.princeton.edu), specialized domain ontologies (e.g., the GoodRelations ontology for e-commerce - http://www.heppnetz.de/projects/goodrelations/), or approaches to word sense disambiguation (Ide & Veronis, 1998).

Alternative Implementation

We do not change or delete any aspect of the UML specification when called for by Evermann and Wand, but provide alternative implementations in those cases. This is because Evermann and Wand's proposed ontological rules are not currently part of the UML. Consider Corollary 21. Currently, there is no mechanism in UML to specify whether a state is stable or not. We use an alternative solution for this corollary. To determine if a state is stable or unstable, our program first gets all transitions with this state as the source state in SC0. Then each of these transitions is checked to see whether it has a trigger event. If any transition has no trigger, it can happen spontaneously. Thus, this state is unstable and the program shows a violation warning.

CONCLUSION AND FURTHER RESEARCH

We have developed a general (i.e., not CASE tool specific) implementation approach for most of the ontological rules proposed by Evermann and Wand. We have done so for 35 rules and 26 corollaries. Of these, 3 rules and 11 corollaries are realized by enabling, disabling or modifying mechanisms (features) in the UML specification; 32 rules and 15 corollaries are realized by a critiquing mechanism that operates in real time as diagrams are being constructed. We have implemented algorithms for these (complete details are given in (Lu, 2004)). We found that the remaining 1 rule and 13 corollaries did not need to be implemented. Of these, 1 rule and 8 corollaries are covered by others (i.e., they can be deduced from other rules and corollaries.), 2 corollaries are actually the solution of violations of others, 1 corollary is inconsistent with the UML specification, and 1 corollary is always true and thus redundant. We did not find any internal inconsistencies or contradictions among the rules.

Of the rules and corollaries that were implemented, our analysis shows that these can be divided into four categories, depending on their importance and the ease with which they can be detected. The requirement to implement an artifact that supports the rules led to the categorization of levels of support in Table 2. Such a classification cannot be deduced from the theoretical analysis underlying the rules proposed by Evermann and Wand. A summary of the status of Evermann and Wand's rules in our implementation is provided in Appendix 2.

Evermann and Wand proposed a set of rules to ensure the ontological soundness of UML diagrams constructed for conceptual modeling purposes. However, they did not consider the usability of the rules in the sense of being able to implement them in a working UML CASE tool. We have been able to evaluate whether and how these rules can be implemented. In doing so, we shed light on differences among the rules in terms of whether they need to be implemented and, if so, the strategies needed to implement them effectively. Our contribution comes in answering the following questions: (1) How can the rules be implemented in a UML tool to support conceptual modeling? (2) Are there any redundancies in the rules? (3) Are any of the rules already implied by the UML specification? (4) Are there any internal inconsistencies or contradictions among the rules? We classify the rules and corollaries

accordingly, based on these questions. Thus, we have empirically demonstrated their feasibility and pruned them to a more compact set. In addition, by considering implementation issues, we have identified some redundancies among the rules and inconsistencies with the UML specification, which otherwise would be difficult to detect. This kind of approach is an alternative to providing a formal specification of the underlying ontology (e.g., Evermann, 2009), to which a theorem proving approach could then be applied to detect redundancies and inconsistencies.

The UML is recognized to lack theoretical foundations. Evermann and Wand propose rules that can be used to ensure that UML diagrams constructed for conceptual modeling purposes adhere to certain ontological principles. We have shown that most of these rules can be supported within a UML case tool. Thus, Evermann and Wand's and our work sets the stage for empirical (experimental or field-based) research to test the effectiveness or value of providing this kind of support. One critical question that can be examined in future research is whether modelers following ontological rules (either manually or supported by a tool such as ours) produce models that are in some sense "better" than those who construct models without ontological support. Related questions for future research involve developing an understanding of ease of use and satisfaction associated with using a tool that supports the enforcement of the rules.

Table 2. Categories of implemented rules

Rule Type	Implementation Approach	Explanation
Must Be; Simple to correct	CRITICAL	User is prevented from proceeding in the construction of a diagram until the violation is corrected.
Must Be; Difficult to correct	HIGH	User is warned once of the violation, and the violation is added to a reminder list with high priority.
Must Have	MED	There is no popup indicating the violation. Instead, the potential violation is added to a reminder list with medium priority.
Relates to non-existing UML component	LOW	The user is queried about the issue and asked whether he/she wants to keep this reminder. Based on the answer, either a low priority reminder is added to the reminder list, or the reminder is discarded.

Finally, it would be useful to compare the effects of notifying modelers immediately on detection of a rule violation (other than CRITICAL violations) versus simply tracking such violations and having the modeler review them after a draft model is completed.

We contend that the approach used in this research is a useful way of evaluating modeling rules developed from a theoretical foundation. The approach can be used to assess the feasibility, coverage, and consistency of rules. In addition, it contributes to a better understanding of how such rules interact with tools that might ultimately be used to implement them. Such an approach can be applied to other research areas in which rules are proposed to support various aspects of information systems development.

REFERENCES

Benevides, A., & Guizzardi, G. (2009). A Model-based Tool for Conceptual Modeling and Domain Ontology Engineering in OntoUML. In *Proceedings of the International Conference on Enterprise Information Systems*, Milan, Italy (LNBIP 24, pp. 528-538).

Booch, G., Rumbaugh, J., & Jacobson, I. (2005). *The Unified Modeling Language User Guide* (2nd ed.). Reading, MA: Addison-Wesley.

Bunge, M. A. (1977). Ontology I: The Furniture of the World: *Vol. 3. Treatise On Basic Philosophy*. Dordrecht, Holland: D. Reidel Publishing Company.

Bunge, M. A. (1979). Ontology II: A World of Systems: *Vol. 4. Treatise On Basic Philosophy*. Dordrecht, Holland: D. Reidel Publishing Company.

Burton-Jones, A., & Meso, P. (2006). Conceptualizing Systems for Understanding: An Empirical Test of Decomposition Principles in Object-Oriented Analysis. *Information Systems Research*, *17*(1), 101–114. doi:10.1287/isre.1050.0079.

Burton-Jones, A., & Weber, R. (1999). Understanding Relationships With Attributes in Entity-Relationship Diagrams. In *Proceedings of the 20th International Conference on Information Systems*, Charlotte, NC (pp. 214-228).

CollabNet, Inc. (2003). *ArgoUML User Manual*. Retrieved September 2003, from http://argouml.tigris.org/

Degen, W., Heller, B., Herre, H., & Smith, B. (2001). GOL: A General Ontological Language. In Welty, C., & Smith, B. (Eds.), *Formal Ontology and Information Systems* (pp. 34–46). New York: ACM Press.

Dobing, B., & Parsons, J. (2006). How UML is Used. *Communications of the ACM*, *49*(5), 109–113. doi:10.1145/1125944.1125949.

Dobing, B., & Parsons, J. (2008). Dimensions of UML Use: A Survey of Practitioners. *Journal of Database Management*, *19*(1), 1–18.

Evermann, J. (2003). *Using Design Languages for Conceptual Modeling: The UML CASE*. Unpublished doctoral dissertation, The University of British Columbia, Vancouver, Canada.

Evermann, J. (2009). A UML and OWL Description of Bunge's Upper Level Ontology Model. *Software and Systems Modeling*, *8*(2), 235–249. doi:10.1007/s10270-008-0082-3.

Evermann, J., & Wand, Y. (2001a). An Ontological Examination of Object Interaction. In *Proceedings of the Eleventh Workshop on Information Technologies*, New Orleans, LA (pp. 91-96).

Evermann, J., & Wand, Y. (2001b). Towards Ontologically based Semantics for UML Constructs. In *Proceedings of the 20th International Conference on Conceptual Modeling (ER'2001)*, Yokohama, Japan (pp. 354-367).

Evermann, J., & Wand, Y. (2006). Ontological Modelling Rules for UML: An Empirical Assessment. *Journal of Computer Information Systems*, *46*(5), 14–19.

Gemino, A., & Wand, Y. (2004). A Framework for Empirical Evaluation of Conceptual Modeling Techniques. *Requirements Engineering, 9*(4), 248–260. doi:10.1007/s00766-004-0204-6.

Gemino, A., & Wand, Y. (2005). Complexity and Clarity in Conceptual Modeling: Comparison of Mandatory and Optional Properties. *Data & Knowledge Engineering, 55*(3), 301–326. doi:10.1016/j.datak.2004.12.009.

Green, P., & Rosemann, M. (2000). Integrated Process Modeling: An Ontological Evaluation. *Information Systems, 25*(2), 73–87. doi:10.1016/S0306-4379(00)00010-7.

Guizzardi, G. (2005). *Ontological Foundations of Structural Conceptual Models*. Amsterdam, The Netherlands: Telematica Instituut.

Guizzardi, G., & Wagner, G. (2010). Using the Unified Foundational Ontology (UFO) as a Foundation for General Conceptual Modeling Languages. In Poli, R., Healy, M., & Kameas, A. (Eds.), *Theory and Application of Ontologies*. Heidelberg, Germany: Springer Verlag. doi:10.1007/978-90-481-8847-5_8.

Ide, N., & Vernis, J. (1998). Introduction to the Special Issue on Word Sense Disambiguation: The State of the Art. *Computational Linguistics, 24*(1), 2–40.

Irwin, G., & Turk, D. (2005). An Ontological Analysis of Use Case Modeling Grammar. *Journal of the Association for Information Systems, 6*(1), 1–36.

Kobryn, C. (2002). UML 2 for System Engineering. In *Proceedings of the INCOSE 2002 Symposium*.

Lu, S. (2004). *Enforcing Ontological Rules in Conceptual Modeling Using UML: Principles and Implementation*. Unpublished master's thesis, Memorial University of Newfoundland, St. John's, Canada.

Object Management Group (OMG). (2003). *OMG Unified Modeling Language Specification, Version 1.5*. Retrieved September 2003, from http://www.uml.org

Opdahl, A. L., & Henderson-Sellers, B. (2002). Ontological Evaluation of the UML Using the Bunge–Wand–Weber Model. *Software Systems Modeling, 1*, 43–67.

Parsons, J., & Cole, L. (2004). An experimental examination of property precedence in conceptual modeling. In *Proceedings of the first Asia-Pacific Conference on Conceptual Modeling,* Dunedin, New Zealand (CRPIT 59, pp. 101-110).

Parsons, J., & Wand, Y. (1997). Using Objects for Systems Analysis. *Communications of the ACM, 40*(12), 104–110. doi:10.1145/265563.265578.

Parsons, J., & Wand, Y. (2008). Using Cognitive Principles to Guide Classification in Information Systems Modeling. *Management Information Systems Quarterly, 32*(4), 839–868.

Siau, K., & Cao, Q. (2001). Unified Modeling Language: A Complexity Analysis. *Journal of Database Management, 12*(1), 26–34.

Wand, Y. (1989). A Proposal for a Formal Model of Objects. In Kim, W., & Lochovsky, F. (Eds.), *Object-oriented Concepts, Databases, and Applications* (pp. 537–559). New York: ACM Press.

Wand, Y., & Weber, R. (1990). An Ontological Model of an Information System. *IEEE Transactions on Software Engineering, 16*(11), 1282–1292. doi:10.1109/32.60316.

Wand, Y., & Weber, R. (1993). On the Ontological Expressiveness of Information Systems Analysis and Design Grammars. *Journal of Information Systems, 3*, 217–237. doi:10.1111/j.1365-2575.1993.tb00127.x.

ENDNOTES

[1] Note that this example is a simplification used simply to illustrate how attribute values determine states. To fully specify states such as "Work," it would be necessary to jointly specify values of other (possibly composite) attributes. For example, being located at ones office would have to be combined with other state variables (e.g., including mental activity) to determine a state of "work."

[2] We are grateful to an anonymous reviewer for pointing this out.

[3] We also use this approach to deal with some structures in UML that have not yet been implemented in the tool we used for our implementation (ArgoUML).

APPENDIX 1: LISTING OF ONTOLOGICAL RULES AND COROLLARIES

(Source: Evermann, 2003)

Rule 1: Only substantial entities in the world are modelled as objects.

Rule 2: Ontological properties of things must be modeled as UML-attributes.

Corollary 1: Attributes in a UML-description of the real world cannot refer to substantial entities.

Rule 3: Sets of mutual properties must be represented as attributes of association classes.

Corollary 2: An association class cannot represent substantial entities or composites of substantial entities.

Corollary 3: If an association class of an n-ary association is intended to represent substantial things, the association should instead be modelled as one with arity (n+1).

Corollary 4: An association class representing a composite must instead be modelled as a composite with attributes representing emergent intrinsic properties.

Corollary 5: An association class cannot possess methods or operations.

Corollary 6: An association class cannot be associated with a state machine.

Corollary 7: An association class must possess at least one attribute.

Corollary 8: An association class must not be associated with another class.

Corollary 9: An association class must not participate in generalization relationships.

Rule 4: If mutual properties can change quantitatively, methods and operations that change the values of attributes of the association class must be modelled for one or more of the classes participating in the association, objects of which can affect the change, not for the associations class.

Rule 5: An association class represents a set of mutual properties arising out of the same interaction.

Rule 6: A composition relation must not be modelled.

Rule 7: Every UML-aggregate must possess at least one attribute which is not an attribute of its parts or participate in an association.

Rule 8: All UML-classes must possess at least one attribute or participate in an association.

Rule 9: Object ID's must not be modelled as attributes.

Rule 10: The set of attribute values (representing mutual and intrinsic properties) must uniquely identify an object.

Rule 11: Every attribute has a value.

Corollary 10: Attribute multiplicities greater than one imply that the order of the different individual attribute value components is semantically irrelevant.

Rule 12: Classes of objects that exhibit additional behaviour, additional attributes or additional association classes with respect to other objects of the same class must be modelled as specialized sub-classes.

Corollary 11: An object acquiring additional behaviour or properties must be destroyed as instance of the general class and created as instance of the specialized class that is modelled with the relevant operations or association classes.

Corollary 12: Re-classification occurs only within a generalization/specialization hierarchy.

Rule 13: Every UML-aggregate object must consist of at least two parts.

Rule 14: An instance of a class that by virtue of additional aggregation relationships acquires emergent properties or emergent behaviour must be modeled as an instance of a specialized class which declares the corresponding attributes and operations.

Rule 15: Object creation occurs when an entity acquires a property so that it becomes a member of a different class.

Corollary 13: Object destruction occurs when an entity loses a property that is necessary for membership in a particular class.

Rule 16: Attributes with class scope should instead be modelled as attributes of an aggregate representing the objects of the class.

Rule 17: If a class that is specialized is declared as abstract, the specialization must be declared to be 'complete.'

Rule 18: A class that is not specialized cannot be declared abstract.

Rule 19: A specialized class must define more attributes, more operations or participate in more associations than the general class.

Rule 20: Every ordinary association must be an association class.

Rule 21: A UML-state represents a specific assignment of values to the attributes and attribute of association classes of the objects for which the state is defined.

Corollary 14: A UML-transition must change the value of at least one attribute used to define the state space.

Rule 22: For every level of refinement of a state C, there must be an additional set of attributes in the class description or in participating association classes that change as the object transitions among the sub-states.

Corollary 15: For all immediate substates of a super-state, the values assigned to attributes describing the super-state are invariant and are equal to those defining the super-state.

Corollary 16: Concurrent sub-states require mutually disjunct sets of additional attributes in the class description or in participating association classes.

Rule 23: Guard conditions on transitions from the same state to nonconcurrent sub-states must be mutually disjunct.

Rule 24: Action states are super-states of a set of sub-states. The object transitions among these while in the action state. State charts must reflect this fact.

Corollary 17: States must not be associated with any actions. Sub-states corresponding to different models should be used instead.

Corollary 18: All states in an activity diagram must be states of the same object.

Corollary 19: If the partitions of an activity diagram represent different objects, they must be part of a composite which is shown in the class diagram.

Rule 25: The quantitative object behaviour (for each model) is entirely describable by top-level state chart (SC0).

Rule 26: All UML-transitions in SC0 must correspond to an operation of the object which SC0 is associated with.

Corollary 20: Every object must have at least one operation.

Corollary 21: States in SC0 are stable.

Corollary 22: All UML-transitions in SC0 must be associated with a UML event.

Rule 27: An object must exhibit additional operations expressing qualitative changes, if a super- or subclass is defined and instances can undergo changes of class to the super- or sub-class.

Rule 28: Methods may be described by state charts other than top-level state charts.

Corollary 23: A state chart describing a method must begin and end with those states in SC0 which the operation that the method implements is a realization of.

Corollary 24: State transitions out of the first state of a method realizing an operation must be associated with the same event that is associated with the transition in SC0 which represents that operation.

Corollary 25: A state chart either expresses the external behaviour of an object (SC0), a method, a signal reception or is a composite state contained in another state machine.

Rule 29: An operation is not directly specified by state machines. Instead, the methods that implement an operation are specified by state machines.

Corollary 26: A state machine that specifies the behaviour of a class or a method is not contained in other state machines.

Corollary 27: The method corresponding to a state chart must modify the attribute values of the object corresponding to the values defined for the initial and final state of the method.

Rule 30: An operation must be associated with the declaration of signal reception.

Rule 31: The event associated with an operation must be identical to the event associated with the signal associated with the reception.

Corollary 28: The state machines associated with a reception and with a method specifying the implementation of an operation which is in turn associated with that reception, must possess the same initial and final states.

Rule 32: Acquisition (loss) of independent properties leads to expansion (contraction) of the things top-level state space SC0 by an orthogonal region.

Corollary 29: Every object must be capable of at least one state transition or be able to undergo change of class to a super- or sub-class.

Rule 33: For every class of objects between which message passing is declared, there exists an association class.

Rule 34: Every object must be the receiver and sender of some message.

Rule 35: For every attribute there exists a constraint which relates this attribute to some other attribute.

Corollary 30: An association class cannot be sender or receiver of a message.

Rule 36: A constraint relates attributes of a single class or attributes of association classes the class participates in.

Corollary 31: A UML-state transition associated with an action must modify an association class attribute's value.

Corollary 32: For every interaction between UML-objects, there must exist a corresponding UML-state transition in both interacting UML-objects.

Corollary 33: A state transition associated with an event must modify an association class attribute's value.

Corollary 34: A signal event may only be associated with a transition in a top-level state chart and the initial transition of a method implementing this.

Corollary 35: A call event may only be associated with a transition in a top-level state chart or the initial transition of a method implementing this.

Corollary 36: Synchronous communication of objects implies transition to a state which cannot be left except through a state transition associated with the return signal.

Corollary 37: Asynchronous communication of objects with expected response implies the existence of at least one state transition caused by the object acted upon, signifying the return interaction after the state transition signifying the original communication.

Corollary 38: The final state transitions of any method implementing an operation that may be invoked through a call action must cause a return action.

Corollary 39: For the state machine of a method to contain a state transition whose effect is a return action, there must exist a corresponding state transition in a state machine of some other object whose effect is a corresponding call action.

APPENDIX 2

Table A1. Implementation Status of Ontological Rules (R) and Corollaries (C)

Not Implemented	Enforced by another Rule	R29, C2, C5, C7, C12, C22, C29, C30, C36
	Solution	C3, C4
	Unnecessary	C10, C11, R15, C13, C17, C27, C37
	Redundant	C15
Implemented via Critiquing Function in ArgoUML	Critical	R1,R2, C1, C5
	High	R3, C6, C8, C9, R4, R5, R6, R9, R12, R14, R16, R17, R18, R23, C23, C24, C25, R32, C34
	Medium	R7, R8, R13, R19, R20, R24, R25, R26, C20, C21, R27, R30, R33, R34
	Low	R21, R22, C16, C18, C19, R28, C26, R30, R31, C28, R35, R36, C31, C32, C33

Note: Rules 10, 11, and 15 and Corollaries 11, 12, 13, 14, 17, 27, 35, 37, 38, and 39 were implemented by enabling, disabling, or modifying mechanisms in the UML specification.

This work was previously published in the International Journal of Information System Modeling and Design (IJISMD), Volume 2, Issue 1, edited by Remigijus Gustas, pp. 24-44, copyright 2011 by IGI Publishing (an imprint of IGI Global).

Chapter 9
A Longitudinal Study of Fan-In and Fan-Out Coupling in Open-Source Systems

Asma Mubarak
Brunel University, UK

Steve Counsell
Brunel University, UK

Robert M. Hierons
Brunel University, UK

ABSTRACT

Excessive coupling between object-oriented classes is widely acknowledged as a maintenance problem that can result in a higher propensity for faults in systems and a 'stored up' future problem. This paper explores the relationship between 'fan-in' and 'fan-out' coupling metrics over multiple versions of open-source software. More specifically, the relationship between the two metrics is explored to determine patterns of growth in each over the course of time. The JHawk tool was used to extract the two metrics from five open-source systems. Results show a wide range of traits in the classes to explain both high and low levels of fan-in and fan-out. Evidence was also found of certain 'key' classes (with both high fan-in and fan-out) and 'client' and 'server'-type classes with high fan-out and fan-in, respectively. This paper provides an explanation of the composition and existence of such classes as well as for disproportionate increases in each of the two metrics over time. Finally, it was found that high fan-in class values tended to be associated with small classes; classes with high fan-out on the other hand tended to be relatively large classes.

DOI: 10.4018/978-1-4666-4161-7.ch009

INTRODUCTION

Excessive class coupling has often been related to the propensity for faults in software (Briand et al., 1997). It is widely believed in the object-oriented (OO) community that excessive coupling between classes creates a level of complexity that can complicate subsequent maintenance and represents a 'stored up' maintenance problem. In practice, a class that is highly coupled to many other classes is an ideal candidate for re-engineering or removal from the system to mitigate both current and potential future problems. A problem that immediately arises however for the developer when considering re-engineering of classes with high coupling is: 'Do those classes have prohibitively large dependencies?' If so, then are those coupling dependencies 'incoming' or 'outgoing' dependencies? In theory, it is more difficult to modify a target class with high incoming and low outgoing coupling, since the former requires detailed and careful scrutiny of each of the many 'incoming' dependent classes and the possible side-effects of change.

In this paper, we investigate versions of five Open Source Systems (OSS) focusing on two well-known coupling metrics - 'fan-in' (i.e., incoming coupling) and 'fan-out' (i.e., outgoing coupling). We used an automated tool to extract each of the coupling metrics from those five systems. The research questions we explore are first, is it the case that classes with large incoming coupling naturally have low outgoing coupling and second, does this relationship worsen over time? In other words, does the potential maintenance problem become worse in terms of fan-in and fan-out values? Results showed a wide range of characteristics in the classes to account for high and low levels of fan-in and fan-out. Evidence was found of 'key' classes, comprising high fan-in and fan-out as well as 'client' and 'server'-type classes comprising high fan-out and fan-in, respectively. We explore the composition of the classes and reasons for the existence of such classes as well as for changes

over time in the two metrics. We also found that high fan-in class values were associated with small classes; on the other hand, classes with high fan-out were comparatively large.

The main message that emerges from the research is that every system is likely to contain classes with relatively large amounts of coupling (whether fan-in, fan-out or both). The task of the developer is to ensure that such classes are monitored and a proactive stance taken to the possible re-engineering or refactoring of those classes. A strong link has been found between excessive coupling and faults (Briand et al., 1997) and it is widely acknowledged that too much coupling is harmful. The study presented is a first step to understanding the traits of this feature of systems at a broad level.

MOTIVATION AND RELATED WORK

The research in this paper is motivated by a number of factors. Firstly, previous research (Mubarak et al., 2008) has shown that there is a trade-off between coupling types – in particular, that between coupling through imported packages and the introduction of 'internal-to-the-package' coupling. In this paper, we explore the potential characteristics and trade-offs between fan-in and fan-out metrics over time. Second, we would always expect potentially problematic classes to be re-engineered by developers through techniques such as refactoring (Fowler, 1999); however, the practical realities of limited time and resources at their disposal means that only when classes exhibit particularly bad 'smells' (e.g. excessive coupling) (Fowler, 1999; Mantyla et al., 2006) are they dealt with. In this paper, we explore, over time, whether smells given by too much coupling do become 'smellier' and, if so, in what proportions. Third, it is likely that there are special types of class with either large fan-in or fan-out values (or both). Understanding the nature of these classes could help to understand the reason for these characteristics and even how and why these classes evolve as they do. Finally, the research is motivated by previous research (Mubarak et al., 2008) which showed that the fan-in and fan-out metrics tended to be relatively small for classes removed from a system. In other words, classes with either high fan-in and/or fan-out may be difficult to move or remove from a system. This question has inspired further examination of trends in the two metrics presented. The original fan-in and fan-out metrics were developed in early software metrics texts dealing with coupling and cohesion and structured programming (Stevens et al., 1974). Yet, very few studies have used fan-in and fan-out as a basis for empirical studies of coupling. A key objective of the research presented is to redress this imbalance in a small way.

In terms of related work, the research presented relates to areas of software evolution, coupling metrics and the use of OSS (Briand et al., 1999; Chapin et al., 2001; Counsell et al., 2003; Ferenc et al., 2004; Godfrey et al., 2001). In terms of software evolution, the laws of Belady and Lehman (1976) provide the backdrop for many past evolutionary studies. One could easily argue that these laws (originally intended to apply to the procedural paradigm) are as relevant today as they have been in the past. Evolution has also been the subject of simulation studies (Smith et al., 2006) and this has allowed OSS evolution to be studied in a contrasting way to that empirically. The research presented in this paper delves into specific evolutionary coupling features (in this case using fan-in and fan-out metrics). In terms of coupling, a framework for its measurement was introduced by Bartsch and Harrison in (2006) embracing different programming styles. Li and Henry (1993) support the view that excessive coupling makes maintenance and tracing more difficult. As a violation of encapsulation, C++ friends - an improper form of coupling, have also been shown to reflect higher fault rates in software (Briand et al., 1997). The role of method invocation (a form of coupling between classes)

in creating faults is also highlighted by the work of Briand et al. (1998). Chidamber and Kemerer proposed six OO metrics amongst which were the Response for a Class (RFC) and Coupling between Objects (CBO) metrics (Chidamber et al., 1994; Fenton et al., 1997). These metrics have been used extensively since. Neither of the metrics however, gives a coarse-grained feel for the incoming and outgoing coupling that fan-in and fan-out provide.

The research in this paper is also inspired by previous work on FIN and FOUT by the authors (Mubarak et al., 2009) on an 80:20 coupling relationships (80% of coupling occurs in 20% of classes). In that same paper only one of FIN and FOUT appeared consistently to have an 80:20 relationship (FIN). Evidence suggested that in fact FIN and FOUT had a complementary relationship. In this paper, we also address the issue of potential re-engineering and view coupling as a key contributor to the decision on whether and when to re-engineer (classes) or not over the lifetime of a system. There is some previous evidence to suggest that 'peaks and troughs' occur in software maintenance (Mubarak et al., 2007), suggesting that developer activity comprises a set of high and low activity periods. This suggests that excessive coupling is a continuous problem addressed only by spurious and frenzied re-engineering activity.

Finally, this study contributes to an empirical body of knowledge on coupling and longitudinal analysis of which more studies have been urged (Kemerer et al., 1999a, 1999b). The basis of the research presented in this paper is that of a previous study by the same authors (Mubarak et al., 2010) in a line of research on coupling. In that paper, preliminary results from the systems were presented. The notion of 'client' and 'server' classes were introduced and studied for the same systems. The same paper did not include any treatment of the effect that size might have on the results presented; size is recognized as a confounding factor which needs to be considered in any study where coupling is a feature (El Emam et al., 2002).

SYSTEMS AND METRICS

The explicit selection criteria for systems studied herein was that first, for consistency of comparison, they all had to be entirely Java and second, sufficient versions of the systems were available (for a longitudinal study). Systems were selected according to the number of downloads they had enjoyed from sourceforge.net only on the basis that the popular systems *might* have enjoyed more developer maintenance activity (e.g., coupling additions, deletions and modification due to the contributions by developers). The following five systems were used as a basis of our study:

1. **Jasmin:** A Java assembler which takes ASCII descriptions of Java classes and converts them into binary Java class files suitable for loading into a Java Virtual Machine. The system comprised 5 versions. It started with 5 packages and had 110 classes and 5 packages and 130 classes by the latest version.
2. **SmallSQL:** A Java DBMS for Java desktop applications. It has a JDBC 3.0 interface and offers many ANSI SQL 92 and ANSI SQL 99 features. The system comprised 9 versions. It started with 130 classes in the first version and had 177 classes in the latest version.
3. **DjVu:** Provides an applet and desktop viewer Java virtual machine comprising 8 versions. It started with 12 packages and 77 classes in the first version with 14 packages and 79 classes in the latest version.
4. **pBeans:** Provides automatic object/relational mapping (ORM) of Java objects to DB tables. Comprised 10 versions, 4 packages and 36 classes in version 1 (10 packages and 69 classes in the latest version).
5. **Asterisk:** Consists of a set of Java classes that allow you to easily build Java applications that interact with an Asterisk PBX Server. This system includes 6 versions. It started

with 12 packages and 222 classes in the first version and ended with 14 packages and 277 classes in the final version.

For each of the five systems, we collected the fan-in and fan-out coupling metrics automatically using the JHawk tool (Counsell et al., 2007). The definition of these two metrics according to JHawk is: 'Fan out is defined as the number of other classes referenced by a class. Fan in is the number of other classes that reference a class'. Henceforward, we refer to fan-in as 'FIN' and fan-out as 'FOUT'. The JHawk tool collects metrics from the source code directories and consequently, the FIN and FOUT metrics collected represent a high-level, broad view of coupling; we note that the tool does not afford an analysis of the different coupling types. In other words, the JHawk tool does not extract coupling through for example aggregation or that of parameter types or any lower-level definition of coupling.

DATA ANALYSIS: 80% SELECTION

In the following analysis, we consider only the largest packages from each system. A package was considered as 'large' if it contained more than ten classes (for statistical validity purposes, we wanted to ensure that the number in each package was relatively high and ten seemed a sensible threshold). We ranked the classes in each of these packages according to their descending FIN values and then took the set of classes from each package that contained 80% of the FIN total. We chose the classes comprising 80% of FIN for a single reason. A previous study has shown that an 80/20 rule applies to coupling in Java classes (Mubarak et al., 2009). In other words, 80% of FIN occurs in just 20% of classes. To be true to the spirit of that earlier study, we adopted the same strategy for selection of classes. Moreover, we wanted to focus on classes with a high FIN and choice of classes comprising 80% of the FIN, when ordered in descending FIN, captures classes with the highest FIN.

Additionally, choosing classes comprising 80% of FIN would also allow us to compare (i.e. correlate) the FIN of those classes with the FOUT of the same set of classes to establish overall relationships between the two metrics and to uncover biases in class make-up and disparity between the two metrics. In particular, we would like to explore the presence of 'key' classes (characterised by a high FIN and high FOUT value) as well as to distinguish 'server' classes that have a high FIN (i.e. those used by many classes) but a low FOUT (i.e. they, correspondingly, do not use many other classes themselves). The profile of these types of classes from an evolutionary perspective is also an interesting research topic and is one that we explore.

The mean of the FIN and FOUT *across the whole package* was also calculated to allow a comparison of the differences between the selected classes and the summary values of FIN and FOUT *for all classes* on an evolutionary package basis. For each of the packages and the set of classes (across all versions) therefore obtained, we asked two questions:

Research Question 1: Is there a significant correlation between FIN and FOUT? If the correlation is negative, then this suggests that, over time, an inverse relationship exists between the two metrics. In other words, as FIN increases there is a decrease in the value of FOUT and *vice versa*. On the other hand,

a positive correlation between the two metrics would imply that both FIN and FOUT increase as a system evolves. As a developer, we would want to choose classes/packages for re-engineering in the former category and preferably when FOUT is increasing (and FIN decreasing).

Research Question 2: Over time, does the relationship between FIN and FOUT worsen (i.e. do both FIN and FOUT increase or does one predominate)?

We note that in the following, we use three correlation coefficients. Spearman's and Kendall's coefficients are non-parametric in nature and assume a non-normal distribution in the data (appropriate for most software engineering data). For completeness however, we have also included Pearson's correlation values – a parametric value which assumes a normal distribution of the data. The FIN and FOUT values for all selected classes and for each version were used as a basis of the correlation analysis.

The Jasmin System

We first consider the set of classes comprising the 80% of FIN. Table 1 shows the correlation between the FIN and FOUT over the five versions (V1-V5) for the Jasmin system on a package basis (the 2 packages chosen using the aforementioned selection criteria in this case were Jas and Jasmin, the latter coincidentally sharing its name with the system from which it is taken). Extracting classes containing 80% of FIN from the Jas package gave

Table 1. Correlations FIN vs. FOUT (Jasmin)

Package	No. of Classes	Pearson's	Kendall's	Spearman's
Jas	50	0.024	0.287**	0.394**
Jasmin	10	-0.973**	-0.619*	-0.788**

*Correlation is significant at the 0.05 level (1-tailed).
**Correlation is significant at the 0.01 level (1-tailed).

a sample of 50 classes for that package and 10 classes for the Jasmin package.

The most striking feature of the values in Table 1 is the significant positive correlation between the two metrics for the Jas package (Kendall's and Spearman's), while the correlation values are strongly and significantly negative for the Jasmin package. There is a simple, yet interesting explanation for each set of correlation values. For the Jas package while the values of FIN are large, the values of FOUT are correspondingly large (Figure 1). Many of these classes are therefore those *used by* many other classes, but also *themselves* use high numbers of other classes. We could thus view this type of class as both a coupling 'source' and 'sink' classes since they use equal measures of both FIN and FOUT. The

dependence of many classes on these types of class alone may make them problematic from a re-engineering perspective. Indeed, Figure 1 shows very few classes where both the FIN is low and FOUT high which would be one possible and sensible criterion for re-engineering. For the Jasmin package on the other hand, the FIN and FOUT metrics are in complete contrast (Figure 2). Classes with high FIN values in this package tend to have low FOUT values and vice versa. The classes in this latter category would be far preferable for re-engineering – since high values for FOUT alone pose less of a problem from a maintenance perspective - the dependencies are outgoing rather than incoming.

From a correlation perspective, both packages present opportunities for re-engineering, but the

Figure 2. FIN/FOUT for the Jasmin package

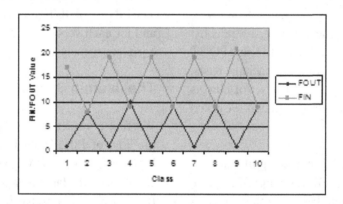

Figure 1. FIN/FOUT for the Jas package

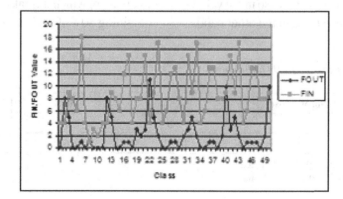

negative correlations for the Jasmin package provide the best opportunity in this sense and the Jas only limited opportunities. In other words, analysis of coupling through extraction of FIN and FOUT has provided an insight in to which classes might be targeted for re-engineering. This would not be the case had we just collected coupling on a far coarser scale using for example, the CBO (Chidamber et al., 2004). The CBO makes no distinction between input coupling and output coupling.

We next consider the set of *all* classes in each of the two packages. The summary data for FIN and FOUT in Table 2 shows the mean, median and maximum values for *every* class in each of the studied packages over the five versions (V1-V5).

Table 2 shows the values of FIN across all the classes of Jas to be relatively small and so too the

values of FOUT. (We note that the values of FIN in each package have been italicised to distinguish them from FOUT values.) There is a clear upward trend in the values of FIN and FOUT in both packages. However, the median values (column 3) do not change significantly throughout and this suggests further that in each package there are certain outliers that subvert the true picture of the FIN and FOUT metrics (i.e., those in Figures 1 and 2).

The values in Table 2 indicate that although FIN and FOUT increase over time, these increases are relatively small. The average values of FOUT in the Jasmin package are significantly higher than that for FIN, again suggesting that classes in this package would be preferable and more amenable to re-engineering than Jas. In answer to the question posed, we see a similarity between the growth in values of FIN and FOUT as they evolve, but not alarmingly so.

The SmallSQL System

Table 3 shows the same correlation values we showed for Jasmin for the SmallSQL system. Only one package was considered for this system, namely 'Database'. The number of the classes comprising the 80% of FIN is 25 classes from a total 135 classes across the nine versions giving a total sample correlation size of (9*25=225). A positive correlation between the FIN metric and the FOUT is evident from Table 3. However, the correlation is weaker for Kendall's and Spearman's, while there is no significant correlation for Pearson's.

Figure 3 shows the values of FIN and FOUT over the nine versions for SmallSQL system on a

Table 2. FIN and FOUT per package (Jasmin)

Package	Metric (Ver)	Mean	Median
Jas	FOUT (V1)	0.67	0
	FOUT (V2)	0.84	0
	FOUT (V3)	1.23	0
	FOUT (V4)	1.35	0
	FOUT (V5)	1.44	0.5
	FIN (V1)	*1.35*	*0*
	FIN (V2)	*1.61*	*0*
	FIN (V3)	*1.86*	*0*
	FIN (V4)	*2.03*	*0*
	FIN (V5)	*2.03*	*0*
Jasmin	FOUT (V1)	6.64	2
	FOUT (V2)	7.17	1.5
	FOUT (V3)	7.23	1
	FOUT (V4)	8.08	1.5
	FOUT (V5)	8.08	1.5
	FIN (V1)	*2.55*	*0*
	FIN (V2)	*2.58*	*0*
	FIN (V3)	*2.38*	*0*
	FIN (V4)	*2.58*	*0*
	FIN (V5)	*2.75*	*0*

Table 3. Correlations FIN vs. FOUT (SmallSQL)

Package	Pearson's	Kendall's	Spearman's
Database	0.041	0.130**	0.175**

**Correlation is significant at the 0.01 level (1-tailed).

Figure 3. FIN/FOUT for the database package

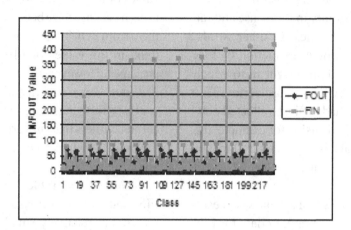

package basis. From Figure 3 it can be seen as was seen for the Jasmin system, that there are some classes with exceptionally large values of FIN. One class that is particularly noticeable is the Utils class, which started with a FIN of 245 in V1 and by V9 had a FIN of 416. In contrast, its FOUT started in version 1 with a value of just 12 and rose to only 19 by version nine.

A class such as Utils (as its name suggests) is likely to be used (i.e., 'utilised') and in great demand increasingly as a system evolves and as more classes are added to the system. A Date class for example is found in java.util – a class which is likely to be used by many other classes. Interestingly, the number of methods in this class and its size in terms of lines of executable code (LOC) did not change significantly. It started with 25 methods and 211 LOC in V1 and in V9 had 34 methods and 257 LOC. In other words, the class itself did not change, but the number of classes *using that class* grew significantly. While the benefits of such a class are clear, classes such as Utils could conceivably pose a problem for developers. With a high FIN, it becomes difficult to modify such a class and this might explain why its size in terms of methods and LOC changed only marginally over the nine versions. This type of class could also be seen as a *key* class to the functioning of the system and while stable in some

senses, might be exceptionally difficult to re-engineer. On the other hand, the fact that it has not changed significantly over the versions studied may mean that it does not need to be re-engineered – so the potential danger outlined is not relevant.

Table 4 presents a summary of the FIN and FOUT for all classes in the Database package of SmallSQL and again gives the value of the mean and median values.

The interesting feature of Table 4 is the drop in both the FIN and FOUT metrics in the transition from V5 to V6. This was not accompanied by any noticeable reduction in the size of the classes; there was some reduction in coupling however, suggesting that between these versions there may have been some effort devoted to re-engineering (with the consequent drop in coupling). Both FIN and FOUT seemed to mirror each other's movements. This again was interesting since it meant that if FIN changed, then FOUT would be changed as a result and also as the system was re-structured. It might also be the case that some active refactoring was undertaken to eliminate inter-class coupling; a natural result of eliminating inter-class coupling is the elimination of total coupling since dependency 'tangling' is simplified overall. In keeping with the Jasmin system, the values of FIN and FOUT remain

Table 4. FIN and FOUT per package (SmallSQL)

Metric (Ver)	Mean	Median
FOUT (V1)	10.32	3
FOUT (V2)	10.53	3
FOUT (V3)	10.31	3
FOUT (V4)	10.38	3
FOUT (V5)	10.42	3
FOUT (V6)	9.96	3
FOUT (V7)	9.98	3
FOUT (V8)	10.13	3
FOUT (V9)	10.19	3
FIN (V1)	*6.92*	*0.5*
FIN (V2)	*8.19*	*0.5*
FIN (V3)	*7.90*	*0*
FIN (V4)	*7.96*	*0*
FIN (V5)	*8.03*	*0*
FIN (V6)	*7.48*	*0*
FIN (V7)	*7.69*	*0*
FIN (V8)	*7.94*	*0*
FIN (V9)	*8.08*	*0*

relatively static. The system does contain a number of classes that are central to the functioning of the system (e.g., Utils).

The DjVu System

Table 5 shows the data for the DjVu system. The number of classes comprising 80% of the FIN was 8 out of 40 across the 9 versions for the Djvu package (the package shares its name with the system from which it is taken), 2 out of 10 for

Table 5. Correlations FIN vs. FOUT (Djvu)

Package	Pearson's	Kendall's	Spearman's
Djvu	-0.088	-0.151	-0.248*
Anno	-0.572*	-0.436*	-0.462*
Toolbar	0.988**	0.914**	0.950**

*Correlation is significant at the 0.05 level (1-tailed).
**Correlation is significant at the 0.01 level (1-tailed).

Anno package and 2 out of 9 for Toolbar package. The number of classes for which we calculated the correlations between FIN and FOUT was 64 for Djvu and 16 apiece for Anno and Toolbar. The first question relates to the nature of the correlations. Negative correlations between FIN and FOUT are evident for the Djvu and Anno packages. There is positive correlation between the metrics for the Toolbar package over the same 8 versions of the DjVu system.

Figure 4 shows the values of FIN and FOUT for the Djvu package. The values of FIN are consistently higher than that of FOUT. *The lines in the graph do not overlap at all and are totally disjoint.* This feature contrasts with all the graphs shown for the previous two systems.

The class which, over the course of the eight versions was consistently high in its FIN was the GRect class; this class started with a FIN value of 59 and ended with a FIN of 81. It had one of the lowest FOUT values for that package however (value of just 4) throughout the versions studied, compared with a mean of 5.67 for the remaining classes. Again, this might be a class for manipulating GUIs which might be critical to system functionality (i.e., a key class). Based on the fact that the Djvu system is a graphically-oriented system – we would expect a shape-oriented class to be the subject of significant use by other classes in the system and this might explain its high FIN. It also gives an insight into the way this type of system evolves. A key class does not see any rise in FOUT, but does in terms of its FIN as more classes use the class. GRect thus acts as a server class to other classes.

Figure 5 shows the FIN and FOUT values for the Anno package. It is interesting that there is a striking difference between the FIN and FOUT values towards later versions of the system studied. The class with the FIN of 11 was the Rect class. The values of FOUT remain static between V4 and V5. It seems that in two packages in this system, the same types of class (i.e., rectangle-based) are both prominent classes (GRect and Rect). This

Figure 4. FIN/FOUT for the Djvu package

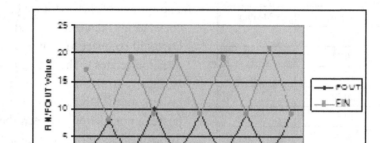

Figure 5. FIN/FOUT for the Anno package

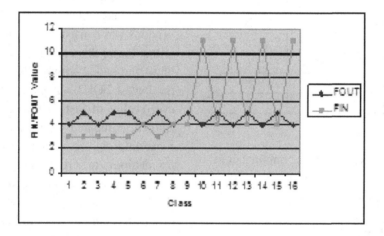

supports our view that there are certain classes whose FIN increases because of their popularity and whose FOUT remains relatively static at the same time. One conclusion that we could draw from our study is therefore that an increasing FIN is not necessarily a sign of decay as such. Some classes become increasingly used by other classes for the functionality they provide. A class whose FIN increases while its FOUT remains stable is a possible sign of one of these types of class.

Figure 6 shows the same data for the Toolbar package. In contrast with any other packages/ systems studied, the values of FOUT are significantly *higher* than that of FIN. There is a strong correspondence between the FIN and FOUT for this package and the values of FIN and FOUT mirror each other; that is, each rises and falls correspondingly. This type of class is characterized by the feature that as incoming coupling is added to it, so too is added outgoing coupling and this is in contrast to classes such as Rect and GRect just described. This feature may be due to the graphical processing nature of the classes in the DjVu system requiring input from other GUI-based classes, and feeding the output to further GUI-based classes – e.g. processing *x* and *y* co-ordinate classes which feature heavily in this system. This would certainly be a plausible explanation. On

Figure 6. FIN/FOUT for the Toolbar package

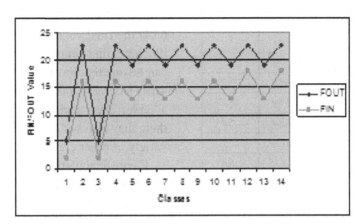

the other hand, it might be a sign of a relatively balanced system that the FIN and FOUT are correspondingly large.

Table 6 shows a summary data for the FIN and FOUT metrics over the different versions for all classes in those packages. (We note that when versions have the same mean and median FOUT or FIN, we list those versions in a single row of the table rather than duplicate a row; see, for example, row 1 of the data in Table 6, pertaining to the FOUT for V1 and V2.)

The Toolbar package is the most striking since both the FIN and FOUT metrics remain relatively static throughout. This is in complete contrast to the Djvu package where FIN rises rapidly and FOUT only marginally. The fluctuation in FIN and FOUT values is also evident for the Anno package (Figure 5). The noticeable feature of Table 6 is the relatively high values of FOUT compared with FIN throughout. In theory, classes with a high FOUT are easier to modify than classes with a high FIN. From the systems studied so far, this system is certainly the most contrasting in terms of its FIN and FOUT values and presents the best opportunity for re-engineering of classes.

The pBeans System

Table 7 shows the correlation data for the pBeans system. We considered two packages for this system – pBeans (again a package that shares its name with the system in which it is located) and the Data package. We calculated the correlations between FIN and FOUT for 37 classes for pBeans package and 30 classes in the Data package (this is how many classes comprised 80% of the FIN across the whole package). A negative correlation between the FIN and FOUT for the pBeans package is evident; however there is no significant correlation between the two metrics for the Data package. Both sets of correlations are negative but only in some cases are they significant. The data in Table 7 suggests that in this system there is a mixture of classes in terms of FIN and FOUT given by the inconsistent pattern of correlations.

Figure 7 shows the values of the FIN and FOUT values for the pBeans package over the versions studied. The peak noticeable for this system was for the StoreException class, which started with a FIN value of 52 which reached 95 by the sixth version. The pBeans package presents an interesting case where the FOUT is significantly larger than FIN in some cases (evident from Figure 7). In particular, the class with the high FOUT was called 'Store' and comprised 88 methods and 690

Table 6. FIN and FOUT per package (DjVu)

Package	Metric (Ver)	Mean	Median
Djvu	FOUT(V1,V2)	6.21	5
	FOUT (V3)	6.5	5
	FOUT(V4,V5,V6)	6.53	5
	FOUT (V7)	6.97	5
	FOUT (V8)	6.89	5
	FIN (V1,V2)	10.29	7.5
	FIN (V3,V4)	13.15	10
	FIN (V5,V6)	13.23	10
	FIN (V7,V8)	15.71	10.5
Anno	FOUT (V1,V2)	9.43	4
	FOUT (V3,V4)	7.78	4
	FOUT (V5)	12.86	11
	FOUT (V6)	16.5	11.5
	FOUT (V7)	14.5	3.5
	FOUT (V8)	8	3
	FIN (V1,V2)	1.14	0
	FIN (V3,V4)	1.33	0
	FIN (V5)	7.57	5
	FIN (V6)	9.17	4.5
	FIN (V7)	4.67	3
	FIN (V8)	2.55	3
Toolbar	FOUT (V1)	25	15.5
	FOUT (V2)	14.56	12
	FOUT (V3,V4)	14.89	12
	FOUT (V5)	14.89	12
	FOUT V6,V7,V8	15.11	12
	FIN (V1)	4.2	1
	FIN (V2)	2.33	1
	FIN (V3,V4)	3.78	1
	FIN (V5)	3.89	1
	FIN (V6, V7, V8)	4.11	1

Table 7. Correlations FIN vs. FOUT (pBeans)

Package	Pearson's	Kendall's	Spearman's
Pbeans	-0.064	-0.271*	-0.355*
Data	-0.676**	0.052	0.087

*Correlation is significant at the 0.05 level (1-tailed).

**Correlation is significant at the 0.01 level (1-tailed).

LOC. The mean number of methods was just 11 and mean LOC 64. The FOUT for this class was 65 at the final version with FIN of just 30. This illustrates that a class, perhaps crucial to a system, can be one that has a high FOUT but not necessarily a correspondingly high FIN. In contrast to a server class such as GRect described earlier, there may also be 'client' classes that use a wide variety of other classes.

Figure 8 shows the values of the FIN and FOUT for the Data package. The remarkable feature is the exceptionally low values of FOUT across the classes. One of the explanations for such a low FOUT and high FIN might be that many of the classes are 'descriptor' classes which many classes would want to use, but equally classes that would not ordinarily use classes themselves. These classes are again server classes that provide a service to other client classes.

Table 8 presents a summary for the FIN and FOUT metrics over the released versions for all classes in the two packages in the pBeans system. The value of the maximum number for FIN over the ten versions is that for the StoreException class in the pBeans package and for FieldDescriptor in the Data package. However, the value of the FOUT metrics for these classes is zero. Table 8 shows fluctuating values in FIN and FOUT and in contrast to previous systems there appears to be little pattern to these fluctuations. Bearing in mind the inconsistent trends in FIN and FOUT (Figures 7 and 8), this might have been expected.

The Asterisk System

Table 9 shows the correlation data for the Asterisk system. There are three packages considered for this system: Fastagi, Manager and Manager.event. The numbers of the classes that we used to calculate the correlations between FIN and FOUT were 29, 42 and 123 classes for the Fastagi, Manager and Manager.event packages, respectively. There is a negative correlation between the FIN and FOUT for the Fastagi package and a positive correlation

Figure 7. FIN/FOUT for the pBeans package

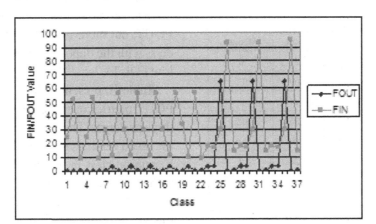

Figure 8. FIN/FOUT for the data package

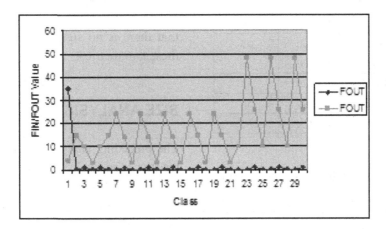

between these metrics for the Manager and Manager.event packages over the seven versions of the Asterisk system. Again, there is no consistency amongst the correlation values in terms of their direction.

Figure 9 shows the FIN and FOUT values for the Fastagi package and explains the negative correlations found for this package in Table 9. There are exceptionally high values of FIN and correspondingly low values of FOUT. One salient feature of the Fastagi is the number of exception handling classes, each of which has an exceptionally large FIN and low FOUT. The same classes are also relatively small, containing only a few

methods. For example, the AGIException class has 2 methods, a value of 109 for FIN and value 0 for FOUT. Figure 10 shows the FIN and FOUT values for the Manager package. The values of FIN and FOUT correspond to a greater extent in this package. Again, we see the existence of server classes with a very high FIN but low FOUT. The Fastagi package is an interesting case from a FIN and FOUT point of view – the classes with the highest FIN are all of a certain type – namely exception handling classes. In practice, it makes sense to group these types of classes together, but this did not seem to be a feature of any of the other systems studied.

Table 8. Summary of FIN and FOUT per package (pBeans)

Package	Metric (Ver)	Mean	Median
pBeans	FOUT (V1,V2)	7.21	0
	FOUT (V3,V4,V5)	6.69	0.5
	FOUT (V6)	6.94	1
	FOUT (V7)	5.85	0.5
	FOUT (V8,V9,V10)	9.19	1.5
	FIN (V1,V2)	*8.21*	*4*
	FIN (V3,V4,V5)	*8.56*	*4*
	FIN (V6)	*8.06*	*2*
	FIN (V7)	*8.15*	*6*
	FIN (V8,V9,V10)	*9.58*	*5*
Data	FOUT (V1,V2)	4.53	2
	FOUT (V3,V4,V5)	5.53	2
	FOUT (V6,V7)	6	2
	FOUT (V8,V9,V10)	5.31	0.5
	FIN (V1,V2)	*2.33*	*0*
	FIN (V3,V4,V5)	*2.65*	*0*
	FIN (V6,V7)	*2.42*	*0*
	FIN (V8,V9,V10)	*6.56*	*1.5*

Table 9. Correlations FIN vs. FOUT (Asterisk)

Package	Pearson's	Kendall's	Spearman's
Fastagi	-0.209	-0.276**	-0.326**
Manager	0.025	0.417**	0.471**
Manager.event	0.254**	0.215**	0.244**

**Correlation is significant at the 0.01 level (1-tailed).

Figure 11 shows the FIN and FOUT values for the Manager.event package. The relatively high FIN values of 28 belong to a class called ManagerEvent. Again the high value of FIN and relatively low value of FOUT for this class makes sense since many classes would want to access this class for the critical functionality it offers (that of event handling).

From the five systems studied, we see that there are certain classes with a low FIN and high FOUT, but more frequent is the occurrence of a class with the opposite characteristics (high FIN, low FOUT).

Table 10 presents a summary for the FIN and FOUT metrics over the released versions for the three packages. The maximum value for FIN over the seven versions is actually the FIN for the Agi-Exception class in Fastagi, for the Channel class in the Manager package and for the ManagerEvent class in the Manager.event package. However, the values of the FOUT metrics for these classes are trivially small. There is a wide fluctuation in mean values for the two metrics over the versions studied. However, in keeping with most of the previous systems – the median values suggest that there is no significant change in terms of these two metrics.

SIZE ANALYSIS

The preceding analysis has pin-pointed characteristics of individual classes and the FIN/FOUT therein. One aspect of the systems that we have analysed only briefly thus far is the 'size' of classes and the relationship that this plays in terms of FIN and FOUT values. We could argue that, from a software engineering perspective, classes with a high FIN should in theory be small classes, since such classes (being used by many other classes) fulfil a specific single function and that specificity implies the class will be both cohesive and small. In the subsequent sections, we therefore explore whether classes with high FIN tend to be small classes. We will use two metrics for this purpose – the number of methods in a class (NOM) and LOC. The NOM metric includes all methods (public, private and protected). The LOC metric includes executable (non-comment) lines.

Figure 9. FIN/FOUT for the Fastagi package

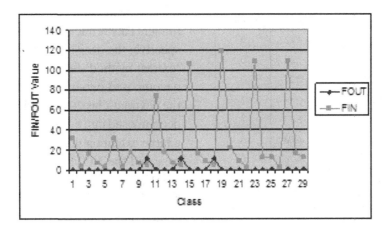

Figure 10. FIN/FOUT for the Manager package

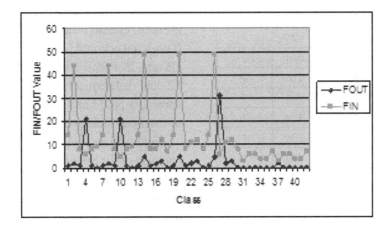

Figure 11. FIN/FOUT for the Manager.event package

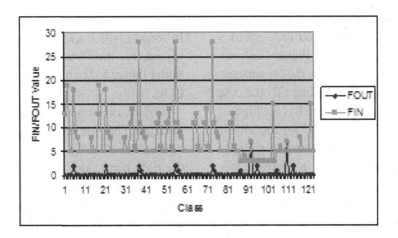

Table 10. FIN and FOUT per package (Asterisk)

Package	Metric (Ver)	Mean	Median
Fastagi	FOUT (V1,V2)	1.83	0
	FOUT(V3,V4,V5)	2	0
	FOUT (V6,V7)	2.21	0
	FIN (V1,V2)	*3*	*1*
	FIN (V3)	*5.17*	*1*
	FIN (V4)	*6.08*	*0*
	FIN (V5)	*6.76*	*0*
	FIN (V6,V7)	*7.21*	*0*
Manager	FOUT (V1,V2)	3.67	0
	FOUT(V3,V4,V5)	4.23	1
	FOUT (V6)	0.64	0
	FOUT (V7)	6.17	0
	FIN (V1,V2)	*3.55*	*0*
	FIN (V3,V4,V5)	*3.26*	*0*
	FIN (V6,V7)	*3*	*3*
Manager Event	FOUT (V1,V2)	0.04	0
	FOUT V3,V4,V5	0.05	0
	FOUT (V6,V7)	0.15	0
	FIN (V1,V2)	*3.18*	*1*
	FIN (V3,V4,V5)	*2.99*	*1*
	FIN (V6)	*1.83*	*1*
	FIN (V7)	*3.48*	*3*

Classes with High FIN

For each of the packages scrutinised, we ordered the set of classes on descending number of FIN. We then extracted the NOM and LOC metrics from that ordered set of classes. Figure 12 shows the NOM and LOC for classes in the Jas package of the Jasmin system on descending FIN (i.e., the left most class (class 1) therefore has the highest FIN and right-most class (class 50) the lowest FIN). There is a clear trend from the figure for classes with a high FIN to have a relatively low NOM and LOC. The median NOM and LOC for classes 1-24 from Figure 12 is 6.5 and 25; the corresponding value for classes 25-50 is 5 for NOM and 39 for LOC. In other words, while

the NOM for classes with high FIN is also high, the LOC values for such classes are significantly higher. This is interesting from a refactoring perspective; the decision as to whether to apply the 'extract method' refactoring (where a method is decomposed into one or more other methods) or the 'extract class' refactoring (where a class is decomposed into one or more classes) depends to a large extent on the size of a method in the first case and the NOM in the second case. In other words, we justify the use of NOM and LOC on the basis that they show different aspects of size and could conceivably lead to the choice of different refactorings. (We need to be mindful of the fact that Figure 12 and all subsequent figures in this section represent classes over different versions of the systems. In other words, Figure 12 represents the set of classes ordered on descending FIN only. It does not account for the evolution of FIN in the classes. In a sense, this makes the trend in Figure 12 and subsequent figures more illuminating since low NOM and LOC are a feature of classes *throughout* their evolution).

Figure 13 shows the same data for the Database package of the SmallSQL system. It is interesting that some of the highest values of NOM and LOC are for mid-range FIN values (as evidenced by the high peaks towards the middle of the figure). From the 233 classes used, the median NOM and LOC for classes 1-116 from Figure 13 are 28 and 156, respectively; the corresponding values for classes 117-233 are 15 for NOM and 59 for LOC. In keeping with Jas, and contrary to what we might expect, for the Database package, classes with high FIN tended to have both a higher NOM and LOC.

Figure 14 shows the same data for the DjVu package. The striking feature of the figure is the high values of LOC at low values of FIN (towards the right hand side of the figure). In contrast to the previous two packages, this evidence clearly supports the stance that high FIN is associated with relatively low values of NOM and LOC (and classes with low FIN tend to have high values of

Figure 12. NOM and LOC for the Jas package (Jasmin)

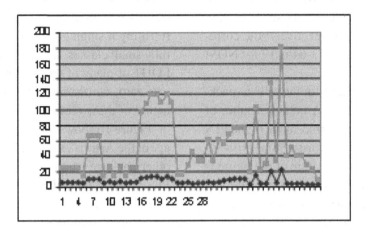

Figure 13. NOM and LOC for the Database package (SmallSQL)

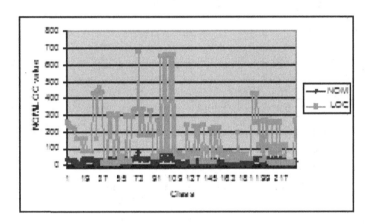

Figure 14. NOM and LOC for the DjVu package (DjVu)

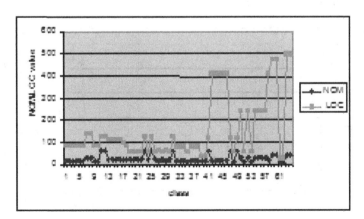

both NOM and LOC). From the 64 classes used, the median NOM and LOC for classes 1-32 from Figure 14 is 21 and 82, respectively; the corresponding value for classes 33-64 is 17 for NOM and 116 for LOC.

Figure 15 shows the data for the pBeans package in the pBeans system. A notable feature of the figure is the peak in the mid-range of the FIN values. This belonged to class: Store with 85 methods. Another notable feature of the figure is the high number of very low values in NOM and LOC. It is interesting that the class with the highest FIN (95) comprised just 3 NOM and 4 LOC. This was class StoreException. In fact, many of

the classes from Figure 15 were exception-based classes which many other classes *used* but by fulfilling a single, cohesive function were naturally small classes. It is also worth noting that the FOUT of many of these exception-based classes was zero, confirming the sink-like, server-type nature of these classes.

Figure 16 shows the data for the Fastagi package of the Asterisk system. In common with every other package studied, classes with a very high FIN have a relatively low NOM and LOC, but there is a spike at mid-range FIN values. Most interesting from the figure is the 1:1 correspondence between the NOM and LOC.

Figure 15. NOM and LOC for the pBeans package (pBeans)

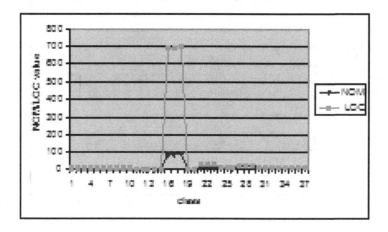

Figure 16. NOM and LOC for the Fastagi package (Asterisk)

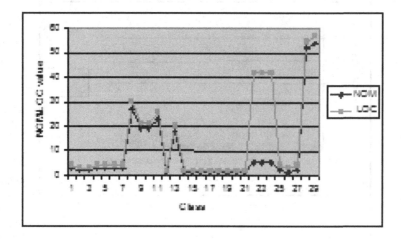

Inspection of the relevant classes revealed that, in keeping with the DjVu package, the classes tended to be exception-based classes with methods containing only a single LOC. It is clear from the preceding analysis that classes with the highest FIN represent some of the smallest classes in the system. In the next section, we explore some of the questions raised by the study including that of whether FOUT exhibits an opposite effect to that of FIN i.e., are some of the largest classes also classes with the largest FOUT?

DISCUSSION

The study presented raises a number of outstanding issues. First, given the evidence presented, what do the results mean for class development? It would appear that classes with a high FIN value tend to be small classes which perform a specific function, usually related to exception/error handling. We found evidence of error and exception handling classes with high values of FIN and invariably with a zero-valued FOUT. The question that naturally arises from this is whether classes with a high FOUT have specific characteristics. To explore this issue, we ranked classes in each of the packages on descending FOUT. Figure 17

shows the values of NOM and LOC for the Jas package in the Jasmin system. The figure shows the opposite effect to that of Figures 12, 14 and 16. High values of FOUT (given at the left-hand side of the figure) appear to be associated with high values of NOM and LOC as opposed to low values of each that we found for FIN.

Figure 18 shows the values of NOM and LOC for the Database package in the SmallSQL system. The same trend is evident – high values of FOUT are associated with high values of NOM and LOC.

From the preceding analysis, we could conclude that if a class has a high FIN value then it will tend to be a relatively small class in terms of its NOM and LOC values. If a class has a high FOUT, then it will tend to be a relatively large class in terms of its NOM and LOC values.

So the question arises as to how this knowledge could be used by a developer? It is clear that classes with a high FIN are usually 'server' classes that provide a specific function. Classes with a high FOUT are candidates for refactoring. The aim of such refactoring would be to eliminate some of the FOUT. In many cases observable from Figures 17 and 18, the NOM is relatively static, while the LOC is less so. For example, the standard deviation of the LOC values in Figure 18 is 158.12. The standard deviation of NOM values is just 15.17. We could

Figure 17. NOM/LOC values for Jas package (Jasmin)

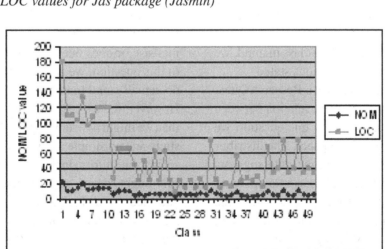

Figure18. NOM and LOC for the Database package (SmallSQL)

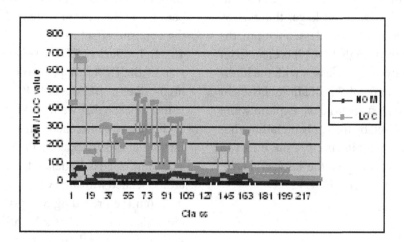

suggest that initially both the 'Extract Method' (Fowler, 1999) and 'Extract Class' (Fowler, 1999) would be appropriate refactorings for classes with high FOUT values. In the former case, the purpose would be to decompose one method into one or more new methods. The purpose of the latter refactoring would be to decompose a class into one or more other classes. We would also have to consider the possibility that classes with high FOUT also suffer from the 'Feature Envy' bad smell (Fowler, 1999). This arises when a class X relies too much on the features of other classes. Elements of the class X should therefore be moved to those classes to reduce coupling. One result of FIN and FOUT analysis is therefore to identify potential refactorings; we could eliminate candidate classes with high FIN values in most cases. With these three types of class in mind, we re-visit our two research questions stated.

The first question we re-visit is Research Question 1. Is there a significant correlation between FIN and FOUT? In answer to this question we return to the findings in the paper. The distribution of FIN and FOUT from the data suggests three broad categories of class: a) classes with high FIN and low FOUT (server classes), b) the opposite, with high FOUT and low FIN (client classes) and c) classes with high amounts of both

FIN and FOUT – the high end of which could be considered 'key' classes. In previous work (Mubarak et al., 2009) a complementary (negatively correlated) relationship appeared to exist between FIN and FOUT. Our study thus supports this viewpoint, albeit that it does not recognise the existence of type c) classes. For type a) and b) classes however, this viewpoint can be supported. It would appear that the relationship between FIN and FOUT can vary depending on the nature of the class. We could conclude that there are positive, significant correlations and significant negative correlations in situations where either FIN or FOUT predominates.

Next we re-consider Research Question 2. Over time, does the relationship between FIN and FOUT worsen (i.e. do both FIN and FOUT increase or does one predominate)? In response to this question, we suggest that FIN and FOUT do actually tend to increase as a system evolves. However, the exact picture is more complicated than we might have envisaged when we started the study and no simple answer exists. The increases seem to be uniform in the sense that in some cases, FIN might remain stable while FOUT increases and vice versa. In the first case, this might be reflective of a class which becomes increasingly dependent on other classes. In the latter case (i.e., when FOUT remains stable and FIN increases), this reflects a situation where a class is becoming increasingly depended upon by other classes. The research question could be said to be true where both FIN and FOUT increase and we did find evidence of this in any many cases.

The results from the systems show that coupling is a multi-faceted feature of systems about which it is difficult to make predictions. While we might be able to identify classes likely to exhibit increased coupling – it is only by observing a system over time, noting any danger signs early on and refactoring those classes that a 'bad' situation can be prevented from worsening. It is interesting that in the cases of classes with a high FIN, it would be difficult to justify the effort required for its refactoring. All that refactoring a large class (with high FIN) might achieve is to spread the same coupling amongst a small set of 'new' classes; doing so might actually introduce more coupling as a result. Equally, refactoring a class with a high FOUT might present an easier task. However, we have to consider the view point of 'better the Devil you know'; in other words, knowing where classes with high FOUT are actually located and can be monitored might be far preferable to decomposing classes to form a range of new classes, whose location, functionality and control is less clear.

One interesting 'holistic' question that arises from the study is that the OO paradigm was introduced to encourage developers to think about classes as self-contained units that communicate minimally with other classes. In theory, classes should remain relatively stable in terms of the maintenance effort required to keep the system up and running. Yet, in the study presented, we saw evidence of widespread changes to classes as they evolve. The message seems to be, in accordance with Lehman's principles of Evolution (Belady et al., 1974) that whether object-oriented or procedural, a system will need to be changed throughout its lifetime to accommodate new requirements and/or correct faults. The notion of an

object's composition remaining stable after design does not seem to have been realised as a result of the OO paradigm. Coupling is necessary and unfortunately, when used excessively, can create highly complex systems which are difficult to maintain. A message from the study presented is that coupling should be therefore be 'managed' in a pragmatic and sensible way.

Finally, it is useful to consider the implications of the research from the perspective of the developer and that of the end user. In the case of the former, it is clear that a small subset of classes in a system is likely to contain either: high FIN, high FOUT or both (i.e. high FIN and high FOUT). In the experience of the authors, every system will typically contain classes of each of these three types. That said, the developer needs to be mindful of the facts that a) these classes should be monitored to ensure that they do not become the source of a disproportionate number of faults as they evolve and b) the decision to re-engineer these classes should be weighed against the benefits of doing so. The extent of coupling in a class should also be considered relative to its size; a small class with high coupling is, in some senses, a more eligible candidate for re-engineering than a larger class with the same level of coupling.

It is incumbent on us to also consider the implications of the research on the end user. After all – it is largely they who are affected if a system is overly fault-prone and/or inefficient. From the perspective of the end user, the quality of a system is informed directly by the quality of its design and how 'stable' it is (i.e., subject to change). Put another way, if a system is constantly being revised and re-released, then this reflect poor initial requirements analysis, poor initial design and a poorly implemented system. In terms of quality factors of real interest to end users, reliability and efficiency would be of immense importance. The value of the work described in this paper to an end user is that monitoring coupling and being aware of the type of classes (and potential dangers associated with such classes) by developers can have a direct, positive effect on the efficiency of the implementation; by minimising coupling there is the benefit of a potential reduction in faults. With that in mind, a conscious and consistent monitoring effort on the part of developers and project manager to prevent classes becoming problematic would be a sensible strategy. One monitoring policy that could be adopted is to define threshold values for coupling, beyond which decisions on what to do with the class (e.g., re-engineer it) should be made.

THREATS TO VALIDITY

We also have to consider the threats to the validity of the study. First, the generalisability of the results on a number of platforms could be questioned. We have used five systems as a basis of our empirical study and we could therefore be criticised because this only represents a small sample of the many OSS freely available. In our defence, we see the study presented as a first step towards a body of empirical knowledge about trends in FIN and FOUT. We could also argue that we would be subject to exactly the same criticism had we chosen thirty or even one hundred OSS systems. Limited time and resources prevent such a study, but we invite other researchers to undertake similar studies to ours. A further criticism is that we have chosen systems of *different* application domains and sizes. We could have chosen systems of the same application domain and size, but while our results might be more focused as a result, the generalisability of such a study possibly compromised even more. By choosing different application domains, we feel we obtain a much richer source of data and a greater ability to identify future avenues for future research.

Second, the study may be criticised for using OSS and not proprietary software. It is true to say that a number of issues are raised by the study of each 'type.' The first issue is that it is difficult to obtain data from a large number of proprietary systems as we are able to do using OSS. The authors have been active in studying data from proprietary systems in the last few years (Gatrell et al., 2009), but usually these are studies have a far more specific research question than coupling *per se*. Furthermore, both OO and OSS have recently been the subject of a great deal of empirical research (Advani et al., 2006; Capiluppi et al., 2004a, 2004b) and a wide range of research issues and research questions remain unanswered in both, one of which is a greater understanding of coupling issues. It is also true to say that many organisations are using OSS as part of their development strategy; by studying OSS we are therefore appealing to industry users and also informing the practices of industry. One of the dangers of industry using OSS is lack of knowledge about the quality of 'free' software.

Third, we have assumed that high levels of FOUT are harmful. Generally speaking this is true – excessive coupling is complexity that can lead to seeding of faults; however, we have to accept that some forms of Java coupling (e.g., interfaces and inheritance) and their evolution (Harrison et al., 2000) are a necessary part of the language without which large systems could not be built. A level of coupling is necessary in any system and some classes by their nature provide features required by many other classes (and are therefore highly coupled through FIN). Equally, some classes need to use many other classes and as such will, by their nature, have high FOUT values. In other words, a 'one size fits all' approach to coupling is a slightly naïve view.

Fourth, a further criticism that could be levelled at the study is that FIN and FOUT give a broad picture of coupling in a system; more insight into system coupling might have been provided had we been able to decompose the two metrics into the different forms of coupling, e.g., inheritance, aggregation and parameter reference types. From a pragmatic perspective, the JHawk tool does not collect coupling other than at a broad level.

It does collect the CBO and RFC of Chidamber and Kemerer (1994), but these represent equally broad views of coupling and do not represent a decomposition of coupling as such. From the perspective of the original purpose of the study, a conscious decision was made to study coupling through the FIN and FOUT metrics and at that level. We justify this stance on two bases; a) these two metrics were among the original coupling metrics proposed by Stevens et al. (1974) and yet have not been the subject of significant empirical research. Our study represents a hard look at the value of empirical trends in these metrics. We feel that a project manager would prefer to have a broad-brush view of coupling in the first instance and then to drill-down further should they need to; b) the purpose of the study was to highlight trends at a high-level as a coarse means of identifying re-engineering and refactoring opportunities. We justify this stance on the following basis: many of the refactorings and code 'smells' identified by Fowler (1999) are based on coarse levels of coupling. For example, the 'Feature Envy' smell is based on the over-dependency of one class on the features of another class. To all intents and purposes, this is coupling at a broad level. Equally, the 'Move Method' refactoring is applicable when a method is being used by another class more than it is being used in its current class. It should be moved to the former; again, this is form of general and unspecific coupling.

Fifth, we have to consider the possibility that a decrease in FIN, for example might automatically mean an increase in the FOUT value for any single class and vice versa. In other words, there is an inverse relationship between the two metrics. In this study, we have considered the FIN and FOUT for a single class without considering the effect that change in either might have on other classes. Of course, this is a valid research question to ask and a particularly interesting research question. However, the logistics of examining the changes in one class that affect other classes (on a large scale) we would view as a future research project; the task of establishing whether (and how) changes in FIN or FOUT for a specific class influences other classes in a system is a non-trivial one. For example, to establish the net effect of a reduction in the FIN of a class would require analysis of the change/revision logs to determine the set of changes that accompanied that reduction on all affected classes. A tool assistant might be needed for a study along these lines.

CONCLUSION AND FUTURE WORK

In this paper we have investigated the relationship between the FIN and FOUT in five open-source systems. A number of findings arose from the analysis. The key finding was that for most of the systems there is a correlation between the changes in the FIN and FOUT. This correlation was negative for some packages; but positive for most other packages – this informed our interpretation of the two metrics. We also asked two salient questions. First, what was the nature and characteristics of classes exhibiting the highest FIN values? Second, do FIN and FOUT increase in corresponding and consistent amounts over time? Our analysis revealed a wide range of traits in the classes to explain high and low levels of FIN and FOUT. We found evidence of certain 'key' classes with high FIN and FOUT; we also found evidence of classes with just high FIN ('server'-type) classes. In certain cases, the size of a class revealed its purpose as much as the values of FIN and FOUT. Evolutionary aspects also showed evidence of a range of parallel changes in FIN and FOUT metrics as they evolved; in other cases, we found unilateral and independent evolution with respect to the two metrics studied. Finally, we observed that high FIN values tended to be associated with classes with specific responsibilities (e.g., error and exception handling). These classes also tended to be small classes in terms of methods and lines of code. Classes with high FOUT on the other hand tended to be classes with high numbers of methods and lines of code.

Above all, the research presented tells us that there is no such thing as completely common trends in systems as far as coupling is concerned and that there are multiple reasons why classes may be highly or minimally coupled through FIN, FOUT or a combination of both. That said, there are other class characteristics that play a crucial part in determining the level of FOUT, such as size and associated with that, the level and type of functionality. 'Key' and 'server' classes it would appear are a fundamental feature in the evolution of a system and its functioning.

We believe that the results presented in this paper are of relevance, since software systems (and developers) spend most of their 'life' in maintenance mode. Coupling in its different forms is a facet of maintenance that has always presented and will continue to present a challenge to developers. Understanding where and how coupling tends to be located helps predict future maintenance activity and also to target scarce refactoring resources to areas where most benefit will be observed. Of course, we would ideally like to have an 'optimal' level of coupling (FIN and FOUT) against which we could compare class coupling; that however is an elusive target, despite some efforts in this area (El Emam et al., 2002).

Future work will focus on first exploring the opportunities and effects of applying refactorings to classes that appear to have a high FOUT; it will also consider a finer-grained analysis of the different types of coupling inherent in the classes studied and a coupling analysis 'normalised' by class size. An analysis of the different forms of coupling might provide insights not afforded by the study of FIN and FOUT. Finally, a interdependence analysis of the effect of a reduction or increase in FIN/FOUT on related classes might reveal further interesting insights. In other words, the question as whether there is an inverse relationship between FIN and FOUT is germane to the study presented. We would encourage further empirical studies into the areas explored to refute, support or complement the results in this paper; to that end; all the data used in this paper can be obtained for replication purposes and other analyses on request from the lead author.

REFERENCES

Advani, A., Hassoun, Y., & Counsell, S. (2006). Extracting refactoring trends from open-source software and a possible solution to the 'related refactoring' conundrum. In *Proceedings of the ACM Symposium on Applied Computing*, Dijon, France (pp. 1713-1720).

Bartsch, M., & Harrison, R. (2006, April). A coupling framework for AspectJ. In *Proceedings of the 10th International Conference on Evaluation and Assessment in Software Engineering*, Keele, UK.

Belady, L., & Lehman, M. (1976). Model of large program development. *IBM Systems Journal, 15*, 225–252. doi:10.1147/sj.153.0225.

Briand, L., Daly, J., Porter, V., & Wuest, J. (1998). Predicting fault-prone classes based on design measures in object-oriented systems. In *Proceedings of the 9th International Symposium on Software Reliability Engineering*, Paderborn, Germany (pp. 334-343).

Briand, L., Daly, J., & Wust, J. (1999). A unified framework for coupling measurement in object-oriented systems. *IEEE Transactions on Software Engineering, 25*, 91–121. doi:10.1109/32.748920.

Briand, L., Devanbu, P., & Melo, W. (1997). An investigation into coupling measures for C++. In *Proceedings of the 19th International Conference on Software Engineering*, Boston, MA (pp. 412-421).

Capiluppi, A., Morisio, M., & Ramil, J. (2004a). Studying the evolution of open source systems at different levels of granularity. In *Proceedings of the 12th International Workshop on Program Comprehension*, Bari, Italy (pp. 172-182).

Capiluppi, A., & Ramil, J. (2004b). Studying the evolution of open source systems at different levels of granularity: Two case studies. In *Proceedings of the 7th International Workshop on Principles of Software Evolution*, Kyoto, Japan (pp. 113-118).

Chapin, N., Hale, J., Kham, K., Ramil, J., & Tan, W. (2001). Types of software evolution and software maintenance. *Journal of Software Maintenance: Research and Practice*, *13*(1), 3–30. doi:10.1002/smr.220.

Chidamber, S., & Kemerer, C. (1994). A metrics suite for object oriented design. *IEEE Transactions on Software Engineering*, *20*, 476–493. doi:10.1109/32.295895.

Counsell, S., Hassoun, Y., Johnson, R., Mannock, K., & Mendes, E. (2003). Trends in java code changes: The key to identification of refactorings? In *Proceedings of the International Conference on the Principle and Practice of Programming in Java*, Ireland (pp. 45-48).

Counsell, S., Loizou, G., & Najjar, R. (2007). Quality of manual data collection in Java software: An empirical investigation. *Empirical Software Engineering*, *12*(3), 275–293. doi:10.1007/s10664-006-9028-y.

El Emam, K., Benlarbi, S., Goel, N., Melo, W., Lounis, H., & Rai, S. (2002). The optimal class size for object-oriented software. *IEEE Transactions on Software Engineering*, *28*(5), 494–509. doi:10.1109/TSE.2002.1000452.

Fenton, N., & Pfleeger, S. (1997). *Software metrics: A rigorous and practical approach* (2nd ed.). Boston, MA: Course Technology.

Ferenc, R., Siket, I., & Gyimothy, T. (2004, September). Extracting facts from open source software. In *Proceedings of the 20th International Conference on Software Maintenance*, Chicago, IL (pp. 60-69).

Fowler, M. (1999). *Refactoring: Improving the design of existing code*. New York, NY: Pearson Education.

Gatrell, M., Counsell, S., & Hall, T. (2009, October). Design patterns and change proneness: A replication using proprietary C# software. In *Proceedings of the IEEE Working Conference on Reverse Engineering*, Lille, France.

Godfrey, M., & Tu, Q. (2001). Growth, evolution, and structural change in open source software. In *Proceedings of the 4th International Workshop on Principles of Software Evolution*, Vienna, Austria (pp. 103-106).

Harrison, R., Counsell, S., & Nithi, R. (2000). Experimental assessment of the effect of inheritance on the maintainability of object-oriented systems. *Journal of Systems and Software*, *52*(2-3), 173–179. doi:10.1016/S0164-1212(99)00144-2.

JHawk tool. (2011). *Virtual machinery*. Retrieved from http://www.virtualmachinery.com/jhawk-prod.htm

Kemerer, C., & Slaughter, S. (1999a). Need for more longitudinal studies of software maintenance. *Empirical Software Engineering: An International Journal*, *2*, 109–118. doi:10.1023/A:1009741031615.

Kemerer, C., & Slaughter, S. (1999b). An empirical approach to studying software evolution. *IEEE Transactions on Software Engineering*, *25*, 493–509. doi:10.1109/32.799945.

Li, W., & Henry, S. (1993). Object oriented metrics that predict maintainability. *Journal of Systems and Software*, *23*, 112–122. doi:10.1016/0164-1212(93)90077-B.

Mäntylä, M., & Lassenius, C. (2006). Subjective evaluation of software evolvability using code smells: An empirical study. *Journal of Empirical Software Engineering, 11*(3), 395–431. doi:10.1007/s10664-006-9002-8.

Mubarak, A., Counsell, S., & Hierons, H. (2008). An empirical study of "removed" classes in Java open-source. In *Proceedings of the Fourth International Joint Conferences on Computer, Information, and Systems Sciences, and Engineering.*

Mubarak, A., Counsell, S., & Hierons, R. (2008). Empirical observations on coupling, code warnings and versions in Java open-source. In *Proceedings of the Third IFIP TC2 Central and East European Conference on Software Engineering Techniques*, Brno, Czech Republic.

Mubarak, A., Counsell, S., & Hierons, R. (2009). Does an 80:20 rule apply to Java coupling? In *Proceedings of the International Conference on Evaluation and Assessment in Software Engineering*, Keele, UK.

Mubarak, A., Counsell, S., & Hierons, R. (2010, May 19-21). An evolutionary study of fan-in and fan-out metrics in OSS. In *Proceedings of the Fourth International Conference on Research Challenges in Information Science*, Nice, France.

Mubarak, A., Counsell, S., Hierons, R., & Hassoun, Y. (2007). Package evolvability and its relationship with refactoring. In *Proceedings of the Third International ERCIM Symposium on Software Evolution*, Paris, France.

Smith, N., Capiluppi, A., & Fernandez-Ramil, J. (2006). Agent-based simulation of open source evolution. *Journal of Software Process - Improvement and Practice, 11*, 423-434.

Stevens, W., Myers, G., & Constantine, L. (1974). Structured design. *IBM Systems Journal, 13*(2), 115–139. doi:10.1147/sj.132.0115.

This work was previously published in the International Journal of Information System Modeling and Design (IJISMD), Volume 2, Issue 4, edited by Remigijus Gustas, pp. 1-26, copyright 2011 by IGI Publishing (an imprint of IGI Global).

Section 4
Goal and Actor Modeling

Chapter 10
A Method for Eliciting Goals for Business Process Models based on Non-Functional Requirements Catalogues

Evellin Cardoso
Federal University of Espírito Santo, Brazil

João Paulo A. Almeida
Federal University of Espírito Santo, Brazil

Renata S. S. Guizzardi
Federal University of Espírito Santo, Brazil

Giancarlo Guizzardi
Federal University of Espírito Santo, Brazil

ABSTRACT

While traditional approaches in business process modeling tend to focus on "how" the business processes are performed (adopting a behavioral description in which business processes are described in terms of procedural aspects), in goal-oriented business process modeling, the proposals strive to extend traditional business process methodologies by providing a dimension of intentionality to business processes. One of the key difficulties in enabling one to model goal-oriented processes concerns the identification or elicitation of goals. This paper reports on a case study conducted in a Brazilian hospital, which obtained several goal models represented in i*/Tropos, each of which correspond to a business process also modeled in the scope of the study. NFR catalogues were helpful in goal elicitation, uncovering goals that did not come up during previous interviews prior to these catalogues' use.

DOI: 10.4018/978-1-4666-4161-7.ch010

INTRODUCTION

The increasing competitiveness drives organizations to promote change in an attempt to improve the quality of the services and products they offer. In recent years, many of the efforts related to managing change in organizations have been conducted in the scope of Business Process Reengineering (Hammer, 1990; Hammer & Champy, 1993). This is based on the assumption that change in business processes should generate radical improvements in critical performance measures (such as cost, quality, service and speed) (Hammer & Champy, 1993). Moreover, it is believed that implementing radical changes in business processes is the way to achieve dramatic and satisfactory results (Hammer, 1990; Hammer & Champy, 1993).

Business Process Modeling is the activity which provides a deep understanding about the organizational processes, so as to grasp how to promote the aforementioned improvements (Hammer, 1990; Hammer & Champy, 1993). However, predicting how a given enterprise environment should respond to changes by simply adopting a business-process centered view is unfeasible since there is a large number of issues to be considered, such as infrastructure, power and politics, organizational culture, etc. (Yu, 1995). Given this multitude of issues, understanding an organizational setting often requires a number of perspectives (Yu, 1995).

While traditional approaches in business process modeling tend to focus on "how" the business processes are performed (adopting a behavioral description in which business processes are described in terms of procedural aspects), in goal-oriented business process modeling (Yamamoto et al., 2006; Neiger & Churilov, 2004), the proposals strive to extend traditional business process methodologies by providing a dimension of intentionality for the business processes (Kavakli & Loucopoulos, 2003). The Zachman (1987) framework also highlights the importance of "motivation" as a driver for enterprise management and system development. Therefore, in the context of business process modeling, goal modeling is extended not only to capture concerns and motivations of the stakeholders in the achievement of business processes, but to incorporate issues related with the strategy of the enterprise as a whole.

Recently, goal-oriented approaches have been largely addressed in the literature of Requirements Engineering (RE), focusing on how these approaches support requirements analysis and modeling for system development (Kavakli & Loucopoulos, 2003). In this context, goals are defined as objectives that should be achieved by the system and its environment (Lamsweerde, 2001). When goals are decomposed and the responsibility to achieve a goal is allocated to the system (as opposed to its environment) a goal becomes a requirement on the system (Lamsweerde, Darimont, & Letier, 1998). If the object under consideration is not a software system but a business process embedded in its organizational environment, goals for business processes may be regarded as objectives to be achieved by the execution of a business process in its environment. Following this analogy, as goals guide the design of the target system in goal-oriented RE, goals guide the creation of business processes in goal-oriented business process engineering. In this scenario, goal elicitation is a key activity as it will helps us understand if the activities carried out truly relate to the organization's strategy.

Most of research initiatives related to goals focuses on goal modeling and analysis, while the area of goal elicitation has remained largely neglected. As a result, goal elicitation remains a challenging activity with problems with respect to methodological guidance (some problems are for example identified in Halleux, Mathieu, and Andersson (2008) and Singh and Woo (2008)). We have experienced this firsthand while conducting a case study in a Rheumatology Department of a hospital in Brazil. The problems we encountered in goal elicitation motivated us to study this subject in further depth. As a result, we propose in this article a systematic way to identify goals in a given organization, thus contributing to the area of goal elicitation. In this case, goals are elicited as part of the so-called AS-IS model, i.e. a stage in which both goals and business processes are aimed at identifying the organization as it is today (in other words, prior to potential business process change). In particular, we investigate here the use of Non-Functional Requirement (NFR) catalogues (Chung et al., 2000; Cysneiros, 2009) in order to tackle the difficulty in identifying business goals. We have observed that a number of non-functional requirements defined in the scope of the NFR framework can be abstracted and extrapolated to identify (soft)goals which have strategic relevance for business process models and that had not been previously identified with other techniques.

This paper is structured as follows: initially, we situate the reader in relation to the approaches for goal elicitation in the context of RE and introduce the proposed method of goal elicitation for business process models. Subsequently, we illustrate the application of this method, discussing some limitations and benefits of the proposed approach. Finally, we conclude this work, presenting our agenda for future work.

GOAL ELICITATION IN THE CONTEXT OF REQUIREMENTS ENGINEERING

Goal-oriented techniques arose in the RE field due to the difficulties presented by traditional systems analysis approaches when dealing with increasingly complex software systems (Lapouchnian, 2005). This issue led practitioners and researches to move their focus to methods and techniques for developing systems which are better aligned with the organizational strategy, introducing some notion of intentionality in these methods and techniques. This section is split in two sub-sections, the first one dealing with several techniques related to goal elicitation, some of which we ap-

plied in the context of our work (e.g. refinement and abstraction techniques). We then dedicated a special section for the NFR Framework, which had a greater impact in our research.

Overview of Existing Approaches

Although the goal elicitation is an active concern in the RE field, many problems related with goal discovery and refinement are still to be solved in literature. For instance, problems related to goal elicitation have been firstly addressed by the RE literature, but essentially the same problems arise within the business process modeling area. Examples include:

1. Goals are difficult to formulate (often these formulations become vague and highly abstract) (Halleux, Mathieu, & Andersson, 2008);
2. The existing approaches for goal elicitation lacks detailed systematic structures (Singh & Woo, 2008), besides being high level and abstract in nature (e.g. asking how, why and how else questions);
3. The involved parties are unable to explicitly state their views (Dardenne, Lamsweerde, & Fickas, 1993);
4. Even when the stakeholders are capable of stating their views, the elicited goals can be conflicting (even when goals are drawn from the same individual) (Alexander, 2002);
5. Analysts have limited knowledge about the environment (Dardenne, Lamsweerde, & Fickas, 1993);
6. Stakeholders do not know how to set tactical and operational goals that accurately reflect the strategic goals (Singh & Woo, 2008);
7. Although stakeholders know about their individual obligations, they are seldom aware of how their role contributes to the realization of business-wide objectives (Kavakli, 2004);
8. Stakeholders do not know how to define goal attributes (for example specificity, difficulty,

acceptance, and commitment) (Singh & Woo, 2008);

9. Often, there is confusion about the fundamental distinction between what to achieve (the goal) and the manner to achieve it (the strategy). This makes it more difficult to discover alternative ways of achieving a goal (Nurcan et al., 2005).

Given this difficulty in eliciting goals, we surveyed the state-of-art in the area of RE for goal discovery. Among the sources which could potentially provide goals for analysts, the literature in *goal-oriented requirements engineering* cites (1) stakeholders who can explicitly state them; (2) preliminary material about the organization; (3) preliminary analysis of the current system (in this case, a preliminary analysis of the current organizational setting) with the identification of problems and deficiencies which lead to TO-BE goals (Lamsweerde, 2001; Lapouchnian, 2005); and (4) policies, strategies, products, processes, models of the organization (Basili, Caldiera, & Rombach, 1994) and mission statements (Koubarakis & Plexousakis, 2000).

Once a preliminary set of goals has been identified (using the aforementioned sources), refinement and abstraction techniques can be applied to identify other goals (Lamsweerde, 2001). With the *refinement technique*, one can find out sub-goals of the parent goal by asking "HOW questions" about the goals already identified (Lamsweerde, 2001). With the *abstraction technique*, more abstract goals can be identified by asking "WHY questions" about the goals previously modeled (Lamsweerde, 2001; Koubarakis & Plexousakis, 2000). In other words, on the one hand, the refinement strategy consists in selecting some of the abstract goals of the organization, which are then further refined to make explicit sub-goals whose satisfaction would entail the satisfaction of these abstract goals. This top-down goal analysis is useful in the cases where the analyst elicits the

goal of the organizational managers, who tend to express high-level goals. On the other hand, the abstraction strategy prescribes the detection of the actors that participate in the organization, along with the elicitation of their goals and operations. This bottom-up goal analysis is useful in the case where the analyst elicits the goal of the organizational actors who tend to express low-level goals.

More sophisticated techniques for goal identification and abstraction include *scenarios*. The large amount of works on this topic can be explained by the complementary characteristics of scenarios and goals. While the former are concrete, narrative, procedural, and leave intended properties implicit, the latter are abstract, declarative, and make intended properties explicit (Lamsweerde, 2001). Furthermore, scenarios are useful means for communicating with stakeholders, offering a natural way to illustrate how their needs may be satisfied or hindered in a given situation (Kavakli, 2004).

Among some specific works in the area, the GBRAM (The Goal-Based Requirements Analysis Method) (Antón, 1997) extensively addresses the problem of identifying goals for system development. It is a methodology for initial identification and abstraction of goals from various sources of information, assuming that no goals have been previously elicited. The method contemplates two complementary activities: goal analysis and goal refinement.

Goal analysis comprehends the exploration of information sources for goal identification followed by organization and classification of goals. This activity is further divided into three types of sub-activities, namely: *explore activities* (which refers to the exploration of the available information, such as interviews, policies, requirements, transcripts, workflow diagrams, corporate goals and mission statements); *identify activities* that are about identifying and extracting goals, identifying stakeholders, identifying agents and their responsibilities from the information provided by the previous explore activities; and *organize activities* that classify and organize goals according to goal dependency relations.

Goal refinement concerns the evolution of goals from the moment they are first identified to the moment they are translated into operational requirements for the system specification. Goal refinement activities can be summarized as follows: *refine activities*, which involve the pruning of the goal set; *elaborate activities*, which refer to the process of analyzing the goal set by considering possible goal obstacles and constructing scenarios to uncover hidden goals and requirements; and *operationalize activities*, which represent the translation of goals into operational requirements. The output of the GBRAM is always a software requirements document (SRD) with the functional and nonfunctional requirements, thus extending beyond goal elicitation.

The Non-Functional Requirements (NFR) Framework

In our experience, we faced several of the problems described in the previous subsection (specifically (1), (2), (3), (5) and (6)). The use of Non-Functional Requirements (NFR) catalogues helped us overcome some of these problems, allowing us to elicit goals in a more efficient way. The NFR Framework is one of the most prominent solutions proposed to address the problem of identifying non-functional requirements in RE (Cysneiros,

2007; Chung et al., 2000). The insight that led us to employ the NFR framework was based on the observation that while catalogues address quality attributes in a system development activity, similar quality attributes could help us to raise details related to the *quality aspects* of the organization and its business processes.

The NFR framework proposes a series of catalogues, which serve different purposes, such as providing guidelines for: (a) the representation and operationalization of NFRs; and (b) the prioritization and decomposition during the design process.

The Softgoal Interdependency Graphs (SIGs) represent particular kinds of NFRs, along with their decomposition structures and possible design alternatives to embody the requirement in the future system. Furthermore, SIGs also represent the interdependencies between the NFRs and their operationalizations. An application of SIGs within a real example is presented in (Chung et al., 2000), having *security* as an important NFR for developing a credit card system. Figure 1 illustrates this example, showing that to incorporate *security* in a given account, three subtypes of NFRs are necessary: *integrity, confidentiality* and *availability*. In turn, to incorporate *integrity* on credit card accounts, two additional NFRs are needed: *completeness* and *accuracy*.

The process of decomposing some NFR may be guided (and thus facilitated) by adopting these catalogues since they are helpful in reasoning

Figure 1. Decomposition of a security softgoal

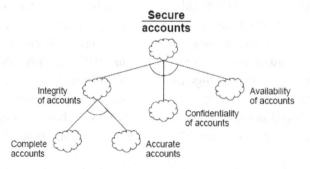

about what qualities the system to-be is expected to meet.

NFRs play an important role in the research reported by Doerr et al. (2005) which is closely related to our work. The authors propose a systematic approach to elicit NFRs, describing three case studies where this approach has been applied. The main difference regarding our work is the fact that they deal with system requirements, while we apply the catalogues to help us elicit process requirements instead of system requirements. Further, Adams and Doerr (2007) have acknowledged the importance of applying NFRs also to elicit goals related to business processes, and propose a metamodel to show the relations between goals and business processes. However, they do not propose a systematic approach to elicit goals, mentioning this as future work. We address this gap here: the following section describes our elicitation approach and illustrates its application.

A GOAL ELICITATION METHOD TO DEEPEN THE UNDERSTANDING OF BUSINESS PROCESS MODELS

This section describes our method for goal elicitation inspired by the needs of our case study. Further, the current state of the art in goal

literature (described as an overview of the existing approaches) has also influenced our work. Basically, the method comprises two consecutive phases, depicted in Figure 2: (1) *Preliminary Goal Elicitation* to collect an initial version of goal models and (2) *Goal Elicitation with Catalogues* to supplement and refine the previously derived goal models by means of NFR.

Preliminary Goal Elicitation

This preliminary goal elicitation and modeling effort was divided in four stages according to the source of information and technique used to interact with the process stakeholders. In the first and second stages, we captured both hardgoals and softgoals.

In a first stage, the available documentation about the organizational processes was assessed. This revealed some organizational characteristics such as: organizational structure and human resources, routines, business processes (with a brief textual explanation in natural language about these processes) and physical space. From the organization structure, we could infer internal actors and the business process they carry out. This documentation also provided goals previously achieved by the department (along with their impacts) and goals which were yet to be achieved

Figure 2. Goal elicitation method

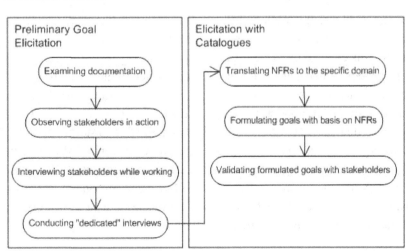

by the department, giving us some insight about the nature of the business processes under consideration and about some relevant goals (stated in natural language). Further, a first interview was undertaken with a physician (who does not belong to the organization), who served as an expert to help us understand general concepts about the medical domain. Additionally, concepts related with rheumatology (diseases, medicines and other technical terms) were briefly surveyed in online information sources.

In a second stage, we obtained a preliminary goal model along with a preliminary business process model. The approach used here consisted in observing the process performers during business process execution, i.e., we observed the daily routine of the organization and captured goals for each stakeholder involved in the business process. While this approach allowed us to understand how actors interact and how actor dependency relationships are established in practice, the actors' focus on getting the work done prevents one from revealing most of the intention and motivation behind their practices.

A third stage focused on eliciting requirements by interviewing the organizational actors while observing them in action. No specific questions have been used in this phase; we solely focused on understanding the actors' practices and their rationale. This helped to reveal the goals of specific activities as well as goals related to a process as a whole. Thus, the model generated in previous stages could be incremented through refinement/abstraction techniques (refer to an overview of the existing approaches). This enabled us to capture the rationale (more general goals) behind more specific goals. It is a fact that the interviews during the process execution provided a more strategic dimension, in the sense that they have captured details related with the organization's strategy in a lower level of abstraction. However, in spite of that, the goal models obtained were strongly related to the business process models, not capturing knowledge about the enterprise setting as a whole. In other words, stakeholders have a great difficulty in formulating goals, tending to state that their goals are to perform their personal activities! This deficiency in goal formulation was addressed in a fourth stage.

In this fourth stage, we concentrated on "dedicated interviews" not only with the business process actors but also with the department manager (by "dedicated interviews" we mean that the interviewees devoted all attention to the elicitation process as opposed to being fully involved in activity execution). The elicitation interviews in this stage focused on raising internal problems of the organization, as well as problems associated with the relationship between the department and external organizations, highlighting all kinds of conflicting interests. The problems and deficiencies that the stakeholders believed to exist in the organization provided not just additional goals to enrich the models, but also some obstacles for goal realization, reasons for non-achievement of goals and possible solutions for these obstacles.

Goal Elicitation with Catalogues

Although we found it hard to deepen the goal analysis in the preliminary phase, during the four stages we have reported in the previous subsection, we had the opportunity to understand the organization's context, its problems, deficiencies and so forth. By observing the execution of the business process, interviewing the stakeholders and observing the organizational setting, we could keep direct contact with implicit factors that underlie the organizational context. These previous stages were thus crucial to provide insights about new concerns that could be added. An important function of these insights regarded the fact that they guided us to suggest which NFR types could be extracted from NFR catalogues (Chung et al., 2000; Cysneiros, 2009; Rilston & Castro, 2002; O'Sullivan, Edmond, & ter Hofstede, 2002) and subsequently adapted to the organizational context.

The fact is that having applied the aforementioned goal elicitation techniques, we observed that a large number of goals seemed to have remained unidentified. The basis for this observation was that a number of business processes seemed to be unrelated to strategic goals after the preliminary phase, which could indicate that (1) a large number of processes had no strategic relevance or that (2) the goals were incomplete or defined at an inadequate level of abstraction. The former situation (1) would indicate a serious issue for the organization and in fact, reveal a blatant disconnection between operational practices and strategic directions. Given the common difficulties in goal elicitation as reported in the literature, and the apparent success of the organization in conducting its business, we have opted to formulate a hypothesis based on (2), which has motivated us to perform a second goal elicitation effort.

In this second effort, we employed the NFR framework (Chung et al., 2000; Cysneiros, 2009; Lamsweerde, 2000). We observed that a number of non-functional requirements defined in the scope of the NFR framework can be abstracted and extrapolated to identify (soft)goals which have strategic relevance for business process models and that had not been previously identified. The insight that led us to employ the NFR framework was based on the observation that while catalogues address quality attributes in a system development activity, similar quality attributes could help us to raise details related to the *quality aspects* of the organization and its business processes. Fortunately, this insight has been confirmed after the application of the catalogues in the goal elicitation activity.

In accordance with the NFR types catalogues, we formulated additional goals for the business process, initially without participation of the stakeholders. The translation from *NFR types* in the catalogues to *goals* was highly related to the knowledge acquired in previous stages, i.e., to adequately refine the NFRs we had to consider the meaning of the NFRs' refinement in the context of the domain under consideration. After incorporating these additional goals into the model, we applied the same techniques of abstraction/ refinement previously applied for identifying additional goals. For the sake of brevity, we concentrate here on some relevant portions of the resulting goal models.

APPLICATION OF THE METHOD OF GOAL ELICITATION FOR BUSINESS PROCESS MODELS

In this section, we elaborate on the application of the method proposed in this article to the case study. Subsequently, we describe the case study and discuss the results of a preliminary phase of goal elicitation. Finally, we explain how we have employed NFR catalogues to refine the goals elicited in the preliminary phase.

Case Study: Goal Elicitation in the Rheumatology Department of a University Hospital

The case study was conducted in the Rheumatology Department of Cassiano de Moraes University Hospital (HUCAM Hospital) which is part of the Federal University of Espírito Santo in Vitória, Brazil. This case study had the main purpose of supporting us on the creation of a systematic method to align goals and business processes.

In the context of the hospital, the department has the following functions: (1) providing educational training to form specialists in rheumatology; (2) providing outpatient medical care; and (3) developing research to investigate the incidence of rheumatologic conditions in population. This department is composed of six specialists in rheumatology, two nurses and two physiotherapists, among other professionals to help hosting patients. Rheumatology residents and interns temporarily join the department for educational purposes, also assisting in the daily routine. The department performs fifteen business processes, such as outpatient care, drugs infusion, among others and performs an average rate of five thousand and seven hundred outpatient medical care instances per year.

The Project team was composed by: (1) enterprise modelers: one analyst (junior researcher), two consultants (senior researchers); and (2) hospital clients: one doctor, one resident, one member of administrative staff, and a few patients. As a result, we developed a total of eight sets of Tropos (Bresciani et al., 2004) models (eight Tropos actor models, each one relating to a Tropos goal model). Each set of Tropos models corresponds to a business process, also modeled in the scope of this study. Besides, a ninth Tropos models has been elaborated to capture organizational issues which are relevant for many business processes. It is relevant to say that many draft models had been elaborated in several cycles (involving elicitation, analysis and modeling) before these resulting models were finalized.

The results we achieved so far only cover the first phase of the project (i.e. AS-IS). All goals and process models have been fully validated by the head doctor (seen as the person responsible for this project, the one who has a broader view of the organization) and partially validated by the other hospital members. The TO-BE part of this project is ongoing work and should be the subject of future publications.

Results of the Preliminary Goal Elicitation Method

Figure 3 exhibits a Tropos diagram depicting the goals of a physician who conducts the diagnosis business process.

Summarizing the constructs and techniques applied in Figure 3, we have that in Tropos diagrams, actors are represented as circles, goals as oval shapes and softgoals as cloud shapes. Moreover, (soft)goals can be related with three kinds of relationships: means-end link, contribution link and AND/OR decomposition link.

The physician provides medical care to a patient ("Provide medical care to patient" goal) through a medical consultation ("Provide medical care in scheduled medical consultation" goal). During consultation, the physician diagnoses the patient's health state ("Diagnose health state" goal) and prescribes the treatment ("Prescribe patient's treatment" goal which uses, in turn, a "Drugs prescription").

The main goal of the physician is to "Diagnose patient's health state". During the process of diagnosis, the physician can find either rheumatologic or non-rheumatologic conditions ("Diagnose rheumatologic conditions" goal and "Diagnose non-rheumatologic conditions" goal). After diagnosing the patient's heath state, the physician is able to select the most suitable treatment for the disease ("Select the most suitable treatment for patient" softgoal). For this reason, "Diagnose patient's health state" is a mean for "Select the most suitable treatment for patient."

The physician must have accurate knowledge so as to discover the presence/absence of diseases ("Acquire technical skills" softgoal). He/she must also access the patient's data for being able to determine how the patient health condition is evolving along the time ("Obtain access to patient's clinical history and data" goal). One of the means for accessing the patient's data and thus to know its clinical history is to obtaining access to patient's records ("Obtain access to patient's records during medical consultation" goal).

A last remark about the model refers to a goal prioritization. Although "Diagnose patient's health state" is the main Physician's goal, there is no prioritization of this goal (or any other of this model) by the stakeholders in a strict sense. Indeed, as we have noticed along the interviews, since the physician constantly pursue the diagnosis of the patient's health state, this entails that the other goals are articulated around this goal in an attempt of contributing to its satisfaction.

Figure 3. Goal model resulted from the preliminary goal elicitation activities

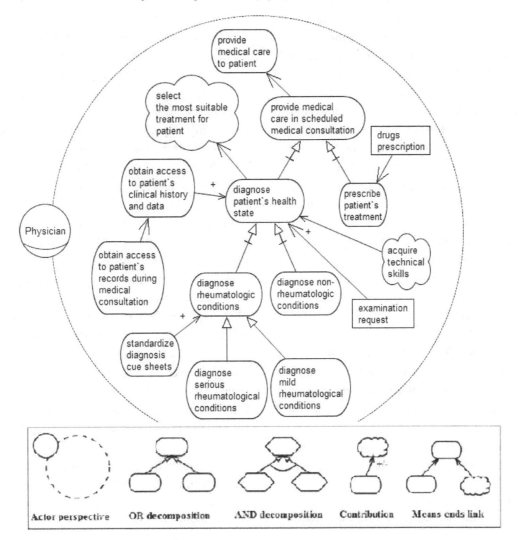

Results of the Goal Elicitation with Catalogues

Before discussing the outcomes related with the use of the catalogues with the stakeholders, we have translated the NFR types to (soft)goals in the context of the domain under consideration. This translation is necessary since the NFR types suggested by the catalogues are highly generic (even in the context of systems development) and an adaptation is required to express the meaning of each NFR type in terms of the context of the domain.

In catalogues, softgoals are classified according to a NFR type, which indicates the particular NFR, such as security or performance, addressed by the softgoal. The softgoals also have a *subject matter* or *topic* which represents the object to which the NFR type refers. Then, in one step of the NFR framework (step 2.4 of the NFR framework (Chung et al., 2000)), to specify some softgoal, the analyst must specify the NFR type and its "topic". For example, in the "good performance for account" softgoal, the NFR type is "performance" and the topic is "account."

Similarly, in our case, the translation step follows the same rationale. For instance, if we consider the NFR type "confidentiality", we must also regard what represents "confidentiality" in the health-care domain (in particular, in the health-care domain of our organization). To properly specify what represents "confidentiality" in this domain, then we must specify the topic which this NFR type refers to. In our case, we have identified the need of confidentiality for the patient's information. Once specified the NFR type and the topic, we have the "Maintain healthcare information private" softgoal.

After we have applied the translation step for all the chosen NFR types of our case study, the NFR types originated the following goals:

1. **Accessibility:** "Obtain access to medical care" (Rilston & Castro, 2002).
2. **Confidentiality:** "Maintain healthcare information private" (Rilston & Castro, 2002).
3. **Completeness:** "Obtain complete information about patient's treatment" (Rilston & Castro, 2002).
4. **Accuracy:** "Obtain accurate information about patient's treatment" (Rilston & Castro, 2002).
5. **Traceability (process and data):** "Obtain traceability for information in patient's treatment" refined into "Obtain traceability in investigation of patient's condition", "Obtain traceability in relation to treatment administered to patient" and "Obtain traceability in relation to physicians who prescribed patient's treatment" (Rilston & Castro, 2002; Cysneiros, 2009).
6. **Integrability:** "Coordinate patient care with other healthcare providers" refined into "Coordinate patient care with specialists in areas related to rheumatology", "Coordinate patient care with municipal and state health services" (to obtain what is called "integrated treatment" exploring the benefits of information integration) and "Coordinate patient care

with other hospital departments" (Rilston & Castro, 2002).
7. **Trust and confidence to the provider (assurance):** "Trust physician" (not shown in Figures 4 and 5 since this goal belongs to the patient's perspective) (O'Sullivan, Edmond, & ter Hofstede, 2002).
8. **Empathy (level of caring and personalized attention provided to the requestor):** (O'Sullivan, Edmond, & ter Hofstede, 2002). "Show empathy to patient"

The use of NFR catalogues is a technique generally applied in the elicitation of non-functional requirements (thus, represented as softgoals in i*/ Tropos). However, in our case, focusing on the NFR types led us to elicit goals which could be objectively evaluated, i.e. hardgoals instead of softgoals (goals that have no objective satisfaction criteria and that are "subject to interpretation" (Yu, 1995), "imprecise, subjective, context-specific and ideal" (Jureta, Faulkner, & Schobbens, 2006)). For instance, the requirement of Accessibility has led to the identification of the hardgoal "Obtain access to medical care" (in other words, this represents the patient's intention to obtain a vacancy in the healthcare service). Besides, the translation seems to be highly domain-dependent. For example, traceability refers to the capacity of tracing patient's data along the treatment. As we have noticed, another particularity concerned with the translation is that different NFR types are mapped to the same goal in the organization. Distributivity (capacity of reaching all decision-makers (Rilston & Castro, 2002)) and integrability (capacity of adequately and efficiently integrating operational information (Rilston & Castro, 2002)) mean the same in this context (in the sense that both mean the information must be integrated so as to reach all decision-makers caring about that information). Privacy and confidentiality are also mapped to the same goal.

With respect to the goals added, we were able to identify goals which had remained implicit in the preliminary study (Figure 4). Most of these goals were either associated with quality aspects of the previously modeled goals ("Obtain complete information about patient's treatment" softgoal and "Obtain accurate information about patient's treatment" softgoal) or with quality aspects for the service as a whole ("Obtain access to medical care" and "Coordinate patient care with other healthcare providers" softgoal and the softgoals originated from its refinements). The fact that most of the elicited goals address quality attributes of the organizational setting can be accounted by the issue that the NFR catalogues are also concerned about quality attributes (in the system development activity). Observe that, in this case, the usage of catalogues can be compared with some kind of abstraction strategy which complements the existent technique of abstraction (which uses the WHY-questions). This abstraction strategy had allowed us to concentrate on the identification of quality metrics for assessing how the operational goals are achieved along the time so that they

support the achievement of the strategic goals of the organization.

We also have noticed that some of the elicited (soft)goals address exceptional situations, for example, the softgoal "Coordinate patient care with specialists in areas related to rheumatology" is relevant only in the case the rheumatologist needs to clarify further details about the diagnosis with other specialists (for example, a dermatologist or ophthalmologist) in the hospital.

After applying the catalogues, we could notice that some of the goals spontaneously mentioned are actually goals for implementing mechanisms for the attainment of more abstract goals. This had remained implicit when applying the abstraction technique, but was finally revealed through the use of the catalogues. For instance, in Figure 4, we suggested three types of traceability: "Obtain traceability in relation to treatment administered to patient" softgoal (obtain information about the drugs prescribed along the treatment), "Obtain traceability in relation to physicians who

Figure 4. Portion of the goal model obtained in goal elicitation activities with catalogues (1)

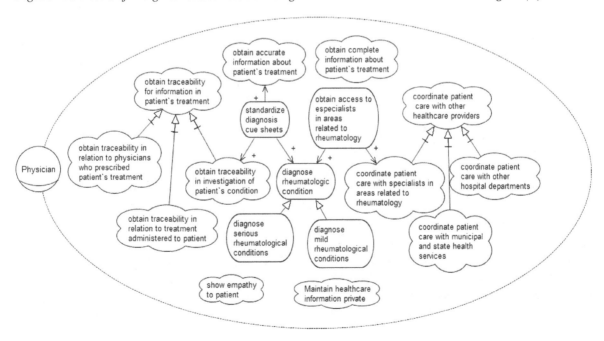

prescribed patient's treatment" softgoal (obtain information about the physicians who had already prescribed treatment to the patient) and "Obtain traceability in investigation of patient's condition" softgoal (obtain information about the conditions which had already been investigated previously by the physician). Actually, this last goal was the motivation for the standardization of diagnosis cue sheets (previously modeled). The standardization of diagnosis cue sheets was one of many means towards achieving traceability in the investigation of diseases.

Finally, all goals suggested through the use of catalogues were validated by the stakeholders in a validation interview. They acknowledged the need of these goals and were also able to spontaneously mention other goals (for example the refinements of the "Provide medical care to patient" goal,

shown in Figure 5). The goal "Provide medical care to patient" can be achieved in three forms: by achieving a consultation appointment (in this consultation, the physician examines the patient and prescribes the treatment); by providing attendance for assessment of high cost drug (the physician examines the patient and in the case of the need of a high cost drug, he/she issues a certificate) and by an informal meeting (the goals which denote these situations are, respectively: "Provide medical care in scheduled medical consultation" goal, "Provide attendance for assessment of high cost drug" goal and "Provide informal meeting" goal). In these informal meetings, the physician can examine a patient who reports the presence of symptoms, or the physician just issues some document required by the patient (a medical certificate, a medical report or a prescription of

Figure 5. Portion of goal model obtained in goal elicitation activities with catalogues (2)

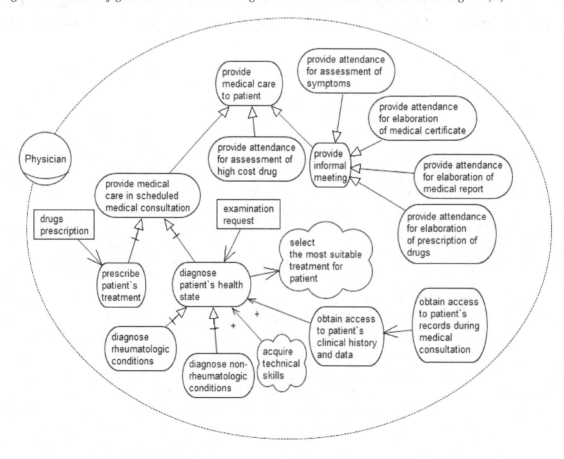

drugs). The goals which denote these situations are, respectively: "Provide attendance for assessment of symptoms" goal, "Provide attendance for elaboration of medical certificate" goal, "Provide attendance for elaboration of medical report" goal and "Provide attendance for elaboration of prescription of drugs" goal. Furthermore, we were able to refine the "Obtain access to medical care" goal in terms of two other goals, namely, "Obtain access to medical" care (to internal patients) goal and "Obtain access to medical care" (to external patients) goal (not shown in the Figures 4 and 5 since this goal is a dependency relation from the patient to the receptionist).

It is essential to emphasize here that all kinds of goal relations, such as goal refinement/abstraction, conflicts, and so forth have not been identified by the stakeholders (in the elicitation with catalogues). Hence, these goal relations are expressed in the models after the approval of the stakeholders of our suggestions. With respect to the goal conflicts, we have also suggested resolutions for them. Again, models reflect stakeholders' decisions after assessing the potential trade-offs of our suggestions.

DISCUSSION

Benefits of the Proposed Approach

In relation to our method, we have found the preliminary goal elicitation activities useful in addressing our need to understand the organizational setting. This has enabled not only to capture details about the enterprise and its business processes, but also to provide proper understanding about the domain under consideration. However, we have found the preliminary stages to be deficient in the identification of *strategic concerns* related to the organization's goals since the focus was concentrated on operational activities. This difficulty was partly addressed through stakeholder interviews. Although these interviews addressed

many organizational issues, much knowledge still remained implicit. With respect to that, the catalogues provided by the NFR framework have shown to be useful as a complementary tool to elicit goals.

Before discussing the nature of the additional goals identified with the support of catalogues, we must highlight some particularities about translating NFR types to goals. We have observed that the translation is highly domain-dependent, i.e., one must take into account how a NFR must be mapped to some goal in the organization domain such that this goal makes sense regarding the organizational context, as we have illustrated in the previous section. Further, one must define whether a NFR type should be represented as a soft or hard goal. As observed in (Daneva et al., 2007), analysts tend to treat NFRs as softgoals, however, as demonstrated in the case study, some NFRs could be objectively specified in the context of the domain.

In relation to the goals uncovered with the help of catalogues, we believe that goals have enabled us to reason about the organization from a more strategic point of view. This can be confirmed by the fact that some additional goals referred to quality attributes; either for specifying qualitatively a hardgoal or for specifying quality metrics for the business process as a whole. We have observed in this case study, that stakeholders have difficulties in explicitly stating quality attributes for business processes (the same difficulty is often reported to elicit requirements in system development (Cysneiros, 2007)). In that respect, the catalogues here employed provided guidelines for identifying these attributes in a systematic way.

We also observed that, in certain cases, stakeholders formulate goals which are highly dependent on the current operationalization of the organization's objectives, i.e., much emphasis is given to the goal of applying successfully a particular solution for a problem. Catalogues partially helped to overcome this issue, revealing higher level goals not easily identified by the abstraction technique. Further, some of the goals uncovered through catalogues had initially been deemed an inherent organizational characteristic by stakeholders, and thus had not been spontaneously mentioned.

At first sight, the technique we have employed seems highly dependent on the experience of analysts in conducting the elicitation effort (experience in the sense that analysts must have broad knowledge about the domain). This issue (of acquiring the knowledge about domain) has been addressed in the preliminary stages with the immersion inside the organization. We believe this is the case partly because of the need to translate NFRs into goals which are specific to the organization's domain. Further investigation in NFR type catalogues for business process in a particular business domain may prove to be fruitful to reduce the dependency on analyst experience and improve goal elicitation in general. In this sense, NFR type catalogues can be seen as design patterns in goal modeling. The compilation of these catalogues in a format of design patterns would allow one to reuse the knowledge by making available methodological connections which are tacit in an experienced modeler's mind and which are not typically available to the novice.

Limitations of the Proposed Approach

We have faced two main difficulties with respect to the elicitation activities reported here. The first one concerns the knowledge-intensive characteristic of the health care domain. Some incorrect details of business process have been identified since these details are specific to medical business processes. This issue has been mastered in the third and forth stages with the support of the interviews.

The second difficulty seems to be an inherent challenge for elicitation activities in most realistic settings, and relates to the limited access of the analysts to stakeholders and the bounded resources allocated for elicitation. In our study in particular, we have not been able to access all the stakeholders of the chain who are indeed interested in the elicited goals. For example, the Rheumatology Department is inserted into a very complex structure in which the department itself is solely one of many "leaf nodes." The stakeholders at higher levels, such as the public administrators, the physicians of other public health services have not been covered, limiting the identification of higher-level goals of the whole system. Such higher-level goals were only inferred by an indirect analysis (i.e., by analyzing the goals which we were able to capture and inferring how the higher-level goals from the whole system might be related with lower-level goals).

CONCLUSION AND FUTURE WORK

This paper has described our efforts in proposing a method for goal elicitation within the context of AS-IS business process modeling. We have presented and exemplified the proposed method by discussing a case study contacted in a Rheumatology Department of a Hospital in Brazil. Next to this, we have discussed the potentials and limitations we identified in our work.

The catalogues provided by the NFR framework are shown to be useful as a complementary tool to elicit goals. More specifically, a number of non-functional requirements defined in the scope of the NFR framework can be abstracted and extrapolated to identify both hard- and soft-goals which have strategic relevance for business process models. As a result, goal models were more complete after employing the technique. The main limitation of the approach seems to be related to the inherent challenge for elicitation activities in most realistic settings, and relates to the limited access of the analysts to stakeholders and the bounded resources allocated for elicitation.

Further research steps will be necessary to associate particular goals with guidelines for business process (re-)design. Additionally, in our future work, we intend to investigate suitable representation and semantics to relate goal models and business process models (especially in the presence of softgoals). Moreover, we aim at investigating the impact this approach of eliciting additional goals through the use of NFR catalogues shall have in business process structures as well as in the systematic redesign of business processes.

ACKNOWLEDGMENT

This research is funded by the Brazilian Research Funding Agencies FAPES (grants number 45444080/09 and 37274554/2007) and CNPq (grants number 481906/2009-6 and 309059/2008-9). We thank all physicians, interns, residents and patients at the Cassiano de Moraes University Hospital for their cooperation in this research. In particular, we are grateful to Prof. Dr. Valéria Valim and Érica Serrano, MD, for providing invaluable assistance in the execution of this research.

REFERENCES

Adam, S., & Doerr, J. (2007). On the notion of determining system adequacy by analyzing the traceability of quality. In *Proceedings of the 19th International Conference on Advanced Information Systems Engineering*, Trondheim, Norway (pp. 325-329).

Alexander, I. (2002). Modelling the interplay of conflicting goals with use and misuse cases. In *Proceedings of the 8th International Workshop on Requirements Engineering: Foundation for Software Quality* (pp. 145-152).

Andersson, B., Bergholtz, M., Edirisuriya, A., Ilayperuma, T., Jayaweera, P., Paul, J., et al. (2008). Enterprise sustainability through the alignment of goal models and business models. In *Proceedings of the 3rd International Workshop on Business/IT-Alignment and Interoperability CEUR Workshop.*

Andersson, B., Bergholtz, M., Edirisuriya, A., Ilayperuma, T., Johannesson, P., & Zdravkovic, J. (2007). *Using strategic goal analysis for enhancing value-based business models.* Paper presented at the Second International Workshop on Business/IT Alignment and Interoperability, Workshop at the 19th International Conference on Advanced Information Systems Engineering.

Anton, A., & Potts, C. (1998). The use of goals to surface requirements for evolving systems. In *Proceedings of the 20th International Conference on Software Enginering*, Kyoto, Japan (pp. 157-166).

Antón, A. I. (1997). *Goal identification and refinement in the specification of software-based information systems.* Unpublished doctoral dissertation, Georgia Institute of Technology, Atlanta.

Asnar, Y., Giorgini, P., Massacci, F., & Zannone, N. (2007). From trust to dependability through risk analysis. In *Proceedings of the Second International Conference on Availability, Reliability and Security*, Vienna, Austria (pp. 19-26).

Basili, V. R., Caldiera, G., & Rombach, H. D. (1994). The goal question metric approach. In Marciniak, J. (Ed.), *Encyclopedia of software engineering* (Vol. 2, pp. 528–532). New York, NY: John Wiley & Sons.

Boardman, A., & Shapiro, D. (2004). A framework for comprehensive strategic analysis. *Journal of Strategic Management Education, 1*(2).

Bresciani, P., Giorgini, P., Giunchiglia, F., Mylopoulos, J., & Perini, A. (2004). Tropos: An agent-oriented software development methodology. *Journal of Autonomous Agents and Multi-Agent Systems*, 203-236.

Cardoso, E., Guizzardi, R., & Almeida, J. P. (in press). *Goal models and business process models in a health environment.* Vitoria, Brazil. *Federal University of Espírito Santo.*.

Chung, L., Nixon, B., Yu, E., & Mylopoulos, J. (2000). *Non-functional requirements in software engineering.* Dordrecht, The Netherlands: Kluwer Academic Publishers.

Cysneiros, L. M. (2007). Evaluating the effectiveness of using catalogues to elicit non-functional requirements. In *Proceedings of the 10th Workshop on Requirements Engineering* (pp. 107-115).

Cysneiros, L. M. (2009). *Catalogues on non-functional requirements.* Retrieved from http://math.yorku.ca/~cysneiro/nfrs/nfrs.htm

Daneva, M., Kassab, M., Ponisio, M. L., Wieringa, R., & Ormandjieva, O. (2007). *Exploiting a goal decomposition technique to prioritize non-functional requirements.* Paper presented at the 10th International Workshop on Requirements Engineering, Toronto, ON, Canada.

Dardenne, A., Lamsweerde, A. v., & Fickas, S. (1993). Goal-directed requirements acquisition. *Science of Computer Programming, 20,* 3–50. doi:10.1016/0167-6423(93)90021-G.

Doerr, J., Kerkow, D., Koenig, T., Olsson, T., & Suzuki, T. (2005) Non-functional requirements in industry: Three case studies adopting an experience based NFR method. In *Proceedings of the 13th IEEE International Conference on Requirements Engineering*, Paris, France (pp. 373-382).

Estrada, H., Martínez, A., & Pastor, O. (2003). Goal-based business modeling oriented towards late requirements generation. In G. Goos, J. Hartmanis, & J. van Leeuwen (Eds.), *Proceedings of the 22nd International Conference on Conceptual Modeling* (LNCS 2813, pp. 277-290).

Frankel, D. (2003). *Model driven architecture: Applying MDA to enterprise computing.* Indianapolis, IN: Wiley Publishing.

Halleux, P., Mathieu, L., & Andersson, B. (2008). *A method to support the alignment of business models and goal models.* Paper presented at the 3rd International Workshop on Business/IT-Alignment and Interoperability CEUR Workshop.

Hammer, M. (1990). Reengineering work: Don't automate, obliterate. *Harvard Business Review, 68*(4), 104.

Hammer, M., & Champy, J. (1993). *Reengineering the corporation: A manifesto for business revolution.* London, UK: Nicholas Brealey Publishing.

Kavakli, E. (2004). Modeling organizational goals: Analysis of current methods. In *Proceedings of the ACM Symposium on Applied Computing*, Nicosia, Cyprus (pp. 1339-1343).

Kavakli, E., & Loucopoulos, P. (1999). Goal-driven business process analysis application in eletricity deregulation. *Information Systems, 24,* 187–207. doi:10.1016/S0306-4379(99)00015-0.

Kavakli, E., & Loucopoulos, P. (2003). *Goal driven requirements engineering: Evaluation of current methods.* Paper presented at the 8th Workshop on Evaluation of Modeling Methods in Systems Analysis and Design, Velden, Austria.

Koliadis, G., & Ghose, A. (2006). Relating business process models to goal-oriented requirements models in KAOS. In *Proceedings of the Pacific Knowledge Acquisition Workshop on Advances in Knowledge Acquisition and Management* (pp. 25-39).

Koubarakis, M., & Plexousakis, D. (2000). A formal model for business process modelling and design. In *Proceedings of the Conference on Advanced Information System Engineering* (pp. 142-156).

Kueng, P., & Kawalek, P. (1997). Goal-based business process models: Creation and evaluation. *Business Process Management Journal, 3*, 17–38. doi:10.1108/14637159710161567.

Lamsweerde, A. (2000). Requirements engineering in the year 00: A research. In *Proceedings of the 22nd International Conference on Software Enginnering* (pp. 5-19).

Lamsweerde, A. (2001). Goal-oriented requirements engineering: A guided tour. In *Proceedings of the 5th IEEE International Symposium on Requirements Engineering* (pp. 249-262).

Lamsweerde, A., Darimont, R., & Letier, E. (1998). Managing conflicts in goal-driven requirements engineering. *IEEE Transactions on Software Engineering, 24*(11), 908–926. doi:10.1109/32.730542.

Lapouchnian, A. (2005). *Goal-oriented requirements engineering: An overview of the current research*. Toronto, ON, Canada: University of Toronto.

Markovic, I., & Kowalkiewicz, M. (2008). Linking business goals to process models in semantic business process modeling. In *Proceedings of the 12th IEEE International Enterprise Distributed Object Computing Conference* (pp. 332-338).

Mylopoulos, J., Chung, L., Yu, E., & Nixon, B. (1992). Representing and using non-functional requirements: A process-oriented approach. *IEEE Transactions on Software Engineering, 18*(6), 483–497. doi:10.1109/32.142871.

Neiger, D., & Churilov, L. (2004). *Goal-oriented business process engineering revisited: A unifying perspective*. Paper presented at the First International Workshop on Computer Supported Activity Coordination, Porto, Portugal.

Neiger, D., & Churilov, L. (2004). Goal-oriented business process modeling with EPCs and value-focused thinking. *Business Process Management*, 98-115.

Nurcan, S., Etien, A., Kaab, R., & Zouka, I. (2005). A strategy driven business process modelling approach. *Journal of Business Process Management, 11*(6), 628–649. doi:10.1108/14637150510630828.

O'Sullivan, J., Edmond, D., & ter Hofstede, A. (2002). What's In a service? Towards accurate description of non-functional service properties. *Distributed and Parallel Databases, 12*(2-3), 117–133. doi:10.1023/A:1016547000822.

Pastor, O., & Molina, J. (2007). *Model-driven architecture in practice: A software production environment based on conceptual modeling*. Berlin, Germany: Springer-Verlag.

Rilston, F., & Castro, J. (2002). *Enhancing data warehouse quality with the NFR framework*. Paper presented at the 5th Workshop on Requirements Engineering.

Rolland, C., Souveyet, C., & Camille, B. A. (1998). Guiding goal modeling using scenarios. *IEEE Transactions on Software Engineering, 24*(12), 1055–1071. doi:10.1109/32.738339.

Singh, S. N., & Woo, C. (2008). *A methodology for discovering goals at different organizational levels*. Paper presented at the Third International Workshop on Business/IT Alignment and Interoperability held in conjunction with the International Conference on Advanced Information Systems Engineering, Montpellier, France.

Soffer, P., & Wand, Y. (2005). On the notion of softgoals in business process modeling. *Business Process Modeling*, 663-679.

Yamamoto, S., Kaiya, H., Cox, K., & Bleistein, S. (2006). Goal oriented requirements engineering: Trends and issues. *IEICE Transactions on Information and Systems, 89*(11), 2701–2711. doi:10.1093/ietisy/e89-d.11.2701.

Yu, E. (1995). *Modeling strategic relationships for process reengineering.* Unpublished doctoral dissertation, University of Toronto, ON, Canada.

Zachman, J. (1987). A framework for information systems architecture. *IBM Systems Journal*, 276–292. doi:10.1147/sj.263.0276.

This work was previously published in the International Journal of Information System Modeling and Design (IJISMD), Volume 2, Issue 2, edited by Remigijus Gustas, pp. 1-18, copyright 2011 by IGI Publishing (an imprint of IGI Global).

Chapter 11
An Approach for E-Service Design Using Enterprise Models

Martin Henkel
Stockholm University, Sweden

Paul Johannesson
Stockholm University, Sweden

Erik Perjons
Stockholm University, Sweden

ABSTRACT

Organisations demand new business models for value creation and innovation that require collaboration with customers and vendors in agile and flexible networks. To realise such networks, organisations are embracing service oriented models and architectures using e-services for business communication. A major issue for a service oriented organisation is to design and offer e-services that are adapted to the needs, wants, and requirements of customers and vendors. This is a challenging task as different customer groups and vendors will have different requirements, which may vary over time, resulting in a large number of e-services. In this paper, the authors suggest enterprise models as being adequate instruments for design and maintenance of e-services. More specifically; an approach for designing e-services based on value and goal models, which will ensure that the constructed e-services will satisfy the needs and wants of customers. A project from the Swedish health care sector is used to demonstrate and evaluate the proposed approach.

INTRODUCTION

Organisations of today demand new models for value creation and innovation. The target of an organisation can no longer only be customers on the mass market. Instead, the individual customer will be put on centre stage where he/she takes on new roles in the creation of value and innovation together with the organisation. In other words, customers are no longer only consumers but active co-producers of value in a value network. In such networks, a flexible cooperation with multiple

DOI: 10.4018/978-1-4666-4161-7.ch011

vendors and other business partners is needed in order to provide tailored solutions for each individual customer (Prahalad & Krishnan, 2008). The role of organisations will be to continuously reconfigure networks of customers, vendors, and other business partners.

In order to realise agile and flexible networks, organisations are turning to service oriented models and architectures. From an external perspective, services offer service consumers to focus on how to make use of the service for his/her specific business. The consumer does not have to deal with typical ownership responsibilities, like infrastructure management and maintenance. Thereby, the consumer can concentrate his/her resources on things that make his/her business successful. From an organisational internal perspective, a service oriented infrastructure will facilitate for an organisation to align its business and IT support. Thereby, an organisation that wants to change its business strategy can more easily do that by developing new services and combining existing ones. This means that services provide many opportunities for organisations to become more focused, flexible, and agile.

As a consequence, many organisations are beginning to embrace service oriented approaches for their enterprise and IT architectures. In such service oriented approaches, e-services are used as a mean both for flexible integration of business and IT systems internally within an organisation, and for supporting external communication between organisations.

A major issue for a service oriented organisation is to design and offer e-services that are adapted to the requirements of customers and business partners. This is a challenging task as different customer groups and vendors will have different requirements, which may also vary over time, resulting in a large number of e-services. These e-services also have to be maintained and evolved in order to adapt to changing requirements. Thus, the organisation needs to manage a large, complex and continually evolving set of e-services.

This task requires a set of instruments, including models and methods, for managing the complex environment. We suggest that enterprise models, in particular value models and goal models, are adequate instruments by offering a basis for analysing customers' and vendors' requirements as well as solution and e-service designs. A main advantage of value models is that they provide an easily understandable overview of actors in a value network as well as the resources and benefits they offer to each other, thereby enabling e-service design based on customers' and vendors' requirements. Furthermore, goal models provide a more detailed view by describing the goals of the actors in a value network, which makes it possible to relate and align e-services to these goals.

In this paper, we propose an approach for designing e-services based on value and goal models. As a first step, we use value modelling to capture high-level resource transfers between actors. Based on the resulting value models, we define top-level goals, which are then refined into a set of lower level goals. These goals are the base for identifying candidate e-services aligned with the goals. Finally, the e-services are refined into the desired granularity level.

The work presented here is based on experiences from a project in the health care domain, the REMS project (Henkel, Perjons, & Zdravkovic, 2006). The main aim of the REMS project was to create a number of e-services that could be used to create, manage and transfer health care referrals between St. Erik's Eye Hospital (an eye specialist clinic), primary health care units, opticians, and private eye specialists in the Stockholm area. Health care referrals are one of the key instruments used when health care providers collaborate in the treatment of patients. The management of health care referrals spans geographical, organisational and IT system boundaries; thus, the project contains ample examples of complex business as well as IT interactions. A systematic approach, supported by an IT infrastructure, was thus required in order to design e-services that support the distribution and management of a large number of health care referrals, as well as support the desired business values and goals of the involved actors, including the patients.

The rest of the paper is structured as follows. In the following two sections, we discuss related research and present an overview of the proposed approach. Value models are described, followed by the description of linking value models with goal models. The goal models are then further refined into e-services. Next, we describe how the identified e-services can be refined to a preferable granularity level. After this, the application of the approach is described, as well as an evaluation of the approach used in the REMS project. Finally, in the last section, we summarise our contribution and discuss the subjects of further work.

RELATED RESEARCH

Identifying, designing and implementing e-services introduce many new challenges for business and IT architects. Compared to traditional information systems, service providers and users interact much more closely in order to create value. Instead of a single set of requirements on an information system, there are distributed requirements on e-services in networks of providers and users. Furthermore, e-service design is tightly interwoven with service use, as feedbacks from users contribute to the evolution of service oriented systems on an ongoing basis. These issues have been addressed in the new subarea of requirements engineering that investigate service design, as evidenced by for example the requirement engineering for services (REFS) workshop series (REFS, 2010). The main approaches in this new area make use of business processes, business functions, business models, and goals when designing e-services.

Many authors have considered *business processes* as a basis for designing service-based systems, see for example Piccinelli et al. (2002)

and Papazoglou and Yang (2002). However, as these are focused on an operational processes perspective, they have omitted the connection between services and business values and goals that we address in this paper.

The notion of *business functions* has also been used to drive the development of e-services. The IBM research community has proposed the Component Business Model (CBM) for creating a structured representation of the business as an organised collection of business components (Cherbakov et al., 2005). In CBM the components correspond to business functions. To support the exchange of information across a network of business actors each business component provides one or more business services. In comparison, the approach proposed in this paper is not driven by business functions. Instead, we use high-level business values as our starting point.

Recent research (Gordijn et al., 2008; Hruby, 2006; Andersson et al., 2005; Gordijn, Akkermans, & Vliet, 2000) employ enterprise *business models* as a foundation to create IT systems. A business model describes *what* is offered by an actor to another actor rather than *how* these offerings are negotiated, contracted and fulfilled among the actors, as explained by a process model. In Osterwalder (2004) and Wieringa and Gordijn (2005), an approach is suggested in which a business model is taken as a starting point for aligning business requirements with executable processes. The approach emphasises that IT solutions need to be derived from business models, validated with particular value propositions and exchanges, and accepted by all the participating actors. We utilise business models in our study, but the business model that we propose, called value model, in addition to the exchange of economic resources, also captures the concept of the actors' intended effects of receiving economic resources, see also the discussion in Weigand et al. (2006). This means that we make a difference between the *economic resource* transferred between actors and the *intended effect* experienced by an actor.

Thus, in the approach proposed in this paper, value models are differentiated from business models by including both the exchange of economic resources and the intended effects that actors experience by receiving economic resources. Examples of intended effects are *increased knowledge* and an *increased feeling of safety*.

Several studies consider *goal-oriented* analysis as a starting point for the design of e-services. In Gordijn, Yu, and Raadt (2006) and Gordijn, Petit, and Weiringa (2006), the i* model for goal modelling and e3 value model for business modelling are combined in order to analyse and design e-service business models. According to Gordijn, Yu, and Raadt (2006), the use of the i* model will reveal the strategic goals behind the value exchanges described in the e3 model, while the e3 value model can be used for profitability analysis for the involved actors. In the approach proposed in this paper, we utilise a goal-modelling method as a bridge between value models on the one hand and e-services on the other. Thereby, the goals are created based on a certain value model configuration, i.e. a certain configuration of customer and vendors in a value network and their resource transfers, and the created goals are then used to identify individual e-services. That is, the goals in the approach presented here are not strategic as in i*, and the purpose is not a general profitability analysis, as described in Gordijn, Yu, and Raadt (2006); Another approach using goal models in presented in Bleistein (2006). In the approach several levels of both goal and context diagrams are combined to analyze requirements on e-business systems. A similarity with the approach we present here is that it starts with high-level goals and an analysis of the collaborating business partners. However, no clear guidelines on how the levels are to be refined and how goals relate to the context diagrams are provided.

In Levi and Arsanjani (2003), e-services are coupled to goals using a modelling method, similar to the approach proposed in this paper. The method described in Levi and Arsanjani (2003) uses high-level business goals, identified by business executives, business owners and business modellers, which are decomposed into a hierarchy of sub-goals. Finally, e-services provided by existing software components can be identified that satisfy these sub-goals. The difference, compared to the approach presented here, is that there is no structured way to start the goal modelling, as it directly starts with high-level business goals.

OVERVIEW OF THE APPROACH

The main aim of the approach proposed in this paper is to drive the design of e-services from a business value and goal perspective by using value and goal models. In order to do this, we utilise four distinct steps: value modelling, top-level goal identification, goal-driven identification of e-services, and e-service refinement (Figure 1). In each step, we apply a set of instruments to create the desired results:

1. **Value Modelling:** A *value model* is used to capture high-level economic resource transfers between actors as well as the different actors' intended effects, such as increased knowledge and increased safety, as a result of transfers of the economic resources.

    Result. A value model, depicting the main actors in the domain and their interchange of economic resources, such as money, business services, and products, as well as the intended effects that the actors strive for receiving economic resources.

    Provided Instruments. Value modelling, including the modelling of actors' intended effects.

2. **Top-Level Goal Identification:** A goal model is used to further refine transfers in the value model. As a starting point for the goal model, we use a set of guidelines to derive top-level goals from the value model.

Figure 1. Overview of the approach

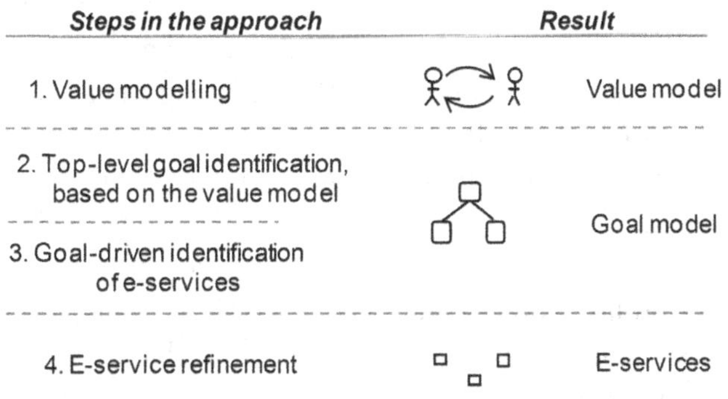

Steps in the approach		Result
1. Value modelling		Value model
2. Top-level goal identification, based on the value model		Goal model
3. Goal-driven identification of e-services		
4. E-service refinement		E-services

Result. Top-level goals based on economic resources and intended effects which are described in the value model.

Provided Instruments. A set of guidelines, outlining the use of value enhancers to aid in defining top-level goals based on resource transfers in the value model.

3. **Goal-Driven Identification of E-Services:** The goal model is refined, leading to e-services as means to fulfil sub-goals. As an extension to the goal model, we introduce an *e-service level*, specifically enabling the identification of e-services that support goal fulfilment.

Result. Refined goal models, with the top-level goal refined into sub-goals, forming a goal hierarchy. The bottom level in this hierarchy consists of e-services that fulfil the desired goals.

Provided Instruments. Goal modelling, with additional e-service goal level.

4. **E-Service Refinement:** To aid the service analyst to select and structure the e-services that are the result of the goal modelling, we provide *granularity guidelines*. These guidelines aid the service analyst to refine the e-services to the desired granularity level.

Result. Refined e-services, of appropriate granularity to be implemented.

Provided Instruments. Granularity guidelines, in the form of a list of top-down and bottom-up principles for selecting granularity levels.

The proposed approach both adds concepts to existing models (for example intended effects, top-level goals and a service level in goal models), as well as providing methodical support for linking values, goals and e-services together.

VALUE MODELLING

Many different kinds of models exist for representing and visualising the architecture, actions, and environment of an enterprise. One recent type of model is the business model that focuses on actors, resources, and resource exchanges (Gordijn, Akkermans, & Vliet, 2000; Wieringa & Gordijn, 2005; Weigand, 2006; Gordijn & Akkerman, 2001). A business model is different from other types of models used in enterprise modelling. In particular, a business model is different from process models, since it gives a high-level view of the actions taking place in and between organisations by identifying actors, resources and the exchange of resources between the actors. So, a business model focuses on the *what* in business. A process model, on the other hand, focuses on the how, as it deals with the operational and procedural aspects of business communication, including control flow, data flow and message passing (Gordijn, Akkermans, & Vliet, 2000; Johannesson, 2010). In other words, a business model takes a declarative view, while a process model takes a procedural view.

Our approach to business modelling is in line with the e3-value language (Gordijn, Akkermans, & Vliet, 2000; Gordijn & Akkerman, 2001). However, to cater for the analysis needs of the health care domain, we extend the e3-value language with the notion of internal resource and intended effects, which makes it possible to capture softer values like knowledge and safety. In the rest of this section, we give an overview of the main concepts in the value models we use.

Actor

An actor is someone who is able to participate in resource transfers and conversions (see below). An actor is typically a legal entity, such as a person or a company.

Economic and Internal Resources

A resource is an object that is viewed as being valuable by some actor. A resource is typically scarce, otherwise an actor would not consider it valuable. For example, ice would not count as a resource at the North Pole where it is abundant, neither would sand in the Sahara. Some concrete examples of resources are books, cars, movies, haircuts, and medical treatments. However, resources can also be of a more social and psychological nature, such as status, beauty, pleasure, health state, honour, and a feeling of safety. To distinguish between these different kinds of resources, we identify two categories of resources: economic resources and internal resources. Intuitively, an economic resource is a resource that can be transferred between actors. More precisely, an economic resource is a resource that can be under the control

of an actor, in the meaning that the actor may have legal rights on the resource. As a basis for analysing economic resources, we have identified the following categories:

- Goods, which are physical objects, like cars, refrigerators, and cell phones.
- Information, which is data in a certain context, like blueprints, referrals, and customer databases.
- Services, which are economic resources that encapsulate other resources and are used to increase the value of some other resource. Examples of services are haircuts and eye treatments. A hair cut can increase the beauty and an eye treatment can give a better health state.
- Money and vouchers, which are media for exchange. A voucher is a certificate that can be exchanged for another specific economic resource, e.g., a good or a service. Usually, a voucher can be exchanged only with some pre-specified actor(s). Money can be viewed as the most general form of voucher without any restriction on economic resources and actors.

In addition to economic resources, there are also internal resources that, intuitively, cannot be directly transferred between actors. More precisely, an *internal resource* is a resource that is not an economic resource. Some obvious examples of internal resources are beauty, health state, honour, and glory. It is not meaningful to talk about legal rights on these resources, neither is it possible to transfer any of these resources from one actor to another. Another example of an internal resource is knowledge. At first sight, it might seem that it is possible to transfer knowledge from one actor to another. However, this cannot be done directly, but only through an intermediary economic resource, e.g., a book (goods) or a lecture (service). Internal resources are often desired by people for their own sake, e.g., someone might desire more knowledge without any intention to use it in a particular way. Someone else might desire knowledge in order to make money through lecturing or other knowledge services, i.e., he/she use knowledge as an instrument for producing some other resource. Thus, internal resources can be seen both as ends in themselves or as instruments for other purposes. Economic resources, on the other hand, are only valuable as instruments for producing other resources.

Conversions

Resources can be used as instruments to produce or modify other resources. We define conversion as an action in which an actor uses some input resources to produce new or modify existing resources. For example, water and flour can be used as input economic resources in a baking conversion to produce the economic resource bread. Another example is an eye treatment (input economic resource) that is used to improve the health state (output internal resource) of a patient. Thus, in some cases, a conversion produces a brand new resource (bread), while in other cases the conversion modifies an existing resource (health state). In other words, a conversion can have two different results: a new resource or a modified resource.

Transfers

Transfers occur when actors want to acquire control of economic resources. Consider the question "What is transferred in a transfer?" This question may seem trivial, as the answer could just be "an economic resource." For example, if someone buys a book at a book store, then a book (goods, which is an economic resource) is transferred to him. Similarly, if someone borrows a book at a library, then again a book is transferred to him, but this book still belongs to the library. Thus, these examples indicate that the simple answer may in fact be too simple. There is clearly a difference between buying a book and borrowing one. If

you buy a book, you are entitled to read it or use it for any other purpose, give it to someone else, or even destroy it. In contrast, if you borrow a book, you are still entitled to read it, but neither to give it away nor to destroy it. So, just saying that a book is transferred when you buy a book is not sufficient – we need to spell out how you are allowed to use the book. In other words, buying a book means to get certain rights on the book. Therefore, we define a transfer as an action in which the rights on an economic resource are handed over from one actor to another.

To summarise, an actor, for example a health care organisation or a patient, can increase and decrease resources by either conversions, in which an actor uses resources (economic or internal resources) to produce new or modify existing resources (economic or internal resources), or by transfers, in which an actor hands over the rights on a resource (economic resource) to another actor or receives the rights on a resource (economic resource) from another actor.

Intended Effect

It is often important to make explicit why an actor wants to acquire a resource in a transfer. To capture this, we introduce the notion of intended effect of a value transfer, which is an increase or decrease of an internal resource that the receiving actor wants to achieve by using the transferred economic resource in one or more conversions. Examples of intended effects are: better health state, increased knowledge on health condition and increased feeling of safety.

Graphical Notation

Based on the above notions, we can now define a simple graphical form of value models. We base our notation on the e3 value language, which has a defined graphical notation. However we simplified this notation in order to limit the number of concepts to the ones presented earlier. This means that e3 concepts such as value interface and value ports are not used in our models. The simple graphical notation of the models makes them easy to introduce to key business stakeholders. A value model is here shown by means of a directed graph representing actors, transfers, and resources (see Figure 2):

- Actors are represented by the nodes of the graph and are shown as stick person icons.
- Transfers are represented by labels on the directed edges of the graph. The label for a transfer consists of three parts:
  - The economic resource being transferred.
  - The category of the economic resource (put within square brackets).
  - The intended effects of the use of the economic resource in one or more conversions (put within ordinary brackets).

  An example of a label for a transfer is:
- Eye treatment [service] (improved health state, increased feeling of safety).

If several conversions are needed in sequence in order to obtain the intended effect, we prefix it with "potentially." Note that the value model does not depict the ordering of the resource transfers, or the event that triggers the transfers. This kind of sequencing can be shown in a process model.

Referral Case from the REMS Project

The concepts presented above are applied to a real case from the REMS project. Figure 2 illustrates an excerpt of a value model defined in the scope of the REMS project. The figure is explained below. First, the transfers between the primary health care and the patient are described, and then the transfers between the patient and the primary health care, and so on. Note that we do not present any intended effects when the resource category is money or a voucher for money, since actors can receive money with many different intended effects.

Figure 2. An excerpt of a value model created in the REMS project

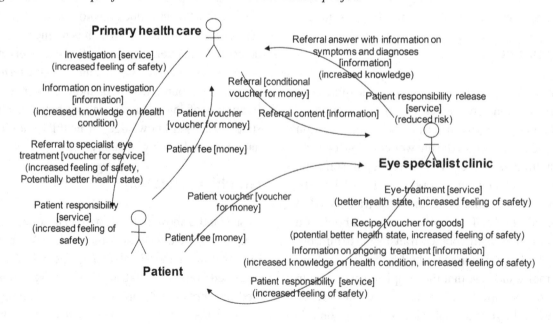

From Primary Health Care to Patient

When a patient experiences an eye health problem, he/she will visit a primary health care provider. The basic resource this provider offers is an investigation service. The intended effect of this investigation is that the patient gains an increased feeling of safety, since the investigation will reduce anxiety as the patient knows that she/he will receive professional care. Note that a service can encapsulate other economic resources, such as information, vouchers, and other services, which can also be visualised as transfers in the value model. In this example, the investigation provides a basis for an information transfer, where the provider informs the patient about his/her health status. This information has the intended effect that the patient will gain an increased knowledge of his/her health condition. If the patient needs further treatment, either the primary care provider will carry out the treatment (a service, which is not shown in Figure 2) or the provider refers the patient to an eye care specialist at a hospital clinic who is able to provide advanced treatments. To do this, the provider provides a referral to eye specialist treatment, which is a voucher for an eye treatment (voucher for service). There are two intended effects as a result of the transfer of the referral to the patient. The first effect is direct: the patient will gain an increased feeling of safety, since the patient knows that the referral can be used for advanced treatment and this will reduce anxiety as the patient knows that she/he will receive professional care. The other effect is indirect: if the patient uses the referral, the treatment at the hospital clinic may improve the health state of the patient, i.e. another intended effect of the referral is a potentially better health state. Furthermore, when the primary care provider starts investigating the patient, the primary care gains a responsibility for the patient's health, i.e., the provider is responsible for carrying out the required actions in order to maintain or improve the patient's health state (depending on the diagnosis). The intended effect of this responsibility transfer is, again, that the patient gains an increased feeling of safety, since he/she knows that a professional health care provider has "promised" the health care system to carry out the required actions for the patient. Note that the responsibility will remain on the primary care provider until the responsibility is explicitly handed over to another health care provider, e.g., an eye specialist clinic.

Patient to Primary Health Care

When the patient visits the primary health care provider, the following resources are transferred from the patient to the provider: patient fee and patient voucher. The patient fee is the money that the patient pays when visiting the primary care, while the patient voucher is a voucher for money that enables further reimbursement for the expenses from the city council (not shown in Figure 2).

From Primary Health Care to Eye Specialist Clinic

The referral that the patient received is also sent from the primary health care to the eye specialist clinic. For the eye specialist clinic, the referral functions as a conditional voucher for money that gives the clinic a right to be reimbursed money from the city council. The voucher is conditional since the clinic can only be reimbursed by the city council if the patient visits the clinic for treatment. Furthermore, the referral also contains referral content which is information that the eye specialist clinic uses to assess how urgent the patient's treatment is, as well as to plan and allocate resources at the clinic.

From Eye Specialist Clinic to Patient

When the patient visits the hospital clinic, he/she will receive an eye treatment service from the clinic. The intended effects of the treatment are twofold: a better health state and an increased feeling of safety. Furthermore, the treatment encapsulates other resources. First, it encapsulates an information transfer, i.e., information on the ongoing treatment, with the intended effect of increased knowledge on the health condition. Secondly, in some cases, the patient also needs certain medicine. The eye specialist clinic provider will then transfer a recipe, which is a voucher for goods; the patient can use the recipe at a pharmacy store and receive the needed medicine. There are two intended effects as a result of the transfer of the recipe. The first effect is direct: the patient will gain an increased feeling of safety, since the patient knows that the recipe can be used in exchange for medicine, which may improve his/her health state. The other effect is indirect: if the patient exchanges the recipe for medicine and also uses the medicine, the medicine may actually improve the health state of the patient, i.e., another effect of the recipe is a potentially better health state. Finally, when the eye specialist clinic starts the treatment, the clinic gets the responsibility for the patient's health, which gives the patient an increased feeling of safety.

From Patient to Eye Specialist Clinic

When the patient visits the eye specialist clinic, the clinic will receive the patient fee and patient voucher. The patient fee is the money that the patient pays when visiting the eye specialist clinic, while the patient voucher is a voucher for money that enables further reimbursement for the expenses from the city council.

From Eye Specialist Clinic to Primary Health Care Provider

When the eye specialist clinic starts treating the patient, it will explicitly take over the responsibility for the patient's health state from the primary health care. Therefore, the primary care provider will receive the resource responsibility release,

with the intended effect: reduced risk. Furthermore, when the eye specialist clinic has treated the patient, the clinic sends a referral answer back to the primary care unit with information on symptoms, diagnoses and carried-out treatments. This information does not lead to any direct actions at the primary care unit. Instead, the referral answer is mainly used to increase knowledge about eye health care for the physicians and nurses at the primary health care unit.

VALUE-DRIVEN IDENTIFICATION OF TOP-GOALS

While value models are used to analyse the high-level transfers of resources among actors, goal models are applied to identify instruments in the form of e-services for: a) realising, and b) improving these transfers.

There are several reasons for choosing goals as mediators between resource transfers on one side and e-services on the other. First, goal models are easy to understand and introduce for stakeholders of an organisation, which together can develop such models (for example, in a participative modelling session). Secondly, goal models enable stakeholders to be creative and innovative, since goal models do not focus on existing solutions. Instead, new and alternative means can be identified to fulfil goals. Thirdly, goal models can be used for measuring the goal fulfilment of processes and services. This makes it attractive to use goals for the management and evaluation of the business and supporting IT systems based on e-services.

Goal models have been used in requirements engineering to understand a problem domain and to map out the interests of different stakeholders. One of the most widely known languages for goal modelling is i* (Mylopoulos, Chung, & Yu, 1999), which provides constructs for modelling goals, tasks, resources, and dependencies between actors. While i* holds a strong position in the academic community, there are also goal modelling languages with a more practical orientation. One of these languages is the Business Motivation Model, BMM (OMG, 2008). A basic notion in BMM is that of a goal, which expresses something a business seeks to accomplish, a desired state of affairs or condition. Examples of goals are being the market leader in an industry or having a profit of more than 1 million euros. Goals can be decomposed, i.e. one goal can be a part of another goal. The decomposition forms a hierarchy where top-level goals are broken down into sub-goals.

Furthermore, BMM includes the notion of *means*, i.e., instruments that can be used to achieve a goal. Means can take different forms, as they can be capabilities, methods, techniques, or even devices. When breaking down a goal into a goal hierarchy, the goals become more concrete further down in the hierarchy until the means are reached.

In the approach proposed in this paper, we use the BMM to identify potential e-services. The e-services that we model are aligned with the concept of means in the BMM, as they are seen as the IT instruments of the enterprise for achieving sub-goals in the bottom-level of the goal hierarchy.

In addition to the goal hierarchy (denoted as the *"sub-goals" layer* in Figure 5 and Figure 6), we have distinguished the following novel layers to the goal model:

- The resource layer describes the starting point for the goal model.
- The top-goal layer is derived from the resource layer such that the top-goals represent desired improvements of the resources.
- The e-service layer describes e-services that can aid in the fulfilment of bottom-level sub-goals.

The first layer, the resource layer, is directly created from the value model, by considering the transferred economic resources in the value model. The remainder of this section will describe guidelines for creating the second layer, the top-goal layer.

The second, top-goal, layer is created transparently from the first layer by considering the interests of the actors involved in a business model envisaged in the form of transferred economic resources. More precisely, the top-level goals are created from the requirements for each single resource transfer to a) obtain the intended effects and b) to exchange the economic resource with certain, desired features. This leads to two guidelines for identifying the top-level goals of an actor:

- Intended effect guideline, which guides the creation of top-level goals based on internal resources. These goals express the relationship between resource transfers and their intended effects; more precisely, they specify that the acquisition of a transferred resource should result in a conversion of an internal resource. An example is "The eye treatment shall give rise to an increased feeling of safety."
- Resource enhancer guideline, which focuses on the features of transferred resources and guides the creation of top-level goals based on a number of resource enhancers. A resource enhancer expresses either a desirable feature of a resource or a desirable feature of the way in which the resource is delivered to the recipient. By applying the resource enhancers, we obtain a number of goals that concern the properties of an economic resource, as well as the adequacy of its delivery. Examples are "The delivery of the eye treatment shall be fast" and "The transferred information shall be correct and up to date."

Applying the described guidelines will result in a number of top-level goals for an actor. These goals reside on a high and abstract level, and as such cannot directly suggest any concrete actions to take. Therefore, there is a need to decompose these goals further until concrete means are identified.

It should be emphasised that when eliciting e-services an actor could use the two outlined guidelines independently and complementarily. In the latter case, the goals and sub-goals from the two guidelines may conflict with each other; it is then up to the goal designer to decide which goal to include or exclude, using common prioritising techniques. Also, duplicated goals and e-services are easily removed. However, note that the two outlined guidelines can result in the identification of e-services on different granularity levels.

Intended Effect Guideline

The intended effect guideline is as follows:

For each transfer of an economic resource (ER) with an intended effect (IE), introduce the goal "ER should give rise to IE."

Using as an example the resource transfer for the giving of eye treatment by a specialist clinic to a patient (see Figure 2), and then by applying the intended effect guideline, we obtain the following top-level goals (see Figure 3):

- The eye treatment (ER) shall give rise to a better health state (IE).
- The eye treatment (ER) shall give rise to an increased feeling of safety (IE).

Figure 3 illustrates a goal model that is derived from the outlined example. The intended effect

guideline is applied for discovering goals in the cases when the effect of the use of an economic resource is important for the involved actors. The use of top goals in this manner thus put emphasis on the consumer side of the resource transfer, this is similar to what (Baida et al., 2005) refers to as properties derived from consumer demand.

Resource Enhancer Guideline

The resource enhancer guideline is as follows:

For each transfer of an economic resource (ER), introduce a number of top-level goals based on the resource enhancers according to the table below.

A *resource enhancer* expresses either a desirable feature of an economic resource itself, or a desirable feature of the way in which the economic resource is delivered to the recipient, making the resource more valuable for an actor. The list of resource enhancers is open-ended, but in a number of case studies we have found the following to be the most fundamental ones: *fast*, *high quality*, *flexible*, *low cost*, and *secure*. This list also matches the critical success factors of business processes as suggested in Mende, Brecht, and Osterle (1994), with the exception of secure. The selected resource enhancers is also in line with the more elaborate quality dimensions than can be found in the SERVQUAL framework (Parasuraman et al., 1988).

When a certain enhancer is applied to a resource, or its delivery, the desired condition is formulated and viewed as a goal of an actor. Fol-

Figure 3. Identified top-goals based on the resource transfer "eye treatment" using the intended effect guideline

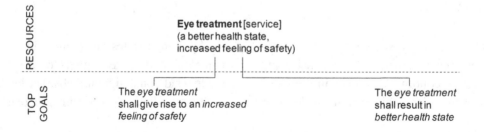

lowing this, in Table 1, we summarise the top-level goals for different types of resources, for each of the resource enhancers.

Some examples of goals obtained by applying the resource enhancer guideline given in Table 1 are the following:

- The information (ER) shall be correct and up to date (property of the resource, when the *high quality* enhancer is applied).
- The waiting time for the eye operation (ER) shall be short (property of the delivery of the resource, when the *fast* enhancer is applied).

Figure 4 shows top-goals that are derived from the example of the transfer of the economic resource *eye treatment* from the *hospital clinic* to the *patient* (this resource transfer is visualised in Figure 2). Figure 4 is only describing identified goals when one resource enhancer, i.e., *fast*, is applied to the service eye treatment. This results in two top-level goals, one for the delivery of the service and one for the property of the service (see Table 1). As with the intended effect guideline, the obtained top-level goals are further decomposed into sub-goals until e-services are elicited. We explain this process in detail in the following section.

Table 1. Resource enhancers and derived top-level goals for different types of economic resources

	Delivery of Resource Types	Properties of the Resource Types
Fast	■ The delivery of the *information/goods/money* to the recipient shall be fast. ■ The delivery, i.e., the waiting time for the *service*, shall be short.	■ The enactment time of the *service* shall be short. ■ N/A for *information/goods/money/voucher*.
High quality	■ The delivery of the *information/goods/money/ service* shall be reliable, i.e., the goods/ information/money/service shall always reach the recipient and the recipient shall always be informed about delays.	■ The *information* shall be correct, relevant, and up to date, and/or according to specifications. ■ The *goods* shall be fit for their use, and/or according to specifications. ■ The *service* shall be enacted fit for use and/or according to specifications. ■ N/A for *money*.
Flexible	■ The delivery of the *information* shall be customisable, i.e., information shall be delivered in different forms, e.g., paper, digital file sent via the Internet. Further, the presentation of the information shall be adapted to the needs of the recipient. ■ The delivery of the *goods* to the recipient shall be customisable, i.e., different forms of delivery shall be provided, e.g. home delivery, delivery to the nearest post office. ■ The delivery of the *money* can be in the form of cash, a check, or sent to an account. Further, the cash can also be delivered in different currencies. ■ The delivery of the *service* to the recipient shall be customisable in space and time, i.e. different forms of delivery shall be provided, e.g. heath care services at home, at health care units close to home, as well as the waiting time being adaptable depending on needs and demand.	■ The *information* shall be customisable to the needs of the recipient, e.g., an XML file will be more customisable than HTML (since the XML schemas can be changed). ■ The *goods* shall be customisable to the needs of the recipient, e.g., a chair is adjustable to fit the user. ■ The enactment of the *service* shall be customisable to the recipient. ■ N/A for *money*.
Low cost	■ The delivery of the *information/goods/ money/service* shall be provided at a low cost.	■ The *information/goods/service* shall be provided at a low cost. ■ N/A for *money*.
Secure	■ The delivery of the *information/goods/ money/service* shall be provided with high confidentiality, high integrity, and accountability.	■ The *goods* shall be safe in intended as well as unintended use. ■ N/A for *information, money and voucher*, and *services*.

Figure 4. Identified top-goals based on the resource transfer "eye treatment" and the value enhancer "fast" using the resource enhancer guideline

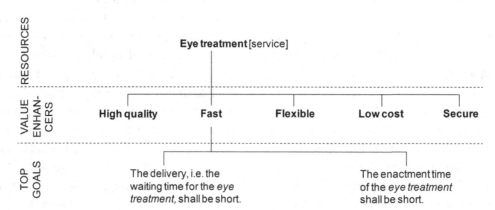

GOAL REFINEMENT AND IDENTIFICATION OF E-SERVICES

The top-level goals identified through the analysis of exchanged economic resources serve as a starting point in the goal modelling session, carried out in a participative manner including different stakeholders. The goal modelling session is performed in two basic steps:

1. Refinement of the top-level goals into sub-goals, forming a goal hierarchy, thereby creating the sub-goal layer in the goal model.
2. Identification of e-services, based on the sub-goals, thereby creating the e-services layer in the goal model.

Each of the above steps requires input from the stakeholders, who are experts in the domain. As described in the following, a goal modelling session leader can guide the overall process.

During the first step, a top-level goal is further refined to create a goal hierarchy. If desired, the modelling of the goal hierarchy can be guided by the goal modelling session leader, by posing a set of guiding questions, see for example Liakos et al. (2006).

During the second step, candidate e-services are identified based on the created sub-goals. When

the bottom-level sub-goals have been identified, it is usually straightforward for the stakeholders to determine candidate e-services that might support these goals. A key question to guide the identification of candidate e-services from bottom-level goals is "Can this goal be achieved using an e-service?"

An example of goal refinement in this manner can be found in Figure 5, where the top-level goal "The waiting time for the eye treatment shall be short" is refined. One of the sub-goal (see Figure 5) states that unused time slots in the hospital shall be decreased, and a sub-goal of this goal is to minimise the number of patients who do not use their allotted time slots. During the goal modelling session, means to achieve this bottom-level sub-goal were discussed. One possible way, as seen in Figure 5, is to introduce an e-service that reminds the patients via e-mail.

Another example of goal refinement can be found in Figure 6, where the top-level goal "The eye treatment shall give rise to an increased feeling of safety" is refined. One of the sub-goal (see Figure 6) to this top-goal states that the patient shall have information about his/her own case before and after treatment. A sub-goal of this goal states that the patient shall be able to monitor the flow of his/her referrals and answers. One possible way of achieving such a sub-goal, as seen in Figure 6,

Figure 5. Goal refinement and e-service identification based on the top-goal "The waiting time fast for the eye-treatment shall be short"

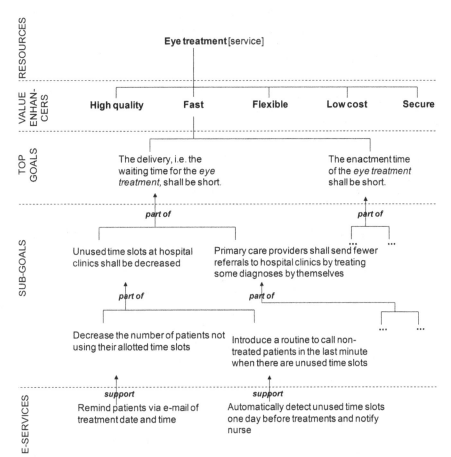

is to introduce an e-service that makes it possible to search and view referrals via the Internet.

Each identified e-service needs, upon implementation, to be coupled to a provider. A simple solution to identifying the providing actor is, by using the value model, to look at which actor provides the resource on which the top-level goal is based. For example, the reminder e-service introduced in Figure 5 is supporting the transfer of the eye-treatment resource from the specialist to the patient. It is thus natural that the specialist becomes the provider of the e-service. However, this simple selection of provider is not suitable in all cases. For example, actors might already have existing systems that can be easily extended to include new services, or the e-services might

be provided by a third party. In the REMS case, the constructed e-services were provided by the eye-specialist clinic at St. Erik's Eye Hospital, because they already had e-services related to referral handling.

The goal refinement described in this section can result in a hierarchy of both quantitative and qualitative goals. In our approach we do not advocate the sole use of either of these types of goals. However, to measure goal fulfilment there is a need to introduce quantitative goals. One approach to combine qualitative and quantitative goals (referred to as objectives) is discussed in BMM (OMG, 2008). For example, the qualitative goal "The waiting time for the eye treatment shall be short" can be related to an objective: "The

Figure 6. Goal refinement and e-service identification based on the top-goal "The eye treatment shall give rise to an increased feeling of safety"

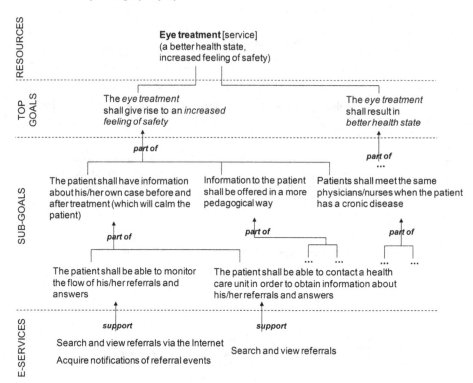

average waiting time for the eye treatment shall be less than one month during 2011". By introducing such objectives in the goal hierarchy, it is possible to use the resulting goal hierarchy to measure the goal fulfilment in business terms.

The goal refinement presented in this section is resulting in a set of e-services. The identified e-services may need to be restructured to a granularity level of convenience, which is discussed in the next section.

E-SERVICE REFINEMENT

Before implementing the e-services that were identified during the goal modeling sessions there is a need to see to that the services are refined such that they are coherent in relation to each other, and that they are aligned with the existing infrastructure. For example, two similar e-services

dealing with the same business concepts might be joined into a larger, more coherent, e-service. The technical infrastructure also needs to be examined. For example, there might be existing e-services that can be reused or existing legacy systems that might be able to provide the needed functionality. Thus, the focus of the refinement is not to identify new e-services, but to adjust the identified services to better fit into a context of business use and technical infrastructure. Central to this refinement is the *granularity* of the e-services, that is, how much functionality they encompass.

Depending on how the goal-modelling sessions were carried out, the identified e-services will be specified on different granularity levels. There will simply be e-service candidates ranging from quite small features (such as "document the patient symptoms") to larger services (such as "prioritise and route the referral to a clinic"). Therefore, a discussion among the business and systems developers about a preferred granularity level needs to be performed. This discussion will be similar to identifying the granularity of UML use cases, which are important modelling artifacts in the Rational Unified Process. For example, Cockburn (2001) distinguishes between, and also presents guidelines for identifying, use cases on different granularity levels, i.e., kite, sea, and fish level.

During the discussion about the granularity level of the e-services, we recommend specifying on which criteria the choice of granularity level will be based. There are two basic approaches to defining the granularity level for the identified e-services: top-down refinement and bottom-up refinement. A top-down approach will use business level concepts as a guide to refine e-services. A bottom-up approach tries to align new e-services with the existing IT infrastructure. Typically, the bottom-up approach fits the desired functionality into the existing systems, while a top-down approach aligns the services with existing business concepts and processes. Although a top-down approach is necessary during analysis to achieve a good overview of the complete set of e-services (Erl, 2007), a bottom-up approach is vital for the alignment with the existing IT assets within an organisation.

To refine the result of the goal modelling, we apply two guidelines: top-down and bottom-up. The top-down refinement guideline is as follows:

Use top-down refinement principles, as defined below, to refine the identified e-services according to business level concepts, such as business activities in a business process.

We have identified three *refinement principles* for the identified e-services from a top-down approach:

1. **Process Descriptions:** The e-services shall be refined according to process descriptions of an organisation or standardised process models presented by a standardisation body.

For example, the services identified by the European health care standard Healthcare Information Service Architecture (HISA, 2007) are based on the process standard SAMBA (SAMBA, 2003). Examples of process steps in SAMBA are deciding referral, refer, renew health care mandate, and perform treatment. These steps can be seen as potential e-services.

In Anzböck and Dustdar (2004), the use of pre-specified workflow transactions between two actors from the Integrating the Healthcare Enterprise (IHE) technical framework is recommended for the identification of e-services. Examples of such workflow transactions are patient identity feed, query registry, retrieve document, find personnel white pages, test results management.

2. **Work Assignment (task):** The e-services shall be refined according to a definition of what constitutes a work assignment, i.e., an e-service is something that fulfils all the steps in a specified work assignment.

For example, in Cockburn (2001), such a work assignment is defined as the steps that a user will fulfill before he/she will take a small ("coffee") break. For example, to refer a patient to an eye specialist is a work assignment, while a step such as finding an eye specialist and addressing the referral to an eye specialist are actions that are too small to constitute one work assignment. They should rather be seen as sub-steps in the work assignment "refer a patient to an eye specialist".

3. **Sell/Buy:** The e-services shall be refined according to a set of other e-service products supplied for the market.

E-services may be designed for a product sold on the market, for example the health care market. Therefore, they need to be adapted for that market or for different market segments.

The bottom-up refinement guideline is as follows: Use bottom-up refinement principles stated below to refine the identified e-services according to the existing infrastructure.

We have identified two *refinement principles* for the identified e-services from a bottom-up approach:

1. **Legacy System:** The e-services shall be refined in order to adapt to the existing legacy systems and their functionality.

   The different e-services will work as wrappers for an existing legacy system (Cheesman & Daniels, 2001).

2. **Reuse:** The e-services shall be refined so that they can be reused by other e-services. In this case, the least common denominator of the requirements from other e-services' use may direct the level of granularity.

To summarise, the above guidelines and principles are used to refine the e-services that are to be implemented. Services on a finer granularity level might be implemented as features (or functions) of other (larger) e-services. For the final implementation there is also a need to cover a finer detail of requirements than what can be done using the goal modelling. For example, non-functional requirements need to be specified for individual services, such as scalability and performance. Another example of details that need to be added is user-interface design requirements. As the focus of the approach here is the identification of e-services, specifying these detailed equipments is out of the scope for the approach.

APPLICATION AND EVALUATION OF THE APPROACH IN THE REMS PROJECT

This section describes the application and evaluation of the approach proposed in this paper, as well as an evaluation of the resulting e-services.

Application of the Approach

The approach for designing e-services based on value and goal models has been applied in a health care project, called REMS (Henkel, Perjons, & Zdravkovic, 2006). As described in the introduction, the aim of the REMS project was to create a number of e-services that could be used to create, manage and transfer health care referrals between several health care providers in the Stockholm region. The project resulted in a number of web-based e-services implemented in a prototype system, hosted by the St. Erik's Eye Hospital.

The REMS projects was a joint research project with:

- Researchers in information systems, responsible for applying the value and goal based approach for designing e-services.
- System developers from an IT company, responsible for gathering requirements on, designing and implementing the e-services.
- Executives at S:t Eriks Eye Hospital, responsible for choosing e-services to implement, from a number of identified candidate services.
- Users of the prototype and e-services, i.e., physicians at an eye specialist clinic at at S:t Eriks Eye Hospital, physicians at primary health care units, opticians at optician companies and physicians at private specialist providers.

The following steps outline how the approach for designing e-services based on values and goals was applied in the REMS project:

1. **Value model creation:** As a starting point, the researchers introduced value modelling to executives at St. Erik's Eye Hospital and physicians at an eye specialist clinic at the hospital. The executives and physicians developed an as-is value model based on

their experiences of eye heath care in the Stockholm region. The resulting value model showed the economic resources that were transferred between patients, primary health care units, eye specialist clinics, opticians, and private specialist units, as well as the intended effects that motivated each economic resource transfer. Initially, there was a mix of economic resources, internal resources, and intended effects in the developed model. Therefore, the initial value model was re-structured by the researchers by transforming internal resources to intended effects, and assigning (at least) one intended effect to each economic resource transfer. The re-structured value model was verified by the executives and physicians at St. Erik's Eye Hospital.

2. **Goal model creation, including identifying candidate e-services:** The transformation of the developed value model into e-services using goal models, was carried out by a number of user representatives. That means that the modelling group in this step was larger than the group in the first step, also including physicians from another hospital, primary care units and private eye specialist units, and opticians from different optician companies (in total six to eight persons in each modelling session). The starting point for the goal modelling session was the top-level goals generated from the value models. Each representative identified a number of sub-goals given the top-level goals. The identified sub-goals were then structured in a number of goal hierarchies, i.e., goal models, by the modelling group, one goal model for each top-level goal. The resulting goal models were refined by the researchers by further interviewing the different representatives. During these interviews also the candidate e-services supporting the goals were identified.

3. **Development of e-services prototypes:** From the identified e-services, the executives at S:t Eriks Eye Hospital need to choose the e-services to implement in the prototype. This choice was based on the goal models, and discussions with user representatives and systems developers. The final chosen e-services were: "Write referral", Send referral, including addressing", "Forward referral, including find available eye specialist", "Receive and review referral", "Re-sent referral", "Send referral answer". Finally, the e-service prototype was implemented by the system developers, and used by physicians at the eye specialist clinics, primary health care units, and private specialist units, as well as opticians at optician companies during a month period before two evaluation activities were performed.

Evaluation of the Approach

After the implementation of the e-services, an evaluation of the value and goal based approach for designing e-services was carried out by the researchers. More specifically, the benefits and drawbacks of the value and goal based approach were evaluated. To structure the evaluation we focused on the ability of the approach to represent the entities of interest in a domain (*expressiveness*), and the degree to which the approach is able to support the design of e-services (*efficiency*). Note that the evaluation of the output of the approach, the e-services, is covered in the next section. In addition to the criteria mentioned above, the approach was intended to allow the active participation from stakeholders. Thus, we also emphasized that the approach should be understood by the key stakeholders (*comprehensibility*). To summarise we have three evaluation criterias that were used to structure the evaluation; *expressiveness, efficiency, comprehensibility*.

The evaluation of the approach was carried out using semi-structured interviews. We interviewed the CEO of S:t Eriks Eye Hospital, and two system developers, which have been responsible for gathering the requirements on the e-services, as well as carrying out the design and implementation of the e-services.

The result of the evaluation is described below by first presenting the value model creation part of the approach and then the goal model creation and e-service identification part. Note that the use of the service refinements criteria is not covered in the evaluation since these criteria were not developed in full when the evaluation was carried out.

The evaluation of the value model creation part, showed several benefits and no direct drawbacks. According to the interviewees, the value model gave an easily *comprehensible* overview of the transfers of resources in the network of health care actors as a whole. The classification of economic resources into goods, services, money and information facilitates *efficient* identification and understanding of the transfers. Beneficial was also the possibility to *express* "soft" aspects such as the desire for safety and knowledge in the form of intended effects. This fits well with the health care domain where such intended effects are essential. These comments points towards that the value model creation part of the approach offers *expressiveness, efficiency* and *comprehensibility*.

The evaluation of the goal model creation and e-service identification part of the approach, showed both benefits and drawbacks. A benefit that was pointed out was that the approach provided a clear, *comprehensible*, link between the values, goals and e-services, i.e., the approach shows how e-services support goals and values. Another benefit that was pointed out was that the *expressiveness* of the goal model supported prioritisation among e-services, when choosing e-services to implement among a number of candidate services. A third benefit was

the use of a set of pre-generated top-level goals which was viewed as an *efficient* and inspiring means for the modelling group in order to identify sub-goals and e-services. However, the use of pre-generated top-level goals was also mentioned as a potential *efficiency* drawback, as they could hinder thinking "outside of the box." Another *efficiency* drawback that was mentioned was that there is no way to be sure that the goal models are complete, in the sense that it covers all possible ways to improve the resource exchanges in the value model. However, the use of both intended effect guideline and resource enhancer guideline seems to support the completeness requirement on top-level goals. A third drawback was that the approach did not *express* concrete means for the prioritisation of the e-services, by relating benefits or revenues to each goal in the goal model, and relating costs for development and maintenance to the e-services.

These comments point towards that the goal model and e-service identification part of the approach offers *expressiveness, efficiency* and *comprehensibility*, although the expressiveness could be extended by adding a prioritisation mechanism when choosing e-services to implement. The comments also indicated that approach might not be *efficient* when it comes to thinking "out of the box" and to ensure that the goal model is complete.

Evaluation of the Resulting E-Services

The goal fulfilment of the implemented e-services was also evaluated by interviewing users of the e-services. Since we had no practical possibility to compare the e-services with e-services designed using another approach, we opted for evaluating how well the implemented services fulfilled the goals stated in the created goal models. Thus, the evaluation is focused on the actual alignment of the goal models with the final e-services. If there is no such alignment, the approach would have failed to influence the design of the e-services.

Six persons that have used the e-prototype were interviewed: two opticians from an optician company, one primary care physician, one private eye specialist and one eye specialist from eye specialist clinic at St. Eriks Eye Hospital. The main result of the evaluation of the implemented e-services showed that the e-services helped the users to achieve goals as specified in the goal models:

- The e-service "Write referral" enforced the primary care physicians and opticians to specify the patients eye symptoms according to a predefined list of eye health issues and possible states of the issues. This supported the receiver of the referral, the physicians at the eye specialist clinic at St. Eriks Eye Hospital, to achieve better quality in the prioritisation of referrals. For example, patients with emergent needs could easier be identified by the specialists.

- The e-service "Forward referral, including finding available eye specialist" made it easier for the physicians at the eye specialist clinic at St. Eriks Eye Hospital to forward referrals to another eye specialist, according to a list of available eye specialists. This was necessary if another health care region or hospital should be responsible for the patient, or that eye specialist clinic temporary lacked resources. To forward referrals manually was a resource intensive activity, involving several persons at the eye specialist clinic.

- The e-service "Send referral answer" enforced the eye specialist to specify investigations and treatments carried out, as well as the result of the treatments, before sending the referral answer back to the primary care physicians or opticians that primarily wrote and send the referrals. Both primary care physicians and opticians stated that

well specified referral answers were an important source to gain more knowledge about eye health care.

As a drawback the lack of system integration with external journal systems were mentioned. This caused some extra work for the users of the e-services, because they needed to copy some patient data between systems.

CONCLUSION

In this paper we have proposed and evaluated an approach that combines the use of value and goal models in order to design e-services. While value models capture high-level resource exchanges between actors, goal models enable a structured approach for defining concrete e-services. The approach consists of several novel contributions in the form of an enhanced value model, defined guidelines to derive top-level goals from value models, and finally a set of refinement guidelines used to structure the designed e-services.

An *enhanced value model* was used to depict actors, their transfers of resources, and the intended effects of these transfers. The value model enables us to represent, explore and relate traditional economic resources, such as goods and services as well as internal resources such as safety and knowledge. Internal resources are important in the health care sector to capture and refine the notion of values for patients.

A set of *high level goal derivation guidelines* that assist in the derivation of high level goals from a value model. To capture business goals pertaining to improvements on both economic and internal resources we defined two sets of guidelines, intended effect guideline and resource enhancer guideline. Applying these guidelines will result in a set of high level goals that are grounded in the value model, thereby linking goals to resource transfers in the value model. The high level goals can then be broken down into sub-goals and e-services that can be used to fulfill these sub-goals.

A set of *e-service refinement guidelines* was finally devised to structure the e-services that were identified during the goal modeling. These guidelines aid designers to select an appropriate granularity for the e-services that should be implemented.

The presented approach allows traceability between e-services, goals and resource transfers. Thus, the identified e-services can be motivated by their ability to support the goals in the goal models, and by their support of the resource transfers in the value model.

The approach was applied and evaluated in a case study in the Health care sector. The evaluation of the approach showed that the models were easy to understand, and allowed a clear overview of the actor's transfers of resources as well as a clear link between resource transfers, goal and e-services. However it was pointed out by the interviewees that the approach could be extended with instruments for the prioritisation of the resulting e-services, since there are seldom possible to implement them all.

ACKNOWLEDGMENT

The REMS project was funded by the Swedish Agency for Innovation Systems (VINNOVA), the Stockholm County Council and St. Erik's Eye Hospital. The authors would like to thank the representatives participating in the modelling sessions and the IT specialists at OOPix AB, Sweden.

REFERENCES

Andersson, B., Bergholtz, M., Edirisuriya, E., Ilayperuma, T., & Johannesson, P. (2005). A Declarative Foundation of Process Models. In *Proceedings of the 17th Conference on Advanced Information Systems Engineering,* Montpellier, France (LNCS 3520, pp. 233-24). New York: Springer Verlag.

Anzböck, R., & Dustdar, S. (2004). Modeling Medical E-services. In *Proceedings of the Business Process Management: Second International Conference (BPM 2004)*, Potsdam, Germany (LNCS 3080, pp. 49-65). New York: Springer Verlag.

Baida, Z., Gordijn, J., Akkermans, H., Saele, H., & Morch, A. Z. (2005). Finding e-Service Offerings by Computer-supported Customer Need Reasoning. *International Journal of E-Business Research, 1*(3), 91–112.

Bleistein, S., Cox, K., Verner, J., & Phalp, K. (2006). Requirements engineering for e-business advantage. *Requirements Engineering, 11*(1), 4–16. doi:10.1007/s00766-005-0012-7.

Cheesman, J., & Daniels, J. (2001). *UML Components. A Simple Process for Specifying Component-Based Software.* Reading, MA: Addison-Wesley.

Cherbakov, L., Galambos, G., Harishankar, R., Kalyana, S., & Rackham, G. (2005). Impact of Service Orientation at the Business Level. *IBM Systems Journal, 44*(4). doi:10.1147/sj.444.0653.

Cockburn, A. (2001). *Writing Effective Use Cases.* Reading, MA: Addison-Wesley.

Erl, T. (2007). *SOA Principles of Service Design.* Upper Saddle River, NJ: Prentice Hall.

Gordijn, J., & Akkermans, H. (2001). E3-value: Design and Evaluation of e-Business Models. *IEEE Intelligent Systems, 16*(4), 11–17. doi:10.1109/5254.941353.

Gordijn, J., Akkermans, J. M., & van Vliet, J. C. (2000). Business Modeling is not Process Modeling. Conceptual Modeling for e-Business and the Web. In *Proceedings of ER 2000 Workshops on Conceptual Modeling Approaches for E-Business and the World Wide Web and Conceptual Modeling*, Salt Lake City, UT (LNCS 1921, pp. 40-51). New York: Springer Verlag.

Gordijn, J., de Kinderen, S., Pijpers, V., & Akkermans, H. (2008). E-Services in a Networked World: From Semantics to Pragmatics. In *Proceedings of Future Internet Symposium (FIS 2008)*, Vienna, Austria.

Gordijn, J., Petit, M., & Wieringa, R. (2006). Understanding Business Strategies of Networked Value Constellations Using Goal and Value Modeling. In *Proceedings of the 14th IEEE International Conference on Requirement Engineering (RE 2006)*, Minneapolis/St.Paul, MN (pp. 126-135). Washington, DC: IEEE Computer Society.

Gordijn, J., Yu, E., & Raadt van der, B. (2006). e-Service Design Using i* and e3 value Modeling. *IEEE Software, 23*(3), 26-33.

Henkel, M., Perjons, E., & Zdravkovic, J. (2006). A Value-based Foundation for Service. In Modelling. In *Proceedings of the European Conference on Web Services (ECOWS'06)*, Zurich, Switzerland (pp. 129-137). Washington, DC: IEEE.

HISA. (2007). *Health Informatics – Service Architecture (HISA), Part 1: Enterprise Viewpoint* (CEN/TC 215/prEN 12967-1). Retrieved April 2010, from www.kith.no/upload/4120/ISOTC215_pCD_12967-1_HISA-20070208.doc

Hruby, P. (2006). *Model-Driven Design of Software Applications with Business Patterns*. New York: Springer Verlag.

Johannesson, P., Andersson, B., & Weigand, H. (2010). Resource Analysis and Classification for Purpose Driven Value Model Design. *International Journal of Information System Modeling and Design, 1*(1).

Levi, K., & Arsanjani, A. (2003). A Goal–driven Approach to Enterprise Component Identification and Specification. *Communications of the ACM, 45*(10), 45–52.

Liaskos, S., Lapouchnian, A., Yu, Y., Yu, E., & Mylopoulos, J. (2006). On Goal-based Variability Acquisition and Analysis. In *Proceedings of the Conference on Requirements Engineering (RE'06)*, Minneapolis, MN (pp. 79-88). Washington, DC: IEEE Computer Society.

Mende, M., Brecht, L., & Osterle, H. (1994). Evaluating Existing Information Systems from a Business Process Perspective. In *Proceedings of the 1994 Computer Personnel Research Conference on Reinventing IS*, Alexandria, VA (pp. 289-296). New York: ACM.

Mylopoulos, J., Chung, L., & Yu, E. (1999). From Object-Oriented to Goal-Oriented Requirements Analysis. *Communications of the ACM, 42*(1). New York: ACM.

OMG. (2008). *Business Motivation Model (BMM), version 1* (ormal/2008-08-02). *Object Management Group*. Retrieved April 2010, from http://www.omg.org/spec/BMM/1.0/PDF

Osterwalder, A. (2004). *The Business Model Ontology*. Unpublished dcotoral dissertation, HEC Lausanne, Switzerland.

Papazoglou, M. P., & Yang, J. (2002). Design Methodology for Web Services and Business Processes. In *Proceedings of the Third International Workshop on Technologies for E-Services (TES 2002)*, Hong Kong, China (LNCS 2444, pp. 54-64). New York: Springer Verlag.

Parasuraman, A., Zeithaml, V. A., & Berry, L. L. (1988). SERVQUAL: a multiple-item scale for measuring consumer perception of service quality. *Journal of Retailing, 64*(1), 12–40.

Piccinelli, G., Emmerich, W., Zirpins, C., & Schütt, K. (2002). Web Service Interfaces for Inter-Organisational Business Processes – An Infrastructure for Automated Reconciliation. In *Proceedings of the 6th International Enterprise Distributed Object Computing Conference (EDOC 2002)*, Lausanne, Switzerland (pp. 285-292). Washington, DC: IEEE Computer Society.

Prahalad, C. K., & Krishnan, M. S. (2008). *The New Age of Innovation. Driving Cocreated Value Through Global Networks*. New York: McGraw-Hill.

REFS. (2010). *IEEE International Workshop on Requirements Engineering For Services (REFS 2010)*. Retrieved April 2010, from http://compsac. cs.iastate.edu/cc_workshops.php

SAMBA. (2003). *Structured Architecture for Medical Business Activities (SAMBA), version 1.1*. Retrieved April 2010, from http://www.contsys. eu/documents/samba/samba_en_short_1_3.pdf

Weigand, H., Johannesson, P., Andersson, B., Bergholtz, M., Edirisuriya, E., & Ilayperuma, T. (2006). On the Notion of Value Object. In *Proceedings of the 18th Conference on Advanced Information Systems Engineering*, Luxembourg (LNCS 4001, pp. 321-335). Berlin: Springer Verlag.

Wieringa, R. J., & Gordijn, J. (2005). Value-Oriented Design of Service Coordination Processes: Correctness and Trust. In *Proceedings of the 2005 ACM Symposium on Applied Computing*, Santa Fe, NM (pp. 1320-1327). New York: ACM.

This work was previously published in the International Journal of Information System Modeling and Design (IJISMD), Volume 2, Issue 1, edited by Remigijus Gustas, pp. 1-23, copyright 2011 by IGI Publishing (an imprint of IGI Global).

Section 5
Methodology and Tools for Analysis and Design

Chapter 12
What Practitioners Think of Inter–Organizational ERP Requirements Engineering Practices:
Focus Group Results

Maya Daneva
University of Twente, The Netherlands

Niv Ahituv
Tel-Aviv University, Israel

ABSTRACT

Empirical studies on requirements engineering for inter-organizational enterprise resource planning (ERP) systems have demonstrated that the ERP vendor-provided prescriptive models for ERP roll-outs make tacit assumptions about the ERP adopter's context. This, in turn, leads to the implementation of suboptimal solutions. Specifically, these models assume that ERP implementations happen within a single company, and so they pay only scant attention to the stakeholders' requirements for inter-organizational coordination. Given this backdrop, the first author proposed 13 practices for engineering the ERP co-ordination requirements in previous publications. This paper reports a confirmatory study evaluating those practices. Using an online focus group, the authors collected and analyzed practitioners' feedback and their experiences to understand the extent to which the proposed practices are indeed observable. The study indicated very low variability in practitioners' perceptions regarding 12 of the 13 practices, and considerable variability in their perceptions regarding the role of modeling inter-organizational coordination requirements. The contribution of the study is twofold: (1) it adds to the body of knowledge in the sub-area of RE for ERP; and (2) it adds to the practice of using qualitative research methods in empirical RE.

DOI: 10.4018/978-1-4666-4161-7.ch012

INTRODUCTION

The elicitation, documentation, and negotiation of the requirements for systems based on ERP software packages have formed an important sub-area of Requirements Engineering (RE) in the last decade (Daneva & Wieringa, 2010). ERP solutions are, more often than not, large and multi-component systems that provide cross-functional services to a business. They often impact data semantics and business processes across more than one functional area of an organization. This sub-area of RE is becoming even more important, as ERP solutions are increasingly responding to the reality of modern companies networking with others to form inter-firm partnerships (also called 'extended enterprises'). For such companies, the use of ERP is a central component of their strategy for the proper management, coordination, and control of inter-organizational relationships (Nicolaou, 2008). An inter-firm partnership is a business collaboration composed of multiple companies or business units, which together accomplish the mission of bringing a product or service to market. Engineering the coordination requirements for an inter-organizational ERP solution to support an inter-firm partnership is, however, a difficult task. The current RE approaches to ERP are based on prescriptive models that are provided by ERP vendors and their implementation partners (Ahituv et al., 2002). These models do not explicitly draw on practices perceived as useful from the standpoint of the stakeholders in the ERP-adopting organizations that have formed a partnership. A 2010 survey by Daneva and Wieringa (2010) on state-of-the-art ERP RE approaches reveals that, while the prescriptive RE models explicitly address business process, data, and interface requirements, they tacitly assume a project environment where an ERP package is implemented within the walls of one organization. As a result, only scant attention is paid to the requirements for inter-organizational coordination that stakeholders expect the ERP solution to meet. This, in turn, leads to the implementation of systems that are suboptimal from the perspective of some stakeholders, as the resulting ERP requirements definitions lack an explicit part on what the solution-to-be should do to properly support the inter-firm partnership's needs and intentions for inter-organizational coordination and collaboration. Many inter-firm partnerships therefore seek to extend the vendor-provided RE models by adding practices that address the requirements for inter-organizational coordination (Daneva & Wieringa, 2010). In the inter-organizational context, the solution-to-be may well include diverse ERP configurations, each of which matches the needs and intentions of a particular partner, which, in turn, implies the presence of coordination mechanisms unique to each configuration. Companies therefore justifiably assume that, if they identify, document, and validate their needs and intentions for ERP-supported coordination early enough, it is more likely that the right ERP-solution will be delivered to them (Prakash, 2010).

In our earlier research by the first author (Daneva & Wieringa, 2006b; Daneva 2010), we investigated the following issues: (1) how to engineer the requirements for inter-organizational coordination in ERP projects; and (2) what constitutes good engineering practices with respect to the coordination requirements for shared ERP solutions. This research was accomplished by reviewing the published literature; specifically, case studies representing the experiences of a broad array of companies that had implemented inter-organizational ERP solutions in the past 15 years. We found that the coordination among companies in an extended enterprise takes place at four different levels of complexity. Considering these levels, we proposed 13 RE practices, along with an early indication of the benefits that can be expected from introducing each RE practice in an extended enterprise. While in our earlier publications (Daneva & Wieringa, 2006b; Daneva 2010), we reported on our motivation to search for the RE practices and on the research process that helped us derive them, in this paper, we focus on the need to evaluate them. Specifically, our goal is to carry out an initial evaluation of the practices based on ERP practitioners' feedback. This paper provides a detailed account of how we used an asynchronous online focus group approach to do this. This study represents the first step of the many we have planned to empirically evaluate RE practices.

The research presented in this paper contributes to the body of knowledge in RE for ERP in two ways. First, we are adding to the literature in RE for ERP, by making RE knowledge explicit and providing information on which practice works in what context, and providing evidence suggesting that 12 of the 13 proposed practices for coordination requirements make sense for practitioners and can perhaps be considered good candidates for inclusion in RE process models for inter-organizational ERP projects.

Second, we are adding to the body of empirical software engineering (SE) studies in general, and to the body of empirical studies in RE in particular. This contribution is twofold: (1) we directly respond to the call (Sjøberg et al., 2007) of the empirical SE community for more empirical research on which SE process to use in what specific context. We also respond to the particular call (Cheng & Atlee, 2007) of the RE community for more empirical research in the sub-areas of RE. The existing literature on empirical SE provides very little guidance on the practical steps of using focus groups to evaluate good SE practices (and RE practices in particular). Kontio et al. (2004) and Lehtola et al. (2004) have published three focus group studies on RE topics, these authors being among the very few who have ever used the focus group research method in the field of RE and who have also provided guidelines (Kontio et al., 2008) for using focus groups in empirical SE. We therefore reflect on our focus group-based validation experiences and distill from them some lessons learned about the strengths and weaknesses of using focus groups as a research approach, hoping it will be of value to the research community.

In the following narrative, we first present related work on judging SE practices. We then provide the theoretical and empirical background of our study and describe our focus group plan, along with the justification for the decisions about the way in which we set up our focus group process. We then report on our focus group execution and its outcomes. Lastly, we discuss the results and limitations of the study, reflect on our experiences, and present our future research activities.

RELATED WORK

Below, we review the published literature sources on two topics: (1) the ways in which SE practices are judged in general; and (2) the approaches that have been used in empirical SE to evaluate the validity of specific practices that have been deemed 'good' or 'best' in a specific SE sub-area (e.g. RE).

The topic of judging practices as good or best in SE has been treated in almost all SE sub-disciplines, for example RE (Sommerville & Sawyer, 1997; Beecham et al., 2005; Schoemaker, 2007), software modeling (Le Gloahec et al., 2008), portfolio management (Jeffery & Leliveld, 2004), software testing (Chilarege, 1999; Kaner et al., 2001), software project management (Brown et al., 2000), software maintenance (April & Abran, 2008), and software estimation (Jones, 2007). This topic has also been treated from the perspective of specific paradigms (e.g. agile SE, object-oriented software development, component-based software development), and of specific application areas (e.g. global software development, cloud computing, outsourcing, service-oriented architecture, business process redesign (Mansar et al., 2010). SE authors search for good practices from a variety of sources, including research papers, experience reports, guides, standards, books, and company-specific repositories (Fraser et al., 2007).

We think that it is not surprising that the volume of literature on this topic is remarkably large, because the software industry is well aware that the capacity of the enterprise to prosper is based on its ability to capture, use, and address good practices (Fraser et al., 2007; Jones, 2009). We must note, however, that, while the literature sources that we referred to in this paragraph did propose specific packages of practices which the authors deemed good or best in their respective sub-areas of study (e.g. RE), only a relatively small minority of these proposals was subjected to a systematic evaluation regarding the validity of the claims that the authors made about the practices in the proposals. In these published sources, we observe that there is agreement among almost all authors that a practice labeled 'good' or 'best' is one that successful organizations tend to use frequently in their projects. The premise that the authors use in judging these practices is an understanding that successful software (or IT) projects follow sound engineering principles, while failing projects do not. We have observed, however, that, despite the continual effort of the SE community to reflect on SE excellence and best practices by using well-founded quantitative analyses (Jones 2009), at the present time, for the majority of practices deemed good or best, the good practice status (or best practice status) has been assigned based exclusively on anecdotal evidence in successful software organizations. For the majority of the practices proposed in the cited sources, there is no statistically representative evidence of the 'goodness' of the practices in question. This is especially true for SE sub-areas with a relatively short history (e.g. agile SE, cloud computing), and also for RE, which has existed as a separate sub-discipline for 15-20 years.

Our review also reveals that there is no agreement on what a 'valid' practice is, or on what 'validity' means and how to demonstrate it. As we will see in the remainder of this section, researchers have used a variety of definitions of validity, each serving the purpose of a specific study. Validity has also been approached by using a variety of research techniques, ranging from quantitative (Basili et al., 1992; Jones, 2009) to qualitative e.g. Sommerville & Sawyer, 1997; Fraser et al., 2007). This variety of definitions and approaches to the validity of SE practices is not surprising, because, as von Wangenheimer et al. (2010) indicate, at the present time there is little methodological support for how to systematically plan and execute the validation of practices in particular, and of maturity models (i.e. the collections of SE practices) in general. In their recently published systematic review of the empirical evaluation of maturity models (von Wangenheimer et al., 2010), these authors found very few studies that report on the possible effects of practices on the intended quality and performance goals.

Because we wanted to review examples of studies that explicitly deal with the validation/ evaluation of SE practice, we had to complete a narrower search of published literature. We deliberately chose to look into four specific groups of sources that not only make proposals for packages of good/best SE practices (as the authors of many of the previously mentioned references had done), but also describe, in more detail, the analytical arguments that practitioners used to substantiate their conclusions about what represents a 'good' or a best practice. These groups of sources include examples of authors who placed SE excellence on a sound quantitative basis (Basili et al., 1992, Jones, 2009), and also of authors who have carried out systematic qualitative evaluation studies on the validity of SE practices:

1. The literature on maturity models in SE, because these models represent a "vast body of knowledge about good software practices" (von Wangenheim et al., 2010) and possibly explain the justification for what practices to include in a model and why (El-Emam & Jung, 2001).

2. The literature on the deployment of the experience factory approach (Basili et al.,

1992, Basili, 1995, Boehm et al., 2005) in organizations, because this approach is one of the earliest key vehicles proposed by the empirical SE community to enable evolutionary learning from organizational experience.

3. The literature on lessons learned (Schneider et al., 2002; Fraser et al., 2007; Jones, 2009) in SE, because leveraging these lessons is a well-known common sense approach in software companies where good practice is distilled to enable its reuse.

4. The literature on the results (Jones, 2000) of the efforts of software practice benchmarking communities and industry peer networks (Sgourev & Zuckerman, 2006), because they are actively involved in the definition and dissemination of good, as well as innovative, practices.

Our review of these studies suggests that, in most of them, the authors seek to demonstrate or evaluate a possible relationship between the uses of one or more practices on the one hand, and some important project or process outcomes on the other, e.g. reduced cost, improved client satisfaction, increased quality, and reduced rework. Furthermore, we observe that the degree to which the authors present their research on this relationship transparently and comprehensibly (e.g. in such a way that other researchers could replicate the published study in new contexts) vary widely. This observation agrees with von Wangenheim et al. (2010), who found that very few practices were evaluated as part of a maturity model validation effort, and whatever evaluation took place was through expert reviews with "varying degree of participation."

Below we summarize, in chronological order, those previously published approaches to validity evaluation of software practices that provide much detail on how the authors' conclusions about validity are substantiated.

Basili et al. (1992) were among the very first who sought to demonstrate a connection between the incremental adoption of learning experiences (these are good practices) in an organization and important project outcomes (namely, cost per line of new code, reliability, "manageability", and effort expended in rework). The conclusions of these authors regarding the impact of good practices have been substantiated through numerous experimental studies carried out in their respective organizations: NASA, the University of Maryland, and the Computer Sciences Corporation.

Jones (2000, 2009) has been using benchmark studies to derive and evaluate best SE practices pertaining to a number of critical SE sub-fields. The benchmark datasets on which Jones's analysis relies contain quantitative data, which are structured according to application type and application size, and collected across software projects in numerous organizations, in a variety of business sectors, and in 24 countries. His evaluation is based on statistical techniques, as well as on comparative analysis techniques that help to quantitatively demonstrate the relative superiority of a specific practice over other practices in an SE sub-area. (We note that the author and his colleagues have been in the software benchmarking business since 1985, working exclusively on quantitative indicators for managing software projects and processes, as well as improving software products.) An important, and unique, aspect of Jones's evaluation on best practice is his definition of specific criteria for including or excluding tools and technologies from best practice status. For example, the author explicitly recommends that any technology considered a potential best practice needs empirical results from at least 10 companies and 50 projects.

El-Emam and Jung (2001) carried out a questionnaire-based survey among software process maturity assessors to validate the SPICE (Software Process Improvement and Capability Determination) model. Their study draws on the accumulated experiences of assessors, while carrying out SPICE trials. The objective of the study was "to determine how good the model is, whether it was useable, useful, whether the rating scheme was meaningful, and whether there were general weaknesses in its architecture."

Jeffery and Leliveld (2004) used an online survey complemented with in-depth interviews to evaluate software portfolio management practices and the maturity levels with which they are associated. The survey data were used to test hypotheses regarding the relationship between relative organizational performance gains and the use of best practices in project portfolio management. The interviews were used to formulate the characteristics of the maturity levels of the author's model.

Beecham et al. (2005) aimed to demonstrate the suitability of RE practices for inclusion in an RE maturity model, and devised a RE-practice validation approach that deployed multiple research techniques, namely an expert panel and a survey. These authors formed a group of 23 experts (which was deemed to be representative of the population of experts in CMM and RE), and then ran a survey-based process to judge how well an RE good practice model met a set of predefined criteria for success. The authors' conclusion was that the range of responses by the experts "formed a good basis for the researchers to gauge how their model might be viewed in practice."

The combination of an expert panel and a survey was also the approach used by Ramasubbu et al. (2005) to validate practices for managing distributed software development. These practices formed key process areas and were meant as an extension of the CMM for the global development context. Like Beecham et al. (2005), Ramasubbu et al. (2005) used the survey data to run statistical techniques and obtain sound results that substantiate their claims.

Mansar and Reijers (2005) presented an approach that used two empirical research techniques, a case study and a survey, in the validation of the best practices for business process redesign projects. In this study, the concept of validity was defined in a range of terms, namely duration, flexibility, quality, productivity, and cost. Using these, the authors referred to: (1) criteria the practices have to meet (e.g. relevance to practitioners); and (2) specific impacts of the practices on project outcomes. The case study technique was applied to evaluate the relevance of the best practices and the extent of their applicability. The survey was used to validate the impact of the best practices as perceived by practitioners. The survey data served as quantitative input to test two hypotheses referring to whether or not "the practices cover all possible aspects practitioners look for," and whether or not "the practices are indeed applied extensively by practitioners" (Mansard & Reijers, 2005). The authors wanted to find out how much practitioners focus on a practice while they are redesigning a business process.

Abba et al. (2009) used a factor analysis-driven approach to evaluate the effectiveness of 58 agile practices for the purpose of forming a guide for agile process improvement. Their goal was to provide assistance to practitioners in choosing the right combination of agile practices based on company-specific needs. The research approach these authors used consisted of: (1) a survey, as the quantitative data collection method; and (2) factor analysis (Field, 2005), as the technique to help explain the maximum amount of common variance in a correlation matrix using the smallest number of explanatory concepts. Factor analysis also formed the core of the research approach of So and Scholl (2009), who investigated the social-psychological effects of 8 agile SE practices.

THEORETICAL AND EMPIRICAL BACKGROUND

As indicated in the Introduction, the overall objective of this study is to evaluate ERP RE practices from the perspective of practicing ERP professionals. This section provides background on these practices, on the concept of validity we have used, and on the overall research approach chosen. The purpose of the section is to help the readers understand the rest of the paper and to avoid any misunderstandings.

The Object of Study: Practices for Inter-Organizational Coordination Requirements

The object of study in this paper is a package of 13 practices for engineering the coordination requirements in an inter-organizational ERP project. For the purposes of our research, we call 'coordination requirements' those requirements that are concerned with two aspects of the inter-organizational relationships: (1) what partner companies in an extended enterprise share; and (2) how they share it (Daneva & Wieringa, 2006b). Engineering inter-organizational coordination requirements means getting stakeholders from the partner companies to explicitly discuss and document their intentions with respect to (1) and (2). Two characterizing properties of the coordination requirements in an inter-organizational ERP project are: (1) that these requirements be derived from the overall business goal of the extended enterprise; and (2) that they be decided at the "intentional level" (Prakash, 2010), which means that, once the partner companies agree on the intentions of the inter-organizational ERP solution-to-be, they have to ensure that the goals of the individual partners come together to satisfy these intentions. In other words, the goals of the partner organizations must support each other. For example, a number of case studies on the implementation of inter-organizational ERP in extended enterprises (Champy, 2002; Saliola & Zanfei, 2009; Simatupang, Wright, & Sridharan, 2002; Simatupang, Sandroto, & Lubis, 2004; Xu & Beamon, 2005) refer to the project setting in which a large company forms a collaboration with other companies to achieve the goal of raising the productivity of its supply chain. Typically, this goal is achieved through a transformation of

the supply chain based on the integration of the company's suppliers into a shared ERP system. Essentially, in forming the extended enterprise, such a company reframes the way it regards its suppliers: as Champy puts it, "the suppliers are no longer regarded as mere producers of parts but as adders of value to the shared enterprise."

Once all the partner companies commit to collaborating towards achieving this goal, each partnering 'adder of value' has to make decisions regarding, for example, how each partner's processes must change to fit the shared system, and for what benefits. Also, partners more often than not have to adopt a shared terminology and information semantics for those areas of business activity in which they want to do things together. This is key, as, without establishing a common understanding about the meaning of the information to be shared, its content could not be used efficiently and accurately. For the purposes of clarification, we have narrowed down the discussion to one particular case that was cited in the literature, and to which we referred in this section (Champy, 2002). It is the case of Wal-Mart, who formed an extended enterprise with its suppliers and also with its customers. This collaboration allowed Wal-Mart to sell, much more quickly, items that had previously been known to take up a disproportionate amount of space in its stores, such as patio furniture and appliances (Champy, 2002). For the suppliers, this collaboration led to increased sales, and for customers it meant speedier execution of orders. For those suppliers and customers who committed to collaborating with Wal-Mart in a shared enterprise, this collaboration required the customers and the suppliers to develop a much deeper understanding of each other's processes. In certain cases, the customer simply demanded that the suppliers adjust their processes to match those of the customer. In other cases, Wal-Mart and a supplier shared a single process to ensure quality, so it became difficult at times to distinguish who works for which partner organization. This variety of ways to share processes and collaborate towards a shared goal required that the inter-organizational ERP system include a variety of ERP configurations, each matching the coordination intentions of a particular partner (or group of partners). Addressing the inter-organizational coordination requirements (e.g. those in the case of Wal-Mart) as explicitly as possible is important, because they are deemed critical (Champy, 2002; Marcotte, Grabot, & Affonso, 2008) to the successful implementation of the multi-enterprise business model (e.g. value collaboration model, customer-centric network) that coordinates all players in an inter-firm partnership. (For a more detailed description of an example of intentional alignment in inter-organizational systems projects in supply chain management, we refer interested readers to the paper by Prakash, 2010).

In earlier research (Daneva & Wieringa, 2006a), we found that four types of coordination requirements are relevant to partners in an extended enterprise: (1) those that refer to the partners' agreements on the goals and benefits of business coordination; (2) those that are concerned with establishing end-to-end inter-organizational business processes—for example, client order fulfillment processes or product provisioning processes; (3) those that address information semantics (the definition and use of common meanings of key information entities); and (4) those that are concerned with achieving interoperable automated processes and data flows. We also carried out literature studies (Daneva & Wieringa, 2006b; Daneva 2010) that resulted in the identification of 13 practices for engineering these requirements in ERP projects.

Moreover, we also found evidence suggesting that these 13 practices are not applicable to all ERP adopting organizations, and we used the notion of 'coordination complexity level' to indicate which practice is suitable for what ERP coordination context in an organization. By 'coordination complexity', we mean the extent to which a company participates in an extended enterprise. This term is based on Champy's analysis of the ways in which

companies participate in inter-firm partnerships (Champy, 2002). In Daneva and Wieringa (2006b), we defined four levels of coordination complexity, each reflecting how extensively a company lets other companies collaborate in and share its own business processes.

Every level of coordination complexity is characterized by the types of partner companies involved, unique inter-organizational coordination goals, areas of sharing, and the coordination mechanisms used. The notion of coordination level, thus reflects the understanding that the more diverse the business partners in an extended enterprise are, and the larger their number, the greater the coordination challenge (Champy, 2002; Daneva, 2010; Prakash, 2010). Level 1 represents the least challenging coordination scenario, with the least complex alignment requirements (Prakash, 2010), while Levels 2, 3, and 4 progress to increasingly challenging coordination processes and more complex alignment requirements. The levels are defined as follows:

Level 1: A company aligns its own processes. The goal of an ERP adopter at this level is to improve internal coordination among departments. No inter-organizational challenges or inter-organizational coordination requirements are addressed at this level (Prakash, 2010).

Level 2: An organization aligns its processes along with the processes of one other type of organization. The goal of an ERP adopter at this level is to improve coordination with this type of organization, whether as a client or as a supplier (Daneva 2010).

Level 3: A company aligns its processes along with the processes of two other types of organizations. The goal of an ERP adopter at this level is to improve coordination with two more company types, e.g. suppliers and clients (Champy, 2002).

Level 4: A company aligns its processes with the processes of organizations of three other types of organizations. The goal of an ERP adopter at this level is to work to improve coordination with three other types of organizations. It is not uncommon for these networks to change the coordination mechanisms in an entire business sector (Babiak, 2009; Holland, Shaw, & Kawalek, 2005).

To help companies make a choice on which of the 13 RE practices to use in their ERP project, we associated each practice with one or more of the above-mentioned levels of coordination complexity. So, we assume that if an ERP-adopting organization is aware of its level of coordination complexity, it would be possible for it to pick up those RE practices suitable for a project that targets the achievement of that particular level of coordination. The RE practices and their relevant levels of coordination complexity are presented in

Table 1. We note that there is no one-to-one mapping between practices and levels. This means that a practice can be associated with more than one level of coordination complexity (Daneva, 2010).

Research Questions and Motivation for Choosing the Research Approach

The purpose of our focus group study is to evaluate, from the perspective of ERP practitioners, the 13 practices and their association with specific complexity levels. Our plan also includes the evaluation of our focus group experiences with a view to understanding the limitations of this early validation study itself.

Our focus group study is a confirmatory in nature, and represents an early assessment exercise in which we set out to clarify two questions:

Table 1. The RE practices to be evaluated

RE Practice	Complexity level at which it is appropriate for organizations to use the practice
P1. Define how work is divided among partner companies	2,3,4
P2. For each network partner, document data, processes, and communication channels to be shared and with whom	2,3
P3. Document the values and goals to be shared and with whom	4
P4. Collect enough knowledge about the ERP-supported internal processes before aiming for cooperative ERP scenarios	4
P5. Document what separately kept application data of partner companies will be shared via interfaces to a common ERP system	3
P6. Align what is shared to what is kept separate	4
P7. Discover and document the market-making mechanisms and common learning models for partners to share	3,4
P8. Understand how ERP-supported coordination mechanisms will be used	3
P9. Assess the compatibility of partner companies' values and beliefs	2,3,4
P10. Make a business coordination model	2,3,4
P11. Map the business coordination model to a set of ERP-supported coordination mechanisms	2,3,4
P12. Use the reference architecture for the package provided by the ERP vendor	2,3,4
P13. Validate the coordination models and their execution	2,3,4

Question 1: Is what we think of as a good inter-organizational ERP RE practice something that ERP architects observe in their project realities?

Question 2: If architects observe a practice, at what complexity level would they place it?

To answer them, we selected the focus group research method, for the following reasons: (1) it is a suitable technique for an inquiry like ours, e.g. obtaining initial feedback on new concepts and helping to clarify the findings that resulted from using other methods; (2) it is well known for its cost-effectiveness (Kontio et al., 2000), which was essential in this first validity evaluation, as we needed to collect a concentrated set of observations within a short time span and on a limited budget; and (3) the resulting data offer a robust alternative (Massey, 2010) to more traditional survey methods, when the number of participants is less important than a rich investigation of content.

Specifically, our plan was to use an online asynchronous focus group (Gaiser, 1997; Orgad, 2005; Kivits, 2005), which is a focus group organized using Internet resources. We selected the online asynchronous form of focus group because: (1) it is extremely useful when the participants are located in multiple time zones and it is difficult to organize a time for geographically far-flung focus group members to participate synchronously; (2) it provides ready-to-use transcribed data; (3) it is flexible, so that our focus group members in various time zones can contribute when it is most convenient for them; (4) it encourages candid exchanges and reduces issues related to the 'interviewer' effect, as focus group members cannot "see" each other; and (5) it allows members' responses to be lengthier and more measured than does the synchronous mode (Orgad, 2005).

Note that, in addition to the focus group approach, we also considered three other research approaches for obtaining answers to our two research questions. These were the Delphi method, which is based on a panel of experts (Brown, 1968), the

online survey method (Simsek & Veiga, 2000), and the in-depth interview approach (King & Horrocks, 2010). We ruled out these three approaches, based on the suggestion of methodologists (Simsek & Veiga, 2000; Morgan, 1997; King & Horrock, 2010; Krueger & Cassey, 2008) that there be a trade-off between the following two criteria when a researcher chooses a research approach: (1) the suitability of the approach to produce the type of data that are appropriate for the purpose of our study; and (2) the estimated costs/efforts to use the approach.

Regarding the first criterion, our starting point was the need to obtain information on a range of views in a short time. Specifically, we needed collective feedback on our proposed package of practices, and we needed this feedback to come from a dialog between the participating practitioners themselves, and not between the researcher and each of the participants individually (which would have been the case with the Delphi approach and the survey method, in which each expert fills out a survey questionnaire, and the case with the in-depth interview approach in which the researcher converses with the experts on a one-on-one basis). We considered it essential to be able to observe the extent and nature of participants' agreements and disagreements regarding the contexts in which our RE practices apply, as these observations would presumably bring us an understanding of the kind of follow-up research that would warrant further efforts. The focus group approach was preferred over both the in-depth interview and the survey approaches, because it relies on group dynamics and helps explore and clarify the participants' views in ways that would be less easily accessible in personal in-depth interviews or in a survey.

Regarding the second criterion, we were conscious of the constraints we faced in terms of available resources. Scheduling, carrying out, and transcribing one-on-one interviews—across time zones and over the phone—would have been a long, coordination-intensive, and prohibitively expensive process. We also note that designing and piloting a survey, as well as engaging a representative sample, would have been challenging in the light of the resource constraints we faced. This is why we had to rule out the survey option, even though this approach would have produced the data we needed.

The Focus Group Research Method

A focus group is a group discussion on a particular topic, which is monitored, facilitated, and recorded by a researcher. It is a way to better understand what people think about an issue, a practice, a product, or a service. Focus groups were first used in the United States before and during World War II to understand how war propaganda broadcast on radio was received. As research procedures, the focus group techniques were widely and systematically refined in the 1950s by R. Merton and his team (Merton, 2005). For the past 40 years, focus groups have been used extensively in business-oriented market and consumer research, as well as in academic business research, in communication studies, and in studies in education, public health, and political science.

The term 'focus group' is derived from the term 'focus group discussion.' In essence, the researcher provides the focus of the discussion, and the data come from the group interaction. This means that the focus group serves both to collect information on a range of ideas and to illuminate variations in perspectives between individuals. Because interaction is at the heart of the focus group method, the researcher is primarily interested in how experts react to each other's statements and points of view, how they build bridges between their different perspectives, and how they build up shared understanding during the discussion. Krueger and Casey (2008) indicate that it is this particular type of interaction that gives the method a high level of validity, because the thoughts and views that each participant expresses can be confirmed or refuted during the group discussion itself.

As a qualitative research technique, focus groups can serve the purpose of both exploratory and confirmatory studies (Krueger & Casey, 2008; Morgan, 1997). The key steps in the focus group-based research process include the following (Kontio et al., 2008):

1. Defining the research questions related to a research problem,
2. Planning the focus group session,
3. Selecting focus group participants,
4. Executing the session,
5. Analyzing the data, and
6. Reporting the results.

The next section reports on the particular way we implemented these steps.

RUNNING THE FOCUS GROUP RESEARCH PROCESS

The Focus Group Plan

To plan our focus group study, we implemented the guidelines proposed by Krueger and Casey (2008). The decision to follow their approach was made after extensive reading on qualitative research literature, specifically literature which compared focus groups with other qualitative techniques, e.g. surveys and in-depth interviews (Morgan 1996), as well as personal consultation with other fellow researchers.

Our research questions (stated in the previous section) drove our choices in composing the focus group. We conducted it with practicing ERP architects from companies who were interested in exploring similar questions from their companies' perspectives. Our focus group plan included 18 ERP solution architects from four telecommunications services providers, two financial services companies, two retail businesses, and one real estate corporation. We applied a purposive sampling approach to selecting these participants. The focus group members were selected because: (1) they had characteristics in common, which pertained to the topic of the focus group: and (2) they had the potential to offer information-rich experiences. We note that focus groups do not gather to vote or to reach a consensus (Morgan, 1997). The intent is to promote self-disclosure, and that is what we were after in this study. According to (Morgan, 1997), the research procedure we planned to implement is known as 'a participatory focus group'. It collects data through group interaction of people of various backgrounds, but with common professional values and common roles in which they execute their professional duties. We also note that, according to focus group research methodologists (Krueger & Casey, 2008; Morgan, 1997), focus groups are not used to provide statistically generalizable results applicable to all people similar to the practitioners in a specific study. The intention of the focus group is not to infer, but to understand, and not to generalize, but to determine a possible range of views. Therefore, in this study we will adopt, based on the methodologists' recommendations, the criterion of transferability as a useful measure of validity. Transferability requires that the results be presented in such a way that allows other researchers to evaluate whether or not the findings apply to their research context.

All 18 ERP architects had the following characteristics:

- They were all in charge of inter-organizational projects that had stakeholders and users at locations distributed in at least four Canadian provinces, namely Quebec, Ontario, Alberta, and British Columbia.
- Each architect (1) has at least six years of experience in inter-organizational ERP RE; (2) is familiar with inter-organizational coordination issues; and (3) has made proposals to improve his/her company's ERP RE process.

- Thirteen architects have experience with the SAP's ERP package only. One architect has experience in Oracle only. Two architects have experience with SAP and Peoplesoft, and the other two with SAP and Oracle.
- Five architects had been working in Coordination Complexity Level 2 organizations, eleven architects were employed by Level 3 ERP adopters, and two architects were working for Level 4 ERP adopters.

All architects were known to the first author, as she had worked with them on a professional basis from 1995 to 2004. (Note that the first author worked as an SAP process analyst in a large company in North America prior to joining the university.) As recommended by Krueger and Casey, 2008, the moderator (in this case, the researcher) "should be similar to the respondents," meaning from the same population. Using purposive sampling, the first author chose the focus group members, based on her knowledge of their typicality. The author chose them from among a large group of colleagues based on her judgment as to whether or not they met the requirement that they be professionals with "the greatest amount of insights on the topic," as Krueger and Casey (2008) recommend.

Deciding on the level of moderator involvement in the focus group discussion is the second important design choice next to the choices related to group composition. In our focus group plan, the definition of the role of the moderator was driven by the research questions and the purpose of our study. We planned our focus group to be a structured one with regard to the questions being asked during the session, which means that the moderator was the one to control what topics would be discussed and in what order.

However, we chose to keep our focus group much less structured with respect to the moderator's involvement, in terms of the way in which the participants interacted. This means that the moderator adopted a passive role, and let the practitioners develop the discussion. To achieve this: (1) we set up policies for responding to the participants' messages, communicated the policies up-front, and made sure that the participants were well aware of them; and (2) we specified that the moderator would intervene in the discussion only if a participant violated these policies. This setup is also known as a 'self-managed' focus group (Morgan, 1997), and we opted for it because it served the purpose of the study well, which was to collect feedback on specific RE practices (i.e. the practices associated with engineering the coordination requirements) in a specific project context (in our case, inter-organizational ERP).

The Execution

The focus group members were contacted on a personal basis by the first author using e-mail. Before opening the discussion, this researcher provided the background of the study and presented the 13 practices as a checklist. The focus group members then worked in two stages, dealing with one research question at each stage. This was to ensure that the group members were not overwhelmed with a long list of inquiries at the start of the process.

In executing the focus group process, the first author served as the moderator. Her responsibility was to review the feedback of the participants, to probe deeper when necessary, and to paraphrase participants' points to ensure that misunderstandings were avoided. This researcher made sure that everyone had a chance to express themselves, but without pressuring any expert to write when they were not willing to do so.

Once the data were collected, preliminary analysis was undertaken immediately. This included reading the transcribed online conversations and applying a procedure for ensuring the quality of

the collected evidence. This procedure consisted of four steps, as recommended in (Krueger & Casey, 2008), and was designed to pose the following questions while each answer was read by a focus group member:

Step 1: Did the ERP architect directly address the question being asked? If so, proceed to Step 3. If not, go to Step 2. If the answer to this question is unclear, mark the text with red and review it later.

Step 2: Did the ERP architect address a different question in the focus group? If so, move the text fragment to the question it addresses. If not, go to Step 3.

Step 3: Does the ERP architect's comment say anything important about the topic? If so, move it to the related question. If not, mark it with a label 'set aside.'

Step 4: Does this comment say something that had already been said earlier? If so, add this text fragment to the stack of similar quotes. If not, start a separate stack.

Reiterating this procedure meant sifting through the data and sorting out quotes that provide evidence of the presence of each practice in the practitioner's observations. The information was then sorted in a way that made sense in relation to the two research questions. We describe the data analysis in more detail in the next section.

Data Analysis and Outcomes: Stage 1

In the first stage, the architects were asked to review the checklists and mark those practices that they either used personally, or witnessed someone else on their RE team using, in the early stages of their ERP projects. Specifically, the researcher asked each architect to provide one of the following types of evidence regarding the use of a practice:

1. An example of the practice being used in a project, and the context details that help reveal the presence of a practice, or
2. A brief explanation of exactly how the practice worked; this was to make sure that the researcher understood that the practice was indeed 'practiced' during a project, and had received convincing evidence of that fact.

The feedback of the focus group members took the form of story-telling, and provided transcribed conversations in which they shared their experiences. An example of a transcribed textual fragment by three focus group members regarding practice P5 is presented in Table 2. The grayed text in the second column of Table 2 identifies quotes that are similar across focus group members. These similarities are marked with codes (see the third column). The codes were instrumental in navigating through the transcribed conversations and identifying similar text fragments.

The responses of the 18 ERP architects are summarized in Table 3. For each practice, we report the number of architects who observed it at least once in a real-life setting. Table 3 indicates that 12 of the 13 practices make sense to practitioners, and were actually observed in real-life projects.

Table 3 shows that five practices, namely P1, P5, P6, P8, and P12, were observed by all 18 focus group members. Four other practices (P2, P3, P9, and P 13) were observed by at least 9 of the 18 focus group members. Two practices (P4 and P11) were observed by 8 and by 6 of 18 focus group members respectively. One practice (P7, Table 3) was not observed at all, but the architects attributed this to the fact that this practice referred to coordination with intermediaries, and no focus group member had worked on a project with an intermediary business.

Table 2. Text transcribed during stage 1: practice P5, contribution by 3 focus group members

Line Number	Transcription	Code
150	**Interfacing is connecting two or more different entities.** In our case, it is connecting one or	5-1
151	more systems with SAP. Now extending our previous example, you are replacing some	
152	legacy applications, but **there are some applications that you don't want to replace yet.**	5-2
153	**You need to somehow pass data back and forth between SAP and these remaining**	
154	**systems at the value partners' sites.** Make sure everyone involved knows **what pieces of**	
155	**data must be going one way or the other way or both ways.** That's **critical,** because you	5-3
156	will still need to do some data transformations/translations, etc. to make the data	
157	understandable to the receiving system. **This will continue as long as you want to keep the**	
158	**systems running alongside SAP.**	5-4
159	**In heterogeneous IT landscapes, you've got to specify the data being passed back and**	5-2
160	**forth between what is in these landscapes and the big shared SAP, otherwise you have no**	
161	**way to get a handle on failure points between technologies.** If your client strives to become	5-4
162	more real-time, and more collaborative, then you've got to move integration closer to the	
163	applications of both your client and their suppliers. What I do is **to make a list of those**	
164	**apps that will go on the SAP Exchange Infrastructure,** the vehicle that's bringing you the	5-3
165	ability to connect all relevant applications, regardless of whether it is an application from	
166	SAP or from a 3rd party.	
167	I think **a good practice in this case is to set up a life cycle for your interfaces.** We do it this	5-3
168	way because **the interfaces cost us a significant effort in development, design and**	5-4
169	**implementation.** What I do is this: first **I get a Data Designer to work with the business**	5-3
170	**owners to determine the data mapping** and complete the functional design. 2.If the	
171	interface is automated, the Technical Designer converts it into a technical specification for	
172	the interface program. 3.The developer used the design to build and test the interface	
173	program. And **I have five rounds of tests done until they migrate the interface to the**	5-2
174	**production environment.**	

Table 3. Inter-organizational ERP RE practices observed by 18 ERP architects

RE Practice	Number of architects observing it
P1. Define how work is divided among partner companies	18
P2. For each network partner, document data, processes, and communication channels to be shared and with whom	17
P3. Document the values and goals to be shared and with whom	11
P4. Collect enough knowledge about the ERP-supported internal processes before aiming for cooperative ERP scenarios	8
P5. Document what separately kept application data of partner companies will be shared via interfaces to a common ERP system	18
P6. Align what is shared to what is kept separate	18
P7. Discover and document the market-making mechanisms and common learning models for partners to share	0
P8. Understand how ERP-supported coordination mechanisms will be used	18
P9. Assess the compatibility of partner companies' values and beliefs	9
P10. Make a business coordination model	12
P11. Map the business coordination model to a set of ERP-supported coordination mechanisms	6
P12. Use the reference architecture for the package provided by the ERP vendor	18
P13. Validate the coordination models and their execution	10

Data Analysis and Outcomes: Stage 2

In the second stage, we excluded the practice that no one had observed (P7, Table 3). We randomly sorted the list of 12 remaining practices and asked the architects to position them at the four coordination complexity levels. We then compared how the architects associated the practices with the levels and how we (the researchers) did so (Table 4). For each practice, we assessed its mapping to a complexity level by using the percentage occurrences of those architects' rankings that coincided with ours (Table 4). We adopted a cut-off of 75% as an acceptable matching level, as recommended in previous validation studies of SE practices (Krishnan et al., 2005; Ramasabbu et al., 2005). The data in Table 4 suggest that our mappings match well with the architects' mappings. However, we observed four pairs of practices and their associated levels which did not meet the 75% cut-off level. These are the practices labeled P2, P6, P10, and P12, and they all refer to the role of modeling in inter-

organizational ERP RE. They were subjected to a second review by the architects. The outcomes of this review are summarized in the section that follows Table 4.

Focus Group Members' Review of the Practices below the 75% Cut-Off Level

Practices P2 and P6: The focus group accepted practices P2 and P6 for all complexity levels. In the original proposal (Daneva & Wieringa, 2006) (Table 1), these two practices had been associated with Coordination Complexity Levels 2 and 3 only. We had not associated these practices with Level 4, because the literature suggests that, in a competitive collaboration (that is, an inter-firm partnership made up of competing companies in the same sector), the more the competitors share, the more this weakens one partner vis-à-vis the others. However, the focus group members provided observations about those cases in which the benefits of sharing can far outweigh the disadvan-

Table 4. Inter-organizational ERP RE associated with complexity levels by 18 ERP architects

RE Practice	Complexity Level in Table 1	Architects' Rankings for a Level 2 Match	Architects' Rankings for a Level 3 Match	Architects' Rankings for a Level 4 Match	Architects' Rankings for Levels 2 and 3 Match	Architects' Rankings for Levels 3 and 4 Match	Architects' Rankings for Levels 2,3, and 4 Match	Correct (%)
P1. Define how work is divided among partner companies	2,3,4	-	-	-	-	-	18	100.00
P2. For each network partner, document data, processes, and communication channels to be shared and with whom	2,3	1	1	1	-	-	15	5.55
P3. Document the values and goals to be shared and with whom	4	-	-	15	-	3	-	83.33
P4. Collect enough knowledge about the ERP-supported internal processes before aiming for cooperative ERP scenarios	4	-	-	14	-	4	-	77.77
P5. Document what separately kept application data of partner companies will be shared via interfaces to a common ERP system	3	2	14	-	2	-	-	77.77
P6. Align what is shared to what is kept separate	4	-	1	1	-	1	15	5.55
P8. Understand how ERP-supported coordination mechanisms will be used	3	-	15	-	3	-	-	83.33
P9. Assess the compatibility of partner companies' values and beliefs	2,3,4	-	-	-	-	3	15	83.33
P10. Make a business coordination model	2,3,4	-	-	-	5	-	9	50.00
P11. Map the business coordination model to a set of ERP-supported coordination mechanisms	2,3,4	-	-	-	-	1	17	94.44
P12. Use the reference architecture for the package provided by the ERP vendor	2,3,4	-	-	6	-	10	2	11.11
P13. Validate the coordination models and their execution	2,3,4	1	1	-	-	-	16	88.88

tages. Our focus group members' arguments for associating these practices with Level 4 (and not only with Levels 2 and 3, as was the case in our original proposal) are as follows:

- Practices P2 and P6 create opportunities for each company in an extended enterprise to learn from their partners. According to the ERP architects, learning from each other is at the core of successful competitive collaborations.

- A company is willing to use competitive collaboration outside the formal agreements, and diffuse new knowledge through competitive tactics (not only through shared goals, as is the case with practice P3).

- Being explicit on what is shared is a way to control the unintended release of sensitive information between competing partner companies.

- In competitive collaborations, understanding what is shared helps competitors get close enough to predict the behavior of their rivals when the partnership unravels or has run its course.

These points led us to conclude that we need a deeper analysis of practices P2 and P6, and also an analysis at a finer level of granularity. We think that these two practices are interdependent, and may also depend on the choice of other practices. So, we decided to analyze the possible scenarios in which practices can be combined, so that we can clearly obtain incremental complexity stratification. This constitutes a line of enquiry for future research.

Practice P10: The focus group was divided according to three standpoints on positioning practice P10. Nine architects thought that documenting inter-organizational coordination processes should be conducted by Level 4 ERP adopters, because this is a very expensive effort and its pay-offs are much less tangible for Level 2 or 3 organizations.

These architects witnessed Level 2 and 3 organizations modeling inter-organizational processes only when the costs for this are split among the partner companies in the network. When there is no consensus on cost-sharing, each partner takes the responsibility of modeling their own part of the process using their own preferred modeling techniques and tools. Special attention is paid, then, to the partnering companies' process interface points. This is where process ownership changes, or where one company hands over process execution to another.

Furthermore, five experts associated practice P10 to Level 2 and Level 3, and argued that modeling prior to architecture design is critical: (1) to the remaining implementation stages; and (2) to the architects' ability to connect the inter-organizational solution built now with the one to be built in the future. The attitude of these architects converged with findings published by Roser et al. (2006) on the importance of explicit modeling of inter-organizational business processes for the solution architecture. These authors investigated an inter-organizational system development environment in which the model transformation approach was used to design a shared system, and concluded that, unless inter-organizational processes are modeled, "model transformation results are likely to be of poor quality." In their study, the authors maintain that different types of architectural concepts rely to a different extent on the existence of explicit models of the inter-organizational business process. We therefore hypothesize that the experiences of the five architects might well refer to the implementation of a solution architecture that might have been highly dependent on the existence of models. We were not able however, to discuss this point with the five architects during the study, as the publication of Roser et al. (2006) was identified after the focus group process was over. Nevertheless, we feel motivated to initiate a follow-up research effort in the near future to gain a deeper understanding of the point raised by these five architects.

Four architects insisted that modeling is a "Level 1 organization's business" (as one architect put it), and therefore should not be part of the discussion on inter-organizational coordination. Another participant added, "You either invest in modeling tools and standards within your own organization and you know why you are doing this, or you do not invest in them at all. If you invest in them, you do this because it's of value to your organization, not because of the collaboration. You either have the stomach for models, or you do not. And if you do not, then you write text; and the most important thing is that everyone else can understand your text. That's what counts most. And not whether you have models or not." The four focus group members also claimed that, unless an organization has an established modeling culture, coordination process modeling would not make much sense, as it may even be perceived as sunk costs from a high level management perspective. Two architects went on to give multiple examples of inter-firm partnerships in which large companies that were pushy and domineering with respect to their partners tried to make those partners adopt complex business process modeling tools (namely the ARIS toolset and LiveModel) and instill the discipline of business process modeling in what they refer to as a "mega-project setting" ('mega-project' is the term they use to describe a very large project). These ERP adopters threw large budgets into hiring external consultants, who created "tons of models that became shelfware eight months after the project was over." The following are two examples of mechanisms through which this happened. In one case, the executive who championed the introduction of the (SAP) modeling standards and tools in a partner company left the organization shortly after the system went live. His departure triggered a chain of restructuring actions that ended with job changes for the business managers, who were initially active supporters of the modeling effort. Once the modeling process had lost its support,

the company staff reverted to their old way of "getting their documentation done." In the second case, the company had a culture of agile ERP adoption. They had a few trained and dedicated modeling analysts, but they specialized in another modeling approach ("light-weight" and "more flexible and creative", relying on story-telling that is similar to business process analysis in the agile project). Also, the business managers who were experienced in using this approach perceived that the SAP modeling notation was not intuitive and too rigid in their culture. They felt no incentive to spend time on modeling (e.g. to report on changes in the SAP models, or to validate the models on a regular basis), as the hours spent on these tasks would be considered as overtime "on top of their other commitments." Because modeling was not linked to their job performance objectives, business managers perceived it as "a big company's thing" that did not warrant their time and attention. Moreover, the two architects also shared that on some occasions they received explicit instructions from their directors to consider shared process fragments and data objects within the shared ERP system as "a black box", and to focus exclusively on those pieces of text documentation that "add business value to the project stakeholders." According to one of these architects: "You might think you would need the models later on, but if your partners do not care about models, then creating models will be an impediment to quickly delivering the working solution."

What all the focus group members agreed on was that modeling the current coordination requirements has key implications in terms of handling requirements for follow-up ERP projects in three categories: (1) ERP upgrades, (2) system consolidation, and (3) maintenance projects. So, we decided to leave the practice mapped to Levels 2, 3, and 4 (as it was in the original proposal (Daneva, 2010) (Table 1), but flag this practice as a subject for follow-up studies. The fact that this practice divided the focus group members into three sub-groups and received controversial reactions from multiple perspectives made us think that it is worthwhile investigating two research questions: (1) why do these variations in perspective exist; and (2) why does variation exist, even among the ERP architects who shared a common position regarding the complexity level with which this practice should be associated.

Practice P12: The fourth practice below the 75% cut-off level was P12. Sixteen architects found P12 to be the most controversial activity in ERP project implementation. Six of the sixteen architects associated it with Level 4 ERP adopters, because, in their opinion, reference models are truly beneficial in extended enterprises among competitors. Ten architects argued that reference models do not capture shared data control flows and that this is a key roadblock to using them efficiently in organizations with a complexity level higher than 2. Their key concerns were that: (1) to efficiently use the reference models, representatives of all the partner companies must spend time and budget to learn the modeling notation embedded in the ERP-package-specific tools and become skilled at using them; this alone was deemed unrealistic, because in inter-organizational ERP projects there is no single authority to make decisions on investing resources in the common skills of the partner companies' employees; (2) rolling out extended, enterprise-wide modeling standards and managing the licenses for any special reference modeling tools is perceived as a project in itself, and very few extended enterprises would put it high on their priority list; and (3) external consulting resources are expensive, because the inter-organizational project would need someone with knowledge of the reference models, of the tool that helps adapt them, and of the business of the extended enterprise itself, and such expertise is always pricey. Reflecting on practice P12 left the focus group unconvinced at the end of the discussion on where to place it. So, we decided to set this question aside to be researched in the future.

LIMITATIONS OF THE STUDY

We considered the possible threats to the validity (Krueger & Casey, 2008; Morgan, 1997) of our results. The major limitation of our focus group setup is that it is centered on a single focus group, which restricts the extent to which generalizations can be drawn from its outcomes. This limitation is offset by the opportunity to gain a deeper understanding of the association between coordination RE practices and coordination complexity levels. As Morgan states (1997), generalizations are likely appropriate only for professionals in settings similar to that of our focus group members. In this respect, we consider the data as "incompletely collected" (Morgan, 1997), meaning that what has been collected is the experience of the architects.

Furthermore, we acknowledge that a plan for at least three focus groups, as the methodologists suggest (Krueger & Casey, 2008; Morgan, 1997), would have brought us much richer results. However, we could not complete it because of resource constraints. We consider this as our most important issue, and therefore it tops our agenda for consideration in future research. We plan to replicate the focus group in two other countries, namely the United States and The Netherlands, until we reach a saturation point, that is, the point at which we have collected the full range of ideas fed back to us and we are not receiving any new information (Krueger & Casey, 2008; Morgan, 1997). (Note that we did not consider tracking inter-rater agreements, because, according to Krueger and Casey (2008), it is not the goal of focus group members to come to a consensus.)

We also acknowledge the inherent weakness of focus group techniques, which is that they are driven by the researcher, meaning that there is always a residual threat to the accuracy of what focus group members say. However, we believe that this threat was significantly reduced in our study, because all the comments made online by the focus group members were transcribed in their entirety and every single e-mail exchange in the focus group was available for reference purposes.

Another validity concern in focus group studies is that the researcher influences the group interaction. However, a study by Morgan (1997) indicates that "in reality, there is no hard evidence that the focus group's moderator's impact on the data is any greater than the researcher's impact in participant observation or individual interviewing." We were also conscious that the focus group members can influence the data they produce, for example, by means of an imbalance in the level of participation of the focus group members. We made sure that the focus group was not dominated by a small number of very active participants, and that everyone had a chance to write. This was achieved by establishing policies on: (1) how to respond; and (2) what level of elaboration is expected in a response. For example, we established a one-message-at-a-time policy, according to which a focus group participant may write only one answer to a message in which there was no pointed question. We also established the policy that the researcher would approach individual focus group members any time she felt that participants did not provide detailed enough answers to pointed questions.

REFLECTION ON OUR EXPERIENCE

As per our plan, once the focus group process was over, we all reflected together on our focus group experiences for the purpose of distilling from them some lessons learned that could possibly be of benefit to other empirical RE and SE researchers undertaking focus group research. We approached the participants in order to collect their views on how they had felt throughout the focus group process. We also reflected on what worked well and why it worked well. In addition, we considered what did not work as we had expected, and why. In this reflection process, we constructed mind maps of our experiences and associated parts of these maps with what could be strengths or weaknesses of the focus group approach. While this reflection was more qualitative in nature, it allowed some lessons to crystallize, which we share below.

Strengths of the Focus Group Approach

Our experience revealed six important strengths of the online asynchronous focus group:

1. No pressure for spontaneous reactions and sufficient time for well-thought out responses. In our experience, the choice of allowing the focus group members to work asynchronously ensured that the participants could take their time to think and to organize their thoughts before responding. They deemed it important to have the opportunity to digest the views of their fellow focus group members and formulate a response without any pressure. In the view of our participants, this choice brought the following benefits:
   a. New viewpoints arose as a result of taking enough time to think over their responses. Five architects shared their opinion that if they had responded spontaneously, these viewpoints would have remained unspoken.
   b. There was consistently no divergence from the topics. So, the responses to our questions were much more distilled.
   c. More in-depth responses were elicited. Our participants (again) attributed this to the time they had to reflect when formulating their answers. They agreed that taking sufficient time to think thorough the information prepared them to share, and to provide the examples they considered appropriate to illustrate their points.
2. Absence of hierarchy among the participants. The researcher ensured everyone's

anonymity while running and reporting on the focus group. Because the participants were unaware of the identities of the others, they were prepared to challenge each other's views if they disagreed. This was how we obtained access to dissonant views (e.g. regarding practice P10). Also, the absence of visual cues that indicate dominance of opinions and positions in our face-to-face focus group seemed to enhance the participants' level of engagement. In the view of the authors, the idea of being part of a group whose solidarity on particular issues might be at stake simply did not apply.

3. Inclusiveness. We had participants across time zones, and we had to ensure equal access for all the participants in the discussion. Therefore, we allowed the focus group members the flexibility to drop in and out of conversations at their convenience, and to return to points of interest as further relevant comments were made. Once the questions at each stage had been aired, the transcribed conversations were made available for the duration of the discussion, so that everyone else could respond.

4. Revised role of the moderator. The first author of this paper, who served as the moderator, found that her role was not interventionist, and was actually less directive than she had expected, once the environment was set up and the rules and policies of the discussion had been established. Her experience was that carefully reading the participants' answers, as well as interjecting with probing and elucidating questions, replaced the steering role of the face-to-face moderator (which is discussed in the methodological literature on focus group research (Krueger & Casey, 2008; Morgan, 1997; Kontio et al., 2008; Orgad, 2005; Kivits, 2005). The focus group members said that they felt comfortable with the policies, and so they were willing to comply with them. They

thought that this way of running the focus group would save them time, and also help the researcher to get the information she needed as quickly as possible.

5. No logistical costs. An indisputable advantage of the online focus group is the absence of logistical and coordination costs (which would otherwise be borne by the researcher) and the absence of travel time for the participants. Organizing a face-to-face group meeting is potentially a burden for the researcher, in terms of booking a facility, finding a time that is convenient to everyone to hold a meeting, and handling any problems that might crop up (e.g. bad weather or traffic jams which could interfere with the timely start of the focus group). None of this is of any concern for an online asynchronous focus group.

6. Volume of information. An interesting, and unexpected, observation by the focus group participants was that they considered the volume of information. Fifteen of the participants indicated that they felt comfortable logging on between three and six times over the duration of the focus group (which was 10 business days), once they had made a commitment to join, and providing up to an hour's worth of comments each. We compared this to face-to-face groups, which last an average of 90 minutes (Krueger & Casey, 2008) and have 7-8 participants. We found that the average contribution of an online focus group member was much longer than that of a face-to-face group member (which would be 10 minutes, on average).

7. Combining the focus group with other qualitative research techniques. In our study, we identified a range of perspectives on some specific topics, e.g. those referring to practice P10, which motivated us to plan follow-up research using in-depth interviews to explore specific perspectives in more depth. This plan leverages the ability of the focus

group method to be used in combination with other qualitative techniques (in-depth interviews, in our case). We consider this ability to be important for SE researchers, as they may need to design research setups that build on focus group insights and are aimed at responding to research questions that lend themselves to other qualitative research techniques.

8. Learning is an important incentive for practitioners to participate. As indicated earlier, some investment of time on the part of focus group members is required for the focus group to happen. Although our participants had the feeling that they were donating their time for a good cause, namely, helping a researcher make ERP RE knowledge explicit, and, thus, adding value to the knowledge chain, we think it is important that the researcher offer some specific incentives for the focus group members to participate. We found that the greatest incentive for our participants was the sharing itself, i.e. sharing of ideas and experiences. The focus group members felt that they would not have shared the information in their emails, if they had not been part of a process that was initiated and moderated by a neutral party (the researcher). This sharing process allowed them to express themselves in a way in which daily professional life rarely affords them. They referred to this sharing experience, as "a learning experience," "knowing what's going on at other sites," and "understanding that we do not do things as badly as we thought."

Weaknesses in Using the Focus Group Approach

Based on our experience, we can glean three important challenges from running an asynchronous online focus group, which, if not addressed, could render the focus group research process inefficient.

1. Lengthy analysis of the transcripts. If the researcher who is acting as a moderator wants to, or needs to, share the transcribed data with other researchers who were not originally involved in the research process, this needs to be handled with special care, and time should be allocated for these researchers to learn about the focus group process and become familiar with the information in the transcripts. Even for a senior researcher, if he or she was not involved at the start of the focus group, it could turn out to be time-consuming to read and reread the data, in order to gain an adequate understanding of it and actively contribute to the data analysis process. The first researcher planned for two Master's students to complete two follow-up projects that would take the transcribed data as input and apply sophisticated coding (Morgan, 1997) techniques to them. However, this idea was abandoned, as the junior researchers, who were unfamiliar with qualitative analysis techniques, found it very difficult to read and make sense of the information in the long transcripts. To remedy the situation, an experienced senior researcher became involved, which made the research process costlier than originally planned. However, we think that planning early and estimating the need for sharing the knowledge produced through the focus group is key to having data analysis performed by multiple researchers.

2. The moderator and the participants need to have a common background. As the focus group members tell short stories about their everyday professional lives, they have a tendency to use their own idiomatic language, which is at times project-specific or ERP-specific. For example, the terms 'production environment' and 'development box' have specific, unambiguous meanings among SAP consultants. However, a researcher in RE or in SE who has never worked as an

SAP consultant may not be able to make sense of these terms while reading the conversations. On the one hand, the researcher cannot follow up with each individual focus group member on the semantics of terms that, from the practitioners' perspective, have well-established meanings. Doing this would mean a number of clarification interactions, each one taking time. On the other hand, the researcher cannot proceed with a focus group in which he/she is behind in his/her understanding of the conversations going on. In this focus group, the moderator shared professional ground with the focus group members (as she had spent 9 years in ERP implementation project roles). However, we think it is important for the researcher to plan time to become familiar with the professional vocabulary of the practitioners and acquire basic skills in understanding the stories that will be part of their conversations.

3. Dependence on experts' availability in balancing the research design choices. There are no precise rules for a researcher to follow to determine the level of homogeneity among the participants of a focus group. It is "a judgment call" (Krueger & Casey, 2008) on the part of the researcher, based on his/her knowledge of the context and the types of participants. The focus group approach assumes that the researcher: (1) is aware of the need to strike a balance between homogeneity and variation among the participants; and (2) knows how to achieve this balance. The balance is important for two reasons: first, because it ensures that the discussion can yield contrasting positions that represent interesting insights for the researcher; and second, establishing balance means setting, up-front, the degree to which thoughts will be shared in the group discussion. It is our belief that researchers unfamiliar with the focus group method are dependent on the availability of a more senior researcher, who should consult with them on the soundness of the research design choices they make and the implications of those choices for the achievement of balance.

CONCLUSION

This paper presents the application an asynchronous online focus group-based approach to evaluating 13 practices for engineering the coordination requirements for inter-organizational ERP systems. We explored two questions regarding these practices: (1) whether or not what we think is a good inter-organizational ERP RE practice is observed by ERP architects in their project realities; and (2) if architects do observe a practice, then at what complexity level would they place it. It was our intention to describe the extent of supporting evidence for the conclusions that we drew.

Regarding the first question, our findings suggest that 12 of the 13 practices were indeed experienced by our focus group members. The practice that the focus group members could not identify as one that happens in their project realities was deemed "too project-specific." It is a practice that addressed inter-organizational coordination in an intermediation business, and no practitioner in our focus group had had exposure to ERP projects in this business setting.

Regarding the second question, we found that, overall, the focus group members associated the practices with the levels of coordination complexity in a way that converged with ours. With respect to four practices, we found a variation between the practitioners' experience and reasoning and what we expected. We looked into why, according to the practitioners, these variations existed. Analyzing this helped us identify implications of our findings for future research. In particular, the results of our study motivated the following questions for the future:

1. What combinations of practices for engineering coordination requirements are characteristic to inter-firm partnerships that are competitive collaborations by nature (meaning ERP-adopting organizations of Level 4 coordination complexity)? What combinations of practices work best for this specific setting?

2. What are the underlying mechanisms in the inter-organizational ERP project context that are responsible for the variations in the roles that inter-organizational process modeling could play at the RE stage of the project? In which cases is this practice a good RE practice, and in which cases would it hamper the project?

3. In which inter-organizational contextual settings would reference models be a roadblock rather than an asset? How can stakeholders in an inter-firm partnership handle the trade-off between potential value and the costs of deploying reference models in RE for inter-organizational ERP?

We note that, while the use of counts in our study served an important purpose, our focus group was not about counting. We used the simplest counting scheme possible (Krishnan & Kellner, 2005), considering the number of times a practice was observable. This does not render our focus group a quantitative study. It remains qualitative one, and the methodology does not provide for our counts in Table 4 being considered as anything more than the relative results of the particular makeup of our focus group.

We have reflected on our experience of the asynchronous online focus group study. We have discussed the limitations of our research approach, and identified eight strengths and three challenges in using this research method in SE/RE research.

Last, but not least, in this paper we included detailed justifications for the more important re-search design choices we made. We did this not only because being explicit about our decisions in setting up our research process helps readers to understand the results, but also because we wanted to act on the calls (Sjøberg et al., 2007, Cheng & Atlee, 2007) of the empirical SE and RE communities for more empirical research in SE and RE. As Morgan (1997) indicates, explicit documentation on the motivation for our decisions – why we do what we do in one specific way and not in another – is a prerequisite for the growth of empirical research in a specific area (in our case, it is RE).

ACKNOWLEDGMENT

This research was financially supported by The Netherlands' Organization for Scientific Research (NWO) under the Jacquard project "QuadREAD" and the Joint Project "Evaluation and Selection of Complex Software Systems" between the Institute of Mathematics and Informatics BAS and the Faculty of Management, Tel Aviv University.

REFERENCES

Abbas, N., Gravell, A., & Wills, G. (2010). Using factor analysis to generate clusters of agile practices. In *Proceedings of the IEEE AGILE Conference* (pp. 11-20). Washington, DC: IEEE Computer Society.

Ahituv, N., Neumann, S., & Zviran, M. (2002). A system development methodology for ERP systems. *Journal of Computer Information, 42*(3), 56–67.

April, A., & Abran, A. (2008). *Software maintenance management: Evaluation and continuous improvement.* Hoboken, NJ: John Wiley & Sons.

Babiak, K. M. (2009). Criteria of effectiveness in multiple cross-sectoral inter-organizational relationships. *Evaluation and Program Planning*, *32*(1), 1–12. doi:10.1016/j.evalprogplan.2008.09.004.

Basili, V. R. (1995). The experience factory and its relationship to other quality approaches. *Advances in Computers*, *41*, 65–82. doi:10.1016/S0065-2458(08)60231-4.

Basili, V. R., Caldiera, G., McGarry, F. E., Rajerski, R., Page, G. T., & Waligora, S. (1992). The software engineering laboratory: An operational software experience factory. In *Proceedings of the International Conference on Software Engineering* (pp. 370-381). New York, NY: ACM Press.

Beecham, S., Hall, T., Britton, C., Cottee, M., & Rainer, A. (2005). Using an expert panel to validate a requirements process improvement model. *Journal of Systems and Software*, *3*, 251–275. doi:10.1016/j.jss.2004.06.004.

Boehm, B., Rombach, H. D., & Zelkovitz, M. (2005). *Foundations of empirical software engineering: The legacy of Victor R. Basili*. Berlin, Germany: Springer-Verlag. doi:10.1007/3-540-27662-9.

Brown, B. B. (1968). *Delphi process: A methodology used for the elicitation of opinions of experts*. Santa Monica, CA: RAND Corporation.

Brown, W., McCormick, H. W., & Thomas, S. W. (2000). *Antipatterns in project management*. Hoboken, NJ: John Wiley & Sons.

Champy, J. (2002). *X-engineering the corporation: The next frontier of business performance*. New York, NY: Warner Books.

Cheng, B. H. C., & Atlee, J. M. (2007). Research directions in requirements engineering. In *Proceedings of the International Conference on Software Engineering and the Workshop on the Future of Software Engineering* (pp. 285-303). Washington, DC: IEEE Computer Society.

Chilarege, R. (1999). *Software testing best practices (Tech. Rep. No. RC 21457 Log 96856 4/26/99)*. Armonk, NY: IBM Research.

Daneva, M. (2010). Engineering the coordination requirements in cross-organizational ERP projects. In Parthasarathy, S. (Ed.), *Enterprise information systems and implementing IT infrastructures: Challenges and issues* (pp. 1–19). Hershey, PA: IGI Global. doi:10.4018/978-1-61520-625-4.ch001.

Daneva, M., & Wieringa, R. J. (2006a). A requirements engineering framework for inter-organizational ERP systems. *Requirement Engineering Journal*, *11*(3), 194–204. doi:10.1007/s00766-006-0034-9.

Daneva, M., & Wieringa, R. J. (2006b). Engineering the coordination requirements in inter-organizational ERP projects: A package of good practices. In *Proceedings of the IEEE International Conference on Requirements Engineering* (pp. 311-314). Washington, DC: IEEE Computer Society.

Daneva, M., & Wieringa, R. J. (2010). Requirements engineering for enterprise systems: What we know and what we do not know? In Nurcan, S., Salinesi, C., Souveyet, C., & Ralyté, J. (Eds.), *Intentional perspectives on information systems engineering* (pp. 115–136). Berlin, Germany: Springer-Verlag. doi:10.1007/978-3-642-12544-7_7.

El Emam, K., & Jung, H. (2001). An empirical evaluation of the ISO/IEC 15504 assessment model. *Journal of Systems and Software*, *59*(1), 23–43. doi:10.1016/S0164-1212(01)00046-2.

Eriksson, P., & Kovalainen, A. (2008). *Qualitative methods in business research*. Thousand Oaks, CA: Sage.

Field, A. (2005). *Discovering statistics using SPSS*. Thousand Oaks, CA: Sage.

Fragidis, G., & Tarabanis, K. (2006). From repositories of best practices to networks of best practices. In *Proceedings of the International Conference on Management of Innovation and Technology* (pp. 370-374). Washington, DC: IEEE Computer Society.

Fraser, F., Ambler, S. W., Bornstein, G., Dubinsky, Y., & Succi, G. (2007). Learning more about "software best practices." In *Proceedings of the 8ᵗʰ International Conference on Agile Processes in Software Engineering and Extreme Programming (XP)* (pp. 271-274).

Gaiser, T. (1997). Conducting online focus groups: A methodological discussion. *Social Science Computer Review*, *15*(2), 135–144. doi:10.1177/089443939701500202.

Holland, C. P., Shaw, D. R., & Kawalek, P. (2005). BP's multi-enterprise asset management system. *Information and Software Technology*, *47*(15), 999–1007. doi:10.1016/j.infsof.2005.09.006.

Jeffery, M., & Lelifeld, I. (2004). Best practices in IT portfolio management. *MIT Sloan Management Review*, 41-49.

Jones, C. (2000). *Software assessments, benchmarks, and best practices*. Reading, MA: Addison-Wesley.

Jones, C. (2007). *Estimating software costs: Bringing realism to estimating*. New York, NY: McGraw Hill.

Jones, C. (2009). *Software engineering best practices: Lessons from successful projects in the top companies*. New York, NY: McGraw Hill.

Kaner, C., Back, J., & Prettichord, B. (2001). *Lessons learned in software testing*. Hoboken, NJ: John Wiley & Sons.

King, N., & Horrock, C. (2010). *Interviews in qualitative research*. Thousand Oaks, CA: Sage.

Kivits, J. (2005). Online interviewing and the research relationship. In Hine, C. (Ed.), *Virtual methods: Issues in social research on the Internet* (pp. 35–49). Oxford, UK: Berg Publishers.

Kontio, J., Bragge, J., & Lehtola, L. (2008). The focus group research method as an empirical tool in software engineering. In Schull, F., Singer, J., & Sjøberg, D. I. K. (Eds.), *Guide to advanced empirical software engineering* (pp. 93–116). Berlin, Germany: Springer-Verlag. doi:10.1007/978-1-84800-044-5_4.

Kontio, J., Lehtola, L., & Bragge, J. (2004) Using the focus group method in software engineering: obtaining practitioner and user experiences. In *Proceedings of the International Symposium on Empirical Software Engineering* (pp. 271-280). Washington, DC: IEEE Computer Society.

Krishnan, M. S., & Kellner, M. I. (2005). Measuring process consistency: Implications for reducing software defects. *IEEE Transactions on Software Engineering*, *25*(6), 800–815. doi:10.1109/32.824401.

Krueger, R. A., & Casey, M. A. (2008). *Focus groups: A practical guide for applied research*. Thousand Oaks, CA: Sage.

Le Gloahec, V., Fleurquin, R., & Sadou, S. (2008). Good practices as a quality-oriented modelling assistant. In *Proceedings of the International Conference on Quality Software* (pp. 345-348). Washington, DC: IEEE Computer Society.

Lehtola, L., Kauppinen, M., & Kujala, S. (2004). Requirements prioritization challenges in practice. In F. Bomarius & H. Iida (Eds.), *Proceedings of the International Conference on Product Focused Software Process Improvement* (LNCS 3009, pp. 497-508).

Mansar, S. L., & Reijers, H. A. (2005). Best practices in business process redesign: Validation of a redesign framework. *Computers in Industry, 56*(5), 457–471. doi:10.1016/j.compind.2005.01.001.

Marcotte, F., Grabot, B., & Affonso, R. (2008). Cooperation models for supply chain management. *International Journal of Logistics Systems and Management, 5*(1-2), 123–153.

Massey, O. T. (2010). A proposed model for the analysis and interpretation of focus groups in evaluation research. *Evaluation and Program Planning, 34*(1), 21–28. doi:10.1016/j.evalprogplan.2010.06.003.

Merton, R. (2005). The focused interview and focus groups. *Public Opinion Quarterly, 51*(4), 550–566. doi:10.1086/269057.

Morgan, D. L. (1997). *Focus group as qualitative research method* (2nd ed., *Vol. 16*). Thousand Oaks, CA: Sage.

Nicolaou, A. I. (2008). Research issues on the use of ERP in inter-organizational relationships. *International Journal of Accounting Information Systems, 9*(4), 216–226. doi:10.1016/j.accinf.2008.09.003.

Orgad, S. (2005). From online to offline and back: Moving from online to offline relationships with research informants. In Hine, C. (Ed.), *Virtual methods: Issues in social research on the Internet* (pp. 51–65). Oxford, UK: Berg Publishers.

Prakash, N. (2010). Intentional alignment and interoperability in inter-organization information systems. In Nurcan, S., Salinesi, C., Souveyet, C., & Ralyté, J. (Eds.), *Intentional perspectives on information systems engineering* (pp. 101–113). Berlin, Germany: Springer-Verlag. doi:10.1007/978-3-642-12544-7_6.

Ramasubbu, N., Kompalli, P., & Krishnan, M. S. (2005). Leveraging global resources: A process maturity model for managing distributed development. *IEEE Software, 22*(3), 80–86. doi:10.1109/MS.2005.69.

Roser, S., Bernhard Bauer, B., & Müller, J. (2006). Model- and architecture-driven development in the context of cross-enterprise business process engineering. In *Proceedings of the International Conference on Services Computing* (pp. 119-126). Washington, DC: IEEE Computer Society.

Schneider, K., von Hunnius, J.-P., & Basili, V. R. (2002). Experience in implementing a learning software organization. *IEEE Software, 19*(3), 46–49. doi:10.1109/MS.2002.1003453.

Schoemaker, M. L. (2007). *Requirements patterns and antipatterns: Best (and worst) practices for defining your requirements*. Reading, MA: Addison-Wesley.

Sgourev, S. V., & Zuckerman E. W. (2006). Improving capabilities through industry peer networks. *MIT Sloan Management Review*, 33-38.

Simsek, Z., & Veiga, J. F. (2000). The electronic survey technique: An integration and assessment. *Organizational Research Methods, 3*(1), 93–115. doi:10.1177/109442810031004.

Sjøberg, D. I. K., Dybå, T., & Jørgensen, M. (2007). The future of empirical methods in software engineering research. In *Proceedings of the International Conference on Software Engineering and the Workshop on the Future of Software Engineering* (pp. 358-378). Washington, DC: IEEE Computer Society.

So, C., & Scholl, W. (2009). Perceptive agile measurement: New instruments for quantitative studies in pursuit of the social-psychological effect of agile practices. In *Proceedings of the International Conference on Agile Processes in Software Engineering and Extreme Programming* (pp. 83-93).

Sommerville, I., & Sawyer, P. (1997). *Requirements engineering: A good practice guide.* Hoboken, NJ: John Wiley & Sons.

von Wangenheim, C. G., Hauck, J. C. R., Zoucas, A., Salviano, C. F., McCaffery, F., & Shull, F. (2010). Creating software process capability/maturity models. *IEEE Software, 27*(4), 92–94. doi:10.1109/MS.2010.96.

This work was previously published in the International Journal of Information System Modeling and Design (IJISMD), Volume 2, Issue 3, edited by Remigijus Gustas, pp. 49-74, copyright 2011 by IGI Publishing (an imprint of IGI Global).

Chapter 13

The Impact of Regulatory Compliance on Agile Software Processes with a Focus on the FDA Guidelines for Medical Device Software

Hossein Mehrfard
Concordia University, Canada

Abdelwahab Hamou-Lhadj
Concordia University, Canada

ABSTRACT

The difficulty of complying with different regulations has become more evident as a large number of regulated businesses are mandated to follow an ever-increasing set of regulations. These regulations often drive significant changes in the way organizations operate to deliver value to their customers. This paper focuses on the impact of the Food and Drug Administration (FDA) regulations on agile software development processes, which in many ways can be considered as just another type of organizational processes. Particular focus is placed on the ability for Extreme Programming (XP) to support FDA requirements. Findings show that XP fails to meet many of the FDA guidelines for medical device software, which increases the risks of non-compliance for organizations that have adopted XP as their main software process. The results of this study can lead the work towards designing an extension to XP for FDA regulations.

DOI: 10.4018/978-1-4666-4161-7.ch013

INTRODUCTION

Recently, there has been a significant increase in attention to regulatory compliance and its impact on the way organizations are managed and controlled. This increase is driven by several factors including the recent corporate scandals such as the ones that involved some of the major U.S. organizations (e.g., Enron, WorldCom), the new challenges that Information Technology (IT) pose on protecting and securing sensitive information, and a higher need for business continuity in an ever-changing business world.

As a result, more regulations, laws, standards, and guidelines are introduced every year driving significant changes in the way companies are managed (Hamou-Lhadj & Hamou-Lhadj, 2007). These changes vary in scope and impact ranging from the introduction of new business processes to changes at the governance and strategic level. Hamou-Lhadj et al. characterize these changes in the form of a compliance support framework that can help effective handling of regulatory compliance requirements (Hamou-Lhadj & Hamou-Lhadj, 2007). The framework is composed of four main components: Governance, People, Process, and Technology. The aim of the governance component is to provide the strategic direction that will guide an effective delivery of end-to-end compliance support activities, while ensuring that these activities are aligned with the company's vision and business objectives. The people component revolves around the proper selection, training, and retention of human potential that will operate the compliance support framework. The process component (the topic of this paper) is concerned with the need to adapt existing business processes (or creating new ones) for the handling of compliance requirements at the operational level. Finally, the technology component emphasizes the need for the proper tools and techniques in order to automate the delivery of compliance support activities.

In this paper, we particularly focus on the impact of regulatory compliance on the process by which software systems, used by regulated companies, are developed, maintained, and tested. Software processes can be seen as just another type of organizational processes since they are used by software companies to carry on the development of software products. As such, the paper has the broader objective of looking into the issue of how regulatory compliance impacts organizational processes used by software companies during product development.

More specifically, we target software systems used to control medical devices. These systems are subject to heavy regulations from government organizations to ensure that their design is carried out based on sound software engineering practices. One of the most predominant set of regulations in North-America that regulate the way software systems used to control medical devices should be developed is the Food and Drug Administration (FDA) regulations.

The FDA is a U.S. government agency that protects consumers by enforcing the U.S. Federal Food, Drug, and Cosmetic Act (FDA, 2009b). It regulates more than $1 trillion worth of consumer goods, about 25% of consumer expenditures in the U.S. (FDA, 2009b). The cost of not complying with FDA regulations can be considerably high, which makes its regulations some of the most important ones that should be on the priority list of a strategic compliance management initiative of any organization subject to the FDA laws.

The FDA also regulates the design and use of medical devices. There are several guidelines that have been issued by the FDA (2002) on how to monitor the manufacturing of safe and reliable medical devices. This also includes the software systems that control these medical devices. Due to complexity and criticality of medical devices, the FDA sets high demands on how to develop software for medical devices. Most of the FDA requirements are directly related to the process activities (e.g., requirement analysis, design, implementation, etc.) used by an organization to develop software. In addition, the FDA expects sufficient level of auditability within the software process itself. In other words, certain aspects of the development life cycle need to be tracked to allow external auditors to assess whether the system is FDA-compliant or not.

However, the requirements imposed by the FDA on the development process are very stringent, and may not be easily attainable. These requirements have been developed to overcome the difficulty of assessing the safety and reliability of software through traditional testing techniques. Additional verification and validation techniques as part of a broader and systematic process have to be applied. As such, The FDA requirements often translate into documenting and following specific guidelines to certify that the system is built, verified, and validated in a systematic manner and according to proven software engineering practices (FDA, 2002).

Therefore, from a risk management perspective, it is important for an organization to understand whether a particular software process meets the FDA requirements or not. Areas where the process fails to meet FDA should also be clearly indicated. In this paper, we chose to study the capability of the Extreme Programming (XP) software process, an agile process, to support these requirements. We choose to focus on XP due to the fact that it embeds most values of the agile movement. As such, we believe that the results presented in this paper can be easily generalized to other agile processes.

This paper is a continuation of previous work in which we discussed how XP can be extended to support one aspect of the FDA requirements which pertains to user studies and understanding user characteristics (Mehrfard et al., 2010). In this paper, we cover all aspects of the FDA requirements ranging from requirement analysis to testing, passing by design and implementation.

More precisely, the main contributions of this paper are as follows:

- We present in detail all the FDA requirements for medical device software. These requirements cover a large spectrum of process activities including requirement analysis, design, implementation, and testing. We believe that this contribution can be used as a reference work for many organizations who struggle to meet FDA requirements due to their ambiguity.

- We study the capability of XP to meet FDA requirements for device medical software. We uncover areas of XP that do not meet FDA requirements. We do this by mapping XP practices and work products to FDA guidelines for each software process activity. Ways to extend XP to meet the FDA requirements can be derived from the mapping table.

FDA GUIDELINES FOR MEDICAL DEVICE SOFTWARE

In this section, we start by presenting our generic approach for mapping a software process to FDA regulations for medical device software. Then, we show the application of this approach for extracting the software process requirements for medical devices from the regulations and guidelines provided by the FDA. We map each of these requirements to XP practices. By doing this, we uncover places where XP lacks support for FDA guidelines.

Mapping Approach

Our approach for mapping a software methodology to FDA guidelines and requirements is shown in Figure 1, and encompasses the following steps:

1. We select among FDA guidelines, the ones that relate to software development.

Figure 1. The framework for mapping a development process to FDA requirements for medical device software

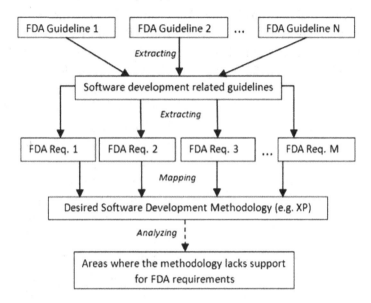

2. We study these requirements from the software engineering process perspective and present typical software practices and documentation that can help developers follow the guidelines.

3. According to the suggested practices and documentation, we investigate the capabilities of our desired software development methodology, i.e., XP, for supporting these requirements.

Step 2 is particularly important since many FDA guidelines and requirements for software development are defined in a way that is too generic to be applied to a development process, which often causes ambiguities for software developers since no specific development methodology can abide by the provided guidelines. For example, the FDA requests the medical device software developers to build safe and reliable software while no specific methods on how safety and reliability should be carried out are explicitly provided by the FDA.

Furthermore, the FDA often uses terms that are not too specific and may have different meanings

depending on the context. That is, a single term can be used in more than one field while having many completely different meanings. For instance, "risk analysis" can refer to an activity in both software requirements engineering and project management. This also can cause confusion in the intended meaning of a term making it difficult for development companies to comply with these guidelines as the developers do not know what they specifically have to follow.

One of objectives of this paper is, therefore, to clarify FDA guidelines and relate them common software process engineering concepts. Once this is done, we map each FDA requirement to XP to assess whether it supports it or not.

The FDA guidelines and requirements are grouped into four categories depending on the process activity to which the guidelines apply:

• Requirement analysis
• Design
• Coding and construction
• Testing

Requirements Analysis

The FDA has issues several guidelines on how the requirement gathering and analysis phase should be carried out (FDA, 2002). These guidelines can be further described based on the following sub-phases:

- Requirements Elicitation
- Requirements Evaluation
- Requirements Traceability Analysis
- System and Acceptance Test Plan

Requirements Elicitation

FDA guidelines require a complete documentation that clarifies the software inputs, a software requirements specification (SRS) document, and the expected software outputs. For instance, developers are required to illustrate all ranges, limits and default values which are acceptable as software inputs, a detailed description of the functions of the system (part of the SRS), and the expected results of applying these inputs to the system, i.e., software outputs (FDA, 2002). Documenting software inputs and outputs helps understand the boundary of the system which is necessary for requirements elicitation (Paetsch et al., 2003).

It also important to clearly define the non-functional requirements (NFR) such as performance, reliability, security and the safety features of software. A particular emphasis is put on safety requirements since an unsafe medical device may cause loss of human lives (FDA, 1997, 2002).

In addition, the FDA requires that all communication points between the software in question and other software systems, hardware, and persons be well defined. These communication points are known as interfaces. For instance, the communication point between the software and users is the user interface (FDA, 2002, 2009).

Another key requirement mandated by the FDA is to identify requirements that are related to human factors such as how the system will be used by end users. This requires studying the characteristics of the various users of the system using Human Factors Engineering (HFE) concepts. In particular, the FDA guidelines suggest many activities including observations, interviews, and conducting focus groups to understand HFE requirements (Sawyer, 1996). To this end, the SRS should describe all the user characteristics based on user's knowledge, ability, expectation, and limitation.

XP provides a number of techniques to elicit requirements. Story cards, for example, are used to capture the software features expected by end users. User stories are written by customers with the help of an XP programmer (who plays the role of an interaction designer). User story is comparable to use cases since both aim to capture the user's needs.

The high involvement of customers in XP is another effective factor for eliciting requirements. After writing user stories, the customer is involved during the "iterations to release" phase and helps break down the user story into multiple tasks. In addition, brainstorming is another elicitation technique that is encouraged in XP with the help of customers and domain experts (Paetsch et al., 2003). This customer involvement also results in better definition of HFE requirements.

However, there is no specific activity in XP that deals with documenting the different interfaces of the system as required by the FDA. As for the functional requirements, they are described in XP by developers during the "iterations to release" phase based on user stories. The non-functional requirements, on the other hand, are dealt with in XP the same way as the functional requirements, i.e., during the "iteration to release" phase. There is a common belief that XP tends to neglect the representation of non-functional requirements during the requirement gathering phase. This is due to the fact that XP tends to focus more on the functionality requested by the customers and less on non-functional requirements. Most of these requirements are only dealt with during the implementation phase. The level of documentation of the requirements in XP is less than what is expected by the FDA. XP, for example, does not require the presence of an SRS. The XP as an agile process tends to maximize team communication in detriment of documentation. The user story is the only document during the requirement elicitation stage used as the requirements document.

Requirements Evaluation

The FDA seeks from organizations to establish ways to evaluate and document requirements through written policies and procedures to resolve any incomplete, ambiguous, inconsistent and conflicting requirements. In addition, the requirements should be evaluated against possible risks. The FDA considers the possibility of applying requirements evaluation in multiple steps (i.e., incrementally) to arrive to clear functional and non-functional requirements (FDA, 2002).

Requirement risk analysis focuses on potential risks that may cause the project to fail. The FDA puts a particular emphasis on risks due to misunderstanding of HFE requirements. Risk management is planned and conducted before entering the requirement phase, i.e., at the project level (FDA, 2002). The FDA also recommends a formal review of the requirements before starting extensive software design (FDA, 2002).

From the software engineering perspective, the term requirements evaluation from the FDA perspective carries many similarities with the concepts of requirement analysis and validation found in software requirements engineering. There exist many techniques to evaluate requirements including formal review meetings, risk analysis, requirements inconsistency management, requirements prioritization, evaluation of alternative options in requirements, requirement verification, and prototyping (Paetsch et al., 2003; Sommerville, 2004).

Due to the incremental nature of XP, requirements are evaluated within different iterations and releases. In fact, the product resulting from an XP iteration or release is seen in XP as a prototype that can be evaluated by customers (Abrahamsson et al., 2002). Requirement prioritization, which includes risk analysis, is a constant practice in XP during the planning phase and the "iteration to release" phase. During the planning phase, the customer selects the story cards for the next release based on its business values which is documented in the release plan. He is also responsible for choosing the story cards for each iteration during the "iteration to release" phase and document these stories in an iteration plan. This practice is done with the help of developers during these phases (Larman, 2003).

A general rule for agile processes is that they deal with the most probable risks to the project during the first release and primary iteration of each release (Larman, 2003). However, there is no specific method in XP for analyzing the risks in requirements. Moreover, XP does not support formal review meetings to evaluate requirements.

The FDA guidelines also suggest the presence of a documented mechanism for evaluating requirements. However, XP does not support the presence of any documentation for requirements evaluation.

Requirements Traceability Analysis

Traceability analysis is an essential activity during the entire development process and is required by the FDA regulations. Traceability analysis defines the relationship between the software development artefacts to keep the logical order of these artefacts. This logical order becomes more evident when we are transiting from one development phase to another one (FDA, 2002, 2009).

The FDA puts an emphasis on traceability analysis during the requirement analysis phase by requiring from regulated organizations to establish, in a documented way, the following relationships:

- Software requirements and system requirements (and vice versa).
- Software requirements and the risk analysis results.

In addition, the relationship of the requirements with recognized risks coming from the risk analysis results must also be determined. In software requirement engineering, requirement traceability analysis is considered as part of the requirement management activities. Requirement management is usually supported by CASE tools during software development. To achieve this, different traceability matrices are suggested such as source traceability, requirement traceability, design traceability and other traceability matrices based on the expected level of quality (Sommerville, 2004).

XP is completely blind with respect to traceability analysis. There is not practice or process artefact that account for having traceability matrices in any of the development phases.

System and Acceptance Test Plan

At this stage, the FDA requires to develop the system and acceptance test plans. According to ANSI/IEEE standard 829, a test plan is defined as "the documentation of scope, approaches, resources, and schedule of intended testing activities. This document should identify test items, the features to be tested, the testing tasks, responsibilities, and any risks requiring contingency planning" (FDA, 2002, 2009a).

An acceptance test plan is documented based on a set of acceptance criteria provided by the customer to approve the final product. It is usually created through a close collaboration between customers and developers (FDA, 2002; Pressman, 2003). A system test plan is written with respect to criteria for testing the software product on a specific operating platform to detect performance issues, and situations of stress (FDA, 2002; Pressman, 2003).

In XP, customers are asked to explain the acceptance criteria of the system before each release (Larman, 2003). These criteria are used to generate acceptance tests which are later executed either by the customer or the developer. In XP, the acceptance test plan is known as the customer test document (Larman, 2003). System testing is supported in XP at the end of each release. The XP programmer (who plays the role of an architect) is responsible for performing system testing (Beck & Andres, 2004). A System test plan is written by an architect and put in practice with the help of an XP tester.

Design Phase

The FDA defines the design phase as the process of translating the user requirements into their related logical components to be implemented. Due to the complexity of medical devices, it suggests to have both a high-level and detailed design. The design activity and associated FDA requirements can be further divided into the following sub-phases (FDA, 2002):

- Design for Usability
- Software Design Evaluation
- Design Traceability Analysis
- Updating the Test Plans
- Test Design Generation

Design for Usability

The FDA guidelines highlight the importance of usability analysis during the design process to improve human performance in using medical equipments based on their abilities (Sawyer, 1996). It recognizes that the design for safety of medical devices should take into account human factors. The reason is that according to the FDA Center for Devices and Radiological Health (CDRH), the lack of attention to human factors during product development may lead to errors that can potentially cause serious patient injuries or even death (Sawyer, 1996). A number of guidelines have been proposed on how to deal with HFE during the design of software including following Human Computer Interface (HCI) guidelines, improving software usability, and performing software design coordinated with hardware design. To improve software usability, the FDA suggests a number of usability tests such as scenario-based testing, and testing the product by users per iteration of software development (Sawyer, 1996).

In XP, the user interface design (UI) is done during the "iterations to release" phase, but XP does not suggest any guideline for UI design. In addition there is no specific practice in XP that supports usability inspection or any other form of usability testing. However, due to the fact that XP tends to be a user-centered process by working with users throughout the process to obtain constant feedback and that it favours communication with customers, one can assume that XP considers the usable aspect of the final product although at a limited extent (Kowalczykiewicz & Weiss, 2002).

During the exploration phase, there is no specific practice in XP that mandates the use of usability design patterns or evaluate usability at the design or architectural level. To design the software system architecture, XP suggests building a system prototype during the exploration phase to evaluate different architectures. The final architecture is consolidated during the first release (Abrahamsson et al., 2002; Beck & Andres, 2004). There are two practices in XP that affect the design of the system architecture: System metaphors and simple design. System metaphors are shared stories that describe how the system works and the simple design principle aims to make easier to understand each design component (Nord et al., 2004). Despite the existence of the XP interaction designer, there is no explicit guideline in XP with respect to following specific architectural patterns and assessing the usability of the system at the architectural level.

Software Design Evaluation

The software design evaluation is considered as an integral part of the design process. The objective is to validate correctness, completeness, consistency, and maintainability of the design (FDA, 2002). The FDA guidelines define two categories of design evaluation activities: Design review, and design verification and validation (FDA, 1997). During the evaluation of the design, activities such as analysis of control flow, data flow, complexity, timing, memory allocation, and criticality analysis should be supported (FDA, 2002). Moreover, the FDA puts an emphasis on analysing component interfaces during the design evaluation to ensure that all the defined interfaces in the requirement phase suit well the proposed design.

Design review meetings are required by the FDA to support the fact that a design inspection has taken place. The focus of these meetings is to identify different concerns of software design and their potential side-effects, possible solutions, and the corresponding corrective actions in software design. During these meetings, designers present their design to the design reviewers. There are three types of design review: preliminary design review, critical design review, and system design review. The process is conducted in an iterative manner until potential problems are explored and solutions have been proposed (FDA, 1997, 2002, 2009).

The FDA defines design verification as a confirmation by examination that a specific requirement has been fulfilled. This requires documenting the design verification process. The FDA suggests using some verification techniques such as fault tree analysis, and worst case analysis. In design control document, the FDA references the ISO 9001:1994 standard, where activities such as prototype evaluation, demonstration, simulation and comparing the design with other similar proven designs are considered as software design verification activities (FDA, 1997).

Design validation is the examination that a design responds to user needs or the intended use of the product. The FDA requires documenting the design validation process. Design validation should be executed under actual or simulated use condition. It also needs to follow a successful verification to ensure that each user requirements is fulfilled. For this purpose, the FDA requires to provide a validation plan, validation methods and validation review. Some of the design validation techniques recommended by the FDA include analysis and inspection methods, compilation of relevant scientific literature, and provision of historical evidence that similar designs are clinically safe (FDA, 1997).

The design in XP is kept as simple as possible and is informally documented. XP does not account for activities that deal with analysis of communication links among the system interfaces, control flow, and data flow as required by FDA. Also, the design review in XP is significantly different from the FDA design review, because there is no formal design document in XP to review. Instead of having formal meetings, design review is limited to pair programming. It is recognized that an iterative cycle of pair programming provides continuous analysis and review of the design to improve and simplify it (Abrahamsson et al., 2002). The development teams using pair programming have reported good quality of design with fewer lines of code as they worked together on both the design and the implementation (Cockburn & Williams, 2001). However, XP does not support any specific practices which are required by the FDA for design verification and validation.

Design Traceability Analysis

As mentioned in the requirement phase, the FDA requires traceability analysis throughout the entire development process. In the design phase, tractability analysis is conducted to verify that the entire design components are traceable to the software requirements and that all requirements can be mapped to a software design (FDA, 2002). For this reason, there should be a design traceability matrix which relates software requirements documents to design specification.

There is overlap between design traceability analysis and design verification. Both of them put an emphasis on conformance of design with the requirements while traceability aims only to show the relations between the requirements and the design. XP does not support any traceability matrix during the design to show this relation.

Updating the Test Plans

The FDA requires updating existing test plans by generating module and integration test plans during the design phase. A module test plan should be created to test specific units of the system. On the other hand, the integration test plan should be updated to test the flow of control and data between program units (FDA, 2002).

In addition, the acceptance and system test plans, which are created during the requirements phase, should also be updated considering HFE criteria defined during the software requirements and design phases.

Both unit testing and integration testing are performed within iteration in XP. But there is no mention in XP about having a specific test plan. The nature of testing in XP is explained in the testing section.

Test Design Generation

After preparing the test plan, the FDA requires from the development team to start generating test procedures and test cases for unit, integration, system and acceptance test based on the results of requirement and design phases. These tests should be completed and finally executed during the coding and test phases (FDA, 2002).

In XP, unit tests cases are generated after the design within an iteration. In addition, acceptance tests which are already generated by customers before the iteration starts are automated by an XP tester to be executed after an iteration is completed. Furthermore, integration tests executed by an XP programmer (who assumes the role of an integrator) at the end of an iteration before acceptance testing so as to integrate the pieces of the code developed during the iteration (Abrahamsson et al., 2002; Larman, 2003).

System test is done per release and supported by an XP programmer (architect). As XP architect is the person who is charge of designing the system structure. He is responsible for developing system test cases during multiple iterations (Beck & Andres, 2004). These activities show that XP supports developing test cases before coding as requested by the FDA. However, XP does not require documenting the test procedures.

Coding and Construction Activities

In this phase, the detailed design specification should be implemented as a computer program. The construction is done either by directly start programming or assembling code components. The selection of the programming language and builder tools (i.e. assembler, linker or compiler) should be based on the availability of debugging and testing tools (FDA, 2002). The coding and construction activities regulated by the FDA are:

- Source Code Evaluation
- Source Code Documentation Evaluation
- Code Traceability Analysis
- Source code Interface Analysis

Source Code Evaluation

Source code is evaluated before compilation to make sure that it follows design specification and coding standards. The FDA recommends using desk checking techniques to evaluate the software code. Desk checking methods include code audit, code inspection, code walkthrough, and code review (FDA, 2009). During code inspection, the author of the code explains statement by statement what the code is supposed to do in a meeting convened to analyze the program logic and its conformance to coding standards. During code walkthrough, developers manually trace the source code with small set of test cases. Code audit is a review of the source code by an independent person, or team to make sure that the source code follows software design and programming standards. A code review consists of organizing meetings, where the software code is presented to project personnel, managers, and customers for feedback and approval (FDA, 2002, 2009).

XP does not support any of the formal desk checking practices required by FDA. Instead, XP claims that pair programming is more successful than any inspection and formal review methods. According to experimental studies, the pair programming technique has been shown to be effective in uncovering errors in the code while programming, saving costs since errors are discovered before compilation (Cockburn & Williams, 2001). Therefore, it is reasonable to assume that pair programming satisfies FDA requirements with respect to source code evaluation without the need of having formal desk checking techniques.

Source Code Documentation Evaluation

The FDA requires documenting the coding and the construction process. In most software projects, the commented code and the generated html or text files from the source code by tools are considered sufficient for documenting the code. However, the FDA requires documentation for each implemented module or function to show its agreement with coding standards and quality policies, defined within the organization. In addition, the existing errors after coding and construction have to be documented. Moreover, the whole process of compilation should be documented (errors found, solutions and unsolved errors and warnings) (FDA, 2002).

XP does not support the production of any documentation needed to satisfy the FDA recommendations such as documenting modules, errors, the compilation process, and the used tools and techniques.

Code Traceability Analysis

The FDA requires having a traceability matrix to show the relation between the source code modules and the design specification and vice versa (FDA, 2002). In addition, the traceability matrices to show the relation of the test cases and the source code as well as the test cases and the design specification is also needed (FDA, 2002).

XP does not support the development of traceability matrices from source code-to-design, from test cases-to-source code, from test cases-to-design, from test cases-to-risk analysis, and from source code-to-risk analysis as required by the FDA.

Source Code Interface Analysis

The implementation of the interfaces between the system modules should be clearly specified in the source code to ensure that the implemented communication links are well integrated with the software implementation. This aims to increase the safety of the final software product.

There is no specific guideline in XP on how to analyze different interfaces of the subsystems for implementing and integrating the various parts of the code.

Test Generation

Besides the test procedures and test cases created to test the software design, the new test cases and their corresponding test procedures are generating based on the implementation. The new test cases can be unit, integration, acceptance, and system testing.

There are two types of test cases in XP that are possible to map to the design: unit and integration test cases. XP follows the test-driven development method (TDD), in which test cases are design before coding starts. Therefore, unit test cases are generated as the result of TDD after the design and before coding. Integration test cases are generated at the end of an iteration once a new piece of code is adding to the collective codebase. These two test cases have the potential to map to the code and the design. For the acceptance test, it is not possible to map it to elements of the design or code. In addition, dividing XP into small iterations and having simple design enables developers to relate the elements of a design to code and therefore create a code-to-design traceability matrix. System test cases are generated during the whole release to be executed during the production phase.

The Testing Phase

The FDA focuses extensively on software testing during the development process to ensure the reliability and safety of the software product. It lists a number of software testing principles to examine software effectively such as the importance of what is to be tested rather than how to apply the test, anticipating the results expected from the testing process, ensuring the independence of the testing process from coding, and documenting the tests. The FDA guidelines highlight four types of testing activities that need to be supported: structural testing, functional testing, statistical testing, and regression testing (FDA, 2002; 2009a).

Structural or white box testing evaluates the internal code structure. The amount of structural test coverage is defined based on common metrics such as coverage of statements, branches, loops, conditions, and data flows (FDA, 2002).

Functional testing is a black box testing technique which is conducted to evaluate the program functionality and program interfaces. The FDA divides functional testing into four different types: normal case, output forcing, robustness, and combinations of inputs (FDA, 2002).

Regression testing is another type of testing technique to manage the changes during the software development life cycle. Regression testing ensures that changes to the system do not negatively impact the other parts of the system (FDA, 2002, 2009).

Test Documentation

Documenting test activities is an important concern for the FDA during the testing process. The documents that the FDA requires during the testing process include a test plan, test procedures, test cases, test reports, and test logs (IEEE Standards Association, 1983; FDA, 2002, 2009).

Test plan, as defined in the requirement phase, should be created early in the process to identify the testing tasks during each development stage. A test procedures document is generated from the test plan. It contains instructions about each test on how to setup the test and evaluate the results. Test cases are designed and implemented depending on the type of testing (i.e. structural, functional, statistic, and regression). This document should identify system inputs, expected results, and a set of execution conditions for test. A test log is defined as a record of the test execution (FDA,

2009). For instance, all detected errors during test execution should be logged. Once test execution is finished, the direction and results of the test should be recorded (FDA, 2002, 2009).

Except a limited number of documents that are created to reach a running product, XP attempts to minimize the amount of efforts on documentation as one of its values. Among the testing documents created in XP, the test cases exist usually in a form that is readable by automatic testing tools.

Test Execution

The FDA requires the following testing activities: unit testing, integration testing, system testing and acceptance (FDA, 2002).

In unit testing, the program is divided to smaller components (modules). Then, the structure and functionality of each component is examined early in program testing (FDA, 2002). Integration testing is one level higher than unit testing. Integration testing concentrates on the flow of control and data between units (FDA, 2002). The system level testing, all aspects of functionality and performance of the software product are tested. This test is done on working software products and developers should consider the requirements that exist at the level of the operating environment. The FDA highlights some aspects of software to examine during system testing such as performance issues, responses to stress conditions, security features, effectiveness of software recovery, HFE and usability, accuracy of documentation, and compatibility with other software products (FDA, 2002).

Finally, for user site testing, the FDA requires the conduct of user site testing as the last step of the testing activity of the software product. It defines user site testing as any testing through actual or simulated use of software as the part of installed system configuration at the user's site. As mentioned in the requirement phase, the FDA assumes that user site testing is the same as the installation testing, beta testing, site validation, installation verification, and user acceptance test.

XP supports unit testing. Unit tests are generated in each iteration based on the design to test subsequent code. Then, after writing the code, the unit tests are executed to find probable faults (Maximilien & Laurie, 2003). In addition, XP supports integration testing by continuous integration whenever new code is written, added to the collective codebase, and unit tested (Abrahamsson et al., 2002).

There is system test in XP with a scope limited to testing the system structure. An XP programmer (architect sub-role) is responsible for providing the system tests to examine the architecture during the production phase for each release (Beck & Andres, 2004).

Test Traceability Analysis

The FDA requires several traceability matrices to link unit tests to detailed design, integration tests to high-level design, and system tests to software requirements (FDA, 2002).

There is no support in XP for traceability matrices from unit tests to detailed design, from integration tests to high-level design, and from system tests to software requirements. But developing such traceability matrix for unit test to detailed design should be straightforward since the unit tests are developed based on the design and before coding starts.

Summary

Tables 1, 2, 3, and 4 summarize for each process activity the recommended practices according to the FDA guidelines for medical device software. The tables also show the documentation that is required to be generated throughout the process for the system to be FDA compliant. Areas where XP fails to meet the FDA requirements as shown in bold. As shown in these tables, many projects that adopt XP run high-risk of non-compliance with the FDA regulations because of the inability of XP to meet several FDA required practices.

Table 1. Mapping between FDA and XP – requirement phase

Requirement Phase	FDA Recommended Practices	FDA Required Documentation	XP Practices	XP Documentation
Requirements Elicitation	Interviews, use cases, observation and social analysis, focus group, brainstorming, and prototyping	Software Requirements Specification (SRS)	User story card writing, High customer involvement, Eliciting requirements in number of iterations	**User stories are the only documentation of requirements in XP**
Requirements Evaluation	Formal review meetings, risk analysis, requirements inconsistency management, requirements prioritization, evaluation of alternative options in requirements, requirement verification, prototyping, requirements risk analysis	Result of the evaluation needs to be documented	System prototype, Building software functionality in number of iterations, Handling possible risks early in the development process	**The process of evaluating requirements is not documented in XP**
Requirements Traceability Analysis	Create traceability matrices	Software requirements and system requirements traceability matrix, software requirements and the risk analysis result traceability matrix	**There is no practice in XP for traceability analysis**	**There is no documentation that relates different artefacts**
Test Plan	Working on acceptance and system test plans	Acceptance test plan, system test plan	Customers are involved in the writing of acceptance tests, The XP architect is responsible for creating a system test plan	Both system and acceptance test plans are documented

Table 2. Mapping between FDA and XP – design phase

Design Phase	FDA Recommended Practices	FDA Required Documentation	XP Practices	XP Documentation
Design for usability	Usability testing, usability inspection, usability inquiry, usability design patterns, scenario-based assessment of architecture	Documentation on design decisions that relate to making the system more usable	System prototyping to obtain feedback for the end users.	The prototype itself is the only evidence that prototyping took place
Software Design Evaluation	Prototype evaluation, demonstration, simulation, comparing the design with other similar proven designs, analysis and inspection methods, compilation of relevant scientific literature, provision of historical evidence that similar designs are clinically safe	Design review document, design verification document, design validation document, Software Design Specification (SDS)	Pair Programming, Refactoring	**Design evaluation is not documented**
Design Traceability Analysis	Create traceability matrices	Requirement-to-design traceability matrix	**There is no practice in XP for traceability analysis**	**There is no documentation that relates different artefacts**
Update Test Plan	Working on unit and integration test plans	Unit and integration test plans	Updating test plans taking into account design elements	Unit and integration test plans
Test Design Generation	Generating test cases for unit, integration, acceptance and system testing	Test cases and test procedures	Generating test cases for unit, integration, acceptance and system testing	Unit test cases, integration test cases, acceptance test cases, and system test cases

Table 3. Mapping between FDA and XP – coding phase

Coding Phase	FDA Recommended Practices	FDA Required Documentation	XP Practices	XP Documentation
Source Code Evaluation	code audit, code inspection, code walkthrough, code review	Documentation that shows that code has been reviewed	Pair programming	**No documentation is produced**
Source Code Documentation Evaluation	Although there is no specific practices defined in the FDA guidelines, the FDA requires that the source code be documented and that the evaluation of this documentation should be performed	Source code document	**There is not support for this activity**	**Since the code does not need to be documented, the evaluation of the documentation does not apply.**
Code Traceability Analysis	Create traceability matrices	Traceability matrices for: source code to design specification, test cases to source code, test cases to design specification, test cases to risk analysis results, source code to risk analysis results	**There is no practice in XP for traceability analysis**	**There is no documentation that relates different artefacts**
Source Code Interface Analysis	Interface checking	Documents that show that interfaces between the system components have bee verified	**There is no support for this activity**	**No documentation is created**
Test Generation	Updating test cases for unit, integration, acceptance and system testing	Document that describes test cases and test procedures	Updating test cases for unit, integration, acceptance and system testing	Unit test case, Integration test case, Acceptance test case, System test case

Table 4. Mapping between FDA and XP – testing phase

Testing Phase	FDA Recommended Practices	FDA Required Documentation	XP Practices	XP Documentation
Test Documentation	The FDA requires documenting the testing process	Test plan, test procedures, test cases, test report, and test logs	XP is a test-driven approach and there are many practices and roles that are dedicated to testing	Test plans, test procedures, test logs, and test cases
Test Execution	Execution of unit tests, integration tests, system tests, and user site testing	Document that describes the results of executing the tests	Tests are executed	Test logs are kept for debugging purposes
Test Traceability Analysis	Create traceability matrices	Traceability matrices for: unit tests to detailed design, integration tests to high level design, and system tests to software requirements	**There is no practice in XP for traceability analysis**	**There is no documentation that relates different artefacts**

To address this issue, there is a need to extend XP for projects that requires FDA compliance by explicitly addressing the missing requirements (Tables 1 through 4. This extension will require adding new roles, practices and work products (documentation). However, we believe that any extension to XP should consider the following points:

- The XP values should not be affected by the extension. These include increased communication among team members, pair programming, collective ownership of the code, rapid iteration, light-weight documentation, etc. These practices have been shown to be useful in many software projects.
- There should be a compromise between keeping the process agile and meeting the FDA requirements. This is particularly difficult to achieve since XP roles are defined in such a way that optimizes the time it takes to produce a release. Adding new practices to XP may XP time to market norms. Tradeoffs that balance agility and auditability need to be investigated.

CONCLUSION AND FUTURE DIRECTIONS

In this paper, we discussed the changes that regulatory compliance can have on software processes with a particular focus on agile practices such as XP. We particularly looked into the requirements imposed by the FDA on the way medical device software is built, tested, and maintained. Some of the contributions of the paper include extracting the requirements that FDA imposes on software processes by focusing on process activities, and analyzing the capability for XP (an agile process) to support FDA requirements. We uncovered areas where XP fails to support many of the FDA key requirements. We suggested that one way of meeting the FDA requirements is to extend XP by adding new roles, practices, and artefacts. However, this extension should be carefully designed so as to (1) minimize the impact on the XP values, and (2) balance the agility of XP with the need to satisfy the FDA requirements.

The immediate future work would be to investigate ways to extend XP to meet the FDA requirement and experiment with this extension in practice. We anticipate that designing an extension to XP while keeping its agility could be a challenging task. Another future direction would be to apply the techniques presented in this paper to other agile processes such as Scrum, FDD, and others.

REFERENCES

Abdeen, M. M., Kahl, W., & Maibaum, T. (2007). FDA: Between process and product evaluation. In *Proceedings of the Joint Workshop on High Confidence Medical Devices, Software, and Systems and Medical Device Plug-and-Play Interoperability* (pp. 181-186). Washington, DC: IEEE Computer Society.

Abrahamsson, P., Salo, O., Ronkainen, J., & Warsta, J. (2002). Agile software development methods: Review and analysis. Kajaan, Finland: VTT Publications.

Beck, K., & Andres, C. (2004). Extreme programming explained: Embrace change (2nd ed.). Reading, MA: Addison-Wesley.

Cockburn, A., & Williams, L. (2001). The costs and benefits of pair programming. In G. Succi & M. Marchesi (Eds.), Extreme programming examined (pp. 223–248). Reading, MA: Addison-Wesley.

FDA. (1997). *Design control guidance for medical device manufacturers.* Retrieved from http://www.fda.gov/downloads/MedicalDevices/Device-RegulationandGuidance/ GuidanceDocuments/UCM070642.pdf

FDA. (2002). General principles of software validation: Final guidance for industry and FDA staff. Retrieved from http://www.pacontrol.com/download/General-Principles-of-Software- Validation.pdf

FDA. (2009a). *Glossary of computer systems software development terminology.* Retrieved from http://www.fda.gov/iceci/inspections/inspection-guides/ucm074875.htm

FDA. (2009b). *Guidelines: Regulatory information.* Retrieved from http://www.fda.gov/RegulatoryInformation/Legislation/default.htm

Forsström, J. (1997). Why certification of medical software would be useful? International Journal of Medical Informatics, 47(3), 143–151. doi:10.1016/S1386-5056(97)00098-1 doi:10.1016/S1386-5056(97)00098-1.

Hamou-Lhadj, A. K., & Hamou-Lhadj, A. (2007). Towards a compliance support framework for global software companies. *The IASTED International Conference on Software Engineering and Applications* (pp 31-36).

IEEE Standards Association. (1983). *IEEE standard for software test documentation.* Retrieved from http://standards.ieee.org/reading/ieee/std_public/description/se/829-1983_desc.html

Kowalczykiewicz, K., & Weiss, D. (2002). Traceability: Taming uncontrolled change in software development. Foundations of Computing and Decision Sciences, 27(4), 239–248.

Larman, C. (2003). Agile and iterative development: A manager's guide. Reading, MA: Addison-Wesley.

Maximilien, E. M., & Laurie, W. (2003). Assessing test-driven development at IBM. In *Proceedings of the International Conference on Software Engineering,* Portland, OR (pp. 564 - 569). Washington, DC: IEEE Computer Society Press.

Mehrfard, H., Pirzadeh, H., & Hamou-Lhadj, A. (2010). Investigating the capability of agile processes to support life-science regulations: The case of XP and FDA regulations with a focus on human factor requirements. In R. Lee, O. Ormandjieva, A. Abran, & C. Constantinides (Eds.), Software engineering research, management and applications (pp. 241–255). Berlin, Germany: Springer-Verlag. doi:10.1007/978-3-642-13273-5_16 doi:10.1007/978-3-642-13273-5_16.

Nord, R. L., Tomayko, J. E., & Wojcik, R. (2004). *Integrating software-architecture-centric methods into extreme programming (XP)* (Tech. Rep. No. CMU/SEI-2004-TN-036). Pittsburgh, PA: Carnegie-Mellon University.

Paetsch, F., Eberlein, A., & Maurer, F. (2003). Requirements engineering and agile software development. In *Proceedings of the International Workshop on Enabling Technologies: Infrastructure for Collaborative Enterprises*, Linz, Austria (pp. 308 - 313). Washington, DC: IEEE Computer Society.

Pressman, R. (2003). Software engineering: A practitioner's approach (6th ed.). New York, NY: McGraw-Hill.

Sawyer, D. (1996). *Do it by design: An introduction to human factors in medical devices.* Retrieved from http://www.fda.gov/downloads/MedicalDevices/DeviceRegulationandGuidance/GuidanceDocuments/UCM095061.pdf

Sommerville, I. (2004). Software engineering (7th ed.). Reading, MA: Addison-Wesley.

This work was previously published in the International Journal of Information System Modeling and Design (IJISMD), Volume 2, Issue 2, edited by Remigijus Gustas, pp. 67-81, copyright 2011 by IGI Publishing (an imprint of IGI Global).

Chapter 14
Predicting OSS Development Success:
A Data Mining Approach

Uzma Raja
University of Alabama, USA

Marietta J. Tretter
Texas A&M University, USA

ABSTRACT

Open Source Software (OSS) has reached new levels of sophistication and acceptance by users and commercial software vendors. This research creates tests and validates a model for predicting successful development of OSS projects. Widely available archival data was used for OSS projects from Sourceforge. net. The data is analyzed with multiple Data Mining techniques. Initially three competing models are created using Logistic Regression, Decision Trees and Neural Networks. These models are compared for precision and are refined in several phases. Text Mining is used to create new variables that improve the predictive power of the models. The final model is chosen based on best fit to separate training and validation data sets and the ability to explain the relationship among variables. Model robustness is determined by testing it on a new dataset extracted from the SF repository. The results indicate that end-user involvement, project age, functionality, usage, project management techniques, project type and team communication methods have a significant impact on the development of OSS projects.

INTRODUCTION

Software development is an expensive endeavor and the risk of failure is high. In this scenario, users are looking for reliable but cheap alternatives to expensive software systems. Open source software (OSS) that is developed online by vol-

unteer participants, offers one such alternative (Roberts, Hann, & Slaughter, 2006). These projects are distributed publicly with free and open access to their source code. Many organizations are accepting OSS projects as an inexpensive and reliable alternative to commercial Closed Source Software (CSS) projects. Some commercial soft-

DOI: 10.4018/978-1-4666-4161-7.ch014

ware development companies adopt existing OSS projects, while others launch their own projects in OSS communities (Cearley, Fenn, & Plummer, 2005). A few OSS projects are headed towards the stock market offering a new venue of high tech investment (Ricadela, 2007). However, the success rate of OSS projects is not any higher than CSS projects (Chengalur-Smith & Sidorova, 2003; Krishnamurthy, 2002). Therefore, as the use of OSS projects increases, it is critical to have performance evaluation models for these projects.

To understand why some OSS projects are more successful than others, it is critical to understand the development process and the factors that impact successful project development. The process model underlying software system success, as proposed by DeLone and McLean (1992), has three steps to it: system creation, system use and consequences. This research focuses on the very first step of system creation and analyzes factors that promote successful system creation or completion. The goal of this study is to address two vital questions:

- Can we predict successful OSS development?
- Can we identify the factors that lead to successful OSS development?

Data archives of OSS projects are publicly available. These archives contain rich project lifecycle information. There has been a move towards automation of software development metric collection and analysis (German, 2004). Mokus, Fielding, and Herbsleb (2002) studied two large scale OSS developments i.e. Apache and Mozilla, using the development archives. The availability of data archives for OSS projects invites the use of mining techniques. Williams and Hollingsworth (2005) demonstrated how data mined from source code repositories can improve static analysis tools. Jensen and Scacchi (2005) used data mining techniques for studying OSS development communities by combining Text

Mining and link analysis to discover update patterns. Dinh-Trong and Bieman (2005) analyzed the maintenance process by mining repositories of a long-lived open source project, FreeBSD. Zimmerman et al. (2005) developed an approach to use association rule mining on CVS data to recommend source code that is potentially relevant to a given code fragment. Ying, Murphy, Ng, and Chu-Carroll (2004) developed a mining approach on the change history of source code to identify relevant code for change task.

OSS projects evolve in cyberspace and their growth models do not follow the traditional CSS developed through organized resources. Godfrey and Tu (2001) conducted one of the first analyses of Linux code evolution and compared it to the existing laws of software evolution. Robles et al. (2006) built on their work to test the model on a newer dataset and found evidence of OSS evolution being different than CSS evolution. Paulson, Succi, and Eberlein (2004) compared the evolution of OSS and CSS projects using linear approximation techniques. Koch (2007) found that the nature of OSS evolution largely depends on the size of the project. Software evolution studies have also facilitated study of software maintenance, since they provide a framework for analyzing OSS projects. While the studies in OSS evolution have focused on growth patterns of projects, there are also studies that have examined the overall success of OSS projects.

Crowsten, Annabi, and Howison (2003) presented a framework for OSS success. Several studies have since focused on various aspects of OSS success. Stewart, Ammeter, and Maruping (2006) explore effects of license choice on OSS development; defining OSS success in terms of number of downloads. Mokus, Fielding, and Herbsleb (2002) have studied OSS success from the point of view of downloads as well. Other studies have investigated success form the point of view of the social network that is supported by the project (Grewal, Lilien, & Mallapragada, 2006; Singh, Tan, & Mookerjee, 2007). The number of CVS commits is another factor that has been used in some studies. Subramaniam, Sen, and Nelson. (2009) explored OSS success in terms of developer interest, project activity and user participation. While study of software project success is critical, particular attention needs to be paid to successful development of software systems. This research is focused on the factors lead to successful completion or progression of a project that is still under development.

Majority of the OSS studies have been conducted on small sample of large-scale OSS projects or explored a small set of independent variables. Robles, Gonzalez-Barahona, and Merelo (2006) emphasize the significance of artifacts beyond source code for studying OSS projects and use a wider variety of files for analysis of OSS development. There is need for a complete set of constructs for model development (Rai, Lang, &Welker, 2002; Sabherwal, Jeyaraj, & Chowa, 2006). It is imperative to consider a broad range of constructs to assure that the resulting model is complete. This work extends on prior studies by considering a wider range of factors and by using multiple statistical techniques.

Given the wide range of variables available in OSS repositories and access to techniques that enable analyzing large samples, this study adds to the body of knowledge by using a large sample of OSS projects and utilizes the power of data mining techniques by using large data archives, building models from data and then testing the model on another sample of data. This allows development of a robust model that can be generalized to a larger population of OSS communities.

This research has important implications for OSS communities that wish to provide high quality projects for public use, for users who prefer a cost effective and reliable alternative to CSS projects and for commercial organizations that take the risk of launching their projects in OSS communities. The rest of the paper proceeds as follows. First we present the conceptual background. Research methods, data and techniques used are discussed next. We then present the analysis followed by results. We discuss threats to validity and implications for research and practice and conclude the paper.

CONCEPTUAL FRAMEWORK

Research on CSS software development has focused on three types of characteristics: Process, Product and Resource. OSS development is characterized by a close interaction between the end user and the development team (Crowston, Annabi, & Howison, 2003). End users can report and resolve defects, submit feature requests, and participate in discussions on message boards. This creates a unique role of the end user in project development and maintenance process (Feller & Fitzgerald, 2002). Therefore, the framework adopted for this study identifies relevant constructs from the End-User characteristics of OSS projects, in addition to the Product, Process, and Resource characteristics to create a model for OSS development success.

Product-related factors refer to the attributes of the software product. Effects of product characteristics on the project outcomes have been established in CSS research (Abdel-Hamid & Madnick, 1983; Banker, Davis, & Slaughter, 1998). Increase in product functionality is attained through new releases over project lifecycle (Boehm, 1984). In OSS projects new versions are released as project grows and functionality is added (Stamelos, Angelis, Oikonomou, & Bleris, 2002). Another product characteristic that is widely investigated is the number of defects occurring in operational software. In CSS projects a higher number of defects are attributed to poor quality. However, in OSS projects, the process of defect detection and removal is different and could be indicative of how widely the product is used. The number of downloads have been a key attribute to determine product usage and success (Crowston, Annabi, & Howison, 2003; Stewart & Gosian, 2006). Prior research in OSS has also analyzed the effects of license choices on the OSS project development (Stewart, Ammeter, & Maruping, 2006). Considering the evolving nature of software systems, it is important to consider the ability of software to operate in changing environments (Stewart & Gosian, 2006). Compatibility refers to the multiple operating environments supported by the software (Fenton & Pfleeger, 1991). OSS projects that offer support over multiple platforms would likely attract a diverse audience and would benefit in terms of defect detection and removal. Lastly, the inherent nature of the application being developed has to be considered to investigate if certain types of applications are more likely to flourish in OSS development environment.

Evaluation of software development process provides insights into the project outcomes (Harter, Krishnan, & Slaughter, 2000; Niazi, Wilson, & Zowghi, 2005). One widely used process evaluation method is the Capability Maturity Model (CMM). While CMM cannot be directly mapped to OSS domain; many of the process characteristics that affect project outcomes can be examined in OSS domain. OSS projects are developed through non-traditional organizations, yet there is evidence of management and control in OSS development communities (Jensen & Scacchi, 2005). Teams have the option to use project management tools. Since OSS projects are developed and maintained by teams that are not physically co-located, the ability to communicate effectively through use of multiple channels could affect the process quality and the development process outcomes. Another process related characteristic for OSS projects is the response time to resolve the issues that occur in software; e.g. software defect, feature or patch requests submitted to the project developers. The response time indicates how quickly a team can react to these issues. For defect reports, the inability of the team to remove them is related to the development process. Thus the number of unresolved defects is considered a process characteristic.

Resource characteristics for software development include personnel (individuals or teams), tools and cost (Fenton & Pfleeger, 1991). The size and experience of the team can affect the overall process of software development. Lack of trained programmers can result in production delays or poor software quality (Fenton & Pfleeger, 1991). The tools available for software development facilitate the development process. Online development of OSS projects is facilitated by the availability of mail messaging and news groups that keep the developers and end users connected to projects related events. Therefore, these characteristics are explored for their potential impact on OSS development. Traditionally, cost is considered an important resource characteristic. However, project cost has little relevance in OSS domain because of the volunteer nature of participation and free licensing.

User-related factors refer to attributes of the end users of the project. Sabherwal, Jeyaraj, and Chowa (2006) urged the need of studying end user participation in systems development. In CSS, a project is developed for a known user with predefined requirements (Hoffer, George, & Valacich, 1996) and the end user does not take a direct part in project development. On the other hand, OSS projects are usually initiated by an individual programmer or group of programmers, trying to solve a problem that is of their own interest (Feller & Fitzgerald, 2002). OSS projects do not have predefined clients or users. However, once a project is launched it is available for public use and a user community emerges. Project source code is available to users, who may detect, identify and report defects to the development team. Users are also free to propose solutions, contribute code and make function/feature requests (Crowston, Li, Wei, Eseryel, & Howison, 2007). Anecdotal references to active user communities have been made in literature, but there is no empirical testing of its effects on project performance. Using the argument that end users impact project performance, we explore the effects of user community size and the extent of their participation in OSS development.

In addition to the factors discussed above, we include two control factors: project size and age as used in prior software development models (Barry, Kemerer, & Slaughter, 2006). Controlling for size assures that the analysis is valid for all projects, irrespective of their size. Controlling for age enables us to use time dependent factors in the model.

RESEARCH METHODS

Online development results in the creation of rich transactional datasets on all aspects of OSS projects. Public access to these data archives provides an opportunity for knowledge extraction and model building. If we were to apply existing theories and test the CSS models in OSS domain, there would be a fear of loss of information that is unique to OSS. Therefore, we develop an explor-atory study of OSS development process using Data Mining (DM). Use of exploratory methods for predictive models has become an acceptable empirical method (Delone & McLean, 1992). Mining of data repositories reveals detailed logs of software evolution and development (Williams & Hollingsworth, 2005) and can also predict software maintenance outcomes (Zimmermann, Zeller, Weissgerber, & Diehl, 2005).

DM provides the ability to build robust models using large amount of data and variables. Domain knowledge is required to develop an understanding of the data and to identify relevant variables. Data preprocessing involves exploring missing values and determining the suitability of available variables for model building. Additional variables can be extracted using transformations and computations. Once acceptable data is prepared, several available DM techniques can be employed on samples of data to develop models. The results are then interpreted to create useful knowledge about the phenomenon under examination. Figure 1 shows the steps involved in DM. Following

Figure 1. Data mining process

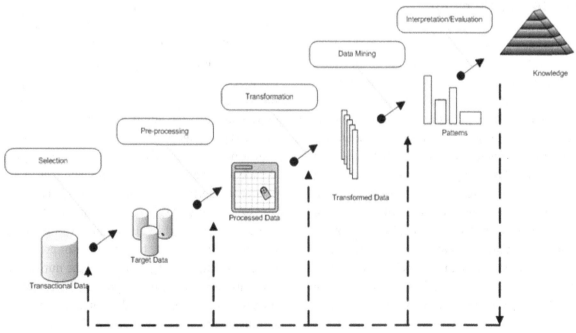

subsections describe the data source used for the analysis, the independent variables identified from the data source, the technique used for analysis.

Data Source

SourceForge.net (SF) is the world's largest OSS development web site, with the largest repository of OSS projects. Owned and operated by OSTG, Inc., SF enables OSS developers to host, develop and maintain their projects. SF is a database driven web site, with over 100,000 projects and records of over 1 million registered users' activities. OSTG has shared certain SF data with the research community for the sole purpose of supporting academic and scholarly research on the OSS phenomenon. We use the data archives starting November 1999 through May 2006 for this research through a research initiative with the University of Notre Dame. The entity relationship diagram of the warehouse along with a data dictionary, available at the research site, provides an insight into the available measures that can be used in analysis.

Data Collection and Variable Identification

Prior research in software engineering highlights a distinction between development and maintenance phase issues associated with software projects (Banker & Kemerer, 1989; Banker, Davis, & Slaughter, 1998). Analysis of a small random sample of OSS projects without any consideration of project lifecycle phases can fail to discover significant relationships (Krishnamurthy, 2002; Stewart, 2004). Therefore, we categorize the available OSS projects in either the development or the maintenance phase, using the lifecycle phase information maintained at SF. For this research, we exclusively focus on projects in development phase. Analysis is restricted to the projects that were launched at least one year prior to our data

extraction. This assures that each project in the analysis has had enough time to evolve.

The list of the independent variables for this research was identified after studying the available attributes in the SF data model. We study each table in detail to determine its usability for our analysis. Domain knowledge is critical in effective model building because it ensures that a relevant list of initial variables is identified. If too many variables are used, the resulting model could be irrelevant to the domain. On the other hand, choice of too few variables can result in exclusion of significant factors (Sabherwal, Jeyaraj, & Chowa, 2006). A list of initial variables was created based on prior research. A detail of these variables is presented in Table 1 and a brief discussion of related data extraction is presented here.

The functionality of a software project can be derived from the number of total modules (Lehman, Perry, & Ramil, 1998). The count of total modules (*Cnt_Mod*) for each project is computed. The artifact repository contains data on various artifact types. The defect artifact type for each project is determined using the *project_ID* and information on all the defects reported is extracted. Besides a distinct ID, every defect submission contains the time stamp of time reported and time resolved. The SF *user_ID* of the person reporting the defect is also available. The total lifecycle defect reports (*Cnt_Def*) are computed for individual projects using their defect report identifiers. The popularity of the project is operationalized as the number of downloads (*Dwnlds*) and the page views (*Pg_Vws*). The project profile maintains information on the License type. We identify whether a project was using the Open Source Initiative (OSI) or not; thus creating a binary variable (*OSI*). The compatibility of a project is evaluated by the number of operating systems (*Cnt_OS*), the total number of programming languages (*Cnt_prglng*) and the number of translations (*Cnt_Tran*) it supports. To categorize the project type, the variable available at SF was initially evaluated. However, SF allows a project

Table 1. Product, process, resource and user related variables identified for analysis

Variable	Source (Units)	Symbol
Modules	The total number of modules in the program (count)	Cnt_Mod
Defects	The total number of defect reports for each project (count)	Cnt_Def
Downloads	Number of times the project has been downloaded (count)	Dwnlds
Page_Views	Number of times the project pages have been viewed(count)	Pg_Vws
License type	Is the project releases under OSI license or not (boolean)	OSI
Operating Systems	Count of the operating system the project supports (count)	Cnt_OS
Programming languages	Number of programming languages used in the project (count)	Cnt_prglng
Translations	Number of languages the project is translated in(count)	Cnt_Tran
Project Type	The textual data on project description is used to create a numbered categorization (categorical)	Prj_{Typ}
Project Management	OSS projects can opt to use a project manager. This is an option the projects can choose to use or not (Boolean)	Use_PM
Communication Frequency	Total messages posted on the projects forums (count)	Cnt_Msg
Reaction Time	The Mean time to resolve an issue (defect, feature request or patch) to the artifact repository (Number of days)	MTTR
Defect Removal	Number of unresolved (open) defects, after one month of reporting (count)	Open_Def
Team Size	Number of SF members in project development team(count)	Team_Size
Communication Tools	This is a Boolean indication of whether the project uses the mail messaging or not (Boolean)	Use_Mail
Configuration Management Tools	Use of CVS to for project version control(Boolean)	Use_CVS
User Community Size	Size of the end user community is computed by the number of distinct users reporting messages or artifacts, who do not belong to the project team, identified by the user group table. (count)	Usr_Size
User Participation	User participation in the defect detection process is measured by the count of defects reported by non-team members (count)	Usr_Rpt
Age	Time elapsed since project start (Days)	Age
Size	Source Line of Code of the project (Number)	Size

to self-select multiple project types. This can be problematic in model building, where we need a single value to represent the type of project. To address the problem of multiple categorizations, we create a new variable representing project type.

Each OSS project provides a 200-word project description. The text includes details about the nature and purpose of the project. This information is useful for text mining. Therefore, we use Text Mining to perform an analysis of the project description text. We generate the Singular Value Decomposition (SVD) terms and cluster the projects using an exception maximization algorithm (Raja & Tretter, in press). As a result, each project is placed in a distinct cluster (i.e. has only one project type). An overview of the clusters is shown in Table 2.

Cluster #1 has general-purpose OSS terms. Cluster #2 has terms referring to database and game projects, cluster #3 has terms associated with operating systems, cluster #4 has terms related to network communication, cluster #5 refers to tool and application development while cluster #6 has terms related to project development and design. We create a new variable called project type (*Prj_Typ*), based on the cluster number. This enables us to investigate the impact of project type on OSS development and to see if OSS environment is suitable for specific types of projects.

A Boolean variable representing whether an OSS project uses project managers or not is extracted from the profile for each project hosted at SF (*Use_PM*). Communication frequency is another process related measure. OSS projects

Table 2. Descriptive terms of the cluster analysis results of the project type data

Cluster	Descriptive Terms	Frequency	Percentage
1	Source, Open Source, Program	648	6
2	MySql, base, game, web video	2188	21
3	Windos, Drivers, OS, Support, Run	1405	13
4	Server, Client, irc, file, protocol, write	743	7
5	Java tool, application, language	3094	29
6	Support, information, design, develop, project, management	2534	24

maintain forums. The SF repository holds data for all the interactions at these forums. The count of total messages exchanged over the forums is computed for each project (*Cnt_Msg*). Registered SF users can report defects and make feature or patch requests at the project site. Each report is time stamped along with the *SF_ID* of the member initiating the request. Once the issue is resolved, the time stamp, along with the member closing the issue, is stored. For every project we compute resolution time, as the mean time to resolve an issue (*MTTR*). The count of unresolved defects is computed from the artifact-reporting repository by identifying the defects that do not have a resolution date/time (*Open_Def*). Defects reported within the past one month were not included in this count.

The size of development team is computed by a count of the registered SF users who are identified as group members of the project (*Team_Size*). The use of communication tools is a boolean indicating whether mail messaging option is used by the team or not (*Use_Mail*). The use of configuration management tools is also a boolean that is determined by extracting information on whether the team uses CVS option available to SF projects or not (*Use_CVS*).

The size of the user community (*Usr_Size*) is computed by identifying all issue reports or forum messages that are associated to users who are not members of the development team (as indicated by the group member information). Data is revisited to ensure there is no duplication of *user_ID*. The participation of the user is computed in terms of

participation to the development process. Therefore all the defect reports or patch submissions made by users who are not a member of the development team, are counted to indicate the user participation (*Usr_Rpts*).

The age of project is computed as the number of days from the registration date (Age). Projects that had been registered for less than a year were excluded from the analysis. The size of project is measured in the kilo source lines of code (*SLOC*).

Dependent Variable

This study purely focuses on OSS development in terms of project completion or its evolution towards completion. During the development phase, the biggest challenge for software projects is the continued growth and transition through the development phases (Crowston & Scozzi, 2002). Considering the high failure rates of software development projects, mere completion of a project is considered a measure of success (Ewusi-Mensah, 1997). Due the iterative nature of OSS development, progression of lifecycle phase is a better measure of completion (Crowston & Scozzi, 2002). We use the transition of an OSS project from one phase of development to the next phase as an indicator of project development.

For each project we examine if there was a change in the lifecycle phase. Some projects indicate multiple phase transitions (e.g. alpha and pre alpha), on the same date. To remove this anomaly, we select the highest level of development for each project on a given date. We use queries to detect multiple phase transitions. There are only three projects that evolved through more than two phases while hosted by the SF community. The dependent variable is set to one (*Dev = 1*) for projects that evolve while hosted at SF and is set to zero (*Dev=0*) for projects that never transition to the next phase. Only 17.7% of all the projects in the development phase exhibit a change in their development status. This number is similar to findings in prior studies (Krishnamurthy, 2002).

Data Cleaning

The next step is to clean the dataset. Transactional data archives often have missing or inconsistent values. This can affect the integrity of DM models. We examine the dataset for missing or inconsistent values. The total number of projects in development phases is *58689*. A careful analysis of the attributes of these projects indicates that not all the project numbers are valid. Many projects do not maintain a defect repository and therefore do not have any data on maintenance activities. We also find that many projects, although registered at SF, do not have any development activity. These projects were never initiated or were active for less than a month. We remove the projects that do not have active repositories and do not have any usable archival data available. To ensure that the analysis has complete data, project that were registered within a year of the analysis are excluded. This ensures that the lack of development activity is not due to the project age. We recode the data to accommodate the discussed exclusions and get a data sample of 10612.

Data Sampling

To build models using DM it is very important to use different samples for model building, validation and testing (Fayyad, Piatetsky-Shapiro, & Smyth, 1996). If the same data is used for model creation and validation, the resulting model will likely be biased to the sample and thus not acceptable. Therefore, we split the dataset into training, validation and testing samples. We use 40% training, 30% validation and 30% testing sample ratio. Initially we build a model using the training dataset. Once an acceptable training model is built, we use the validation set to evaluate the model. We then use specific diagnostics e.g. lift charts, to check how well the training model holds for the validation sample. After several iterations of re-training, a reasonable model is selected. The validation dataset can no longer be used to test the accuracy of this model. To create a robust model, we test the model with the test sample. The accuracy of the model on the test data gives a realistic estimate of the performance of the model for OSS projects in general.

Predictive Modeling

We use three most commonly used supervised DM methods: Logistic Regression (LR), Decision Trees (DT) and Neural Networks (NN) for building the model. Each method allows us to create predictive models that can be compared to each other for various fit characteristics. The best-suited model depends upon model fit and its suitability for the given domain. All three types of models have advantages and disadvantages. We use competing models to help account for all types of linear and nonlinear relationships in the data.

Results of each 'train and validate' iteration are examined to see if one model is performing better than another. By carefully examining the performance of each model we get insight into the variables and into how the more desirable model might be modified to get the best results. NN models have the advantage of high predictive power because they can fit models of any shape. The disadvantage of this technique, especially for academic research, is the difficulty in interpretation of its results. In exploratory research, where the factors affecting the outcome are not completely known, the use of NN as the final model is not recommended (Berry & Linoff, 2004). The *DT* results in a sequence of English language rules that are easy to describe and understand. They provide the fit statistics and the prediction of new values. However, the individual variable significance and contributions to the model are not easy to interpret.

LR is suitable when the outcome variable is binary or dichotomous. There are a few differences between Linear Regression and LR models and their assumptions (Hosmer & Lemeshow, 2000). *LR* fits a linear model to the log of the odds of the response, the logit transformation. The logit transformation forces the predicted values for the fitted model to be between 0 and 1, thus giving a predicted probability for the different levels of the binary variable. The LR represents a model in the form of an equation. The significance of the regression coefficients explains the phenomenon under study. Thus the LR regression model is the most desirable model for interpretation but it required insight from the DT and NN models to transform variables and improve its predictive ability.

We use all three techniques simultaneously in the model formulation phase. Results from the DT are insightful into the interactions between independent variables. The NN model provides a base line for detecting complex non-linear relationships. Next section explains how DT and NN results improve the performance of the LR model.

ANALYSIS

The process flow of the model building process is shown in Figure 2. We use SAS Enterprise Miner 5.2 and SAS Text Miner 4.3 for the analysis. After extracting the variables from the SF dataset, we explore the descriptive statistics, identify missing or inconsistent values and perform collinearity analysis (insight node). The text analysis node performs the categorization of the projects based on their textual description. Once the dataset is ready, the sampling node creates three samples of data (text miner node). We then perform initial runs using LR, NN and DT nodes. The results from

Figure 2. Process flow diagram of the model building process

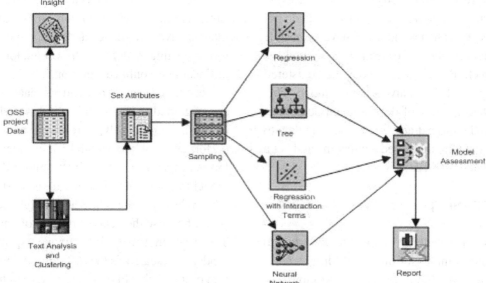

each of the technique are compared, using the fit statistics and other model comparison criteria e.g. lift charts (Assessment node). Once the best model is identified, we generate the detailed report for the selected model (Report node).

Considering the small percentage of projects that experienced a phase transition, we use stratified random sampling to create the three splits into training validation and test data sets. Thus each spilt is an accurate representation of the actual population. We use the training dataset to create models using predictive modeling techniques of LR, DT and NN. We use the stepwise method to select variables for the LR model. Although stepwise regression is not recommended for theory testing, it is widely used in exploratory research; where there is no a-priori assumptions regarding the relationships between the variables, and the goal is to discover relationships (Hosmer & Lemeshow, 2000; Menard, 2002; Berry & Linoff, 2004). The initial results indicate that the NN model and the DT models are better than the LR model. The lift charts of this analysis are shown in Figure 3 (lift shows improvement of

the model over using no model-higher lift is better). The poor performance of the first LR model (LR1) indicates missing variables.

The NN results indicate that the effects of age could be non-linear. Therefore, we perform optimal binning on the continuous variable Age into three categories: *Age_low*, *Age_med* and *Age_high*. *Age_high* indicates that the project was registered at SF, more than three years from the date of data extraction. *Age_low* indicates projects registered within the past two years. The cutoff point was selected based on the relationship to the dependent variable.

The *DT* results indicate a persistent partitioning based on the type of project and the use of mail messaging. Thus we create interaction terms for these two variables for the LR model (*LR2*). After adding the newly created interaction and binned terms, we perform another LR analysis (This new node is represented in Figure 2 as Regression with interaction terms).

We use the values of the Akaike Information Criteria (AIC) and Lift Charts to select the best model. The AIC is a measure of goodness of fit;

Figure 3. Comparative lift charts for LR, NN, DT and LR1 models

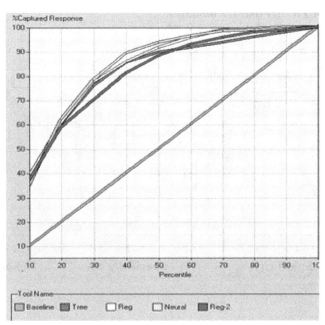

the model with the lowest AIC is usually the best model (Bozdogen, 1987). The Receiver Operating Characteristic (ROC) Charts are similar to lift charts i.e., the larger the area under the ROC curve the better the model: a diagonal line represents no model. A ROC chart is traditionally used in signal detection theory to show how the receiver operates on the existence of signal in the presence of noise. It is a plot of the probability of detecting the true signal (sensitivity) and the false signal (1-sensitivity) for an entire range of possible cutoff points. In DM, ROC curves are used to plot the true positive responses against the false positives (identified by the model). The closer the curve follows the left-hand border and the top border of the *ROC* space, the more accurate the test. The closer the test comes to the 45-degree line, the less accurate the test is. The area under the ROC curve measures the accuracy of the test. If the area under curve is greater than 0.8 (The entire area being 1.00), the resulting model is considered to be acceptable. Comparing the ROC curve for all techniques in Figure 4 shows that the second Logistic Regression (LR2) model has the highest overall lift and is thus considered the best model.

Final Model

The LR model provides the best fit and the lowest AIC, of all three predictive modeling techniques used in the analysis. The formulation of the LR equation is shown below (1). It contains all the variables and the interactions that are significant in the final model. P_{Dev} represents if the outcome is successful development or not.

$$P_{Dev} = \mu + \beta_1(Cnt\_Mod) + \beta_2(Cnt\_Def) + \beta_3(Dwnlds) + \beta_4(Prj_{typ}) + \beta_5(Open\_Def) + \beta_6(Use\_PM) + \beta_7(Cnt\_Msg) + \beta_8(Team\_Size) + \beta_9(Usr\_Rpts) + \beta_{10}(Prj\_type * Use\_mail) + \beta_{11}(Age_{low}) + \beta_{12}(Age_{med}) \tag{1}$$

We select the variables for our final model at 5% significance level and test the model across all three data splits. The selected model statistics are for a sample of 3183 observations. The statistical profile of the variables selected for the final model is shown in Tables 3 and 4.

Figure 4. ROC curves for LR, NN and DT models

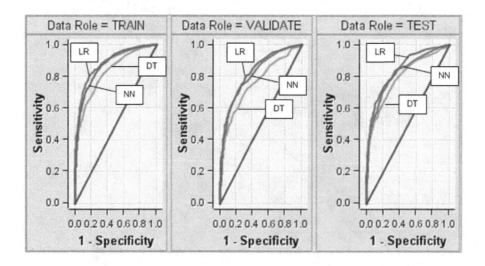

Table 3. Fit statistics of the train, test and validate samples of the LR model

Description	Train	Validate	Test
Akaike's Information Error	1335.930		
Average Squared Error	0.097	0.108	0.102
Average Error Function	0.330	0.417	0.356
Mean Square Error	0.098	0.108	0.102
Root Average Sum of Squares	0.312	0.329	0.319
Root Mean Squared Error	0.313	0.329	0.319
Sum of Squared Errors	384.230	319.931	300.510
Misclassification Rate	0.131	0.137	0.133
ROC Estimates	0.851	0.834	0.840

Data Integrity and Diagnostic Checks

A variety of specification tests are recommended for LR models (Hosmer & Lemeshow, 2000; Menard, 2002). We test our final model according to these recommendations. We examine the Pearson Residuals and Deviance Residuals for case wise effect on the fit and did not detect any violations (Hosmer & Lemeshow, 2000; Menard, 2002). The highest condition number of the model is 1.9, which is well within the recommended cutoff limit. The Variance Inflation Factor (VIF) of the independent variables is below 5, suggesting that multicollinearity is not affecting the estimates (Belsley, Kuh, & Welsch, 1980; Neter, Wasserman, & Kutner, 2004).

To test the fit of the final model, the first step is to ascertain that the model contains all required variables, entered in the correct functional form. The next step is to evaluate the goodness-of-fit of the model. Thus knowing the values of all the independent variables in the model allows an accurate prediction of outcome, better than in case of no information in the independent variables. The next step is to evaluate how well the group of independent variables explains the outcome. In

Table 4. Analysis of maximum likelihood estimate of the LR coefficients

Parameter	Estimate	Std Error	Wald Chi-Sq	Pr> Chi-Sq
Intercept	-24081	0.12	358.35	<0.001
Cnt_Mod	12.19	14.48	70.81	< 0.0001
Cnt_Def	20.89	6.13	11.6	0.00007
Dwnlds	1.16	4.54	6.52	0.016
PType$_1$	0.316	0.33	0.9	0.345
PType$_2$	-0.395	0.23	3	0.0835
PType$_3$	0.127	0.21	0.36	0.5497
PType$_4$	0.526	0.26	4.12	0.0423
PType$_5$	-0.877	0.32	7.54	0.006
Use_PM	0.278	0.08	10.13	0.0015
Cnt_Msg	9.041	3.79	5.69	0.00171
Open_Def	-6.505	3.17	4.21	0.0401
Team_Size	0.057	0.02	14.25	0.002
Usr_Rpt	0.018	0.007	6.09	0.0136
PType$_1$* Use_Mail	0.849	0.33	6.68	0.0098
PType$_2$* Use_Mail	-0.364	0.23	2.61	0.1065
PType$_3$* Use_Mail	0.006	0.21	0	0.9758
PType$_4$* Use_Mail	-0.029	0.26	0.01	0.9082
PType$_5$* Use_Mail	-0.659	0.33	4.13	0.0422
Age$_{low}$	1.178	0.11	125.44	<0.0001
Age$_{med}$	-0.329	0.11	8.97	0.0027

LR models, the Log Likelihood (LL) criteria are used to select model parameters. We assess model fit by comparing the *-2LL* of the model with and without the independent variables. Reduction in the value of *-2LL* with and without the covariates, determines the fit of the model. The results show that the model is significant at *5%* significance level (*p < 0.0001*). The results of this test are shown in Table 5.

The area under the ROC curve tests the accuracy of the LR model. As a rule, the area under

Table 5. Likelihood ratio test for global null hypothesis

-2 Log Likelihood		Likelihood Ratio Chi-Sq	Df	Pr > Chi-Sq
Intercept Only	**Intercept & Covariate**			
1803.960	1292.126	511.834	20	< 0.0001

the curve indicates how well the model provides discrimination between the high and low values of the target variable. If ROC is 0.5 or less, it implies that the model offers no discrimination. A value of ROC in the range of 0.7 to 0.8 indicates that the model provides an acceptable discrimination between projects that develop and the ones that do not. If the ROC is between 0.8 and 0.9, it indicates that the model provides an excellent discrimination and ROC of higher than 0.9 indicates that the model provides outstanding discrimination between projects. Our final model has an area under the ROC curve of 0.839 on the test data. This indicates that the selected model provides excellent discrimination between OSS projects that developed and the ones that did not.

We also test the model for all three data samples and the area under ROC is over *0.8* for all three samples The ROC curve for the final model for the train, validate and test samples is shown in Figure 5. It shows that all fits are acceptable for the final model indicating a robust model that can be generalized over the population.

Additional fit statistics were also tested on the model. Figures 5 and 6 show Cumulative Lifts and Lift Chart for all three samples of train validate and test, respectively. If the model had not been robust, there would be notable differences among the training, validation and test plots. The charts show that the fit is acceptable for the final model selected and thus the model is robust.

Figure 5. Cumulative lift for all train, validate and test samples

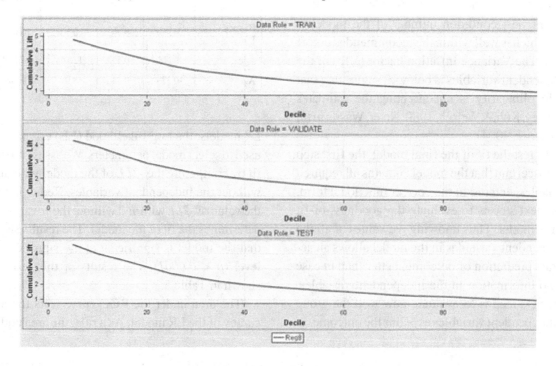

Figure 6. Lift charts for all train, validate and test samples

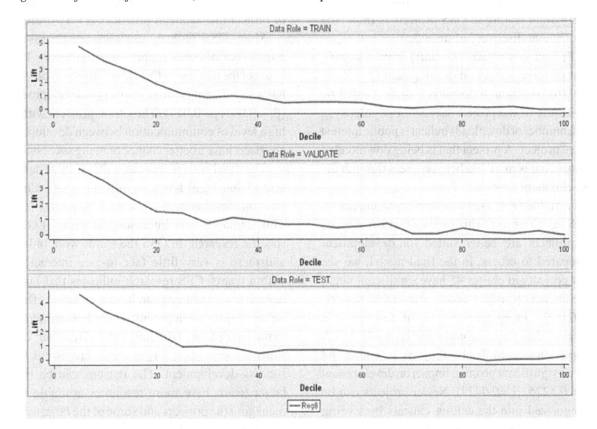

RESULTS

We now discuss the variables that are significant in the model and discuss how these factors impact OSS projects during development phase. The independent variables are selected at the significance level of 5%. The form of the estimation equation of the final model is shown in (2).

The count of the new modules (*Cnt_Mod*) is an indicator of the increase in the functionality of OSS project. As a project develops and new functionality is added the number of new modules increases. Although the sample of development projects contains only those projects that had been in the OSS community for over a year, the increase in functionality can vary with time. Therefore, the functionality of the projects is normalized for time. The functionality of the project (*Cnt_Mod*) has a

significant positive impact on development ($\beta_1=$ *12.9, p <0.0001*). This indicates the importance of continuous improvement in the project functionality considering the high level of competition in OSS projects.

The project defect count (*Cnt_Def*) has a significant positive relationship with project development ($\beta_2= 20.89, p= 0.007$). At first glance, this appears counter intuitive. However, a deeper look into the OSS development process indicates that the identification and reporting of defects cannot be an indicator of low quality. Mere reporting of defects indicates that the project is being used and the faults are being reported. In fact, the process of detecting and reporting defects has been one of the processes of OSS that has been associated with its success. This claim however had never been empirically tested. Therefore, this research provides the empirical evidence that the process of software testing in OSS projects is improved by efficient discovery of defects.

Project downloads (*Dwnlds*) have a significant positive impact on development ($\beta_3 = 1.16$, p=0.0106). Though downloads alone cannot be a measure of the project success or popularity, a high number of downloads indicates public interest in the project. A project that is being downloaded more often is more likely to progress through the development process.

Variable (*Prj_Typ*) has significant impact on OSS development. This implies that some types of projects are better suited for development compared to others. In the final model, we see that projects in cluster #5 have significant negative impact on project development ($\beta = -0.8799$, p=0.006). From the analysis of keywords, it appears that these projects are typically JAVA Applications and Tools. Projects in cluster #4 have a significant positive impact on development ($\beta = 0.5226$, p =0.0423). Newer projects can be categorized into the exiting clusters by scoring them based on the project description and the effects of the project type on project development can be analyzed.

Although the number of defects reported has positive influence on development, the number-of-defects-open (*Open_Def*) has a significant negative influence ($\beta_5 = -6.5052$, p =0.04). This indicates that whereas the reporting of the defects is a contributor to project development, the inability to remove the defects leads to decline in development. Thus if defects are being discovered but not removed, the odds of project development is reduced. There can be several reasons for this, e.g. large number of defects open can be indicative of the lack of sufficient effort. High complexity of the code and low maintainability can also cause the count of defects-open to increase.

The use of project management (*Use_PM*) has a significant positive impact on OSS development ($\beta_6 = 0.2787$, p=0.0015). Although OSS projects are developed through non-traditional methods of

software development, this result indicates that use of project management practices is very useful.

Many OSS projects use message boards as a means of discussion and communication. The count of the messages (*Cnt_Msg*) on project boards has a significant positive impact on development ($\beta_7 = 9.041$, p=0.017). Therefore, projects with a high level of communication between developers and users have a better chance of being successful.

The final model indicates that a large team size (*Team_Size*) has a significant positive impact on development ($\beta_8 = 0.0573$, p=0.0002). This finding is very interesting in terms of OSS specific research. In OSS the teams work online and there is very little face-to-face interaction within teams. CSS research indicates that large team sizes sometimes can have a negative effect on the project development, if members are added in the later phases (Boehm, 1987). However, our study indicates that larger teams are useful for success development. The reasons can be that larger teams have more resources available for managing the projects and some of the large team issues encountered in CSS are not applicable in OSS. In OSS, the participation in a project is voluntary. Therefore, the creation of teams takes place over time, depending upon the interest and expertise of the programmers. Once a team is formed, typical issues of conflict management and task distribution that occur in CSS are not directly valid in the OSS domain.

The number of defects reported by the end users (*Usr_Rpt*) of the project has a positive impact on project development ($\beta_9 = 0.0186$, p= 0.013). This reveals that OSS project end user can facilitate the development process by being an active member of the development process. The significant positive relationship provides support of the claim that the large community is an advantage that OSS holds over CSS projects.

There is a significant interaction effect of the project type and use of mail messaging. We find that use of mail in cluster # 1 projects has a significant positive impact on project development ($\beta = 0.8497$, $p=0.0098$). However, the use of mail messaging for projects in cluster #5 has a significant negative impact on development ($\beta = -0.6588$, $p=0.0422$). This finding emphasizes the significance of the newly created variable project type. It indicates that the nature of the project is very critical in the successful OSS development. It also indicates the importance of project domain specific practices in successful development.

Age of the project is used as a control variable. We find that projects registered more recently have a higher probability of progression in development compared to older projects. *Age_low* has a significant positive impact on project development ($\beta_{11} = 1.177$, $p <0.0001$). *Age_high* has a significant negative impact on project development ($\beta_{12} = -0.329$, $p=0.002$). This can be explained in two ways. The first explanation is based on literature in software evolution. Software evolution laws assert that as a software system ages, it declines in performance (Lehman & Ramil, 2001, 2002). Godfrey and Tu (2001) tested these laws in the OSS domain using Linux data. The scope of the current research does not encompass the complex questions about laws of software evolution, but variation in the pattern of development, based on the age, is indicative of an interesting future research question. Another explanation is that, as the OSS movement has matured so, has the processes and tools of project development and management. Therefore younger projects use advanced resources and have a higher chance of surviving.

DISCUSSION

We posed two questions in the beginning of this paper. The first question was if the successful development of OSS projects could be predicted. Building a predictive model of OSS development that can classify a given project correctly to an acceptable precision, answers this question affirmatively. The next question was to identify the

factors that impact OSS project development. Our analysis identifies a list of variables that impact OSS development. Projects that offer increased functionality; have more downloads and fewer unresolved issues are more likely to develop in OSS domain. Teams that use project management and have frequent communication between developers and users have a better chance of producing successful projects. The inability of a project team to remove defects can hamper development. We also found that OSS domain is well suited to specific types of projects. We also found that the end users can play a role in project development by actively participating in the process of defect detection.

Threats to Validity and Limitations

Establishing validity ensures that a study is reliable and repeatable. The main areas of validity are: Internal, Construct and External. Internal validity establishes that the changes in the dependent variable maybe due to other variations in a third variable. However the process of DM eliminates such threats by considering all the available variables it the initial analysis. Thus using a wide range of starting variables encounters the confounding threat. Selection bias is another threat of internal validity that is caused if the sample is not selected as a reflection of the actual population. Stratified random sampling was used to create the train, test and validate sets. The threat of maturation was removed by excluding projects registered within a year of data collection. Experimenter bias could have potential impact in Text Analysis, where subjective judgment is required to interpret the clusters. A researcher, not involved in the study performed a review of the key terms in clusters to ensure the integrity of results and to remove any selection bias.

Construct validity in traditional deductive research establishes that the measures correlate the theoretical constructs. However, in inductive research, the analysis is carried out at the measure level, refereed to first order constructs. The first order constructs in this case are at the operational level, similar to the concept of "inquiry from the inside" where the researcher is investigating the phenomenon at first order. However, we believe that there is room for further triangulation of our results that would lead to identification of second order constructs and construct validity in its traditional form. Therefore the methodology itself removes the threat to construct validity. We can however establish face validity given the nature of the measures and the attributes they reflect i.e. product, process, resource or user context.

The projects launched at least a year before the cut-off for data extraction was included in the analysis. This cut-off had to be implemented to ensure that there was sufficient number of contributions, defects and patches to conduct analysis. We acknowledge that the cut-off time might not be suitable for the entire OSS population. However, given the large sample size of the projects, we believe that the impact of this constraint would be minimal.

Implications

The results provide evidence that end user participation can promote project development. Using the project types created in this research, projects, tasks and users could be mapped for fitness. A study on these lines might be more useful for project that are already complete and are in the maintenance phase. The results also indicate the complex nature of project aging. Software evolution, aging and maturity have been a well-researched topic in CSS domain. Further studies in OSS domain are needed to explain how software matures with age and at some time in the lifecycle, starts to deteriorate. There is a need for predictive models to identify the lifecycle phases that affect software aging. As the OSS communities become more established, we need further studies on interplay between the development of an OSS project and the community that hosts it.

The model created in this research can be used as an evaluation tool to monitor or select OSS projects. The model allows developing a scoring mechanism for new projects. Using the data for the factors identified in the results, the chances of successful development of any OSS project can be predicted to 87% accuracy. This provides the user community with a mechanism to evaluate the available OSS projects and to make informed decisions regarding spending their effort, resources and capital on an OSS project. OSS project development teams can use this model to monitor project performance. They can keep track of their project by examining the critical factors that impact project success. Effective management of these factors could lead to successful project development.

Future Research

This model is robust and has an excellent predictive power. However, we need to recognize its limitations to improve future developments. Perhaps the most significant limitation of the current model is that it was developed using data only from the SF repository. Although SF is the largest community of OSS projects, it is by no means the only one. While we see no reason why the results could not be generalized to other OSS development communities, it still remains an empirical question. One way to address this limitation would be to test the model in other community environments. With access to other OSS communities, we can test this model over a wider range.

Second, we only considered direct relationship between the independent factors and project development. We did not look at complex mediating effects that might exist. For example, we looked at the direct impact of team experience on development, which was insignificant. However, we cannot rule out that it would have impact on other factors like the size and quality of the project. Similarly, there are many other factors that could have an indirect impact on project success. Future studies can explore multistage models.

Third, this was a cross-sectional analysis of the SF dataset. To examine the development lifecycle, a longitudinal study of a few projects or panel data analysis of a group of projects could provide further insight into OSS development. We believe that the variable project type could be useful to conduct analysis on specific type of OSS projects and could be used to identify a homogenous population for future research.

Finally, as discussed previously, many projects do not use the SF repository for defect reporting. All such projects were eliminated from the analysis to avoid missing data. Further studies are needed to evaluate the projects that do not have complete archives available through SF. However, access to the data archives can be a potential barrier in this case.

CONCLUSION

This model adds to the existing body of knowledge in OSS project development. To the best of our knowledge, this is the first empirical investigation into the effects and significance of end user involvement on OSS development. The model provides a quantitative tool to compare the performance of various OSS projects. It also identifies some key factors that contribute to OSS development. The identification of these factors is very important to the practitioner and research community. The development teams can better monitor the performance of their projects and adjust the independent variables to achieve the desired outcome. For businesses that wish to adopt OSS projects, this model allows them to study potential projects and make better decisions regarding adoption. For the research community the model provides a deeper understanding of the phenomenon of OSS development and a better way to predict software project outcomes. It provides

support for arguments made in many of the prior models. It also identifies some new factors that have not been used in prior research, therefore raises some questions for future research in OSS domain. This study also demonstrates the use of multiple predictive modeling techniques in model formulation process.

REFERENCES

Abdel-Hamid, T., K., & Madnick, S. E. (1983). The dynamics of software project scheduling. *Communications of the ACM, 26*(5), 340–346. doi:10.1145/69586.358135.

Banker, R. D., Davis, G. B., & Slaughter, S. A. (1998). Software development practices, software complexity and software maintenance performance. *Management Science, 44*(4). doi:10.1287/mnsc.44.4.433.

Banker, R. D., & Kemerer, C. F. (1989). Scale economies in new software development. *IEEE Transactions on Software Engineering, 15*(10), 1199–1205. doi:10.1109/TSE.1989.559768.

Barry, E. J., Kemerer, C. F., & Slaughter, S. A. (2006). Environmental volatility, development decisions, and software volatility: A longitudinal analysis. *Management Science, 52*(3), 448–464. doi:10.1287/mnsc.1050.0463.

Belsley, D. A., Kuh, E., & Welsch, R. E. (1980). *Regression diagnostics: Identifying influential data and sources of collinearity*. New York, NY: John Wiley & Sons.

Berry, M. J. A., & Linoff, G. S. (2004). *Data mining techniques: For marketing, sales and customer relationship management*. Indianapolis, IN: Wiley Publishing.

Boehm, B. (1984). Software engineering economics. *IEEE Transactions on Software Engineering, 1*(1), 4–21. doi:10.1109/TSE.1984.5010193.

Boehm, B. (1987). Improving software productivity. *IEEE Computer*, *20*(1), 43–57.

Bozdogen, H. (1987). Model selection & Akaike's information criterion (AIC): The general theory and its analytical extensions. *Psychometrika*, *52*, 345–370. doi:10.1007/BF02294361.

Cearley, D. W., Fenn, J., & Plummer, D. C. (2005). *Gartner's positions on the five hottest IT topics and trends in 2005*. Stamford, CT: Gartner Inc..

Chengalur-Smith, S., & Sidorova, A. (2003). Survival of open-source projects: A population ecology perspective. In *Proceedings of the 24th International Conference of Information Systems*, Atlanta, GA.

Crowston, K., Annabi, H., & Howison, J. (2003) Defining open source project. In *Proceedings of the International Conference of Information Systems*, Seattle, WA.

Crowston, K., Li, Q., Wei, K., Eseryel, U. Y., & Howison, J. (2007). Self-organization of teams for free/libre open source software development. *Information and Software Technology*, *49*(6), 564–575. doi:10.1016/j.infsof.2007.02.004.

Crowston, K., & Scozzi, B. (2002). Open source software projects as virtual organizations: Competency rallying for software development. *IEEE Software*, *149*(1), 3–17. doi:10.1049/ip-sen:20020197.

Delone, W. H., & McLean, E. R. (1992). Information systems success: The quest for the dependent variable. *Information Systems Research*, *3*(1), 60–95. doi:10.1287/isre.3.1.60.

Dinh-Trong, T. T., & Bieman, J. M. (2005). The freeBSD project: A replication case study of open source development. *IEEE Transactions on Software Engineering*, *31*(6), 481–495. doi:10.1109/TSE.2005.73.

Ewusi-Mensah, K. (1997). Critical issues in abandoned information systems development projects. *Communications of the ACM*, *40*(9), 74–80. doi:10.1145/260750.260775.

Fayyad, U. M., Piatetsky-Shapiro, G., & Smyth, P. (Eds.). (1996). *From data mining to knowledge discovery: An overview*. Menlo Park, CA: AAAI Press.

Feller, J., & Fitzgerald, B. (2002). *Understanding open source software development*. Reading, MA: Addison-Wesley.

Fenton, N. E., & Pfleeger, S. L. (1991). *Software metrics: A rigorous approach*. New York, NY: Chapman & Hall.

German, D. M. (2004). Mining CVS repositories, the softchange experience. In *Proceedings of the 1st International Workshop on Mining Software Repositories* (pp. 17-21).

Godfrey, M., & Tu, Q. (2001). Growth, evolution and structural change in open source software. In *Proceedings of the 4th International Workshop on Principles of Software Evolution*, Vienna, Austria.

Grewal, R., Lilien, G. L., & Mallapragada, G. (2006). Location, location, location: How network embeddedness affects project success in open source systems. *Management Science*, *52*(7), 1043–1046. doi:10.1287/mnsc.1060.0550.

Harter, D. E., Krishnan, M. S., & Slaughter, S. A. (2000). Effects of process maturity on quality, cycle time, and effort in software product development. *Management Science*, *46*(4), 451–466. doi:10.1287/mnsc.46.4.451.12056.

Hoffer, J. A., George, J. F., & Valacich, J. S. (1996). *Modern systems analysis and design*. Reading, MA: Benjamin Cummings Publishing.

Hosmer, D. W., & Lemeshow, S. (2000). *Applied logistic regression*. New York, NY: John Wiley & Son. doi:10.1002/0471722146.

Jensen, C., & Scacchi, W. (2005). Collaboration, leadership, control, and conflict negotiation and the netbeans.org open source software development community. In *Proceedings of the 38th Annual Hawaii International Conference* (p. 196b).

Koch, S. (2007). Software evolution in open source projects - a large-scale investigation. *Journal of Software Maintenance and Evolution: Research and Practice*, *19*(6). doi:10.1002/smr.348.

Krishnamurthy, S. (2002). Cave or community? An empirical examination of 100 mature open source projects. *First Monday*, *7*(6).

Lehman, M. M., Perry, D. E., & Ramil, J. F. (1998). Implications of evolution metrics on software maintenance. In *Proceedings of the International Conference on Software Maintenance* (pp. 208-217).

Lehman, M. M., & Ramil, J. F. (2001). Rules and tools for software evolution planning and management. *Annals of Software Engineering*, *11*, 15–44. doi:10.1023/A:1012535017876.

Lehman, M. M., & Ramil, J. F. (2002). Software evolution and software processes. *Annals of Software Engineering*, *14*, 275–309. doi:10.1023/A:1020557525901.

Menard, S. W. (2002). *Applied logistic regression analysis*. Thousand Oaks, CA: Sage.

Mockus, A., Fielding, R. T., & Herbsleb, J. (2002). Two case studies of open source software development: Apache and Mozilla. *ACM Transactions on Software Engineering and Methodology*, *11*(3), 309–346. doi:10.1145/567793.567795.

Neter, J., Wasserman, W., & Kutner, M. H. (2004). *Applied linear regression models*. New York, NY: McGraw-Hill.

Niazi, M., Wilson, D., & Zowghi, D. (2005). A framework for assisting the design of effective software process improvement implementation strategies. *Journal of Systems and Software*, *78*(2), 204–222. doi:10.1016/j.jss.2004.09.001.

Paulson, J. W., Succi, G., & Eberlein, A. (2004). An empirical study of open-source and closed-source software products. *IEEE Transactions on Software Engineering*, *30*(4). doi:10.1109/TSE.2004.1274044.

Rai, A., Lang, S. S., & Welker, R. B. (2002). Assessing the validity of IS success models: An empirical test and theoretical analysis. *Information Systems Research*, *13*(1), 50–69. doi:10.1287/isre.13.1.50.96.

Raja, U., & Tretter, M. J. (in press). Developing taxonomy of software patches: A text mining approach. *Journal of Software Maintenance and Evolution.*.

Ricadela, A. (2007). The worth of open source: Open question. *Business Week, 1*.

Roberts, J. A., Hann, I.-H., & Slaughter, S. (2006). Understanding the motivations, participation, and performance of open source software developers: A longitudinal study of the Apache projects. *Management Science*, *52*(7), 984–999. doi:10.1287/mnsc.1060.0554.

Robles, G., Gonzalez-Barahona, J. M., & Merelo, J. J. (2006). Beyond source code: The importance of other artifacts in software development (a case study). *Journal of Systems and Software*, *79*, 1233–1248. doi:10.1016/j.jss.2006.02.048.

Sabherwal, R., Jeyaraj, A., & Chowa, C. (2006). Information system success: Individual and organizational determinants. *Management Science*, *52*(12), 1849–1864. doi:10.1287/mnsc.1060.0583.

Singh, P. V., Tan, Y., & Mookerjee, V. (2007). Social capital, structural holes and team composition: Collaborative networks of the open source software community. In *Proceedings of the Twenty Eighth International Conferences on Information Systems*, Montreal, QC, Canada.

Stamelos, I., Angelis, L., Oikonomou, A., & Bleris, G. L. (2002). Code quality analysis in open source software development. *Information Systems Journal, 12*(1), 43–60. doi:10.1046/j.1365-2575.2002.00117.x.

Stewart, K. J. (2004). OSS project success: From internal dynamics to external impact. In *Proceedings of the 4th Workshop on Open Source Software Engineering*, Edinburgh, Scotland.

Stewart, K. J., Ammeter, A. P., & Maruping, L. M. (2006). Impacts of license choice and organizational sponsorship on user interest and development activity in open source software projects. *Information Systems Research, 17*(2), 126–144. doi:10.1287/isre.1060.0082.

Stewart, K. J., & Gosian, S. (2006). The impact of ideology on effectiveness in open source software development teams. *Management Information Systems Quarterly, 30*(2), 1–23.

Subramaniam, C., Sen, R., & Nelson, M. L. (2009). Determinants of open source software project success: A longitudinal study. *Decision Support Systems, 46*(2), 576–585. doi:10.1016/j.dss.2008.10.005.

Williams, C. C., & Hollingsworth, J. K. (2005). Automatic mining of source code repositories to improve bug finding techniques. *IEEE Transactions on Software Engineering, 31*(6), 466–480. doi:10.1109/TSE.2005.63.

Ying, A. T. T., Murphy, G. C., Ng, R., & Chu-Carroll, M. C. (2004). Predicting source code changes by mining change history. *IEEE Transactions on Software Engineering, 30*(9). doi:10.1109/TSE.2004.52.

Zimmermann, T., Zeller, A., Weissgerber, P., & Diehl, S. (2005). Mining version histories to guide software changes. *IEEE Transactions on Software Engineering, 31*(6), 429–445. doi:10.1109/TSE.2005.72.

This work was previously published in the International Journal of Information System Modeling and Design (IJISMD), Volume 2, Issue 4, edited by Remigijus Gustas, pp. 27-48, copyright 2011 by IGI Publishing (an imprint of IGI Global).

Chapter 15
Towards Method Component Contextualization

Elena Kornyshova
Université Paris I – Panthéon Sorbonne, France

Rébecca Deneckère
Université Paris I – Panthéon Sorbonne, France

Bruno Claudepierre
Université Paris I – Panthéon Sorbonne, France

ABSTRACT

Method Engineering (ME) is a discipline which aims to bring effective solutions to the construction, improvement and modification of the methods used to develop Information Systems (IS). Situational Method Engineering (SME) promotes the idea of retrieving, adapting and tailoring components, rather than complete methodologies, to the specific context. Existing SME approaches use the notion of context for characterizing situations of IS development projects and for guiding the method components selection from a repository. However, in the reviewed literature, there is no proposed approach to specify the specific context of method components. This paper provides a detailed vision of context and a process for contextualizing methods in the IS domain. This proposal is illustrated with three case studies: scenario conceptualization, project portfolio management, and decision-making.

INTRODUCTION

An IS development methodology (ISDM) is a set of ideas, approaches, techniques and tools which system analysts use to help them transforming organizational needs into an appropriate Information System. The application areas of these methodologies are various. Because of this diversity, it is now apparent that a universal method that could be applied to deal with any IS development project does not exist. Method engineering (ME) represents the effort to improve the usefulness of ISDM by creating an adaptation framework whereby methods are created to match specific organizational situations. ME aims to find solutions to the construction, improvement and

DOI: 10.4018/978-1-4666-4161-7.ch015

modification of the methods used to develop information systems. One of the ME fundamentals for optimizing, reusing, and ensuring flexibility and adaptability of these methods is their decomposition into modular parts (Harmsen, Brinkkemper, & Han Oei, 1994; Rolland, 2005). This purpose is the object of Situational Method Engineering (SME) which promotes the idea of retrieving, adapting and tailoring components, rather than complete methodologies, to the specific context.

Existing SME approaches consider the notion of context in order to guide the selection of a method component from a repository according to a given situation. They also deal with different kinds of context factors characterizing situations of IS development projects and offer various methodologies for using context. For instance, the method component context is studied in different approaches and is represented as: reuse frame (Mirbel, 2008); interface (Ralyté & Rolland, 2001b); method service context (Guzélian & Cauvet, 2007); contingency factors (Van Slooten & Hodes, 1996; Harmsen, 1997); development situation (Karlsson & Agerfalk, 2004). These approaches foresee different context elements which are the characteristics of method components.

However, the reviewed literature shows that, firstly, there is no approach considering all of the possible characteristics and, secondly, these approaches do not suggest a methodology allowing to define a set of concrete context characteristics for a given method.

In our view, the context is a set of characteristics which describes situations of a method application. The context is defined for an IS development method and its components. Each method component is then described by concrete values of these characteristics. In this paper, we focus on the contextualization of method components. Our goal is to propose (1) a generic model of context based on the state-of-the-art and (2) an IS development methods contextualization process. We introduce the frame of contextualization, we

present the context model, the context typology and the process to construct the context characteristics set for a given method. We illustrate our proposal with three case studies: scenario conceptualization, project portfolio management and decision-making.

All processes in this work are formalized with the MAP model which is commonly used in the ME field (Rolland, Prakah, & Benjamen, 1999). In our proposal, this formalism is used to represent the contextualization process in an intentional way. In the case studies, it is used to represent the organization of the method components (the links between them).

The paper is organized as follows. The notion of method component is described in the second section. Third section surveys a state-of-the-art on the notion of context. The fourth section proposes a context model and a process for the contextualization of method components. We illustrate our proposal with examples in the fifth section. Related works are given in the sixth section. A conclusion and future works are given in the last section.

CONTEXT AND ITS APPLICATION IN METHOD ENGINEERING

Cross Domains Application of Context-Awareness

Bouquet, Ghidini, Giunchiglia, and Blanzieri (2003) state that the study of context was started in the 70s. Since then, many different domains in relation with information systems use the notion of context and give various interpretations of it. For instance, Dey, Abowd, and Salber (2001) defines the notion of context by the information that could be used for characterizing the situation of an entity (person, object or computer), and, more generally, by any element that can influence the IS behavior. Rey and Coutaz (2002) foresee the context from four points of view:

- The context must be defined in terms of an object. It means that "there is no context without context."
- The capture of context is not the goal in itself but the captured data must serve a purpose.
- The context is an information space shared by multiple actors (users and systems).
- The context is infinite and varies with the passing of time.

Context models are multidisciplinary and have been proposed in several areas (Bradley & Dunlop, 2005). The linguistic research is concerned with analyzing the usage context of signs (or words) within a language. Bunt (1997) defines five types of context for communication aspects which are respectively:

- **Linguistic:** Refers to linguistic material.
- **Semantic:** Refers to domain description including objects and properties.
- **Physical:** Refers to the environment description in which action or interaction occurs.
- **Social:** Refers to the interactive situation which occurs between actors.
- **Cognitive:** Refers to the participants' intentions, their evolution relating to perception, production, evaluation and execution.

Context is also formalized using mathematical models. For instance, Coutaz and Rey (2002) propose a cumulative model where the context (Ctx) is a timely aggregation of situations. A situation is a state descriptor for a user (U) performing a task (T) at a specific time (t). The model is depicted by the following formula:

$$Ctx(U,T,t) - \bigcup_{n=1}^{m} (Situation(U,T,t_n))$$

Related to the information technologies field, the context is represented as a model or an ontology. For instance, Gu, Wang, Pung, and Zhang (2004) suggest a more detailed vision of context. It describes a formal context model based on ontology for intelligent environments. This context ontology defines a vocabulary for representing knowledge about context in this field. It includes two levels: upper ontology (capturing general context knowledge) and domain-specific ontologies (detailing basic concepts in application to a given domain). Gu, Wang, Pung, and Zhang (2004) also specifies a way for modeling context classification, dependency between context elements, and quality of context.

In the field of Knowledge Representation and Reasoning (KRR), which is an area of Artificial Intelligence, two types of the context theory have been proposed: (1) *divide-and-conquer*, which sees context as a way of partitioning a global model of the world into smaller and simpler pieces and (2) *compose-and-conquer*, which sees context as a local theory of the world in a network of relations with other local theories (Bouquet, Ghidini, Giunchiglia, & Blanzieri, 2003).

Another term, closely related to the context one, is *context-awareness*. Context awareness is a term originating from pervasive computing, or ubiquitous computing (Schilit, Adams, & Want, 1994). These systems deal with linking changes in the environment with computer systems, which are otherwise static. Although it is a computer science term, it has also been applied to business theory in relation to business process management issues (Rosemann & Recker, 2006).

There are numerous context-awareness applications when human interactions occur. More related to our study, context models are also proposed for business process reengineering (Bessai, Claudepierre, Saidani, & Nurcan, 2008), computer science (Bradley & Dunlop, 2005), service selection (Kirsch Pinheiro, Vanrompay,

& Berbers, 2008) and decision-making within a military situation (Rosen, Fiore, Salas, Letsky, & Warner, 2008; Drury & Scott, 2008). In latter cases, the context model is seen as a way to analyze a given *situation* to guide the way of processing. Thus, context models are mainly used to solve the problem of lacking flexibility and adaptability within processes.

Method Engineering and Method Components

Method Engineering is a discipline which aims to bring effective solutions to the construction, improvement and modification of the methods used to develop information and software systems. Several authors tried to design methods that would be as effective and as adapted as possible to the development needs of information systems (Firesmith & Henderson-Sellers, 2001; Rolland & Cauvet, 1992). This goal was not always reached, especially because the methods were not always well adapted to projects specificities. The situational methods were designed to correct this weakness. The situational approach finds its justification in the practical field analysis which shows that a method is never followed literally (Ralyte, 2001; Mirbel & de Rivieres, 2002). Situational Method Engineering promotes the idea of using components, instead of complete methodologies, to specific situations (Ralyté & Rolland, 2001a). In order to succeed in creating good methodologies that best suit given situations, components (building blocks of methodologies) representation and cataloguing are very important activities. In particular, the components have to be represented in a uniform way that includes all the necessary information that may influence their retrieval and assembling.

The notion of method component is central of SME as it promotes the idea of retrieving, adapting and tailoring modular parts, rather than complete methodologies, to specific situations. There are various representations of modular parts: fragments (Brinkkemper, 1996), chunks (Rolland, Plihon, & Ralyté, 1998), components (Wistrand & Karlsson, 2004), OPF fragments (Henderson-Sellers, 2002) and method services (Deneckère, Iacovelli, Kornyshova, & Souveyet, 2008; Guzélian & Cauvet, 2007; Iacovelli, Souveyet, & Rolland, 2008).

Method Fragment Approach (Brinkkemper, 1996). Fragments are standardized building blocks based on a coherent part of method. A fragment is either a Product or a Process fragment and is stored on a method base from which they can be retrieved to construct a new method following assembly rules (Bunt, 1997). The method component definition consists in encouraging a global analysis of the project while basing itself on contingency criteria. Projects and situations are characterized by means of factors associated with the methods.

Method Chunk Approach (Ralyté, Deneckère, & Rolland, 2003). A chunk is described as a way to capture more of the situational aspects in ME and to appropriately support the retrieval process. A chunk based method aims at associating the reusable components to their description in order to facilitate component research and extraction according to the user's needs. The chunk approach expresses projects requirements (the context) as a requirements map, which is used to test the similarity between requirements and existing components.

Method Component (Wistrand & Karlsson, 2004). Components allow viewing methods as constituted by exchangeable and reusable components. Each component consists of descriptions for process (rules and recommendations), notations (semantic, syntactic and symbolic rules for documentation), and concepts. This approach introduces the notion of method rationale which is the systematic treatment of the arguments and reasons behind a particular method. In the same way, the component description contains its rationale. Its matching with the context is performed by goal analysis.

OPEN Process Framework (OPF) Fragment (Henderson-Sellers, 2002). In the OPEN Process Framework (OPF), the fragment is generated from an element in a prescribed underpinning meta-model. This meta-model has been upgraded with the availability of the international standard ISO/IEC 24744.

Method Service (Guzélian & Cauvet, 2007). This approach offers a repository with a large variety of method fragments, called method services, together with a service composition process. During composition, the process guides developer's choices; it selects method services and delivers a method fragment that achieves developer's requirements. The SO2M meta-model is based on three main principles: service orientation, task ontology for reuse of knowledge on development problems and dynamic construction of method services for generating tailored methods. The method service approach uses an identification part that defines the purpose of the service. The component retrieval is thus done by using goal, actor, process, and product ontologies.

Deneckère, Iacovelli, Kornyshova, and Souveyet (2008) structure the process of SME according to three steps of manipulating method components:

1. The decomposition of methods into components which are stored in a method repository,
2. The retrieval of components that better match the project specificities, and
3. The construction of a new method with these selected components.

According to these steps, different method components could be compared according to the four following criteria: decomposition principle, retrieval/selection principle, matching with situation, and construction technique (Table 1).

First, the methods are decomposed into methods components which are stored in method base (or repository). Thus, we define the criterion *decomposition principle* which deals with different ways to decompose methods into components. This principle predefines the components' description used for their identification during project fulfillment.

Once the methods are decomposed and stored in the base, they could be used in the projects. On the first step, the engineer must find in the method base the components that better match the project specificities. On this basis, we identify two criteria: retrieval/selection principle and matching with situation. The *retrieval/selection principle* defines steps to carry out for identifying an appropriate component. In ME, all approaches are situational, which means they take into account

Table 1. Method components comparison

Criteria	Fragment	Chunk	Component	OPF Fragment	Method Service
Decomposition principle		by intentions	by goal	inheritance, instantiation	Not specified
Retrieval/selection principle	Request	similarity measure	request by goal	request by goal	semantic similarity
Matching with situation	project characterisation	requirements map		by goal and actor	by goal, actor, process, and product ontologies
Construction technique	assembly	assembly, extension	assembly, extension, reduction	agile	assembly without overlapping

the specific project situation by different manners. This aspect is considered within the *matching with situation* attribute.

The next step is to build a new method from the selected components. Based on Nehan and Deneckère (2007), we distinguish the following main manners to use components for *constructing a new method* according to project specificities: assembly, extension, and reduction. By assembly, separate fragments are grouped with regard to the studied specific project to form a unique method (Ralyté, Deneckere, & Rolland, 2003). By applying extension, a basic method is transformed into a new one by addition of new components (Ralyté, Deneckere, & Rolland, 2003). By reduction, some components are removed from the basic method in order to transform it to match the engineer's needs (Wistrand & Karlsson, 2004).

Decomposition Principle. The decomposition principle is quite different following the component type. Method fragment uses a tree decomposition to link all coherent method parts. Chunks are obtained by intentional decomposition of methods (Ralyté, Deneckere, & Rolland, 2003). The OPF fragment is a *clabject*, which is a result of both instantiation and inheritance (Gonzales-Perez, 2007). Components are decomposed by goals (Wistrand & Karlsson, 2004). The method service approach does not specify this attribute value.

Retrieval/Selection Principle. The retrieval and selection of a method fragment are made by different types of queries. Chunks are selected with the application of similarity measures of their descriptors and interfaces. This helps to evaluate the degree of matching between them and the requirements (Ralyté, Deneckere, & Rolland, 2003). On the same way, the method service selection is made by a comparison of the requirements (expressed by intentions) with the service intentional descriptors by ontologies, which allow comparing the semantic similarity (Guzélian & Cauvet, 2007). Differently, OPF fragments, stored on a 'work product tool', are selected with queries on their endeavour (Gonzales-Perez, 2007). Method

fragments are selected by application of request on the goal (Harmsen, Brinkkemper, & Oei, 1994).

Matching with Situation. Approaches don't match the situation with the same techniques. The method fragment definition consists in encouraging a global analysis of the project while basing itself on contingency criteria. Projects and situations are characterized by means of factors associated with the methods. The chunk approach includes projects requirements expressed as a *requirements map* (Ralyté, Deneckere, & Rolland, 2003), which is used to test the similarity between requirements and existing fragments. In component containing its "rational", the matching is performed by goal analysis (Wistrand & Karlsson, 2004). The Method service approach uses an identification part that defines the purpose of the service. The matching is thus done by using goal, actor, process, and product ontologies (Guzélian & Cauvet, 2007).

Construction Technique. The method fragments are assembled for creating a new method. The chunk approach uses assembly (allowing overlapping between different chunks) and extension. In addition to the assembling and extending, the component approach suggests method reduction. The method service construction is based on a composition process that supports the aggregation of services in sequence or in parallel (Guzélian & Cauvet, 2007). In the OPF approach, a new method is constructed by dynamic instantiation of fragments during the project. Hence, the OPF approach suggests an agile construction of methods.

A more detailed comparison of these different kinds of modular parts may be found in Deneckère, Iacovelli, Kornyshova, and Souveyet (2008).

Our view of a component has been described in Deneckère, Iacovelli, Kornyshova, and Souveyet (2008). We based our method component on the method chunk for its intrinsic intentionality as we decompose the methods into method components according to an intentional principle. This part will then be used for retrieving and selecting method components from the method base. We suggest modelling method components as shown in Figure 1.

Method components are expressed at different granularity, at various levels of abstraction. For instance, a component may be an entire method that can be decomposed into other less complex components (which, in turn, may also be decomposed into other more simple components, and so on). They are a representation of the components composition.

The *intention* describes the general purpose of the component. The *product part* corresponds to the description of the component input and output product models. The *source product part* defines the product required for applying the component. The *target product part* defines the result, which must be obtained by the component application. The *process part* contains guidelines which explain how to apply the component in order to obtain the product part.

For instance, a method component *Weighting* is given in Figure 2 for illustrating this model. This component is part of decision-making methods. It allows defining weights to criteria in a given decision-making situation. The Weighting component is described by its ID ant its name. Its intention is to *Define relative importance of criteria*. The source product part is composed of criteria organized into a set. The target product part includes also a weight class. The process part describes the main steps to follow for defin-

ing weights, namely: scale criteria according to their importance, attribute values from 1 to 100 to each criterion, and calculate relative importance. Finally, it shows how to create the corresponding class if necessary.

Method Components Context

Based on the study of different SME approaches dealing with method components, we have identified five main approaches dealing with context in the method engineering field.

- **Reuse Frame:** The reuse frame (Mirbel, 2008) is a framework representing different factors which affect IS development projects. These factors are called *criteria*. Reuse frame allows specifying a context of method fragments reuse, searching method fragments and comparing between them in order to find an alternative fragment to a used one. The reuse frame model includes a reuse situation (which is a set of criteria classified into three dimensions: *organizational*, *technique* and *human*) and reuse *intention*.

- **Interface:** In Ralyté and Rolland (2001b) the method fragment context is defined by its interface which includes a situation and an intention. The situation represents the conditions in which the method frag-

Figure 1. Method component meta-model

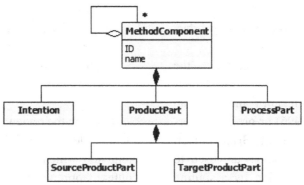

Figure 2. Decision-making method component weighting

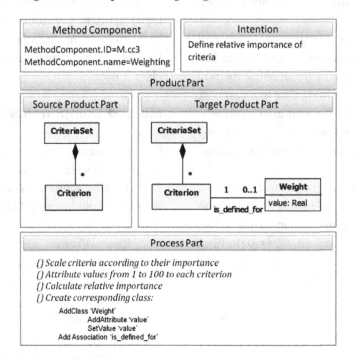

ment can be applied in terms of required inputs product(s). The intention is a goal that the method fragment helps to achieve. Therefore, the interface model includes two elements: the *situation* and the *intention*. These two first approaches have been unified in Mirbel and Ralyté (2006).

- **Method Service Context:** The method service context (Guzélian & Cauvet, 2007) aims at describing the situation in project development for which the method service is suitable and defining the purpose of the service. Its model includes *domain* characteristics (project nature, project domain) and *human* (actor), *process* and *product* ontologies.

- **Contingency Factors:** Situations (the context) are described by a set of characteristics called contingency factors (Van Slooten & Hodes, 1996) or project factors (Harmsen, 1997; Harmsen, Brinkkemper, & Oei, 1994). These factors are used to define the project situation by assigning

values to them. In Van Slooten and Hodes (1996), four categories are given: *domain characteristics* (describing the content of the system), *external factors* (laws and norms), *technical factors* (related to the development platform) and *human factors* (representing the development expertise of people).

- **Development Situation:** Karlsson and Agerfalk (2004) define the development situation as an abstraction of one or more existing/future software development projects with common characteristics. This situation is used to characterize the specific projects and to select configuration packages (method fragments). The development situation model includes a characteristics set.

Based on the review of these five approaches, we have identified height characteristics (context elements) which allow us to compare existing context approaches (Table 2). This compari-

Table 2. Comparative analysis of approaches dealing with context in ME Field: context elements

Approach	Characteristics							
	Goal/ Intention	Organizational	Technical	Human	Domain	External	Process	Product
Reuse Frame	X	X	X	X				
Interface	X							X
Method service context				X	X		X	X
Contingency factors			X	X	X	X		
Development situation	Not specified							

son highlights that there is no approach which consider all possible characteristics. Moreover, the analysis of these context approaches shows that they do not suggest a way to specify context characteristics. For instance, the context of the DM method component illustrated in Figure 2 must be defined in order to state in what kind of situation this component is useful. However, the existing literature does not provide means for defining its context.

CONTEXTUALIZATION OF METHOD COMPONENTS

Our Proposal

In SME, all approaches are situational, which means they take into account the specific project situation (or *Context*). However, the definition or description of this context is often just superficially addressed.

Our proposal uses the context expressiveness to describe the situation in which a component may be applied. It is then based on the *semantic* type of context previously presented. Moreover, our view of a component includes an intention oriented approach which allows representing the *cognitive* aspect of the context.

The preceding comparative analysis of context approaches shows that they address several aspects of context. However, they do not cover all of them and do not help in the context characteristics specification. Our goal is to enhance the definition of the context of IS development method for the further selection of components from a repository according to a given situation. In the following we present our vision of context and a process to define the context for a given method.

Enhanced Definition of Method Context

We propose to consider the context granularity at two levels: the method and method component ones (See Figure 3 for the proposal overview). Each method is available in a given context. As a method is composed of some components, each of them can be also described by specifying its context. Therefore, the method context is an aggregation of contexts associated to its components.

In our proposal, we describe the context as a set of characteristics. These characteristics describe situations of a method application. The detailed context model is presented in Figure 4.

The central element of this model is characteristic. A set of characteristics constitute the context. *Context characteristics* indicate specific

Figure 3. Proposal overview

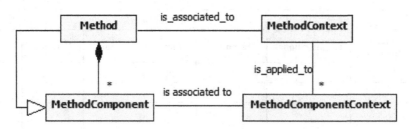

Figure 4. Context model

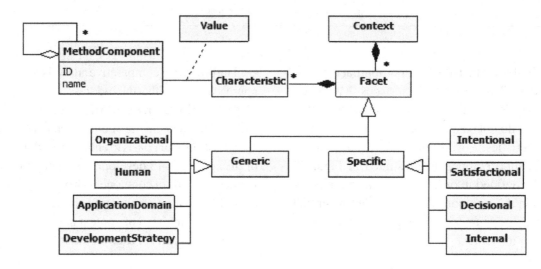

conditions to use the component. Characteristics are organized into *facets* for better representation and comprehension. We distinguish two types of characteristics (and consequently two types of facets): *generic* and *specific*. The first ones are common for most IS engineering projects; the latter ones vary from one project to another. To distinguish between them is important because of their different identification approaches. The context characteristics set is defined for a method component. Therefore, each method component is described by the valuations of these characteristics (*value*).

In the following, we describe different context characteristics by facets.

Generic characteristics. In order to establish the typology of generic characteristics we have used IS development project characteristics

(Kornyshova, Deneckère, & Salinesi, 2007). In this work, a project characteristics typology is proposed in order to guide method components retrieval and to prioritize the selected components.

The suggested typology of context characteristics covers essential aspects of IS engineering projects. Based on Mirbel and Ralyté (2006), Van Slooten and Hodes (1996), and Kornyshova, Deneckère and Salinesi (2007), it includes four facets: organizational, human, application domain, and development strategy.

The *organizational* facet (Table 3) highlights organizational aspects of IS project development. For instance, the *Management Commitment* characteristic represents the management team involvement in the project. Possible values for this characteristic are Low, Normal and High (i.e. a High value means a high involvement and so on).

Table 3. Organizational facet characteristics

a. Characteristic	b. Type	c. Value Domain
d. Management commitment degree	e. Quantative	f. 3-grade scale
	Qualitative	ENUM:{low, normal, high}
Importance degree	Quantative	3-grade scale
	Qualitative	ENUM:{low, normal, high}
Impact degree	Quantative	3-grade scale
	Qualitative	ENUM:{low, normal, high}
Time pressure degree	Quantative	3-grade scale
	Qualitative	ENUM:{low, normal, high}
Shortage of re-sources degree	Quantative	3-grade scale
	Qualitative	ENUM:{low, normal, high}
Level of innova-tion degree	Quantative	3-grade scale
	Qualitative	ENUM:{low, normal, high}
Size	Quantative	3-grade scale
	Qualitative	ENUM:{low, normal, high}
Cost	Quantative	REAL
	Qualitative	ENUM:{low, normal, high}
Nature of limited resources	Qualitative	ENUM:{financial, hu-man, temporal, informational }
Innovation nature	Qualitative	ENUM:{business innovation, technology innovation}
Duration	Quantative	REAL

Table 4. Human facet characteristics

Characteristic	Type	Value Domain
Resistance degree	Quantative	3-grade scale
	Qualitative	ENUM:{low, normal, high}
Conflict degree	Quantative	3-grade scale
	Qualitative	ENUM:{low, normal, high}
Expertise degree	Quantative	3-grade scale
	Qualitative	ENUM:{low, normal, high}
Clarity degree	Quantative	3-grade scale
	Qualitative	ENUM:{low, normal, high}
Stability degree	Quantative	3-grade scale
	Qualitative	ENUM:{low, normal, high}
Expert role	Qualitative	ENUM:{tester, developer, designer, analyst}
User involvement	Qualitative	ENUM:{real, virtual}
Stakeholder number	Quantative	NUMBER

The *human* facet (Table 4) describes the qualities of persons involved in IS project development. For example, the *User involvement* characteristic represents the kind of participation of the users in the project. Its values may be real or virtual.

The *application domain* facet (Table 5) includes indicators characterizing the domain of IS project. For instance, the *Application type* characteristic deals with the different kinds of projects according to the organization structure and can have the following values: intra-organization application, inter-organization application, organization-customer application.

The *development strategy* facet (Table 6) gathers indicators about different characteristics of development strategy. For instance, the *Source system* characteristic represents the origin of the reused elements that may be code, functional domain or interface.

Specific characteristics. Their identification is based on the method description. The method engineer defines them by analyzing different aspects which are organized into four facets: intentional, satisfaction, decisional and internal, like in Harmsen (1997).

The *intentional* facet concerns the method intentions. The *satisfaction* facet indicates the satisfaction degree that the engineer has about the method application results. The *decisional* facet arises from a decision-making process in the method. The *internal* facet concerns the

Table 5. Application domain facet characteristics

Characteristic	Type	Value Domain
Formality degree	Quantative	3-grade scale
	Qualitative	ENUM:{low, normal, high}
Relationships degree	Quantative	3-grade scale
	Qualitative	ENUM:{low, normal, high}
Dependency degree	Quantative	3-grade scale
	Qualitative	ENUM:{low, normal, high}
Complexity degree	Quantative	3-grade scale
	Qualitative	ENUM:{low, normal, high}
Repetitiveness degree	Quantative	3-grade scale
	Qualitative	ENUM:{low, normal, high}
Variability degree	Quantative	3-grade scale
	Qualitative	ENUM:{low, normal, high}
Application type	Qualitative	ENUM:{intra-organization, inter-organization, organization-customer }
Application technology	Qualitative	ENUM:{application to develop includes a database, application to develop is distributed, application to develop includes a GUI}
Dividing project	Qualitative	ENUM:{one single system, establishing system-oriented subprojects, establishing process-oriented subprojects, establishing hybrid subprojects}
Variable artefacts	Qualitative	ENUM:{organisational, human, application domain, and development strategy}

Table 6. Development strategy facet characteristics

Characteristic	Type	Value Domain
Source system	Qualitative	ENUM:{code reuse, functional domain reuse, interface reuse}
Project organization	Qualitative	ENUM:{standard, adapted}
Development strategy	Qualitative	ENUM:{outsourcing, iterative, prototyping, phase-wise, tile-wise}
Realization strategy	Qualitative	ENUM:{at once, incremental, concurrent, overlapping}
Delivery strategy	Qualitative	ENUM:{at once, incremental, evolutionary}
Tracing project	Qualitative	ENUM:{weak, strong}
Goal number	Quantative	NUMBER
	Qualitative	ENUM:{one goal, multi-goals}

Table 7. Specific map characteristics

Characteristic	Type	Value Domain
Goal satisfaction degree	Quantative	3-grade scale.
	Qualitative	ENUM:{low, normal, high}
Goal achievement degree	Quantative	3-grade scale
	Qualitative	ENUM:{low, normal, high}
Section satisfaction degree	Quantative	3-grade scale
	Qualitative	ENUM:{low, normal, high}
Section completeness degree	Quantative	3-grade scale
	Qualitative	ENUM:{low, normal, high}

known criteria associated with the specific project management. For the specific map characteristics see Table 7.

Table 8 shows the correspondence between the proposed typology and the existing context elements (analyzed in the previous section). We can make some remarks to compare them:

- Our typology covers all existing elements.
- We propose to identify more precisely process and product characteristics using our approach instead of using product and process as context characteristics directly.

- We add decisional characteristics which are not presented in the existing typologies.

Our typology indicates the main characteristics that can be defined in function of a given situation. It can be completed if new characteristics arise. Figure 5 illustrates the obtained characteristics typology as an ontology, like in Gu, Wang, Pung, and Zhang (2004).

Table 8. Correspondence between the proposed typology and existing context elements

Proposed Typology	Context Elements (cf. Table 2)
Organizational	Organizational
Human	Human
Application domain	Domain
Development strategy	Technical
Intentional	Goal/ Intention
Satisfaction	External, Process, Product
Decisional	Process, Product
Internal	Technical, Process, Product

Contextualization Methodology

In order to define the context for a given method and its components, we propose an approach based on the contextualization process modeled with the MAP formalism.

Map Formalism

A MAP illustrates a given process of IS engineering. The MAP model (Rolland, Prakash, & Benjamen, 1999) is a representation of process models expressed in intentional terms. It allows specifying process models in a flexible way by focusing on the process intentions, and on the various ways to achieve each of these intentions.

The meta-model of MAP (Rolland & Prakash, 2001) is represented as a UML class diagram (Figure 6).

A Map is a combination of at least two sections. Each Map has a code and a description which allow identifying it. The Map code depends on the Map position according to the refinement levels. The Map description gives a main purpose of the Map, or in other words, its main intention.

The Map model enables to represent non-deterministic sequences of activities. It is expressed through the combination of different intentions and strategies used for achieving these intentions. Actually, an engineer has several intentions or goals that he(she) wants to achieve. Furthermore, there are several ways of achieving these intentions. The Map model allows considering intentions and strategies in ISE processes in order to perform them in a flexible manner.

An *Intention* is a goal that can be achieved by the performance of an activity. Each map has two special intentions, *Start* and *Stop*, to begin and

Figure 5. Characteristics ontology

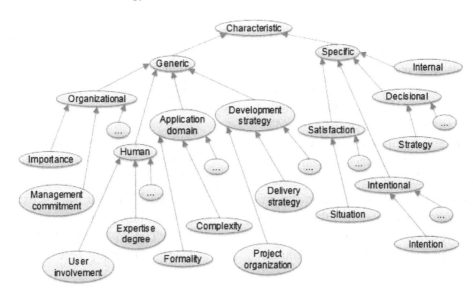

Figure 6. Map Meta-model

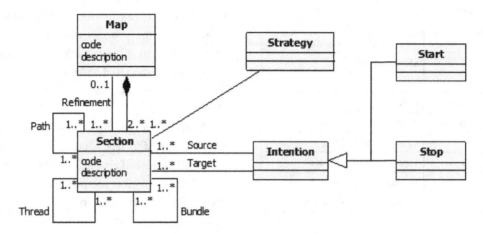

to end the map respectively (Rolland & Prakash, 2001). Prat (1997) suggests a model to describe the intention in details. This model has already been applied to the method engineering field in order to represent the intention of the method chunks (Ralyte, 2001). Following this model, the intention is expressed in natural language and is composed of a verb and at least one parameter. Each parameter has a particular role with regard to the verb. An example is the *Identify DM Requirements* intention. The detailed description of the intention elements could be found in Prat (1997) and Ralyte (2001).

A *Strategy* is an approach, a manner to achieve an intention (Rolland & Prakash, 2001). Each strategy relates two intentions. The strategy concept allows, firstly, separating the goal and the manner to achieve this goal and, secondly, expressing alternative approaches for the goals achievement. An example is the *By problem exploring* strategy.

A *Section* is the main element of the Map model. It represents a combination of two intentions and a strategy relating these intentions. In other words, a section encapsulates knowledge about an activity in a triplet <Source intention; Strategy; Target intention>, in other terms, knowledge corresponding to a particular process step to achieve an intention (the target intention)

from a specific situation (the source intention) following a particular technique (the strategy). A section is characterized by a code and a description. The Sections code depends on its position on the Map. The Section description embodies the triplet <Source intention; Strategy; Target intention>. An example can be mentioned: <*Start; By problem exploring; Identify DM Requirements*>.

A section of a map can be refined by another map. This is shown through the refinement relationship between the section and the map. Refinement is an abstraction mechanism by which a complex assembly of sections at level $i+1$ is viewed as a unique section at level i. This relationship introduces levels in the process representation as each map may be represented as a hierarchy of maps.

Sections in a map are related to each other by three kinds of relationships namely thread, path and bundle.

- A *thread relationship* shows the possibility for a target intention to be achieved in several ways from the same source intention. Each of these ways is expressed as a section in the map.
- A *path relationship* establishes a precedence relationship between sections. For

a section to succeed another, its source intention must be the target intention of the preceding one.

- A *bundle relationship* shows the possibility for several sections having the same source and target intentions to be mutually exclusive.

A Map is graphically presented as a directed diagram, where *intentions* are nodes and *strategies* are edges, and each *section* corresponds to two nodes related to each other by an edge (Figure 7). The directed nature of this diagram shows the precedence links between intentions. An edge enters a node if its associated strategy can be used to achieve the target intention (the given node).

An example of a map is given in Figure 8.

This map contains three intentions, namely: *Start, Identify DM Requirement*, and *Stop*. There are four strategies: *By problem exploring, By variability exploring, Tool-based strategy*, and *By expertise* which correspond to the four sections:

<Start; By problem exploring; Identify DM Requirements>;

<Start; By variability exploring; Identify DM Requirements>;

<Identify DM Requirements; Tool-based strategy; Stop>;

<Identify DM Requirements; By expertise; Stop>.

Each map is completed by a set of guidelines that help engineers in navigating through the map. There are three types of guidelines: simple, tactical and strategic. A *simple* guideline may give informal content advice on how to proceed in handling the situation in a narrative form. A *tactical* guideline is a complex guideline, which uses a tree structure to link its sub-guidelines. A *strategic* guideline is a complex guideline which shows that a section of a map can be refined by another map. This relationship implies that each map may be represented as a hierarchy of maps.

Figure 7. Map model graphical representation

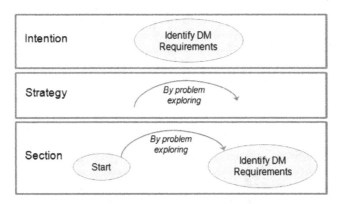

Figure 8. Map example

The MAP model defines the process through the combination of observable situations in which a certain number of specific intentions can be achieved. The work to be made is described in the process as depending on both situation and intention. In other words, it depends on the context in which a method engineer must act at a given point in time. By modelling *intentions* and the ways (*strategies*) to reach them, the process has the ability to represent the *cognitive* context as defined by Bunt. Moreover, by relating method service (Rolland, 2008) (or method component (Ralyté, Deneckère, & Rolland, 2003) to a section, Rolland extends the context expressiveness of the MAP to the *semantic* context of Bunt. This approach allows identifying several context aspects. More precisely, this model includes a set of guidelines which help an engineer navigate through the process model. The navigation is carried out by *arguments* that allow the engineer to choose the adapted variant within the process model. These arguments express the context of a given process model.

Contextualization Map

The Map model is used in our approach for modeling the contextualization process (Figure 9). This process includes two possible ways to define the context: top-down or bottom-up. By the top-down approach, the engineer defines the method context and then instantiate it for each method component. By the bottom-up approach, the engineer specifies the contexts of all method components and assemblies them into the method context.

Both method and method component contexts can be defined following two strategies: *By deduction* and *By generation*. It depends on the characteristic type. The generic characteristics are *deduced* from the generic context typology and the specific ones are *generated* from method description. These strategies could be applied as many times as possible characteristics exist.

This MAP has two main intentions: *Define method context* and *Define method component context*. The achievement of these intentions implies the definition of the context characteristics set for method or for method components respectively. The definition of method components contexts includes also the attribution of values to the defined characteristics.

Figure 9. Contextualization map

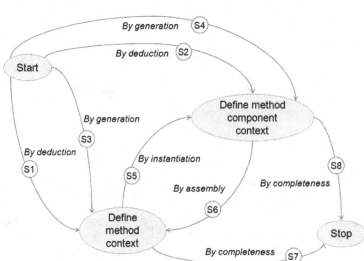

The contextualization Map includes eight sections, as shown in Table 9.

All these sections are explained below. Operators are defined for each section in order to indicate how to proceed for carrying out its execution.

<Start, By deduction, Define method context>. The generic characteristics deduction is based on the context typology. This section gives a selection of characteristics carried out by the IS method engineer. The result of this strategy is a sub-set of generic characteristics available for a given project. The corresponding operator is:

```
Select Context Characteristic ()
```

<Start, By deduction, Define method component context>. This section includes the selection of characteristics form generic typology like the previous one and includes furthermore the attribution of values to these characteristics. The result of this strategy is a sub-set of generic characteristics available for a given project with corresponding values. Two following operators are applied consecutively:

```
Select Context Characteristic ()
Attribute a Value to Context
Characteristic ()
```

<Start, By generation, Define method context>. The specific characteristics generation is based on the method description. The method engineer defines them by analyzing different aspects which are organized into four facets: intentional, satisfaction, decisional and internal. This section includes four operators. Each of the following operators is applied depending on the corresponding characteristic's facet:

```
Analyze Method Goal ()
Measure Method Satisfaction ()
Analyze Method Argumentation ()
Measure Method Characteristics ()
```

Table 9. Contextualization map sections

Section	<Source Intention, Strategy, Target intention >
S_1	<Start, By deduction, Define method context>
S_2	<Start, By deduction, Define method component context>
S_3	<Start, By generation, Define method context>
S_4	<Start, By generation, Define method component context>
S_5	<Define method context, By instantiation, Define method component context>
S_6	<Define method component context, By assembly, Define method context>
S_7	<Define method context, By completeness, Stop>
S_8	<Define method component context, By completeness, Stop>

<Start, By generation, Define method component context>. The definition of specific characteristics for method components context is the same as for method context (the previous section) but also requires the attribution of characteristics values. This section uses the same four operators and adds another one that deals with the attribution of values to the characteristics. This last one is applied after each of the first four operators for defining concrete values of the identified specific characteristics.

```
Analyze Method Goal () [for
intentional facet]
Measure Method Satisfaction () [for
satisfaction facet]
Analyze Method Argumentation () [for
decisional facet]
Measure Method Characteristics ()
[for internal facet]
Attribute a Value to Context
Characteristic () [for all facets]
```

<Define method context, By instantiation, Define method component context>. The context characteristics instantiation is common for both characteristics types and is applied in the

353

top-down approach. This section allows defining a sub-set of generic and specific method characteristics with an associated value for each method component separately. Several functions may be applied (sum, maximum, minimum, average, weighted sum, and so on) for attributing values to the method context. This section contains two operators applied consecutively:

```
Retain Context Characteristic ()
Attribute a Value to Context
Characteristic ()
```

<Define method component context, By assembly, Define method context>. In the case of the bottom-up approach, the strategy *By assembly* follows the definition of the method component context *By deduction* or *By generation*. The method engineer groups method components characteristics together. As a result, the method context includes all characteristics of its components contexts. The application of this strategy allows also defining characteristics' values for the method context. This section is carried out by the following operator:

```
Group Characteristics ()
Attribute a Value to Context
Characteristic ()
```

<Define method context, By completeness, Stop> and **<Define method component context, By completeness, Stop>.** These sections are the same in both top-down and bottom-up approaches and include verification of completeness and coherence of the described context. The associated operator is:

```
Verify Context Completeness ()
```

All these operators are resumed in Table 10.

APPLICATION: THREE CASE STUDIES

In this section, we illustrate our proposal by applying the contextualization methodology to three cases: scenario conceptualization, project portfolio management and decision-making.

Table 10. Operators' description

Operators	Description
Select Context Characteristic ()	Helps to select each of the pertinent characteristics of the context.
Attribute a Value to Context Characteristic ()	For each characteristic selected, a value corresponding to the project context has to be defined.
Analyze Method Goal ()	Helps to define the characteristics of the intentional facet which concerns the method intentions (the method goals).
Measure Method Satisfaction ()	Helps to measure the satisfaction degree on the results obtained by the engineer and concerns the satisfaction facet.
Analyze Method Argumentation ()	The decisional facet needs this operator in order to describe a decision-making situation with the definition of the arguments to take into account in the DM process.
Measure Method Characteristics ()	This operator is used to give values to the characteristics associated with the specific project management.
Retain Context Characteristic ()	Helps to define a subset of characteristics (generic or specific characteristics) and to give them values adapted to the project.
Group Characteristics ()	This operator allows to group all the characteristics together in the same set which corresponds to the context.
Verify Context Completeness ()	Helps to study the completeness and the coherency of the context set of characteristics.

We use the Map model for representing methods and for organizing method components into methods in our examples. The key concept of a Map is the notion of Section. When dealing with methods modeled by maps, each method component is represented by a map section. Thus, each Map section is linked to a particular method component, as shown in Figure 10.

Each case study describes a particular map organizing method components. We then show how the engineer may use the contextualization map in order to create the context of the method/components.

Case Study #1: Scenario Conceptualization

Case Study Description

The first example is based on the map defined in the Crews-L'écritoire approach (Ralyté, Rolland, Plihon, & Ralyté, 1999). This map is given in Figure 11.

This map was created to support the elicitation of functional system requirements in a goal-driven manner and to conceptualize them using textual devices such as scenarios or use cases. It provides guidelines to discover functional system requirements expressed as goals and to concep-

Figure 10. Section and method component correspondence

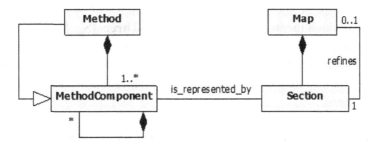

Figure 11. Crews-L'écritoire Approach Map (CL Map)

355

tualize these requirements as scenarios describing how the system satisfies the achievement of these goals. This map contains three main intentions, namely 'Elicit a Goal', 'Write a Scenario' and 'Conceptualize a Scenario'. There are twelve separate sections which allow the engineer to navigate through the map. Each of these sections is expressed as a specific component which is saved into a repository.

Contextualization Process

The engineer executes the contextualization map. He decided to select the top-down approach of the contextualization process. This specific way to navigate through the map will guide the engineer first through the definition of the method characteristics and then through the definition of the components ones. Figure 12 shows the path used in the navigation through the map in order to define the method components contexts.

This selected path contains three sections of the Contextualization Map and may be resumed on the three following steps:

1.   Definition of the method Context (S_1),
2.   Definition of the method components contexts (S_5), and
3.   Verification of the context completeness (S_8).

Step One (S_1: Definition of the method context): The engineer had studied the set of possible generic characteristics to specify the context of its method. He has applied the operator *Select Context Characteristic ()* in order to define a sub-set of generic context characteristics according to the given project. In this example, he has selected three indicators: *Expertise degree*, *Formality degree* and *Duration* (Table 11).

Step Two (S_5: Definition of the method components context): The method context defined previously is instantiated in this step for each component (each section of the CL map). It means that a value has to be affected to each characteristic. The following operators are applied to each method characteristic: *Retain Context Characteristic ()* and *Attribute a Value to Context Characteristic ()*. Table 12 shows the values of these criteria applied to each section of the CL map.

Step Three (S_8: Verification of the context completeness): The engineer has decided that the identified context characteristics are sufficient by applying the operator *Verify Context Completeness ()*.

Case Study #2: Project Portfolio Management

Case Study Description

The second example deals with Information Technology Project Portfolio Management (IT-PPM). Figure 13 shows the IT-PPM intentional

Figure 12. Path used in the contextualization map for the CL map case study

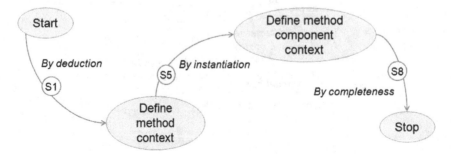

Table 11. Generic facet values

Characteristic	Value Fomain
Human Facet	
Expertise degree	3-grade scale
Application Domain Facet	
Formality degree	3-grade scale
Organisational Facet	
Duration	REAL

map which describes the ways to manage a project within a portfolio.

This Map is a refinement of the section < Define Risks, By Project Planning, Align IT and Business Process > of the map dealing with IT governance presented in Claudepierre and Nurcan (2009). This map contains three main intentions: 'Identify project', 'Evaluate project', and 'Prioritize project' and ten associated sections. The related components are saved into a method base which includes their description and methodological guidelines for their application.

Contextualization Process

The engineer has selected the top-down approach of the contextualization process. It guides the engineer through the definition of the method characteristics before the definition of method component characteristics. Figure 14 shows the path used in the navigation through the contextualization map in this particular case study.

This path contains four sections of the Contextualization Map that we represent within the three following steps:

1. Definition of the method Context (S_1 and S_3),
2. Definition of the method components contexts (S_5), and
3. Verification of the process completeness (S_8).

Step One (S_1, S_3: Definition of Method Context):
This step contains the execution of two sections of the Contextualization Map: S_1 and S_3.

Definition of the generic characteristics (S_1). The engineer uses the characteristics presented in

Table 12. CL map indicators

	Section	Expertise Degree	Formality Degree	Duration
S1	<Start; Initial goal identification strategy; Elicit a goal>	1	1	10 mn
S2	<Elicit a goal; Goal structure driven strategy; elicit a goal>	1	2	15 mn
S3	<Elicit a goal; Template driven strategy; elicit a goal>	1	3	15 mn
S4	<Elicit a goal; Linguistic strategy; elicit a goal>	1	1	15 mn
S5	<Elicit a goal; Template strategy; write a scenario>	2	3	10 mn
S6	<Elicit a goal; Free prose strategy; write a scenario>	1	1	15 mn
S7	<Write a scenario; Manual strategy; conceptualize a scenario>	2	1	15 mn
S8	<Write a scenario; Computer supported strategy; conceptualize a scenario>	1	3	5 mn
S9	<Conceptualize a scenario; Alternative discovery strategy; Elicit a Goal>	1	1	20 mn
S10	<Conceptualize a scenario; Composition discovery strategy; Elicit a Goal>	2	2	20 mn
S11	<Conceptualize a scenario; Refinement discovery strategy; Elicit a Goal>	2	2	20 mn
S12	<Conceptualize a scenario; Completeness strategy; Stop>	1	1	5 mn

Figure 13. IT-PPM Map

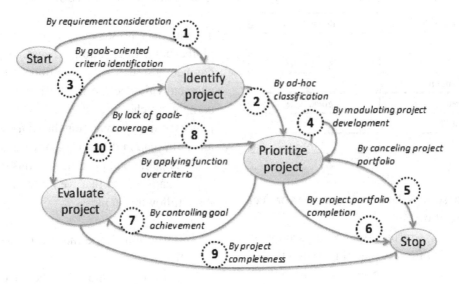

Figure 14. Path used in the contextualization map for the IT-PPM case study

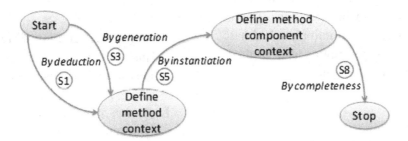

Table 4 and Table 5 as generic characteristics to specify the context of the method. The engineer has applied the operator *Select Context Characteristic ()* in order to define a sub-set of generic context characteristics according to the given project. He has selected three generic characteristics for this example: *Expertise degree, Expert role* and *Application type* (Table 13).

Definition of the specific characteristics (S_3). The engineer also uses *specific* context characteristics (cf. Table 14). This specific context is depicted by the constraints of the business environment (the design *situation*), the *intention* of the designer and the *strategy* for reaching the intention. So, the three operators were applied to identify the specific characteristics. *Analyze*

Method Goal () is used to identify the *Intention* which is related to the intentional type of specific characteristic. *Measure Method Satisfaction ()* allows defining the *Situation* in the Satisfactional facet (as it describes the satisfaction degree

Table 13. Generic characteristics

Characteristic	Value Domain
Human Facet	
Expertise degree	{low, normal, high}
Expert role	{tester, developer, designer, analyst}
Application Domain Facet	
Application type	{intra-organization application, inter-organization application, organization-customer application}

Table 14. Specific characteristics

Characteristic	Value Domain
Intentional Facet	
Intention	TEXT
Satisfactional Facet	
Situation	TEXT
Decisional Facet	
Strategy	TEXT

of the previous intention). Finally, *Analyze Method Argumentation ()* defines the *Strategy* in the decisional facet of the specific characteristic.

Step Two (S$_5$: Definition of Method Components Context): The method context defined at the previous step is now instantiated for each component. A value is affected to each characteristic in order to help the case process execution guidance. The following operators are applied to each method characteristic: *Retain Context Characteristic ()* and *Attribute a Value to Context Characteristic ()*. The results are presented in Table 15.

Step Three (S$_8$: Verification of the process completeness): The engineer has decided that the identified context characteristics are sufficient to allow a satisfying guidance through the portfolio project management by the operator *Verify Context Completeness ()* application.

Table 15. Specific characteristics instantiation

	Section	Expertise Degree	Expert Role	Appli. Type	Situation	Intention	Strategy
S1	<Start; By goals-oriented criteria identification; Identify project>	Normal	Analyst Designer	Intra-Org.	Problem statement	Identify project	By requirement consideration
S2	<Identify project; By ad-hoc classification; Prioritize project>	Low	Analyst Designer	Intra-Org.	Project identified	Prioritize project	By ad-hoc classification
S3	<Identify project; By goals-oriented criteria identification; Evaluate project>	High	Analyst Designer	Intra-Org.	Project identified	Evaluate project	By goals-oriented criteria identification
S4	<Prioritize project; By modulating project development; Prioritize project>	High	Designer	Intra-Org.	Project prioritized	Prioritize project	By modulating project development
S5	<Prioritize project; By cancelling project portfolio; Stop>	Low	Designer	Intra-Org.	Project prioritized	Stop	By canceling project portfolio
S6	<Prioritize project; By project portfolio completion; Stop>	Low	Designer	Intra-Org.	Project prioritized	Stop	By project portfolio completion
S7	<Prioritize project; By controlling goal achievement; Evaluate project>	Low	Designer	Intra-Org.	Project prioritized	Evaluate project	By controling goal achievement
S8	<Evaluate project; By applying function over criteria; Prioritize project>	Normal	Analyst	Intra-Org.	Project evaluated	Prioritize project	By applying function over criteria
S9	<Evaluate project; By project completeness; Stop>	Low	Designer	Intra-Org.	Project evaluated	Stop	By project completeness
S10	<Evaluate project; By lack of goals-coverage; Identify project>	Normal	Analyst	Intra-Org.	Project evaluated	Identify project	By lack of goal coverage

Case Study #3: Decision-Making

Case Study Description

The third example allows defining context for the Decision-making (DM) generic process. The map model of the DM generic process is given in Figure 15.

The DM Method Family describes the generic DM process including the main activities used for DM. It can be used each time an IS engineer meets a DM situation. The DM map is a collection of DM method components organized into a generic process (a kind of multi-method) for their easier usage in practice. DM components represent detailed guidelines for DM activities associated to the specific context of their use. The DM map contains four main intentions: 'Define Alternatives', 'Define Criteria', 'Evaluate Alternatives', and 'Make Decision' and twenty six sections, or DM method components.

Contextualization Process

The engineer executes the contextualization map and selects the bottom-up approach of the contextualization process as he is able to qualify each DM component. In this case, the engineer specifies the contexts of all method components and assemblies them into the method context. The used path in the Contextualization Map is shown in Figure 16.

This selected path contains four sections of the Contextualization Map and may be resumed on the three following steps:

1. Definition of the method components contexts (S_2 and S_4),
2. Definition of the method Context (S_6), and
3. Verification of the context completeness (S_7).

Figure 15. DM generic process map (DM map)

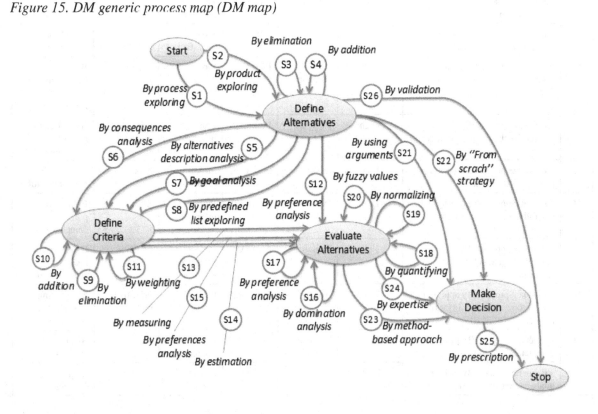

Figure 16. Path used in the contextualization map for the DM map case study

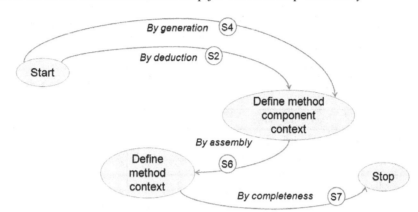

Step One (S_2, S_4: Definition of Method Component Context): This step contains the execution of two sections of the Contextualization Map: S_2 and S_4.

Definition of the generic characteristics (S_2). The engineer uses the characteristics presented in Table 4 and Table 5 as generic characteristics to specify the context of the DM components. He has applied the operator *Select Context Characteristic ()* in order to define a sub-set of generic context characteristics according to the given project. The engineer has selected two generic characteristics: *Expertise degree*, and *Complexity degree* (Table 16).

Then, the engineer attributes values to each DM method components using the *Attribute a Value to Context Characteristic ()* operator (Table 18).

The engineer has attributed values to twenty three DM components. The other three components (N/E – not evaluated values in Table 18) cannot be evaluated according to these characteristics as they depend significantly on the given situation.

Definition of the specific characteristics (S_4). The engineer also uses *specific* context characteristics (cf. Table 17) leading him to qualify method components. An operator was applied to identify the specific characteristics: *Analyze Method Goal ()* for identifying the *Intention*.

The engineer also attributes an intention to each DM method components using the *Attribute a Value to Context Characteristic ()* operator (Table 18).

Step Two (S_6: Definition of the method context): In order to define the context characteristics of the DM method, the engineer uses the *Group Characteristics ()* operator. For this, he takes all characteristics, specified for all components. Then he applies the *At-*

Table 16. Generic characteristics

Characteristic	Value Domain
Application Domain Facet	
Complexity degree	3-grade scale
Human Facet	
Expertise degree	3-grade scale

Table 17. Specific characteristic

Characteristic	Value Domain
Intentional Facet	
Intention	TEXT

Table 18. Specific characteristics instantiation

	Section	Complexity Degree	Expertise Degree	Intention
S1	<Start; By process exploring; Define alternatives>	2	2	Define alternative list
S2	<Start; By product exploring; Define alternatives>	2	2	Define alternative list
S3	<Define alternatives; By elimination; Define alternatives>	1	1	Refine alternative list
S4	<Define alternatives; By addition; Define alternatives>	1	1	Refine alternative list
S5	<Define alternatives; By alternatives description analysis; Define criteria>	2	1	Define criteria list
S6	<Define alternatives; By consequences analysis; Define criteria>	2	1	Define criteria list
S7	<Define alternatives; By goal analysis; Define criteria>	1	1	Define criteria list
S8	<Define alternatives; By predefined list exploring; Define criteria>	1	1	Define criteria list
S9	<Define criteria; By elimination; Define criteria>	1	2	Refine criteria list
S10	<Define criteria; By addition; Define criteria>	1	2	Refine criteria list
S11	<Define criteria; By weighting; Define criteria>	2	1	Define relative importance of criteria
S12	<Define alternatives; By preferences analysis; Evaluate alternatives>	2	1	Evaluate alternatives
S13	<Define criteria; By measuring; Evaluate alternatives>	2	1	Evaluate alternatives
S14	<Define criteria; By estimation; Evaluate alternatives>	2	1	Evaluate alternatives
S15	<Define Criteria; By preferences analysis; Evaluate alternatives>	2	1	Evaluate alternatives
S16	<Evaluate alternatives; By domination analysis; Evaluate alternatives>	2	2	Discard dominated alternatives
S17	<Evaluate alternatives; By preferences analysis; Evaluate alternatives>	2	2	Refine alternative evaluations
S18	<Evaluate alternatives; By quantifying; Evaluate alternatives>	1	2	Quantify alternative values
S19	<Evaluate alternatives; By normalizing; Evaluate alternatives>	1	2	Normalize alternative values
S20	<Evaluate alternatives; By fuzzy values; Evaluate alternatives>	3	3	Define fuzzy values of alternatives
S21	<Define alternatives; By using arguments; Make decision>	N/E	N/E	Make decision
S22	<Define alternatives; By "From scratch" strategy; Make decision>	N/E	N/E	Make decision
S23	<Evaluate alternatives; By method-based approach; Make decision>	3	3	Make decision
S24	<Evaluate alternatives; By expertise; Make decision>	N/E	N/E	Make decision
S25	<Make decision; By prescription; Stop>	1	2	Prescribe decision
S26	<Define alternatives; By validation; Stop>	1	3	Validate decision

tribute a Value to Context Characteristic () operator for evaluating the method context characteristics.

In order to attribute values to the method context (Table 19), he chooses the maximal value for the characteristics Complexity degree and Expertise degree, and for intention, he takes the main intention which is the Make Decision intention (This intention is on the top of the taxonomy of the DM intentions).

Step Three (S$_8$: Verification of the context completeness): The engineer has decided that the identified context characteristics are sufficient by applying the operator *Verify Context Completeness ()*.

Lessons Learned

The three case studies have shown that the contextualization approach can be used in various areas of information system engineering.

Closely related to the method at hand, it requires the strong degree of the engineer commitment into methodological processes. The engineers' intervention is highly required at all steps of the contextualization process. In addition, it allows taking into account the specificity of each studied method, that is to say the context-awareness. The last one is one of the most important issues in the current science of IS engineering. In this manner, these three examples show how the contextualization approach can contribute to resolve this issue.

The main usages of the contextualization results are the following: a more simple navigation through the map (in the case of Scenario conceptualization); a better 'context-aware' selection

Table 19. Method context values

Characteristic	Value
Complexity degree	3
Expertise degree	3
Intention	Make Decision

of method components (in the case of PPM); an easier customization of the generic process (in the case of DM); and, finally, means for identifying situations in which a given component is useful (three case studies). For instance, the *Weighting* DM method component (Figure 2) is useful in the situation characterized by the level 2 of complexity (normal), requiring the level 1 of expertise (low), and when the goal is to define the relative importance of criteria.

However, these case studies have made obvious that it is more easily to use the generic characteristics of context then to try to find some specific characteristics. It means that the operators for identifying specific characteristics must be enhanced.

RELATED WORKS

The current work was motivated by a need to formalize an approach for specifying context of methods and method components. It is related to the following fields of information system engineering: situational method engineering (SME), decision-making in information system engineering, and process variability.

SME approaches. Several works has been done to define the concept of method component in order to obtain flexible methods. The different kind of method components present in the literature are the method fragment (Brinkkemper, 1996), the method chunk (Ralyté, Deneckère, & Rolland, 2003), the method component (Wistrand & Karlsson, 2004), the OPF fragment (Henderson-Sellers, 2002) and the method service (Guzélian & Cauvet, 2007). Some details on these method components are given in section 2.2. In this field, the paper contributes to the methodology of identifying and evaluating method context characteristics.

Decision-making methods in ISE. With regard to IS engineering, the issue of DM has already been explored with respect to requirements engineering (Ngo-The & Ruhe, 2005), to method engineering

(Aydin, 2006), and, more generally, to systems engineering (Ruhe, 2003). Ruhe emphasizes the importance of DM in SE along the whole life cycle (Ruhe, 2003). However, DM in IS engineering has several lacks: (1) decisions are not formalized in terms of alternatives and criteria, their consequences are not analyzed, decisions are not transparent, (2) at intuitive and ad hoc decisions overshadow method-based ones, (3) and there is no tool which covers a complete DM process even if DM tools exist. To overcome these drawbacks, some studies are made, for instance a generic DM process is proposed at Figure 15 and an ontology of the DM concepts is elaborated (Kornyshova & Deneckère, 2010).

Process variability and the MAP process model. Variability has proved to be a central concept in different engineering domains to develop solutions that can be easily adapted to different organizational settings and different sets of customers at a low price. The MAP formalism has a high level of variability as it is expressed in an intentional manner through goals and strategies. As a high level of variability means a high number of variation points, a process customization is then required to offer a better guidance. In a parallel way to the Product lines concept which has appeared within the management of variability and customization of products, a new concept has arise to represent the processes that may be customized to a given project: the *Process lines* (Deneckère & Kornyshova, 2010a). In Deneckère and Kornyshova (2010b), Maps are considered as Process lines and a typology of characteristics is used to configure the line in order to obtain a process adapted to the project at hand.

DISCUSSION AND CONCLUDING REMARKS

The situational method engineering field aims at considering methods as a set of method components. Different approaches have been defined to consider this concept of method component (method fragment, method component, method services, method chunk, and OPF fragment). Each of these approaches mainly focus on the definition of what is a method component and how to assemble them in order to create a new method adapted to the project at hand. All of these approaches hint the fact that the notion of context has to be used to enhance the method component retrieving as they use several context related notions (interface, contingency factors, development situation, and so on). However, the process of how to identify and evaluate the method context is not suggested and our proposal is (1) to give a strong definition of a method component context and (2) to offer a contextualization process which will help engineers to define the method components context with ease.

Strong definition of a method component context. We have studied the literature in order to define the criteria that may be used to characterize the situation in which method components may be used. This leads us to define a typology of characteristics which we have structured in different facets (each considering a special view of a project). We then related these characteristics to the method component concepts.

Contextualization process. We have identified two possible ways to use these characteristics for defining context (the top-down and the bottom-up approaches) in order to propose a contextualization process that may be adapted to several situations. We modeled this process with the MAP formalism in order to keep a high level of flexibility in the process utilization.

This proposal can be applied in different IS engineering situations such as the selection of a component for enhancing the existing IS engineering method (for instance, extension-based approaches) or a selection of several components for constructing a new one (for instance, assembly-based approaches).

We have applied the proposed model on three case studies as follows.

- **Scenario Conceptualization:** This case is based on a well know process used on the project *'Crews L'Ecritoire'*. The case study use the contextualization process to help the engineer to navigate through the process and select the right components following its degree of expertise, the duration of each performed component and its formality degree (which are generic characteristics of the typology).
- **IT Project Portfolio Management:** This case study contributes to the study of the relatively unexplored domain of IT governance from the SME point of view. The engineer selects more characteristics than in the first case study as he chooses also specific characteristics (characteristics to apply on a specific process model, in this case the MAP process model).
- **Decision Making:** The contribution of this case study is twofold: the validation of the contextualization methodology and the application of the SME principles to a field issue from the operational research. Firstly, the DM case study has shown how to describe the context of DM components using three characteristics (complexity degree, expertise degree, and intention) and to identify the method context from the context of its components. Secondly, this case has demonstrated that the SME approach (identification of method components and their contextualization) is successfully applied to the DM methods for their further utilization in the IS engineering field.

Our future work aims at: (1) enhancing the approach for a more simple identification of specific context characteristics; (2) ensuring the adaptability of methods with regards to context specificities; and (3) proposing a method for a formalized selection of method components following their characteristics values.

REFERENCES

Aydin, M. N. (2006). *Decision-making support for method adaptation*. Enschede, The Netherlands: University of Twente.

Bessai, K., Claudepierre, B., Saidani, O., & Nurcan, S. (2008). Context-aware business process evaluation and redesign. In *Proceedings of the International Workshop Business Processing Modeling Development* (pp. 1-10).

Bouquet, P., Ghidini, C., Giunchiglia, F., & Blanzieri, E. (2003). Theories and uses of context in knowledge representation and reasoning. *Journal of Pragmatics*, *35*(3). doi:10.1016/S0378-2166(02)00145-5.

Bradley, N. A., & Dunlop, M. D. (2005). Toward a multidisciplinary model of context to support context-aware computing. *Human-Computer Interaction*, *20*(4). doi:10.1207/s15327051hci2004_2.

Brinkkemper, S. (1996). Method engineering: Engineering of information systems development method and tools. *Information and Software Technology Journal, 38*(7).

Bunt, H. (1997). Context and dialogue control. In *Proceedings of the CONTEXT Workshop*.

Claudepierre, B., & Nurcan, S. (2009). ITGIM: An intention driven approach for analyzing the IT governance requirements. In *Proceedings of the International Workshop on Requirements, Intentions and Goals in Conceptual Modeling*.

Coutaz, J., & Rey, G. (2002). Recovering foundations for a theory of contextors. In *Proceedings of the 4th ICCADUI Conference*, Valenciennes, France.

Deneckère, R., Iacovelli, A., Kornyshova, E., & Souveyet, C. (2008). From method fragments to method services. In *Proceedings of the Evaluation of Modeling Methods in Systems Analysis and Design Conference*, Montpellier, France.

Deneckère, R., & Kornyshova, E. (2010a). *La variabilité due à la sensibilité au contexte dans les processus téléologiques*. Marseille, France: Informatique des Organisations et Systèmes d'Information et de Décision.

Deneckère, R., & Kornyshova, E. (2010b). Process line configuration: An indicator-based guidance of the intentional model MAP. In I. Bider, T. Halpin, J. Krogstie, S. Nurcan, E. Proper, R. Schmidt, & R. Ukor (Eds.), *Proceedings of the 11th International Workshop on Enterprise, Business Process and Information Systems Modeling*, Hammamet, Tunisie (LNBI 50, pp. 327-339).

Dey, A., Abowd, G., & Salber, D. (2001). A conceptual framework and toolkit for supporting the rapid prototyping of context-aware applications. *Human-Computer Interaction, 16*(2-4), 97–166. doi:10.1207/S15327051HCI16234_02.

Drury, J. L., & Scott, S. D. (2008). Awareness in unmanned aerial vehicle operations. *International C2 Journal, 2*(1).

Firesmith, D., & Henderson-Sellers, B. (2001). *The OPEN process framework: An introduction*. Reading, MA: Addison-Wesley.

Gonzales-Perez, C. (2007). Supporting situational method engineering with ISO/IEC 24744 and the work product tool approach. In *Proceedings of the International IFIP WG8.1 Working Conference on Situational Method Engineering: Fundamentals and Experiences*, Geneva, Switzerland (pp. 7-18).

Gu, T., Wang, X. H., Pung, H. K., & Zhang, D. Q. (2004). An ontology-based context model in intelligent environments. In *Proceedings of the Communication Networks and Distributed Systems Modeling and Simulation Conference* (pp. 270-275).

Guzélian, G., & Cauvet, C. (2007). SO2M: Towards a service-oriented approach for method engineering. In *Proceedings of the World Congress in Computer Science, Computer Engineering and Applied Computing*, Las Vegas, NV.

Harmsen, A. F., Brinkkemper, J. N., & Oei, J. L. H. (1994). Situational method engineering for information systems project approaches. In *Proceedings of the International IFIP WG8.1 Conference on Methods and Associated Tools for the Information Systems Life Cycle*.

Harmsen, F. (1997). *Situational method engineering*. Cambridge, UK: Ernst & Young.

Henderson-Sellers, B. (2002). Process meta-modelling and process construction: Examples using the OPF. *Annals of Software Engineering, 14*(1-4).

Iacovelli, A., Souveyet, C., & Rolland, C. (2008). Method as a service (MaaS). In *Proceedings of the International Conference on Research Challenges in Information Science*, Marrakech, Morocco (pp. 371-380).

Karlsson, F., & Agerfalk, P. J. (2004). Method configuration: Adapting to situational characteristics while creating reusable assets. *Information and Software Technology, 45*, 619–633. doi:10.1016/j.infsof.2003.12.004.

Kirsch Pinheiro, M., Vanrompay, Y., & Berbers, Y. (2008). Context-aware service selection using graph matching. In *Proceedings of the ECOWS Workshop* (Vol. 411).

Kornyshova, E., & Deneckère, R. (2010). Decision-making ontology for information system engineering. In *Proceedings of the International Conference on Conceptual Modeling*, Vancouver, BC, Canada.

Kornyshova, E., Deneckère, R., & Salinesi, C. (2007). Method chunks selection by multicriteria techniques: an extension of the assembly-based approach. In *Proceedings of the International IFIP WG8.1 Working Conference on Situational Method Engineering: Fundamentals and Experiences*, Geneva, Switzerland (pp. 64-78).

Mirbel, I., & de Riviere,s V. (2002). Adapting analysis and design to software context: The jecko approach. In *Proceedings of the 8th International Conference on Object Oriented Information Systems.*

Mirbel, I. (2008). *Contributions à la modélisation, la réutilisation et la flexibilité des systèmes d'information.* Unpublished HDR thesis, Nice University, Nice, France.

Mirbel, I., & Ralyté, J. (2006). Situational method engineering: Combining assembly-based and roadmap-driven approaches. *Requirements Engineering, 11*(1), 58–78. doi:10.1007/s00766-005-0019-0.

Nehan, Y. R., & Deneckère, R. (2007). Component-based situational methods - A framework for understanding SME. In *Proceedings of the International IFIP WG8.1 Working Conference on Situational Method Engineering: Fundamentals and Experiences*, Geneva, Switzerland.

Ngo-The, A., & Ruhe, G. (2005). Decision support in requirements engineering. In Aurum, A., & Wohlin, C. (Eds.), *Engineering and managing software requirements* (pp. 267–286). Berlin, Germany: Springer-Verlag. doi:10.1007/3-540-28244-0_12.

Prat, N. (1997). Goal formalisation and classification for requirements engineering. In *Proceedings of the Third International Workshop on Requirements Engineering: Foundations of Software Quality*, Barcelona, Spain (pp. 145-156).

Ralyte, J. (2001). *Method chunks engineering.* Unpublished doctoral dissertation, University of Paris 1-Sorbonne, Paris, France.

Ralyté, J., Deneckere, R., & Rolland, C. (2003). Towards a generic model for situational method engineering. In J. Eder & M. Missikoff (Eds.), *Proceedings of the 15th International Conference on Advanced Information Systems Engineering* (LNCS 2681, p. 1029).

Ralyté, J., & Rolland, C. (2001a). An assembly process model for method engineering. In *Proceedings of the International Conference on Advanced Information Systems Engineering*, Interlaken, Switzerland.

Ralyté, J., & Rolland, C. (2001b, November). An approach for method reengineering. In H. Kunii, S. Jajodia, & A. Solvberg (Eds.), *Proceedings of the 20th International Conference on Conceptual Modeling*, Yokohama, Japan (LNCS 2224, pp. 471-484).

Ralyté, J., Rolland, C., & Plihon, V. (1999). Method enhancement with scenario based techniques. In M. Jarke & A. Oberweis (Eds.), *Proceedings of the 11th International Conference on Advanced Information System Engineering* (LNCS 1626, pp. 103-118).

Rey, G., & Coutaz, J. (2002). Le Contexteur: une abstraction logicielle pour la réalisation de systèmes interactifs sensibles au contexte. In *Proceedings of the IHM Conference* (pp. 105-112).

Rolland, C. (2005). L'ingénierie des méthodes: une visite guidée. *E-revue en Technologies de l'Information (e-TI).*

Rolland, C. (2008). Method engineering: Towards methods as services. In *Proceedings of the International Conference on Software Process*, Leipzig, Germany.

Rolland, C., & Cauvet, C. (1992). Object-oriented conceptual modelling. In *Proceedings of the International Conference on Management of Data*, Bangalore, India.

Rolland, C., Plihon, V., & Ralyté, J. (1998). Specifying the reuse context of scenario method chunks. In *Proceedings of the 10th International Conference on Advanced Information Systems Engineering*, Pisa, Italy.

Rolland, C., & Prakash, N. (2001). Matching ERP system functionality to customer requirements. In *Proceedings of the 5th IEEE International Symposium on Requirements Engineering*, Toronto, ON, Canada.

Rolland, C., Prakash, N., & Benjamen, A. (1999). A multi-model view of process modeling. *Requirements Engineering*, 4(4), 169–187. doi:10.1007/s007660050018.

Rosemann, M., & Recker, J. (2006). Context-aware process design: Exploring the extrinsic drivers for process flexibility. In *Proceedings of the Workshops and Doctoral Consortium in the 18th International Conference on Advanced Information Systems Engineering*, Luxembourg (pp. 149-158).

Rosen, M. A., Fiore, S. M., Salas, E., Letsky, M., & Warner, N. (2008). Tightly coupling cognition: Understanding how communication and awareness drive coordination in teams. *International C2 Journal*, 2(1).

Ruhe, G. (2003). Software engineering decision support – Methodology and applications. In Tonfoni, G., & Jain, C. (Eds.), *Innovations in decision support systems: International series on advanced intelligence* (*Vol. 3*, pp. 143–174). Adelaide, Australia: Advanced Knowledge International.

Schilit, B., Adams, N., & Want, R. (1994). Context-aware computing applications. In *Proceedings of the IEEE Workshop on Mobile Computing Systems and Applications*, Santa Cruz, CA (pp. 89-101).

Van Slooten, K., & Hodes, B. (1996). Characterising IS development projects. In *Proceedings of the IFIP WG8.1 Conference on Method Engineering*.

Wistrand, K., & Karlsson, F. (2004). Method components: Rationale revealed. In *Proceedings of the International Conference on Advanced Information Systems Engineering*, Riga, Latvia (pp. 189-201).

This work was previously published in the International Journal of Information System Modeling and Design (IJISMD), Volume 2, Issue 4, edited by Remigijus Gustas, pp. 49-81, copyright 2011 by IGI Publishing (an imprint of IGI Global).

Compilation of References

Abbas, N., Gravell, A., & Wills, G. (2010). Using factor analysis to generate clusters of agile practices. In *Proceedings of the IEEE AGILE Conference* (pp. 11-20). Washington, DC: IEEE Computer Society.

Abdeen, M. M., Kahl, W., & Maibaum, T. (2007). FDA: Between process and product evaluation. In *Proceedings of the Joint Workshop on High Confidence Medical Devices, Software, and Systems and Medical Device Plug-and-Play Interoperability* (pp. 181-186). Washington, DC: IEEE Computer Society.

Abdel-Hamid, T., K., & Madnick, S. E. (1983). The dynamics of software project scheduling. *Communications of the ACM, 26*(5), 340–346. doi:10.1145/69586.358135.

Abrahamsson, P., Salo, O., Ronkainen, J., & Warsta, J. (2002). Agile software development methods: Review and analysis. Kajaan, Finland: VTT Publications.

Acerbis, R., Bongio, A., Brambilla, M., & Butti, S. (2007). Web ratio 5: An eclipse-based case tool for engineering web applications. In L. Baresi, P. Fraternali, & G.-J. Houben (Eds.), *Proceedings of the 7th International Conference on Web Engineering* (LNCS 4607, pp. 501-505).

Adam, S., & Doerr, J. (2007). On the notion of determining system adequacy by analyzing the traceability of quality. In *Proceedings of the 19th International Conference on Advanced Information Systems Engineering*, Trondheim, Norway (pp. 325-329).

Advani, A., Hassoun, Y., & Counsell, S. (2006). Extracting refactoring trends from open-source software and a possible solution to the 'related refactoring' conundrum. In *Proceedings of the ACM Symposium on Applied Computing*, Dijon, France (pp. 1713-1720).

Agarwal, S., Handschuh, S., & Staab, S. (2005). Annotation, composition and invocation of semantic web services. *Journal of Web Semantics, 2*(1).

Ahituv, N., Neumann, S., & Zviran, M. (2002). A system development methodology for ERP systems. *Journal of Computer Information, 42*(3), 56–67.

Akkiraju, R., Farrell, J., Miller, J., Nagarajan, M., Schmidt, M., Sheth, A., & Verma, K. (2005). *Web service semantics – WSDL-S*. Retrieved from http://lsdis.cs.uga.edu/projects/METEOR-S/WSDL-S

Alexander, I. (2002). Modelling the interplay of conflicting goals with use and misuse cases. In *Proceedings of the 8th International Workshop on Requirements Engineering: Foundation for Software Quality* (pp. 145-152).

Altintas, I., Barney, O., & Jaeger-Frank, E. (2006). Provenance collection support in the kepler scientific workflow system. In *Proceedings of the IPAW Conference* (pp. 118-132).

Andersson, B., Bergholtz, M., Edirisuriya, A., Ilayperuma, T., Jayaweera, P., Paul, J., et al. (2008). Enterprise sustainability through the alignment of goal models and business models. In *Proceedings of the 3rd International Workshop on Business/IT-Alignment and Interoperability CEUR Workshop*.

Andersson, B., Bergholtz, M., Edirisuriya, A., Ilayperuma, T., Johannesson, P., & Zdravkovic, J. (2007). *Using strategic goal analysis for enhancing value-based business models*. Paper presented at the Second International Workshop on Business/IT Alignment and Interoperability, Workshop at the 19th International Conference on Advanced Information Systems Engineering.

Andersson, B., Bergholtz, M., Edirisuriya, E., Ilayperuma, T., & Johannesson, P. (2005). A Declarative Foundation of Process Models. In *Proceedings of the 17th Conference on Advanced Information Systems Engineering,* Montpellier, France (LNCS 3520, pp. 233-24). New York: Springer Verlag.

Antón, A. I. (1997). *Goal identification and refinement in the specification of software-based information systems.* Unpublished doctoral dissertation, Georgia Institute of Technology, Atlanta.

Anton, A., & Potts, C. (1998). The use of goals to surface requirements for evolving systems. In *Proceedings of the 20th International Conference on Software Engineering,* Kyoto, Japan (pp. 157-166).

Antoniol, G., Canfora, G., de Lucia, A., & Casazza, G. (2000). Information retrieval models for recovering traceability links between code and documentation. In *Proceedings of the International Conference on Software Maintenance* (p. 40). Washington, DC: IEEE Computer Society.

Anzböck, R., & Dustdar, S. (2004). Modeling Medical E-services. In *Proceedings of the Business Process Management: Second International Conference (BPM 2004),* Potsdam, Germany (LNCS 3080, pp. 49-65). New York: Springer Verlag.

April, A., & Abran, A. (2008). *Software maintenance management: Evaluation and continuous improvement.* Hoboken, NJ: John Wiley & Sons.

Asnar, Y., Giorgini, P., Massacci, F., & Zannone, N. (2007). From trust to dependability through risk analysis. In *Proceedings of the Second International Conference on Availability, Reliability and Security,* Vienna, Austria (pp. 19-26).

Avison, D. E., & Fitzgerald, G. (1995). *Information systems development: Methodologies, techniques and tools.* New York, NY: McGraw Hill.

Awad, A., Polyvyanyy, A., & Weske, M. (2008). Semantic querying of business process models. In *Proceedings of the Conference on Enterprise Distributed Object Computing* (pp. 85-94). Washington, DC: IEEE Computer Society.

Aydin, M. N. (2006). *Decision-making support for method adaptation.* Enschede, The Netherlands: University of Twente.

Azeez, A. (2008). *Axis2 popularity exponentially increasing.* Retrieved from http://afkham.org/2008/

Baader, F., Horrocks, I., & Sattler, U. (2002). Description logics for the semantic web. *Künstliche Intelligenz, 16*(4), 57–59.

Babiak, K. M. (2009). Criteria of effectiveness in multiple cross-sectoral inter-organizational relationships. *Evaluation and Program Planning, 32*(1), 1–12. doi:10.1016/j.evalprogplan.2008.09.004.

Baida, Z., Gordijn, J., Akkermans, H., Saele, H., & Morch, A. Z. (2005). Finding e-Service Offerings by Computer-supported Customer Need Reasoning. *International Journal of E-Business Research, 1*(3), 91–112.

Bajracharya, S., Ossher, J., & Lopes, C. (2009, May). Sourcerer: An internet- scale software repository. *In Proceedings of the ICSE Workshop on Search-Driven Development-Users, Infrastructure, Tools and Evaluation* (pp. 1-4). Washington, DC: IEEE Computer Society.

Ballinger, K., Ehnebuske, D., Ferris, C., Gudgin, M., Liu, C. K., Nottingham, M., et al. (2006). *WS-I basic profile version 1.1.* Retrieved from http://www.ws-i.org/Profiles/BasicProfile-1.1.html

Banker, R. D., Davis, G. B., & Slaughter, S. A. (1998). Software development practices, software complexity and software maintenance performance. *Management Science, 44*(4). doi:10.1287/mnsc.44.4.433.

Banker, R. D., & Kemerer, C. F. (1989). Scale economies in new software development. *IEEE Transactions on Software Engineering, 15*(10), 1199–1205. doi:10.1109/TSE.1989.559768.

Barry, E. J., Kemerer, C. F., & Slaughter, S. A. (2006). Environmental volatility, development decisions, and software volatility: A longitudinal analysis. *Management Science, 52*(3), 448–464. doi:10.1287/mnsc.1050.0463.

Bartsch, M., & Harrison, R. (2006, April). A coupling framework for AspectJ. In *Proceedings of the 10th International Conference on Evaluation and Assessment in Software Engineering,* Keele, UK.

Basili, V. R., Caldiera, G., McGarry, F. E., Rajerski, R., Page, G. T., & Waligora, S. (1992). The software engineering laboratory: An operational software experience factory. In *Proceedings of the International Conference on Software Engineering* (pp. 370-381). New York, NY: ACM Press.

Basili, V. R. (1995). The experience factory and its relationship to other quality approaches. *Advances in Computers, 41*, 65–82. doi:10.1016/S0065-2458(08)60231-4.

Basili, V. R., Caldiera, G., & Rombach, H. D. (1994). The goal question metric approach. In Marciniak, J. (Ed.), *Encyclopedia of software engineering* (*Vol. 2*, pp. 528–532). New York, NY: John Wiley & Sons.

Beck, K., & Andres, C. (2004). Extreme programming explained: Embrace change (2nd ed.). Reading, MA: Addison-Wesley.

Beco, S., Cantalupo, B., Giammarino, L., Matskanis, N., & Surridge, M. (2005). OWL-WS: A workflow ontology for dynamic grid service composition. In *Proceedings of the First International Conference on e-Science and Grid Computing* (pp. 148-155). Washington, DC: IEEE Computer Society.

Beecham, S., Hall, T., Britton, C., Cottee, M., & Rainer, A. (2005). Using an expert panel to validate a requirements process improvement model. *Journal of Systems and Software, 3*, 251–275. doi:10.1016/j.jss.2004.06.004.

Beeri, C., Eyal, A., Kamenkovich, S., & Milo, T. (2006). Querying business processes. In *Proceedings of the 32nd International Conference on Very Large Data Bases* (p. 343-354).

Belady, L., & Lehman, M. (1976). Model of large program development. *IBM Systems Journal, 15*, 225–252. doi:10.1147/sj.153.0225.

Belhajjame, K., & Brambilla, M. (2009). Ontology-based description and discovery of business processes. In *Proceedings of the 10th Workshop on Business Process Modeling, Development, and Support* (LNBIP 29, pp. 85-98).

Belsley, D. A., Kuh, E., & Welsch, R. E. (1980). *Regression diagnostics: Identifying influential data and sources of collinearity*. New York, NY: John Wiley & Sons.

Ben Khalifa, H., Khayati, O., & Ghezala, H. (2008, December 15). A behavioral and structural components retrieval technique for software reuse. In Proceedings of Advanced Software Engineering and its Applications (pp. 134–137). Washington, DC: IEEE Computer Society. doi:doi:10.1109/ASEA.2008.45 doi:10.1109/ASEA.2008.45.

Beneventano, D., Bergamaschi, S., Guerra, F., & Vincini, M. (2001). The MOMIS approach to information integration. In *Proceedings of the International Conference on Enterprise Information Systems* (pp. 194-198).

Benevides, A., & Guizzardi, G. (2009). A Model-based Tool for Conceptual Modeling and Domain Ontology Engineering in OntoUML. In *Proceedings of the International Conference on Enterprise Information Systems*, Milan, Italy (LNBIP 24, pp. 528-538).

Berry, M. J. A., & Linoff, G. S. (2004). *Data mining techniques: For marketing, sales and customer relationship management*. Indianapolis, IN: Wiley Publishing.

Bessai, K., Claudepierre, B., Saidani, O., & Nurcan, S. (2008). Context-aware business process evaluation and redesign. In *Proceedings of the International Workshop Business Processing Modeling Development* (pp. 1-10).

Bider, I. (2002). *State-oriented business process modeling: Principles, theory and practice*. Unpublished doctoral dissertation, Royal Institute of Technology, Stockholm, Sweden.

Blaha, M., & Rumbaugh, J. (2005). *Object-Oriented Modeling and Design with UML*. London: Pearson.

Bleistein, S., Cox, K., Verner, J., & Phalp, K. (2006). Requirements engineering for e-business advantage. *Requirements Engineering, 11*(1), 4–16. doi:10.1007/s00766-005-0012-7.

Boardman, A., & Shapiro, D. (2004). A framework for comprehensive strategic analysis. *Journal of Strategic Management Education, 1*(2).

Bochner, S., & Chandrasekharan, K. (2001). *Fourier transforms*. Princeton, NJ: Princeton Book Company.

Bodart, F., Patel, A., Sim, M., & Weber, R. (2001). Should Optional Properties be used in Conceptual Modeling? A Theory and three Empirical Tests. *Information Systems Research, 12*(4), 384–405. doi:10.1287/isre.12.4.384.9702.

Boehm, B. (1984). Software engineering economics. *IEEE Transactions on Software Engineering, 1*(1), 4–21. doi:10.1109/TSE.1984.5010193.

Boehm, B. (1987). Improving software productivity. *IEEE Computer, 20*(1), 43–57.

Boehm, B., Rombach, H. D., & Zelkovitz, M. (2005). *Foundations of empirical software engineering: The legacy of Victor R. Basili*. Berlin, Germany: Springer-Verlag. doi:10.1007/3-540-27662-9.

Booch, G., Rumbaugh, J., & Jacobson, I. (2005). *The Unified Modeling Language User Guide* (2nd ed.). Reading, MA: Addison-Wesley.

Bose, R., & Frew, J. (2005). Lineage retrieval for scientific data processing: A survey. *ACM Computing Surveys, 37*(1), 1–28. doi:10.1145/1057977.1057978.

Botha, R. A. (2002). *CoSAWoE - a model for context-sensitive access control in workflow environments*. Unpublished doctoral dissertation, Rand Afrikaans University, Johannesburg, South Africa.

Bouquet, P., Ghidini, C., Giunchiglia, F., & Blanzieri, E. (2003). Theories and uses of context in knowledge representation and reasoning. *Journal of Pragmatics, 35*(3). doi:10.1016/S0378-2166(02)00145-5.

Bozdogen, H. (1987). Model selection & Akaike's information criterion (AIC): The general theory and its analytical extensions. *Psychometrika, 52*, 345–370. doi:10.1007/BF02294361.

Bradley, N. A., & Dunlop, M. D. (2005). Toward a multidisciplinary model of context to support context-aware computing. *Human-Computer Interaction, 20*(4). doi:10.1207/s15327051hci2004_2.

Brambilla, M., Butti, S., & Fraternali, P. (2010). Web ratio BPM: A tool for designing and deploying business processes on the web. In B. Benatallah, F. Casati, G. Kappel, & G. Rossi (Eds.), *Proceedings of the 10th International Conference on Web Engineering,* (LNCS 6189, pp. 415-429).

Brambilla, M., Deutsch, A., Sui, L., & Vianu, V. (2005). The role of visual tools in a web application design and verification framework: A visual notation for LTL formulae. In D. Lowe & M. Gadedke (Eds.), *Proceedings of the 5th International Conference on Web Engineering* (LNCS 3579, pp. 557-568).

Brambilla, M., Dosmi, M., & Fraternali, P. (2009). Model-driven engineering of service orchestrations. *In Proceedings of the IEEE World Conference on Services-I* (pp. 562-569). Washington, DC: IEEE Computer Society.

Braun, U., Shinnar, A., & Seltzer, M. (2008). Securing provenance. In *Proceedings of the 3rd Conference on Hot Topics in Security*, Berkeley, CA (pp. 1-5).

Bray, T., Paoli, J., Sperberg-McQueen, C. M., Maler, E., Yergeau, F., & Cowan, J. (2004). *Extensible markup language (XML) 1.1*. Retrieved from http://www.w3.org/TR/2004/REC-xml11-20040204/

Bresciani, P., Giorgini, P., Giunchiglia, F., Mylopoulos, J., & Perini, A. (2004). Tropos: An agent-oriented software development methodology. *Journal of Autonomous Agents and Multi-Agent Systems*, 203-236.

Brewka, G. (2001). On the relationship between defeasible logic and well-founded semantics. In T. Eiter, W. Faber, & M. Truszcynski (Eds.), *Proceedings of the 6th International Conference on Logic Programming and Nonmonotonic Reasoning*, Vienna, Austria (LNCS 2173, pp. 121-132).

Briand, L., Daly, J., Porter, V., & Wuest, J. (1998). Predicting fault-prone classes based on design measures in object-oriented systems. In *Proceedings of the 9th International Symposium on Software Reliability Engineering*, Paderborn, Germany (pp. 334-343).

Briand, L., Devanbu, P., & Melo, W. (1997). An investigation into coupling measures for C++. In *Proceedings of the 19th International Conference on Software Engineering*, Boston, MA (pp. 412-421).

Briand, L., Daly, J., & Wust, J. (1999). A unified framework for coupling measurement in object-oriented systems. *IEEE Transactions on Software Engineering, 25*, 91–121. doi:10.1109/32.748920.

Brinkkemper, S. (1996). Method engineering: Engineering of information systems development method and tools. *Information and Software Technology Journal, 38*(7).

Brown, B. B. (1968). *Delphi process: A methodology used for the elicitation of opinions of experts*. Santa Monica, CA: RAND Corporation.

Brown, P. J., Bovey, J. D., & Chen, X. (1997). Context-aware applications: From the laboratory to the marketplace. *IEEE Personal Communications, 4*(5), 58–64. doi:10.1109/98.626984.

Brown, W., McCormick, H. W., & Thomas, S. W. (2000). *Antipatterns in project management*. Hoboken, NJ: John Wiley & Sons.

Bubenko, J. A. Jr, Brash, D., & Stirna, J. (1998). *EKD user guide*. Stockholm, Sweden: Stockholm University.

Bunge, M. A. (1977). Ontology I: The Furniture of the World: *Vol. 3. Treatise On Basic Philosophy*. Dordrecht, Holland: D. Reidel Publishing Company.

Bunge, M. A. (1979). Ontology II: A World of Systems: *Vol. 4. Treatise On Basic Philosophy*. Dordrecht, Holland: D. Reidel Publishing Company.

Bunge, M. A. (1979). Treatise on Basic Philosophy: *Vol. 4. Ontology II: A World of Systems*. Dordrecht, The Netherlands: Reidel Publishing Company.

Bunt, H. (1997). Context and dialogue control. In *Proceedings of the CONTEXT Workshop*.

Burke, W. W. (1994). *Organisational development - a process of learning and changing*. Reading, MA: Addison-Wesley.

Burton-Jones, A., & Weber, R. (1999). Understanding Relationships With Attributes in Entity-Relationship Diagrams. In *Proceedings of the 20th International Conference on Information Systems*, Charlotte, NC (pp. 214-228).

Burton-Jones, A., & Meso, P. (2006). Conceptualizing Systems for Understanding: An Empirical Test of Decomposition Principles in Object-Oriented Analysis. *Information Systems Research, 17*(1), 101–114. doi:10.1287/isre.1050.0079.

Capiluppi, A., Morisio, M., & Ramil, J. (2004). Studying the evolution of open source systems at different levels of granularity. In *Proceedings of the 12th International Workshop on Program Comprehension*, Bari, Italy (pp. 172-182).

Cardoso, E., Guizzardi, R., & Almeida, J. P. (in press). *Goal models and business process models in a health environment*. Vitoria, Brazil. *Federal University of Espírito Santo.*.

Cardoso, J., & Sheth, A. (Eds.). (2006). *Semantic web services, processes and applications (Semantic web and beyond: Computing for human experience)* (*Vol. 3*). New York, NY: Springer. doi:10.1007/978-0-387-34685-4.

Cavalcanti, M. C., Targino, R., Baião, F., Rossle, S., Bisch, P. M., & Pires, P. F. et al. (2005). Managing structural genomic workflows using Web services. *Data & Knowledge Engineering, 53*, 45–74. doi:10.1016/S0169-023X(04)00112-0.

Cearley, D. W., Fenn, J., & Plummer, D. C. (2005). *Gartner's positions on the five hottest IT topics and trends in 2005*. Stamford, CT: Gartner Inc..

Ceri, S., Fraternali, P., Bongio, A., Brambilla, M., Comai, S., & Matera, M. (2002). *Designing data-intensive web applications*. San Francisco, CA: Morgan Kaufmann.

CGXML. (2008). *Framework for conceptual knowledge processing*. Retrieved from http://tockit.sourceforge.net/cgxml/index.html

Champy, J. (2002). *X-engineering the corporation: The next frontier of business performance*. New York, NY: Warner Books.

Chapin, N., Hale, J., Kham, K., Ramil, J., & Tan, W. (2001). Types of software evolution and software maintenance. *Journal of Software Maintenance: Research and Practice, 13*(1), 3–30. doi:10.1002/smr.220.

Charfi, A., & Mezini, M. (2004). Hybrid web service composition business process meet business rules. In *Proceedings of the 2nd International Conference on Service-Oriented Computing*.

Cheesman, J., & Daniels, J. (2001). *UML Components. A Simple Process for Specifying Component-Based Software*. Reading, MA: Addison-Wesley.

Chein, M., & Mugnier, M. L. (1992). Conceptual graphs: Fundamental notions. *Revue d'Intelligence Artificielle*, *6*(4), 365–406.

Chen, K., Madhavan, J., & Halevy, A. (2009). Exploring schema repositories with schemr. In *Proceedings of the 35th SIGMOD International Conference on Management of Data* (pp. 1095-1098).

Cheng, B. H. C., & Atlee, J. M. (2007). Research directions in requirements engineering. In *Proceedings of the International Conference on Software Engineering and the Workshop on the Future of Software Engineering* (pp. 285-303). Washington, DC: IEEE Computer Society.

Chengalur-Smith, S., & Sidorova, A. (2003). Survival of open-source projects: A population ecology perspective. In *Proceedings of the 24th International Conference of Information Systems*, Atlanta, GA.

Cherbakov, L., Galambos, G., Harishankar, R., Kalyana, S., & Rackham, G. (2005). Impact of Service Orientation at the Business Level. *IBM Systems Journal*, *44*(4). doi:10.1147/sj.444.0653.

Chidamber, S., & Kemerer, C. (1994). A metrics suite for object oriented design. *IEEE Transactions on Software Engineering*, *20*, 476–493. doi:10.1109/32.295895.

Chilarege, R. (1999). *Software testing best practices (Tech. Rep. No. RC 21457 Log 96856 4/26/99)*. Armonk, NY: IBM Research.

Chopra, A. K., Mylopoulos, J., Dalpiaz, F., Giorgini, P., & Singh, M. P. (2010). Requirements as Goals and Commitments Too. In *Intentional Perspectives on Information System Engineering* (pp. 137–153). Berlin: Springer. doi:10.1007/978-3-642-12544-7_8.

Chopra, V., Li, S., & Genender, J. (2007). *Professional apache tomcat 6*. New Delhi, India: Wiley.

Chung, L., Nixon, B., Yu, E., & Mylopoulos, J. (2000). *Non-functional requirements in software engineering*. Dordrecht, The Netherlands: Kluwer Academic Publishers.

Claudepierre, B., & Nurcan, S. (2009). ITGIM: An intention driven approach for analyzing the IT governance requirements. In *Proceedings of the International Workshop on Requirements, Intentions and Goals in Conceptual Modeling*.

Clifford, B., Foster, I., Voeckler, J.-S., Wilde, M., & Zhao, Y. (2008). Tracking provenance in a virtual data grid. *Concurrency and Computation*, *20*(5), 565–575. doi:10.1002/cpe.1256.

Cockburn, A., & Williams, L. (2001). The costs and benefits of pair programming. In G. Succi & M. Marchesi (Eds.), Extreme programming examined (pp. 223–248). Reading, MA: Addison-Wesley.

Cockburn, A. (2001). *Writing Effective Use Cases*. Reading, MA: Addison-Wesley.

CollabNet, Inc. (2003). *ArgoUML User Manual*. Retrieved September 2003, from http://argouml.tigris.org/

Counsell, S., Hassoun, Y., Johnson, R., Mannock, K., & Mendes, E. (2003). Trends in java code changes: The key to identification of refactorings? In *Proceedings of the International Conference on the Principle and Practice of Programming in Java*, Ireland (pp. 45-48).

Counsell, S., Loizou, G., & Najjar, R. (2007). Quality of manual data collection in Java software: An empirical investigation. *Empirical Software Engineering*, *12*(3), 275–293. doi:10.1007/s10664-006-9028-y.

Coutaz, J., & Rey, G. (2002). Recovering foundations for a theory of contextors. In *Proceedings of the 4th ICCADUI Conference*, Valenciennes, France.

Crowston, K., Annabi, H., & Howison, J. (2003) Defining open source project. In *Proceedings of the International Conference of Information Systems*, Seattle, WA.

Crowston, K., Li, Q., Wei, K., Eseryel, U. Y., & Howison, J. (2007). Self-organization of teams for free/libre open source software development. *Information and Software Technology*, *49*(6), 564–575. doi:10.1016/j.infsof.2007.02.004.

Crowston, K., & Scozzi, B. (2002). Open source software projects as virtual organizations: Competency rallying for software development. *IEEE Software*, *149*(1), 3–17. doi:10.1049/ip-sen:20020197.

Cysneiros, L. M. (2007). Evaluating the effectiveness of using catalogues to elicit non-functional requirements. In *Proceedings of the 10th Workshop on Requirements Engineering* (pp. 107-115).

Cysneiros, L. M. (2009). *Catalogues on non-functional requirements*. Retrieved from http://math.yorku.ca/~cysneiro/nfrs/nfrs.htm

Dadam, P., & Reichert, M. (2009). The ADEPT project: A Decade of research and development for robust and flexible process support - challenges and achievements. *Computer Science, 23*(2), 81–97.

Daneva, M., & Wieringa, R. J. (2006). Engineering the coordination requirements in inter-organizational ERP projects: A package of good practices. In *Proceedings of the IEEE International Conference on Requirements Engineering* (pp. 311-314). Washington, DC: IEEE Computer Society.

Daneva, M., Kassab, M., Ponisio, M. L., Wieringa, R., & Ormandjieva, O. (2007). *Exploiting a goal decomposition technique to prioritize non-functional requirements*. Paper presented at the 10th International Workshop on Requirements Engineering, Toronto, ON, Canada.

Daneva, M. (2010). Engineering the coordination requirements in cross-organizational ERP projects. In Parthasarathy, S. (Ed.), *Enterprise information systems and implementing IT infrastructures: Challenges and issues* (pp. 1–19). Hershey, PA: IGI Global. doi:10.4018/978-1-61520-625-4.ch001.

Daneva, M., & Wieringa, R. J. (2006). A requirements engineering framework for inter-organizational ERP systems. *Requirement Engineering Journal, 11*(3), 194–204. doi:10.1007/s00766-006-0034-9.

Daneva, M., & Wieringa, R. J. (2010). Requirements engineering for enterprise systems: What we know and what we do not know? In Nurcan, S., Salinesi, C., Souveyet, C., & Ralyté, J. (Eds.), *Intentional perspectives on information systems engineering* (pp. 115–136). Berlin, Germany: Springer-Verlag. doi:10.1007/978-3-642-12544-7_7.

Dardenne, A., Lamsweerde, A. v., & Fickas, S. (1993). Goal-directed requirements acquisition. *Science of Computer Programming, 20*, 3–50. doi:10.1016/0167-6423(93)90021-G.

Davenport, J., & Keane, M. T. (1999). Similarity and structural alignment: You can have one without the other. In *Proceedings of the Twenty First Annual Conference of the Cognitive Science Society* (pp. 132-137).

Davenport, T. H. (1993). *Process innovation: Reengineering work through information technology*. Boston, MA: Harvard Business School Press.

David, P., & Spence, M. (2007). *Designing institutional infrastructure for e-science*. Retrieved from http://www.stanford.edu/group/siepr/cgi-bin/siepr/?q=system/files/shared/pubs/papers/pdf/07-23.pdf

Davis, G. B. (1982). Strategies for information requirements determination. *IBM Systems Journal, 21*(1), 1982. doi:10.1147/sj.211.0004.

Dayal, U., Whang, K.-Y., Lomet, D., Alonso, G., Lohman, G., Kersten, M., et al. (Eds.). (2006, September 12-15). In *Proceedings of the 32nd International Conference on Very Large Data Bases,* Seoul, Korea. New York, NY: ACM Press.

De Marco, T. (1979). *Structured Analysis and System Specification*. Upper Saddle River, NJ: Prentice Hall.

Degen, W., Heller, B., Herre, H., & Smith, B. (2001). GOL: A General Ontological Language. In Welty, C., & Smith, B. (Eds.), *Formal Ontology and Information Systems* (pp. 34–46). New York: ACM Press.

Deiters, W., Löffeler, T., & Pfenningschmidt, S. (2003). The information logistical approach toward a user demand-driven information supply. In Spinellis, D. (Ed.), *Cross-media service delivery* (pp. 37–48). Boston, MA: Kluwer Academic.

Delone, W. H., & McLean, E. R. (1992). Information systems success: The quest for the dependent variable. *Information Systems Research, 3*(1), 60–95. doi:10.1287/isre.3.1.60.

Deneckère, R., & Kornyshova, E. (2010). Process line configuration: An indicator-based guidance of the intentional model MAP. In I. Bider, T. Halpin, J. Krogstie, S. Nurcan, E. Proper, R. Schmidt, & R. Ukor (Eds.), *Proceedings of the 11th International Workshop on Enterprise, Business Process and Information Systems Modeling*, Hammamet, Tunisie (LNBI 50, pp. 327-339).

Deneckère, R., Iacovelli, A., Kornyshova, E., & Souveyet, C. (2008). From method fragments to method services. In *Proceedings of the Evaluation of Modeling Methods in Systems Analysis and Design Conference*, Montpellier, France.

Deneckère, R., & Kornyshova, E. (2010). *La variabilité due à la sensibilité au contexte dans les processus téléologiques*. Marseille, France: Informatique des Organisations et Systèmes d'Information et de Décision.

Dey, A. K. (2000). *Providing architectural support for building context-aware applications*. Unpublished doctoral dissertation, Georgia Institute of Technology, Atlanta, GA.

Dey, A., & Abowd, G. (2000, April). Towards a better understanding of context and context-awareness. In *Proceedings of the Workshop on the What, Who, Where, When and How of Context-Awareness*, Hague, The Netherlands.

Dey, A., Abowd, G., & Salber, D. (2001). A conceptual framework and toolkit for supporting the rapid prototyping of context-aware applications. *Human-Computer Interaction*, *16*(2-4), 97–166. doi:10.1207/S15327051HCI16234_02.

Dietz, J. L. G. (2006). *Enterprise Ontology: Theory and Methodology*. Berlin: Springer. doi:10.1007/3-540-33149-2.

Dijkman, R., Dumas, M., & Ouyang, C. (2008). Semantics and analysis of business process models. *Information and Software Technology*, *50*(12), 1281–1294. doi:10.1016/j.infsof.2008.02.006.

Dimitrov, M., Simov, A., Stein, S., & Konstantinov, M. (2007). A BPMO based semantic business process modelling environment. In *Proceedings of the Workshop on Semantic Business Process and Product Lifecycle Management* (Vol. 251).

Dinh-Trong, T. T., & Bieman, J. M. (2005). The freeBSD project: A replication case study of open source development. *IEEE Transactions on Software Engineering*, *31*(6), 481–495. doi:10.1109/TSE.2005.73.

Do, H. H. (2006). *Schema matching and mapping-based data integration*. Unpublished doctoral dissertation, Universität Leipzig, Leipzig, Germany.

Doan, A., Madhaven, J., Domingos, P., & Halevy, A. (2004). Ontology matching: A machine learning approach. In Staab, S., & Studer, R. (Eds.), *Handbook on ontologies* (pp. 397–416). New York, NY: Springer.

Dobing, B., & Parsons, J. (2006). How UML is Used. *Communications of the ACM*, *49*(5), 109–113. doi:10.1145/1125944.1125949.

Dobing, B., & Parsons, J. (2008). Dimensions of UML Use: A Survey of Practitioners. *Journal of Database Management*, *19*(1), 1–18.

Doerr, J., Kerkow, D., Koenig, T., Olsson, T., & Suzuki, T. (2005) Non-functional requirements in industry: Three case studies adopting an experience based NFR method. In *Proceedings of the 13th IEEE International Conference on Requirements Engineering*, Paris, France (pp. 373-382).

Dori, D. (2002). *Object-process methodology*. Berlin, Germany: Springer-Verlag.

Drury, J. L., & Scott, S. D. (2008). Awareness in unmanned aerial vehicle operations. *International C2 Journal, 2*(1).

Du, X., Song, W., & Munro, M. (2007, August 29-31). Semantic service description framework for addressing imprecise service requirements. In *Proceedings of the 16th International Conference on Information System Development*, Galway, Ireland.

Du, X., Song, W., & Munro, M. (2008, August 25-27). A method for transforming existing web service descriptions into an enhanced semantic web service framework. In *Proceedings of the 17th International Conference on Information System Development*, Paphos, Cyprus.

Dumas, M., Garcia-Banuelos, L., & Dijkman, R. M. (2009). Similarity search of business process models. *A Quarterly Bulletin of the Computer Society of the IEEE Technical Committee on Data Engineering, 32*(3), 23–28.

Dustdar, S., & Schreiner, W. (2005). A survey on web services composition. *International Journal of Web and Grid Services*, *1*(1), 1–30. doi:10.1504/IJWGS.2005.007545.

Editor, O. W. L.-S. (2008). *Related projects*. Retrieved from http://owlseditor.semwebcentral.org/related.shtml

Ehrig, M. (2005). *Foam - framework for ontology alignment and mapping*. Retrieved from http://www.aifb.uni-karlsruhe.de

Ehrig, M., Haase, P., Stojanovic, N., & Hefke, M. (2005) Similarity for ontologies - a comprehensive framework. In *Proceedings of the 13th European Conference on Information Systems*.

Ehrig, M., Koschmider, A., & Oberweis, A. (2007). Measuring similarity between semantic business process models. In *Proceedings of the Fourth Asia-Pacific Conference on Conceptual Modelling*, Darlinghurst, Australia (pp. 71-80).

El Emam, K., Benlarbi, S., Goel, N., Melo, W., Lounis, H., & Rai, S. (2002). The optimal class size for object-oriented software. *IEEE Transactions on Software Engineering*, *28*(5), 494–509. doi:10.1109/TSE.2002.1000452.

El Emam, K., & Jung, H. (2001). An empirical evaluation of the ISO/IEC 15504 assessment model. *Journal of Systems and Software*, *59*(1), 23–43. doi:10.1016/S0164-1212(01)00046-2.

Elsayed, I., Han, J., Liu, T., Woehrer, A., Khan, F. A., & Brezany, P. (2008). Grid-enabled non-invasive blood glucose measurement. In M. Bubak, G. Dick van Albada, J. Dongarra & P. M.A. Sloot (Eds.), *Proceedings of the 8th International Conference on Computational Science, Part I* (LNCS 5101, pp. 76-85).

Eriksson, P., & Kovalainen, A. (2008). *Qualitative methods in business research*. Thousand Oaks, CA: Sage.

Erl, T. (2007). *SOA Principles of Service Design*. Upper Saddle River, NJ: Prentice Hall.

Estrada, H., Martínez, A., & Pastor, O. (2003). Goal-based business modeling oriented towards late requirements generation. In G. Goos, J. Hartmanis, & J. van Leeuwen (Eds.), *Proceedings of the 22nd International Conference on Conceptual Modeling* (LNCS 2813, pp. 277-290).

Euzénat, J., Loup, D., Touzani, M., & Valtchev, P. (2004). Ontology alignment with OLA. In *Proceedings of the 3rd EON Workshop at the 3rd International Semantic Web Conference*.

Euzénat, J., & Shvaiko, P. (2007). *Ontology matching*. Berlin, Germany: Springer-Verlg.

Evermann, J. (2003). *Using Design Languages for Conceptual Modeling: The UML CASE*. Unpublished doctoral dissertation, The University of British Columbia, Vancouver, Canada.

Evermann, J., & Wand, Y. (2001). An Ontological Examination of Object Interaction. In *Proceedings of the Eleventh Workshop on Information Technologies*, New Orleans, LA (pp. 91-96).

Evermann, J., & Wand, Y. (2001). Towards Ontologically based Semantics for UML Constructs. In *Proceedings of the 20th International Conference on Conceptual Modeling (ER'2001)*, Yokohama, Japan (pp. 354-367).

Evermann, J. (2009). A UML and OWL Description of Bunge's Upper Level Ontology Model. *Software and Systems Modeling*, *8*(2), 235–249. doi:10.1007/s10270-008-0082-3.

Evermann, J., & Wand, Y. (2006). Ontological Modelling Rules for UML: An Empirical Assessment. *Journal of Computer Information Systems*, *46*(5), 14–19.

Evermann, J., & Wand, Y. (2009). Ontology Based Object-Oriented Domain Modeling: Representing Behavior. *Journal of Database Management*, *20*(1), 48–77.

Ewusi-Mensah, K. (1997). Critical issues in abandoned information systems development projects. *Communications of the ACM*, *40*(9), 74–80. doi:10.1145/260750.260775.

Falconer, S., Noy, N., & Storey, M. A. (2006). Towards understanding the needs of cognitive support for ontology mapping. In *Proceedings of the Workshop on Ontology Matching at the International Semantic Web Conference*.

Fayyad, U. M., Piatetsky-Shapiro, G., & Smyth, P. (Eds.). (1996). *From data mining to knowledge discovery: An overview*. Menlo Park, CA: AAAI Press.

FDA. (1997). *Design control guidance for medical device manufacturers*. Retrieved from http://www.fda.gov/downloads/MedicalDevices/DeviceRegulationandGuidance/GuidanceDocuments/UCM070642.pdf

FDA. (2002). General principles of software validation: Final guidance for industry and FDA staff. Retrieved from http://www.pacontrol.com/download/General-Principles-of-Software- Validation.pdf

FDA. (2009). *Glossary of computer systems software development terminology*. Retrieved from http://www.fda.gov/iceci/inspections/inspectionguides/ucm074875.htm

FDA. (2009). *Guidelines: Regulatory information*. Retrieved from http://www.fda.gov/RegulatoryInformation/Legislation/default.htm

Feller, J., & Fitzgerald, B. (2002). *Understanding open source software development*. Reading, MA: Addison-Wesley.

Fensel, D., Lausen, H., Polleres, A., Bruijn, J., & Stollberg, M. Roman, D., & Domingue, J. (2007). Enabling semantic web services: The web service modeling ontology. New York, NY: Springer.

Fensel, D., & Bussler, C. (2002). The web service modeling framework WSMF. *Electronic Commerce Research and Applications, 1*(2), 113–137. doi:10.1016/S1567-4223(02)00015-7.

Fenton, N. E., & Pfleeger, S. L. (1991). *Software metrics: A rigorous approach*. New York, NY: Chapman & Hall.

Fenton, N., & Pfleeger, S. (1997). *Software metrics: A rigorous and practical approach* (2nd ed.). Boston, MA: Course Technology.

Ferenc, R., Siket, I., & Gyimothy, T. (2004, September). Extracting facts from open source software. In *Proceedings of the 20th International Conference on Software Maintenance*, Chicago, IL (pp. 60-69).

Ferrario, R., & Guarino, N. (2008). Towards an Ontological Foundation for service Science. In *Proceedings of the First Future Internet Symposium (FIS 2008)*, Vienna, Austria (pp. 152-169). Berlin: Springer.

Field, A. (2005). *Discovering statistics using SPSS*. Thousand Oaks, CA: Sage.

Finkelstein, C. (2004). Enterprise Integration Using Enterprise Architecture. In Linger, H., (Eds.), *Constructing the Infrastructure for the Knowledge Economy* (pp. 43–82). New York: Kluwer Academic/Plenum Publishers.

Firesmith, D., & Henderson-Sellers, B. (2001). *The OPEN process framework: An introduction*. Reading, MA: Addison-Wesley.

Fluit, C., Sabou, M., & van Harmelen, F. (2004). Supporting user tasks through visualization of light-weight ontologies. In Staab, S., & Studer, R. (Eds.), *Handbook on ontologies* (pp. 415–434). New York, NY: Springer.

Flynn, D., & Jazi, M. D. (1994). Organisational and information systems modeling for information systems requirements determination. In P. Loucopoulos (Ed.), *Proceedings of the 13th International Conference on Entity-Relationship Approach* (LNCS 881, pp. 79-93).

Forsström, J. (1997). Why certification of medical software would be useful? International Journal of Medical Informatics, 47(3), 143–151. doi:10.1016/S1386-5056(97)00098-1 doi:10.1016/S1386-5056(97)00098-1.

Fowler, M. (1999). *Refactoring: Improving the design of existing code*. New York, NY: Pearson Education.

Fox, G., & Gannon, D. (2006). Workflow in grid systems. *Concurrency and Computation*, 1009–1019. doi:10.1002/cpe.1019.

Fragidis, G., & Tarabanis, K. (2006). From repositories of best practices to networks of best practices. In *Proceedings of the International Conference on Management of Innovation and Technology* (pp. 370-374). Washington, DC: IEEE Computer Society.

Frakes, W. B., & Nejmeh, B. A. (1987). Software reuse through information retrieval. *SIGIR Forum, 21*(1-2), 30–36. doi:10.1145/24634.24636.

Frankel, D. (2003). *Model driven architecture: Applying MDA to enterprise computing*. Indianapolis, IN: Wiley Publishing.

Fraser, F., Ambler, S. W., Bornstein, G., Dubinsky, Y., & Succi, G. (2007). Learning more about "software best practices." In *Proceedings of the 8th International Conference on Agile Processes in Software Engineering and Extreme Programming (XP)* (pp. 271-274).

Freire, J., Koop, D., Santos, E., & Silva, C. T. (2008). Provenance for computational tasks: A survey. *Computing in Science & Engineering, 10*(3), 11–21. doi:10.1109/MCSE.2008.79.

Gaiser, T. (1997). Conducting online focus groups: A methodological discussion. *Social Science Computer Review, 15*(2), 135–144. doi:10.1177/089443939701500202.

Gane, C., & Sarson, T. (1979). *Structured System Analysis*. Upper Saddle River, NJ: Prentice Hall.

Gansner, E. R., & North, S. C. (2000). An open graph visualization system and its applications to software engineering. *Software, Practice & Experience, 30*(11), 1203–1233. doi:10.1002/1097-024X(200009)30:11<1203::AID-SPE338>3.0.CO;2-N.

Gatrell, M., Counsell, S., & Hall, T. (2009, October). Design patterns and change proneness: A replication using proprietary C# software. In *Proceedings of the IEEE Working Conference on Reverse Engineering*, Lille, France.

Gemino, A. (1998). To be or maybe to be: An empirical comparison of mandatory and optional properties in conceptual modeling. In *Proceedings of the Ann. Conf. Admin. Sci. Assoc. of Canada* (pp. 33-44). Saskatoon, Canada: Information Systems Division.

Gemino, A., & Wand, Y. (2004). A Framework for Empirical Evaluation of Conceptual Modeling Techniques. *Requirements Engineering*, 9(4), 248–260. doi:10.1007/s00766-004-0204-6.

Gemino, A., & Wand, Y. (2005). Complexity and Clarity in Conceptual Modeling: Comparison of Mandatory and Optional Properties. *Data & Knowledge Engineering*, 55(3), 301–326. doi:10.1016/j.datak.2004.12.009.

Gerede, C. E., & Su, J. (2007). Specification and verification of artifact behaviors in business process models. In B. Krämer, K.-J. Lin, & P. Narasimhan (Eds.), *Proceedings of the 5th International Conference on Service-Oriented Computing* (LNCS 4749, pp. 181-192).

German, D. M. (2004). Mining CVS repositories, the softchange experience. In *Proceedings of the 1st International Workshop on Mining Software Repositories* (pp. 17-21).

Gibb, F., McCartan, C., O'Donnell, R., Sweeney, N., & Leon, R. (2000). The integration of information retrieval techniques within a soft-ware reuse environment. *Journal of Information Science*, 26(4), 211–226. doi:10.1177/016555150002600402.

Gilson, O., Silva, N., Grant, P. W., & Chen, M. (2008). From web data to visualization via ontology mapping. *Computer Graphics Forum*, 27(3). doi:10.1111/j.1467-8659.2008.01230.x.

Giunchigli, F. Shvaiko, P., & Yatskevich, M. (2004). S-match: An algorithm and an implementation of semantic matching. In C. J. Bussler, J. Davies, D. Fensel, & R. Studer (Eds.), *Proceedings of the First European Semantic Web Symposium on the Semantic Web: Research and Applications* (LNCS 3053, pp. 61-75).

Glinz, M. (2000). Problems and Deficiencies of UML as a Requirements Specification Language. In *Proceedings of the 10-th International Workshop on Software Specification and Design,* San Diego (pp. 11-22).

Goderis, A., Li, P., & Goble, C. A. (2006). Workflow discovery: The problem, a case study from e-science and a graph-based solution. In *Proceedings of the International Conference on Web Services* (pp. 312-319). Washington, DC: IEEE Computer Society.

Godfrey, M., & Tu, Q. (2001). Growth, evolution and structural change in open source software. In *Proceedings of the 4th International Workshop on Principles of Software Evolution*, Vienna, Austria.

Goldkuhl, G., & Cronholm, S. (1993, June 14-16). *Customizable CASE environments: A framework for design and evaluation.* Paper presented at the COPE IT/Nord-DATA Workshop, Copenhagen, Denmark.

Goldkuhl, G. (1999). *The grounding of usable knowledge: An inquiry in the epistemology of action knowledge.* Linköping, Sweden: Linköping University.

Goldkuhl, G., Lind, M., & Seigerroth, U. (1998). Method integration: The need for a learning perspective. *IEEE Software*, 145(4).

Goldstone, R. L., & Son, J. (2005). Similarity. In Holyoak, K., & Morrison, R. (Eds.), *Cambridge handbook of thinking and reasoning* (pp. 13–36). Cambridge, UK: Cambridge University Press.

Gomes, P., Pereira, F. C., Paiva, P., Seco, N., Carreiro, P., & Ferreira, J. L. et al. (2004). Using wordnet for case-based retrieval of uml models. *AI Communications*, 17(1), 13–23.

Gonzales-Perez, C. (2007). Supporting situational method engineering with ISO/IEC 24744 and the work product tool approach. In *Proceedings of the International IFIP WG8.1 Working Conference on Situational Method Engineering: Fundamentals and Experiences*, Geneva, Switzerland (pp. 7-18).

Gordijn, J., Akkermans, H., & van Vliet, H. (2000). Business Process Modeling is not Process Modeling. In Conceptual Modeling for E-Business and the Web (LNCS1921, pp. 40-51). New York: Springer.

Gordijn, J., Akkermans, J. M., & van Vliet, J. C. (2000). Business Modeling is not Process Modeling. Conceptual Modeling for e-Business and the Web. In *Proceedings of ER 2000 Workshops on Conceptual Modeling Approaches for E-Business and the World Wide Web and Conceptual Modeling*, Salt Lake City, UT (LNCS 1921, pp. 40-51). New York: Springer Verlag.

Gordijn, J., de Kinderen, S., Pijpers, V., & Akkermans, H. (2008). E-Services in a Networked World: From Semantics to Pragmatics. In *Proceedings of Future Internet Symposium (FIS 2008)*, Vienna, Austria.

Gordijn, J., Petit, M., & Wieringa, R. (2006). Understanding Business Strategies of Networked Value Constellations Using Goal and Value Modeling. In *Proceedings of the 14th IEEE International Conference on Requirement Engineering (RE 2006)*, Minneapolis/St.Paul, MN (pp. 126-135). Washington, DC: IEEE Computer Society.

Gordijn, J., Yu, E., & Raadt van der, B. (2006). e-Service Design Using i* and e3 value Modeling. *IEEE Software, 23*(3), 26-33.

Gordijn, J., & Akkermans, H. (2001). E3-value: Design and Evaluation of e-Business Models. *IEEE Intelligent Systems, 16*(4), 11–17. doi:10.1109/5254.941353.

Goyal, S., & Westenthaler, R. (2003). *RDF gravity (RDF graph visualization tool)*. Retrieved from http://semweb.salzburgresearch.at/apps/rdf-gravity/index.html

Green, P., & Rosemann, M. (2000). Integrated Process Modeling: An Ontological Evaluation. *Information Systems, 25*(2), 73–87. doi:10.1016/S0306-4379(00)00010-7.

Greenwood, M., Goble, C., Stevens, R., Zhao, J., Addis, M., Marvin, D., et al. (2003). Provenance of e-science experiments – experience from bioinformatics. In *Proceedings of the UK e-Science All Hands Meeting* (pp. 223-226).

Greenwood, M., Glover, K., Pocock, M. R., Wipat, A., & Li, P. (2004). Taverna: A tool for the composition and enactment of bioinformatics workflows. *Bioinformatics (Oxford, England), 20*(17), 3045–3054. doi:10.1093/bioinformatics/bth361.

Grewal, R., Lilien, G. L., & Mallapragada, G. (2006). Location, location, location: How network embeddedness affects project success in open source systems. *Management Science, 52*(7), 1043–1046. doi:10.1287/mnsc.1060.0550.

Grosso, E., Eriksson, H., Fergerson, R., Tu, S., & Musen, M. (1999). Knowledge-modeling at the millenium the design and evolution of Protégé-2000. In *Proceedings of the 12th International Workshop on Knowledge Acquisition, Modeling and Management.*

Gruber, T. (1993). A translation approach to portable ontology specifications. *Knowledge Acquisition, 5*(2). doi:10.1006/knac.1993.1008.

Gu, T., Wang, X. H., Pung, H. K., & Zhang, D. Q. (2004). An ontology-based context model in intelligent environments. In *Proceedings of the Communication Networks and Distributed Systems Modeling and Simulation Conference* (pp. 270-275).

Guha, R., McCool, R., & Fikes, R. (2004, November). Contexts for the semantic web. In S. A. McIlraith, D. Plexousakis, & F. van Harmelen (Eds.), *Proceedings of the Third International Semantic Web Conference*, Hiroshima, Japan (LNCS 3298, pp. 32-46).

Guizzardi, G. (2007). Modal Aspects of Object Types and Part-Whole Relations and the de re/de dicto distinction. In *Proceedings of the 19th International Conference on Advanced Information Systems Engineering,* Trondheim, Norway (LNCS 4495). Berlin: Springer Verlag.

Guizzardi, G. (2005). *Ontological Foundations of Structural Conceptual Models*. Amsterdam, The Netherlands: Telematica Instituut.

Guizzardi, G., & Wagner, G. (2010). Using the Unified Foundational Ontology (UFO) as a Foundation for General Conceptual Modeling Languages. In Poli, R., Healy, M., & Kameas, A. (Eds.), *Theory and Application of Ontologies*. Heidelberg, Germany: Springer Verlag. doi:10.1007/978-90-481-8847-5_8.

Gustas, R. (2010). A Look behind Conceptual Modeling Constructs in Information System Analysis and Design. *International Journal of Information System Modeling and Design, 1*(1), 79–108.

Gustas, R., & Gustiene, P. (2008). Pragmatic – Driven Approach for Service-Oriented Analysis and Design. In *Information Systems Engineering: From Data Analysis to Process Networks* (pp. 97–128). Hershey, PA: IGI Global.

Gustas, R., & Gustiene, P. (2009). *Service-Oriented Foundation and Analysis Patterns for Conceptual Modeling of Information Systems. Information System Development: Challenges in Practice, Theory and Education* (Vol. 1). New York: Springer.

Guzélian, G., & Cauvet, C. (2007). SO2M: Towards a service-oriented approach for method engineering. In *Proceedings of the World Congress in Computer Science, Computer Engineering and Applied Computing*, Las Vegas, NV.

Halleux, P., Mathieu, L., & Andersson, B. (2008). *A method to support the alignment of business models and goal models*. Paper presented at the 3rd International Workshop on Business/IT-Aligment and Interoperability CEUR Workshop.

Hammer, M. (1990). Reengineering work: Don't automate, obliterate. *Harvard Business Review, 68*(4), 104.

Hammer, M., & Champy, J. (1993). *Reengineering the corporation: A manifesto for business revolution*. London, UK: Nicholas Brealey Publishing.

Hamou-Lhadj, A. K., & Hamou-Lhadj, A. (2007). Towards a compliance support framework for global software companies. *The IASTED International Conference on Software Engineering and Applications* (pp 31-36).

Harel, D., & Rumpe, B. (2004). Meaningful Modeling: What's the Semantics of 'Semantics'? *IEEE Computer*, 64-72.

Harel, D. (1987). Statecharts: A Visual Formalism for Complex Systems. *Science of Computer Programming, 8*, 231–274. doi:10.1016/0167-6423(87)90035-9.

Harmon, P. (2009). The scope and evolution of business process management. In vom Brocke, J., & Rosemann, M. (Eds.), *Handbook on business process management*. New York, NY: Springer.

Harmsen, A. F., Brinkkemper, J. N., & Oei, J. L. H. (1994). Situational method engineering for information systems project approaches. In *Proceedings of the International IFIP WG8.1 Conference on Methods and Associated Tools for the Information Systems Life Cycle*.

Harmsen, F. (1997). *Situational method engineering*. Cambridge, UK: Ernst & Young.

Harrison, R., Counsell, S., & Nithi, R. (2000). Experimental assessment of the effect of inheritance on the maintainability of object-oriented systems. *Journal of Systems and Software, 52*(2-3), 173–179. doi:10.1016/S0164-1212(99)00144-2.

Harter, D. E., Krishnan, M. S., & Slaughter, S. A. (2000). Effects of process maturity on quality, cycle time, and effort in software product development. *Management Science, 46*(4), 451–466. doi:10.1287/mnsc.46.4.451.12056.

Haselhoff, S. (2001). Optimising information flow by means of context: Models and architecture. In *Proceeding of the Informatik Conference* [Wirtschaft und Wissenschaft in der Network Economy].

Hella, L., & Krogstie, J. (2010). A structured evaluation to assess the reusability of models of user profiles. In *Proceedings of the Conference on Exploring Modeling Methods in Systems Analysis and Design*.

Henderson-Sellers, B. (2002). Process meta-modelling and process construction: Examples using the OPF. *Annals of Software Engineering, 14*(1-4).

Henkel, M., Perjons, E., & Zdravkovic, J. (2006). A Value-based Foundation for Service. In Modelling. In *Proceedings of the European Conference on Web Services (ECOWS'06)*, Zurich, Switzerland (pp. 129-137). Washington, DC: IEEE.

Hepp, M., Leymann, F., Domingue, J., Wahler, A., & Fensel, D. (2005). Semantic business process management: A vision towards using semantic web services for business process management. *In Proceedings of the IEEE International Conference on e-Business Engineering* (pp. 535-540). Washington, DC: IEEE Computer Society.

Hevner, A. R., March, S. T., Park, J., & Ram, S. (2004). Design science in information systems research. *Management Information Systems Quarterly, 28*(1), 75–105.

Hidders, J., Dumas, M., Van der Aalst, W. M. P., ter Hofstede, A. H. M., & Verelst, J. (2005). When are two workflows the same? In *Proceedings of the Australasian Symposium on Theory of Computing* (pp. 3-11).

HISA. (2007). *Health Informatics – Service Architecture (HISA), Part 1: Enterprise Viewpoint* (CEN/TC 215/prEN 12967-1). Retrieved April 2010, from www.kith.no/upload/4120/ISOTC215_pCD_12967-1_HISA-20070208.doc

Hoffer, J. A., George, J. F., & Valacich, J. S. (1996). *Modern systems analysis and design*. Reading, MA: Benjamin Cummings Publishing.

Holland, C. P., Shaw, D. R., & Kawalek, P. (2005). BP's multi-enterprise asset management system. *Information and Software Technology, 47*(15), 999–1007. doi:10.1016/j.infsof.2005.09.006.

Holmes, R., & Murphy, G. C. (2005). Using structural context to recommend source code examples. In *Proceedings of the 27th International Conference on Software Engineering* (pp. 117-125). New York, NY: ACM Press.

Honda, K., Yoshida, N., & Carbone, M. (2008). Multiparty asynchronous session types. In *Proceedings of the 35th Annual ACM SIGPLAN-SIGACT Symposium on Principles of Programming Languages* (p. 273-284). New York, NY: ACM Press.

Horkoff, J., & Yu, E. (2010). Interactive Analysis of Agent-Goal Models in Enterprise Modeling. *International Journal of Information System Modeling and Design, 1*(4).

Hosmer, D. W., & Lemeshow, S. (2000). *Applied logistic regression*. New York, NY: John Wiley & Son. doi:10.1002/0471722146.

Hruby, P. (2006). *Model-Driven Design of Software Applications with Business Patterns*. New York: Springer Verlag.

Humphrey, W. S. (2007). Software process the improvement – a personal view: How it started and where it is going. *Software Process Improvement and Practice, 12*, 223–227. doi:10.1002/spip.324.

Iacovelli, A., Souveyet, C., & Rolland, C. (2008). Method as a service (MaaS). In *Proceedings of the International Conference on Research Challenges in Information Science*, Marrakech, Morocco (pp. 371-380).

Ide, N., & Vernis, J. (1998). Introduction to the Special Issue on Word Sense Disambiguation: The State of the Art. *Computational Linguistics, 24*(1), 2–40.

IEEE Standards Association. (1983). *IEEE standard for software test documentation*. Retrieved from http://standards.ieee.org/reading/ieee/std_public/description/se/829-1983_desc.html

Ingram, S. F. (2005). *An interactive small world graph visualization*. Retrieved from http://www.cs.ubc.ca/~sfingram/cs533C/small_world.pdf

Ingwersen, P. (1992). *Information retrieval interaction*. London, UK: Taylor Graham.

Inoue, K., Yokomori, R., Yamamoto, T., Matsushita, M., & Kusumoto, S. (2005). Ranking significance of software components based on use relations. *IEEE Transactions on Software Engineering, 31*(3), 213–225. doi:10.1109/TSE.2005.38.

Irwin, G., & Turk, D. (2005). An Ontological Analysis of Use Case Modeling Grammar. *Journal of the Association for Information Systems, 6*(1), 1–36.

Jacobson, I., & NG, P.-W. (2005). *Aspect-Oriented Software Development with Use Cases*. Upper Saddle River, NJ: Pearson Education.

Janciak, I., Kloner, C., & Brezany, P. (2008, September 29-October 1). Workflow enactment engine for WSRF-compliant services orchestration. In *Proceedings of the 9th IEEE/ACM International Conference on Grid Computing* (pp. 1-8).

Jayasinghe, D. (2008). *Quickstart apache axis2*. Birmingham, UK: Packt Publishing.

Jeffery, M., & Lelifeld, I. (2004). Best practices in IT portfolio management. *MIT Sloan Management Review*, 41-49.

Jensen, C., & Scacchi, W. (2005). Collaboration, leadership, control, and conflict negotiation and the netbeans.org open source software development community. In *Proceedings of the 38th Annual Hawaii International Conference* (p. 196b).

JHawk tool. (2011). *Virtual machinery*. Retrieved from http://www.virtualmachinery.com/jhawkprod.htm

Johannesson, P., Andersson, B., & Weigand, H. (2010). Resource Analysis and Classification for Purpose Driven Value Model Design. *International Journal of Information System Modeling and Design, 1*(1), 56–78.

Jones, C. (2000). *Software assessments, benchmarks, and best practices*. Reading, MA: Addison-Wesley.

Jones, C. (2007). *Estimating software costs: Bringing realism to estimating*. New York, NY: McGraw Hill.

Jones, C. (2009). *Software engineering best practices: Lessons from successful projects in the top companies*. New York, NY: McGraw Hill.

Jonkers, H., Lankhorst, M., van Buuren, R., Bonsangue, M., & van der Torre, L. (2004). Concepts for Modeling Enterprise Architectures. *International Journal of Cooperative Information Systems*, *13*(3), 257–287. doi:10.1142/S0218843004000985.

Kalfoglou, Y., & Schorlemmer, M. (2002). Information flow based ontology mappings. In *Proceedings of the 1st International Conference on Ontologies, Databases and Application of Semantics.*

Kalman, R. E. (1960). A new approach to linear filtering and prediction problems. *ASME - Journal of Basic Engineering.*

Kaner, C., Back, J., & Prettichord, B. (2001). *Lessons learned in software testing*. Hoboken, NJ: John Wiley & Sons.

Karlsson, F., & Agerfalk, P. J. (2004). Method configuration: Adapting to situational characteristics while creating reusable assets. *Information and Software Technology*, *45*, 619–633. doi:10.1016/j.infsof.2003.12.004.

Kavakli, E. (2004). Modeling organizational goals: Analysis of current methods. In *Proceedings of the ACM Symposium on Applied Computing*, Nicosia, Cyprus (pp. 1339-1343).

Kavakli, E., & Loucopoulos, P. (2003). *Goal driven requirements engineering: Evaluation of current methods*. Paper presented at the 8th Workshop on Evaluation of Modeling Methods in Systems Analysis and Design, Velden, Austria.

Kavakli, E., & Loucopoulos, P. (1999). Goal-driven business process analysis application in eletricity deregulation. *Information Systems*, *24*, 187–207. doi:10.1016/S0306-4379(99)00015-0.

Kemerer, C., & Slaughter, S. (1999). Need for more longitudinal studies of software maintenance. *Empirical Software Engineering: An International Journal*, *2*, 109–118. doi:10.1023/A:1009741031615.

Kemerer, C., & Slaughter, S. (1999). An empirical approach to studying software evolution. *IEEE Transactions on Software Engineering*, *25*, 493–509. doi:10.1109/32.799945.

Kerdiles, G., & Salvat, E. (1997). A sound and complete proof procedure based on tableaux and projection. In D. Lukose, H. Delugach, M. Keeler, L. Searle, & J. Sowa (Eds.), *Proceedings of the Fifth International Conference on Conceptual Structures: Fulfilling Peirce's Dream* (LNCS 1257, pp. 371-385).

Khan, F. A., Han, Y., Pllana, S., & Brezany, P. (2008). Provenance support for grid-enabled scientific workflows. In *Proceedings of the International Conference on Semantics, Knowledge and Grid* (pp. 173-180).

Kiefer, C., Bernstein, A., Lee, H. J., Klein, M., & Stocker, M. (2007). Semantic process retrieval with iSPARQL. In *Proceedings of the 4th European Conference on the Semantic Web: Research and Applications* (pp. 609-623).

King, N., & Horrock, C. (2010). *Interviews in qualitative research*. Thousand Oaks, CA: Sage.

Kirsch Pinheiro, M., Vanrompay, Y., & Berbers, Y. (2008). Context-aware service selection using graph matching. In *Proceedings of the ECOWS Workshop* (Vol. 411).

Kivits, J. (2005). Online interviewing and the research relationship. In Hine, C. (Ed.), *Virtual methods: Issues in social research on the Internet* (pp. 35–49). Oxford, UK: Berg Publishers.

Klyne, G., Reynolds, F., Woodrow, C., Ohto, H., Hjelm, J., Butler, M. H., et al. (2004). *Composite capability/preference profiles (CC/PP): Structure and vocabularies 1.0*. Retrieved from http://www.w3.org/TR/2004/REC-CCPP-struct-vocab-20040115/

Kobryn, C. (2002). UML2 for System Engineering. In *Proceedings of the INCOSE 2002 Symposium.*

Koch, S. (2007). Software evolution in open source projects - a large-scale investigation. *Journal of Software Maintenance and Evolution: Research and Practice*, *19*(6). doi:10.1002/smr.348.

Koliadis, G., & Ghose, A. (2006). Relating business process models to goal-oriented requirements models in KAOS. In *Proceedings of the Pacific Knowledge Acquisition Workshop on Advances in Knowledge Acquisition and Management* (pp. 25-39).

Kontio, J., Lehtola, L., & Bragge, J. (2004) Using the focus group method in software engineering: obtaining practitioner and user experiences. In *Proceedings of the International Symposium on Empirical Software Engineering* (pp. 271-280). Washington, DC: IEEE Computer Society.

Kontio, J., Bragge, J., & Lehtola, L. (2008). The focus group research method as an empirical tool in software engineering. In Schull, F., Singer, J., & Sjøberg, D. I. K. (Eds.), *Guide to advanced empirical software engineering* (pp. 93–116). Berlin, Germany: Springer-Verlag. doi:10.1007/978-1-84800-044-5_4.

Kornyshova, E., & Deneckère, R. (2010). Decision-making ontology for information system engineering. In *Proceedings of the International Conference on Conceptual Modeling*, Vancouver, BC, Canada.

Kornyshova, E., Deneckère, R., & Salinesi, C. (2007). Method chunks selection by multicriteria techniques: an extension of the assembly-based approach. In *Proceedings of the International IFIP WG8.1 Working Conference on Situational Method Engineering: Fundamentals and Experiences*, Geneva, Switzerland (pp. 64-78).

Kotinurmi, P. (2001). *User profiles and their management*. Retrieved from http://www.tml.tkk.fi/Studies/Tik-111.590/2001s/papers/paavo_kotinurmi.pdf

Kotis, K., & Lanzenberger, M. (2008). Ontology matching: Current status, dilemmas and future challenges. In *Proceedings of the International Conference on Complex, Intelligent and Software Intensive Systems* (pp. 924-927).

Koubarakis, M., & Plexousakis, D. (2000). A formal model for business process modelling and design. In *Proceedings of the Conference on Advanced Information System Engineering* (pp. 142-156).

Kowalczykiewicz, K., & Weiss, D. (2002). Traceability: Taming uncontrolled change in software development. Foundations of Computing and Decision Sciences, 27(4), 239–248.

Krishnamurthy, S. (2002). Cave or community? An empirical examination of 100 mature open source projects. *First Monday*, 7(6).

Krishnan, M. S., & Kellner, M. I. (2005). Measuring process consistency: Implications for reducing software defects. *IEEE Transactions on Software Engineering*, 25(6), 800–815. doi:10.1109/32.824401.

Krogstie, J. (1999). Using quality function deployment in software requirements specification. In *Proceedings of the Fifth International Workshop on Requirements Engineering: Foundations for Software Quality*.

Krogstie, J., & Jørgensen, H. D. (2002). Quality of interactive models. In A. Olive, M. Yoshikawa, & E. S. K. Yu (Eds.), *Proceedings of the First International Workshop on Advanced Conceptual Modeling Techniques* (LNCS 2784, pp. 351-363).

Krogstie, J., Lindland, O., & Sindre, G. (1995). Towards a deeper understanding of quality in requirements engineering. In J. Iivari, K. Lyytinen, & M. Rossi (Eds.), *Proceedings of the 7th International Conference on Advanced Information Systems Engineering* (LNCS 932, pp. 82-95).

Krogstie, J. (2001). Using a semiotic framework to evaluate UML for the development of models of high quality. In Krogstie, J. (Ed.), *Unified modeling language: Systems analysis, design and development issues* (pp. 89–106). Hershey, PA: IGI Global. doi:10.4018/9781930708051. ch006.

Krogstie, J., & Arnesen, S. (2004). Assessing enterprise modeling languages using a generic quality framework. In Krogstie, J., Siau, K., & Halpin, T. (Eds.), *Information modeling methods and methodologies*. Hershey, PA: IGI Global. doi:10.4018/978-1-59140-375-3.ch004.

Krueger, R. A., & Casey, M. A. (2008). *Focus groups: A practical guide for applied research*. Thousand Oaks, CA: Sage.

Kueng, P., & Kawalek, P. (1997). Goal-based business process models: Creation and evaluation. *Business Process Management Journal*, 3, 17–38. doi:10.1108/14637159710161567.

Künzle, V., & Reichert, M. (2009). *Towards object-aware process management systems: Issues, challenges, benefits.* Paper presented at the 10th International Workshop on Business Process Modeling, Development, and Support, Amsterdam, The Netherlands.

Künzle, V., & Reichert, M. (2009). Integrating users in object-aware process management systems: Issues and challenges. In S. Rinderle-Ma, S. Sadiq, & F. Leymann (Eds.), *Proceedings of the 5th International Workshop on Business Process Design* (LNBIP. 43, pp. 29-41).

Küster, J., Ryndina, K., & Gall, H. (2007). Generation of business process models for object life cycle compliance. In G. Alonso, P. Dadam, & M. Rosemann (Eds.), *Proceedings of the 5th International Conference on Business Process Management* (LNCS 4714, pp. 165 -181).

Lambrix, P., & Tan, H. (2006). Sambo - a system for aligning and merging biomedical ontologies. *Journal of Web Semantics, 4*(3), 196–206. doi:10.1016/j.websem.2006.05.003.

Lamsweerde, A. (2000). Requirements engineering in the year 00: A research. In *Proceedings of the 22nd International Conference on Software Enginnering* (pp. 5-19).

Lamsweerde, A. (2001). Goal-oriented requirements engineering: A guided tour. In *Proceedings of the 5th IEEE International Symposium on Requirements Engineering* (pp. 249-262).

Lamsweerde, A., Darimont, R., & Letier, E. (1998). Managing conflicts in goal-driven requirements engineering. *IEEE Transactions on Software Engineering, 24*(11), 908–926. doi:10.1109/32.730542.

Lankhorst, M. M., Proper, H. A., & Jonkers, H. (2010). The Anatomy of the Archimate Language. *International Journal of Information System Modeling and Design, 1*(1), 1–32.

Lanzenberger, M., & Sampson, J. (2006) Alviz - a tool for visual ontology alignment. In *Proceedings of the 10th International Conference on Information Visualization* (pp. 430-440).

Lapouchnian, A. (2005). *Goal-oriented requirements engineering: An overview of the current research.* Toronoto, ON, Canada: University of Toronto.

Lara, R., Roman, D., Polleres, A., & Fensel, D. (2004). A conceptual comparison of WSMO and OWL-S. In L.-J. Zhang & M. Jeckle (Eds.), *Proceedings of the European Conference on Web Services* (LNCS 3250, pp. 254-269).

Larkey, L. B., & Markman, A. B. (2005). Processes of similarity judgment. *Cognitive Science, 29*(6), 1061–1076. doi:10.1207/s15516709cog0000_30.

Larman, C. (2003). Agile and iterative development: A manager's guide. Reading, MA: Addison-Wesley.

Larman, C. (2009). *Applying UML and Patterns: An Introduction to Object-Oriented Analysis and Design and Iterative Development* (3rd ed.). Upper Saddle River, NJ: Pearson Education.

Le Gloahec, V., Fleurquin, R., & Sadou, S. (2008). Good practices as a quality-oriented modelling assistant. In *Proceedings of the International Conference on Quality Software* (pp. 345-348). Washington, DC: IEEE Computer Society.

Lehman, M. M., Perry, D. E., & Ramil, J. F. (1998). Implications of evolution metrics on software maintenance. In *Proceedings of the International Conference on Software Maintenance* (pp. 208-217).

Lehman, M. M., & Ramil, J. F. (2001). Rules and tools for software evolution planning and management. *Annals of Software Engineering, 11*, 15–44. doi:10.1023/A:1012535017876.

Lehman, M. M., & Ramil, J. F. (2002). Software evolution and software processes. *Annals of Software Engineering, 14*, 275–309. doi:10.1023/A:1020557525901.

Lehtola, L., Kauppinen, M., & Kujala, S. (2004). Requirements prioritization challenges in practice. In F. Bomarius & H. Iida (Eds.), *Proceedings of the International Conference on Product Focused Software Process Improvement* (LNCS 3009, pp. 497-508).

Levi, K., & Arsanjani, A. (2003). A Goal–driven Approach to Enterprise Component Identification and Specification. *Communications of the ACM, 45*(10), 45–52.

Liaskos, S., Lapouchnian, A., Yu, Y., Yu, E., & Mylopoulos, J. (2006). On Goal-based Variability Acquisition and Analysis. In *Proceedings of the Conference on Requirements Engineering (RE'06)*, Minneapolis, MN (pp. 79-88). Washington, DC: IEEE Computer Society.

Lillehagen, F., & Krogstie, J. (2009). *Active knowledge modeling of enterprises*. New York, NY: Springer.

Lindland, O. I., Sindre, G., & Solvberg, A. (1994). Understanding Quality in Conceptual Modeling. *IEEE Software, 11*(2). doi:10.1109/52.268955.

Lind, M., & Seigerroth, U. (2003). Team-based reconstruction for expanding organisational ability. *Journal of the Operational Society, 54*, 119–129. doi:10.1057/palgrave.jors.2601474.

Lin, Y., Sampson, J., & Hakkarainen, S. (2004). An evaluation of UML and OWL using a semiotic quality framework. In Siau, K. (Ed.), *Advanced topics in database research* (Vol. 4, pp. 178–200). Hershey, PA: IGI Global.

Liu, R., Bhattacharya, K., & Wu, F. Y. (2007). Modeling business contexture and behavior using business artifacts. In J. Krogstie, A. Opdahl, & G. Sindre (Eds.), *Proceedings of the 19th International Conference on Advanced Information Systems Engineering* (LNCS 4495, pp. 324-339).

Li, W., & Henry, S. (1993). Object oriented metrics that predict maintainability. *Journal of Systems and Software, 23*, 112–122. doi:10.1016/0164-1212(93)90077-B.

Ljung, L. (1999). *System identification - theory for the use*. Upper Saddle River, NJ: Prentice Hall.

Llorens, J., Fuentes, J., & Morato, J. (2004). UML retrieval and reuse using XMI. In *Proceedings of the IASTED International Conference on Software Engineering* (pp. 740-746).

Lu, R., & Sadiq, S. (2006). Managing process variants as an information resource. In *Proceedings of the 4th International Conference on Business Process Management* (pp. 426-431). Washington, DC: IEEE Computer Society.

Lu, S. (2004). *Enforcing Ontological Rules in Conceptual Modeling Using UML: Principles and Implementation*. Unpublished master's thesis, Memorial University of Newfoundland, St. John's, Canada.

Ludäscher, B., Altintas, I., Berkley, C., Higgins, D., Jaeger, E., & Jones, M. et al. (2006). Scientific workflow management and the Kepler system: Research articles. *Concurrency and Computation, 18*, 1039–1065. doi:10.1002/cpe.994.

Ludwig, S., & Reyhani, S. (2005). Semantic approach to service discovery in a grid environment. *Journal of Web Semantics, 3*(4).

Lundqvist, M., Sandkuhl, K., Seigerroth, U., & Stirna, J. (2008). Method requirements for information demand analysis. In *Proceedings of the 2nd International Conference on Adaptive Business Systems*.

Lundqvist, M., Seigerroth, U., & Stirna, J. (2008). *InfoFlow application case: Experiences from modelling activities at SYSteam management*. Jönköping, Sweden: Jönköping University.

Maamar, Z., Benslimane, D., Thiran, P., Ghedira, C., Dustdar, S., & Sattanathan, S. (2007). Towards a context-based multi-type policy approach for web services composition. *Data & Knowledge Engineering, 62*(2), 327–351. doi:10.1016/j.datak.2006.08.007.

Maamar, Z., Mostefaoui, S. K., & Yahyaoui, H. (2005). Toward an agent-based and context-oriented approach for web services composition. *IEEE Transactions on Knowledge and Data Engineering, 17*(5), 686–697. doi:10.1109/TKDE.2005.82.

Mansar, S. L., & Reijers, H. A. (2005). Best practices in business process redesign: Validation of a redesign framework. *Computers in Industry, 56*(5), 457–471. doi:10.1016/j.compind.2005.01.001.

Mäntylä, M., & Lassenius, C. (2006). Subjective evaluation of software evolvability using code smells: An empirical study. *Journal of Empirical Software Engineering, 11*(3), 395–431. doi:10.1007/s10664-006-9002-8.

Marcotte, F., Grabot, B., & Affonso, R. (2008). Cooperation models for supply chain management. *International Journal of Logistics Systems and Management, 5*(1-2), 123–153.

Markovic, I., & Kowalkiewicz, M. (2008). Linking business goals to process models in semantic business process modeling. In *Proceedings of the 12th IEEE International Enterprise Distributed Object Computing Conference* (pp. 332-338).

Markovic, I., Pereira, A. C., & Stojanovic, N. (2008, February). *A framework for querying in business process modelling*. Paper presented at the Multikonferenz wirtschaftsin- formatik.

Martin, D., Burstein, M., Hobbs, J., Lassila, O., McDermott, D., Mcllraith, S., et al. (2004). *OWL-S: Semantic mark-up for web services.* Retrieved from http://www.daml.org/services/owl-s/1.0/owl-s.html

Martin, J., & Odell, J. J. (1998). Object-Oriented Methods: A Foundation (UML ed.). Upper Saddle River, NJ: Prentice-Hall.

Massey, O. T. (2010). A proposed model for the analysis and interpretation of focus groups in evaluation research. *Evaluation and Program Planning, 34*(1), 21–28. doi:10.1016/j.evalprogplan.2010.06.003.

Maximilien, E. M., & Laurie, W. (2003). Assessing test-driven development at IBM. In *Proceedings of the International Conference on Software Engineering*, Portland, OR (pp. 564 - 569). Washington, DC: IEEE Computer Society Press.

McGuinness, D., Fikes, R., & Wilder, S. (2000). An environment for merging and testing large ontologies. In *Proceedings of the 7th International Conference on Principles of Knowledge Representation and Reasoning* (pp. 483-493).

Medjahed, B., & Atif, Y. (2007). Context-based matching for web service composition. *Distributed and Parallel Databases, 21*(1), 5–37. doi:10.1007/s10619-006-7003-7.

Mehrfard, H., Pirzadeh, H., & Hamou-Lhadj, A. (2010). Investigating the capability of agile processes to support life-science regulations: The case of XP and FDA regulations with a focus on human factor requirements. In R. Lee, O. Ormandjieva, A. Abran, & C. Constantinides (Eds.), Software engineering research, management and applications (pp. 241–255). Berlin, Germany: Springer-Verlag. doi:10.1007/978-3-642-13273-5_16 doi:10.1007/978-3-642-13273-5_16.

Meissen, U., Pfennigschmidt, S., Voisard, A., & Wahnfried, T. (2004). Context- and situation-awareness in information logistics. In W. Lindner, M. Mesiti, C. Turker, Y. Tzitzikas, & A. I. Vakali (Eds.), *Proceedings of the Workshops on Current Trends in Database Technology* (LNCS 3268, pp. 448-451).

Menard, S. W. (2002). *Applied logistic regression analysis.* Thousand Oaks, CA: Sage.

Mende, M., Brecht, L., & Osterle, H. (1994). Evaluating Existing Information Systems from a Business Process Perspective. In *Proceedings of the 1994 Computer Personnel Research Conference on Reinventing IS*, Alexandria, VA (pp. 289-296). New York: ACM.

Merton, R. (2005). The focused interview and focus groups. *Public Opinion Quarterly, 51*(4), 550–566. doi:10.1086/269057.

Miller, S., & Xu, H. (2001) Integrating a heterogenous distributed data environment with a database specific ontology. In *Proceedings of the International Conference on Parallel and Distributed Computing Systems.*

Mindswap. (2008). *OWL-S API.* Retrieved from http://www.mindswap.org/2004/owl-s/api/

Mirbel, I. (2008). *Contributions à la modélisation, la réutilisation et la flexibilité des systèmes d'information.* Unpublished HDR thesis, Nice University, Nice, France.

Mirbel, I., & de Riviere, s V. (2002). Adapting analysis and design to software context: The jecko approach. In *Proceedings of the 8th International Conference on Object Oriented Information Systems.*

Mirbel, I., & Ralyté, J. (2006). Situational method engineering: Combining assembly-based and roadmap-driven approaches. *Requirements Engineering, 11*, 58–78. doi:10.1007/s00766-005-0019-0.

Mitra, P., Kersten, M., & Wiederhold, G. (2000). Graph oriented model for articulation of ontology independencies. In *Proceedings of the 7th International Conference on Extending Databases Technology.*

Mitra, P., Noy, N., & Jaiswal, A. (2005). Ontology mapping discovery with uncertainty. In Y. Gil, E. Motta, R. Benjamins, & M. A. Musen (Eds.), *Proceedings of the 4th International Semantic Web Conference* (LNCS 3729, pp. 537-547).

Mockus, A., Fielding, R. T., & Herbsleb, J. (2002). Two case studies of open source software development: Apache and Mozilla. *ACM Transactions on Software Engineering and Methodology, 11*(3), 309–346. doi:10.1145/567793.567795.

Montes-y-Gómez, M., Gelbukh, A., López-López, A., & Baeza-Yates, R. (2001). Flexible comparison of conceptual graphs. In H. C. Mayr, J. Lazansky, G. Quirchmayr, & P. Vogel (Eds.), *Proceeding of the 12th International Conference and Workshop on Database and Expert Systems Applications* (LNCS 2113, pp. 102-111).

Moody, L. D. (2009). The "physics" of notation: Towards a scientific basis for constructing visual notations in software engineering. *IEEE Transactions on Software Engineering, 35*(6), 756–779. doi:10.1109/TSE.2009.67.

Moreau, L., Clifford, B., Freire, J., Futrelle, J., Gil, Y., & Groth, P. et al. (2010). The open provenance model core specification (V1.1). *Future Generation Computer Systems, 27*(6), 743–756. doi:10.1016/j.future.2010.07.005.

Morgan, D. L. (1997). *Focus group as qualitative research method* (2nd ed., *Vol. 16*). Thousand Oaks, CA: Sage.

Mubarak, A., Counsell, S., & Hierons, H. (2008). An empirical study of "removed" classes in Java open-source. In *Proceedings of the Fourth International Joint Conferences on Computer, Information, and Systems Sciences, and Engineering*.

Mubarak, A., Counsell, S., & Hierons, R. (2008). Empirical observations on coupling, code warnings and versions in Java open-source. In *Proceedings of the Third IFIP TC2 Central and East European Conference on Software Engineering Techniques*, Brno, Czech Republic.

Mubarak, A., Counsell, S., & Hierons, R. (2009). Does an 80:20 rule apply to Java coupling? In *Proceedings of the International Conference on Evaluation and Assessment in Software Engineering*, Keele, UK.

Mubarak, A., Counsell, S., & Hierons, R. (2010, May 19-21). An evolutionary study of fan-in and fan-out metrics in OSS. In *Proceedings of the Fourth International Conference on Research Challenges in Information Science*, Nice, France.

Mubarak, A., Counsell, S., Hierons, R., & Hassoun, Y. (2007). Package evolvability and its relationship with refactoring. In *Proceedings of the Third International ERCIM Symposium on Software Evolution*, Paris, France.

Muehlen, M., & Recker, J. (2008). How much language is enough? Theoretical and practical use of the business process modeling notation. In Z. Bellahsène & M. L éonard (Eds.), Advanced Information Systems Engineering (LNCS 5074, pp. 465-479).

Mugnier, M. (2000). Knowledge representation and reasonings based on graph homomorphisms. In G. Mineau & B. Ganter (Eds.), *Proceedings of the 8th International Conference on Conceptual Structures* (LNAI 1867, pp. 172-192).

Müller, D., Reichert, M., & Herbst, J. (2007). Data-driven modeling and coordination of large process structures. In R. Meersman & Z. Tari (Eds.), *Proceedings of the 15th International Conference on Cooperative Information Systems* (LNCS 4803, pp. 131-149).

Mutschler, B., Weber, B., & Reichert, M. (2008). Workflow management versus case handling: Results from a controlled software experiment. In *Proceedings of the 23rd Annual ACM Symposium on Applied Computing, Special Track on Coordination Models, Languages and Architectures* (pp. 82-89).

Mylopoulos, J., Chung, L., & Yu, E. (1999). From Object-Oriented to Goal-Oriented Requirements Analysis. *Communications of the ACM, 42*(1). New York: ACM.

Mylopoulos, J., Chung, L., Yu, E., & Nixon, B. (1992). Representing and using non-functional requirements: A process-oriented approach. *IEEE Transactions on Software Engineering, 18*(6), 483–497. doi:10.1109/32.142871.

Nehan, Y. R., & Deneckère, R. (2007). Component-based situational methods - A framework for understanding SME. In *Proceedings of the International IFIP WG8.1 Working Conference on Situational Method Engineering: Fundamentals and Experiences*, Geneva, Switzerland.

Neiger, D., & Churilov, L. (2004). *Goal-oriented business process engineering revisited: A unifying perspective.* Paper presented at the First International Workshop on Computer Supported Activity Coordination, Porto, Portugal.

Neter, J., Wasserman, W., & Kutner, M. H. (2004). *Applied linear regression models.* New York, NY: McGraw-Hill.

Ngo-The, A., & Ruhe, G. (2005). Decision support in requirements engineering. In Aurum, A., & Wohlin, C. (Eds.), *Engineering and managing software requirements* (pp. 267–286). Berlin, Germany: Springer-Verlag. doi:10.1007/3-540-28244-0_12.

Niazi, M., Wilson, D., & Zowghi, D. (2005). A framework for assisting the design of effective software process improvement implementation strategies. *Journal of Systems and Software*, 78(2), 204–222. doi:10.1016/j.jss.2004.09.001.

Nicolaou, A. I. (2008). Research issues on the use of ERP in inter-organizational relationships. *International Journal of Accounting Information Systems*, 9(4), 216–226. doi:10.1016/j.accinf.2008.09.003.

Nigam, A., & Caswell, N. S. (2003). Business artifacts - an approach to operational specification. *IBM Systems Journal*, 42(3), 428–445. doi:10.1147/sj.423.0428.

Nord, R. L., Tomayko, J. E., & Wojcik, R. (2004). *Integrating software-architecture-centric methods into extreme programming (XP)* (Tech. Rep. No. CMU/SEI-2004-TN-036). Pittsburgh, PA: Carnegie-Mellon University.

Noy, N., & Musen, M. (2001). Anchor-prompt: Using non local context for semantic matching. In *Proceedings of the Workshop on Ontologies and Information Sharing at IJCAI*.

Noy, N., & Musen, M. (2003). The prompt suite: Interactive tools for ontology merging and mapping. *International Journal of Human-Computer Studies*, 59(6), 983–1024. doi:10.1016/j.ijhcs.2003.08.002.

Nurcan, S. (2008). A survey on the flexibility requirements related to business processes and modeling artifacts. In *Proceedings of the 41st Annual Hawaii International Conference on System Science* (p. 378).

Nurcan, S., Etien, A., Kaab, R., & Zouka, I. (2005). A strategy driven business process modelling approach. *Journal of Business Process Management*, 11(6), 628–649. doi:10.1108/14637150510630828.

Nysetvold, A. G., & Krogstie, J. (2006). Assessing business process modeling languages using a generic quality framework. In Siau, K. (Ed.), *Advanced topics in database research series* (Vol. 5, pp. 79–93). Hershey, PA: IGI Global. doi:10.4018/978-1-59140-935-9.ch005.

O'Sullivan, J., Edmond, D., & ter Hofstede, A. (2002). What's In a service? Towards accurate description of non-functional service properties. *Distributed and Parallel Databases*, 12(2-3), 117–133. doi:10.1023/A:1016547000822.

OASIS. (2007). *The WS-BPEL 2.0 specification*. Retrieved from http://www.oasis-open.org/committees/download.php/10347/wsbpel-specification-draft-120204.htm

Object Management Group (OMG). (2003). *OMG Unified Modeling Language Specification, Version 1.5*. Retrieved September 2003, from http://www.uml.org

Object Management Group (OMG)/Business Process Management Initiative. (BPMI) (2007). *Business process management notation (BPMN) 2.0*. Retrieved from http://www.bpmn.org

Öhgren, A., & Sandkuhl, K. (2008). Information overload in industrial enterprises - results of an empirical investigation. In *Proceedings of the ECIME Conference*, London, UK.

Oinn, T. M. (2003). Talisman - rapid application development for the grid. *Bioinformatics (Oxford, England)*, 19(1), 212–214. doi:10.1093/bioinformatics/btg1028.

OMG. (2008). *Business Motivation Model (BMM), version 1* (ormal/2008-08-02). *Object Management Group*. Retrieved April 2010, from http://www.omg.org/spec/BMM/1.0/PDF

OMG. (2010). *Unified Modeling Language Superstructure, version 2.2*. Retrieved January 19, 2010, from www.omg.org/spec/UML/2.2/

Opdahl, A. L., & Henderson-Sellers, B. (2002). Ontological Evaluation of the UML Using the Bunge–Wand–Weber Model. *Software Systems Modeling*, 1, 43–67.

Orgad, S. (2005). From online to offline and back: Moving from online to offline relationships with research informants. In Hine, C. (Ed.), *Virtual methods: Issues in social research on the Internet* (pp. 51–65). Oxford, UK: Berg Publishers.

Orriens, B., Yang, J., & Papazoglou, M. P. (2003). A framework for business rule driven web service composition. In *Proceedings of the 4th International Workshop on Conceptual Modeling Approaches for e-Business Dealing with Business Volatility*.

Osterwalder, A. (2004). *The Business Model Ontology*. Unpublished dcotoral dissertation, HEC Lausanne, Switzerland.

Ouyang, C., Dumas, M., Van Der Aalst, W. M. P., ter Hofstede, A. H. M., & Mendling, J. (2009). From business process models to process-oriented software systems. *ACM Transactions on Software Engineering and Methodology, 19*(1), 1–37. doi:10.1145/1555392.1555395.

Paetsch, F., Eberlein, A., & Maurer, F. (2003). Requirements engineering and agile software development. In *Proceedings of the International Workshop on Enabling Technologies: Infrastructure for Collaborative Enterprises*, Linz, Austria (pp. 308 - 313). Washington, DC: IEEE Computer Society.

Pallas Athena. (2002). The Pallas Athena BV: *Flower user manual*. Apeldoorn, The Netherlands: Buscador-Word. Retrieved from http://word.bienesyautos.com/word-YAWL-Editor-15/2.php

Paolucci, M., Kawamura, T., Payne, T., & Sycara, K. (2002). Semantic matching of web services capabilities. In I. Horrocks & J. Hendler (Eds.), *Proceedings of the 1st International Semantic Web Conference* (LNCS 2342, pp. 333-347).

Paolucci, M., Sycara, K., & Kawamuwa, T. (2003, May 20-24). Delivering semantic web services. In *Proceedings of the Conference on World Wide Web*, Budapest, Hungary (pp. 829-836).

Papazoglou, M. P., & Yang, J. (2002). Design Methodology for Web Services and Business Processes. In *Proceedings of the Third International Workshop on Technologies for E-Services (TES 2002)*, Hong Kong, China (LNCS 2444, pp. 54-64). New York: Springer Verlag.

Parasuraman, A., Zeithaml, V. A., & Berry, L. L. (1988). SERVQUAL: a multiple-item scale for measuring consumer perception of service quality. *Journal of Retailing, 64*(1), 12–40.

Parsons, J., & Cole, L. (2004). An experimental examination of property precedence in conceptual modeling. In *Proceedings of the first Asia-Pacific Conference on Conceptual Modeling,* Dunedin, New Zealand (CRPIT 59, pp. 101-110).

Parsons, J., & Wand, Y. (1997). Using Objects for Systems Analysis. *Communications of the ACM, 40*(12), 104–110. doi:10.1145/265563.265578.

Parsons, J., & Wand, Y. (2008). Using Cognitive Principles to Guide Classification in Information Systems Modeling. *Management Information Systems Quarterly, 32*(4), 839–868.

Pastor, O., Fons, J., Torres, V., & Pelechano, V. (2004). Conceptual modelling versus semantic web: the two sides of the same coin? In *Proceedings of the Workshop on Application Design, Development and Implementation Issues in the Semantic Web.*

Pastor, O., & Molina, J. (2007). *Model-driven architecture in practice: A software production environment based on conceptual modeling*. Berlin, Germany: Springer-Verlag.

Paulson, J. W., Succi, G., & Eberlein, A. (2004). An empirical study of open-source and closed-source software products. *IEEE Transactions on Software Engineering, 30*(4). doi:10.1109/TSE.2004.1274044.

Pesic, M. (2008). *Constraint-based workflow management systems: Shifting control to users*. Unpublished doctoral dissertation, Eindhoven University of Technology, The Netherlands.

Piccinelli, G., Emmerich, W., Zirpins, C., & Schütt, K. (2002). Web Service Interfaces for Inter-Organisational Business Processes – An Infrastructure for Automated Reconciliation. In *Proceedings of the 6th International Enterprise Distributed Object Computing Conference (EDOC 2002)*, Lausanne, Switzerland (pp. 285-292). Washington, DC: IEEE Computer Society.

Platzer, C., & Dustdar, S. (2005). A vector space search engine for web services. In *Proceedings of the Third European Conference on Web Services* (p. 62). Washington, DC: IEEE Computer Society.

Prahalad, C. K., & Krishnan, M. S. (2008). *The New Age of Innovation. Driving Cocreated Value Through Global Networks*. New York: McGraw-Hill.

Prakash, N. (2010). Intentional alignment and interoperability in inter-organization information systems. In Nurcan, S., Salinesi, C., Souveyet, C., & Ralyté, J. (Eds.), *Intentional perspectives on information systems engineering* (pp. 101–113). Berlin, Germany: Springer-Verlag. doi:10.1007/978-3-642-12544-7_6.

Prat, N. (1997). Goal formalisation and classification for requirements engineering. In *Proceedings of the Third International Workshop on Requirements Engineering: Foundations of Software Quality*, Barcelona, Spain (pp. 145-156).

Pressman, R. (2003). Software engineering: A practitioner's approach (6th ed.). New York, NY: McGraw-Hill.

Rai, A., Lang, S. S., & Welker, R. B. (2002). Assessing the validity of IS success models: An empirical test and theoretical analysis. *Information Systems Research, 13*(1), 50–69. doi:10.1287/isre.13.1.50.96.

Raja, U., & Tretter, M. J. (in press). Developing taxonomy of software patches: A text mining approach. *Journal of Software Maintenance and Evolution.*.

Rajbhandari, S., Wootten, I., Ali, A. S., & Rana, O. F. (2006). Evaluating provenance based trust for scientific workflows. In *Proceedings of the Sixth IEEE International Symposium on Cluster Computing and the Grid* (pp. 365-372).

Ralyte, J. (2001). *Method chunks engineering*. Unpublished doctoral dissertation, University of Paris 1-Sorbonne, Paris, France.

Ralyté, J., & Rolland, C. (2001). An assembly process model for method engineering. In *Proceedings of the International Conference on Advanced Information Systems Engineering*, Interlaken, Switzerland.

Ralyté, J., & Rolland, C. (2001b, November). An approach for method reengineering. In H. Kunii, S. Jajodia, & A. Solvberg (Eds.), *Proceedings of the 20th International Conference on Conceptual Modeling*, Yokohama, Japan (LNCS 2224, pp. 471-484).

Ralyté, J., Backlund, P., Kühn, H., & Jeusfeld, M. A. (2006). Method chunks for interoperability. In D. W. Embley, A. Olivé, & S. Ram (Eds.), *Proceedings of the 25th International Conference on Conceptual Modeling* (LNCS 4215, pp. 339-353).

Ralyté, J., Deneckere, R., & Rolland, C. (2003). Towards a generic model for situational method engineering. In J. Eder & M. Missikoff (Eds.), *Proceedings of the 15th International Conference on Advanced Information Systems Engineering* (LNCS 2681, p. 1029).

Ralyté, J., Rolland, C., & Plihon, V. (1999). Method enhancement with scenario based techniques. In M. Jarke & A. Oberweis (Eds.), *Proceedings of the 11th International Conference on Advanced Information System Engineering* (LNCS 1626, pp. 103-118).

Ramasubbu, N., Kompalli, P., & Krishnan, M. S. (2005). Leveraging global resources: A process maturity model for managing distributed development. *IEEE Software, 22*(3), 80–86. doi:10.1109/MS.2005.69.

Recker, J. (2010). Opportunities and constraints: The current struggle with BPMN. *Business Process Management Journal*, 181–201. doi:10.1108/14637151011018001.

Recker, J., Indulska, M., Rosemann, M., & Green, P. (2010). The ontological deficiencies of process modeling in practice. *European Journal of Information Systems, 19*(5), 501–525. doi:10.1057/ejis.2010.38.

Recker, J., Rosemann, M., Indulska, M., & Green, P. (2009). Business process modeling: A comparative analysis. *Journal of the Association for Information Systems, 10*(4), 333–363.

Redding, G., Dumas, M., ter Hofstede, A. H. M., & Iordachescu, A. (2008). Transforming object-oriented models to process-oriented models. In A. Ter Hofstede, B. Benatallah, & H.-Y. Paik (Eds.), *Proceedings of the 3rd International Workshop on Business Process Management* (LNCS 4928, pp. 132-143).

REFS. (2010). *IEEE International Workshop on Requirements Engineering For Services (REFS 2010)*. Retrieved April 2010, from http://compsac.cs.iastate.edu/cc_workshops.php

Reijers, H. A., Liman, S., & Van der Aalst, W. M. P. (2003). Product-based workflow design. *Management Information Systems, 20*(1), 229–262.

Rey, G., & Coutaz, J. (2002). Le Contexteur: une abstraction logicielle pour la réalisation de systèmes interactifs sensibles au contexte. In *Proceedings of the IHM Conference* (pp. 105-112).

Ricadela, A. (2007). The worth of open source: Open question. *Business Week, 1*.

Rilston, F., & Castro, J. (2002). *Enhancing data warehouse quality with the NFR framework*. Paper presented at the 5th Workshop on Requirements Engineering.

Rinderle-Ma, S., & Reichert, M. (2007). A formal framework for adaptive access control models. In S. Spaccapietra, P. Atzeni, F. Fages, M.-S. Hacid, M. Kifer, J. Mylopoulos et al. (Eds.), Journal on Data Semantics 9 (LNCS 4601, pp. 82-112).

Roberts, J. A., Hann, I.-H., & Slaughter, S. (2006). Understanding the motivations, participation, and performance of open source software developers: A longitudinal study of the Apache projects. *Management Science, 52*(7), 984–999. doi:10.1287/mnsc.1060.0554.

Robles, G., Gonzalez-Barahona, J. M., & Merelo, J. J. (2006). Beyond source code: The importance of other artifacts in software development (a case study). *Journal of Systems and Software, 79*, 1233–1248. doi:10.1016/j.jss.2006.02.048.

Rock, A. (2000). *Deimos: Query answering defeasible logic system*. Retrieved from http://www.cit.gu.edu.au/~arock/defeasible/Defeasible.cgi

Rolland, C. (2005). L'ingénierie des méthodes: une visite guidée. *E-revue en Technologies de l'Information (e-TI)*.

Rolland, C. (2008). Method engineering: Towards methods as services. In *Proceedings of the International Conference on Software Process*, Leipzig, Germany.

Rolland, C., & Cauvet, C. (1992). Object-oriented conceptual modelling. In *Proceedings of the International Conference on Management of Data*, Bangalore, India.

Rolland, C., & Prakash, N. (2001). Matching ERP system functionality to customer requirements. In *Proceedings of the 5th IEEE International Symposium on Requirements Engineering*, Toronto, ON, Canada.

Rolland, C., Plihon, V., & Ralyté, J. (1998). Specifying the reuse context of scenario method chunks. In *Proceedings of the 10th International Conference on Advanced Information Systems Engineering*, Pisa, Italy.

Rolland, C., Prakash, N., & Benjamen, A. (1999). A multi-model view of process modeling. *Requirements Engineering, 4*(4), 169–187. doi:10.1007/s007660050018.

Rolland, C., Souveyet, C., & Camille, B. A. (1998). Guiding goal modeling using scenarios. *IEEE Transactions on Software Engineering, 24*(12), 1055–1071. doi:10.1109/32.738339.

Rosemann, M., & Recker, J. (2006). Context-aware process design: Exploring the extrinsic drivers for process flexibility. In *Proceedings of the Workshops and Doctoral Consortium in the 18th International Conference on Advanced Information Systems Engineering*, Luxembourg (pp. 149-158).

Rosemann, M., & zur Mühlen, M. (1998). Modellierung der aufbauorganisation in workflow-managementsystemen: Kritische bestandsaufnahme und gestaltungsvorschläge. *EMISA-Forum, 3*(1), 78–86.

Rosemann, M., & zur Mühlen, M. (2004). Organizational management in workflow applications: Issues and perspectives. *Information Technology Management, 5*(3-4), 271–291.

Rosen, M. A., Fiore, S. M., Salas, E., Letsky, M., & Warner, N. (2008). Tightly coupling cognition: Understanding how communication and awareness drive coordination in teams. *International C2 Journal, 2*(1).

Roser, S., Bernhard Bauer, B., & Müller, J. (2006). Model- and architecture-driven development in the context of cross-enterprise business process engineering. In *Proceedings of the International Conference on Services Computing* (pp. 119-126). Washington, DC: IEEE Computer Society.

Röstlinger, A., & Goldkuhl, G. (1994). *På väg mot en komponentbaserad metodsyn*. Paper presented at the VITS Höstseminarium, Linköping, Sweden.

Ruhe, G. (2003). Software engineering decision support – Methodology and applications. In Tonfoni, G., & Jain, C. (Eds.), *Innovations in decision support systems: International series on advanced intelligence* (Vol. 3, pp. 143–174). Adelaide, Australia: Advanced Knowledge International.

RuleML (2008). *The rule markup initiative*. Retrieved from http://www.ruleml.org/

Ryan, N., Pascoe, J., & Morse, D. (1997). Enhanced reality fieldwork: The context-aware archaeological assistant. In Gaffney, V., van Leusen, M., & Exxon, S. (Eds.), *Computer applications in archaeology*. Oxford, UK: British Archeological Reports.

Sabherwal, R., Jeyaraj, A., & Chowa, C. (2006). Information system success: Individual and organizational determinants. *Management Science*, *52*(12), 1849–1864. doi:10.1287/mnsc.1060.0583.

Sadiq, S., Orlowska, M. E., Sadiq, W., & Schulz, K. (2005). When workflows will not deliver: The case of contradicting work practice. In *Proceedings of the 8ᵗʰ International Conference on Business Information Systems* (pp. 69-84).

Sadiq, S., Sadiq, W., & Orlowska, M. (2005). A framework for constraint specification and validation in flexible workflows. *Information Systems*, *30*(5), 349–378. doi:10.1016/j.is.2004.05.002.

SAMBA. (2003). *Structured Architecture for Medical Business Activities (SAMBA), version 1.1*. Retrieved April 2010, from http://www.contsys.eu/documents/samba/samba_en_short_1_3.pdf

Sampson, J. A. (2007). *Comprehensive framework for ontology alignment quality*. Unpublished doctoral dissertation, Norwegian University of Science and Technology, Trondheim, Norway.

Sampson, J. A., & Lanzenberger, M. (2006). Visual ontology alignment for semantic web applications. In J. F. Roddick, V. R. Benjamins, S. Si-said Cherfi, R. Chiang, C. Claramunt, R. A. Elmasri et al. (Eds.), *Proceedings of the 1st International Workshop on Advances in Conceptual Modeling: Theory and Practice* (LNCS 4231, pp. 405-414).

Saracevic, T. (1975). Relevance: A review of and a framework for the thinking on the notion in information science. *Journal of the American Society for Information Science and Technology*, *26*(6).

Saracevic, T. (1996). Relevance reconsidered. In Ingwersen, P., & Pors, N. O. (Eds.), *Information science: Integration in perspective* (pp. 201–218). Copenhagen, Denmark: Royal School of Library and Information Science.

Sawyer, D. (1996). *Do it by design: An introduction to human factors in medical devices*. Retrieved from http://www.fda.gov/downloads/MedicalDevices/DeviceRegulationandGuidance/GuidanceDocuments/UCM095061.pdf

Schilit, B., Adams, N., & Want, R. (1994). Context-aware computing applications. In *Proceedings of the IEEE Workshop on Mobile Computing Systems and Applications*, Santa Cruz, CA (pp. 89-101).

Schneider, K., von Hunnius, J.-P., & Basili, V. R. (2002). Experience in implementing a learning software organization. *IEEE Software*, *19*(3), 46–49. doi:10.1109/MS.2002.1003453.

Schoemaker, M. L. (2007). *Requirements patterns and antipatterns: Best (and worst) practices for defining your requirements*. Reading, MA: Addison-Wesley.

Schroeder, B. A. (1995). On-line monitoring: A tutorial. *Computer*, *28*(6), 72–78. doi:10.1109/2.386988.

Schroeder, R. (2008). e-Science as research technologies: Reconfiguring disciplines, globalizing knowledge. *Social Sciences Information. Information Sur les Sciences Sociales*, *47*(2), 131–157. doi:10.1177/0539018408089075.

Seacord, R. C., Hissam, S. A., & Wallnau, K. C. (1998). Agora: A search engine for software components. *IEEE Internet Computing*, *2*(6), 62–70. doi:10.1109/4236.735988.

Senger, M., Rice, P., & Oinn, T. (2003). Soaplab - a unified Sesame door to analysis tools. In *Proceedings of the UK e-Science All Hands Meeting* (pp. 509-513).

Setten, M., Veenstra, M., & Nijholt, A. (2002). Prediction strategies: Combining prediction techniques to optimize personalization. In *Proceedings of the Conference on Adaptive Hypermedia - Personalization in Future TV*, Malaga, Spain.

Settimi, R., Cleland-Huang, J., Ben Khadra, O., Mody, J., Lukasik, W., & De- Palma, C. (2004). Supporting software evolution through dynamically retrieving traces to UML artifacts. In *Proceedings of the 7th International Workshop on Principles of Software Evolution* (pp. 49-54). Washington, DC: IEEE Computer Society.

Sgourev, S. V., & Zuckerman E. W. (2006). Improving capabilities through industry peer networks. *MIT Sloan Management Review*, 33-38.

Siau, K., & Cao, Q. (2001). Unified Modeling Language: A Complexity Analysis. *Journal of Database Management*, *12*(1), 26–34.

Siau, K., & Rossi, M. (2008). Evaluating techniques for system analysis and design modelling methods – a review and comparative analysis. *Information Systems Journal, 21*(3), 249–268. doi:10.1111/j.1365-2575.2007.00255.x.

Silver, B. (2009). *Case management: Addressing unique BPM requirements*. Aptos, CA: BPMS Watch. Retrieved from http://www.global360.com/xres/uploads/resource-center-documents/Case_Management_WP_final.pdf

Simmhan, Y. L., Plale, B., & Gannon, D. (2005). A survey of data provenance in e-science. *SIGMOD Record, 34*, 31–36. doi:10.1145/1084805.1084812.

Simmhan, Y. L., Plale, B., & Gannon, D. (2008). Karma2: Provenance management for data-driven workflows. *International Journal of Web Services Research, 5*(2), 1–22. doi:10.4018/jwsr.2008040101.

Simsek, Z., & Veiga, J. F. (2000). The electronic survey technique: An integration and assessment. *Organizational Research Methods, 3*(1), 93–115. doi:10.1177/109442810031004.

Singh, P. V., Tan, Y., & Mookerjee, V. (2007). Social capital, structural holes and team composition: Collaborative networks of the open source software community. In *Proceedings of the Twenty Eighth International Conferences on Information Systems*, Montreal, QC, Canada.

Singh, S. N., & Woo, C. (2008). *A methodology for discovering goals at different organizational levels*. Paper presented at the Third International Workshop on Business/IT Alignment and Interoperability held in conjunction with the International Conference on Advanced Information Systems Engineering, Montpellier, France.

Sintek, M. (2007). *Ontoviz tab: Visualizing protégé ontologies*. Retrieved from http://protegewiki.stanford.edu/index.php/OntoViz

Sjøberg, D. I. K., Dybå, T., & Jørgensen, M. (2007). The future of empirical methods in software engineering research. In *Proceedings of the International Conference on Software Engineering and the Workshop on the Future of Software Engineering* (pp. 358-378). Washington, DC: IEEE Computer Society.

Smirnov, A., Pashkin, M., Chilov, N., & Levashova, T. (2005). Ontology–based knowledge repository support for healthgrids. In *Proceedings of Healthgrid* (pp. 47–56). From Grid to Healthgrid.

Smith, N., Capiluppi, A., & Fernandez-Ramil, J. (2006). Agent-based simulation of open source evolution. *Journal of Software Process - Improvement and Practice, 11*, 423-434.

So, C., & Scholl, W. (2009). Perceptive agile measurement: New instruments for quantitative studies in pursuit of the social-psychological effect of agile practices. In *Proceedings of the International Conference on Agile Processes in Software Engineering and Extreme Programming* (pp. 83-93).

Soffer, P., & Wand, Y. (2005). On the notion of softgoals in business process modeling. *Business Process Modeling*, 663-679.

Soffer, P., Wand, Y., & Kaner, M. (2007). Semantic analysis of flow patterns in business process modeling. In G. Alonso, P. Dadam, & M. Rosemann (Eds.), *Proceedings of the 5th International Conference on Business Process Management* (LNCS 4714, pp. 400-407).

Soffer, P., & Wand, Y. (2005). On the notion of soft-goals in business process modeling. *Business Process Management Journal, 11*(6), 663–679. doi:10.1108/14637150510630837.

Sommerville, I. (2004). Software engineering (7th ed.). Reading, MA: Addison-Wesley.

Sommerville, I., & Sawyer, P. (1997). *Requirements engineering: A good practice guide*. Hoboken, NJ: John Wiley & Sons.

Song, W., & Li, X. (2005). A conceptual modeling approach to virtual organizations in the grid. In H. Zhuge & G. C. Fox (Eds.), *Proceedings of the Fourth International Conference on Grid and Cooperative Computing* (LNCS 3795, pp. 382-393).

Song, W., Du, X., & Munro, M. (2009). A concept graph approach to semantic similarity computation method for e-service discovery. *International Journal of Knowledge Engineering and Data Mining, 1*(1).

Sowa, J. F. (1984). *Conceptual structures: Information processing in mind and machine*. Reading, MA: Addison-Wesley.

SRML. (2001). *Simple rule markup language*. Retrieved from http://xml.coverpages.org/srml.html

Stamelos, I., Angelis, L., Oikonomou, A., & Bleris, G. L. (2002). Code quality analysis in open source software development. *Information Systems Journal*, *12*(1), 43–60. doi:10.1046/j.1365-2575.2002.00117.x.

Stevens, W., Myers, G., & Constantine, L. (1974). Structured design. *IBM Systems Journal*, *13*(2), 115–139. doi:10.1147/sj.132.0115.

Stewart, K. J. (2004). OSS project success: From internal dynamics to external impact. In *Proceedings of the 4th Workshop on Open Source Software Engineering*, Edinburgh, Scotland.

Stewart, K. J., Ammeter, A. P., & Maruping, L. M. (2006). Impacts of license choice and organizational sponsorship on user interest and development activity in open source software projects. *Information Systems Research*, *17*(2), 126–144. doi:10.1287/isre.1060.0082.

Stewart, K. J., & Gosian, S. (2006). The impact of ideology on effectiveness in open source software development teams. *Management Information Systems Quarterly*, *30*(2), 1–23.

Stirna, J., Persson, A., & Sandkuhl, K. (2007). Participative enterprise modelling: Experiences and recommendations. In J. Stirna, A. Persson, & K. Sandkuhl (Eds.), *Proceedings of the 19th International Conference on Advanced Information Systems Engineering* (LNCS 4495, pp. 546-560).

Storey, M., Musen, M., Silva, J., Best, C., Ernst, N., Fergerson, R., et al. (2001). Jambalaya: Interactive visualization to enhance ontology authoring and knowledge acquisition in Protégé. In *Proceedings of the International Workshop on Interactive Tools for Knowledge Capture*.

Strang, C. J. (2005). Next generation systems architecture —The matrix. *BT Technology Journal*, *23*(1). doi:10.1007/s10550-005-0107-1.

Subramaniam, C., Sen, R., & Nelson, M. L. (2009). Determinants of open source software project success: A longitudinal study. *Decision Support Systems*, *46*(2), 576–585. doi:10.1016/j.dss.2008.10.005.

Tan, W.-C. (2004). Research problems in data provenance. *A Quarterly Bulletin of the Computer Society of the IEEE Technical Committee on Data Engineering*, *27*(4), 45–52.

Taylor, I. J., Deelman, E., Gannon, D. B., & Shields, M. (Eds.). (2006). *Workflows for e-science: Scientific workflows for grid*. New York, NY: Springer.

Van der Aalst, W. M. P. (2003). Inheritance of business processes: A journey visiting four notorious problems. In H. Ehrig, W. Reisig, G. Rozenberg, & H. Weber (Eds.), Advances in Petri net Technology for Communication-Based Systems (LNCS 2472, pp. 383-408).

Van der Aalst, W. M. P., & Pesic, M. (2006). DecSerFlow: Towards a truly declarative service flow language. In F. Leymann et al (Eds.), Dagstuhl Seminar Proceedings: The Role of Business Processes in Service Oriented Architectures (LNCS 4184, pp. 1-23).

Van der Aalst, W. M. P., Barthelmess, P., Ellis, C. A., & Wainer, J. (2000). Workflow modeling using proclets. In O. Etzion & P. Scheuermann (Eds.), *Proceedings of the 7th International Conference on Cooperative Information Systems* (LNCS 1901, pp. 198-209).

van der Aalst, W. M. P., ter Hofstede, A. H. M., & Weske, M. (2003). Business process management: A survey. In M. Weske (Ed.), *Proceedings of the International Conference on Business Process Management* (LNCS 2678, p. 1019).

Van der Aalst, W. M. P., ter Hofstede, A., & Weske, M. (2003). Business process management: A survey. In *Proceedings of the 1st International Conference on Business Process Management* (pp. 1-12).

Van der Aalst, W. M. P., & Basten, T. (2002). Inheritance of workflows: An approach to tackling problems related to change. *Theoretical Computer Science*, *270*(1-2), 125–203. doi:10.1016/S0304-3975(00)00321-2.

Van der Aalst, W. M. P., ter Hofstede, A., Kiepuszewski, B., & Barros, A. (2003). Workflow patterns. *Distributed and Parallel Databases*, *14*(1), 5–51. doi:10.1023/A:1022883727209.

Van der Aalst, W. M. P., Weske, M., & Grünbauer, D. (2005). Case handling: A new paradigm for business process support. *Data & Knowledge Engineering*, *53*(2), 129–162. doi:10.1016/j.datak.2004.07.003.

Van Glabbeek, R. (2001). The linear time - branching time spectrum I: The semantics of concrete, sequential processes. In Berstra, J. A., Ponse, A., & Smolka, S. A. (Eds.), *Handbook of Process Algebra* (pp. 3–99). Amsterdam, The Netherlands: Elsevier. doi:10.1016/B978-044482830-9/50019-9.

van Griethuisen, J. J. (1982). *Concepts and Terminology for the Conceptual Schema and Information Base (Rep. No. ISO TC97/SC5/WG5, No 695)*. ISO.

van Ham, F., & van Wijk, J. J. (2004). Interactive visualization of small world graphs. In *Proceedings of the IEEE Symposium on Information Visualization* (pp 199-206).

Van Slooten, K., & Hodes, B. (1996). Characterising IS development projects. In *Proceedings of the IFIP WG8.1 Conference on Method Engineering*.

Vanderfeesten, I., Reijers, H. A., & Van der Aalst, W. M. P. (2008). Product-based workflow support: Dynamic workflow execution. In Z. Bellahsene & M. Leonard (Eds.), *Proceedings of the International Conference on Advanced Information Systems Engineering* (LNCS 5074, pp. 571-574).

Vitvar, T., Kerrigan, M., van Overeem, A., Peristeras, V., & Tarabanis, K. (2006). Infrastructure for the semantic pan-european e-government services. In *Proceedings of the AAAI Spring Symposium on the Semantic Web meets eGovernment*.

Vockler, J. S., Mehta, G., Zhao, Y., Deelman, E., & Wilde, M. (2006). Kickstarting remote applications. In *Proceedings of the 2nd International Workshop on Grid Computing Environments in conjunction with Super-Computing* (pp. 76-85).

von Wangenheim, C. G., Hauck, J. C. R., Zoucas, A., Salviano, C. F., McCaffery, F., & Shull, F. (2010). Creating software process capability/maturity models. *IEEE Software, 27*(4), 92–94. doi:10.1109/MS.2010.96.

Wand, Y. (1989). A Proposal for a Formal Model of Objects. In Kim, W., & Lochovsky, F. (Eds.), *Object-oriented Concepts, Databases, and Applications* (pp. 537–559). New York: ACM Press.

Wand, Y., & Weber, R. (1990). An Ontological Model of an Information System. *IEEE Transactions on Software Engineering, 16*(11), 1282–1292. doi:10.1109/32.60316.

Wand, Y., & Weber, R. (1993). On the Ontological Expressiveness of Information Systems Analysis and Design Grammars. *Journal of Information Systems, 3*, 217–237. doi:10.1111/j.1365-2575.1993.tb00127.x.

Weber, B., Reichert, M., & Rinderle-Ma, S. (2008). Change patterns and change support features - enhancing flexibility in process-aware information systems. *Data & Knowledge Engineering, 66*(3), 438–466. doi:10.1016/j.datak.2008.05.001.

Weigand, H., Johannesson, P., Andersson, B., Bergholtz, M., Edirisuriya, E., & Ilayperuma, T. (2006). On the Notion of Value Object. In *Proceedings of the 18th Conference on Advanced Information Systems Engineering*, Luxembourg (LNCS 4001, pp. 321-335). Berlin: Springer Verlag.

Wieringa, R. J., & Gordijn, J. (2005). Value-Oriented Design of Service Coordination Processes: Correctness and Trust. In *Proceedings of the 2005 ACM Symposium on Applied Computing*, Santa Fe, NM (pp. 1320-1327). New York: ACM.

Williams, C. C., & Hollingsworth, J. K. (2005). Automatic mining of source code repositories to improve bug finding techniques. *IEEE Transactions on Software Engineering, 31*(6), 466–480. doi:10.1109/TSE.2005.63.

Wistrand, K., & Karlsson, F. (2004). Method components: Rationale revealed. In *Proceedings of the International Conference on Advanced Information Systems Engineering*, Riga, Latvia (pp. 189-201).

Wombacher, A., & Rozie, M. (2006). Evaluation of workflow similarity measures in service discovery. In Service Oriented Electronic Commerce (LNCS 4275, pp. 51-71).

Wu, D., Parsia, B., Sirin, E., Hendler, J., & Nau, D. (2003). Automating daml-s web services composition using shop2. In *Proceedings of the 2nd International Semantic Web Conference* (pp. 195-210).

Wu, S., Sheth, A., Miller, J., & Luo, Z. (2002). Authorization and access control of application data in workflow-systems. *Journal of the Association of Intelligent Information Systems, 18*(1), 71–94. doi:10.1023/A:1012972608697.

Yamamoto, S., Kaiya, H., Cox, K., & Bleistein, S. (2006). Goal oriented requirements engineering: Trends and issues. *IEICE Transactions on Information and Systems, 89*(11), 2701–2711. doi:10.1093/ietisy/e89-d.11.2701.

Yang, Q. (1997). *Intelligent planning: A decomposition and abstraction based approach*. Berlin, Germany: Springer Verlag.

Ying, A. T. T., Murphy, G. C., Ng, R., & Chu-Carroll, M. C. (2004). Predicting source code changes by mining change history. *IEEE Transactions on Software Engineering, 30*(9). doi:10.1109/TSE.2004.52.

Yourdon, E., & Constantine, L. L. (1979). *Structured Design*. Upper Saddle River, NJ: Prentice Hall.

Yu, E. (1995). *Modeling strategic relationships for process reengineering*. Unpublished doctoral dissertation, University of Toronto, ON, Canada.

Yu, E. (1997). Towards Modeling and Reasoning Support for Early-Phase Requirements Engineering. In *Proceedings of the 3rd IEEE International Symposium on Requirements Engineering* (pp. 226-235). Washington, DC: IEEE Press.

Zachman, J. (1987). A framework for information systems architecture. *IBM Systems Journal*, 276–292. doi:10.1147/sj.263.0276.

Zachman, J. A. (1996). *Enterprise Architecture: The Issue of the Century*. Database Programming and Design Magazine.

Zhang, J., Zhang, S., Cao, J., & Mou, Y. (2004, September 15-18). Improved HTN planning approach for service composition. In *Proceedings of the IEEE International Conference on Services Computing* (pp. 609-612).

Zhao, J., Goble, C., Greenwood, M., Wroe, C., & Stevens, R. (2003). Annotating, linking and browsing provenance logs for e-science. In *Proceedings of the Workshop on Semantic Web Technologies for Searching and Retrieving Scientific Data* (pp. 158-176).

Zhao, J., Goble, C., Stevens, R., & Turi, D. (2008). Mining Taverna's semantic web of provenance. *Concurrency and Computation, 20*(5), 463–472. doi:10.1002/cpe.1231.

Zhuge, H. (2002). A process matching approach for flexible workflow process reuse. *Information and Software Technology, 44*(8), 445–450. doi:10.1016/S0950-5849(02)00022-8.

Zimmermann, T., Zeller, A., Weissgerber, P., & Diehl, S. (2005). Mining version histories to guide software changes. *IEEE Transactions on Software Engineering, 31*(6), 429–445. doi:10.1109/TSE.2005.72.

About the Contributors

John Krogstie holds a PhD (1995) and an MSc (1991) in information systems from the Norwegian University of Science and Technology (NTNU), where he is currently a full professor in information systems. He is also the Vice Dean of the faculty, responsible for the thematic area ICT at NTNU. John Krogstie is the Norwegian representative for IFIP TC8 and chair of IFIP WG 8.1 on information system design and evaluations. His research interests are information systems modelling, quality of models and modelling languages, eGovernment and mobile information systems. He has published around 150 refereed papers in journals, books and archival proceedings since 1991.

* * *

Niv Ahituv is the Academic Director of Netvision Institute of Internet Studies and the Marko and Lucie Chaoul Chair for Research in Information Evaluation at Tel Aviv University. From 1999 to 2002 he served as Vice President and Director General (CEO) of Tel Aviv University. From 1989 to 1994 he served as the Dean of Graduate School of Business Administration at Tel Aviv University. In 2005 he was awarded a *Life Time Achievement Award* by ILLA, The Israeli Association for Information Technology. Professor Ahituv represents the Israeli Government in UNESCO in issues related to Information Technology.

Khalid Belhajjame is a researcher at the school of computer science of the University of Manchester. He obtained his Ph.D from the University of Grenoble. His general research areas are information and knowledge management, where he has contributed to research proposals on data integration, knowledge engineering of semantic web services, scientific workflows and data provenance.

Marco Brambilla is assistant professor at Politecnico di Milano. He got his PhD at Politecnico di Milano in 2005. His research interests include conceptual models, tools and methods for Web applications, services, and search; user interaction, semantic Web and business processes. He has been visiting researcher at Cisco Systems and at UCSD (University of California, San Diego) and he participated to several national and international research projects. He is coauthor of the book "Designing Data-Intensive Web Applications" (Morgan-Kauffman, 2002).

Peter Brezany is a professor at the Institute of Scientific Computing, University of Vienna, Austria. He received his PhD in Computer Science in 1980 from the Slovak Technical University Bratislava, Slovakia. He began research in 1976 on the design of parallel programming languages and their compilers. Since 1990 he has worked on automatic parallelization of scientific and engineering applications for distributed-memory systems, parallel input/output support for high-performance computing, and large-scale parallel and distributed data mining. His current research focus is knowledge discovery and data management on Computational Grids and Clouds, especially in the context of e-Science applications.

Bruno Claudepierre is a PhD student at the University of Paris 1 Panthéon-Sorbonne (CRI - Centre de Recherche en Informatique) under the direction of Pr. Colette Rolland and Dr. Selmin Nurcan. His research purposes are focused on Information Systems engineering methods and their adaptations in order to comply with the new requirements of IT Governance. He usually works with CRI staff members on connected research areas like Business Process Redesign, Method Engineering, Business/IT alignment and Information System Design.

Steve Counsell is a Senior Lecturer in the Department of Information Systems and Computing at Brunel University. He received his PhD from Birkbeck, University of London in 2002 and his research interests relate to empirical software engineering; in particular, refactoring, software metrics and the study of software evolution. He worked as an industrial developer before his PhD.

Maya Daneva is an Assistant Professor with the Information Systems Department, University of Twente, the Netherlands. She leads a company-university research program on requirements engineering and architecture design for large enterprise systems projects. Prior to this, Maya was a business process analyst in the Architecture Group of TELUS Corporation in Toronto, Canada's second largest telecommunication company, where she consulted on ERP requirements processes, architecture reuse, and sizing methods for SAP projects. Maya also was a researcher at the University of Saarbruecken, Germany, involved in improving process modeling methods for SAP. Maya authored more than 70 research and experience papers.

Rébecca Deneckere is affiliated to the CRI (Centre de recherche en Informatique) at the university of Paris 1 Panthéon-Sorbonne. Her domain of research is the Method Engineering field, especially Situational Method Engineering. She is also working on Decision-making in Information System Engineering. Her last field of research is the processes context-awareness and the configuration of method lines.

Xiaofeng Du received the PhD degree in computer science in 2009 from the Durham University, United Kingdom. Currently, he is a research fellow at the School of Computer Science, Birmingham University and the Business Modelling and Field Management Research Centre, British Telecom. His research interests include Web services, semantic Web services, service composition, and process mining. He is a member of the British Computer Society.

Remigijus Gustas is a full professor in the Department of Information Systems at Karlstad University (Sweden). He is the head of the research group on enterprise and system architecture design. Remigijus Gustas holds a diploma in system engineering (1979), a doctor (1986) and a docent (1991) in the area of information systems. In 1999, he was granted a habilitated doctor degree in the area of information system engineering. His main teaching subjects are system analysis and design, advances in information system modeling, object-oriented modeling, database systems, and enterprise modeling. Remigijus Gustas has been involved in a number of industrial and European information technology projects. Remigijus Gustas is a member of IFIP WG 8.1. He was leading projects in the area of enterprise modeling, service-oriented analysis and design, e-business modeling, and software technologies. Remigijus Gustas has acted as a reviewer of contributions for several journals. He was chairing and serving as a program committee member in a number of international conferences. Remigijus Gustas is the author of one monograph and around 70 research publications. His research interests lie in the area of conceptual modeling, semantic and pragmatic aspects of service architectures, information system analysis and design, enterprise modeling and integration. Remigijus Gustas is editor-in-chief of the International Journal of Information System Modeling and Design.

Abdelwahab Hamou-Lhadj, PhD, is an Assistant Professor in the Department of Electrical and Computer Engineering (ECE) at Concordia University, Montreal, Canada. His research interests include software engineering, software behaviour analysis, software compliance engineering, and information technology. Dr. Hamou-Lhadj is the founder and the leader of the Software Behaviour Analysis Lab. He has published numerous articles in renowned conference and journal proceedings. He has also been involved in the organization and the program committees of several international conferences. Dr. Hamou-Lhadj holds a PhD degree in Computer Science from the University of Ottawa, Canada. He is also an OMG certified expert in Business Process Management. He is a member of IEEE, IEEE Computer Society, ACM, and the American Society for Quality (ASQ).

Martin Henkel is an assistant professor at Stockholm University, Stockholm, Sweden, in the area of information systems. The focus of his research is service oriented systems, business process and model driven development of information systems. He is and has been involved in several research projects on health care and the analysis and design of e-services. Currently Martin is in the program committee of several conferences, among these the European Conference on Web Services.

Rob Hierons received a BA in Mathematics (Trinity College, Cambridge), and a Ph.D. in Computer Science (Brunel University). He then joined the Department of Mathematical and Computing Sciences at Goldsmiths College, University of London, before returning to Brunel University in 2000. He was promoted to full Professor in 2003.

Sardar Hussain is currently pursuing a PhD at the National e-Science Centre (NeSC), at the University of Glasgow in the area of fine-grained security with specific emphasis on the definition and enactment of security-oriented workflows comprising heterogeneous services from multiple autonomous and security conscious providers and related issues including provenance. He received his M.Sc in Computer Science from the Quaid-i-Azam University, Islamabad in 2005. Currently, Sardar serves as a faculty member for University of Malakand, Khyber Pakhtoonkhwa Pakistan.

Ivan Janciak is a senior researcher at the Department of Scientific Computing, University of Vienna, Austria. His research interests include workflow enactment engines, distributed data mining, and ontologies. He received his PhD from the Department of Scientific Computing, University of Vienna in 2010.

Paul Johannesson holds a position as professor at Stockholm University, where he works in the area of information systems. Johannesson has worked on federated information systems, languages for conceptual modelling, schema integration, the use of linguistic instruments in information systems, process integration, IT in health care, e-commerce systems design, and value and business modelling. Johannesson is and has been a member of several international program committees; among these are the ER conference and the CAiSE conference.

Fakhri Alam Khan is a PhD candidate at the Department of Scientific Computing, University of Vienna, Austria. His research interests includes scientific workflows provenance, nature inspired metaheuristic algorithms, and workflow parameters significance measurement. He received his M.Sc. from the Quaid-i-Azam University Islamabad in 2005 and worked at the central bank of Pakistan (State Bank of Pakistan).

Elena Kornyshova is a PhD student at the University of Paris 1 Panthéon-Sorbonne (CRI - Centre de Recherche en Informatique) under the direction of Pr. Colette Rolland and Dr. Rébecca Deneckère. Her research domains are Method Engineering, Process Engineering, Enterprise Architecture and Decision-making in Information System Engineering. Her PhD research aims to propose a Method Engineering approach to improve Decision-making in Information System Engineering.

Vera Künzle finished her Diploma in CS in August 2005. Since then she has been working as software engineer at Persis – a company developing software systems for human resource management. At Persis she is responsible for talent management and recruitment application software. Since 2008 Vera has been additionally working on her PhD under the supervision of Manfred Reichert at the University of Ulm. Her major research interests include object-aware process management and access control.

Shan Lu is employed by Around America Aviation Group and works closely on projects involving Canada and China. He holds a Bachelor of Engineering degree from Wuhan University of Technology, as well as both a Master of Science degree and an MBA from Memorial University of Newfoundland. His research has been presented at conferences, including *Evaluating Modeling Methods in Systems Analysis and Design (EMMSAD)*. Shan has considerable work experience in information systems, having worked in the information systems departments of CRC group in Shenzhen, China, and the iNews network in Canada.

Magnus Lundqvist currently holds an MSc (2001) and a Licentiate (2007) degree in computer science from Linköping's institute of Technology (Sweden). He is now in the final stage of his PhD studies in informatics and will therefore in a near future defend his dissertation on Information Demand Analysis. Magnus has worked for several years at Linköping University and Jönköping University as a teacher focusing on courses in software engineering, information security, Internet technologies, document and workflow management, knowledge modelling, and information logistics. Magnus's research focus is mainly directed towards the understanding of needs and requirements for information management in enterprises.

Hossein Mehrfard received his Master's degree in Electrical and Computer Engineering from Concordia University, Montreal (QC), Canada. His research interests include agile software development, software process improvement and modeling, software compliance, requirements engineering, and traceability analysis. He is currently working on investigating the impact of regulatory compliance on software development with a focus on agile software processes.

Asma Mubarak received the PhD from the Department of Computing at Brunel University in 2010 and is currently a Lecturer in Computing at the University of Damascus in Syria. Her research interests are empirical software engineering, incorporating coupling metrics, system re-engineering and refactoring.

Malcolm Munro is a professor of software engineering in the Department of Computer Science at the University of Durham, UK. His main research focus is software visualization, software maintenance and evolution, and program comprehension. He is also involved in research in Software as a Service and the application of Bayesian networks to software testing and program comprehension.

Jeffrey Parsons is Professor of Information Systems and Associate Dean (Research) in the Faculty of Business Administration at Memorial University of Newfoundland. He holds a PhD in Information Systems from the University of British Columbia. His interests include systems analysis and design, data management, and electronic commerce. His research has been published in journals such as *Nature, Management Science, MIS Quarterly, Information Systems Research, Journal of Management Information Systems, Communications of the ACM, ACM Transactions on Database Systems,* and *IEEE Transactions on Software Engineering.* Dr. Parsons is a senior editor for the *Journal of the Association for Information Systems* and an associate editor for *Information Systems Research.* He has served as Program Co-Chair for the 2010 International Conference on Conceptual Modeling, the 2008 Americas Conference on Information Systems, and the 2001 Workshop on Information Technologies and Systems.

Erik Perjons is a research engineer in the area of information systems at Stockholm University, Stockholm, Sweden. His research focus is enterprise modeling, business process management, and model driven development of information system. He has participated in several research projects in health care, analyzing and designing health care processes within and between health care organizations, as well as integrating and designing information system support.

Uzma Raja is an assistant professor of management information systems at the University of Alabama in the Department of Information Systems, Statistics, and Management Science. She received her Ph.D. in information systems from Texas A&M University in 2006. Her research interests are in the areas of information systems evolution, open source software, data/text mining applications, and health information systems. Her research has been published in IEEE Transactions on Software Engineering, Information Resource Management Journal, Journal of Software Maintenance and Evolution, Information Technology and Management, and Journal of Health Information Management Systems.

Manfred Reichert holds a PhD in CS and a Diploma in Mathematics. Since January 2008 he has been appointed as full professor at the University of Ulm. Before, he was working as Associate Professor at the University of Twente where he was also leader of the strategic research orientation on e-health and a member of the Management Board of the Centre for Telematics and Information Technology. His major research interests include next generation process management technology (e.g., adaptive processes, management of process variants, data-driven processes), service-oriented architectures (e.g., service interoperability, service evolution), and advanced applications for ICT solutions (e.g., e-health). Together with P. Dadam he pioneered the work on the ADEPT process management technology. Manfred was PC-Co-Chair of the BPM'08 conference in Milan and General Co-Chair of the BPM'09 conference in Ulm.

Jennifer Sampson received her PhD in Computer Science from the Norwegian University of Science and Technology. In her work she pioneered the use of whole ontology visualization techniques for alignments. Jennifer now works in industrial IT at Statoil in Norway doing large scale data integration.

Kurt Sandkuhl is a full Professor of business information systems at the University of Rostock, Germany, and affiliated Professor of information engineering at Jönköping University, Sweden. He received his MSc and PhD in computer science from Berlin University of Technology (Germany), and the post-doctoral lecturing qualification from Linköping University (Sweden). Before joining the University of Rostock in 2010, Kurt Sandkuhl was a scientific employee at Berlin University of Technology (1988-1994), department manager (1996-2000) and division manager (2000-2002) at Fraunhofer-Institute for Software and Systems Engineering in Berlin, and Professor at Jönköping University, Sweden (2002-2010). Kurt Sandkuhl has taught courses in software engineering, development of distributed applications, computer-supported collaborative work, system analysis, information modeling, software quality management, information logistics and graduate seminars in information systems. His research interests are in enterprise modeling, information logistics and ontology engineering. Kurt Sandkuhl published three books and more than 100 papers in journals and international conferences.

Ulf Seigerroth is assistant professor in informatics with specialisation in enterprise modelling at School of Engineering, Jönköping University (JTH). Ulf received his bachelor degree in 1994, Licentiate degree in 1999 and PhD in 2003. In 2004 he was appointed as head of the informatics department at Jönköping International Business School for 3.5 years. During this time Ulf was the co-founder and co-director of CenIT (Centre of Evolving IT in Networked organisations) and he was also the co-founder of the graduate school of informatics (GSI). Ulf is since 2010 acting as research director for a research group in information engineering. Ulf´s current research direction is towards issues concerning business and IT-alignment and transformation. Within this area more specific issues of interest are enterprise modelling, enterprise architecture, information logistics, and method engineering. His research is characterised by empirically driven and theory- and method informed development (action research).

William Song is Associate Prof. of Computer Science and Director of Research Group of Web Intelligence, Services, and Agent Technologies at Durham University, United Kingdom. His major research interests include database systems and development, conceptual modelling, semantic web technology, web services, web mining, requirements engineering, business modelling, e-business, service science and web science. He has pursued in the research and development of contextual conceptual modelling for many years and published many research papers on this topic. He is a member of the IEEE Computer Society and ACM.

Marietta J. Tretter is a professor at the Department of Information and Operations Management, Texas A&M University. She has conducted research on data mining applications, as well as on topics involving statistical computing and mathematical programming. Her work has appeared in journals such as Management Science, Operations Research, Math Programming, Academy of Management and the Annals of Statistics. She teaches courses in basic Business statistics and Data Mining for Business. Her research interests are related to aspects of GIS, Data Mining applications and Software Engineering.

Csaba Veres received his PhD in Cognitive Science from the University of Arizona, where he studied the relationship between conceptual semantics and natural language. He subsequently gained experience in data modeling, and formed strong research interests in the relationship between technical information systems, conceptualizations of those systems, and the artificial languages used to describe them. Csaba has been actively researching semantic web technologies for the past 10 years, always maintaining that a strong connection between cognitive sciences and computer science is necessary for a complete understanding of the challenges we face in systems interoperability. Csaba has applied semantic technologies in projects involving knowledge management, tourism, linked data, and metadata driven search. He is currently Associate Professor at the University in Bergen.

Barbara Weber obtained her Ph.D. in Economics at the Institute of Information Systems, University of Innsbruck (Austria). Since 2004, she is researcher at the Department of Computer Science at the University of Innsbruck where she currently completed her habilitation in Computer Science. She is a member of the Quality Engineering (QE) research group and head of the research cluster on business processes and workflows at QE. Her main research interests are flexible processes and intelligent user support in extensible systems. This spans several technology areas including process-aware information systems, case-based reasoning, process-oriented knowledge management, enterprise information systems, process mining, and agile software development. She has published more than 60 research papers and articles, among others in Data and Knowledge Engineering, Science of Computer Programming and the International Journal of Cooperative Information Systems.

Index

A

abstract business process (ABP) 34
abstraction 2, 7, 26, 31, 34, 44, 100, 145, 147-148,
      159, 228-229, 232-233, 237, 239-240, 343-344,
      350, 367
acceptance test 302, 304, 307-309
actor 32, 88, 155, 157, 250
aggregative information 12-13
Akaike Information Criteria (AIC) 325
AlViz 99, 102, 110-111, 113-119, 121
ArchiMate 147, 150, 172, 174
ArgoUML 182, 192, 194
atomic service 126, 130, 138-141
Axis2 63-67, 69-74

B

batch activity 5, 11, 14, 18-19, 25
best practices 31, 273, 275, 294-296
bioinformatics 35, 40-41, 47, 74-75
black-box activity 2, 5, 10-13, 17, 24
bundle 351
Bunge, Mario 155, 164, 180-181, 192
business process 2, 32
business process modeling (BPM) 31
Business Process Reengineering 78, 227, 339

C

case 32
Case Handling (CH) 22
catalogue 226, 228, 230-233, 235-242
Chimæra 100-101, 103-104
classification dependency 157
closed source software (CSS) 315
compose-and-conquer 339
comprehensibility 151, 263-264
conceptual graph (CG) 127

conceptual modeling 97, 114, 120-121, 144-146,
      148-151, 154-156, 160, 164, 167, 172-174,
      177-180, 188, 191-193, 242-243, 267, 365-367
constraint 32
contact person 151, 154, 157-159, 161-162, 165-
      168, 170-171
context 125, 338
Context-based Semantic Service Description Frame-
      work (CbSSDF) 125-126
context-sensitive activity 5, 11
contingency factor 338, 344, 364
control flow 15, 31-36, 38-41, 159, 164, 250, 305-
      306
conversion 128, 251, 255
coordination complexity 277-278, 281, 284, 288,
      292-293
coordination requirement 270-272, 276-277, 282,
      287, 292-294
coupleness 52, 61-62
coupling 200, 222
      incoming 200, 208
      outgoing 200-201, 208
Coupling between Objects (CBO) 201
creation dependency 12-13

D

data flow diagram (DFD) 148
data mining (DM) 319
dataset cleaning 323
data structure 5, 7, 19, 26
Decision Tree (DT) 323
declarative view 250
decomposition principle 341-342
defeasible logic 126, 143-144
development situation 338, 344, 364
DjVu 202, 207-210, 214-215, 217
domain state 160, 169

E

e3 value language 251
Easychair 2, 4
efficiency 60, 123-124, 129, 136-137, 142, 219-220, 263-264
enactment engine 51-65, 67-68, 72-74
end user 40, 103-104, 126-127, 129, 219, 302, 317-318, 330-331
Enterprise Knowledge Development (EKD) 85
enterprise modeling (EM) 78
enterprise system 149, 164
e-science 47-48, 51-55, 62-63, 68-70, 72-75
e-services 245-249, 254-267
evaluation 101
execution dependency 12-13
expressiveness 127, 193, 263-264, 345, 352
extended enterprise 271, 276, 288

F

first order logic (FOL) 127
flexibility 3, 27, 29, 54-55, 62, 73, 99, 141-142, 146, 151, 171-172, 177, 275, 290, 338, 340, 364, 368
FOAM algorithm 100-101, 103-104, 115-116, 119
focus group 270, 272, 278-284, 286-293, 295-296
Food and Drug Administration (FDA) 298-299
formalization 44
form-based activity 3, 5-6, 8-11, 14, 17, 19, 24, 26
functionality 54, 59, 64-65, 79, 86, 101, 105, 110-111, 118, 149, 152-155, 182, 207-208, 212, 219, 222, 260-262, 302, 309, 315, 317, 320, 329, 331, 368
functional testing (black box) 309

G

General Formalized Ontology (GFO) 178
GLUE 82, 101, 103-104
goal elicitation 226-228, 230-235, 237-240
granularity 11, 15, 18-19, 21-22, 25-26, 147, 152-153, 158, 223, 246-247, 249, 256, 260-262, 266, 286, 343, 345

H

health care 240, 245-247, 250-254, 261-266

I

i* model 148
InfoFlow 83, 86, 88, 92, 95-97

J

Jasmin 202-206, 214-215, 217
J-Tree 110-111, 113, 118

K

Kepler provenance 54, 58
Kickstart 54, 58-59, 62
Knowledge Representation and Reasoning (KRR) 339

L

legacy system 262
listener mode 55, 60
Logistic Regression (LR) 323

M

matching 39
method chunk 340
method engineering (ME) 337
method fragment 340
method services 340-341, 364-365
moderator 281-282, 289-292
monitoring mode 55, 60
myGrid 41

N

natural language 127, 130, 132, 139, 141, 151, 161, 231-232, 350
Neural Network (NN) 323
Non-Functional Requirement (NFR) 228
number of methods (NOM) 212, 214-218

O

object-awareness 2
object life cycle 19

information demand 77-93, 95-97
information logistics 78-79, 81, 96-97
information retrieval (IR) 46
information system development methodology (ISDM) 337
inheritance 36, 45, 50, 155, 157-160, 163, 165, 167, 170, 220, 223, 342
instance-specific activity 5, 11, 19, 25
intended effect 247, 251-257, 263-265
inter-firm partnership 271, 277, 284, 293
interoperability 52, 54, 71, 73, 97, 99-100, 102, 118-119, 241-243, 296, 313

object-process methodology (OPM) 26
ontology 34-35, 37, 41, 99, 103, 110, 112-113, 180
    alignment 99, 101-102, 104-106, 108-110, 113-118
    management 101, 103-105, 113
    merging 103-104, 121
    visualization 105, 112
Ontology Composition (ONION) 104
Ontology Mapping Enhancer (OMEN) 106
OntoUML 178, 192
Open Provenance Model (OPM) 62
open source software (OSS) 315
overlap 36

P

parsing 63-67
passive concept 155, 157, 159-160, 162
pBeans 202, 209-212, 216
pragmatics 101, 106, 108-109, 267, 365
process 32
    authorization 14, 18, 24
    equivalence 36
    specialisation 36
process management system (PrMS) 2
Proclet 19, 28
PROMPT 100-101, 103-104, 121
property precedence 181, 193
Proton 80, 86-87, 89-91, 97
provenance 53

Q

query specification 38, 47

R

Receiver Operating Characteristic (ROC) 326
recruitment 3
refinement 77, 86, 90, 95, 135, 196, 228-230, 232-233, 239, 241, 248-249, 258-262, 265-266, 349-350, 357
regulatory compliance 298-299, 312
requirement engineering for services (REFS) 247
requirements analysis 302
    elicitation 81, 302
    evaluation 302-303
    traceability 302-304, 306-308, 310
Requirements Engineering (RE) 227, 271
resource 250
    economic 247-248, 250-252, 255-257, 263
    enhancer 255-258, 264-265

    internal 250-251, 255
Response for a Class (RFC) 201
reuse frame 338, 343

S

satisfiability 129
Scientific Workflow Management System (SWfMS) 53
scoping 84-86
semantic link 157
semantics 107, 109-110, 113, 118
Semantic Service Description Model (SSDM) 125-126, 129
Semantic Web 49, 75, 99, 102-103, 119-124, 138, 142-145
service interactions 126, 148, 150, 154, 156-159, 167, 172
service query 128-129, 132-133
Service Usage Context (SUC) 124-125, 142
Simple Conceptual Unified Flow Language (SCU-FL) 56
Singular Value Decomposition (SVD) 321
situational method engineering (SME) 337-338, 363
SmallSQL 202, 205-207, 214-215, 217-218
small world graph 110-113, 118, 122
Softgoal Interdependency Graph (SIG) 230
software design 147, 177-178, 303-308
software engineering (SE) 272
software requirements document (SRD) 230
source code 31, 46, 49-50, 202, 307-308, 315-318, 335-336
source code search 31, 46
SourceForge.net 119, 143, 202, 315, 320
state transition 150, 154-155, 160, 181, 196-197
substantial entity 180-181, 188, 190, 195
subsystem 149
supply chain 276-277, 296
swimlane 152
syntax 101, 106, 182

T

Taverna Freefluo 56
thread 350
time complexity 137-138
top-level goal 248-249, 258-259, 263
traceability 47, 236-238, 241, 266, 302-304, 306-308, 310, 313
transfer 251
Tropos model 226, 234, 236, 242
typification 90-91

U

Unified Enterprise Competence Modelling Language (UECML) 85
Unified Foundational Ontology (UFO) 179, 193
Unified Modeling Language (UML) 147, 177-178
usability 54, 73, 191, 304-305, 309, 320
user profile 79, 97, 120

V

validity 273, 331
value model 148, 174, 246-255, 259, 262-267
variability 267, 270, 351, 363-364
Variance Inflation Factor (VIF) 327

Vienna e-Science Provenance System (VePS) 52, 63
Virtual Data System (VDS) 54, 58
visualizer 63-64, 68
voucher 250, 252-254

W

weighting 343-344, 363
workflow 53
workflow similarity 45, 50
worklist 8, 10, 13

Z

Zachman framework 147